BY HIS OWN RULES

BRADLEY GRAHAM

BY HIS

THE AMBITIONS, SUCCESSES, AND

OWN

ULTIMATE FAILURES OF DONALD RUMSFELD

RULES

PUBLICAFFAIRS
New York

Book Design by Trish Wilkinson
Text set in 11-point Minion

Library of Congress Cataloging-in-Publication Data

Graham, Bradley.
    By his own rules : the ambitions, successes, and ultimate failures of
Donald Rumsfeld / Bradley Graham.
        p.   cm.
    Includes bibliographical references and index.
    ISBN 978-1-58648-421-7 (hardcover)
    1. Rumsfeld, Donald, 1932– 2. Cabinet officers—United States—
Biography. 3. United States. Dept. of Defense—Officials and employees—
Biography. 4. War on Terrorism, 2001– 5. Iraq War, 2003– 6. United
States—Politics and government—2001–I. Title.
E840.8.R84G73 2009
355.6092—dc22
[B]   2008055406

First Edition

10 9 8 7 6 5 4 3 2 1

To Seymour and Kalmaine
And to Russell

Contents

Introduction

Face time with the president is political gold in Washington, so Donald Rumsfeld moved quickly after taking charge at the Pentagon to secure regular private meetings with President George W. Bush. Now, nearly six years and many meetings later, the defense secretary arrived in the Oval Office prepared to raise a delicate, personal matter.

His opportunity came as talk that day, in September 2006, turned to Iraq. The conflict there was going badly. Violence had metastasized into a civil war. Plans to begin a major drawdown of U.S. troops had stalled. Iraqi forces still appeared unready to assume charge of security, and the Iraqi government, riven by sectarian strife, was doing little to unite the nation. In Washington, much of the blame for the mess in Iraq had fallen on Rumsfeld. He had failed to plan adequately for the occupation, was slow to develop a counterinsurgency campaign, and had alienated too many people with his combative, domineering personality.

By then, Rumsfeld had hung on to office longer than most of his predecessors in the top Pentagon job. But with congressional elections approaching in the fall, he had become a campaign target, vilified by Democrats and considered a political liability by many Republicans. If, as was increasingly anticipated, Democrats won control of one or both chambers of Congress, it would mean more hearings for Rumsfeld and more punishing interrogations. In recent days, Rumsfeld and his wife, Joyce, had discussed the prospect of his stepping down.

"We said there's no way he would stay if either the House or the Senate went Democratic because he would be the issue," Joyce recalled months later. The criticism "would have been relentless until he was gone."

Sitting with Bush, Rumsfeld broached the possibility of his departure. A "fresh pair of eyes" on Iraq might not be a bad thing, the secretary remarked. He made no explicit offer to resign. Still, his inference was unmistakable.

Or so the president thought. Although Bush didn't pursue the point, he told a senior White House official afterward what Rumsfeld had said. Bush took the comment as a sign of Rumsfeld's own recognition of the political realities closing in on him. "In the president's mind, Rumsfeld had cracked the door open," the official recounted. "And whether the president wanted to kick it open or not was up to him."

———•———

The question of whether to keep Rumsfeld had dogged Bush and his senior advisers for months. It had been raised after the Abu Ghraib prison scandal in early 2004 and several months later in the wake of Bush's reelection. It had come up again as the Iraq War worsened during 2005, and once more in the spring of 2006 when a number of retired generals stepped forward to appeal for Rumsfeld's dismissal.

Each time, Bush resisted letting Rumsfeld go, even rebuffing several suggestions that he do so by his own chief of staff, Andrew Card, and other senior aides and advisers. Bush had still valued Rumsfeld's counsel and also worried that the disruption caused by replacing a secretary in wartime could be risky. Moreover, Rumsfeld had been unfailingly loyal to the president, and he had a powerful ally in Vice President Richard Cheney, who owed his own rise in the administrations of Richard Nixon and Gerald Ford four decades earlier to Rumsfeld. Cheney and his aides liked Rumsfeld's hard-charging style and argued that the secretary had been right on a number of things where others had been wrong.

Importantly, too, the Pentagon leader had championed the administration's signature drive to reform the U.S. military. From the beginning of his tenure, he had proclaimed "transformation" his main slogan and had pushed to create a more agile, adaptable military. He had relentlessly challenged existing assumptions and had advocated new principles of warfare, insisting on the need for change in confronting new and evolving threats to the United States.

He had taken on the Army early, its heavy forces and cumbersome deployments standing as a symbol of the bureaucratic inertia he was determined to overcome. Eventually during his tenure, the Army was restructured into more flexible, more easily deployable units. And he had pressed all the services—Army, Air Force, Navy, and Marine Corps—to work more cooperatively. Before Rumsfeld was finished, his constant churning had led to a rewriting of U.S. war plans to emphasize speed and fewer troops, a repositioning of U.S. forces around the world to shrink bases in Europe and Asia that dated from the Cold War, and a rearrangement of the military's regional and functional commands to fill gaps and adjust to new dangers.

Outside the Pentagon, in interagency deliberations, he had emerged as a forceful conservative voice on a range of national security policies and a fierce guardian of what he considered military prerogatives. Publicly, he had performed as the administration's most spirited spokesman, sparring sharply with the media. All in all, Rumsfeld had become the most powerful secretary of defense since Robert S. McNamara.

But he was also the most controversial. His methods were offensive to many. Senior officers complained that he treated them harshly. Legislators groused that he was either unresponsive to their requests or disrespectful in personal dealings, and senior officials at the State Department and the White House portrayed him as uncompromising, evasive, and obstructive. Despite his reputation as a shrewd politician and skilled bureaucratic operator, Rumsfeld had lost the confidence of so many lawmakers and strained so many relations inside the administration that few were willing to argue for his staying on.

The dismal facts on the ground in Iraq were such that even Rumsfeld, with his customary glass-half-full outlook, couldn't gloss over them. He had acknowledged in other conversations with Bush and presidential aides that things in Iraq weren't going "well enough or fast enough." Josh Bolten, the White House chief of staff, encouraged Bush to work Rumsfeld's phrase into his own public remarks. Bolten was concerned about a disconnect between the administration's stay-the-course message and American public opinion about the war, opinion that had become exceedingly negative during 2006.

Intensified efforts over the summer of 2006 to secure Baghdad by relying on Iraqi forces as well as on U.S. troops had failed to quell the violence for long. The escalating turmoil had called into question Rumsfeld's strategic premise that Iraqi forces could be trained and rushed into service to take over the counterinsurgency fight so that U.S. troops could go home. Bush himself, prompted by his national security adviser, Stephen Hadley, had belatedly begun challenging the course in Iraq that Rumsfeld and U.S. military commanders were pursuing.

As Bush started looking for a new approach, he had to confront the question of whether to retain the secretary so closely associated with what looked like a doomed strategy. By early October, he had all but resolved to let Rumsfeld go. Even so, he was adamant that the announcement of Rumsfeld's departure be postponed until after the elections. He did not want it seen as a politically expedient attempt to boost Republican chances at the polls. Bush's aides, in turn, advised against waiting too long after the elections and running the risk of triggering a Democratic drumbeat for Rumsfeld's head.

A White House rump group was formed to choreograph the probable change in Pentagon leadership in the context of other postelection moves. It included Bolten; Hadley; Karl Rove, the president's top political adviser; and Dan Bartlett, Bush's counselor and communications chief. They settled on making the announcement about Rumsfeld the day after the elections, although the move was contingent on Bush's finding someone to take over at the Defense Department. He started looking seriously at Robert Gates, the president of Texas A&M University, a former CIA director, and a favorite of Bush's dad.

————•————

Rumsfeld suspected his time was running out. But he was not informed of the White House plan. For his part, Bush, hiding his intentions, went so far as to engage in a deliberate deception, telling news service reporters a week before the elections that the defense secretary would be staying on.

The president's feint confused even Rumsfeld's wife, whose own political instincts were keen, to say the least. "I thought, What is that about?" she recalled. "I had kind of been winding down, thinking it's almost over. And then that statement came out, and I thought, Oh, my gosh! So then I started thinking, I've got to get myself—forget Don—I just have to get myself the energy to get through another two years."

The weekend before the elections, as Bush met secretly at his Texas ranch with Gates and decided to make the switch, Rumsfeld rushed to complete an options paper on Iraq for the president. As was his custom with important documents, Rumsfeld asked General Peter Pace, the chairman of the Joint Chiefs of Staff, and Eric Edelman, the head of the Pentagon's policy branch, to help refine it. To prevent copies from circulating outside his office, Rumsfeld insisted that the two senior officials come in person and make changes on the spot. "He really got frantic about it—that it be done and given to the president," said Delonnie Henry, Rumsfeld's personal secretary. "He was just obsessed about this options paper."

Dated November 6, one day before the elections, the memo, titled "Iraq—Illustrative New Courses of Action," showed Rumsfeld coming around to accepting some change in approach. "In my view it is time for a major adjustment," he wrote. "Clearly, what U.S. forces are currently doing in Iraq is not working well enough or fast enough."

But what Rumsfeld had in mind still came nowhere near the magnitude of the shift being contemplated by Bush and the National Security Council staff. He stopped well short of proposing any coherent new plan. Instead, he provided a laundry list of twenty-one "illustrative options," many purely tactical. His aim appeared to be to promote discussion rather than to rally others around a decision. Refraining from endorsing any particulars, he simply divided the options into two groups—one worthy of consideration, which he labeled "above the line," and the other, a less favorable set, placed "below the line."

Those he favored tended to amount to an intensification or acceleration of the existing strategy—more U.S. trainers, more U.S. equipment for Iraqi forces, and more resources for the Iraqi ministries of Defense and Interior. The basic thrust was to draw down U.S. troops and shift to an advisory mission. In the other group of less attractive choices were options pushed by the proponents of doing more—shifting more U.S.

forces into Baghdad to control it, surging more U.S. troops into Iraq, staging a Dayton-like peace process like the one used in the Balkans conflict in 1995, partitioning Iraq, and setting a firm withdrawal date.

———•———

The memo reflected Rumsfeld's predilections and his weaknesses. He liked lists. He often approached problems by spelling out options. He favored analysis. And yet, he was lost. Although he recognized the need for change, he was unable to embrace a bold new initiative and uncertain about just what action to recommend.

There was no small measure of irony in Rumsfeld's poor management of the Iraq War and his other failures as defense secretary. None of his predecessors had come into the job with as much experience or potential. He was the only person ever to get a second shot at being defense secretary, having served once before in the mid-1970s. During stints in several senior government positions under both Nixon and Ford, he had developed a reputation as an able administrator and an effective bureaucratic infighter. In a subsequent career as a corporate chief executive, he had turned struggling businesses into profitable enterprises—and made himself wealthy in the process. Even in his youth he had shown a talent—particularly on the wrestling mat—as a first-rate competitor adept at sizing up opponents and taking them down.

Yet as the war in Iraq grew into the administration's most serious challenge, Rumsfeld remained most dedicated to his military transformation agenda. A hands-on manager in Washington, he inexplicably deferred key decisions in Baghdad on personnel and strategy. He was sluggish in responding to evolving conditions, averse to acknowledging an insurgency, reluctant to recognize that Iraqi forces were not yet ready to take over from U.S. troops, and resistant to the idea of raising U.S. force levels. Even as the chaos and bloodshed in Iraq worsened in the middle of 2006, Rumsfeld remained fixated on finding ways to facilitate the turnover of responsibility to Iraqi troops and to accelerate the withdrawal of U.S. forces.

He was hardly alone in this view. The top U.S. generals in the region—Army general John Abizaid, who oversaw U.S. forces in the Middle East and Southwest Asia, and Army general George Casey Jr., who commanded

U.S. troops in Iraq—strongly supported the idea of continuing to shrink U.S. military involvement in Iraq. They shared Rumsfeld's sense of urgency about placing more responsibility in the hands of the Iraqis and avoiding the risk of greater dependency on U.S. involvement. The Joint Chiefs of Staff, too, under Pace's leadership, did not see how the U.S. military, already badly strained by three years in Iraq, could consider building up there.

This consensus in upper military ranks left little room for alternative views inside the Pentagon. Edelman had mounting reservations about the existing strategy. But he regarded Rumsfeld and his field generals as unreceptive to other opinions. Jack Keane, a retired general and former vice chief of the Army on friendly terms with Rumsfeld, had tried, during a meeting in September 2006, to urge the embattled secretary to change course but had made little headway. "I thought there was a general resignation about him that I hadn't seen before," Keane recalled months later. "I thought probably it was because he was realizing the war was not going well, and people were coming to him and telling him so—not just critics but people he respected."

———•———

Rumsfeld had confided nothing even to his closest Pentagon aides about the possibility that he might soon be gone. His staff joked that they would probably be the last to know. But hints began emerging in mid-October.

Delonnie Henry, Rumsfeld's secretary, noticed an increased interest by her boss in his archives. Rumsfeld kept lots of personal files—and had done so for years—checking from time to time that the records were being properly organized, updated, and digitized. He was a stickler especially for tallies—tallies of when and how long he had conferred with members of Congress, met with the chairman of the Joint Chiefs of Staff, talked to the media. Other records tracked the trips he had taken and foreign dignitaries he had seen.

Measuring things seemed to satisfy a certain compulsion in Rumsfeld and allowed him to gauge progress. He had even devised a way of measuring how he was doing as secretary of defense in a list labeled "accomplishments and initiatives" that was periodically updated. The staff referred to it as "Rumsfeld's greatest hits." Although he had often denied worrying about his legacy, his private record keeping and public touting of achievements suggested otherwise.

Other subtle signs also indicated that Rumsfeld might be anticipating the end. He put a hold on his regular purchase of season tickets for sports events. He seemed less concerned about getting prompt responses back to the many memos he issued to subordinates.

Victor E. "Gene" Renuart Jr., who as a three-star Air Force general was Rumsfeld's senior military assistant at the time, detected a change in the secretary's mood prior to the elections. "He clearly was more thoughtful about things," the general recalled. "I didn't press him, nor did he offer. But you could sense something was on his mind. He was a little more quiet, more reserved, just not quite his normal personality."

After Bush decided on Gates, Cheney called Rumsfeld to deliver the news. Rumsfeld remembers responding, "Fair enough. That makes sense. Let's get on with it." He then proceeded to get his affairs in order.

His thirty-nine-year-old son Nick—the youngest of his three children—had arrived in town with no advance notice to Rumsfeld's staff, which was unusual. The trip was presented as a last-minute thing—a chance to visit with the folks and watch the election returns. Actually, Nick spent Monday, November 6, with Joyce at the family's house in Washington, D.C., preparing a letter of resignation that Rumsfeld had composed. While Joyce entered it into a computer, Nick helped set up the printer using stationery with the letterhead "The Secretary of Defense." The letter consisted of four brief paragraphs:

Dear Mr. President:

With my resignation as Secretary of Defense comes my deep appreciation to you for providing me this unexpected opportunity to serve.

I leave with great respect for you and for the leadership you have provided during a most challenging time for our country. The focus, determination and perseverance you have so consistently provided have been needed and are impressive.

It has been the highest honor of my long life to have been able to serve our country at such a critical time in our history and to have had the privilege of working so closely with the truly amazing young men and women in uniform. Their dedication, professionalism, courage and sacrifice are an inspiration.

It is time to conclude my service. As I do so, I want you to know that you have my continuing and heartfelt support as you enter the final two years of your Presidency.

Respectfully, Donald Rumsfeld

Left unstated was any particular reason for the resignation. Rumsfeld chose not to try to explain. It was simply time to go.

At a meeting with Bush the next afternoon, on November 7, Rumsfeld presented his resignation letter. The election results that evening revealed an overwhelming victory for the Democrats, handing them control of both chambers of Congress for the first time since 1994. American voters had delivered a repudiation of the Bush administration and its Iraq policy.

The next morning, a White House courier arrived at the Pentagon with an envelope for Rumsfeld and instructions not to leave until the secretary of defense had received it. Rumsfeld, attending a briefing on Iraq across the hall from his office, took the envelope and placed it in his briefcase to look at later. It contained a handwritten letter from Bush accepting Rumsfeld's resignation and praising him for his service to the nation.

Shortly before word of his departure was officially announced, Rumsfeld began calling in his most senior aides one by one, telling each the news. Pace walked out of Rumsfeld's office appearing pale. "He looked like he'd seen a ghost," Henry observed. Matt Latimer, the secretary's main speechwriter, teared up. "You've been a star," Rumsfeld told him, sounding unusually effusive. Such expressions of appreciation were not Rumsfeld's style. Stories about how sparing he was in voicing gratitude, let alone praise, were legendary among those who had worked for him. Aides knew they were doing a good job if he didn't tell them they weren't or if he gave them more work to do. "That was just the way it was," Henry said. "But I think at the end there, he was really awkward. He was overwhelmed."

Preparing for a White House appearance with Bush that afternoon, Rumsfeld scribbled some notes for a few remarks on the yellow, legal-sized paper he often used. He faxed a draft to Joyce at home to review. He was particularly concerned his remarks not sound defensive.

———•———

Shortly before 3:00 p.m., Rumsfeld headed to the White House, where, in a brief Oval Office session, Bush declared that "new leadership" and a "fresh perspective" were needed to guide the military through the difficult war in Iraq. He portrayed Rumsfeld's departure as a mutual decision, saying that he and the secretary had held "a series of thoughtful conversations" and that Rumsfeld understood that "Iraq is not working well enough, fast enough."

Bush's reference to a series of talks evidently referred to broader discussions that had taken place between the president and the defense secretary about the situation in Iraq, potential changes in U.S. strategy, and plans to dispatch new U.S. military commanders to the region. There had been no explicit conversation between the two men about Rumsfeld's departure before Bush's decision to pick a replacement.

"The president, at least in his own mind, felt that through some of these conversations about the strategy, Rumsfeld was also giving clear signals that new leadership made sense," one presidential aide explained later. A blunt discussion about Rumsfeld's leaving was not necessary, another White House official suggested. "I think they both understood where they were in the conversation," the official said. Additionally, there was often a certain formality about Rumsfeld, and the president, until he had finally decided the time had come for Rumsfeld to go, may have been reluctant to say something that could have been misunderstood. "Rumsfeld is businesslike and might have interpreted a comment from the president as sending a signal, prompting him to tender his resignation immediately," the official said.

Rumsfeld, for his part, was wary of making a formal offer to resign. He had done so twice in the spring of 2004 following the Abu Ghraib revelations, and he did not want to be seen as someone who kept submitting his resignation as a technique to try to defuse calls for his removal and shore up his political standing. To have talked to Bush this time about stepping down would, in his view, have been final.

When it was Rumsfeld's turn to speak at the White House event, he limited his remarks, thanking the president for the opportunity to serve and praising the professionalism and dedication of U.S. forces. He made no effort to defend his record, nor did he acknowledge any missteps on Iraq. But recognizing the target for blame that he had become, he invoked the words of an earlier civilian warrior who considered himself misunderstood by critics. Paraphrasing Winston Churchill, he said, "I have benefited greatly from criticism, and at no time have I suffered a lack thereof."

He made only one reference to the fighting in Iraq and Afghanistan and the hunt for terrorists worldwide, calling it a "little understood, unfamiliar war, the first war of the twenty-first century—it is not well known; it was not well understood; it is complex for people to comprehend." The comment, coming at the tail end, sounded like a parting shot tinged with the frustration Rumsfeld himself had felt in trying to understand the new global fight and figuring out how best to combat it.

Even with the heated speculation about Rumsfeld before the elections, the defense secretary's exit stunned Washington. In bearing the brunt of attacks for the administration's conduct of the Iraq War, Rumsfeld had to some extent served to shield Bush from criticism. His departure confirmed what a damaging political liability he had become, although Bush was still unwilling to concede publicly that his defense secretary had made serious mistakes. To the contrary, the president praised Rumsfeld for having been "a superb leader during a time of change."

Many of Rumsfeld's friends were offended by the White House's seemingly rushed and unceremonious handling of the announcement of Rumsfeld's resignation. To his supporters, the day-after news conference—which concluded with Bush patting the defense secretary on the shoulder as he ushered him out of the Oval Office—was insensitive and unbefitting of Rumsfeld's long career of public service.

To others, though, the end of Rumsfeld's tenure came too late. A number of Republican lawmakers complained bitterly that Bush had not cut Rumsfeld loose before the elections, when the move might have provided a boost at the polls for some GOP candidates. While presidential aides had anticipated some gripes about the timing, the extent of the anger within party ranks surprised them.

Once away from the Pentagon, the former secretary effectively disappeared from the political scene, rarely appearing in public and declining most requests for interviews. When he initially agreed to see me for this book, he put talk about Iraq off limits. But at our final interview in late 2008, he relented and addressed a number of aspects of the war. Still, he had little to say when asked about regrets, and he scoffed at a question inviting him to acknowledge any mistakes. At times he seemed unsure himself of what to think about certain decisions or events, waiting for some later opportunity to review the facts and to reflect.

The story of Donald Rumsfeld is an exceptional personal drama that has had profound consequences for the United States and the world. It is an instructive tale of what can happen when a man, once considered among the best and brightest of his generation, meets his greatest challenge late in life and ends up being relieved of duty, widely despised and branded a failure.

Hubris and miscalculation, obstinacy and mismanagement, bad advice and bad luck all played a part in bringing Rumsfeld down. Given his leading role in two wars that have become national sinkholes, his association with some of the most shameful incidents in modern U.S. military history, and his personification of the arrogance and misjudgments of the Bush administration, Rumsfeld is likely to remain a deeply controversial figure for many years, easy to caricature and easy to loathe.

But he is more complicated than the common image of him as a pugnacious, inflexible villain. Quiet trips to visit the war wounded at Walter Reed Army Medical Center belied his public stoicism and suggested anguish and pain that few saw. Gruff and imperious in formal settings, he could, in more casual surroundings, be disarmingly genial and fun-loving. At turns brilliant and engaging, charming and generous, highly ethical and deeply committed to public service, he was also defined by his tendency toward confrontational, unyielding, overbearing, and ornery behavior.

For all his complexities—or perhaps because of them—Rumsfeld had an abiding interest in simple rules. During the second half of his life, he composed lists of them to live by and distributed them freely to others. The homespun compendium of lessons for coping with the federal bureaucracy and corporate world drew largely on quips, aphorisms, and adages that Rumsfeld had read or heard elsewhere. But he fused them into an approach to issues and people that was distinctly his own, confident of his way even as some close to him worried, when he struggled as defense secretary, that he was veering badly off course. By the end of 2006, even his rules couldn't save him.

CHAPTER 1

A Bit of a Rascal

The tough-guy image that defined Donald Rumsfeld later in life might suggest a childhood of hard knocks and personal struggle. But Rumsfeld's beginnings, set largely in the quiet, leafy village of Winnetka near the shores of Lake Michigan north of Chicago, contained many positively reinforcing elements—loving parents, close friendships, success in school.

Rumsfeld's parents, George and Jeannette, moved to Winnetka in 1937, when Rumsfeld was five and his sister, Joan, was seven. As a realtor, George saw promise in the burgeoning North Shore suburb. It was not yet the wealthy enclave it would become, but its offer of tranquility and safety, just a forty-five-minute train ride from Chicago's downtown, pointed to a future of growth and prosperity.

Winnetka was far from Sudweyhe in northwestern Germany, which Rumsfeld's ancestors had left in the mid-nineteenth century for America. There, the Rumsfelds had been farmers. Records in Sudweyhe, today a suburb of the port city of Bremen, show a continuous line of Rumsfelds from 1776 on, the names of the firstborn son alternating between Hermann and Heinrich. The line probably extends even further back, but earlier church records were destroyed in a fire at the parish minister's home.

By 1866, Hermann Rumsfeld, then forty-five, was in a bind. His wife Wuebke had died two years earlier after fifteen years of marriage, leaving him with seven children. He worked a family farm—a small corn-growing lot with a straw-roofed house flanked on both sides by barns. With the German economy in depression, many in the area had joined a massive flow of emigrants to the United States, where land could be acquired cheaply. Hoping for better prospects, Hermann sold his farm to a neighbor.

Exactly what he did next is unclear. Some histories show him moving with his six youngest children, ages two to fifteen, to the United States. By this account, the eldest child, Heinrich, stayed home to farm and followed in 1869, a year before his permit for emigration expired. An alternate history has Hermann buying a farm in Ofen, bordering the city of Oldenburg, after selling his property in Sudweyhe. The farm buildings burned down in 1865, but Hermann built new structures. Two of his sons subsequently traveled to the United States to escape being drafted. Hermann sold the farmstead in Ofen in 1876 and followed his sons. The manifest for the SS *Donau*, dated June 24, 1876, lists five Rumsfelds, including "Herm," a farmer age fifty-four, fitting the description of Don Rumsfeld's great-great-grandfather.

After reaching America, the Rumsfeld clan settled in the Chicago area. By the time George was born in 1904, the family was still struggling. His own parents had divorced when he was two, leaving him and his older brother, Henry, with their mother, Lizette, herself an émigré from northwestern Germany. To support her young family, Lizette worked in the mail-order division of the Marshall Field's department store handling shoe orders—a job she held until retirement at age sixty-five.

One Saturday morning when George was thirteen, he walked into the Baird and Warner (B&W) real estate office on Broadway in the Uptown neighborhood of Chicago and approached one of the partners, Warner G. Baird, seeking an after-school job. George explained that his father had died earlier in the year and his mother was having financial difficulty. Impressed with George's sincerity, Baird hired him as an office boy. From 1918 to 1922, George worked summers and after school in B&W's Uptown office.

George again approached Baird as he prepared for college at the University of Illinois in Champaign. He had secured a scholarship that paid for his room and had landed a job waiting tables that covered his meals. But he needed financial help for tuition. Baird provided a loan, and George signed a note for it.

In college, George majored in business and belonged to Alpha Chi Rho. Tall, rather quiet, with soft blond hair, he met Jeannette, a stunning brunette in Chi Omega who had transferred from a school in Normal, Illinois, and was studying for a teaching degree. She could trace her own ancestry back to the American Revolution, but her immediate family had experienced its share of struggle. The youngest of five children, she was, like George, from the Chicago area. She had never really known her mother, who had been quite ill when Jeannette was a toddler and had died before Jeannette's seventh birthday. Her father had been more business- than family-oriented, although she always felt that she was his favorite.

Jeannette's petite frame contrasted with George's wiry height, but together they made a handsome couple. They were married on June 16, 1927. Shortly before his wedding day, George, who was back working at Baird and Warner, went to Baird to pay off the note signed years earlier. As Baird recalled the moment, George had a check in hand to cover the interest and principal. Baird would have been willing to excuse the whole loan, but he said that if it would make George happy, he would accept repayment of just the principal without the interest charge.

—•—

By 1933, George had risen to office manager in the real estate firm's North Michigan Avenue office. The steady employment provided some financial cushion during the Depression. Years later, when Donald Rumsfeld eventually acquired the kind of wealth never known by his forbearers, he sank a fair portion of it into real estate.

Moving his young family from a small apartment in Evanston to a home in Winnetka marked George's first house purchase. The house, at 545 Provident Avenue, had room for George's mother, Lizette, and her mother, Elizabeth Yagle Claussen. An apple tree in the backyard with a thick branch jutting over the garage provided space for a tree house. In the evenings after dinner, Don and Joan played kick-the-can and hide-and-seek with other kids in the neighborhood.

Out of step with Winnetka's sleepiness, Don Rumsfeld emerged as a boy eager to push the boundaries. While studying Native Americans in school and learning about smoke signals, he lit the contents of a wastebasket in his own bedroom and flapped a blanket over the smoke until an alarmed parent rushed in to douse the fire. Not long afterward, playing in a field behind an elementary school in the neighborhood, he put a match to some weeds, then fled the scene on his bike. Fortunately, the fire didn't take. By his own account, he was "a bit of a rascal," sometimes shoplifting gum and candy, and once, with some others, breaking into a convenience store, "not to take anything—just to do it." Rumsfeld's dad summed up his son's behavior this way: "If it doesn't go easy, force it!"

George Rumsfeld also had a deep streak of daring and determination that drove him past customary barriers. At thirty-seven, too old to be drafted for World War II, he wanted desperately to serve and fulfill his duty to country. The Navy refused to take him when he tried to enlist, declaring him underweight. So he downed milk shakes and bananas several times a day to add pounds and applied again in August 1942. Passing the physical exam despite a bad knee, he entered the military and received his lieutenant's commission, completing Officer's Candidate School at Quonset Point, Rhode Island.

George Rumsfeld's war service would have a profound impact on his son. For one thing, it took the family away from Winnetka on a journey around America as Donald, his sister, and his mother followed George from assignment to assignment—first to a blimp base in Elizabeth City, North Carolina, then to a firefighting and gunnery school in Bremerton, Washington, and later to the Pacific coastal towns of Seaside and Astoria in Oregon. From June 1944 to October 1945, when George served as a hangar deck officer on two escort carriers, the rest of the family took up residence in Coronado, California.

While George was at sea, he and Jeannette exchanged long letters filled not only with words of tenderness but also with many details of life both at war and on the home front. In one instance, after Jeannette bought a house in Coronado, she wrote George all about it, describing the house and what everything cost—sometimes to the penny—and assuring him that if he didn't like anything about the deal, they could certainly change it.

Assigned initially to the USS *Bismarck Sea,* George was transferred to another ship, and then was denied a request to be put back on the *Bismarck*, where he had many friends. The *Bismarck* later sank off Iwo Jima after being struck by two kamikaze fighters on February 21, 1945, in an attack that killed 318 sailors, or about one-third of the ship's crew. The tragedy hit George hard. Two months after his promotion to lieutenant commander in October 1945, George left the Navy, having earned both the American Campaign Medal and the Asiatic–Pacific Area Campaign Medal with battle star.

Moving from place to place, changing schools each year, following the war news, knowing his dad was at sea in the Pacific campaign, Don Rumsfeld felt directly affected. "The intensity of a young, bright boy— father gone on a ship—he was tracking the war, he cared desperately about the outcome," his wife Joyce observed.

Rumsfeld took considerable pride in the extra effort his dad had made to enter the Navy and participate in the war. The experience instilled in him a lasting appreciation for government and military service. In tribute to his father, Rumsfeld framed the honorable discharge letter that George received from James Forrestal, then secretary of the Navy and later the first secretary of defense. Millions of others who had served got the same letter, but to Rumsfeld it was a precious memento signifying the patriotism and dedication to public service that he shared with his father. Until Rumsfeld's final days as defense secretary, the letter hung on a wall in his office.

When the Rumsfelds resettled in Winnetka after the war in 1945, Don entered eighth grade at Skokie Junior High School. He was back in familiar surroundings, but he had changed. While away, living in a different region of the country each year, he had been compelled to meet new kids, make new friends, and adjust to new neighborhoods and schools. He had learned to cope with the long absence of a parent and to make his own way.

"I remember asking him if it wasn't difficult moving around so much when his dad was in the service," recalled Judy Koch Merrifield, who was Rumsfeld's first girlfriend in junior high school. "He said, 'Yes, it's difficult, but it sure makes you grow up fast.'"

Rumsfeld's father returned to work after the war at Baird & Warner as a residential real estate salesman. In time he became manager of the Winnetka office and then a company vice president. Along the way he began to acquire houses himself, usually ones that needed work, which he renovated to resell. Sometimes the Rumsfeld family lived in a house while it was being fixed up. As a result, Don changed houses several times during his adolescence, although he remained in the same general area.

With its tree-lined streets, Winnetka was a quaint, small town. The geographic boundaries of Lake Michigan and a nature preserve left little possibility for the town to annex big tracts of land that might have attracted large-scale builders. A prohibition against encroachment by industry ensured Winnetka's residential character and helped preserve older properties. George Rumsfeld seemed to have a particularly good eye for fixer-uppers, houses that were fundamentally in good shape but could use some sprucing up. He tended to favor properties that were near schools and priced toward the lower median end of the market, so they would benefit from higher-priced houses in the area.

Years later, Don Rumsfeld sometimes portrayed himself as having grown up with little money. And it is true that he did not live in the wealthier sections of Winnetka and had to earn whatever he wanted to spend. From the age of ten onward, he held a variety of odd jobs—newspaper delivery boy, golf-course caddy, gardener, rug cleaner, ditch digger, janitor. He was industrious and learned not to take things for granted.

But Rumsfeld's family was more middle class than poor, and in the years after Don left home, his father's acquisition of rental houses yielded a comfortable income. When George Rumsfeld died in 1974, he left a valuable estate containing more than a half dozen properties.

From his father, Rumsfeld drew his more outgoing qualities and his industriousness. He remembered his dad as "a happy person" who laughed a lot, enjoyed life, and often came home whistling. George liked to play golf, but because he worked "day and night," he played quickly, trying to finish nine holes at dusk in about thirty-five minutes. "He never took a warm-up stroke," Rumsfeld recalled years later. "He would just get on that course and hit the ball and go."

George Rumsfeld also had a reputation for being highly ethical—so honest and principled that he would point out flaws in a house to prospective buyers. Critical of those with "one-way pockets," who took from their community without giving back, he believed people should not just make money for themselves but should help the industry in which they were working. To that end, he served on various committees and later as president of the North Shore Board of Realtors, a director of the Winnetka Trust and Savings Bank, and a longtime member of the Winnetka Rotary. In Don Rumsfeld's eyes, his dad was "a standard for his friends, his associates, and his family."

Rumsfeld's mother, who worked as a substitute teacher, was a slight, delicate woman, an intense, bookish personality more straightlaced than her husband. A stickler for precise speech, she served as the family grammarian. "She kept cleaning up my language—or at least trying," Rumsfeld recalled. His own proclivity to nitpick the word choice and phrasing of subordinates, journalists, and others can be traced to her.

Jeannette Rumsfeld also took great pride in her son, keeping scrapbooks of his achievements well into his adult years. "I think his mother was a competitive individual and wanted Don to do well," said Myles Cunningham, a childhood friend.

———•———

Rumsfeld entered New Trier High School in 1946 when the school was gaining prominence as one of the best public secondary institutions in the country. *Life* magazine featured a New Trier student on the cover of a special issue on education several years later, extolling the school's extensive course offerings, elaborately equipped athletic program, and large selection of student clubs. Academically, Rumsfeld was placed on a fast track known as the V (for "velocity") program, which offered advanced courses. "He was smart and he was inquisitive," said Betty Christian, a classmate. "He wasn't afraid to speak up. He would say what he thought."

Rumsfeld held his own in class, although he never did well enough to make the annual Honor Society list. "He was a very good student, but not a scholar," recalled Cunningham, who had classes with Rumsfeld. "He was always capable, always confident. But Don never stood out in the classroom; it wasn't his forte. His recognition really came outside the classroom."

Rumsfeld made his biggest mark in school—and found some of his closest friends and mentors—in athletics. Lacking the height for basketball and the heft for varsity football (although he did end up playing on the junior varsity), he decided to give wrestling a try. The sport was new at the school, having started there only two years before Rumsfeld arrived. The program was led by the school's baseball coach, Dick Clausen, who knew so little about wrestling that he came to practice with a book of pictures showing various moves.

Rumsfeld wrestled in intramural tournaments before making the school team. Strong, quick, agile, and determined, he brought ideal attributes to the sport. He seemed to relish the sense of being out on the mat, matching strength and wits with a single opponent, having no one to rely on but himself. "I think he liked that," said Brad Glass, who was two years ahead of Rumsfeld at New Trier and became one of the school's greatest wrestlers.

By Rumsfeld's junior year, the school had hired a new and more knowledgeable wrestling coach, Al Hurley. Hurley's southern drawl and laid-back, country-boy manner masked the mind of a real wrestling technician. He started teaching moves and holds that the kids had never seen and placed a heavy emphasis on physical conditioning. Rumsfeld threw himself into the sport and the training requirements.

Wrestling provided an outlet for Rumsfeld's aggressiveness and ambition, which were already in evidence in his youth. He enjoyed winning, and having begun something new, he didn't want to stop until he emerged as the best, the champ. "George and I weren't particularly interested in having an athlete as a son, but it was good for Don, we realized, because he had all that energy," Jeannette Rumsfeld once told an interviewer.

Cunningham remembers the sight of Rumsfeld moving around a cinder track in the school's basement that had been set up with hurdles, overhead bars, and other obstacles to resemble a commando course. "I marveled at what he could do," Cunningham said. "He'd tumble through that thing—just flew around it."

Early on, Rumsfeld befriended a teammate named Lenny Vyskocil, who had won the state championship as a freshman. The two had similar builds and were so close in appearance that each could be mistaken for the other from a distance. Vyskocil was arguably the most technically skilled wrestler on the team. Rumsfeld had seen Vyskocil do an impressive takedown move called the fireman's carry. "He came to me and said, I want you to teach me this," Vyskocil recalled. "I couldn't do it during practice, so what I did was stay later with Don for a number of days, after practice, and we worked on it. He wanted to go over and over it to make sure he had every corner of it figured out. In the end, I think he did it better than I did."

The fireman's carry served as Rumsfeld's signature move for the rest of his time as a wrestler, through college and the Navy. Requiring great balance and exact timing, it involves a wrestler taking hold of an opponent's arm, then dropping down, grabbing a leg, picking the opponent up off the mat—like a fireman carrying somebody out of a house—and bringing him down. When it works, it is very effective. But it also is risky and can backfire. "You can get into trouble with it," recalled Bob Nellis, another teammate of Rumsfeld's who, by his own admission, was not good at the move himself. "It requires you to duck under your opponent, and if you don't have yourself positioned right, the opponent can just fall on top of you and crush you."

Rumsfeld could execute the fireman's carry to near technical perfection. But much else about his wrestling style tended to center on speed and brute force. "That's the way Don wrestled," Cunningham said. "Not a lot of subtle moves, not a lot of smoothness, not a lot of technique. Just athleticism. Get the job done." As an example, Cunningham recalled Rumsfeld's approach to escaping from wrestling holds. The team worked on various reversal techniques and other moves that required staying down on the mat. "Don had none of that," Cunningham said. "Don's idea was just to stand up and tear the guy loose. That's all he did. The sooner he could get to his feet and tear him loose—that was it."

Rumsfeld also drove hard not just to score points against his opponents by breaking holds or dropping them to the mat; he wanted to pin them. "He was the most aggressive wrestler I ever saw," said Lex Irvine, another teammate. "A lot of wrestlers will go out and circle the opponent and try for a takedown. Don didn't do that. He'd charge across and tear a guy down to the mat as soon as he could."

Hurley encouraged such aggressiveness. It became a point of pride on the New Trier team to pin opponents. "We would put a half-dollar in a jar, and there were twelve wrestlers, and the one who got the fastest pin got the money," Vyskocil said. "Coach Hurley didn't like us betting, but we did."

Hurley, who succeeded in channeling whatever inner aggression the young Rumsfeld was feeling and inculcating a sense of discipline, had a profound impact on him. His take-no-prisoners style somehow suited Rumsfeld's own drive for the jugular. "Don now says that Coach Hurley turned his life around—not going down the wrong way but demanding discipline and output and so on," said Carolyn Twiname, a former classmate and lifelong friend.

The aggressiveness paid off. In Hurley's first year at New Trier—Rumsfeld's junior year—the high school took second in the state championship. The next year Rumsfeld not only starred on the team, wrestling in the 145-pound class, but served as cocaptain along with Vyskocil. That year also marked the most successful season up to that point for New Trier's varsity wrestling squad. The team swept the suburban league title and went on to take the state championship. In regular season, the squad never lost a single meet and was tied only once, in a match against Moline High School.

But there was one wrestler Rumsfeld had trouble beating: Fred Pearson, a trim, muscular, blond teenager from Tilden High School on Chicago's South Side. Pearson was a more experienced and more accomplished wrestler—he had won the state title his junior year. His style was less aggressive than Rumsfeld's but technically more proficient.

He and Rumsfeld squared off three times in 1950. The first was at a dual meet between the New Trier and Tilden teams, and Pearson beat Rumsfeld 10 to 6. By the state tournament in March—the climax of the wrestling season for suburban and downstate schools—tension had built over the rematch, which occurred in the semifinals. "They just both went out after each other, and it was really exciting," Nellis said. "These guys stalked each other on the mat like a couple of tigers. Neither backed down." Pearson was declared the winner, although New Trier disputed the call.

"The guy was a bull in a China shop," Pearson said of Rumsfeld years later. "But he wasn't a bull without logic. He was in great shape and a smart, capable guy."

Pearson and Rumsfeld locked bodies one last time, in a postseason tournament run by the Central Amateur Athletic Union on Chicago's South Side. There, Rumsfeld triumphed over his archrival, but lost a subsequent match to a five-time tournament champion. "Don was determined to be the best at everything, and he was going to get back at Pearson no matter what it took, and he finally did," Cunningham said. Several decades later, when Rumsfeld and Pearson met at a fund-raising dinner in Chicago, Pearson had virtually forgotten their last match. Rumsfeld never did.

———•———

As a wrestler, Rumsfeld was encouraged to spend a summer at Camp Owakonze on Baril Lake in Ontario, Canada, which was owned by New Trier's athletic director, Duke Childs. A number of New Trier's staff served as counselors, including Hurley and Pete Frantzen, the junior varsity football coach who also was Rumsfeld's adviser throughout high school. The camp lasted eight weeks and offered a rugged experience, filled with canoe trips, woodchopping, and the great outdoors. Against the rules, Rumsfeld sometimes smoked cigarettes; once he asked a younger camper, John Madigan, to hide a pack for him.

"There was an inspection when I wasn't in the cabin," Madigan recalled. "I came back and they told me they had found these and I was in serious trouble and they were going to take it up in the highest councils of the camp. I thought I was going to get sent home, but I didn't, I survived. I never ratted on Don. I've held it over him all these years." Madigan went on to become chairman and chief executive officer of the Tribune Company, on whose board of directors Rumsfeld subsequently served.

Madigan also remembered a canoe trip with Rumsfeld. "I was in his canoe, and he was paddling stern," he said. "We'd get exhausted paddling across these great lakes and stopped to rest maybe every fifteen or twenty minutes. One time as we were stopped, I felt the canoe wobble a little bit and turned around. Don had kicked up into a handstand, holding on to the gunnels of the canoe, which was fully loaded with gear and provisions and everything else. We were in the middle of the lake. It was incredible. That's Don—he didn't feel like resting; he'd rather do a handstand than sit."

Back at home in the summer of 1948 and spending a day at the Maple Street beach on Lake Michigan, Rumsfeld disregarded a No Diving sign and plunged from a pier. He hit a piling or a pipe, cutting his head and gashing his upper torso. "There was a very distinct sign there saying, 'No Diving.' You couldn't miss it," recalled Bill Ryno, a childhood friend. But Rumsfeld had been chasing after a girl. He emerged from the water gushing with blood—a frightening sight to his friends on the scene. He spent days recovering. All told, from the accident and a hernia operation that same summer, he received about one hundred stitches.

Rumsfeld's energetic, fun-loving side endeared him to many friends. For all his competitiveness and intensity, he got along well with peers. Widely known by his nickname "Rummy," he socialized easily, laughed readily, and emerged as one of the most popular students in his high school class.

John Griesser, who captained the football team senior year, remembered Rumsfeld not only as one of the most competitive people he had ever met, but also as someone who was always upbeat, who accepted people for who they were, and who would do anything for a friend. Another classmate, Betty Christian, explained Rumsfeld's appeal flat out: "He was good-looking, he had a great personality, and he was fun to be with."

Joyce Pierson started noticing Rumsfeld during sophomore year of high school. "I was aware that there was fascination or excitement around him and wherever he was," she recalled years later. "He definitely had a dazzle."

Joyce had moved to the North Shore area—a house in the suburb of Wilmette—in 1941 when she was nine years old. Her father, Red Pierson, worked for International Harvester as a sales executive and had shifted his family several times—from Montana to North Dakota to Minnesota to Wisconsin—before settling near corporate headquarters in Chicago.

Slender, blue-eyed, and bubbly, Joyce made friends easily and was popular in high school. "She was kind of a little pixie, always a smile on her face, always happy and good to everybody," recalled Barbara Mayberry, a close friend. In junior year, classmates elected Joyce secretary of the class and Rumsfeld vice president. The two started spending time together in meetings, planning a prom and other events. Joyce was dating a senior on the football team at the time, but the relationship was stormy.

After the summer, Rumsfeld returned to school determined to ask Joyce out. The first Saturday of their senior year, he took her to a play in Chicago. They started dating, but the relationship was stop-and-go, and by the second half of the year, Rumsfeld was going out with someone else. As dazzled as Joyce was by Rumsfeld, she also was wary of him because he had dated—and broken up with—a number of her close friends. "So mine was more of a defensive mode—it's not going to happen to me kind of thing," she recalled. "I was cautious."

Both continued to hold prominent positions in the class during senior year, Rumsfeld as vice president of the Tri-Ship Club, Joyce as head of the Girls Club's Friendly Committee. The committee's mission was to try to break through New Trier's thick network of cliques and include those left out. This kind of social outreach effort seemed to suit Joyce's personality and interests particularly well. Friends considered her typecast for the role—one she would find herself playing countless times by Rumsfeld's side later in life.

———•———

For all his popularity, there also was something that, to a number of his closer friends, appeared to set Rumsfeld apart. He was filled with goals, intense and inwardly driven. "He'd say things like, 'I want to accomplish something,'" Vyskocil recalled. "Don was serious. Even though he was like one of the guys all the time and dating and stuff, there was a very serious side to him. More so than anybody else I'd known."

Rumsfeld openly professed to friends that he intended to be president of the United States someday. Griesser recalled Rumsfeld saying so to a group of boys standing around in a school hallway. The words also stuck in Betty Christian's mind. "When he said that, he wasn't bragging, he wasn't boasting," she recounted. "It just was a statement about something that he was going to achieve. He believed in himself, and he had his mind set. You heard him and in the back of your mind you would think, It could very well be." Joyce said the idea of Rumsfeld becoming president was something they only joked about in high school. In any case, his comment revealed an early interest in public service. "The point is, he was thinking politics, governance, freedom, the country that he loved," she said.

Rumsfeld's image as a clean-cut superachiever was further burnished by a commitment to the Boy Scouts that continued through high school. He rose with a group of eight other boys—members of Explorer Post 25—to the top rank of Eagle Scout in his senior year. "We always were working on merit badges," said Ryno, another member of the group. "We went on campouts all around Illinois. It was a way to keep us out of trouble." Ryno credited a conscientious scoutmaster, Bob Levings, for holding the group together and pushing the boys along.

Rumsfeld once came close to giving up on scouting. At age twelve, after three years as a scout in Illinois, North Carolina, Washington State, and California, he had written his father, who was serving on an aircraft carrier in the Pacific, to say he wanted to quit.

"My dad sent a note back saying, 'That's fine, use your own judgment,'" Rumsfeld recalled in a speech years later. "Go ahead, it's your call. After all, quitting is easy. You can quit one thing, and then you can quit another, and then pretty soon you're a quitter. So you will have defined yourself not by what you've done, what you accomplish in life, but your decisions not to finish what you start."

"Well, even at age twelve, I got the message," Rumsfeld went on. "And I stayed in scouting. And it was one of the best decisions I've made."

For Rumsfeld, scouting became an affirmation not only of persevering and seeing something through to its end but also of honor and duty to God and country—values that carried over later into his military and government service. The experience also had a lasting impact on Rumsfeld in another, more tangible way by introducing him to a part of the United States where he would later sink roots. One summer he attended the Philmont Scout Ranch in Cimarron, New Mexico, and fell in love with the area—its wide-open spaces, rugged terrain, and natural beauty. Decades later, he returned to buy property in the state and made a farm just north of Taos a center of his family life.

———•———

When the time came to decide on college, Rumsfeld's parents hoped their son would pick a school close enough to home that they could attend his wrestling matches. A friend's father, who recruited athletes for the University of Michigan, tried to interest Rumsfeld in the school's wrestling program. But the dean of boys at New Trier was a graduate of Princeton and urged Rumsfeld to consider applying there.

Brad Glass, New Trier's star wrestler, had gone to Princeton. So had two other strong athletes in the class ahead of Rumsfeld—Ned Jannotta and Jim Otis. When the three returned home for winter break in late 1949, they conspired to persuade Rumsfeld to pick Princeton. "We definitely worked him over," Jannotta recalled. "I remember going to New Trier and collaring him in the hall; then we got the dean to give us a room, and the four of us went in and gave him a good pitch about Princeton."

Rumsfeld took a while to make up his mind. He had assumed he would end up wrestling at a Big Ten school, not in the Ivy League. "We had a hard time, it seemed, getting him to make the decision," Otis said. Ultimately, Rumsfeld picked Princeton. Decades later, he told an interviewer that he probably would not have gone to Princeton if it had not had a wrestling program.

He still had feelings for Joyce, or "Bird," as he called her. He had searched her out during the evening of graduation to give her a token of affection—a Boy Scout saddle ring from the West. Joyce carried a flame for Rumsfeld, too, but did not want to attend an eastern school just to be near him if it would mean always waiting for the phone to ring. Instead, she headed west to the University of Colorado along with several friends. "I just thought, Do your own thing," she recalled. In her copy of the New Trier yearbook, Rumsfeld wrote, "Have a good time in Colorado (that play school)."

———•———

In the 1950s Princeton still had many of the qualities of an exclusive, self-perpetuating club, its students drawn largely from wealthy families and boarding schools and its upperclassmen's social life dominated by a hierarchy of seventeen eating clubs. The college had begun a conscious effort after World War II to recruit students from the nation's public schools, but of the 770 men in Rumsfeld's entering class, more than 60 percent still came from prep schools.

As a public school graduate attending Princeton on a scholarship, Rumsfeld felt at a distinct disadvantage. "Back in my day," he told an interviewer, "an awful lot of people had gone to prep school, and the first year those people had taken most of the freshman courses by the time they got there. I hadn't." The transition to college life was not easy for him. "He was an unhappy camper for the first semester," Otis recalled. "He kidded us about the dirty trick we had played, telling him what a great place it was."

To make it through, Rumsfeld allowed himself few diversions, basically leading an intense, austere existence. "I worked hard," he recounted. "I was disciplined, and I managed my time. I got up early and worked and went to class and went to sports, whatever it was that season. And I didn't have any money, so I didn't have dates or anything like that. I had no reason not to be highly focused."

Darkening the outlook for many in Rumsfeld's class was the war in Korea, which had begun in the summer of 1950. Recruiters for the Reserve Officer Training Corps (ROTC) had little trouble meeting their quotas on college campuses amid the patriotic fervor of the period. Sometime in the fall of 1950, Rumsfeld decided to join the Naval ROTC, which provided more scholarship money than did the nonathletic scholarship he had secured from Princeton. But the program came with a major commitment, requiring him to attend training classes during the summers and three times each week, followed by three years of military service after graduation.

Rumsfeld made the decision to join over winter break when he was home with his family. Joyce was there, too, and they discussed it. "I remember him saying, 'This is a big decision,'" said Joyce, who went with him when he mailed the letter of commitment. "I remember that was one of the grown-up decisions where I was with him. He said, 'This means that three years after I graduate, I'm committed.'"

———·———

Rumsfeld eventually fell in with a group of roommates, all athletes, who formed a bond that lasted for decades afterward. There were three whose main sport was football (Richard Stevens, Somers Steelman, and Prewitt Turner), a couple of hockey players (Derek Price and Peter Gall), another couple of tennis players (Sidney Wentz and Michael Weatherly), and a baseball player (Joseph Castle).

They teased each other a lot. Rumsfeld, given his ancestry and his crew-cut look, got kidded about being a "tough German." Weatherly was "Mickman," reflecting his Irish roots. Wentz was "Bear," because, often slouching, he walked like one. Turner was dubbed "Sportyman," a name conveyed by his dad. Stevens was known as "the old philosopher," given his penchant for pulling classmates aside, dropping his voice, and imparting words of wisdom. And Steelman got called "Syd," a reference to a large black bull named Big Syd that he had tried to ride in a rodeo in Atlantic City when he was fourteen years old.

"There was camaraderie, but it was like in the Marine Corps—you couldn't be sensitive," Weatherly recalled. "You had to give as well as you could take. If anybody showed a weakness, he was in trouble. But we also loved each other. I can't remember a serious rift or fight among any of us the whole time."

Rumsfeld also knew how to put on a show for his roommates, becoming famous especially for one-armed push-ups. Stevens, who had seen Rumsfeld do fifty push-ups with his right arm, once bet him five dollars he couldn't do fifty push-ups with his left. Rumsfeld took the bet, did the fifty, then picked up the five dollars and walked out of the room.

"Rumsfeld was a very strong individual, and we used to brag about him," Steelman said. "Every now and then some character would come into the room and say, 'I'm here to see Rumsfeld do his one-handed pushups,' and we'd egg the guy on to put his money where his mouth was. Then Rumsfeld would proceed to take the money."

Rumsfeld is remembered by his roommates as someone who was fun to be around—upbeat, with a good sense of humor, a quick mind, and a big grin. But he remained highly disciplined, always conscious of certain limits. While some of his friends ventured on weekends to New York bars and dance halls, Rumsfeld did not go. He was not the late-night partying type. "Rumsfeld was never one to close the place up," Weatherly said. "He was not on the cutting edge of some crazy things we did. He was a conservative guy—a Midwestern boy, scholarship student, Naval ROTC."

There was also a seriousness about Rumsfeld, a sense of discipline laced with a deep strain of morality, that was striking even in his college days. "As close as we all were, there weren't any moments when Rummy let his guard down," Steelman said. "I mean, he was straight and stayed straight. He had very definite ideas as to right and wrong, and he never deviated. At that young age, a lot of us deviated."

Indeed, thinking back on it, Steelman saw a certain calculation in Rumsfeld's ability to keep such a tight hold on himself. "The guy was thinking," Steelman said. "Do you know what I mean? He wasn't the kind of guy who would stray off and say something or do something that would come back to haunt him. He had that instinct."

———◆———

Academically, Rumsfeld by his account maintained the equivalent of a B average in college. Friends confirmed that Rumsfeld, while not an academic star, did not appear to struggle in class. "He wasn't an intellectual giant but very determined. He was not going to get distracted," recalled Wentz, who met Rumsfeld in the Naval ROTC program and became one of his best friends at Princeton.

Rumsfeld did especially well in math. But he chose to major in politics, which was popular at the time and which he saw as permeating all aspects of life.

When asked years later about his college days, Rumsfeld had fond recollections of two professors: Walter P. "Buzzer" Hall, an authority on modern European history whose entertaining, demonstrative classroom style consistently made him one of the school's most popular lecturers, and Eric F. Goldman, also a historian and a popular lecturer, whose major work, *Rendezvous with Destiny*, a social history of the Progressive Era, was published in 1952 while Rumsfeld was at Princeton.

But for the most part, Rumsfeld recalled little about the courses he took as an undergraduate or the professors whose lectures he attended. He portrayed himself as often questioning what professors said in class and wondering, as he once told the *Princeton Alumni Weekly*, whether what he was hearing was the whole story. "I felt I learned as much or more from my peers and my individual study as I did from the faculty," he said. "Maybe that's a good thing. Maybe it's designed to be that way."

At the time, Rumsfeld characterized his own political leanings as independent, and Wentz remembered him as largely free of any political ideology. "He was not swayed by majority opinion," Wentz said in an interview. "Nor was he always one way or the other. I think he was his own man." That did not mean, however, that Rumsfeld lacked strong preferences for particular candidates or positions on tough issues. "We were both somewhat skeptical of the world, of heroes," Wentz said. "We used to have fairly vigorous debates. I was pro-Eisenhower because he was no-nonsense, but Rumsfeld liked Adlai Stevenson for his articulation, his ability to project ideas."

Rumsfeld was not politically active as an undergraduate. But he and his friends in the spring of their senior year were caught up, like much of the nation, in watching the televised Army-McCarthy hearings, the riveting showdown between the bullying Senator Joseph McCarthy from Wisconsin and the military officials he accused of protecting communists in their ranks. "We were just glued to it. It was so dramatic," he said, recalling his own antipathy toward McCarthy.

———— • ————

Rumsfeld's greatest success at Princeton came outside the classroom, in athletics. He played on the lightweight football team, limited to players weighing less than 150 pounds, and as a senior led it to its most successful season in years. But it was wrestling that remained his main interest in college, as it had been in high school.

The sport had a long if not particularly illustrious history at Princeton. Well into his second decade leading the program when Rumsfeld arrived, head coach Jimmy Reed had a rather mediocre record guiding the Tigers. But the team enjoyed its golden age during Rumsfeld's years there, boosted especially by the exceptional performance of Rumsfeld's high school friend Brad Glass, who became the first National Collegiate Athletic Association (NCAA) wrestling champion in the school's history.

True to form, Rumsfeld in his matches often relied on the fireman's carry. "He was very quick and quite smart, but he did do that carry on everybody—and it worked on almost everybody," said Carlton MacDonald Jr., a teammate. "I said to him once, 'I bet you can't do it on me.' And damn if he didn't. And I even knew he was going to do it!"

Rumsfeld reached his college wrestling peak in 1953, when as a junior he went undefeated during the regular season and rose to the finals of the Eastern Intercollegiate Wrestling Association meet, held that year at Princeton. In the final match, everybody had expected to see Cornell University's Ken Hunt, who had had an undefeated season, face off against Syracuse University's Ed Rooney, considered an excellent leg wrestler (someone who ties up opponents below the waist and then overpowers them). But Rumsfeld eliminated Rooney, 6 to 4, in the semis by getting ahead of him in points early, then keeping his distance and running out the clock.

In the championship bout later that night, it was Rumsfeld against Hunt, whose strategy was to bait Rumsfeld into making the first move. It worked. Rumsfeld "would go in for this so-called takedown, and see that he couldn't get it, and as he backed off, that's when I would go in and take him down with an ankle pickup," Hunt recalled in an interview with the *New Yorker* in 2003. "I took him down three times with that, and that was six points right off the bat." Still, Rumsfeld persisted. "I think I was ahead eight–zip or eight–two, and then I began to run out of gas. I had the feeling that he could taste blood, you know, if he could get me real tired—and I was getting tired," Hunt said. In the third and final period, Rumsfeld gained a few more points but came up short, losing 9 to 5.

Two weeks later, at the national NCAA tournament, Rumsfeld lost in the first round to Jim Ellis of Indiana University. Elected team captain in his senior year, Rumsfeld had another undefeated regular season but didn't manage to do as well in the regional competition as he had done the year before, finishing fourth.

Half a century after Rumsfeld's college wrestling days, Roger Olesen, an accomplished writer about wrestling, coauthored a book on the 1953 season titled *A Turning Point*. He offered a critical assessment of Rumsfeld's style, concluding that it had relied less on technical skill than on sheer bulldog grit. "They've always built Rumsfeld up as being a great wrestler," Olesen said. "But he wasn't. Rumsfeld, I think, was just a plugger. He would keep coming after you even when the final verdict was no longer in doubt."

———•———

Rumsfeld's senior thesis probed President Harry Truman's controversial attempt to forestall a 1952 steelworker's strike by nationalizing the nation's steel mills, and the U.S. Supreme Court's subsequent decision striking the act down as an abuse of executive power. In his conclusion, Rumsfeld endorsed the Court's decision to curb the president's emergency powers, although he threw in a realistic caveat, envisioning situations beyond a labor dispute where other rules might apply to presidential action. "There is much to be said for not tying the hands of the President unduly," he wrote. "No one wishes to injure adequate defense action in the event of an enemy attack or an emergency of similar gravity. But it must not be forgotten that the concept of emergency is elastic."

Still, Rumsfeld ended affirming the importance of limits. He noted that almost anyone could rise to the presidency, a fact he regarded as both good and bad. "With an eye toward its bad aspect, i.e., the Presidency may not always be occupied by a man intelligent enough to use his power sparingly, Jefferson had the correct answer 165 years ago, when he warned: 'In questions of power let no more be said of confidence in man, but bind him down from mischief by the chains of the Constitution.' Let us be thankful that we live in a land where we can demand of those in authority, 'Give an account of thy stewardship.'"

An idealistic speech delivered at Princeton in the spring of his senior year by Adlai E. Stevenson II made a lasting impression on Rumsfeld. At the time, the former governor of Illinois was between his two unsuccessful presidential campaigns, and he appeared reflective during his visit to his alma mater in March 1954. He used his visit to talk about the nature of the U.S. political system and the importance of individual action and involvement in the political process. Addressing the senior class banquet, Stevenson called on members of the class to apply their education to the nation's service.

"You dare not, if I may say so, withhold your attention," Stevenson said. "For if you do, if those young Americans who have the advantage of education, perspective and self-discipline, do not participate to the fullest extent of their ability, America will stumble, and if America stumbles, the world falls."

He spoke about the "broad responsibility" the students had "to protect and improve" what they had inherited and what they would be willing to fight and die to preserve—"the concept of government by consent of the governed as the only tolerable way of life." He observed that the United States had made a "magnificent gamble" in deciding that people should have an opportunity to help guide and direct the country's course. It was a gamble in the sense, he said, that it presumed free people would be able, given sufficient information, to make correct judgments. It also presumed that people would avail themselves of the opportunity to get involved in government affairs, either as active participants or as supporters or monitors of those who were in public life.

In later years, Rumsfeld frequently talked about the inspiration he had drawn from Stevenson's words and how the speech had contributed to his decision to enter government. Decades after he heard it, Rumsfeld could still quote passages from the address. What made a lasting impression was not only Stevenson's call to public service but his tone. Even as the Cold War was dawning, with its threat of nuclear war and sustained struggle against the Soviet Union, Stevenson sounded full of hope and promise.

"You live in a time of historic change and of infinite difficulty," he told the Princeton seniors in a passage Rumsfeld liked to cite. "But do not let the difficulties distract you. Face the problems of your time you must, deal with them you must. But do not allow the alarms and excursions and partisanship of our political scene to distract you. . . . Dare, rather, to live your lives fully, boldly; dare to study and to learn, to cultivate the mind and the spirit."

Rumsfeld stayed in touch with Joyce during their time in college, but they saw each other only intermittently, when both were at home for brief periods. They dated others, although according to his roommates, Rumsfeld did not pursue anyone else intently, whereas Joyce as early as sophomore year accepted a pin from a suitor, indicating a serious relationship. "A lot of guys at CU really thought Joyce was it. She was so darling," recalled Julie Sherman Whitaker, one of the half dozen or so girls from Joyce's New Trier class who joined her at the University of Colorado and in the Kappa Alpha Theta sorority there.

Reflecting Rumsfeld's hold on her mind and her heart, Joyce, who majored in art history, signed up for a couple of courses in U.S. political thought and U.S. foreign policy her senior year. "That's not usually what you take as an art history major," she said. "But in college, he had been writing to me or talking to me, putting thoughts out there that then became of interest to me." One book she recalled Rumsfeld recommending was *Man's Fate*, by André Malraux, a novel about the early days of the Chinese Revolution focusing on the intertwining plights of several characters and their life-and-death struggles. "That was one of his favorite books," Joyce said. Another, by Rumsfeld's account, was Benjamin Franklin's autobiography.

Just before the start of his senior year, Rumsfeld had come out to Boulder, Colorado, to visit Joyce. She then went to Princeton in the spring. "He was writing his thesis and studying for his comprehensives," she recalled. "And so my five days at Princeton, I would go to the library, and he and his friends had a special little study carrel that they would put me in and close the door. Then someone would come and open my door and say, Now you can come and have lunch. So I'd go out and then I would come back to the carrel, same thing, all afternoon. Then they'd let me out again and I'd have dinner. I read five books.

"The pressure of all those guys, the intensity of their study, was fierce. But it was the first time that I had met his gang. I was intimidated, no question. They were just kind of circling, waiting for me. And a lot of teasing. They were funny. They were very close. They were trying to pretend that they weren't scared to death about not graduating. One of them always had the newspaper in front of his books to pretend that he was casual. But they were all under a lot of pressure."

Because the visit went well, Rumsfeld suggested she come back for his graduation. But there was another boyfriend in the picture in Colorado. Joyce intended to move to Chicago after her college graduation, as did her boyfriend. "He was determined," Joyce said. "Even knowing all about Don, he was sure that he was going to win out."

Worried about losing Joyce, Rumsfeld made up his mind by the time of his graduation to ask her to marry him. His roommate Stevens recalled Rumsfeld being intent on tidying up his room before she arrived. "He said, 'I'm going to get engaged but I want to go into this thing the right way,'" Stevens said. "There was all this discipline, all this focus."

Decades later, recalling the moment that Rumsfeld proposed, Joyce searched a bit for the words to describe the event. "He was sure I wouldn't be around much longer, I think, so he was almost mad when he said do you think we should get married or something. He said let's just not continue whatever it was. We were probably taking a walk. I mean, it was just—let's just—it was more matter of fact. So we got engaged, set a date."

Joyce also remembered breaking the news to the Colorado boyfriend. "I wired him and said, This is hard to believe but I'm engaged to the guy who was paying no attention to me for four years. I do remember being panicked that he was going to move before I could get word to him."

Rumsfeld waited to present an engagement ring until he and Joyce returned to Illinois a short time later. "He wanted to wait so I'd be with my parents and he could talk to them and acknowledge what was up," Joyce said. "My parents were stunned. They loved him, but, you know, the storminess of it—no one could figure out if we were together or not. So the fact we were engaged was just a big surprise, I think, to everyone.

"It was just a funny relationship," she went on. "The reality, the bottom line is, I would never have married anyone until he married someone other than me. That had already been fixed in my mind, which shows how crazy I was. I think he thought, Well, this isn't the ideal time. I mean, he would have loved to have a few more years as a bachelor. But he thought, Gee, I'm not going to wake up some day and say why didn't you act faster or sooner. So his was more of an intellectual decision, not knowing that I would have waited."

As Rumsfeld took leave of Princeton, he looked forward to getting married and to serving several years in the Navy. Beyond that, he expected to attend law school. His mother had always wanted him to be a lawyer.

All in all, the Princeton experience had been a positive one for him. He had performed ably in class, excelled in wrestling, and made a number of lifelong friends. But Rumsfeld never overcame the early sense of economic and class division he had felt his freshman year. Even after ending up a member of Cap and Gown, one of Princeton's top-tier eating clubs, Rumsfeld carried a certain lingering disdain of Ivy Leaguers and of the eastern establishment elite. "He'd call them 'reversible names'— people with initials and all that kind of stuff," said Ken Adelman, who met Rumsfeld in Washington in the late 1960s and became a close friend. "We talked about that hundreds of times."

Joyce acknowledges that her husband has harbored a strong aversion to elitism and privilege. "Don always says he went to Princeton on a scholarship," she remarked when asked about this bias. "So he's got that edge. He is wary of those who think they're better."

CHAPTER 2

Developing His Own Tune

Commissioned an ensign after graduation, Rumsfeld in October 1954 reported to Pensacola, Florida, for basic training to become a Navy pilot. He had all the makings of a hotshot aviator—excellent coordination, good judgment, fighting edge, and self-confidence. He trained in an SNJ, a propeller-driven aircraft, and dreamed of earning an assignment flying jets off an aircraft carrier. Such coveted positions went to the Navy's best pilots, and Rumsfeld clearly stood out among his peers. "Coordination was required—a lot of the tests they gave us were based on coordination—and if anybody was coordinated, it was Rummy," recalled Alan Halkett, a UCLA graduate who was in Rumsfeld's pilot-training class.

Rumsfeld completed the basic flight-training course faster than anyone in his group, rushing ahead to conduct carrier-qualifying flights on the USS *Monterey* before the ship was mothballed. (At that time, primary-training students had to complete six landings on an aircraft carrier.) But Rumsfeld never got his wish for a carrier assignment. The Navy sent him instead to fly seaplanes. "I was about as disappointed as any human being could be," he remarked years later during an interview.

It is not clear from the information available whether Rumsfeld's assignment reflected some lack of ability to qualify for carrier duty or simply the luck of the draw. His contemporaries certainly remember him as an excellent pilot, with not only the skills but the tough attitude for at-tack aircraft. "Flying attack jets was a glamour assignment that took an aggressive personality," said Charles Kinnaird, now a Detroit attorney who graduated with Rumsfeld from Princeton and attended flight train-ing with him. "Rummy had that."

It could be that the Navy simply had an urgent need to fill other slots when Rumsfeld's name came up. But other Navy veterans from that period say the service was always ready to place its top pilots in carrier aircraft, and if Rumsfeld really had been a superior aviator, he would have ended up flying jets at sea.

In any case, Rumsfeld's disappointment soured him on the idea of making a career of military service, which he had seriously considered. Had he become a carrier pilot, he might well have made a long-term commitment to the Navy. "I think he would have stayed in," Joyce said, recalling her husband's early career. "But all of a sudden he was flying these huge seaplanes. It just wasn't a fit for him."

Rumsfeld spent six months in advanced training in Corpus Christi, Texas, earning his wings in January 1956. Worried then about being shunted off to seaplane duty for an extended period, he applied to re-turn to Pensacola as a flight instructor. "It was the only way to avoid going to a seaplane squadron," said Walt Halperin, who went through training with him.

Before heading back to Florida, Rumsfeld, who had not given up on his wrestling after donning a military uniform, moved to Norfolk, Vir-ginia, to train on the Navy's wrestling team. He won an All-Navy cham-pionship title in 1956 at 147 pounds, earning him a chance to compete in Annapolis, Maryland, for a spot in the group the Navy would be send-ing to U.S. Olympic team tryouts.

But there again, disappointment struck. During a workout match, he separated his shoulder. The injury was serious enough to force him to drop out of the competition. Even had he remained healthy, there was no guarantee Rumsfeld would have made the cut for the Olympic team. Joseph Gattuso, the three-time eastern collegiate champ whom Rumsfeld was wrestling at the time of the shoulder accident, remembers him as a "spunky" and skillful wrestler, although not one of the best in the group.

In any case, with his wrestling days over, Rumsfeld returned to Pen-sacola in May to teach flying. The job proved to be a challenging test of patience. "He taught formation flying, and every morning he would say, 'Today, I'm not going to scream,'" Joyce recalled. "You have four people in four planes who don't know how to do it, and you're in a chase plane. So he would come home at three or four in the afternoon after an early-morning launch, just barely able to talk. They all would talk with their hands saying, you know, this is what happened, this guy went this way and that guy went that way."

Accidents were a constant worry, especially for spouses on the ground. "In those Navy years, in that three-year period, we lost fifteen really close friends in crashes and training accidents," Joyce remembered. "There'd be a crash, you'd hear the sirens. The minute you'd hear them, the wives, without saying a word, would just stop what they were doing and head home. Two different times the chaplain came down our walk and went to a neighbor. They'd come down the walk and you'd think they're coming to you."

The pilots tended to deal with the danger stoically. At Saufley Field, where Rumsfeld flew, a huge sign in the hangar stated matter-of-factly, "A mid-air collision can spoil your whole day."

Rumsfeld had his own close call once while on a night flight over the Gulf of Mexico from Key West to Corpus Christi in a twin-engine seaplane. It was his final flight as a student pilot, and Rumsfeld was looking forward to receiving his wings the next day. Suddenly, one of the engines failed, and the plane began descending. Rumsfeld and other crew members struggled to jettison everything they could—suitcases, fuel, radar equipment—to lighten the aircraft in hopes of regaining some altitude. Finally, as Rumsfeld recalls, the aircraft leveled off at about nine hundred feet, and they managed to reach a military landing field near Lake Pontchartrain in Louisiana.

Like many young military pilots, Rumsfeld exuded great confidence in his own ability—a characteristic that never seemed to wane through the rest of his life. "Self-assurance, he always had that," Halperin recalled. "Someone else might say cocky. It bordered on that. But he was such a good-natured, happy guy, so much fun, that it didn't bother you that he had that side to his personality, being overly self-assured."

Indeed, Halperin and his wife Willa, who socialized often with the Rumsfelds in those days, remember many enjoyable times. They golfed together, went to the beach, fished. Once, they rented a plane and all went flying, the Halperins seated up front and the Rumsfelds behind.

It was a period in their lives when none of them had much, when they were just starting out. Living conditions on the base were spartan in small, concrete-block houses. "I remember Rummy coming over once, and we ate dinner on an ironing board in our bedroom because it was the only room that was air-conditioned," Willa said. "Nobody lived lavishly."

Before long, too, they all were learning to be parents together as children started to come into the picture. The Rumsfelds welcomed Valerie, their firstborn, in 1956. Their futures were ahead of them.

In November 1957, Rumsfeld left Pensacola and active-duty Navy service. Explaining his reasons for moving on, Rumsfeld told an interviewer later that after three years as a "damn good" Navy pilot, he didn't want to spend the rest of his life being "just another chauffeur" in a military plane.

Acting on an interest in politics that dated back to his college days, he went to Washington looking for a job on Capitol Hill. As he tells the story, he just "knocked on doors" until he found a congressman willing to hire him. He says he had never met a congressman or any politician before that.

Rumsfeld first visited Congress in the late 1930s with his parents. In 1954 he returned with Joyce while in Washington to attend a friend's wedding. They went to the Senate gallery and, by Rumsfeld's account, saw Carl Hayden of Arizona dozing in the majority leader's chair and Wayne Morse of Oregon talking about music to an empty chamber. "I was so excited to be there," Rumsfeld recalled. "And I said to Joyce, 'Isn't that thrilling?' And she said, 'I think you're a little strange.'"

The tale allows him to highlight his own early enthusiasm for one of Washington's great centers of power while also portraying Congress as less than it's cracked up to be. That's certainly how Rumsfeld came to view it over time, although at the outset he just wanted very much to be part of the action.

For him to show up on the doorstep in hopes of just knocking and being let in suggests no small measure of nerve. But chances are he didn't arrive as a total walk-in. His search was likely facilitated by his network of Princeton and Navy connections. So, too, his wrestling background appears to have factored into the decision by David Dennison, a first-term Republican congressman from Ohio's Eleventh District, to hire Rumsfeld as an administrative assistant.

"He had been a wrestler in college, and I had been a wrestler, and he hired me because I had been a wrestler," Rumsfeld recounted once. "I mean, that's how life works. It had nothing to do with my ability to work in his office and do the things he wanted."

A lawyer and former special assistant to Ohio's attorney general, the thirty-nine-year-old Dennison was an especially active first-term member. He championed the first comprehensive federal employee's training bill, supported improvements in the postal service, and promoted pensions for government employees. He also helped reunite a number of separated immigrant families and gave a speech in the House on civil rights that attracted favorable notice from President Dwight Eisenhower. For voters back home, Dennison was at the forefront of efforts to improve Lake Erie harbors in his district.

Until then, Rumsfeld's exposure to politics had been limited to what he had studied in school or watched from afar. He found immersion in Congress overwhelming and excruciating. "Going from being a naval aviator to an administrative assistant to a congressman from Ohio was one of the most wrenching experiences of my lifetime," Rumsfeld said in an interview with Pentagon historians. "I didn't know how to write press releases or radio programs, do legislative research, work in an office, manage a campaign. It was all new and terribly difficult for me. It took an enormous amount of effort and application and hours and anguish trying to do it well."

Complicating matters, Rumsfeld had to manage initially without his wife and daughter at his side. They had remained in Chicago, where Joyce spent months recuperating from hepatitis contracted around the time of the move from Pensacola.

Rumsfeld's family caught up with him in Ohio in 1958 as he was managing Dennison's reelection campaign. The congressman had some strong local support, including an endorsement from the *Warren Tribune Chronicle.* "No member of Congress has been busier or more active in the interest of his district, state and nation than Mr. Dennison in his first two years in the House of Representatives," the paper said. "His diligence has attracted the favorable attention not only of his own constituents but of his colleagues in the national legislature and top political personalities in both parties."

But Dennison faced an uphill fight against a local county attorney, Robert E. Cook, due in large part to a controversial ballot item. A proposal for a constitutional amendment that would ban compulsory union shops had riled the labor unions and triggered a surge in registration of Democratic voters. That didn't bode well for the Republican Dennison.

A whiff of scandal also enveloped Dennison when he was accused of having put his father and his wife on his congressional office payroll. Rumsfeld insists there was nothing to the story. He says Dennison's wife had worked in the office, but only for a few months to fill the gap between the departure of Rumsfeld's predecessor and Rumsfeld's arrival. Dennison's dad had been hired for just a month or two to conduct a study. Nonetheless, the family payroll cases dogged Dennison. The existence of several other scandals involving Republican candidates in neighboring states didn't help Dennison either.

Dennison lost by 967 votes out of a total of 157,969 cast—an extremely narrow defeat that hit Rumsfeld hard. The controversy over Dennison's hiring of family members had made an especially deep impact on the young congressional aide. It prompted Rumsfeld to promise himself to avoid even the appearance of financial impropriety in his own dealings—something he went to considerable lengths to do in the high-level positions he held later in both government and business.

With Dennison out, Rumsfeld returned to Capitol Hill and took a job on the staff of another Republican congressman, Robert Griffin of Michigan, whose office was down the hall from where Dennison's had been in the Cannon House Office Building. Himself a rising star in Congress, Griffin saw promise in Rumsfeld as an intelligent, quick-to-learn staff member. The connection with Griffin would prove exceptionally important as Rumsfeld's own political career developed later.

For now, Rumsfeld concentrated on learning more about the inside operations of Congress. He also began night school at Georgetown University, studying for a law degree. It was something his mother had hoped he might pursue, and he figured a legal education would facilitate his work on legislation. "I wanted to learn the language of law," he told an interviewer. "It bothers me if I don't know the language people about me are speaking." His family also was expanding with the birth in 1960 of a second daughter, Marcy.

But later that year, Dennison, having decided on a comeback effort, appealed to Rumsfeld to help run another campaign. Reluctantly, Rumsfeld agreed, only to witness his candidate again go down in defeat, unable to overcome the coattails effect in Ohio of the presidential campaign of John F. Kennedy. "I remember seeing Rumsfeld when he was helping Dennison in Ohio, and he was complaining there were Kennedys all over the place," Kinnaird said. "He gave me the impression it was an uphill battle against those glamorous types."

After Dennison's second disappointing loss, Rumsfeld moved with Joyce and their two daughters back to the Chicago area to bide his time until his own run for political office. While in Ohio, he had enrolled at Case Western Reserve University to continue his legal education. But in Chicago, drawing on contacts with childhood friends, he lined up a job as a securities salesman with a financial brokerage firm, A. G. Becker and Company, and dropped his plans to earn a law degree.

Rumsfeld had no intention at that point of pursuing a career up some corporate ladder. His ambition was still centered on government service, which was clear in a conversation that Michael Weatherly, a Princeton classmate, recalls having around that time with Rumsfeld and another classmate, Dick Stevens.

"I was in the advertising business, and Stevens was with IBM," Weatherly said. "I remember Rumsfeld asking us what our goals were. Stevens said he wanted to make branch manager, and I said I wanted to make money. Rumsfeld said our goals were so shallow and so different from his. 'That's not what it's about, it's about contributing,' he said." Stevens, when asked about that conversation years later, had no recollection of it but said it sounded like Rumsfeld. "He would take you to task," Stevens remarked.

Rumsfeld did not have to wait long for an opening to get back into politics. In 1961, Republican congresswoman Marguerite Stitt Church, who had represented Rumsfeld's hometown district on Chicago's North Shore for a decade, decided not to seek another term. A lawyer named Marion Burks, who was a state representative with a conservative voting record, quickly emerged as the Republican front-runner, but others also started entering the race for the GOP nomination. Rumsfeld saw his chance.

The Thirteenth District was a mix of older shoreline communities and small inland townships that together formed a reliably Republican voting base with a strong conservative bent. It was largely a bedroom district, with the highest median income and lowest rate of unemployment in the nation. It also vied with two other districts (in California and Virginia) for having the highest median level of education.

That a twenty-nine-year-old first-timer like Rumsfeld could take the Republican Party's nomination ahead of more-seasoned, better-known candidates seemed a long shot. Although he had grown up in the area, Rumsfeld had been gone for ten years. He lacked political or social standing in the community. Nonetheless, Rumsfeld felt he had to try. "Immediately Don decided to run for that office, knowing that unless he took advantage of the opportunity, it would be years before such a chance would happen again," his father later explained in a letter to friends.

Building a political organization from scratch, Rumsfeld tapped into his old network of schoolmates in the area. "We were at a Christmas party at his house," John Mabie said. "He called a bunch of us into his den and said, 'I'm going to run for Congress. Will you guys support me?' We said, 'Sure!' I then told my father, who said, 'You're crazy, he's got no chance.'"

As new as Rumsfeld was to the political game, his friends had even less experience. Rumsfeld at least had spent a little time as a congressional aide and had helped manage two election campaigns in Ohio. His friends were just getting started in their own nonpolitical careers. "The idea of him getting elected was like trying to climb the Empire State Building. In my mind, it looked impossible," said Jim Otis, who was among those enlisted early.

But what Rumsfeld and his friends lacked in experience, they more than made up for with enthusiasm. The underdog nature of the campaign served to give it a what-have-we-got-to-lose spirit, galvanizing the group. "We were all so young then and so enthusiastic and thought we could do almost anything, so we went charging into it," Carolyn Twiname said.

Ned Jannotta signed on as campaign manager, Brad Glass as treasurer. Rumsfeld's dad offered a house in Winnetka for use as a campaign headquarters. Rumsfeld's mother spent all her spare time clipping newspapers for articles about all the issues and about the activities of his opponent. His sister handled bookkeeping of bills and donations.

One of Rumsfeld's biggest hurdles was his age. His brush cut and boyish appearance didn't help. "He looked like he wasn't old enough to vote, let alone be a congressman," Jannotta said. But Rumsfeld sought to turn his youth to an advantage. "If elected, at age thirty, I would have enough years ahead that I could achieve the seniority necessary to move into a position of major responsibility in the Congress," he said in a statement announcing his candidacy. A campaign flyer portrayed him as representing "new hope for the Republican party" and "new vigor for the challenges that confront us at home and abroad."

On the issues, Rumsfeld struck broad conservative themes. There were many subjects on which he had not yet formed strong opinions, but he positioned himself in the Republican mainstream. He warned against the "pressing dangers of communism." He touted a strong U.S. military. He opposed "stifling taxation and federal domination of farming, education, medical care and urban affairs."

His main pitch focused less on issues than on presenting himself as a bright, honest, hardworking young man who would be a very good representative for the district. Campaign photos showed him as a family man, with Joyce and their daughters—Valerie, six, and Marcy, two. Other photos highlighted his continued military connection, featuring him in a flight jacket climbing into a plane as a Navy reservist flying with an antisubmarine squadron. (As a reservist, he piloted the S2F Tracker, a propeller-driven, twin-engine antisubmarine aircraft with a crew of four.)

He also tapped into congressional ties established during his days in Washington. Dennison and Griffin both wrote endorsements. Bob Michel, then a congressman from Peoria, Illinois, and later minority leader, posed for a photo with Rumsfeld. The two had come to know each other when both were administrative assistants on Capitol Hill.

Rumsfeld's first speeches to voters revealed a poor public speaking style. He slouched, lacked force, mumbled, and stumbled. Using a school auditorium, his top campaign aides put Rumsfeld on a stage one day and ran through a tough, blunt critique. "Get your chin up! Don't lean on the podium! Smile! Don't tail off your sentences—you've got to wind up strong!" he was instructed. As Jannotta recalled, the sessions, which lasted for hours, were "brutal," but they "paid huge dividends."

———•———

Rumsfeld campaigned tirelessly. He went to train stations in the North Shore area at dawn to stand on railway platforms shaking hands. He attended countless coffee sessions in private houses to discuss issues. He looked for endorsements wherever he could—area newspapers, local politicians, community business leaders. His small army of volunteers learned the tactics of grassroots movements, putting up signs in yards and atop cars, passing out "Rumsfeld for Congress" matchbooks, sealing envelopes and licking stamps, soliciting funds, and making phone calls.

They could not count on much help from local Republican committeemen or the local GOP's built-in organization. "We didn't know any of the committeemen, we didn't even know what they did," Mabie said. And when they went to meet them, they often got a cold shoulder. "I remember one committeeman saying to Don, 'Sonny, why don't you come back in another ten years,'" Jannotta recalled.

They had an easier time initially wooing some prominent businessmen, using Princeton ties and their parents' connections. Backers included senior executives from Quaker Oats, American Hospital Supply, G. D. Searle, Jewel Food Stores, ACNielsen, Motorola, and Abbott Laboratories. With their support came funds and enhanced respectability for Rumsfeld.

"We did very well with the business community, particularly older business leaders in Winnetka," Jannotta said. "In many ways, senior businesspeople were easier to sell than Rumsfeld's contemporaries because senior businesspeople could see the potential in him, and the district had a history of long-serving representatives. They were particularly attracted to a guy who might be there for a long time, might become speaker of the House."

Twiname's dad, Harold Anderson, who headed the Publishers Newspaper Syndicate that distributed columns, comics, and Gallup poll results, was particularly helpful. He served as a kind of senior adviser to the campaign and used his newspaper links to draw press attention to Rumsfeld, most notably by the *Chicago Sun-Times*. The paper, in an editorial two and a half months before the April 1962 primary, assured voters that Rumsfeld was conservative enough to represent his district. "Rumsfeld's Republicanism is sound," the paper said. "He isn't an extremist. He is what is best described as an intelligent conservative."

With about nine candidates in the race, the field was crowded. As his candidacy gained momentum, Rumsfeld persuaded several competitors to drop out, arguing that he had the best chance of beating the main contender, Burks. Church herself, while declining to endorse anyone, hinted in mid-February that she favored Rumsfeld, saying, "If the Republican party needs anything, it is youth."

Then Rumsfeld caught a lucky break. A story in the *Sun-Times* reported financial irregularities in an insurance firm linked to Burks. The article revealed that months before Burks had entered the congressional race, the state insurance director had quietly reported more than $1.5 million diverted in questionable ways at Central Casualty Company, a five-year-old firm that Burks had helped promote and where he had served as general counsel and then chairman of the board before becoming a candidate in December 1961. The company's financial affairs were so tangled that the only solution appeared liquidation, the state director had concluded.

Burks had no direct financial responsibility for the firm, and state officials were not suggesting he had done anything illegal. Burks maintained that he had known nothing about the financial dealings at issue. But his high-level position in the company, and his role lending his name and prestige to it, cast doubt on his claims.

Burks's campaign manager called the story a "campaign smear" and portrayed it as a "smoke screen" intended to obscure Rumsfeld's inexperience. Rumsfeld and his aides denied any role in planting the story with the *Sun-Times*, and no evidence has since emerged to contradict that. Indeed, some suspected at the time that the story had originated with Burks's other political enemies, notably, committeemen in the townships resentful of the older shoreline communities where Burks drew his principal support.

The fight for the GOP nomination grew increasingly bitter as Republican organizations in the district split between Rumsfeld and Burks. Then, a month before the primary vote, the *Sun-Times* dropped a new bombshell in the insurance case that all but sank Burks.

On March 9, 1962, the paper printed a copy of a Central Casualty check for $200,000 signed by Burks in 1960 to an Evanston bank. The paper also reported another check for $100,000 that Burks had signed. The existence of the two checks contradicted earlier claims by Burks that he had lacked authority to sign company checks for substantial amounts.

When Burks saw the *Sun-Times* report, he initially had no recollection of the checks, but then subsequently discovered that he really had signed them. He said he had forgotten because the checks "were written into the company instead of out of it," representing money from new stock issues sold by Central Casualty and transferred from a stock fund to the company's general fund. Support for Burks quickly eroded. By primary day, he was able to garner only 27 percent of the vote. Rumsfeld won easily with 68 percent.

The allegations against Burks later proved unfounded, and Burks went on to serve as a respected circuit court judge. During the campaign, Rumsfeld had never actually mentioned the purported scandal. He had left it to his operatives, who showed up in places where Burks spoke and tossed questions at him. Years later, Rumsfeld acknowledged that Burks had been wrongly accused. Still, he said, the episode drove home to him the importance of living a life above reproach. "I learned from the incident and from other political errors of the time," he stated. "You had to conduct your affairs in life so they didn't erode your professional efforts."

As the GOP candidate in a heavily Republican district, Rumsfeld went on to capture the general election in November with little problem, winning by a vote of 134,442 to 73,998. Improbable as his candidacy had been at the start, Rumsfeld's come-from-behind victory shook up the area's political establishment and introduced the young, brash, ambitious new congressman as a force to be reckoned with. It also had a significant impact on the lives of a number of Rumsfeld's friends, who had come together in the campaign and achieved something few had thought possible.

"We took a sleepy Republican organization and put some life into it," said Otis, looking back on it all years later. "And it was fun, we really had a good time. Winning the election was a wonderful moment. It was the first thing we ever did that we accomplished all together. It cemented a lot of friendships, not just with Don but with lots of people."

———•———

Rumsfeld's election from the staid, bedrock North Shore was seen as an anomaly. A dissertation written soon afterward by a doctoral candidate in the Chicago area argued that each congressional district produces a perfectly predictable member of Congress. Rumsfeld, the paper went on, represented an exception to the rule, because he was distinguished principally by his total lack of social, financial, or political standing in the community. Rumsfeld received a copy of the paper and, as he tells the story, woke up Joyce as he read it in bed.

"Listen to this," he said to her. "It's terrible."

"Go back to sleep, Don," Joyce replied. "It's tough to argue with."

But Rumsfeld would show himself to be a significant player in Congress. Even before the new congressional session got under way, he turned up in the middle of the political maneuvering for GOP House leadership positions. A group of younger members led by Griffin, Mel Laird of Wisconsin, and Charles Goodell of New York were vying for a larger role in the party's hierarchy and had a plan to unseat Charles Hoeven of Iowa as chairman of the Republican Conference, the third-ranking post in the House Republican leadership. Griffin phoned Rumsfeld and asked if he would organize freshman congressman behind another candidate, Gerald Ford of Michigan, who was seen as more amiable and more open to change. Rumsfeld knew Ford from his earlier time on the Hill, and Ford had campaigned for him. "We looked to Don to bring along the new members," Griffin recalled in an interview. "I had worked with Don and knew a lot about him. He was eager and willing to provide leadership."

The plotters kept their efforts secret until the day of the Republican Conference, then sprang their coup and elected Ford, 87 to 76. Other old-guard leaders held on to their positions—Charles Halleck of Indiana as minority leader and Les Arends of Illinois as GOP whip. But the rebels had won their first major victory. The disgruntled Hoeven told reporters that he was "the scapegoat and fall-guy" of liberal Republicans who were determined to take over the leadership. "You'd better be careful," he warned Halleck. Ford has "just taken my job, and the next thing you know he'll be after yours."

The episode catapulted Rumsfeld to the top of the freshman class of the Eighty-eighth Congress, with a reputation as an energetic reformer. He held regular meetings with his cohorts and some of the party's ranking figures and became identified with a bloc of a dozen or so youthful GOP congressmen who viewed Congress as moribund and were intent on making a difference.

"That congressional class was full of guys with high motivation," said Barbara Ludden, who had worked for Church before Rumsfeld hired her to be his administrative assistant. "These weren't guys who had been precinct captains and other jobs in the party and then got supported to run. These were guys who really felt they'd make a difference when they came to Washington. They came in with high ideals and with an idea that it was time for a change, and I don't mean just a political or party change, but a change in the institution."

Laird, who had entered Congress at Rumsfeld's age a decade earlier, offered the young Illinois lawmaker some advice. "I told him, 'Keep your head down for a while and just get acquainted and be careful your first year,'" Laird recalled.

Indeed, Rumsfeld still even looked too young to be in Congress. "He didn't look much older than some of the page boys flitting down the aisles," noted a *Chicago Tribune* reporter. There "lingered about him the fresh, eager, crew-cut appearance of a college graduate applying for his first job."

On many issues, Rumsfeld shared the views of other young Republican conservatives in the House at the time. Most of them had come to maturity in the shadow of the Korean War and found a world menaced by communist imperialism. They also had inherited a nation with constantly rising taxes, mounting public debt, and an increasingly powerful government bureaucracy. Almost all had small children and were determined to give them a better world in which to live. They were fiercely anticommunist and were stoutly opposed to deficit spending. They objected to federal domination of farming, education, medical care, power resources, and urban affairs as a threat to freedom and economic growth.

But Rumsfeld also had a deep reformist streak, one that would drive him time and again during his life to shake things up in places he landed, whether in government or corporate America. To a degree, he was simply wired to be restless and dissatisfied with the status quo. He even described himself, years later, as "genetically impatient." Congress just happened to be his first target.

Some around him at the time also sensed about Rumsfeld a deep streak of independence and inner direction. He was on a mission that served his nation but was still very much his own. "From the very beginning, Don wasn't marching to the drummer out ahead," Ludden said. "He was developing his own tune and was going to march to that. It just took him a while to get it sorted out."

———•———

When committee assignments were handed out, Rumsfeld received a spot on the Science and Astronautics panel—not exactly the sort of positioning he had hoped for. The science committee was not considered a launch pad for great legislative careers. "I think he would have preferred to be on Ways and Means or Armed Services," Ludden said. But the crusty, aged leaders still in charge of GOP power levers in the House were wary of the obstreperous, brash troublemaker from Chicago's North Shore and were not ready to do him any favors.

In any case, Rumsfeld was determined to make the most of his opportunities and used his posting on the committee to delve into the U.S. space program. As a Navy flier, he felt a certain kinship with astronauts. "It became a little family joke between him and Joyce—that if he weren't a member of Congress, he'd like to be an astronaut," Ludden said.

At the time, the U.S. space effort was focused on putting a man on the moon. By the summer of 1963, Rumsfeld was complaining on the House floor that the military's role in space had been neglected. While the U.S. program aimed for outer space, he warned, the Soviets sought to dominate "inner space"—that is, the area within five hundred miles of the surface of the earth.

With a group of five other junior committee members, Rumsfeld called for a special congressional panel to reevaluate the nation's goals in space. He also sought to curtail what he considered spending excesses in the space budget, winning passage on the House floor of two cost-cutting amendments that went against the recommendations of more-senior party members.

On other occasions, Rumsfeld wasn't averse to using his influence over the space budget to obtain some good, old-fashioned pork for North Shore–area voters. He won approval in March 1964 to give the space agency $4.5 million—more than twice as much as it had asked for—to conduct research into the problem of aircraft noise, a measure of particular interest to his constituents living near Chicago's O'Hare Airport. He also fought, unsuccessfully, to get a new $60 million electronics-research center switched from Boston to Chicago, complaining that the government's research dollars were flowing largely to the East and West coasts.

Overall, Rumsfeld's first-term voting record remained predictably conservative. He advocated military superiority, chastised the Soviets, touted the virtues of fiscal responsibility, and supported programs that emphasized individual responsibility. Such positions earned him a 100 percent rating from the conservative Americans for Constitutional Action. The liberal Americans for Democratic Action gave him a meager 4 percent.

In his zeal, though, to demonstrate his conservative credentials, Rumsfeld erred in a way that would later cause him regret. It led him into a hurtful and embarrassingly erroneous public denunciation of Paul Nitze, one of the Cold War's leading strategists.

In 1963, during Rumsfeld's first year in Congress, Nitze was nominated to be secretary of the Navy, and Rumsfeld, searching for ways of attacking the Kennedy administration as soft on defense, thought he had found a target in Nitze and what appeared, to the young congressman at least, to be an obscure but damning report in Nitze's past. The report was the product of a conference sponsored five years earlier by the National Council of Churches, and it criticized the Eisenhower administration for dragging its feet in pursuit of "the goal of universal disarmament," urging greater reliance on the United Nations and more intense, sincere negotiation with the Soviet Union.

Although Nitze had argued against many of the points in the report, Rumsfeld used it to portray him as dangerously naive in confronting communism. The allegations should have been dismissed as absurd given Nitze's hawkish credentials—among them, authorship of two highly influential government papers in the 1950s, NSC-68 and the Gaither Report, playing up the Soviet threat and advocating a U.S. military buildup.

But those documents, still classified, were not widely known, and Richard Russell, chairman of the Senate Armed Services Committee, picked up Rumsfeld's argument and pressed Nitze on whether he favored a "policy of appeasement." The nomination nearly went down in defeat, passing only at President Lyndon Johnson's urging after President Kennedy's assassination. Years later, Rumsfeld, by then an admirer of Nitze, apologized to him for the episode, but Nitze never quite got over the insult of having had his reputation impugned during the confirmation process.

As much as Rumsfeld sought to play the part of committed conservative after arriving in Congress, his positioning may have stemmed less from any deep-seated political philosophy than from pragmatic calculation. According to friends and associates at the time, Rumsfeld's views on a number of issues were still being formed.

"I don't think he, early on, had carved out firmly held views," said Jannotta, who after managing Rumsfeld's campaign had become part of a small, Chicago-based kitchen cabinet of advisers. "I think he had leanings and instincts. He represented, when he ran for Congress, good raw material—a real good brain, honest and hardworking. But politically I don't think he carried a banner. I think he developed his political views over time."

Until Rumsfeld's own thinking could evolve, his safest course was to vote the party line. "Let's face it, he was a new congressman without a political agenda when he came in," Ludden said. "It would make sense that if you weren't sure of your issues when you came in and you were just getting your footing and you come from one of the most conservative districts in the country, you're not going to start off going against things." Robert Ellsworth, then a young Republican congressman from Kansas, identified Rumsfeld early as more operator than believer. "He wasn't an ideologue but he voted as he should vote being from where he was from," Ellsworth observed.

———•———

Ludden was one of the first people Rumsfeld hired to staff his office— and she agreed to sign on as his administrative assistant even with a pay cut. She had only just received an increase in her annual salary to $11,000 shortly before Church left. Rumsfeld offered her $9,900. "He hadn't made $10,000 in his life, and he couldn't quite bring himself to pay me what I'd been making," she recounted. "My husband said to me, 'Why are you doing this? You could make more money taking a committee position.' And I said, 'Because I think this guy could be president, and I'd like to say I knew him when.'"

In his early congressional days, Rumsfeld acted like "a man with purpose," a man who felt he could make a difference, Ludden recalled. "Neither one of us was sure what exactly that difference would be, but somehow it was going to make things better; we would have an impact."

He was also a man with many questions in search of answers. "He had a favorite saying: 'There's always one more question,'" she recalled. "No matter what issue we were working on, there was always one more question."

He spent long hours on the job and expected his staff to do so as well. And he ran his office tightly. "It was button-down, closely managed," said Bruce Ladd, who served as legislative assistant for several years. "Rumsfeld found delegating hard. He wanted to do things himself because he knew they would be done right that way." Once, on a visit back to the district when Rumsfeld was driving himself in a car, Ladd offered to take the wheel to reduce the chance of Rumsfeld being involved in an accident and drawing unwanted headlines. But Rumsfeld resisted even that.

Rumsfeld was intent on staying abreast of public opinion in his district. He sent questionnaires to constituents each year, typically receiving more than twenty-five thousand responses, which he tabulated and published. He also ensured that any constituents who wrote to him received a prompt reply. "He had a policy that every letter had to be answered within one week of it being received," said Sue Sittnick, who handled the office correspondence. "We got a ton of mail because we had a very informed district, and they liked to write and give their opinions. One night a week, we'd have to stay until every piece of mail was answered."

Rumsfeld checked each letter prepared for his signature. "He was just meticulous about that," Sittnick added. "He would catch the smallest detail, whether a misspelled word or something else. He didn't want anything to go out over his signature that he wasn't totally happy with."

Frugality became a Rumsfeld hallmark as well. He refused to spend all the money allotted to his office by Congress for postage, returning the unused sums to the U.S. Treasury. The same was true of funds for cost-of-living increases for staff salaries. Not surprisingly, this didn't always sit well with his staff. "I remember that, at the time, we really were upset about that because the money was there for him to use," Sittnick said. "But he wasn't just going to take that amount of money and use it all, unless he felt people deserved it."

Similarly, on the few occasions that Rumsfeld traveled on government business, he declined to spend all the per diems provided. On one trip, he refunded foreign currencies to embassies or wrote checks to the Treasury no less than eight times. "He was very punctilious," recalled fellow Princeton wrestling teammate Frank Carlucci, who was a diplomat in Brazil when Rumsfeld visited in 1965. "He wasn't interested in the entertainment side, he was interested in learning about Brazil. He was all business."

Rumsfeld's private life reflected the same deep-seated thriftiness. He drove an old rusty Volkswagen, and he lived with Joyce, two kids, and a dog in a townhouse in Georgetown only thirteen feet wide, reportedly the narrowest in the neighborhood. The place got even more cramped when Rumsfeld's son, Nick, was born in 1967. "He was never about any of the trappings," Sittnick said.

His scrupulous attention to expenses can be traced back to his modest, disciplined upbringing. But it also reflected a deliberate defensiveness arising from his campaign experiences. He had seen what even the smallest suggestion of impropriety had done to the political career of his first congressional boss, Dennison, and to the main opponent in his own first run for Congress, Burks. "He was tremendously careful about avoiding any kind of scandal," Ladd said.

Ludden recalled a day when a lobbyist dropped by the office to leave an envelope for Rumsfeld. "'This is for Don,' he said, and walked out. I could tell it had money in it. When Don came in, he was furious and called the guy on the phone and said, 'Don't you ever come into my office again! Come pick up this package!' And that was it. He wasn't real big on influence peddlers."

—•—

Facing reelection in 1964, Rumsfeld had a decided advantage, being the Republican incumbent in a heavily Republican district. He was unopposed for the nomination in the Republican primary. But the general election campaign was lively and took on a nasty edge.

The Democratic opponent, Lynn A. Williams, the first president of the Great Books Foundation and a vice president of the University of Chicago, zeroed in on Rumsfeld's conservative positions. He accused Rumsfeld of being a far-right-winger, with a voting record "more negative" than that of Senator Barry Goldwater, then the unpopular GOP nominee for president.

Williams pointed out that Rumsfeld had voted against a long list of assistance efforts that included the antipoverty bill, foreign aid, and the creation of an executive department of urban affairs. Rumsfeld had also opposed aid for college construction, medical schools, student loans, mass transit, city and suburban libraries, and air pollution control, as well as the use of surplus food for the needy, Williams asserted. All told, Williams cited thirty-three votes that he said portrayed Rumsfeld as an "extremist."

Rumsfeld protested to the Fair Campaign Practices Committee that Williams had incorrectly identified nine votes in Rumsfeld's record. Meanwhile, he was engaged in some mudslinging himself, reprinting and distributing by the thousands an editorial from the *Skokie News* that, among other things, described Williams as "totally unfit to hold any public office." The Fair Campaign Practices Committee ultimately determined that while Williams had been inaccurate on one vote and had oversimplified some of Rumsfeld's positions, the sum of the inaccuracies was far less significant than the "extremely offensive, highly extravagant . . . venomous utterance" circulated by Rumsfeld's campaign.

In the end, Rumsfeld won by a comfortable margin, 58 percent to 42 percent, although it was a narrower margin than his 2.5-to-1 victory two years earlier over Burks. Years later, Williams recalled Rumsfeld as actually "a bright, decent, pleasant, charming fellow," although one with an extremely conservative voting record.

President Johnson's landslide victory over Barry Goldwater in the 1964 election swept many of Rumsfeld's fellow party members out of office, leaving only 140 Republicans in the House. It was a bleak moment for the GOP, but the young, ambitious Rumsfeld saw opportunity. The electoral disaster could provide the opening for the kind of change in party leadership and structure that he and other young Republicans had been urging. A major obstacle was Charles Halleck, the entrenched minority leader, regarded as too old, too irascible, and too inflexible by the reformers. Any move against Halleck, though, would be risky, since the Indiana Republican had many powerful friends in Congress.

Rumsfeld has credited Tom Curtis of Missouri as the "intellectual leader" behind a group of about half a dozen members who quickly sought to press for reforms. Curtis has identified Rumsfeld as the moving force, and other accounts clearly show him as a main organizer.

"Don Rumsfeld was a catalyst in this," Curtis told an interviewer in 1965. "He called me from Florida right after the election and wanted something to be done. I said I was in the process of writing a letter and it can kind of be the kick-off for calling a conference. Don wanted to change leaders. I said, that isn't my main thrust. I said any one of the twenty guys would be very adequate as leaders if they would only get out ahead of their followers—consult with the other members and then get out ahead."

Rumsfeld flew to Washington to confer with Griffin, Goodell, and others about how to proceed. At that point, by his account, his focus was on effecting certain changes in party rules and structure, not in the party's leadership.

A party conference was convened in December to debate possible reforms and to draft a Republican legislative program. During the seven-hour meeting, Rumsfeld promoted a number of proposals, including some that would open more senior committee and party positions to younger members. His main intention, he said at the time in an unpublished interview, was engineering an end to the Democratic Party's long-standing control of Congress. "I've only got one life to live," he remarked. "I want to build the Republican Party into a majority party and work for its constructive principles."

Afterward, Rumsfeld flew home to Illinois, feeling good that the conference had aired concerns and had reached agreement to study reforms. But Halleck had appeared negative toward many of the proposals, giving fresh impetus to the movement to unseat him. The next day, Rumsfeld's phone started ringing. "It looked like something was on and they wanted me to come back," Rumsfeld recalled.

He caught a plane at ten that evening, arrived in Washington at two in the morning, and by nine was on the Hill meeting with Griffin, Goodell, Minnesota's Albert Quie, and others. The group decided to challenge Halleck and to replace him with Gerald Ford. The plan involved phoning as many House members as possible and asking for their help before Halleck, who was vacationing in Florida, returned to Washington. "We worked hard on it," Rumsfeld said. "I spent probably as much time on it as anybody and ended up really as one of two or three people who kind of managed the thing."

The contest wasn't really about political philosophies. On the substance of legislation, Ford was generally regarded as only slightly less conservative than Halleck. More at issue were personality and leadership styles. The opposition to Halleck fastened on what critics argued had been his indecision in staking out party positions on legislation proposed by the Democratic administration. He hadn't done enough, his critics said, to devise Republican alternatives. He was seen as unsympathetic to expanding the staffs of Republican minorities on House committees and to gaining better committee assignments for young Republicans. Ford was younger, more energetic, and more likable, and had friends on both sides of the aisle. His backers argued that he would bring more vigor and efficiency to organizational problems.

In the final tally, Ford defeated Halleck by a mere six votes, 73 to 67. The episode was a major turning point for Republicans in the House, opening the way to a new manner of leadership. For Rumsfeld personally, it served as a political catapult to prominence at the start of only his second congressional term. He and his group of fellow activists even acquired a nickname, "Rumsfeld's Raiders."

Rumsfeld had established himself as a leading proponent of congressional reform, someone willing to challenge much more senior, powerful politicians and risk his own standing in the process. In the immediate aftermath, the risk appeared to pay dividends. He landed an assignment on the Government Operations Committee and was elected chairman of the 88th Club, an organization of House Republicans who had first served in the previous congressional session.

Backing Ford also helped Rumsfeld secure a relationship with the powerful Michigan lawmaker, who, a decade later when he reached the presidency, would bring Rumsfeld into the pinnacle of White House power with him.

But Rumsfeld's maneuvering made some serious enemies along the way as well. He knew that such Halleck allies as Arends, the GOP whip, would probably be biding their time, waiting for an opportunity to strike back. "Perhaps behind the scenes it has hurt me more than I am aware of," Rumsfeld told an interviewer a few months after the unseating of Halleck. "I have laid back purposely and tried to mend some of my fences."

Rumsfeld agreed with a theory espoused at the time by Goodell about the need to build on plateaus of power, to take things slow between the moves and not constantly be churning things up. "You've got to resort to gluing over the pieces once in a while," Rumsfeld said. But having acknowledged the dangers of continuing to agitate, he still could not seem to help himself and kept pushing. In significant ways, his approach to Congress resembled his approach to wrestling—the same competitiveness, the same tendency to follow his own game plan. At times he seemed driven as much by the love of the fight and the challenge as he did by a deep-seated desire to improve the order of things.

———•———

By the start of Rumsfeld's second term, the U.S. military's involvement in the Vietnam War had begun to escalate. Rumsfeld had voted in favor of the Gulf of Tonkin Resolution in 1964 giving President Johnson, without a formal declaration of war, authorization to use military force in Southeast Asia. But as the war consumed more and more U.S. troops and drove Americans into sharply opposing camps, he came to have many second thoughts about that vote.

"My position, I suppose like a lot of Americans during the period 1963–69, evolved as the situation changed," Rumsfeld told Pentagon historians in a previously undisclosed 1994 interview. By the middle of 1965, Rumsfeld was already taking issue with the Johnson administration for having launched military action without an explicit declaration of war by Congress. "Does the concept of declaring war need updating?"

he asked in testimony before the Joint Committee on the Organization of the Congress in June.

At that point, though, Rumsfeld was raising the question in the context of his ongoing campaign to reform Congress. He was arguing about congressional versus presidential authority, not about the nature of the Vietnam War itself or the wisdom of the U.S. involvement in it.

"What is Congress's proper role today in these areas of foreign policy and undeclared war in view of the advent of nuclear weaponry and the modern technology of warfare and the need for centralized control and decision-making?" Rumsfeld asked in his testimony. "Is Congress effectively exercising its power of appropriation? . . . Is the congressional check on executive action in the increasingly important area of intelligence, counterinsurgency and covert military operations adequate?" Rumsfeld pleaded with Congress to clarify its responsibilities for foreign and military policy. "Congress must be able to do more than merely nod 'yes' or 'no' to presidential proposals—whether out of apelike obedience or uninformed obstinacy," he concluded.

Two years later, Rumsfeld was still focused on the same point. He joined a group of fifty-two House members proposing that Congress reexamine the administration's policies in Vietnam to determine whether there was sufficient authorization for the deepening American involvement in the war. Their resolution did not directly challenge the administration's Vietnam policies. But it suggested that the time had come for Congress to pass formal judgment on the correctness of and constitutional authority for those policies. Backed by forty-eight Republicans and four Democrats, the measure drew an unusual coalition of congressional hawks and doves united by a common concern over whether Congress had been bypassed in the determination of Vietnam policy.

The logistical management of the war also became an issue for Rumsfeld, as he worried that waste and black-market operations were thwarting U.S. effectiveness. A visit he made to Vietnam in May 1966 as a member of a Government Operations subcommittee deepened his concerns about weak monitoring of war supplies, some of which, including chemicals for explosives, were suspected of being resold to the Vietcong and the North Vietnamese, even to Chinese Communists. At the subcommittee's urging, the Pentagon and the State Department tightened controls and moved to audit more closely allegations of graft, collusion, and mismanagement. "The trip was an eye-opener for him," said Bruce Ladd. "Rumsfeld came back with a jolt of realism about Vietnam."

Even more troubling for Rumsfeld than the evident corruption and inefficiency was the deception. "I was floored when I went over there as a member of the Government Operations subcommittee to find that the port that was being built at Cam Ranh Bay was being designed to support a force on the ground of something in the neighborhood of half a million troops, when in fact the administration's comments about what they planned to do were quite different from that," Rumsfeld said in the 1994 Pentagon interview. "I was concerned . . . that there seemed to be a gap between what we were doing and what the American people were being told."

Rumsfeld complained about excessive secrecy surrounding the war, charging that the Johnson administration was withholding information from the public about the situation in Vietnam. He told newspaper editors in February 1966 that although government secrecy was hardly new, "the Johnson administration has been particularly skillful and imaginative in its use of secrecy and news manipulation as a protective device. Within the last few years, increased government secrecy has resulted in a marked loss of confidence by the people in their government."

Similar charges would be leveled four decades later against George W. Bush's administration during the Iraq War. Once again, the government's official statements about a faraway conflict would often contradict what Americans could see and hear from other credible sources. But in that case, Rumsfeld himself would be targeted by the complaints as a main perpetrator.

Back in the 1960s, the issue of the Johnson administration's truthfulness about the Vietnam War played into a more general legislative campaign that Rumsfeld was pursuing, a campaign touting greater openness in government. John Moss, a Democrat from California and chairman of the Government Operations subcommittee on which Rumsfeld began to serve in his second term, had been pushing for more transparency. In early 1965, Moss had introduced legislation that sought to guarantee public access to federal government records.

Rumsfeld became a cosponsor of the measure and, next to Moss, its strongest supporter against strong White House opposition. Johnson administration officials worried the bill would infringe on executive privilege and impair government operations. They insisted that executive agencies must retain the ability to bar public access to whatever information they wanted to suppress and to provide for confidentiality when the national interest required it.

After the Senate passed its version in October 1965, Rumsfeld stepped up efforts to rally Republican support for the measure in the House. He conferred with Ford, who promised to help, and started inserting in the *Congressional Record* dozens of statements, articles, columns, and examples of news management. "I inserted anything I could find to give other people ammunition to use in speeches, to ask questions about, to point up the problem of government secrecy," Rumsfeld recalled. "I encouraged other members of Congress to interest themselves in the subject, and I got the word to the Republican National Committee and the Republican Congressional Committee."

Against the backdrop of an increasingly unpopular war, allegations of excessive government secrecy were bound to resonate even more, and if they could be made to stick, they would have obvious political benefits for Rumsfeld and his fellow Republicans. Rumsfeld kept taunting the Johnson administration. Why should Johnson have pushed the Voting Rights Act of 1965 if he was going to deny access to the kind of information that voters needed to draw informed conclusions? Why should the administration have any objection to ensuring the people's right to know?

Rumsfeld "believed in openness, and that's what got him into the story," Ladd said. "But I think he also saw it to some extent as a good political issue. He was a Republican pushing an issue opposed by a Democratic president."

Recognizing Rumsfeld's efforts to turn the issue into a potent weapon for Republicans in the November election, Moss advised the White House that agreement on the bill had become a political necessity. The administration's opposition fell away, and the legislation passed the House unanimously in June 1966. The Freedom of Information Act was born.

In a speech before the Federal Bar Association in Chicago nearly a year and a half later, Rumsfeld said the new law had proven neither an "immediate cure-all" for the administration's credibility problem nor a "wholly meaningless instrument" but, rather, something in between. Over the long term, he predicted, the measure would help both to spur public demand for integrity in government and to make more information available "so that the public and the press will have to rely less upon what government officials tell them" and "will have independent means of checking for the truth."

But the law could only do so much, he added. "This law deals with secrecy," he said. "It does not pretend to come to grips with the problems of deceit and lack of candor in government pronouncements. The political system, the ballot box, may be the only real answer for the credibility problem."

Those words still rang true in 2006, when voters, acting on a negative view of Republican leadership in Washington, took away Republican control of Congress and triggered the end of Rumsfeld's run as defense secretary.

In the fall of 1966, before the congressional elections, the liberal Americans for Democratic Action gave almost all Illinois Republicans a score of zero. The exception was Rumsfeld, who was awarded 17 out of a possible maximum of 100. At the same time, his standing among the Americans for Constitutional Action, a conservative group, fell to 68.

Increasingly, Rumsfeld was being viewed as a moderate conservative. That reputation stemmed in part from his bent for fighting to reform and modernize the Republican Party. It also reflected his emergence as a strong supporter of civil rights.

As early as his first term, Rumsfeld had sided with many northern Republicans in backing the comprehensive Civil Rights Act of 1964, counteracting the coalition of southern Democratic congressmen and southern Republican conservatives who had resisted the measure. In his second term, a bitter controversy arose over the open-housing section of Johnson's 1966 civil rights bill.

The bill had a provision intended to prevent discrimination in the sale or rental of housing in large apartment buildings and in new subdivisions. That provision wasn't very popular among many Republicans or, indeed, among many of Rumsfeld's constituents, and he had received a lot of mail on the issue, according to Sittnick.

But Rumsfeld voted against a Republican-sponsored proposal to kill the open-housing section. His principled stand on this, as on other civil rights measures, derived from a basic sense of fair play. As a staunch fiscal conservative, he didn't necessarily believe in a helping hand. But he did believe in a level playing field.

His most eloquent expression of this thinking came in the spring of 1968, when the housing issue was again before Congress as part of the Civil Rights Act of 1968. The act was being considered in the wake of protests and rioting triggered by the assassination of civil rights leader Martin Luther King Jr. Proponents argued for urgent passage to prevent further civil disorder. Opponents said the legislation should be opposed lest it be considered a move to appease the rioters.

"My vote today," Rumsfeld declared on the House floor, "will be cast not because of the pressures of the moment, but in spite of them. It will be cast not out of fear, but from conviction and concern. It is based very simply on my conviction that every person in this nation regardless of race, color or creed should have the right and opportunity to live wherever his economic circumstances will permit."

He went on to describe the fair-housing provisions of the bill as being "in complete harmony with the spirit and broad purposes of this country since its inception." He said that passage would make it easier for many black Americans to realize their dreams of better housing and, in the process, would strengthen the nation overall. "I know of no better hope for the future of this nation than for its people, all of its people, to be able to reasonably aspire to fulfill their best hopes for the future," he said. "The dignity of each man requires it. No man should ask for more; no man deserves less."

On several other controversial issues in his second term, Rumsfeld also supported the liberal line. He voted against legislation sponsored by the House Un-American Activities Committee to extend the 1950 Internal Security Act, a move intended to make aiding a hostile power a federal crime when the United States was engaged in "undeclared" or "unconventional" war or "police action." He opposed a reactionary District of Columbia crime bill, and he favored protecting the Federal Trade Commission's authority to require health-hazard warnings in cigarette advertising.

"I don't think he was looking to identify himself as some kind of party maverick," Ladd said. "I know what went into his decision making and his thinking, and he struggled with these issues." Once, Rumsfeld asked Ludden, his administrative assistant, to draft a paper examining whether a member of Congress should vote as a representative of the people or as someone who expressed his beliefs and took his chances that constituents would continue to back him. "I think his thinking was that he would get the best information he could on any issue and then vote his conviction," Ludden recalled.

Socially, too, Rumsfeld did not want to be limited by party affiliations and fixed sets of political beliefs. His ability to connect with people easily extended across party lines and outside politics, encompassing a broad circle of friends that included many Democrats and many nonconservatives. One of his closest ties was with Allard K. Lowenstein, the leading antiwar activist who entered the House as a representative from Long Island, New York, in 1969 toward the end of Rumsfeld's time in Congress. Rumsfeld and Lowenstein had overlapped a bit as congressional aides in the late 1950s. They wrestled together and once planned to go into partnership on a weekly newspaper. "Don's relationships with people had less to do with their political views than with the people themselves," Ludden said.

In his socializing as in much else, Rumsfeld was helped significantly by Joyce. Fun and effervescent, she had none of the edges of her husband and seemed to draw affection and plaudits from everyone. Easy to talk with, she had never lost her knack for reaching out to people and bringing everyone together. And she was discreet, rarely gossiping or telling tales on people.

During Rumsfeld's first term, Joyce had tried spending only half the year in the Washington area and the other half back in the family's house in Glenview, Illinois. But this double life was wearying, so with money borrowed from Rumsfeld's dad, the couple bought the house in Georgetown. After more than two dozen moves in nearly ten years of marriage, Joyce was pleased to be sinking some roots in the capital.

She portrayed herself in a 1964 interview as a stay-at-home mom, more comfortable in that role than as the woman-behind-the-man involved in her husband's career. But others credited her with being Rumsfeld's closest confidante and soul mate. Sittnick observed that Rumsfeld often used Joyce as "a sounding board."

In Rumsfeld's 1966 reelection effort, his opponent, a lawyer named James McCabe, posed little challenge, and Rumsfeld glided to victory with 76 percent of the vote. A *New York Times* editorial at the time, titled "Quality in the House," listed Rumsfeld approvingly among a handful of Republican members. "Certain members stand out as men and women of quality who willingly shoulder responsibility, do their work in committee, participate effectively in debate and generally try to give a lead to the often wayward currents of public and congressional opinion," the editorial reported.

Nonetheless, in January 1967, at the start of a new session, Rumsfeld lost to a fellow member from Illinois, Charlotte Reid, in what the *Chicago Tribune* called "a red hot fight" over a seat on the powerful House Appropriations Committee. Arends, who had not forgotten Rumsfeld's role in ousting Halleck, chose Reid, an avowed conservative who had entered Congress the same year as Rumsfeld and had a near 100 percent party voting record. Rumsfeld was also denied a desired transfer to the Armed Services Committee, although he did make it onto the Joint Economic Committee, becoming the youngest ever to serve on that panel.

Even before the new session of Congress had begun, Rumsfeld was out front again on a sensitive issue, this time the military draft. Discontent with conscription had been mounting with the unpopularity of the Vietnam War and with the soaring number of draftees. Bureaucratically, the draft was becoming a nightmare, and as early as March 1966 Rumsfeld had joined twenty-nine other Republican members of the House in a demand for a congressional investigation of the Selective Service, charging that "bumbling bureaucracy" was making a mess of the draft law.

But conscription also bothered Rumsfeld on another level. Although a firm believer in the importance of serving one's country, he considered the draft inherently unfair and a waste of manpower. His thinking was influenced by Milton Friedman, the nation's leading free-trade economist, who had made the economic and philosophical case for ending the draft and creating an all-volunteer Army.

In December 1966, Rumsfeld was one of several members of Congress who attended a conference on the draft at the University of Chicago. There, Friedman presented a passionate argument against conscription, appealing to the libertarian principles of freedom and efficiency. Impressed, Rumsfeld joined on the spot with Representative Robert Kastenmeier of Wisconsin in calling publicly for replacement of the military draft with fully volunteer armed services. Recalling the moment, Rumsfeld wrote years later that Friedman "was such an enthusiast for the all-volunteer force that it was contagious. Everyone there seized the issue, myself included."

Returning to Washington, Rumsfeld introduced legislation on the all-volunteer force and testified before the House and Senate Armed Services committees—"an intimidating thing to do as a junior congressman," he recounted, "to explain to giants like Eddie Hebert and Richard Russell why the current system was not the right system." It took several more years of political debate and ultimately the backing of President Nixon before conscription was abolished and an all-volunteer force created. But Rumsfeld deserved some of the credit. More than three decades later, he found himself arguing against moves, prompted by the pressures of the Iraq War, to reinstate the draft. The arguments he invoked then were the same ones he had used as a young congressman.

Rumsfeld's voting record during his third term in Congress continued to reflect his evolving conservatism and the views of his suburban constituents. He opposed funding for urban mass transit and anti-poverty programs. He assailed federal education officials for subsidizing the Future Farmers of America Foundation, a private nonprofit corporation, arguing that the federal government had no business financing private youth-education organizations. He led criticism of NASA for faulty spacecraft designs blamed for the fiery death of three astronauts at Cape Kennedy in 1967.

But his signature issue remained congressional reform, which he pursued with typical brashness and determination. His focus was a reform bill containing one hundred recommendations to modernize Congress. Passed by the Senate, the bill was bottled up in the House, where it had drawn fire from a number of directions. Some committee chairmen, for instance, opposed the limits that the bill would place on their traditional ways of doing business—such as conducting closed-door sessions with nonrecord votes or using the proxies of absent members. Members from rural districts objected to a provision that would remove postmasters from the patronage system. Lobbyists also were working against the measure, since it would tighten controls over them as well.

Rumsfeld tried a number of parliamentary tactics to pry the bill— and a companion one on election reform that would restrain fund- raising and impose new disclosure requirements—out of committee. But he was warned by veteran leaders and freshmen alike that he had no chance of forcing the Democratic leadership to schedule the legislation for House action in 1968.

Acknowledging the challenge, Rumsfeld told an interviewer at the time that the measures "are inside bills and enjoy no constituency." But he also sounded determined, expressing confidence that he could pursue measures unpopular with other lawmakers, even if it jeopardized his own ability to operate in the clubby atmosphere of Congress, because he didn't need to seek favors for constituents on other matters. "My district isn't looking for a new dam, and we have no oil or tobacco interests that I have to fear," he said. "I don't have to agree to things I don't believe in, so I can push for things that I'm convinced are right."

In October 1968, Rumsfeld thought he had found an opening to gain leverage and push the reform bills through. It came, though, over a seem- ingly unrelated matter—House consideration of a bill to permit free tele- vision time for debates between presidential candidates. The Democratic nominee, Vice President Hubert Humphrey, was trailing GOP nominee Nixon in the polls and was pressing for debates that would also include third-party candidate George C. Wallace. But Nixon, while willing to de- bate Humphrey, was balking at a three-way event involving Wallace.

Rumsfeld mounted a filibuster against the bill, delaying action through the night. But his interest wasn't really the debates. He made it clear that he and his supporters were holding up House action in order to call attention to the blocked bills for election reform and congressional reorganization. The roll of members was called twenty-eight times, beat- ing the previous record of twenty-two for a single day's session and de- laying movement on the debate bill through the night. Ultimately, the bill passed, but Rumsfeld had made his point.

Going into the 1968 election, Rumsfeld was being mentioned as a pos- sible committee chairman in the next Congress as Republicans looked for new, younger leadership. Given his age and relatively short tenure in Congress, Rumsfeld had come to wield an unusual amount of influence, much of it the result of his sheer energy as well as his willingness to challenge existing authority.

He tended to attribute his success in large part to a strong work ethic. "I'm no intellectual giant but I'll work harder than anybody else," he told Ladd candidly as the two were on one of many trips to Rumsfeld's district. Others saw sheer ambition and a driving, combative style.

Rumsfeld had no trouble winning reelection to a fourth term, beating David C. Baylor, an attorney from Wilmette and self-proclaimed dove on the Vietnam War, by a vote of 186,714 to 69,987. Only one other congressman in the nation won that year by a larger margin.

But a committee leadership post for Rumsfeld did not materialize. House party leaders thwarted his bid to become head of the GOP's Research and Planning Committee. In a 76-to-74 vote, Rumsfeld lost out narrowly to Representative Robert A. Taft Jr. of Ohio.

Rumsfeld's defeat was officially attributed to a need to give the position to a congressman from a state other than Illinois, which already had two members in top leadership posts in the House. But Rumsfeld and his allies saw the rejection as a fresh sign of the old guard maneuvering to keep him from rising up the ranks.

Rumsfeld professed to take the defeat in stride, but Joyce knew better. She hand-lettered a plaque with this legend: "You've worked like hell. You've done all you can—and you blew it!" Rumsfeld hung the plaque on his office wall.

After several terms in the House, Rumsfeld was beginning to recognize that, as bright a star as he was, his future leadership prospects could well remain limited. Besides, he thought, being a legislator might not be his calling after all. It didn't really suit his temperament or his ambitions. He had too much energy, too little patience.

"The legislative process is too slow and turgid for a guy like Rumsfeld," Ellsworth observed years later. "He's too sharp, he's too bright, he's too let's-get-something-done. He was not satisfied. And in those days, you have to remember that none of us ever dreamed the Republicans would be in the majority in the House. We really never thought that the country would drop the Democrats as the dominant party."

CHAPTER 3

Tough Enough

Congress had provided Rumsfeld his undergraduate education in politics. Richard Nixon was about to afford him some graduate-level training. The two men had met only in passing prior to the 1968 presidential race, when Nixon came to speak to the congressional 88th Club, which Rumsfeld headed. But Rumsfeld, facing easy reelection himself in 1968 and seeing a chance to act on a bigger stage, was ready to join Nixon's national campaign. And Nixon, happy to benefit from Rumsfeld's youthfulness and energy, found a place for him as a "surrogate" on the speaking circuit and as one of several assistant floor managers at the GOP National Convention in Miami Beach, Florida.

As Rumsfeld's luck would have it, the Democratic National Convention that year was in his hometown of Chicago. His familiarity with the city helped win him a spot on a team of Republican operatives sent to observe the proceedings and report back to Nixon. There turned out to be much to report.

Months of mounting rage in the country over the war in Vietnam and the assassinations of Martin Luther King Jr. and Robert F. Kennedy exploded in the streets of Chicago as the convention was under way. Police clashed with antiwar protestors amid a swirl of flying rocks, swinging clubs, and clouds of tear gas, producing shocking images of a nation bitterly divided. Headquartered on the nineteenth floor of the Conrad Hilton hotel, the GOP team had a window on the unfolding conflict and chaos below. Rumsfeld provided a running commentary of the urban battle scenes in phone calls to Nixon and his aides, who were in Florida.

"Nixon had the idea of getting someone to observe and report by telephone immediately what he was seeing, and I got Rumsfeld because he's from Chicago," recalled Robert Ellsworth, a former congressman and Rumsfeld friend who worked for Nixon at the time as his national political director. "Nixon just loved that. He was delighted to have these direct reports from Rumsfeld about the rioting going on down on the sidewalks and the streets and the parks."

After the election, Nixon considered naming Rumsfeld chairman of the Republican National Committee. But the new president was also in search of a political operative hard-nosed and daring enough to take on a much more challenging task: running the Office of Economic Opportunity (OEO), the agency responsible for overseeing federal antipoverty efforts. Several others had already declined the job of OEO director or had been sounded out and showed no interest.

Nixon turned to Rumsfeld, who hesitated. It was a risky proposition. Established by the Democrats in 1964 and intended, in Lyndon Johnson's words, to "conquer poverty," OEO had grown into an activist, freewheeling collection of antipoverty programs. Its Community Action groups advocated aggressively at the state and local levels. Its Legal Services lawyers carried the concerns and frustrations of poor communities into courtrooms. The agency's Head Start program addressed preschool education, the Job Corps pursued employment training for young people, and Volunteers in Service to America (VISTA) oversaw a kind of domestic Peace Corps.

The agency evoked images of city-hall picketing and partisan politicking. It also had a reputation for managerial chaos, inefficiency, and scandal. Antipoverty leaders complained OEO wasn't doing enough, but state and local officials and business groups decried it as intrusive and disruptive.

Nixon had promised to rein in the agency, and Rumsfeld looked like the man for the job. He was "rough and ready, willing to tangle," according to Bryce Harlow, a Nixon associate who helped recruit him. "He was the kind of guy who would walk on a blue flame to get a job done."

But Rumsfeld thought he was not quite right for the position and also questioned whether the timing was right for him. No fan of the agency, he had voted against the original Economic Opportunity Act of 1964 that established the War on Poverty program. He worried that if he accepted Nixon's offer and generated a lot of controversy at the poverty agency, it could impair his own long-range political ambitions. He had a very safe congressional seat, which would be easier to give up if he were getting an administration job more prominent than that of OEO director.

Still, the idea of moving to the executive branch tempted Rumsfeld, who recognized that staying in Congress would be frustrating. If he succeeded in the OEO job, he could gain experience running a large organization and enhance his national reputation.

Rumsfeld wanted assurances that if he took the job, he would not be presiding over the dismantling of the agency. Nixon had already announced plans to spin off two of OEO's most important programs— Head Start and Job Corps—to other federal departments. Flown to Florida for a meeting with Nixon at the president's Key Biscayne residence, Rumsfeld received a pledge that OEO would remain intact. Additionally, he was promised a second title as assistant to the president and cabinet-level status. It wasn't the same as running his own cabinet department, but it was a step in that direction.

Rumsfeld's decision to jump to OEO stunned his Capitol Hill colleagues. Some moderate Republican lawmakers were disappointed and viewed Rumsfeld as having sold out to the White House. Others, though, expected that he could at least bring some enlightened attitudes to the new administration. Many antipoverty activists worried that Rumsfeld was being sent to dismantle OEO.

In any case, Rumsfeld was on the move again, switching jobs, embracing a new opportunity. Never staying too long in one position would become a pattern of his life. "He's not the kind of guy who falls in love with a job," said Ned Jannotta, an investment banker who, unlike his longtime friend, has stayed with one firm his entire career. "He thinks of a job as there to get something done, and once he gets it done, he moves on. He does not like to get bored at something. He's a problem-solver. The maintenance of something is not his thing."

Before Rumsfeld's appointment as OEO director could be approved, there was one legal obstacle to overcome. Congress had just raised the

OEO director's salary from $30,000 to $42,500, and as a member of the Congress that had authorized the increase, Rumsfeld was forbidden from receiving it. (The Constitution prohibits a member of Congress from taking a federal post if the salary for the position was raised during the member's time in office.)

A way to circumvent this constitutional hitch was suggested in a memo by a new assistant attorney general, William H. Rehnquist. He proposed that Nixon tie Rumsfeld's salary not to the OEO post but to Rumsfeld's title as assistant to the president. Thus, the path for Rumsfeld's first executive-branch job was cleared by the legal finesse of a future chief justice of the United States.

Nixon had spelled out OEO's new mission earlier in the year, declaring that it would become a kind of "incubator" of programs for the poor. Instead of operating programs, the agency would focus on experimenting with promising antipoverty approaches that other agencies could in turn adopt. Militancy would be played down, and research played up. The pilot project would be favored.

Rumsfeld took on this mission with zeal. He imposed tighter controls on OEO activities. He ordered Community Action offices to shape up, toughened VISTA's hiring standards to favor older, more highly skilled volunteers, and established new evaluation procedures for Legal Services projects. He also strengthened procurement practices and brought in new senior staff.

"Rumsfeld called me in and said the first thing I ought to do was fire all the regional directors," recounted Frank Carlucci, who had been on the Princeton wrestling team two years ahead of Rumsfeld and was an early Rumsfeld hire to run the Community Action program. The order initially stunned Carlucci. Having served as a U.S. diplomat, he had been accustomed to the State Department practice of carrying people over from one administration to the next. But Rumsfeld's approach, as Carlucci came to realize, was to limit the number of holdovers so that senior directors would be beholden to the agency's new leadership for their jobs. "I did dismiss a number of very able people," Carlucci said.

In the face of angry, sometimes militant protests against OEO's new measures, Rumsfeld stood his ground. In one particularly dramatic confrontation at OEO headquarters, several dozen University of Pennsylvania law students—most of them either black or Mexican American—occupied an office in November 1969, holding Terry Lenzner, the Legal Services director, hostage. Decrying what they called "overt racism" in the agency, they demanded that an OEO-financed fellowship in poverty law be transferred from their school to Howard University, the nation's premier historically black university, in Washington, D.C. Rumsfeld refused to negotiate and at one point even tried, unsuccessfully, to walk Lenzner out of the room taken over by the protestors. In the end, police arrested the students.

While working to discipline and scale back OEO, Rumsfeld also proved a surprisingly strong defender of the agency's need to exist, resisting political pressures from the White House and Congress to gut the agency. He lobbied White House budget officials for larger budget appropriations and antagonized some of his former House Republican colleagues by spurning their plan to turn most OEO programs over to state control. With Democratic help and with little presidential support, Rumsfeld won a House vote in December 1969 for a two-year extension of the agency.

Rumsfeld's staunch defense of OEO found a few allies in the administration—among them, Pat Moynihan, the president's counselor on urban affairs, who had helped recruit Rumsfeld for the OEO job, and Arthur Burns, the president's counselor on economics. But others around the president were irritated that Rumsfeld was fighting so hard to preserve the troubled agency.

When Rumsfeld held a news conference at the National Press Club after nearly seven months at OEO, he was immediately asked about a report that he was viewed "with open hostility" in the Nixon White House. Rumsfeld replied that he didn't feel any hostility, nor did he have any regrets about having given up his congressional seat. But he acknowledged it had been a wild ride. "I admit I feel like I'm sitting on a bubbling volcano half the time," he remarked.

Rumsfeld's determination to sustain the antipoverty agency he had once opposed may be explained in part by a belated recognition that some OEO activities were indeed beneficial to the poor. But much of his motivation appears to have been the result of his change of circumstance. He was no longer a young congressman intent on burnishing his conservative credentials. He had become a senior administration official interested in preserving his new bureaucratic domain.

If there was a philosophical element to his defense of OEO, it was overshadowed, at least in the eyes of a number of Rumsfeld's associates, by the image of a young politician on the make. OEO seemed to be little more than a bureaucratic project for Rumsfeld. He was seen as being driven less by any particular political philosophy than by a pragmatic interest in advancing his own career.

"He was not an ideologue," observed Lenzner, an early Rumsfeld hire. "I would describe him as a political philosophy in the making. I saw him as a young congressman who had been thrust into this position and was shaping things as he went along, in terms of what he believed and how he reacted to issues and how he dealt with problems."

———•———

Faced with running his first large institution, Rumsfeld proceeded in a way that would become a pattern for all his future management posts. First he set out to learn all he could about the workings of the agency, talking to top staff people, interviewing some for hours. Then he systematically developed his team. He viewed government as teamwork, a disciplined group effort, so the people he had onboard with him were key.

"One of the most gratifying things for me is to have an assignment and then to go out and find good people and to work with them on the creative things people can do," he once said. "It's great. When I take on a job, I like to—in sequence—engage myself in the different elements. Then—as I'm familiar with them and understand them—to leave them to someone else and go on to another element."

He brought in some friends—Don Lowitz from Chicago and Don Murdoch from Madison, Wisconsin—and he hired Carlucci away from the State Department. Others he picked were new to him but quickly became friends—among them Lenzner, a former football team captain at Harvard University who had worked as a civil rights attorney at the Justice Department and as a fighter of organized crime with the U.S. Attorney's Office in New York.

But his most fateful hire was Richard Cheney, a relative newcomer to Washington. Then a twenty-eight-year-old Capitol Hill staff aide, Cheney became Rumsfeld's right-hand man at OEO, beginning a storied relationship that spanned the Nixon and Ford administrations and that would have major consequences for the presidency of George W. Bush.

Cheney had come to Washington in the late 1960s on a fellowship from the American Political Science Association. Previously a doctoral candidate working on his dissertation, he planned to return to a teaching job at the University of Wisconsin. The fellowship, which enabled him to work for a congressman, offered Cheney a window on Capitol Hill, and one House member he initially approached for a position was Rumsfeld. The two tell somewhat different stories about what happened next.

Cheney maintains that his interview with Rumsfeld went badly. Rumsfeld remembers thinking well of Cheney, but for various reasons, he hired someone else. In any case, Cheney ended up taking a job with another Republican, Representative William Steiger of Wisconsin, who served on the committee that oversaw OEO.

When Rumsfeld was nominated for the agency, Cheney sent him, unsolicited, a twelve-page memo suggesting how he should handle himself in his confirmation hearings and what he ought to do with OEO once he was established. Rumsfeld remembers liking the memo and being impressed with Cheney's demonstrated interest in the agency. Soon afterward, Rumsfeld invited him to become his special assistant.

The two men were a study in contrasts, but in their differences they appeared to balance each other. Cheney's patient, discreet, self-effacing demeanor served as a natural foil for Rumsfeld's tendency to push the ends of envelopes and leave people feeling on edge. "Cheney didn't seek in any way to impose his personality, his role, on anybody," Lenzner recalled. "He was kind of the perfect special assistant to Don." They bonded quickly. "Rumsfeld took to Cheney right away and tended to operate extensively through him," Carlucci said. "If I needed a decision, I found the best way to get it quickly was to go through Cheney."

In time, Rumsfeld lowered the voice, visibility, and activity of OEO while keeping the agency in existence. After more than a year on the job, he told an interviewer, "We've got about two-thirds of the programs working pretty satisfactorily."

But many OEO supporters continued to harbor fears that Rumsfeld had not done enough to ensure the agency's survival—fears that were borne out in Nixon's second term when OEO was dissolved, its remaining programs distributed to other departments. Rumsfeld, according to his critics, had tended to focus more on administrative and bureaucratic matters than on substantive programmatic aspects that might have provided OEO stronger protection against extinction.

Allard Lowenstein, who had initially defended the selection of his friend Rumsfeld for the director's job, was among those expressing disappointment. "The cumulation of events within OEO and the administration within the last year-and-a-half have not produced the kind of results that many of us had hoped would come from him being in that position," he said in late 1970.

But Lowenstein was feeling bitter toward Rumsfeld for a personal reason as well, one that resulted from a choice Rumsfeld had had to make between friendship and political loyalty as he climbed up Washington's power ladder.

Running for reelection to Congress in 1970, Lowenstein had faced a tough opponent who accused him of being a dangerous radical. When Rumsfeld was asked about the charges, he at first defended his friend, saying he considered Lowenstein patriotic and noting that he had never heard him advocate violence. But a week before the election, Rumsfeld endorsed Lowenstein's opponent. Lowenstein, feeling betrayed, never forgave Rumsfeld.

Asked at the time about the episode, Rumsfeld claimed that he had been reluctant to oppose Lowenstein but that, as an assistant to the president, he was no longer an "independent operator" and had to toe the party line. Although he didn't say so explicitly then, he had been instructed to support the Republican candidate. "I guess what happens is," Rumsfeld remarked, "when I left Congress and ceased being a political entity of my own and became a part of an administration, my code says, By golly, I'm part of this administration, and if I don't want to be part of his administration, I can leave it. One man got elected president of the United States, and while he's there you support the dickens out of him."

It was a stark declaration of the importance Rumsfeld placed on loyalty to the president—and conversely, on the limits he put on friendship when up against such political imperatives. Although quite a few in the Nixon administration viewed Rumsfeld as largely out for himself, he took care to show unwavering support for the president, and this would remain an abiding principle of his through all the administrations in which he would take part. As a boss himself, Rumsfeld expected loyalty from subordinates and so knew its value to his own bosses.

———•———

Wearing two hats while at OEO, Rumsfeld divided his time between offices at the antipoverty agency and at the White House. His frequent presence at the White House reflected Nixon's wishes. The president had taken an increased interest in Rumsfeld and made it clear to his staff that he wanted Rumsfeld welcomed into "the inner councils."

As an assistant to the president, Rumsfeld joined a handful of senior aides each morning to discuss challenges facing Nixon and to plan the day ahead. Around the table sat H. R. "Bob" Haldeman, chief of staff; George Shultz, director of the Office of Management and Budget; John Ehrlichman, domestic policy chief; Robert Finch, counselor to the president; and Henry Kissinger, the top adviser on national security affairs.

For Rumsfeld, shifting between such high-level sessions and OEO activities involved a heady balancing act. Half his time was dedicated to managing issues affecting the poor, the other half to contemplating political machinations. As his tenure at OEO wore on, Rumsfeld dedicated more of his time to thinking about ways of shoring up Nixon's political standing and ensuring the president's reelection. "Gradually I could see Rumsfeld's focus was more and more on the White House dealing with White House problems," Lenzner said. "He became less and less visible at the agency."

In the summer of 1970, Nixon considered reassigning Rumsfeld either to head the Office of Management and Budget or to chair the Republican National Committee. Soon after the 1970 congressional elections, in which the Republicans did poorly, Nixon and his team began talking about an administration shake-up. Rumsfeld figured prominently in the restructuring plans.

One suggestion was for Rumsfeld to replace George Romney as secretary of housing and urban development. But Romney refused to leave, and although Nixon and his aides talked about firing Romney, the president couldn't bring himself to do so. Rumsfeld, who saw Romney as too politically important to antagonize, recalls arguing against letting him go.

The next month, in December 1970, Nixon and his aides again tried to persuade Rumsfeld to take over as head of the Republican National Committee. But Rumsfeld wasn't interested. He rejected the suggestion that he run the Committee for the Re-election of the President, which he considered lacking in challenge. "A trained ape could go out there and do that, and I'll be darned if I'm a trained ape," he remembers declaring at the time.

After such unsuccessful attempts to reposition Rumsfeld, Nixon gave him the elevated title of "counselor" and brought him full-time into the White House, where he could be kept on hold for a future cabinet-level post. Carlucci was picked to replace Rumsfeld at OEO. Rumsfeld had hoped that Carlucci, as the new director, would take care of one piece of unfinished business: firing Lenzner, the Legal Services director. But Carlucci insisted that Rumsfeld handle his own housecleaning. "I didn't want to have to fire Terry Lenzner right after I took over," Carlucci recalled. "I said, 'You should do it, he's your man.'"

Rumsfeld's once-close relationship with Lenzner had been worn thin over Rumsfeld's efforts to constrain the agency's legal aid activities, which had become a particular target of conservatives led by Governors Ronald Reagan of California and Claude Kirk of Florida. Although the poverty lawyers dealt mostly in divorce, welfare, and consumer matters, they had with relish dragged governments into court at every level in class-action suits and other cases. Lenzner had strongly defended the activities of his lawyers.

An unbridgeable divide between the two men ultimately arose over a Rumsfeld plan in the summer of 1970 to give regional offices more authority over Legal Services. Lenzner fiercely opposed the move, fearing it would subject OEO lawyers to a host of local politics and pressures. But Lenzner recognized that his own time was running out, particularly after Rumsfeld, in an office meeting, abruptly presented him with a list of dozens of concerns about his performance.

Not long after, Lenzner was summoned to Rumsfeld's office late on a mid-November day. He purposefully took a lit cigar with him, knowing it would irritate Rumsfeld. At the meeting, as Lenzner vividly recalled years later, Rumsfeld got right to the point. "You know, we've got all these problems with you and Legal Services, and you're unable, unwilling, to comply with what we want done, and we'd like you to resign," Rumsfeld said.

It wasn't much of an explanation, Lenzner thought. And Rumsfeld didn't appear to be enjoying the moment. "Don, we've had a problem with communication, but you've been away and part of the problem is of your making," Lenzner said, trying to reason.

But Rumsfeld had made up his mind. "Well, are you going to resign?" he asked.

Lenzner offered to go willingly if his deputy, Frank Jones, could replace him. Rumsfeld responded by firing them both. In a statement, he described the two men as "either unwilling or unable" to carry out his policies and cited instances in which Lenzner had exceeded his authority. Lenzner charged that the real reason for his dismissal lay in his refusal to tailor the Legal Services program to the political aims of the administration. Jones, an African American, left saying OEO had fallen into the hands of right-wingers and bigots.

Looking back after a long career subsequently as an investigative attorney in Washington, D.C., Lenzner expressed mixed feelings about Rumsfeld. "I don't think either of us understood how difficult a program it was going to be," he remarked. "I think we were in the midst of events that we didn't appreciate, that were kind of getting out of control." In Lenzner's view, with all the political battles that were being waged, those tumultuous years at OEO changed Rumsfeld. "I think to some extent he was burned by that experience," he said. "I don't think it was what he had expected, and I don't think he saw it as a real plus in terms of what his future career was going to look like."

Rumsfeld's own assessment not long after moving on reflected just how searing had been his trial by fire. "It was a very tough job," he remarked to a journalist. "I hate to be critical of my predecessors, but it sure was a management nightmare."

———•———

The OEO job had launched Rumsfeld out of the role of rebellious minority congressman and given him his first executive management experience. It had also afforded him some exposure to the inner workings of the White House. With his move to counselor, his tutelage under Nixon intensified, and he quickly settled into playing the part of protégé to one of the country's most skilled political infighters.

Nixon figured that Rumsfeld, still under forty, would get some political seasoning by being brought into the White House full-time as he waited for a cabinet position to open up. A West Wing sinecure, the president thought, could also help incubate Rumsfeld's chances for a return to elective office someday, possibly a run for a Senate seat. Just what tasks Rumsfeld would perform were left unclear. But that didn't seem to matter to the president. "Nixon decided he wanted him in the Executive Branch without really knowing how he wanted to use him," Ehrlichman, Nixon's domestic policy chief, wrote in his memoir. "Rummy Rumsfeld was handsome and bright, and that was enough."

As a former congressman, Rumsfeld also had something that Ehrlichman, Haldeman, Kissinger, and others in the inner circle around Nixon lacked—actual experience as an elected official. Nixon, for all the hard knocks he had endured in politics, felt a certain identification with other politicians and had a high regard for Rumsfeld's skills. While the president's other men were at times put off by Rumsfeld's ambition and self-promotion, Nixon looked past these and admired Rumsfeld's toughness and drive. Nixon also figured Rumsfeld's youthful image and effectiveness as a speaker could be put to good use as a public face for his administration, particularly with young and suburban voters.

White House files from the period, preserved in the Nixon archives, suggest that one way Rumsfeld quickly sought to make himself useful was by providing political advice on a range of matters. He wrote Haldeman, for instance, on January 4, 1971, criticizing a decision to exclude Senator Edmund Muskie of Maine, a leading Democratic candidate for president, from the signing of the Clean Air Act. Rumsfeld said the move, which drew critical press accounts, made Nixon look "non-presidential." In another memo the same day, Rumsfeld strongly recommended that Nixon come out against Pentagon spying on civilians involved in government and public affairs. "There are 150 reasons why it is a bad thing to do under our system of government. The president knows them all," he wrote.

Rumsfeld's memo-writing style—crisp, to the point, but comprehensive—impressed Nixon. In a meeting with Haldeman in February, Nixon referred to a Rumsfeld memo done in advance of a meeting with the Federal Executive Board. "An excellent briefing paper," the president called it, suggesting Haldeman show it to others. "One sentence on every item. One sentence. That's all. Just saying, 'Say this, say that' . . . without going through a whole long detailed business about everything. But he really covered it extremely well."

But Rumsfeld worried about being a senior White House official with no portfolio and was eager to find a more defined role for himself. In February, with efforts under way to end the war in Vietnam, he attempted to interest Nixon and the NSC staff in making him a special envoy who would travel to Southeast Asia and make recommendations for a U.S. role in postwar reconstruction. Such an appointment, Rumsfeld argued in a memo, would help dramatize a shift in emphasis from combat operations to postwar concerns and give Nixon an independent view of developments.

NSC officials dismissed the idea, arguing that it wasn't necessary, would confuse allies, and would lead to a diversion of effort. Nor was Nixon interested, given everything else his administration was doing about Vietnam. "I don't think that you should do anything that appears to be too contrived," he told Rumsfeld when the matter came up in an Oval Office discussion between them in March 1971. "So much is being studied to death in terms of the postwar plans and all that sort of thing." Besides, Nixon predicted, Vietnam would quickly recede, and "we won't give a damn." The only countries or regions "that matter in the world," he explained to his eager counselor, were Japan, China, Russia, and Europe.

Instead, he suggested Rumsfeld take a trip to Europe. And in fact, a trip to Europe and North Africa was later scheduled in the spring for the stated purpose of conferring with foreign leaders, mainly about drug trafficking and health care delivery.

The conversation in March was one of a number of private talks, preserved by the White House taping system, in which Rumsfeld sought to advance his career and also draw political advice from Nixon. Rumsfeld showed little inhibition in sounding out the president about various high-level job possibilities, and Nixon seemed more than willing to offer tips from his own political experience and help plot Rumsfeld's future.

Rumsfeld had begun the March session wanting to know from Nixon whether to regard the counselor's job as a short-term holding position or as something longer term. Nixon offered assurances that he was still hoping to find a cabinet post for Rumsfeld. But he said an earlier plan to make Rumsfeld secretary of housing and urban development had fallen through because Romney hadn't stepped down from the job as expected.

Nixon called Rumsfeld "a good operator" capable of almost any cabinet position. In that sense, he contrasted him with Robert Finch, another presidential counselor who had been brought into the White House after a lackluster performance as secretary of health, education, and welfare. Finch, Nixon said, wasn't really suited for a top department job "because operations aren't his cup of tea."

Nixon told Rumsfeld to consider his counselor post "as temporary, as a very interim period." He said a number of cabinet positions would probably fit Rumsfeld, mentioning Health, Education, and Welfare (HEW), Transportation, Interior, and Commerce in addition to Housing and Urban Development (HUD). He ruled out Defense, State, or Justice, though, and told Rumsfeld, "You wouldn't want Agriculture."

Rumsfeld tossed out another idea. He suggested "something in the trade area"—service on the International Economic Council, perhaps—indicating this could help his plans "down the road" to run for political office in Illinois. Nixon, warming to the mention of an international activity, noted the greater importance and appeal of foreign over domestic affairs. He recalled his own experience running for the Senate in 1950 as a foreign affairs expert.

The president reported that he had tried to find a spot for Rumsfeld at the State Department as undersecretary for development, but Secretary of State William Rogers had objected to Rumsfeld's lack of foreign policy experience. Nixon said the real objection that Rogers had had was taking onboard "a colorful, strong" individual like Rumsfeld. The president subsequently landed on the idea of making Rumsfeld the special trade representative.

Rumsfeld was intrigued. The post could involve travel and would help position him for future jobs at the State or Defense Department. But most importantly, it would give him a specific focus. "You once told me I should be doing something in a line area, and I'm inclined to agree with you. I'd like that," Rumsfeld told the president. "There is a problem potentially of a guy floating around in the White House" because of the risk that "you get into someone else's business."

Nixon agreed that such a danger existed, particularly for an operator like Rumsfeld. The more Nixon thought about making Rumsfeld special trade representative, the more he liked the idea. Rumsfeld was the man for the job—he would be "tough as hell," would "fight like hell for American exports," and could "get along with the Congress."

The next day, Nixon discussed the idea with Haldeman. He spoke of wanting someone in the post who could offset the more liberal, free-trade leanings of Shultz and Pete Peterson, the assistant to the president for international affairs. "I need a man who will be in there fighting," the president said. "That's why putting Rumsfeld in this special trade thing might be a good idea, 'cause at least Rummy is tough enough. He's a ruthless little bastard, you can be sure of that." Nixon's crude reference to Rumsfeld was apparently meant as a compliment. "He's tough enough that if he knows what I want, he isn't going to come in and try to sell me something," Nixon added. "You know, just because the free traders want it."

————•————

But no decision was taken, and Nixon continued to ponder the question of just what to do with his ambitious political ward. Within a few weeks, the president actually fell into a sour mood about Rumsfeld. The talk suddenly turned from promoting Rumsfeld to dismissing him. The issue was Vietnam.

Rumsfeld had first discussed Vietnam with Nixon in early 1969, after the bombing of Cambodia in March that year. As a congressman, Rumsfeld had campaigned against excessive secrecy about the war and had watched the serious erosion in credibility of Johnson's presidency. Now, under Nixon, the bombing was being kept secret out of deference to the political leaderships in Cambodia and Laos and to avoid domestic protests. Rumsfeld believed this was not reason enough for Nixon to risk the new administration's credibility, and he told the president so. "I cautioned him that if there were good reasons for the bombings, fine, let's do them, but let's announce them," Rumsfeld recalled in an interview with Pentagon historians in 1994.

Rumsfeld credits himself with continuing to advocate straight talk about the war in deliberations inside Nixon's White House. When Kissinger announced at a staff meeting that U.S. forces were about to launch an "incursion" into Cambodia, Rumsfeld took issue with the description. "Come on, Henry, it's not an incursion, it's an invasion. Why the hell don't you just call a spade a spade?" Rumsfeld recalled saying. "You've got bad people in there, you're going to go in and do something—a perfectly legitimate thing—but you're trying to gild the lily." Kissinger was not pleased. At times, when he saw Rumsfeld and Joyce, Kissinger would flash the peace symbol in a taunting reference to Rumsfeld's antiwar stance.

By 1971, Rumsfeld had joined a small group of administration officials—all involved in domestic policy—who were questioning in staff meetings why the administration could not move more quickly to end the war. Other members included Finch, Ehrlichman, Shultz, and Clark MacGregor, the counselor for congressional relations. Their appeals for an accelerated solution angered Nixon. "They don't want to think about foreign policy!" Nixon exploded over the phone to Kissinger in reference to them on April 6. "They're only concerned about, frankly, peace at any price, really. . . . All they're concerned about is, well, revenue-sharing and the environment and all that crap, which doesn't amount to anything in my opinion." Kissinger concurred, saying, "They want to take off the immediate pressure, this is their overriding concern."

The next morning, Rumsfeld pressed Kissinger in the presence of other White House staff members as to why the administration couldn't move more rapidly to conclude the war. Afterward, Kissinger grumbled to Nixon that Rumsfeld had never exactly said what he wanted the president to do. Although Rumsfeld had spoken vaguely of setting a date by which the United States would reduce its presence to a "residual force" in Vietnam, he had never called for a "date certain" for getting out.

Nixon's frustration seemed to reach a boiling point at a meeting later that day as he prepared for a prime-time presidential address to the nation on Vietnam. He intended to announce plans to withdraw one hundred thousand Americans from Vietnam by the end of the year but would not set a date to end the war. In a conversation with Kissinger and Haldeman, the president couldn't shake his irritation with Rumsfeld. "I think Rumsfeld may be not too long for this world," Nixon remarked.

The president worried that Rumsfeld might quit first. "He's ready to jump the ship," Nixon said.

"Well, I don't think he's ready to jump," said Haldeman. "And I doubt he ever would, just 'cause it serves his interest more not to. But I sure don't think he's ever going to be a solid member of the ship."

"He just positions himself to be close to the *Washington Post* and the *New York Times*," Kissinger interjected.

Nixon wanted a plan. "Well, then, let's dump him right after this," he said. "Good God, we're sending him and Finch on a two-month holiday to Europe. Shit. For what purpose?"

"To get him out of town," Kissinger replied, a reminder that the trip had originated with Nixon and Kissinger.

Nixon tried to go back to the task of rehearsing that night's speech but couldn't put Rumsfeld out of his mind. "Coming back to the Rumsfeld problem—I'm disappointed in Don, Bob," he told Haldeman. "I don't want to be disappointed. . . . I don't want somebody who's just with us, goddamn, when things are going good, you know what I mean? He thinks we're going down the tubes, and he's just going to ride with us, maybe he's going to take a trip to Europe occasionally. Screw him." What especially galled Nixon was that Rumsfeld, who was viewed as one of the administration's most effective public speakers, refused to go out and defend the Nixon administration to the American people. "He won't step up to anything," Nixon complained. "We have given him, time and time again, opportunities to step up, and he will not step up and hit the ball."

Haldeman agreed. "I used to think at one point he was a potential presidential contender, but he isn't," he told the president.

"He's like Finch," Nixon said. "Finch and he both have the charisma for national office, but neither has got the backbone."

Later that night, after the speech, Nixon in a phone call with Kissinger remarked that he hadn't heard from Rumsfeld, Finch, or Mac-Gregor yet. "I mean, they're all cowering, I suppose, waiting until they see how the polls show." Then in a call with Haldeman, Nixon asked specifically whether there had been any word from Rumsfeld. Haldeman said he hadn't heard from him. "Well, nobody has," Nixon observed, "so he's playing his own little game."

However much it may have irritated Nixon and his inner circle, Rumsfeld's desire to keep a low profile on Vietnam certainly made political sense for him. His experience had been in domestic policy, and his focus remained there. Distancing himself from an unpopular war, especially one that he felt had been waged too secretly, seemed advisable for someone eyeing a run for elective office.

Indeed, while Rumsfeld's stance disappointed the president's top aides, it hardly surprised them. They did not mistake it as an act of principle. They tended to view it in much the same way as they viewed other Rumsfeld actions—that is, as a function of his consuming self-interest. "Eventually the senior staff grew to realize that the ambitious Rumsfeld would decline every assignment that did not enhance his personal goals; but that didn't become clear until he had moved into the West Wing," Ehrlichman wrote in his memoir.

Kissinger appraised Rumsfeld as "ruthless and very much out for himself" in a phone conversation with his friend, Nelson Rockefeller, then governor of New York, not long after the discussion of dumping Rumsfeld. When Rockefeller noted that Rumsfeld was thinking of going back to Illinois, Kissinger replied, "He is in the best tradition of Illinois politicians, from what I have seen." The tradition that Kissinger had in mind was clearly the ends-justifies-means, party-machine kind.

Nixon's own aggravation had eased by mid-April when Rumsfeld, together with Finch, went off to confer with foreign leaders in Europe and North Africa. They visited eleven countries in twenty-three days, seeking support for a U.S. amendment to the 1961 U.N. convention on drugs and for a study on health delivery to be undertaken by NATO countries.

"Confidence in the President among European leaders is high," the two counselors reported on their return. "Several foreign policy questions entered our conversations with foreign leaders. We were, however, struck by how seldom Vietnam was mentioned. It appeared not to be a burning issue in the minds of the officials with whom we met." If there was criticism from the Europeans, it was of U.S. economic management, particularly the exporting of inflation to Europe. "There appeared to be far less respect for U.S. skill and sophistication in economic, monetary and trade matters than was the case with respect to U.S. foreign policy matters," Rumsfeld and Finch wrote in a memo.

In a private meeting with Nixon, Rumsfeld also offered some pointed observations about the U.S. ambassadors he had met during the trip. He described one—Graham Martin in Italy—as "stiff, unpleasant, and cocksure of himself." In general, he told Nixon, he had not been impressed with the career foreign service officers along the way. "I worry about all the experts and political officers who don't know beans about politics," he said. "We've got a State Department filled with people who've never run, never worked in a campaign." Nixon acknowledged the problem.

Over the next few months, Rumsfeld busied himself working on the Property Review Board, making speeches and helping with White House political operations. "I've really been moving around," Rumsfeld told Nixon when they met for another of their one-on-one sessions in July. Rumsfeld counted 110 appearances in the previous three or four months in twelve states and nearly as many foreign countries.

But he still longed for something more high profile. "I recognize that what I'm doing is useful to you, but it's not anything of direct responsibility to you," he remarked to the president, "and it's not been of any great visibility."

With still no cabinet vacancy opening up, Nixon mentioned the possibility of Rumsfeld becoming ambassador to NATO. Nixon called the NATO job "the best ambassadorship" because it "always has substance" and involves the "whole alliance." The idea intrigued Rumsfeld, who saw it helping to "fill a gap" in his résumé. But he wanted to be certain that Nixon and Kissinger would actually use him in the role and not just go over his head. He worried, too, that such an assignment might look like he was "just being kicked upstairs." Nixon assured him that wouldn't be the case.

Rumsfeld had some other job ideas that he threw out, testing Nixon's reaction. He raised the possibility of becoming a "roving ambassador," focusing on parts of the world—Latin America, Asia, and Europe—that tended to receive less attention by Nixon and Kissinger. He also suggested taking over the undersecretary of state's job, which had been filled for a year by John Irwin. In a particularly cheeky moment, Rumsfeld even went so far as to outline how Nixon might approach William Rogers, the secretary of state, about moving Irwin aside.

"It struck me," Rumsfeld began, "that maybe it would be desirable for everyone if . . . you said to Bill, 'Well, we've got a helluva problem in trade and we need a man of his stature as special trade representative, and I want Irwin, and I want to do a favor for the Republican Party by giving our youngest cabinet member some very valuable experience in State that would help the party ten to twenty years from now.' You wouldn't be saying, uh, 'Rogers, you and State need Rumsfeld.' You'd be saying, 'Bill, I want you to do something that conceivably would be helpful to the party down the road.'"

Nixon didn't reject the option, but he didn't jump at it either. That and the other possibilities remained on hold.

———•———

In his conversations with Nixon, Rumsfeld could be heard frequently complimenting the president and sounding very solicitous of his views. Clearly Rumsfeld had become skilled in the practice of currying favor with a superior. His ability to come up with ingratiating comments when they served his interests is all the more noteworthy given Rumsfeld's own reputation as boss for being notoriously sparing with praise for subordinates.

With Nixon, Rumsfeld sometimes seemed to go out of his way to deliver a compliment. Asked once by the president, for instance, for his view of Vice President Spiro Agnew, Rumsfeld contrasted him with the president, portraying Nixon as a superior operator. "You've got so much ease in different experiences and circumstances, and he tends to be rigid and inflexible on things," Rumsfeld said. "You come out like a listener . . . and he comes out like he wants to lecture you."

Rumsfeld also praised Nixon for his contemplative demeanor. "There's something about you that people think you're learning all the time, you're absorbing," Rumsfeld said. On another occasion later in the year, Rumsfeld brought up an address Nixon had recently given in Kansas City. He commended it for being "uplifting in its international message."

Rumsfeld's tendency to be agreeable and attentive to Nixon did land him in an uncomfortable position when, many years later, he was nominated by George W. Bush for defense secretary. As Rumsfeld was waiting to be confirmed, the *Chicago Tribune* published a story highlighting a taped 1971 conversation in which Rumsfeld appeared to affirm disparaging remarks by Nixon about how southerners would view some racial comments by Agnew.

The vice president's unscripted remarks had been a recurring problem for Nixon. In this instance, Agnew, talking with reporters during a trip to Africa, had compared African American leaders unfavorably to three authoritarian African leaders. In a conversation with Rumsfeld about the issue, Nixon was initially critical of Agnew's crass comments, saying, "It doesn't help. It hurts with the blacks. And it doesn't help with the rednecks because the rednecks don't think any Negroes are any good."

"Yeah," Rumsfeld replied.

As for the whole notion that "black Americans aren't as good as black Africans," Nixon went on, "most of them basically are just out of the trees. . . . Now, my point is, if we say that, they say, 'Well, by God.' Well, ah, even the Southerners say [here Nixon adopts a drawl], 'Well, our niggers is just better than their niggers.'"

Rumsfeld laughed.

Nixon: "You know, that's the way they talk!"

Rumsfeld: "That's right."

Nixon: "I can hear 'em."

Rumsfeld: "I know."

Nixon: "It's like when our black athletes—I mean in the Olympics— are running against the other black athletes; the Southerner may not like the black, but he's for that black athlete."

Rumsfeld: "That's right."

Nixon: "Right?"

Rumsfeld: "That's for sure."

Nixon: "Well, enough of that."

Asked about this conversation in his confirmation testimony before the Senate Armed Services Committee in 2001, Rumsfeld denied agreeing with Nixon's racially charged comments and claimed not to have remembered the discussion when it surfaced in the press.

"The tape seems to indicate that I may have agreed with one or more things on that tape," he told the committee, trying to explain his failure to object to Nixon at the time. "To the extent I did agree with anything, I am certain I agreed only with the fact some people talked like that." Rumsfeld added that Agnew "should not have used or thought such derogatory and offensive and unfair and insensitive things about minorities."

The Senate panel did not press Rumsfeld on whether he should have challenged Nixon's characterization of Agnew's remarks. Presumably, he had avoided taking issue with the president because it didn't seem worth making a fuss about and jeopardizing his own position at the White House. No doubt at the time Rumsfeld assumed the conversation would remain between just Nixon and him. He knew Nixon's language could be offensive. He looked past that side of him, just as Nixon often looked past Rumsfeld's less attractive traits. What held their rather curious relationship together was something else—a shared appreciation for the political game, its toughness and its complexities.

The full extent of Rumsfeld's relationship with Nixon has become known only in recent years in the wake of the release of additional White House tapes and new histories of the period. Previously, Rumsfeld had been seen as having little to do with the administration's darker side—its enemies lists, dirty tricks, and secret wiretaps aimed at Nixon's political opponents. Rumsfeld was the Boy Scout, the accomplished wrestler—he fought hard but cleanly.

Contributing to this perception was his timely appointment as ambassador to NATO at the end of 1972 before the Watergate scandal erupted. And indeed, no evidence has surfaced implicating Rumsfeld in any illegal activity related to Watergate. But he did play a role in Nixon's political operations, and while he apparently did not cross any criminal lines, he appears to have been willing to walk along a few questionable ones, whether passing on derogatory information about political opponents or capitalizing on a secret connection with a big-name pollster. He certainly did enough to be regarded highly by John Mitchell and Charles Colson, top figures in Nixon's political apparatus with reputations for playing tough.

In his first months as White House counselor, Rumsfeld's political tasks were minor. He provided Mitchell and Haldeman, for instance, with various political research papers, including reports on the Senate race in Illinois, background information on the main money man behind Democratic senator Birch Bayh of Indiana, and analyses of the political situations in New Jersey, Maryland, and Florida. Rumsfeld also relayed concerns voiced by Nixon supporters that the administration had been insensitive to women on a number of fronts and did not understand what would be required to attract women's support in the 1972 presidential campaign.

But by May, when he returned from his trip to Europe, he showed himself willing to pass on a little dirt about a Nixon adversary. In a briefing on the trip, Rumsfeld informed Nixon that the U.S. ambassador to Spain, Robert C. Hill, had "a file of bad stuff" about Senator Muskie, then the frontrunner for the Democratic presidential nomination. The file, Rumsfeld said, involved Muskie's "extracurricular activities."

Hill had obtained the purportedly damaging material from Maine's attorney general, according to Rumsfeld. Nixon wanted to know what kind of activities. "Business or women? Women won't hurt him, business might," the president said. Rumsfeld didn't indicate which activity was involved. Nixon said he would look at the material.

Rumsfeld's importance to Nixon and his political operatives was significant enough by the summer of 1971 that the president put aside the idea of sending him to NATO. Rumsfeld himself had been reluctant to go abroad anyway before the presidential campaign. But Mitchell also objected, and Nixon himself made it clear that he considered Rumsfeld too useful to lose at that point. "He's young, he's 39 years old. He's a hell of a spokesman, you know," he remarked to Haldeman. A moment later, he added, "NATO is fine, but it pulls him out of the politics. . . . I think Rumsfeld will be more valuable in politics. . . . He's an operator."

That same July day, Nixon discussed with Colson a plan for Rumsfeld to approach the pollster George Gallup Jr., who had been a classmate of Rumsfeld's at Princeton. Haldeman, in a memo to Rumsfeld a few days earlier, had asked him to "assume personal responsibility for weekly calls" to Gallup "concerning poll results." Just where the president and his men thought these contacts might lead is unclear, although Nixon imagined that Gallup could be persuaded to shade his firm's results. "I mean, if the figures aren't up there, we don't want them to lie about it," Nixon told Colson. "But they can trim them a little one way or another."

Nothing on the Nixon tapes suggests Rumsfeld did try to affect any Gallup poll results. But in October 1971, Rumsfeld was able to learn several days in advance about a survey that would show a jump in Nixon's popularity rating. At the same time, Rumsfeld felt uneasy about his Gallup back channel, worried it could compromise the pollster's independent image if it were ever disclosed. He urged Nixon to keep the channel secret. "I kind of want to be awful careful about telling people around this building that I'm talking to him because all he's got in this business is his integrity," Rumsfeld told the president. That is why, Rumsfeld added, he wanted to let Nixon know directly when he talked to Gallup. Nixon concurred.

Another tape-recorded conversation four months later indicates the contacts were still helping. Just before Nixon left for China in February 1972, Haldeman told him that the results of a Gallup poll were being held back, to his benefit. "I can't believe that Gallup would tell . . . Rumsfeld that he would hold the poll," Nixon replied. "Because Gallup was always, 'Jesus Christ, I call them as I see them.'" Haldeman explained that the poll wasn't being discarded; the release of the results was just being delayed until after the China trip.

Asked about the Gallup connection years later in an interview for this book, Rumsfeld recalled obtaining early polling information only once. He had little memory of any other political errands he fulfilled for Nixon, except for an occasional speech.

The archives show that Rumsfeld did draw the line at some tasks. He balked, for instance, in January 1971 when senior White House aides tried to saddle him with the chore of the "cultivation and promotion" of CBS News correspondent Dan Rather, who was a neighbor and friend of

Rumsfeld's. In a memo to Haldeman a month later, Rumsfeld said, "It would not be workable for me to be the prime contact" with Rather.

Reflecting back on his relationship with Nixon, Rumsfeld professed not to fully understand it. "I think he was—I don't know—he clearly thought I had potential," Rumsfeld said. He pointed to his relationship with John Mitchell as one factor contributing to the president's favorable regard. "John Mitchell liked me, and I liked him," Rumsfeld said.

Joyce Rumsfeld, commenting on her husband's connection with Nixon, summed it up this way: "It wasn't a friendship, it was a relationship. It was intellectual. They weren't friends, although Don had enormous respect for his brainpower."

———————

In the summer of 1971, Nixon imposed a ninety-day freeze on wage and price increases. Rumsfeld didn't know it then, but the move would lead soon to a new job for him.

A growing balance-of-payments deficit had allowed foreign governments to accumulate large amounts of dollars, prompting the United States to abandon the gold standard. This threatened to boost the price of imported goods and accelerate an already rising inflation rate. By imposing wage and price controls, Nixon hoped to choke off an inflationary surge while simultaneously increasing the money supply, priming the U.S. economy and boosting employment. Nixon assumed that with new jobs to fill and more money to spend on price-controlled goods, the U.S. public would be more inclined to reelect him in 1972.

As the initial phase of freezes was ending in the fall, Nixon announced a second, more complicated set of controls that constituted the most comprehensive mandatory constraints on the economy since the Korean War. Major businesses and labor unions would be required to ask government permission to raise prices or wages. Medium-sized organizations would have to report promptly any wage or price action and be prepared to have them pared down. Shopkeepers, landlords, and other small concerns would have to abide by wage and price standards. The interim goal was to cut the consumer price index to an annual rate of increase of 2–3 percent by the end of 1972, about half what it had been.

Rumsfeld agreed reluctantly to direct the Cost of Living Council overseeing the postfreeze controls. He didn't really believe in wage and price controls, and he had said so when Shultz asked him to take the job. Shultz was well aware of Rumsfeld's opposition—which was one reason he wanted Rumsfeld to manage the program.

Privately, Shultz had expressed some reservations to Nixon about Rumsfeld's own ability to manage a large organization. "He can't run stuff very well," Shultz had said. But he added that Rumsfeld knew how to compensate. "He gets other people to run stuff. He's good at getting other people to do his work."

In any case, within days of his appointment in October 1971, Rumsfeld was getting high marks from Nixon and senior aides for the job he was doing, making news and shoring up the president's own standing on the economic front. "He's doing beautifully, I must say," Colson remarked to Nixon in a phone call in late October, adding that Rumsfeld even appeared to like the work.

"We've finally found him a niche now," the president said.

Implementing Nixon's new controls proved far more difficult than the simple ninety-day freeze. All told, there were four thousand people developing, administering, and enforcing wage and price controls on about eighty million employees and more than ten million firms. Rumsfeld had little formal training in economics, but the challenges he was up against were as much political as economic. Determining which businesses should be freed from price limits, which workers should be exempted from wage controls, and when such moves should take place were among Rumsfeld's daily considerations.

"Everything I was dealing with was politically very, very sensitive," Rumsfeld recounted. "There were people—let's be honest, Republicans and Democrats—saying to me, 'You should do this because it'll break the unions' or 'You should do this because it'll support the unions' or 'You should do this because it'll remake the health care system of America.'"

Economists criticized the controls for their complexity. Spokesmen for the nation's poor complained that the program was freezing the economic status quo and perpetuating social injustice. Public opinion polls, meanwhile, showed growing misgivings about the fairness and firmness of the methods used to set the controls. But by early 1972, the drastic

measures were beginning to have their intended effect, slowing an inflation rate that had proven resistant to traditional remedies.

"Is the system now perfect? No," Rumsfeld declared at the time. But as
the public anxiously watched each new inflation statistic, Rumsfeld insisted the program would succeed in curbing the rise in prices and wages.

In the process, Rumsfeld and the Cost of Living Council faced off
against some of the country's most powerful businesses and unions. They
denied price hikes to auto and can manufacturers. They expanded price
curbs on unprocessed foods such as eggs, fresh vegetables, fresh fruits, and
raw seafood. They briefly lifted price controls on other items—lumber,
for instance—only to reconsider and reimpose them. Midway through
1972, they exempted millions of small businesses and local governments
from wage and price controls, freeing more than a quarter of the nation's
total workforce and sales.

As the first anniversary of the monumental control effort approached
in August, the economy showed signs of substantial progress in real
growth and higher employment. But advances toward other goals of the
program—reducing inflation and lessening international pressures on
the dollar—were still unclear. Critics contended that however well the
program had worked overall, its application had been unfair—holding
back wages while allowing corporate profits to rise.

"The controls program is not infallible, but it is fair to say that prices
and wages are in better shape today than they would have been if no
hand had been raised to check inflation," Rumsfeld declared. Consumer
prices had increased at an annual rate of 2.7 percent under the program,
compared to an annual 3.9 percent in the seven months preceding it, 5
percent in 1970, and 6 percent in 1969.

Even so, among those Rumsfeld had a hard time convincing was his
wife. "I told my wife food prices have been almost unchanged for the past
few months," Rumsfeld confided to reporters. "She told me, 'Don't tell
anyone that. They will never believe it. My grocery bill is up $10 a week.'"

In the end, Rumsfeld took greatest satisfaction in the fact that he survived his inflation-fighting tenure without a scandal. He recalled only

one allegation of wrongdoing against someone on his staff, "and I sent that over to the Department of Justice in one second; we were scrupulous about it," he said.

But after one year, Rumsfeld was eager to get off the council and out of Washington. As he explains, he was feeling increasingly uncomfortable around some of Nixon's top White House aides—notably, Haldeman, Ehrlichman, and Colson, officials who were eventually implicated in the Watergate scandal. Uncomfortable—and wary. Colson had called Rumsfeld a number of times on the Cost of Living Council to request political favors at Nixon's behest. But Rumsfeld pushed back, worried about the propriety of what was being asked.

"I went to George Shultz and told him I was not enjoying myself and didn't want to continue on in the economic stabilization program," he recounted. "I thought it was time for me to either leave the administration and go into business or to spend some time overseas in a foreign policy post."

Rumsfeld had his eye on the NATO ambassadorship that Nixon had mentioned as a possibility in the summer of 1971. But he also was looking at returning to Illinois, where he could position himself to challenge Senator Adlai E. Stevenson III, who was up for reelection in 1974. In a meeting with Ehrlichman, Rumsfeld seemed to have decided on the Illinois option, only to switch and insist on keeping an administration job for a year when he spoke later with Nixon. The apparent change of mind, Haldeman wrote afterward, was "a complete shock" to Nixon and Ehrlichman, "and typical Rumsfeld, rather slimy maneuver."

Shultz, by then Treasury secretary, helped secure the NATO position for Rumsfeld, smoothing the way with Kissinger, who initially was not enthusiastic about the idea. "I am not one of Rumsfeld's admirers," Kissinger said when Shultz broached the idea in a December 1 phone conversation.

Shultz noted to Kissinger that Rumsfeld had "done quite a good job" directing the Cost of Living Council. "He works at it," Shultz said. "He has a good sense of able young people. He attracts them and gets them working hard. And he thinks outside the boundaries of the particular ruts that the existing bureaucracy has. And he's responsive and loyal—he wants to report in; then if you say, 'All right, now you handle [it],' he's not afraid to go ahead and do it. He's very good to work with."

"All right, well maybe I've got him wrong," Kissinger replied.

"So I wouldn't be surprised but that he'd make a very good ambassador in NATO," Shultz offered.

The two then spoke about other things for a bit, but Shultz returned to the subject of Rumsfeld. "You don't seem as though you feel like saying right now whether he would be acceptable to you," he said to Kissinger.

"Oh hell, I suppose I can live with Rumsfeld—I don't have that much to do with the NATO ambassador," Kissinger responded.

"You would find him quite—he fishes around at you some, but basically he takes orders and carries them out," Shultz added. "He's bright."

"Yeah, he's bright," Kissinger conceded. "I think he is a little—frankly, my objection is I found him to be on the soft side of most issues, and what we need in Europe now is really some stern—but I might be wrong on that."

"I think there—the political side, the thing that appeals politically right now is to be a pretty tough guy. So that being the case, that's the way Rumsfeld is going to be," Shultz said. "Because his basic orientation is to his political future."

The announcement in December 1972 of Rumsfeld's appointment to NATO surprised many in Washington. Here was Rumsfeld, one of the president's favorite protégés, quitting the center of power to take a relatively unglamorous diplomatic post. The move also surprised Rumsfeld's mother. "She thought it would be nice for me to be secretary of transportation," he told an interviewer. "She was a little disappointed when I called her."

Rumsfeld at the time described the NATO move as "kind of a wild card" for him. But he figured it would enable him to gain the foreign experience and perspective he needed. "Throughout my life," he observed, "I've made some strange judgments, based on the idea that you can't lose if you do something that challenges you—no matter what the appearances. They've usually worked out."

It was this instinct that had caused Rumsfeld to give up six years of seniority and a safe Republican House seat in suburban Chicago in 1969 to take on what was thought to be an impossible job as head of OEO. From there, he had moved into a troubleshooter's role as White House counselor and then was named to head the largest peacetime system of wage and price controls ever. Though anything but expert on the antipoverty programs or on economics generally, he had survived in both hot seats. Now he was looking to further round out his education.

"Everything in Rummy's life seemed to come early and easily," observed Robert Hartmann, who would work with Rumsfeld later under President Gerald Ford. "But this was deceptive. He was a cool and careful planner. As a politician, he recognized and respected fate; as a wrestler, he was ever alert for an opening to take fate by the forelock."

The move to NATO was portrayed by some as a kind of finishing school for Rumsfeld amid speculation that he still intended to run for the Senate from Illinois in 1974. But later, when the Watergate scandal crashed over the Nixon administration with Rumsfeld comfortably far away in Brussels, he would be credited with a splendid sense of political timing.

It wasn't the first time he had displayed a knack for keeping one step ahead of disaster or dissolution. He had resigned as head of OEO two years before Nixon began dismantling the agency. He had resigned as head of the Cost of Living Council months before it went out of existence. And although Rumsfeld had continued to be publicly loyal to Nixon as the winds of corruption started to blow from the White House, he appeared astute enough to move farther and farther away.

As much as Rumsfeld had asked to go, packing him off to Brussels was also a neat way for those in Nixon's inner circle who had never warmed to him, suspicious of his ambition, to rid themselves of a possible nuisance. Indeed, he may have been pushed out the door at the same time he reached for it. "I still don't know whether they cut me out or if, by my behavior, I cut myself out," Rumsfeld acknowledged a few years later.

At age forty and without any prior experience in diplomacy or in European affairs, Rumsfeld entered NATO's elite diplomatic club. He was by far the youngest member of the group, which included fourteen other ambassadors, most of them ten or twenty years Rumsfeld's senior. More accustomed to the rough-and-tumble debating methods of the U.S. Congress than to the more refined setting of the NATO Council, Rumsfeld initially came across as excessively blunt and inadequately prepared.

"When Don first arrived, he had very little knowledge of international relations," recalled François de Rose, then the French ambassador to

NATO. "He had never lived abroad and didn't speak any of the European languages. He was really a greenhorn—and very young for the job."

But Rumsfeld quickly learned his way around, helped in large measure by his capacity both for hard work and for warm, interpersonal relations with other ambassadors outside the formal council meetings. He formed important bonds with several veteran European diplomats. André de Staercke, Belgium's ambassador to NATO and the dean of the envoys there, became a mentor to him. De Rose, despite the strains in U.S.-French relations following France's withdrawal in 1966 from NATO's military structure, also developed a strong professional relationship and friendship with the U.S. diplomatic novice. "He impressed us with his will to learn the job and to know the questions that were discussed," de Rose recalled. "He learned very quickly the outside and inside of the issues."

Representing the United States automatically made Rumsfeld influential, and his inside knowledge of the Nixon administration played to his advantage. He also earned the respect of the staff of the U.S. mission at NATO. "He drove his troops pretty hard, but they respected him because he worked hard, too," said a State Department official who watched Rumsfeld at close quarters during his NATO days.

The job gave Rumsfeld his first personal involvement with strategic arms issues and questions involving the balance of forces in Europe. With the Vietnam War winding down and the world's diplomatic focus turning to a series of international negotiations intended to reduce U.S. and Soviet nuclear weapons and rearrange conventional forces, Kissinger had proclaimed 1973 the "Year of Europe."

Rumsfeld found himself involved in the Nixon administration's efforts to resist rising support in Congress for reducing U.S. troop strength in Europe. Such sentiment was being fueled by the worsening U.S. monetary and trade position in the world and by a deepening interest in détente with the Soviet Union. Twice Rumsfeld was called back from Europe to testify before Congress against proposed legislation to withdraw forces from Europe.

Because crises outside Europe had a tendency to have an impact on NATO, Rumsfeld also ended up with a diplomatic role when the Arab-Israeli War erupted in October 1973. He was part of a frustrating Nixon administration effort to gain European support for U.S. policy in the

Middle East. On instructions from Kissinger, Rumsfeld strongly demanded in the first week of the war that the European allies cool their relations with the Soviet Union, which was supporting the Arab side. But the Europeans resisted, sensitive to their oil interests and reluctant to see the Middle East conflict trigger a major East-West confrontation.

Rumsfeld was particularly proud of his role in drafting the NATO declaration of principles that Nixon and other heads of state signed in June 1974, marking the alliance's twenty-fifth anniversary. He had coordinated closely with de Rose to include language recognizing the nuclear forces of France and Britain as contributing to global deterrence.

"This was really important for us because the French nuclear effort had been criticized in the United States and Europe," de Rose said. "But there were many governments who didn't want to give that blessing to the French nuclear effort." De Rose, in an interview, cited the episode as the most significant achievement of his close association with Rumsfeld.

For the most part, though, Rumsfeld as ambassador lacked a central role in the major East-West issues of the time. "My impression was that he felt somewhat out of the loop at NATO because, you know, Kissinger's style and Nixon's was to play it pretty close to the vest," said William G. Hyland, who was then the National Security Council staff official in Washington handling NATO affairs. Hyland recalled Rumsfeld stopping in to consult while on trips back to Washington. "I think he came to visit us mainly to see if he could find out what was going on behind the scenes."

There was little U.S. press coverage of Rumsfeld's tour at NATO. He tended to keep a low profile and avoided the grander trappings of the office. He was acutely discomfited, for instance, by his butler's habit of calling him "Excellency" and got the butler to stop it.

With Europe at his doorstep, Rumsfeld took advantage of opportunities to travel and explore. He ran with the bulls in Spain, went on a walking trip in the southern Sahara to view prehistoric paintings, and toured Malta. In 1973, he drove a rented Volkswagen bus with his mother, wife, and children to Sudweyhe to show his family their ancestral house. Two years later, the house, which had been built in 1764, was torn down to make room for a new development.

"He moved around a lot because he's a curious man," said Étienne Davignon, who headed the political department at Belgium's ministry of foreign affairs at the time and became friends with Rumsfeld. "He wanted to make the most of his assignment and take up all the opportunities that the job gave him."

Nixon, in his memoir, wrote that as the Watergate scandal mushroomed, "Don Rumsfeld called from Brussels, offering to resign as ambassador to NATO and return to help work against impeachment among his former colleagues in Congress." Rumsfeld denies ever making such an offer. What he remembers is a phone call from General Alexander Haig Jr., Nixon's chief of staff, who asked him whether he thought it made sense for him to return to Washington to lend his assistance.

Rumsfeld didn't. "I think you've played musical chairs over here," he told Haig. "I'm the third U.S. ambassador to NATO in the Nixon presidency, and the idea of pulling me out, it seems to me, would be really insulting to Europe. Furthermore, there's not a heckuva lot I could do." Rumsfeld suspects that Haig never relayed Rumsfeld's actual reply. More likely, the president was advised that Rumsfeld had expressed interest in helping but didn't think it made sense to abandon his post to do so.

At the time, some speculated that Rumsfeld's political career might be stunted as a result of his association with Nixon. When, in one of his last acts as president, Nixon visited Brussels for the June 1974 summit, Rumsfeld was asked by a journalist whether he thought his involvement with the disgraced president might prove an insurmountable obstacle in a future quest for public office. "I think people tend to judge candidates on themselves," he said hopefully. He rejected the theory that anyone who had worked for Nixon might be destroyed politically by Watergate. "I'm only 42," he said, smiling. "Lots of people are just starting in politics at my age."

CHAPTER 4

Keep Your Eye on Rummy

In early August 1974, Rumsfeld and his wife were on vacation in the Italian-French Riviera, driving from San Remo to St. Tropez. The Nixon debacle was reaching its climax, and Joyce urged Don to read the newspapers, which were filled with predictions of the president's impending resignation. He did and was surprised by how quickly Nixon's situation had deteriorated. Later that day, Rumsfeld received a summons home. After months of cover-ups, political standoffs, abuses of power, and constitutional dramas, Nixon had resigned in disgrace, and Gerald Ford was stepping into the presidency. Having had no time to prepare, Ford wanted Rumsfeld to coordinate a four-man transition team and help organize a new staff.

Rumsfeld's sudden involvement at the center of one of the most wrenching governmental changeovers in U.S. history might seem odd at first, but Ford had good reason to turn to him. Conveniently out of Washington during the unraveling of Watergate, Rumsfeld was free of taint and yet had been part of Nixon's inner circle and so knew many of the holdover staff. He had garnered a reputation as an able, energetic, and disciplined administrator. And he had an important link to Ford, having spearheaded the rebel group of House Republicans who had dumped Charles Halleck and engineered Ford's rise to minority leader nine years earlier.

Flying back to Washington on August 9, the day Ford was sworn into office, Rumsfeld arrived too late for the ceremony but in time for an afternoon meeting at the White House with Ford and senior staff. Rumsfeld had been greeted at Washington's Dulles Airport by Dick Cheney, then a vice president in the investment firm Bradley Woods and Company, who would again assume a position at Rumsfeld's right hand.

The nation was exhausted by Watergate, nursing deep wounds from the Vietnam War and facing the dreadful economic combination of mounting unemployment, rising prices, and a plummeting GNP. Ford was determined to establish a new tone and quickly set about highlighting his differences from Nixon, promising an open and candid administration in contrast with Nixon's secretive, obstructionist reign.

But the top personnel advising the president had not changed. A firm believer in the collegial approach to decision making, Ford wanted to retain Nixon's entire cabinet and those White House staff members not implicated in the Watergate scandal, most notably Henry Kissinger and Alexander Haig Jr. Ford's own loyalists, from his days as House minority leader and vice president, had not had any time to prepare for managing the presidency. And besides, Ford believed it would not be fair simply to fire those who had had nothing to do with Watergate.

Trying to merge the two staffs was a risky proposition, and tensions arose from the start. Complicating matters was Ford's desire to establish a decentralized management system, relying on an array of senior advisers— what he called a "spokes-of-the-wheel" model—instead of the Nixon model of a single, all-powerful chief of staff.

Rumsfeld doubted that this open-door management style, a holdover from Ford's days in the House, would work in running the White House. He also thought Ford should move quickly to establish his own team of senior officials and step away from the shadow of the Nixon years. While keeping some of Nixon's appointees was practical to give a sense of continuity, Rumsfeld argued that the longer the new president waited to make new choices, the more difficult it would be to change and the less Ford would be perceived as his own man. But he agreed to work with the transition team and to prepare a report on how to proceed. He told Ford that the team—which also included former Pennsylvania governor William Scranton, Interior Secretary Rogers Morton, and Jack Marsh, who had been Ford's national security adviser—would then "go out of business" in a month. "Rumsfeld and the others were acutely aware of the dangers inherent in the role they played," Ford wrote in his memoir. "They didn't want the transition team to 'take over' the government."

One of Ford's immediate decisions was the selection of a vice president. Speculation quickly centered on George H. W. Bush, then the fifty-year-old chairman of the Republican National Committee, and Nelson Rockefeller, former New York governor and multimillionaire GOP liberal. Bush represented the safe choice, the favorite among Republican party officials. Rockefeller offered depth and experience and a chance for Ford to reach beyond the Nixon holdovers, but picking Rockefeller threatened to incite the Right, which detested him.

Ford himself added Rumsfeld to the short list of candidates he asked the FBI to run background checks on. By then, Rumsfeld was being seen as something of a mystery man in the group helping the new president, notably more important than his age and experience would explain. Lacking national stature or a strong political base, he would seem to bring little to a ticket with Ford in 1976. His scant party support was evident in a poor showing among members of Congress, governors, and other Republicans who sent recommendations to Ford about the vice presidential choice. While Bush drew the most mentions, Rumsfeld managed only fifteenth place in the tally. When only first choices were counted among the 910 politicians who offered advice, Bush held the lead with 125 nominations, and Rumsfeld trailed far behind, with just one backer.

Nonetheless, taking advantage of his White House position and the highly unsettled political conditions surrounding the new administration, Rumsfeld promoted his availability. Robert Hartmann, a former congressional aide and vice presidential chief of staff to Ford who had come onboard as White House counselor and had begun to clash with Rumsfeld over access to Ford, noted the involvement of Rumsfeld's supporters in "the clearly coordinated planting with Washington reporters of the fact that Rumsfeld was one of those under consideration."

Ford ultimately settled on Rockefeller, whose celebrity status, the president was betting, would boost his new administration's image. "He'd picked Rockefeller because he had stature and was widely recognized and thought it was a good fit for himself because he wasn't well known," Cheney recalled in an interview. "But he looked on Bush and Rumsfeld as the future of the party."

The selection of Rockefeller was announced on August 20, and the transition team submitted its final report the same day, urging Ford to put his own people in other top jobs as soon as he could. By then, Rumsfeld had told Ford he needed to head back to NATO headquarters to tend to a crisis heating up over Cyprus that threatened to force Greece out of NATO. Rumsfeld figured he had done what he could to help, but the transition period had also been of some benefit to him. His prominent role in the transition and his appearance on Ford's short list for vice president had given him fresh viability as a candidate for national office. While he would have remained had he been offered a cabinet post in the new administration, he recognized none was likely to open up if Ford held to his plan to keep Nixon's cast, and given his sense of ongoing White House dysfunction, Rumsfeld thought it best to stay away.

Shortly afterward, Ford's honeymoon in his new job ended with his shocking and highly unpopular decision to pardon Nixon. And by his second month as president, Ford was increasingly disturbed by the squabbling on his staff between those who had come in with him and the Nixon holdovers. Resolved to recruit someone new to try to get a tighter hold on White House operations, Ford arranged to shift Haig, who had been filling the senior coordinator role, to the post of top NATO commander, and to woo Rumsfeld back.

On September 21, Rumsfeld, in Illinois attending the funeral of his father, who had suffered from Alzheimer's disease and had died a few days before, received a call from Ford inviting him to Washington. The next day the two met in the Oval Office for an hour and a half as Ford tried to persuade a reluctant Rumsfeld to take the top White House staff job.

Rumsfeld had expected that Ford might offer him a cabinet post, where he could have more independence and political visibility. But a senior White House job? He had been there, done that. He was disappointed, moreover, that Ford had not followed his recommendations for the transition. Too many former Nixon people had been retained. And, Rumsfeld told Ford, the spokes-of-the-wheel management model just wasn't going to work.

"I said it just wasn't feasible," Rumsfeld recalled saying. "He could be minority leader that way, but not president of the United States." The only thing that happens where the spokes of the wheel converge, Rumsfeld told Ford, is that the grease gets overheated and has to be changed every few thousand miles.

In their conversation, Ford acknowledged to Rumsfeld that the spokes approach didn't appear to be working. He signaled a willingness to move toward a more traditional chief of staff arrangement, although he deferred doing so since he had only recently announced his plan for more decentralized management.

But Rumsfeld had been enjoying his life in Brussels. He was finally getting the international experience he had wanted to fill out his résumé. He was rubbing shoulders with some of Europe's most skilled diplomats, being mentored by them and forming close friendships with a few. And he was finding the time to be with his family and to travel.

Rumsfeld returned to Brussels and spent several days continuing to resist, but the president persisted, and Rumsfeld finally agreed, finding it impossible to refuse the request of his old friend and new U.S. president—or the attraction of coming back to a powerful, if derivative, position in Washington. Learning soon after that First Lady Betty Ford had been diagnosed with breast cancer made Rumsfeld even more inclined to help, given the additional strain that Ford would be under dealing with his wife's illness.

The administrative and political challenges that Rumsfeld walked into appeared overwhelming. Credibility in the executive branch had to be rebuilt, relations between Nixon and Ford people sorted out, a new leadership team formed, and order imposed on a White House that had been under political siege and seriously adrift for months. Looking back on it, Rumsfeld considers his time as Ford's right-hand man the most daunting assignment of his life.

"Clearly, the toughest job I've ever had," he declared in an interview for this book. "You had a president who'd never run for the office, who'd never been an executive, who didn't have a campaign team, didn't have a platform. And you had a White House that was deemed, unfairly in many respects, not legitimate."

While Rumsfeld had demonstrated administrative talent running OEO and the Cost of Living Council, it was in Ford's White House that he showed a keener skill for organizing and a shrewdness for bureaucratic maneuvering. As he worked to boost the overall efficiency of the president's staff, the experience would enhance his reputation as a disciplined, effective manager. But his clashes with other top officials also furthered an image of him as a combative and manipulative operator focused primarily on advancing his own interests.

Rumsfeld moved quickly, in keeping with Ford's wishes, to erase the imperial image that the presidency had acquired under Nixon and restore a more approachable, down-to-earth look. He eliminated many of the titles that had proliferated in the Nixon administration, cut back sharply on perquisites long available to White House aides, wrote a code of ethics for White House staff members, and reorganized the presidential staff in a way that allowed senior members to be interchangeable with their deputies.

Under Nixon, the chief of staff had tightly controlled access to the president. By contrast, nine senior staff members were to have more or less equal access to Ford. Rumsfeld wasn't called "chief of staff" but "staff coordinator." He portrayed himself as an administrator first and foremost, intent on getting all points of view and options before the president when decisions were pending. "There are people in the White House who are assigned substantive jobs. It happens I am not," he told a seminar at Princeton in the fall of 1975.

In fact, though, Rumsfeld ended up with considerable control over White House activities. He spent more time with Ford than did any other official. His influence extended from operation of the White House dining room to the design of economic policy and the plotting of presidential campaign strategy. He was the chief power broker, the president's trouble shooter, and Ford's ranking adviser.

At his side as his deputy was Cheney, still self-effacing, still willing to take care of many of the mundane chores and spare his boss the trouble. Rumsfeld also placed dependable lieutenants in other critical slots, such as the presidential personnel office and the cabinet secretary's office. Among the loyalists he brought in were Don Murdoch, who was in Madison, Wisconsin, practicing law; Don Lowitz, who had been Rumsfeld's general counsel and who came in from Chicago as a temporary consultant; William Walker, another friend from Chicago, who became head of the White

House personnel office; and William Greener Jr., the deputy press secretary, who had been with Rumsfeld at the Cost of Living Council.

He also drew on a network of allies and friends to fill other government offices, including John Dunlop as secretary of labor, William Coleman Jr. as secretary of transportation, Edward Levi as attorney general, and Howard H. "Bo" Callaway as director of the president's campaign committee.

At the same time, Rumsfeld artfully maneuvered to diminish the clout of potential rivals. The Ford White House was home to much suspicion and sniping, with Rumsfeld often factoring in the middle of real and imagined moves for power, particularly against Kissinger, Rockefeller, and Treasury secretary Bill Simon. All three men pointed to Rumsfeld as the one responsible for planting rumors in the media of Ford's disenchantment with them. And all complained to the president directly about it. Simon later remarked on a noticeable reduction in negative stories about him once Rumsfeld became secretary of defense and finally had his own cabinet position.

Indeed, soon after returning from NATO and sliding into his prominent White House staff position, Rumsfeld was identified in the press as the one to watch. "With his varied background and contacts, with his well-known brashness and informality, Mr. Rumsfeld can be expected to cast a wide net for the president," wrote Leslie Gelb in the *New York Times*. "He is strikingly handsome, energetic, has a good sense of humor, a fast intelligence and the ability to make snap decisions." *New York Times* columnist James Reston noted "strong support" for Rumsfeld among Republicans, who regarded him "as one of the most attractive and capable leaders" of the coming generation. "So it would not be a bad idea to keep your eye on 'Rummy.' He could turn out to be in the right place with the right credentials for much larger things in his party."

Rumsfeld's initial struggles were with members of Ford's entourage—most notably Hartmann, who was suspicious of Rumsfeld as a Nixon holdover. Rumsfeld managed to edge him out in a process that involved limiting Hartmann's duties to speechwriting and some politics and shifting him out of an office that was next to the Oval Office.

Eroding Kissinger's standing took more doing. The enormous authority that Kissinger had amassed under Nixon had carried over into the Ford administration, where he still served as both secretary of state and national security adviser, dominating foreign policy. Rumsfeld worried about Ford being perceived as simply doing Kissinger's bidding and perpetuating the policies of the Nixon administration. Rumsfeld began chipping away at Kissinger's power, balancing papers and memos that Kissinger prepared, for instance, by adding information and arguments from other senior White House assistants.

When White House press secretary Ron Nesson had a minor skirmish with a lower-level Kissinger aide, he was surprised to find that Rumsfeld raised the episode directly with the president. "I had the uneasy feeling that Rumsfeld was using the incident to drag me into a behind-the-scenes struggle to curb the power of Kissinger and the National Security Council," Nesson wrote.

With Rockefeller, the tensions were more personal, rooted in a dislike each had for the other. The assertive, grinning Rockefeller was the public service–minded representative of a true American dynasty. But Rumsfeld saw him as a rich, arrogant bully who browbeat some and lavished money and gifts on others to create his entourage. The vice president would sometimes join with Kissinger, a longtime friend, in ganging up on Rumsfeld. Rockefeller's behavior only aggravated Rumsfeld's own ingrained bias against wealthy easterners.

Aside from these personal considerations, Rockefeller threatened the management system that Rumsfeld had set up. The vice president and his staff considered themselves an independent power inside the White House and had a penchant to write memos and launch initiatives outside Rumsfeld's preferred formal channels. Rumsfeld worried particularly that Rockefeller's desire to play a strong role in domestic policy would undermine Ford's chances of election in the same way that Kissinger's powerful foreign policy role would.

When Rockefeller proposed a Domestic Council modeled after the National Security Council and Ford appointed him head, Rumsfeld managed to take control of the council's day-to-day operations. He sought as well to ensure that papers from Rockefeller's staff outlining positions and proposals got subjected to the regular White House review process. When Rockefeller, for instance, devised a massive $100 billion energy program, Rumsfeld, concerned about the potential creation of a massive quasi-public corporation, made certain the idea was circulated within the administration for comment. The move angered Rockefeller, who viewed it, not incorrectly, as a ploy to sandbag his idea. Rumsfeld claimed that he was simply carrying out Ford's bidding to solicit opinions.

If there is one aspect of his White House experience that Rumsfeld regretted most, it was his inability to get along better with Rockefeller—or so Rumsfeld told an interviewer shortly after the Ford administration ended. He had tried, he said, to make the relationship with Rockefeller work, knowing that Ford liked the vice president. But Rumsfeld and Rockefeller could not coexist peaceably.

It was under Ford that Rumsfeld's signature management style began to show itself in full. It was a style high on energy and intensity and low on frills and compliments. "He was a tough, no-nonsense guy, very purposeful. I mean, he was all business," said Jerry Jones, who had carried over from the Nixon administration in the post of White House staff secretary. "The first day I met with him, after he got back from NATO, he said something to this effect—I don't remember the quote exactly but this is about it—'Jones, I don't want to get to know you; I might like you and I'm going to have to fire you.' It didn't work out that way, but that was the opening gambit."

He worked at a stand-up desk in a large office on the first floor of the West Wing, whisking through the papers that flowed into the White House, composing memos on a Dictaphone that were then transcribed by one of his two secretaries. Most of Rumsfeld's instructions were communicated by memo. "Don generates much more paper than I do," Cheney once remarked of his friend and mentor. "He's more inclined to dictate a memo when he wants something done."

Rumsfeld put in long hours and expected the same of others. His speech was so clipped it bordered on brusqueness. He showed little patience with incompetence. When a subordinate once tarried too long over an explanation, Rumsfeld snapped, "Come back when you have something to say."

Rumsfeld could be charming when he wanted, but more often than not he was abrasive, even insulting in dealing with subordinates. He was known to hang up on aides in mid-conversation, and during one meeting he barked to another cabinet-level official to stand up when asking a question.

He did not flatter, nor did he pass out compliments. Although he knew he should do so, it just wasn't his way. He explained that he considered it a waste of time "going around puffing people's egos up." His praise, he said, came in the form of giving people training, advice, and more work. "And ultimately that's a lot more valuable to a person than a letter on their jacket or a pat on their head," he added.

He did concede his approach had its shortcomings. "Now from the standpoint of human relations," he remarked, "if I'm to be flawed, faulted, there's no question but that the oil can is mightier than the sword. And there's no question but that probably as a human being I would do better if I did take more time to simply praise people. I don't. Maybe I'll develop the ability to do it more easily. I don't have a great need for praise. Therefore, I guess, I unconsciously assume that others don't."

Rumsfeld did have a sense of humor, but it was not the soothing, joke-telling kind. It was more biting wit with an edge—the kind of humor that could make people laugh but still leave them feeling uneasy and on guard. He had a big smile, which helped soften his image, but his toughness came through. And he clearly was no brooder.

"I'll reflect on a decision I've made that might be wrong," he told an interviewer, "but I've never been much for hand-wringing. I don't sit down and ask myself: 'Are you sure you're happy?' I never agonize, because if you do, you won't be able to cope. What you do is just keep establishing priorities, and when the work builds up, you stop, take that which is important, delegate the rest and move on."

Along the way, too, Rumsfeld had acquired an endless vocabulary of hand signals that he used when he spoke. "His active hands move as if blown by every gust in his mind—always shaping, grasping bits of form out of the chaos of power," the author John Hersey wrote in a profile of the Ford White House. Hersey noted in the motions a variety of "stabbings, long-fingered rounding out of abstractions, flat-handed layering of relationships, squarings off, chops, slaps, flicks, pinches, punches, piano playing and a bit of harp work," all employed while Rumsfeld "gives concise and brisk explanations of items he raises, and President Ford, in no hurry, makes decisions as they are needed."

Hersey called Rumsfeld "bright, jealous, crafty and fiercely combative," which seemed to sum up the general view of him. In newspaper profiles of the time, he was frequently characterized as supremely cautious, ambitious, and opportunistic. Of his relationships with the press, Rumsfeld himself said, "I don't badmouth, and I don't leak—and I don't go on 'Meet the Press' to say something I didn't intend to say."

He also didn't like to lose. "I am not going to say I care if I win," he said, "but I never want it written on my tombstone, 'He was a good loser.'" He was speaking at the time of his weekly tennis doubles matches with Ford, although his words clearly had broader application.

That was the public Rumsfeld. In private he could be different— gracious, considerate, fun-loving. He liked to have a good time, and among friends, he was given to clowning. He inspired genuine, lasting friendships—including one with Ford. Rumsfeld's intense, blunt style contrasted sharply with the president's fondness for relaxed good fellowship. But each man had a high regard for the other, and the two got along well.

Rumsfeld's varied personality made him somewhat of an enigma to many. A *Washington Post* profile captured his combination of beguiling traits and inscrutability—a politician, on the one hand, of good looks, abiding intensity, retentive mind, and much humor, and yet, on the other, not entirely knowable.

"There is something distant about Rumsfeld, something in him he doesn't allow most others to know," wrote Judy Bachrach. She quoted people close to Rumsfeld saying they didn't really get him, not deep down. "Rummy always holds back a bit," said Marvin Feldman, who was his assistant director for program development at OEO. Observed Frank Carlucci, "Rumsfeld keeps his cards close to his chest. He's not the kind of person who talks unnecessarily."

To Brent Scowcroft, who worked with Rumsfeld during the Nixon and Ford years and continued to have contact with him over several subsequent decades, he remained perplexing. "To this day, I do not know what Rumsfeld really thinks," Scowcroft said in 2007. "I've had a chance to watch his mind operate. For anybody else with whom I've had that kind of contact, I've gotten a picture of who they are, what makes them work, and so on. I have no idea what makes him work, what makes him the way he is."

But no one disagreed about Rumsfeld's ambitiousness. Indeed, Laurence Leamer, who profiled Rumsfeld in a 1977 book about leading Washington figures, wrote that while Rumsfeld had a number of admirable qualities—honesty, courage, energy, and discipline—there was at his core a ceaseless ambition. Leamer once asked Rumsfeld about this widespread perception of him as an ambitious man. Sitting in a small alcove off his main White House office, Rumsfeld replied that the label was a "sloppy and inaccurate" characterization of what he preferred to view simply as working on something he found interesting and of value and succeeding at it. "I've always been kind of amused by the references," he said.

Rumsfeld has long been a great keeper of lists, a habit of his since grammar school. His ultimate list, which sums up his views on serving and surviving in government, business or life in general, is now a lengthy compendium titled "Rumsfeld's Rules." This didactic collection of dos and don'ts began during Rumsfeld's time with Ford and was meant to inform the White House staff of wise and proper behavior.

"As a youngster, I read a lot, and there were a lot words I didn't know," he recalled in an interview. "I always carried a three-by-five card, and I'd write down a word I didn't know the meaning of and then I'd look it up and write down the definition. I'd use the card as a bookmark in a book or carry it in my pocket. Then for some reason along the way, I started keeping track of anecdotes or statements or sayings or pithy comments that seemed interesting. I kept some of them in a file."

The file grew as Rumsfeld took on different jobs—Navy pilot, congressional aide, member of Congress, White House official, NATO ambassador. He had kept the list to himself during that time. But now as chief of staff, facing the most significant, highest-profile organizational challenge of his career, he was ready to broaden the audience.

He discussed the list with Ford, then distributed it to the White House staff. The "first edition" bears the date December 1, 1974. Split into several sections, the rules numbered about a hundred by the end of the Ford administration. The first mention of them in the press is a December 1976 article in the *Wall Street Journal*. An abridged version containing about a third of the rules showed up a month later in the *Washington Post*. In 1980, Rumsfeld copyrighted the list.

Although it bore his name, Rumsfeld didn't claim any particular pride of authorship over many of the rules on the list. While he did compose some himself, he drew others from a variety of sources—proverbs, aphorisms, jokes, and clever quotations. By the time he left the Pentagon in 2006, the list had grown to more than thirty pages.

At each of the organizations he ran, in government and business, Rumsfeld made a practice of giving his rules to new hires. It became a blueprint for his own managerial style. As domineering and overbearing as he could be, as rough, tough, and gruff, Rumsfeld recognized a certain prescription for how things should be. "Don had some class," Hartmann once wrote about him. "He was ruthless within the rules." They just happened to be his own rules.

The original list already contained a wealth of collected wisdom. One of Rumsfeld's all-time favorite sayings was there, drawn from the flight manual for the Navy's SNJ plane, which Rumsfeld had flown during his time as a student aviator. "If you are lost—'climb, conserve and confess,'" the instruction stated. You climb to get altitude, you conserve gas by throttling back, and you confess on the radio that you are lost. Rumsfeld considered that good advice for anyone lost, no matter the context.

Other rules promoted notions of confidence ("Be yourself."), self-criticism ("If you foul up, tell the President and others fast, and correct it."), caution ("It is easier to get into something than it is to get out of it."), modesty ("Don't begin to believe you are indispensable or infallible."), and integrity ("You and the White House staff must be, and be seen as being, above suspicion.").

Some of the maxims were purely procedural and commented on ways to do the job: "Have a deputy and use him," or, "Learn quickly how to say, 'I don't know.'" Others stressed the importance of maintaining perspective on the job: "Keep your sense of humor. Don't forget General Stilwell's motto, 'The higher a monkey climbs, the more you see of his behind.'"

There was advice on how to deal with inevitable criticism from the press, Congress, and others: "Put your head down, do your job as best you can, and let the 'picking' (and there will be some) roll off." And encouragement to generate some criticism: "If you are not criticized, it could be because you are not doing much that is productive." But also a warning to watch what you say: "Don't speak ill of another member of the Administration." Plus some simple pointers on proper grammar and speech: "Be precise," and, "Never say 'the White House wants'—buildings don't 'want.'"

One rule offered this shrewd tactic for holding on to a job: "Be able to resign. It will improve your value to the President." Another urged knowing when to leave: "Don't stay on the job too long. Change is healthy for everyone." In any case, Rumsfeld counseled, don't let go of your principles: "Don't blindly obey directions from the President with which you disagree, or even when you agree, when you feel he hasn't weighed all sides, without first discussing it with him."

A number of rules applied specifically to White House work. Rumsfeld stressed, for instance, that presidential aides must make sure that the president, cabinet members, and other top staffers are constantly aware of all important problems. "If they are out of the flow of information," he wrote, "decisions will either be poorly made or not made—each is dangerous."

Other points on the list emphasized the importance of cooperating closely with Congress. One reminded staff members that "you will need the support of each member of the House and Senate, regardless of philosophy or party, on some issue at some time." Another even more wisely observed that members of Congress "are not there by accident. Each managed to get there for a reason. Discover it, and you have learned something valuable about our country."

But many of the dos and don'ts were really general management principles, with relevance outside government as well. "Read and listen for what is missing," asserted one. "Many advisers are capable of knowing how to improve what has been proposed. Few will see what isn't there."

Rumsfeld's tough office manner showed up in a rule that decreed: "Don't be afraid of sharp edges. Sometimes they are necessary to leadership." But other precepts on the list indicated Rumsfeld's own awareness of the need to curb one's sense of self-importance in office. "Don't forget," he wrote, "that the fifty or so invitations you receive a week from 'the high and the mighty' are sent not because those people are dying to see you but because of the position you hold. If you don't believe that, ask one of your predecessors how fast they stop."

As much as the list may have grown out of a childhood habit, Rumsfeld's dedication to refining and expanding it reflected his adult view of life as something that could be ordered and structured according to certain prescriptions. It suggested a systematic and rational approach to doing things, a very programmatic attitude. And indeed, that is much of what had made Rumsfeld the archetype of a new breed of professional politician from his early days in Congress. It wasn't just that he was educated and motivated, ethical and incorruptible. Rumsfeld was constantly working on himself, constantly becoming. And the rules were his road map.

"I think Rumsfeld is still too program oriented," Nixon had said of Rumsfeld in a dictated evaluation of him soon after he started at the White House as a presidential counselor. Nixon, who had a sentimental, sometimes maudlin side, considered Rumsfeld, for all his focus and drive, lacking in a certain sentimentality. "He is part of the new, pragmatic, post-war college group who are no-nonsense types and frankly lack the basically idealistic and romantic attitude," the president said.

But Rumsfeld got results, and that is what mattered. He understood bureaucratic power, understood how to get what he wanted. He believed that if certain principles were adhered to, certain proven behavior practiced, the right outcomes would follow. And with his rules, he was laying out the formulas for anyone else interested.

There was more than a little confidence in his act of publicizing them. After all, a number of the sayings were borrowed from others, and together they constituted a kind of collective, folksy wisdom. Yet the list was distinctly his, packaged and marketed with his name on it. And few could argue with Rumsfeld's success to that point. If the rules were what had helped him get to where he was, well, then maybe there was something to them.

———•———

With the 1976 presidential election on the horizon, Ford faced a growing political challenge on his right from Governor Ronald Reagan of

California. The president was under increased pressure to shore up conservative support by abandoning his liberal vice president, Rockefeller, and to define himself more clearly by removing Nixon holdovers from his administration. Against this backdrop, in November 1975 Ford announced a sweeping set of cabinet changes that were viewed by many as intended to strengthen his standing among conservatives. They also appeared to advance Rumsfeld's interests by promoting him to a cabinet job and positioning him as a possible vice presidential running mate in 1976.

The overhaul required Rockefeller, acting on a strong suggestion delivered privately by Ford, to agree to step down at the end of the term. James Schlesinger was removed as defense secretary, and Rumsfeld was named to replace him. William Colby left the CIA, and George H. W. Bush, then chief of the U.S. Liaison Office in China, became the new CIA director. Kissinger, meanwhile, was relieved of his job as national security adviser but continued as secretary of state.

Although Ford maintained that the shake-up was intended to form his own national security team after fifteen months in office, a suspicion took hold widely that Rumsfeld had engineered the whole thing. After all, not only had Rumsfeld ended up with the top Pentagon job, but Kissinger was removed from the West Wing and Bush, by being assigned to the CIA, was effectively out of contention as a possible vice presidential candidate. Further, Cheney, Rumsfeld's alter ego, had been named as the new White House chief of staff.

On the day that the cabinet changes were announced, Rumsfeld was taking a rare break to attend a Washington Redskins football game. His absence served only to enhance his reputation as the leave-no-fingerprints, master maneuverer of the Ford administration.

But subsequent evidence suggests Rumsfeld was less involved in pulling the political strings than rumored. The historical record confirms Ford's insistence that he conceived of the reorganization to assert his own leadership. Ford had been uncomfortable with Schlesinger, whom he considered aloof and frequently arrogant, and he had been bothered by Schlesinger's strained relations with Kissinger and with some in Congress. To balance the dismissal of Schlesinger, who was popular with congressional conservatives, Ford took some power away from

Kissinger, whose efforts at détente and arms control with the Soviet Union were distrusted by conservatives.

As for Bush's CIA appointment, Rumsfeld had not been among those pushing for it, according to internal administration documents. In a memo to Ford in July 1975, Rumsfeld put forward ten other names to replace Colby. The memo included the preferences of eight different Ford advisers. Only three—Cheney; John Marsh, who oversaw congressional relations; and David Packard, the electronics company executive—listed Bush among their recommendations for the new CIA director.

Along with the list of recommendations, Rumsfeld sent Ford brief descriptions of the contenders. Bush was favorably reviewed. Under "pros," the memo cited: "Experience in government and diplomacy; generally familiar with components of the intelligence community and their missions; management experience; high integrity and proven adaptability." Under "cons" was listed only Bush's chairmanship of the Republican National Committee, with the remark, "RNC post lends undesirable political cast."

Rumsfeld learned that Ford intended to move him into Schlesinger's place only eight days before the announcement. "The president sat Kissinger and me down in a chair and said, 'Here's what I'm going to do,'" Rumsfeld recalled years later. Rumsfeld told Ford he was making a mistake. "You're within just a little over a year before the election," he said. "If you wanted to do it, you should have done it early on, not now. And furthermore, Jim Schlesinger is doing a helluva good job, and I wouldn't have any difference with him on policy at all." Rumsfeld also objected to placing himself and Bush in positions where they could not participate in the campaign. He said that he and Bush were both men who had backgrounds in politics and should be kept available to help.

But Ford persisted, and Rumsfeld agreed to think about the offer. The notion that he wasn't very tempted to take it after long aspiring to a cabinet post seems far-fetched. In particular, though, he wanted to consult Paul Nitze, the leading Cold War strategist whose patriotism Rumsfeld, as a young congressman, had once called into question. Rumsfeld had since apologized, and the two had become friends while Rumsfeld was at NATO, when Nitze would stay at the ambassadorial residence during visits. He was now the assistant secretary of defense for international affairs.

Nitze urged Rumsfeld to take the job. "First of all, you'd be good at it," he said, according to Rumsfeld. "Second, you could get confirmed. And third, you have a relationship with the president that will enable you to do the job a lot better. Neither you nor I could name two other people who have the relationship with the president, who could get confirmed, and who could do the job. They just don't exist."

When word leaked of Ford's plans, the president pressed Rumsfeld for a decision. Flying to Florida on November 2, Ford had Cheney call Rumsfeld at the football game for an answer, and Rumsfeld said yes.

On November 18, the Senate confirmed Rumsfeld's nomination on a 95-to-2 vote. The brief debate on the nomination was not so much a discussion of Rumsfeld's merits as it was a tribute to Schlesinger. Senators who rose to support Rumsfeld prefaced their statements with protests over the change and the manner in which it was being handled. Notwithstanding Ford's assertions that Schlesinger's ouster and Rumsfeld's appointment, along with the other cabinet changes, were his idea, the shake-up that made Rumsfeld defense secretary cemented the view of him as a partisan opportunist willing to place his own ambitions ahead of all else in order to dispose of rivals for the vice presidency in 1976.

Rumsfeld's new position was his sixth administration job in six years. But as secretary of defense, he would finally have the kind of authority he had sought in government. The Pentagon's top officers awaited his arrival with some anxiety. The department had been shaken by congressional budget slashes and was apprehensive about strategic arms talks. Schlesinger's dismissal had left everyone stunned.

In his twenty-eight months as secretary, Schlesinger, a former economics-professor-turned-military-analyst, had provided the intellectual and philosophical direction that permitted the military establishment to regroup and rebuild after the turmoil of the Vietnam War. Rumsfeld's background had been in politics, and he had yet to show the necessary breadth of intellect to handle an assignment as complex and demanding as running the nation's defenses. Moreover, at forty-three, Rumsfeld was the youngest defense secretary ever.

A main test of Rumsfeld's ability would come in the area of arms control. With Schlesinger's departure, it was thought that the department had lost its best strategic thinker, the only one in the Pentagon capable of providing a counterweight to Kissinger in the strategic arms negotiations with the Soviet Union. Schlesinger, while not opposed to an arms deal, worried that the United States was sacrificing military security for friendship with the Soviet Union and had wanted a deal on stricter terms than Kissinger sought. At times he was openly critical of Kissinger's bargaining tactics, and he regarded Kissinger as overly willing to make concessions to further his détente policy, which was aimed at relaxing superpower tensions.

There was considerable doubt that Rumsfeld would be a match for Kissinger in strategic theory. Indeed, Rumsfeld's record in the field of national security showed him to be someone who proceeded cautiously and often made points by asking questions. He was expected to be an implementer of White House policy, not an innovator of policy as Schlesinger— or, for that matter, Robert McNamara—had been.

At his confirmation hearing, Rumsfeld faced a barrage of skeptical questions about the policy of improved relations and arms control agreements with the Soviet Union. At the time, détente was under attack by some Democrats, including presidential hopeful Senator Henry "Scoop" Jackson of Washington, as well as by many conservative Republicans, who supported the challenge to Ford being mounted by Reagan. These hard-line advocates had worried that Schlesinger's exit signaled an administration tilt toward Kissinger's pro-détente approach. But Rumsfeld reassured skeptics that he was in basic agreement with Schlesinger's views on the subject.

Indeed, Kissinger was anticipating that the ambitious Rumsfeld would prove a more difficult colleague, since Schlesinger at least had no obvious political ambition, while Rumsfeld would want to avoid risking Ford's standing—or his own—with the Reagan wing by embracing détente. Further, Rumsfeld had the confidence of Ford. And he had learned how to operate at the upper levels of government. After his confirmation hearing, he sent a transcript to Ford along with a note pointing out Jackson's concerns that previous defense secretaries had not been present at crucial meetings at which decisions on strategic arms control negotiations were made. Rumsfeld was signaling that things had to change.

In Ford's first meeting with Rumsfeld as defense secretary along with Kissinger and Brent Scowcroft, the new national security adviser, the president said, "I hope we can overcome the problem that Henry had before"—a reference to Kissinger's strained relations with Schlesinger. Kissinger told the president that he had already arranged with Rumsfeld to take a Pentagon representative with him to Moscow for the next Strategic Arms Limitation Treaty (SALT) negotiations. But he added, "I hope it won't be played as being squeezed out of me."

Kissinger himself had a reputation that rivaled Rumsfeld's for bureaucratic maneuvering. Praised as a foreign policy genius, Kissinger was also known for being duplicitous, secretive, arrogant, and vain. He was already a luminary when Rumsfeld was just starting in the Nixon administration, and he watched as the young Illinois politician steadily climbed Washington's power ladder. "Rumsfeld afforded me a close-up look at a special Washington phenomenon: the skilled full-time politician-bureaucrat in whom ambition, ability, and substance fuse seamlessly," Kissinger wrote in his memoir.

Try as they did after Rumsfeld became secretary of defense, the two were unable to avoid a clash over how hard and fast to push détente with the Soviets. "They were just totally different people with a different frame of reference," said Staser Holcomb, a three-star admiral who was Rumsfeld's military assistant. "Rumsfeld was standing on the brakes and Kissinger standing on the accelerator."

Kissinger's tensions with Rumsfeld were different from those he had with Schlesinger. "Schlesinger was basically an academic who would occasionally fight intellectual battles using political means—though never very comfortably," Kissinger wrote. "Rumsfeld might invoke systems analysis in his battles, but he was more a political leader than an analyst." William Hyland, the NSC director of intelligence and research at the time, put it more succinctly. Schlesinger thought of dispute as "principled disagreement." With Rumsfeld, it was a "bureaucratic contest."

One of Rumsfeld's favorite tactics was to stall when presented with new diplomatic initiatives or military moves. The delay was often interpreted not as a sign of Rumsfeld's uncertainty about how to respond but as an indication of his muffled opposition. "You'd say, 'Well, what do you think of this proposal, Don? Should we go ahead with it?'" Hyland recounted. "And he'd say, 'Well, let me think about it.' And then nothing would happen. That'd go on for sometimes quite awhile, and you'd realize it was deliberate. He would ask a lot of questions that were interesting but not really relevant. He'd say things like, 'How do you know this?' or 'What do you know about that?' Kind of picky stuff. His style was never to say, 'Mr. President, I can't agree to this,' or 'Mr. President, you ought to do that.' I don't remember anything like that. But I have to give him credit—he got his way."

"He had the technique of lying in the weeds," Scowcroft recalled. "For example, I would be developing a strategy for a particular circumstance, and I'd be working and getting it all put together, and then we'd have a meeting to finalize it, and that's when he'd toss a monkey wrench in. 'Well, I don't think that would work,' he would say, or 'How would that work?' and so on. He wouldn't propose an alternative but just gum up the works. And that's why I found him so difficult to work with. He just made my job a lot harder. And he was very good at it."

Rumsfeld knew enough about the inner workings of government to determine how to gather information about his bureaucratic adversaries. To learn more about what the State Department was up to, for instance, he examined the communication traffic between State and Defense soon after arriving at the Pentagon. He told an assistant to get him a listing by month of the "exclusive distribution" and "no distribution" cables from the State Department over the previous two years. From as many as ninety per month, the cables had dwindled to just a few from State in the final months of the Schlesinger period.

"The Pentagon had been effectively tuned out in terms of the flow of information from the State Department to the Pentagon," Rumsfeld recalled in an interview with Pentagon historians. "I had breakfast with Henry and laid the report on the table. He said, 'Yes, we'll fix that.' It slowly started back up."

It was a small but telling example of Rumsfeld's grasp of the bureaucracy and how to make it work for him.

Early in the Ford administration, expectations that an arms control agreement could be reached ran high. The Vladivostock Accords in November 1974 had appeared to pave the way to a deal, setting a limit for the United States and Soviet Union of 2,400 missile systems and bombers each. But the two nations came to an impasse in 1975 over two issues that were not negotiated at Vladivostok: the Soviet Backfire bomber and the U.S. cruise missile. The United States proposed that both systems be allowed in equal numbers above the 2,400 ceiling, but the Soviets didn't want their bomber counted at all, insisting its range was less than U.S. authorities declared and so did not qualify as a strategic weapon.

In January 1976, Kissinger headed to Moscow with some new negotiating proposals. After discussions with Soviet president Leonid Brezhnev, he sensed Soviet interest in a deal that would balance several hundred Backfires against several hundred ship-launched cruise missiles—an option the Pentagon had seemed to endorse. But Rumsfeld and the Joint Chiefs balked, and Kissinger had no room to negotiate further. "I had no choice but to let the opportunity to exploit this breakthrough go by," he wrote exasperatedly in a memo to Ford.

Back in Washington, Kissinger and Rumsfeld remained at odds over acceptable terms for a U.S.-Soviet agreement. In mid-February, Kissinger finally gave up the quest for an agreement before the election. He was convinced defense officials would prolong the options game, and he worried about the divisiveness of the issue. In Kissinger's view, Rumsfeld "in effect permitted and indeed encouraged the bureaucratic process to run into the sand."

Rumsfeld acknowledged as much years later. "I would be like the skunk at the garden party, saying, 'You can't do that, this would have that effect, and I think it's a mistake, and I think you ought to hold off,'" he told Pentagon historians. "I felt that what we were able to get out of it in that time frame wasn't worth our doing."

The lack of agreement among his top national security advisers was deeply frustrating to Ford. In his memoir, Ford blamed the inability to close a deal on a combination of Soviet intransigence and "highly technical" objections by Rumsfeld and the Pentagon. Ford personally delivered a copy of the book to Rumsfeld before publication. "He handed me his book, and he put his hand on my leg and he said, 'You're not going to like it,'" Rumsfeld recalled in an interview for this book. "I said, 'Why is that, Mr. President?' He said, 'Well, because I kind of laid the responsibility for the fact that we didn't get a SALT deal on Brezhnev and you.' And I said, 'Heck, I can live with that.' And he laughed because he knew that I felt strongly about it."

After Ford narrowly lost the 1976 election to Jimmy Carter, some of Ford's associates argued that a foreign policy success such as a strategic arms agreement might have saved their president. They blamed Rumsfeld for undermining the arms talks and eroding Ford's election chances. Other factors, though, also contributed to the defeat, including Ford's pardon for Nixon's crimes and the feeble condition of the economy. In retrospect, Rumsfeld himself, not surprisingly, doubts that an arms control deal would have made a difference.

———•———

Rumsfeld's own motives for remaining wary of détente and thwarting a strategic weapons agreement have been the subject of much speculation. Was he acting out of an ideological conviction that the policy was flawed? Or was he driven by political calculation, eager under pressure from the Right and Reagan's rising candidacy to position himself—and Ford—as more hawkish? In Congress and in the Nixon administration, Rumsfeld had appeared increasingly dovish about the Vietnam War. But in the Ford administration, he had emerged as a leading hawk.

There was little question about Rumsfeld's political ambitions. "He wanted to be Ford's running mate in 1976," said Ken Adelman, who had known Rumsfeld since his days at OEO and worked for him at the Pentagon as a special assistant. "He wasn't maneuvering for it, but he hoped that Ford would call him up." But Adelman also saw Rumsfeld as genuinely believing that the Soviets posed a dangerous threat. When asked years later about his motives, Rumsfeld insisted he was acting out of conviction. "There was no political calculation at all," he said in an interview. "There just wasn't. It's what I believed."

Kissinger and his aides had a mixed view of Rumsfeld's motivations. Scowcroft saw Rumsfeld as a political opportunist, positioning himself on the conservative side for a run for the presidency someday. Hyland figured that both ideology and politics played a part. "I think it was about 50/50," he said.

Kissinger left the question open, suggesting in his memoir of the Ford years that Rumsfeld may have acted out of either a disagreement with the substance of the strategic arms negotiations or a political judgment that it would be unwise to take such a step in an election year. Even if politics was the driver, Kissinger considered that an "honorable" motivation and credited Rumsfeld with a better understanding of the political winds of the day.

What had worried Kissinger most were the threats from the Left— the protests against the Vietnam War, the 1972 Democratic campaign of George McGovern, the movement to reduce U.S. troop levels overseas. Kissinger hoped to co-opt the peace issue from the Left through his dé- tente policy of arms negotiations and general easing of tensions with the Soviet Union. Rumsfeld, by contrast, was eyeing the Right. What he saw rising was a reinforced sense that America needed to reassert itself and what it stood for, remain wary of compromise with communist regimes, and never again suffer military defeat.

"As a veteran of the political wars," Kissinger said, "Rumsfeld understood far better than I that Watergate and Vietnam were likely to evoke a conservative backlash and that what looked like a liberal tide after the election of the McGovernite Congress in fact marked the radical apogee."

In any case, the hawkish posture that Rumsfeld assumed as defense secretary has ended up defining him ever since. He continued to push for a strong U.S. military and to express wariness about arms control treaties and other forms of accommodation with the Soviet Union. The moderate image he had garnered initially in Congress and then sustained in the Nixon administration by his championing of OEO and advocacy of an accelerated end to the Vietnam War gave way under Ford to a harder image more in keeping with his bedrock conservatism—and with where Rumsfeld thought American politics were going.

———•———

Rumsfeld had been at the Pentagon only a couple of months when he introduced a new plan for a surge in defense spending and issued a warning about Soviet military investment. In January 1976, delivering the defense secretary's traditional annual report to Congress, he called for an $8.9 billion increase in defense spending, topping the $100 billion mark for the first time. He somberly declared that military trends were running against the United States. Unless they were reversed by an increased investment in the defense establishment and the development of a new generation of strategic weapons, he predicted a military imbalance.

Schlesinger had begun the push for more money, noting that over the previous decade, Soviet military spending had increased while U.S. investment had declined. Rumsfeld's new twist was to add a warning that the United States could slip into a position of military inferiority.

To sell the budget plan and drive home his message about the Soviet threat, Rumsfeld distributed a package of charts and graphs that showed Soviet and U.S. forces as "roughly equivalent." He also organized a series of briefings at the White House for members of Congress. Held in the Roosevelt Room, the briefings were delivered by John Hughes, a longtime Defense Intelligence Agency officer, who displayed satellite photos revealing recent Soviet accomplishments. Among them: the introduction of three new intercontinental-range ballistic missile systems; the start of a large-scale upgrading of submarines; modernized ground forces; improved tactical air capabilities; and expanded naval capabilities. "Hughes didn't have to say a word," Holcomb recalled. "He just kept flipping through a stack of classified charts and photographs, one after another, telling a story in pictures that words couldn't tell about the Soviet buildup and what the state of play was."

In playing up the specter of communist advance, Rumsfeld and his group tended to exaggerate those parts of the picture that supported their case while playing down offsetting elements. The charts, for instance, that showed the Soviets building ships faster than the Americans neglected to show that the Soviets generally had smaller ships. The charts that showed the Soviets having twice as many soldiers as the Americans omitted mention that the soldiers were defending against the Chinese or were involved in activities more industrial than military. While Rumsfeld spoke of the $40 billion that Congress had cut out of presidential defense budgets in the previous six years, he did not note the $160 billion spent on the war in Vietnam.

The scare talk had little subtlety or complexity. It was intended, purely and simply, to spur defense spending. "In a preeminently political year, Rumsfeld was taking a preeminently political approach," wrote Laurence Leamer a year later in a profile of Rumsfeld. His aim was to portray the United States and Soviet Union locked "not so much in a great struggle of ideals and wills, as some would view it, or a tragic stalemate that defined the new era, as others considered it, but a battle of checkbooks." And the pitch worked. By the autumn of 1976, after about half the Congress had seen the Hughes briefing, Rumsfeld had obtained congressional approval for an increase in defense spending.

For his part, Kissinger had cautioned against exaggerating Soviet power and U.S. weakness. Despite their increased spending, the Soviets remained, according to Kissinger, far behind in any overall assessment of military, economic, and technological strength. But Rumsfeld maintained that highlighting the trends was in the U.S. national interest.

In the wake of the Vietnam War, Rumsfeld had little tolerance for suggestions that the United States should pull back from international engagements and reduce its military posture. At a Pentagon reception in the late 1970s, not long after he had left the secretary's job, Rumsfeld ran into a general he knew who was serving in President Carter's White House. "It's a different era," the general told him, "and we have to significantly modify down our interests in the world to fit our reduced capabilities and our national attitude."

Recounting the story years later to Pentagon historians, Rumsfeld did not identify the general but said the officer had things all wrong. "Instead of saying we needed to do what I was trying to do, which was to present the facts and persuade the American people of the circumstance so that we would have the willingness and steadiness of purpose over time to invest as appropriate to create the kind of deterrence, he was saying we had to give up and stop thinking we could do all that and tuck in, because we did not have the wherewithal to do it, either economically or attitudinally. What utter nonsense. The reality is that we can afford whatever we need as a country, notwithstanding the people who have said to the contrary. It's a matter of choices."

Although intended to shore up Ford's image as being strong on defense, Rumsfeld's hard-sell approach had a boomerang effect. The question of Soviet military dominance became the most emotional issue in the Republican presidential primaries in the spring of 1976 and helped rejuvenate Reagan's campaign. Starting with the North Carolina primary in March, Reagan emphasized a charge that became a central theme in his campaign—that the Ford administration had permitted the United States to slip toward a position of military inferiority to the Soviet Union. Both Ford and Rumsfeld argued in rebuttal that Reagan should be blaming Congress and not the president for any military shortcomings.

Rumsfeld's scare talk about possible Soviet superiority was reminiscent of the "missile gap" days of 1960 when Democratic presidential candidate John F. Kennedy charged the Republican administration with letting the Soviet Union surpass the United States in intercontinental-range ballistic missiles. Rumsfeld stopped short of suggesting that the Soviets were out to achieve military superiority over the United States or to attack the United States in a surprise strike. But other arms specialists, like his friend Nitze, shaped the iron that Rumsfeld had heated by assigning dark intentions to the Russians.

Conservatives complained of a serious U.S. intelligence failure, criticizing CIA assessments of Soviet intentions and military might as too benign and optimistic. Bush as CIA director agreed to appoint a team of outside experts, designated Team B, to produce its own report on the Soviet Union based on a review of the classified data. Delivered at the end of 1976, the team's report sharply contradicted the view that the CIA had been offering. It said the available evidence suggested that most Soviet strategic actions were offensive rather than defensive, aiming at attaining military superiority over the United States, and that some new Soviet weapons programs threatened to change the strategic balance.

Rumsfeld, while not a true believer like some Team B members and associated advisers, found the analysis useful. "I would describe him as a hard-liner but not an ideologue," said retired admiral Bobby Inman, who served under Rumsfeld then as vice director of the Defense Intelligence Agency. "Ideologues in my experience had a solution they were pushing—the Team B group. Worst case. And I don't have the recollection that I would put him in the absolute, worst-case camp. But he was a hard-liner from the standpoint of, You need to compete, you need to confront."

As a precedent, the Team B experience became a useful model for critics of the U.S. intelligence community to invoke when other challenges arose about official assessments, some of which affected Rumsfeld. In 1998, for instance, amid allegations by congressional Republicans that the CIA had underestimated the ballistic missile threat to the United States, a commission inspired by Team B was established to study the threat. It was chaired by Rumsfeld and included Paul Wolfowitz, who as a young defense intellectual had served as a Team B adviser. Later still, during the planning for the Iraq War, Rumsfeld approved a Pentagon group, which Wolfowitz oversaw, to conduct a separate intelligence analysis looking for links between Saddam Hussein and al Qaeda.

The original Team B report also fed Rumsfeld's concerns about the CIA. As secretary of defense the first time, Rumsfeld had taken his own critical view of the CIA's analysis of the Soviets as less menacing than he thought they were. "It bothered me that the CIA seemed to always be wrong on one side—and the wrong side—the side not of safety," he later told Pentagon historians.

In addition to differing with the CIA over assessments of the Soviet Union, Rumsfeld tangled with the agency over budget issues during his first stint as defense secretary. "I was in the middle of some terrible budget arguments," Scowcroft recalled. "A good part of the CIA budget is in defense, and Rumsfeld's position was, 'If it's in my budget and I have to defend it before the Congress, I decide how it's going to be spent.' And I said, 'No you don't.' This was just back and forth."

Underlying the strain, too, was personal tension between the secretary of defense and the CIA director. Bush saw Rumsfeld as having muscled him out of the way. Rumsfeld regarded Bush as a lightweight who was more interested in friendships, public relations, and public opinion polls than in substantive policy. "He didn't credit Bush with knowing what was going on," Holcomb said. "Rumsfeld's sense of confidence and mission and relatedness to the president's purpose was stronger than he thought Bush's was. He just was not giving him any weight in the scheme of things." Robert Ellsworth, who was at the Pentagon at the time in charge of intelligence matters, recalled: "All of us were of the same opinion—we thought maybe Bush was in over his head. We had guys who were just so rigorous and so thorough and so professional, and his guys were not."

Rumsfeld had his own concerns about the Pentagon's intelligence apparatus, which was under heightened congressional scrutiny at the time along with the CIA's. Both the Senate and the House had launched investigations in the wake of disclosures about covert U.S. assassination attempts against foreign leaders and efforts to subvert foreign governments. Intelligence agencies also were reported to have collected information on the political activities of U.S. citizens.

In an effort to avoid time-consuming dealings with Congress on intelligence probes, Rumsfeld used latent authority to establish Ellsworth as a second deputy secretary of defense. (Ellsworth had been serving at the Pentagon as an assistant secretary.) Having a deputy focused largely on intelligence proved helpful to Rumsfeld—all the more so because Rumsfeld did not get along with his other deputy, William P. Clements, a businessman from Texas who had made a fortune selling oil equipment.

Clements had resisted efforts by Ford to move him to another department when Rumsfeld arrived. If forced out, Clements threatened to return to Dallas and call a news conference to declare his departure a "power play" by Rumsfeld. Clements stayed on, but he didn't enjoy it. "As far as I know, Rumsfeld and I never agreed on anything," he told Pentagon historians in a 1996 interview. "It was a very unpleasant period for me."

With the budget increase came funding for a number of new weapons programs. At the top of the price list was the B-1 bomber, the most expensive aircraft ever built at that point. A rash of technical problems, delays, and cost overruns since Nixon commissioned the plane in 1970 had driven critics to press for cancellation. But Rumsfeld affirmed his faith in the project by flying it himself—or at least handling the controls of a prototype during a much-publicized, hour-long flight that was followed by a photo shoot of Rumsfeld in an orange flight suit.

Rumsfeld also used the boost in military spending to build more Trident missile-launching submarines and to develop a new intercontinental land-based missile called the MX, with a range about three times greater than the Minuteman. He provided more funds for lower-flying, long-range cruise missiles and more Navy ships.

Rumsfeld's biggest procurement battle came over the Army's most important weapons program, the design of the M1 tank. Disagreement raged within the Pentagon over what kind of engine to put in the tank. The Army wanted a diesel, but Clements and Malcolm Currie, the Pentagon's director of research and engineering, argued for a more innovative turbine. One evening in the summer of 1976, with no consensus still among his subordinates over which way to go, the contract-award decision was kicked up to Rumsfeld. He was furious that the matter of the engine had not been resolved and refused to decide on the spot, ordering further review.

Among other considerations, in the interest of standardization within NATO, Rumsfeld wanted more done to ensure that the final tank design would allow for interchangeability of key parts with the emerging Leopard 2 tank of West Germany. In the end, Rumsfeld chose the more questionable turbine engine, overruling the Army's preference for the more conventional approach. He also went with a bigger gun—120 mm instead of 105 mm—again rejecting the Army's recommendation.

Critics contended that Rumsfeld's choice of the turbine was politically motivated by an interest in bailing out the ailing Chrysler Corporation, which made the engine. (General Motors had backed the diesel.) But Rumsfeld has denied that helping Chrysler was a factor in his decision. He considered his decision vindicated years later during the 1991 Persian Gulf War when the tank faced its first major combat test and proved itself a machine of staggering capacity to kill, although, at a hefty sixty-seven tons, the armored behemoth also showed a gluttonous thirst for fuel.

In his second term as defense secretary, when he was pushing his agenda to transform the Pentagon, Rumsfeld from time to time recalled his experience with the M1 as an early example of his standing up to military bureaucracy in favor of riskier technology. The episode also reinforced in his mind the importance, when developing new weapons, of trying to leapfrog into an entirely new generation of technology rather than going for a simpler upgrade.

In one Pentagon corridor hang the portraits of the twenty-one people who have served as secretary of defense since the job's creation in 1947. The painting of Rumsfeld during his first stint as secretary stands out; he is the only man shown in shirtsleeves, without a suit jacket—a pose that conveys his down-to-business, nothing fancy, no-standing-on-ceremony attitude. "He'd be out and around in his shirtsleeves," recalled Robin West, who worked as a special assistant to Rumsfeld at the time. "He was not some great, stone-faced secretary of defense. He was animated, he was open."

But this workman style also carried a tough edge as Rumsfeld lived up to his reputation for being demanding, blunt, and direct. Staser Holcomb, then a rear admiral, remembers being summoned for an interview with Rumsfeld, who was looking for a military assistant. Holcomb had never been in the office of the secretary of defense. "I stood by the desk, and he was scribbling away for what seemed to me for a very long time," Holcomb recalled in an interview. "Finally, Rumsfeld looked up and said, 'Here read this,' and he gave me six pages labeled Rumsfeld's Rules. I read them while he continued to scribble and got the gist of them. Another very long silence. And he looked up and said, 'Can you live with that?' I said, 'Yes sir, I think I can.' Another very long silence. And he said, 'Are you liberal or conservative.' And I said, 'You'll probably find me conservative on most things.' Then he said, 'You'll do. Come to work on Monday.'"

Subordinates learned quickly that Rumsfeld was a stickler for details, which made it all the more satisfying, for some of them, at least, when they could prove more right than Rumsfeld. During an evacuation of Lebanon, for instance, the chief of naval operations, Admiral James L. Holloway III, reported to Rumsfeld that 103 civilians had been taken out one day. "That's getting pretty precise," Rumsfeld remarked, according to Holloway. "Are you sure?"

"Knowing you, Mr. Secretary, we're damn sure," Holloway replied, confident of the figure.

The next day, when the ship reached its destination port in Greece, word came back to Rumsfeld that 104 evacuees had been off-loaded. "Got you!" Rumsfeld exclaimed when he next saw Holloway. "When that ship arrived, it had 104 people."

Holloway double-checked and found that a baby had been born on the trip across. When informed that the admiral had been right, Rumsfeld "was a good sport about it," Holloway said. "I think at first he thought we'd made up the number."

Other times, when he was faced with information that didn't suit him, Rumsfeld would find his own novel way around the facts. "I was working on one speech, the 12th version or something, and getting back his rewrites—his chicken scratches—his printing, he can barely write," recalled Ken Adelman. "And I looked at it and took it to him and said, 'Don, you can change what I write and you can change what you yourself write or want to say, but goddamn, I've given you a great Pericles quote. You can't change Pericles.' Don then took the draft and put some more chicken scratches on it. I looked at it, and he had retained his rewrite of the great Athenian general, and penned in 'as Pericles should have said.'"

Power was respected at the Pentagon, and Rumsfeld demonstrated his influence early on. His handling of the redoubtable Kissinger and his success in restoring some of the defense spending cuts made by Congress prior to Schlesinger's departure impressed the staff. But his forceful manner offended some senior officers, much as it would decades later when he again led the Pentagon.

In a memoir published in 2007, Holloway described Rumsfeld as "much more aggressive in his approach to decision-making" than his predecessor had been. "He did ask questions from his subordinates, but as a rule, he received the answers with an undisguised air of cynicism," Holloway wrote. "It was as if he had made up his mind that he should assume that he could not believe what his chiefs were telling him. It soon became obvious that a response at odds with the secretary's preconceived position was to be avoided. This made it uninviting to speak up at one of his conferences. As a result, his decisions would often appear to be quite arbitrary."

In an interview, Holloway recalled a meeting with the chiefs and senior Pentagon civilians in which Rumsfeld blasted him for a public statement about a new military plane. "If you ever do this to me again, you're wiped out; I will not have it; you just can't run free like this," Rumsfeld said angrily, according to Holloway. As it turned out, another senior official, not Holloway, had made the offending remarks.

"We were grown men; we were people who we thought deserved a certain amount of consideration and understanding," Holloway said. But the admiral and the other service chiefs felt that too often Rumsfeld failed to listen to them or simply was unavailable when timely decisions needed to be made. "There was a feeling that Don was just very, very difficult to work with," Holloway said.

"It was a very rocky relationship," confirmed Inman, director of naval intelligence at the time, referring to dealings between Rumsfeld and the Joint Chiefs. "Holloway is a very courteous man and treats everyone—subordinates, seniors—with courtesy. But Rumsfeld was very brusque and occasionally would just seize an opportunity to chew out Holloway or one of the other chiefs in front of everyone else."

One of Holloway's most vivid recollections of working with Rumsfeld was catching up with him in a hallway to get his approval of a message related to a pending action in the western Pacific. When Rumsfeld saw that the message had been drafted as coming from the Joint Chiefs of Staff, he ordered it rewritten to indicate it was coming from the secretary of defense. "This single fact shocked me—that he would tear up a message like this for the simple reason that it was shown coming from the Joint Chiefs of Staff and had to come from the secretary of defense," Holloway said.

In his memoir Holloway criticized Rumsfeld for spending an unusually large amount of his time away from the Pentagon working on political rather than military matters and sometimes, when urgent approval was needed for something, proving hard to reach. "We could not always count on being able to contact him in a time-sensitive situation, and he did not characteristically afford us much latitude in delegated authority," Holloway said. "This could make the working relationships between him and the service chiefs quite uncomfortable, because it was not always clear what the secretary wanted done."

Rumsfeld traveled frequently to areas of the United States where interest in defense issues was high, and he had helped answer warnings from Reagan that the United States was losing its will to maintain a strong military posture. He denied that his motives in these visits and speeches were political, justifying his trips as his own effort to acquaint himself with the department. But Ford subsequently announced that he had ordered Rumsfeld—along with Kissinger and Attorney General Edward Levi—not to campaign, and in the autumn of 1976, Rumsfeld abandoned his plans to visit California and several other politically key states.

———•———

As defense secretary, Rumsfeld took a more active interest in the selection of senior military officers than had his predecessors. Instead of rubber-stamping the recommendations of service chiefs for top positions, he issued instructions that each chief should offer up at least two names for each senior post. Part of Rumsfeld's motivation, according to Holcomb, was to ensure the promotion of more minority candidates. During Rumsfeld's tenure, the Navy announced its first black three-star admiral. When Rumsfeld returned to the Pentagon for his second tour, he involved himself even more deeply in the promotion and assignment of generals and admirals. And Holcomb was brought back from retirement to manage the process.

Rumsfeld's most trying moment with the chiefs came in October 1976 over publication of remarks by Air Force general George Brown, the chairman of the Joint Chiefs of Staff. Brown had a tendency to say the wrong things. (He had been reprimanded by Ford in 1974 after telling a Duke University audience that Jews controlled banks and newspapers in the United States and exerted undue influence in Congress.) In his latest misstep, the general had suggested that Israel was a military burden to the United States, that Britain and its military forces were "pathetic," and that the shah of Iran had "visions of the Persian Empire."

Despite calls for Brown's dismissal, Rumsfeld chose a different approach. He appeared with the general at a news conference where Brown read a two-page statement intended to place his comments in the "proper perspective." Seldom if ever had the nation's top-ranking military officer been put through so public an exercise in clarifying his comments. Rumsfeld considered this chastisement sufficient. He also tried a little humor. As Brown began to speak, Rumsfeld put his hand over the general's mouth and said, "The general has nothing to say." The scene drew laughs.

Rumsfeld also charitably handled the issue of Malcolm Currie, one of his top civilian appointees, who had spent two days at a fishing lodge in the Bahamas owned by Rockwell International, a major defense contractor. Resisting calls in March 1976 to fire Currie, who oversaw the department's research and engineering programs, Rumsfeld issued him a letter of severe reprimand, ordered him to forfeit four weeks' pay, and required him to cover the $3,500 cost of his trip.

Currie's actions over Labor Day weekend in 1975 had been in clear violation of department rules stipulating that defense officials keep their relations with defense contractors "above reproach" and "avoid even the appearance of a conflict of interest" by refusing to accept "hospitality, gratuities or favors from defense contractors." But Currie was highly regarded within the Pentagon as a knowledgeable, effective administrator. Rumsfeld did not want to lose him. Two weeks earlier, he had praised Currie at a news conference as "one of the most talented and able and sound and wise individuals" in government. But Rumsfeld had also declared that he would "land all over individuals" who stepped outside the bounds of proper behavior.

A subsequent *New York Times* report alleged that upon his return from the Bahamas, Currie had gone to bat for Rockwell's troubled weapons system—the Condor air-to-surface missile. Currie was said to have argued in internal Pentagon deliberations against terminating the program, maintaining that further development and tests would overcome technical problems with the weapon. Rumsfeld cleared Currie of any conflict of interest in the case.

Ford's electoral defeat in 1976 brought Rumsfeld's first tenure as defense secretary to an end after only fourteen months. In that time, Rumsfeld felt that his most significant achievement had been to alert Congress and the public that the Soviet Union had grown from a primitive power of the 1960s to a superpower. To ensure that the United States did not lag behind, he had tried to commit the nation to a major military expansion. Before he left office, Rumsfeld had prepared another defense budget, this one—at $110.1 billion—even fatter than the last.

Looking back on his first stint at the Pentagon, Rumsfeld has offered various assessments. "It was a period of accomplishment and hard work, but in an environment which was not unpleasant," he told Pentagon historians in 1994. It helped, he said then, that there had been no U.S. combat casualties and no major scandals that would have brought punishing scrutiny by the media. "That makes your life more pleasant, so that most of your time is spent on things that are constructive and forward-looking rather than defensive and unpleasant. My days were not all downers, in the sense of fighting a rear-guard action someplace or having a lot of Americans killed someplace, or having someone pounding on you in the press for some reason."

He appeared to offer a somewhat different set of impressions in an interview with Bob Woodward in 1989, describing the Pentagon as difficult and almost unmanageable. The job of secretary of defense was "ambiguous," Rumsfeld said then, because there was only "a thin layer of civilian control." He said it was "like having an electric appliance in one hand and the plug in the other and you are running around trying to find a place to put it in." He added, "You can't make a deal that sticks. No one can deliver anything more than their temporary viewpoint." Even the secretary.

There was never enough time to understand the big problems, Rumsfeld said, adding that the Pentagon was set up to handle peacetime issues, such as the political decision about moving an aircraft carrier. In a real war, these would be military questions, and he went so far as to say that in case of war, the country would almost need an organization different from the Pentagon.

The Pentagon press corps graded Rumsfeld's tenure harshly. Out of fourteen defense secretaries assessed in a survey published in August 1979 by the *Armed Forces Journal International*, Rumsfeld fell in last place. Although he received good marks for being candid and likable, they were more than offset by low scores in every other category—competence, honesty, effectiveness, strength, forthrightness, and trustworthiness.

It hadn't helped Rumsfeld that he had succeeded Schlesinger, a very popular figure with journalists. Schlesinger rated second in the survey behind Melvin Laird, who had held the post in the Nixon administration. Bill Greener, Rumsfeld's spokesman at the time, thought his boss's low score also reflected Rumsfeld's tendency to keep his cards close. Additionally, Rumsfeld's tenure had not lasted long enough to show what he could do. After finally reaching one of the top jobs in government, his time was cut short by the democratic election cycle. Nearly a quarter of a century would pass before he would get another shot at a position of government power.

CHAPTER 5

A Politician in the Corporate World

After the end of the Ford administration, Rumsfeld, his wife, and the Cheneys vacationed at a beachfront house on the island of Eleuthera in the Bahamas. Far from Washington, Rumsfeld contemplated his next move. Fourteen years had passed since he had entered government, looking more like a young page than a sitting member of Congress. His rise to the upper reaches of American politics had left him with an impressive résumé of legislative and executive-branch experience, but the taste of power had only fed his ambition. With his eye still on the ultimate prize of the presidency, he hoped someday to return to the political game.

In his final weeks as defense secretary, Rumsfeld was approached by G. D. Searle and Company, a family-run pharmaceutical firm in the Chicago area, about a top management position. Talks were quietly begun between company officers and Rumsfeld's longtime friend, Ned Jannotta, about the possible terms for hiring Rumsfeld. The prospect of running a major corporation in his hometown, where he and Joyce both had family and friends, was highly appealing.

Although government service had been his calling for most of his adult life, Rumsfeld had a high regard for the role of business in U.S. society and considered it useful for people to move back and forth between the worlds of government and business. "He viewed the private sector as the engine of the country," Joyce explained in an interview. "He has always felt that. Government has a very important role, but the innovation, the energy, the dazzle is in the private sector, and he has always had respect for that. He has felt government is better served if it is composed of people who have had private-sector experience."

On their vacation, the Rumsfelds decided to resettle in Chicago. "We got in the plane, we looked at each other and said, 'Let's go home,'" Joyce recalled. "It was that simple."

Through the rest of the winter and into the spring of 1977, Rumsfeld lectured at Northwestern University's Graduate School of Management and Princeton University's Woodrow Wilson School of Public and International Affairs as discussions with Searle progressed. Searle itself was in trouble. Founded in 1888, it had scored big in the early 1960s by pioneering Enovid, the first birth-control pill, and developing a host of innovative drugs, including Dramamine for motion sickness, Matamucil for constipation, and Lomotil for diarrhea. But a series of unprofitable acquisitions aimed at diversifying away from pharmaceuticals in the late 1960s and early 1970s had squandered cash and pulled profits down. Compounding matters, the Food and Drug Administration (FDA) had rescinded approval for the company's promising new sweetener, aspartame, amid indications that Searle had misrepresented test results. The company's stock had plunged from a high of $110 to $11 a share by 1977.

Management of the firm was in the hands of Daniel and William Searle—the great-grandsons of the company's founder—and a brother-in-law, Wesley M. Dixon. Although they were reluctant to look outside the family for a new leader, the trio recognized that their joint management model was floundering. Rumsfeld had no pharmaceutical expertise, or even much experience in business. But the Searles recognized that the key to turning their company around would have more to do with leadership talent and political clout than with technical competence, and Rumsfeld's proven ability to manage complex situations and his capable, clean-cut image seemed just what was needed.

Dan Searle already had a relationship with Rumsfeld stretching back fifteen years when he had served as a major fund-raiser for Rumsfeld's first congressional campaign. But what eventually clinched the CEO position for Rumsfeld was his attitude toward the stock owned by the

Searle family. Another candidate up for the job, concerned that one-third of the firm's common stock was concentrated in the Searle family, had insisted that the shares be put into a voting trust that he would oversee. When Rumsfeld was asked whether he would demand a voting trust, he responded adamantly, "If I felt I had to have a voting trust, I wouldn't even be talking to you!" This trusting, self-confident reply was what the Searles wanted to hear.

The announcement in April 1977 that Rumsfeld would be taking charge of Searle was greeted with skepticism by business analysts, who cited his lack of experience and doubted the Searle family would give him free rein. The move was also puzzling to some political pros who were aware of Rumsfeld's continuing interest in elective office. Even Rumsfeld's mother opposed her son entering a struggling firm, for fear it would mar his reputation.

But many of Rumsfeld's moves over the previous decade had been risky and unconventional. As he himself remarked at the time, "If you look at my career, it would be sheer lunacy to think I had planned it." He did not think of his life as a linear progression from one logical position to another. He had an abiding belief that if he did each job well, other interesting and significant opportunities would open up for him. And so they had.

Besides, at $200,000 a year plus a bonus and benefits, Rumsfeld at Searle stood to earn much more than he ever had and gain a measure of financial stability for the first time in his life. He had yet to acquire any substantial personal wealth. His first congressional campaign had left him with debts that took five years to pay off. He had garnered some savings from the sale of a house in Washington in the early 1970s before moving to Europe, but those funds had been lost in a sinking stock market. When he returned to Washington after his time as ambassador, Rumsfeld had had to rely on money from his parents to buy a house. To help with family finances, Joyce had worked in a Georgetown dress shop. At the time he left the government payroll, Rumsfeld was almost broke.

But more important to Rumsfeld than the financial lure of Searle was the chance to take on a major challenge outside the political world. "What I was looking for was something outside of Washington I could get fully engaged in, something I could become central to," he once explained. "What I wanted was something big, complex and international enough to be challenging."

———•———

Rumsfeld approached his new corporate job the same way he had tackled other management challenges. He sought at first to gather all the information he could—about the company's products, the relevant markets, the potential courses of future action—by talking to current employees, tracking down former ones, and interviewing other experts. He also started putting together his own team of senior subordinates.

"Don hit the ground running, but he knew nothing," Joyce recalled. "He couldn't even pronounce the names of some of the products. Chemistry was not his thing."

In his first days, he formed a task force of inside executives and outside consultants to analyze the company. For five months, they debated the fit, profitability, and cash and management needs of every Searle division and concluded that at least twenty subsidiaries had to be shed. Dismantling much of Searle's earlier diversification effort, Rumsfeld restructured the remaining elements of the firm into three major groups: prescription-only drugs, over-the-counter products, and retail Pearle optical stores. While severing chunks of the company, Rumsfeld built up others, expanding the optical business with additional stores and increasing the research-and-development budget. He also broadened the board of directors, bringing in more members from outside the firm and strengthening his own hand.

The speed at which Rumsfeld acted drew skeptical comment in the industry, but he defended the rapid revamping as necessary to avoid the damage of a prolonged sell-off. He was equally determined about cutting corporate staff. In a matter of months, the payroll shrank from 800 employees to 350. Although severance-pay packages and job counseling were offered, former employees complained the purge was crudely handled. Searle had been a nonunion ship with no recent history of layoffs. "There were some instances where people came to me pleading their cause," Dan Searle recalled. "My stock reply was, 'Look, Don Rumsfeld is chief executive now. Your discussions have to be with him or his staff.'"

To underscore a pledge not to interfere with their new CEO, the two Searle brothers and Dixon had moved out of the company's twelve-story headquarters in Skokie, Illinois, and into an unmarked suite in an adjacent office tower. But Rumsfeld established a binder of up-to-date memos and corporate documents that was made available to the Searles to leaf through at their convenience—a clever gesture that reinforced the family's high regard for him.

This considerate arrangement was indicative of Rumsfeld's management style. For all his assertions of personal authority, he tended to be very mindful of his bosses, whether they were corporate owners or presidents of the United States. He was always careful to keep them apprised of his thinking and to ensure his actions remained transparent to them.

But toward subordinates at Searle, Rumsfeld displayed the same demanding, hard-driving style that he had shown managing the White House and the Pentagon. In high-pressured meetings at the company, he asked question after probing question, with little patience for foot-dragging or ignorance. "You had to have your stuff together before you spoke, and you needed to be concise about it," said Sue Sittnick, who had worked for Rumsfeld when he was a congressman and had joined Searle's public relations office. "I saw him cut off people who didn't know an answer and tried to bluff."

Rumsfeld was insistent that his rules be strictly followed, no matter how seemingly picky. If, for example, materials relevant to a particular meeting did not arrive at least two days ahead of time, Rumsfeld would call off the session. "I remember a meeting which Don just abruptly canceled because the materials arrived late, and he said, 'If you're depending on me to understand materials I just got, forget about it,'" recalled Jim Denny, who served as chief financial officer.

Rumsfeld's tough leadership tactics garnered national attention. In 1980, *Fortune* included Rumsfeld in a lineup of the nation's "ten toughest bosses." The article described Rumsfeld this way: "Fast-paced, urgent . . . when people argue with him—God it can be tough . . . demolishes anyone who blows smoke at him." And it quoted Rumsfeld's own stern appraisal of how to handle a disobedient employee: "You not only let someone who has not been obeying you go, you do it publicly so everyone knows that breaking the rules brings immediate punishment. . . . We got rid of a bunch for the good of the rest."

At a meeting of Searle's stockholders a few weeks after publication of the article, Rumsfeld defended his tough-guy image as inevitable given the steps he had needed to take to improve efficiency at Searle. But he added: "They say I use the stick and not the carrot. The truth is, I use both."

Maybe so, although the stick seemed to predominate. And while Rumsfeld's friends and associates often argued that he didn't place any harder demands on others than he placed on himself, there was too often an unkind edge to Rumsfeld's treatment—a badgering and bullying—that suggested a mean streak. It was a style that Rumsfeld seemed unable or unwilling to change, perhaps because it produced results for him, although it also undercut his ability to inspire loyalty among staff. The same style would get him into trouble when he returned to the Pentagon as defense secretary under Bush.

For his part, Rumsfeld had rationalized the Searle layoffs as ultimately beneficial to the individuals who were let go. Years later, asked about his reputation as a corporate axman, Rumsfeld said in an interview for this book that he had tried to handle the most difficult dismissals himself "because it's just, I think, more decent if I'm the one making the decision." He said that, to soften the blow, whenever possible he attributed a firing to a shift in market conditions or a change in company direction rather than deficiencies on the part of the person being let go.

Further, he portrayed being out of a job as a form of opportunity. "Looking for a job is an assignment that can be enormously satisfying," he said. "It gives you a pause in your life. You've got some severance, you've got a period of time, you can go out and meet new people and think about doing something that fits you."

———•———

In many ways, Rumsfeld found running Searle a liberating experience. The corporate world in general, he thought, didn't have the pressures that existed on politicians to appear to have all the answers. In the political world, senior officials were always having to pump themselves up so that they appeared to know everything and to be doing much. Business executives, in Rumsfeld's view, weren't required to be omniscient or omnipresent. They could delegate. They could admit mistakes. In business, too, there was more of a chance to think, to read, to reflect, and to plan, or so it was for Rumsfeld.

He reflected on the differences between his previous life and his new one in another article in *Fortune* a little more than a year after arriving at Searle. The magazine, which had published a profile of someone who had gone from business into government, asked him to talk about the experience of going the other way. His article was titled "A Politician in the Corporate World."

But for all the new freedom Rumsfeld was enjoying, he had also discovered certain demands in the business world that didn't exist in the political one. Politicians, for instance, could get credit simply for intent, for caring about a problem, for trying to solve it. "In business, you don't get a lot of points for just starting in the right direction," Rumsfeld observed. What counts are results.

In outlining the pros and cons of both worlds, Rumsfeld almost seemed to be wrestling with two sides of himself, looking not for a victory of one over the other but for a way of justifying an existence that would straddle both. His time in government had provided useful experience in the art of crisis management. In fact, he reported finding the move from the Pentagon to Searle much easier than his transition years earlier from Congress to the executive branch. He brushed off the notion that too much time in the complex multilayered world of government could leave a person "so bureaucratized that you forget how to operate any other way."

Still, there was a hint in the article that he wasn't quite yet sure whether he would make it as a businessman. "It's not clear to me that skills are readily transferable between business and government," he said. "I've heard executives who have been successful in the private sector say: 'I want to get into government.' But there's no particular reason why a successful businessman should be successful in government—or the reverse."

———•———

As the head of a drug-manufacturing company that met frequently with federal regulatory authorities, Rumsfeld had actually ended up at a major intersection of business and government. For the firm to survive and prosper, Rumsfeld would have to ensure that regulators approved new drugs, that lawmakers passed favorable legislation, and that administration officials intervened if necessary. He had his own contacts in Washington, of course, but he would need others even more skilled in working the corridors of federal agencies and the halls of Congress. In putting together a new team of associates at Searle, he found it useful to dip back into the political pool for talent.

His most significant hire was John Robson, who came onboard as executive vice president for planning and regulatory affairs. A skilled lawyer who knew Washington's regulatory ropes, Robson had worked as general counsel to the Department of Transportation and, more recently, as head of the Civil Aeronautics Board under President Gerald Ford. Even more important in some respects, he was a close friend to Rumsfeld. The two had overlapped at New Trier High School (Robson was two years ahead), and Robson had served as issues director of Rumsfeld's first congressional campaign. Short, smart, and athletic, Robson had a passion for the arts and a humorous disposition that was welcomed by his colleagues.

Robert Shapiro, Robson's former special assistant in the Transportation Department and an experienced Washington lawyer, was recruited for general counsel. Bill Greener, Rumsfeld's Pentagon spokesman, was hired as vice president for public affairs. And Bill Timmons, who as a congressional aide in the 1960s had become friends with Rumsfeld and who had served with him in the Nixon White House, was tapped to lead Searle's lobbying efforts in Washington.

Another hire who would prove critical didn't come from government but did have a past connection. Jim Denny, a former Princeton classmate (though not a close friend to Rumsfeld there) was installed as Searle's chief financial officer. Rumsfeld, having already hired Robson, was hesitant about bringing another former school buddy on the payroll but agreed after being assured that Denny, who was treasurer of the Firestone Tire and Rubber Company, was the best a search team had turned up.

Before long, Denny and Robson joined Rumsfeld in a close-knit, powerful triumvirate. Spending hours around a conference table, the three men brainstormed and plotted the company's future. Rumsfeld re-lied heavily on Robson to smooth Searle's way in Washington and on Denny to oversee the company's books and to teach him how to inter-pret balance sheets and read income statements. "In going through the financial statements, Don would be back and forth to my office all day long, asking, 'What does this mean? Why did you do it this way?'" Denny recalled.

Rumsfeld's drastic restructuring of Searle and the large sell-off initi-ated during his first year quickly paid off. The company went from a loss of \$28.4 million in 1977 to earnings of \$72.2 million in 1978. Even so, the firm's long-term profitability remained in doubt.

Although Rumsfeld had refocused Searle as essentially a pharmaceu-tical business, its last successful drug patents were due to expire immi-nently, with little in line to replace them. The booming Pearle stores, which sold mass-merchandized prescription eyewear, provided a rela-tively small share of Searle's overall sales. To sustain its growth, Searle would have to develop and market new drugs. "We were struggling to create a strategy for a company that the financial markets would under-stand and buy into," Denny said. "People were basically kind of pes-simistic about what we could do."

———•———

A potential bonanza already lay in the company's hands in the form of a revolutionary product that had been ready to go on sale since 1974. The product, aspartame (better known later by its brand names Nutra-Sweet and Equal), was not a medicine but a low-calorie substitute for sugar with the potential of replacing saccharin as the leading artificial sweetener.

But the FDA was refusing to let aspartame go on the market amid warnings from scientists and consumer advocates that it might produce brain tumors or pose other health risks. The agency had initially granted approval in 1974, then rescinded it in late 1975 when questions arose over Searle's testing data for the product. Complicating matters, Searle also had come under heightened FDA scrutiny for discrepancies in research data involving several other drugs—notably, Aldactone and Aldactazide, two diuretics used to treat hypertension, and Flagyl, a drug for reproductive-tract infections. Clearly, Searle was going to have to do something about the company's lab practices and reporting procedures—and its strained relations with the FDA—if it hoped to bring aspartame and other new drugs to market.

In hopes of reestablishing Searle's credibility with the FDA, one of the first personnel moves Rumsfeld made was to hire a new head of research and development—Daniel L. Azarnoff, a soft-spoken professor of pharmacology at the University of Kansas and a recognized name in the field. He also instituted a new quality-assurance program that included rigorous documentation and research protocols for company products. And he paid a visit to the head of the FDA to see what else could be done to resolve the agency's concerns.

"I said, look, here's a big company, they've got a lot of good products, and they've got a history, a lot of shareholders, and I've been brought in from the outside to figure out how we get it from where it is to where it wants to go, and you folks have been looking at it and have questions about it," Rumsfeld recalled. "Tell me what you recommend, what ought one to do to get us from where we are to where we think we ought to be. I'm game for anything. But what is unhelpful is just uncertainty over a sustained period. We'll deal with any legal issues in the courts. We've got lawyers doing that. I don't know anything about them, but we'll do that."

At one point, Rumsfeld even approached a leading critic of aspartame, a public interest lawyer named James Turner. The two men met at a Washington hotel, where Turner proposed joining forces if Rumsfeld would agree to a full set of tests to be run on aspartame. While earlier research had looked at whether the product carried any risk of causing cancer, Turner wanted to broaden the testing to cover potential impacts on the brain such as dizziness, retardation, and blindness.

"We had a very good, very full and frank exchange," Turner recalled years later in an interview for an online documentary. But Rumsfeld wasn't interested in working out any new testing deal. "His scientists kept jumping up and running around the room and saying there's no problem, there's no problem, there's no problem," Turner said. "Ultimately he made the decision not to find out what the facts were but to move forward on the limited record that they had before them."

For Turner, the experience reinforced an impression of Rumsfeld as someone interested less in pursuing the right means to an end than in getting to the end itself, one way or another. "He's a fixer, he's an operative," Turner said. "You assign him a job and he goes and he does it." Rumsfeld was pursuing other avenues to try to spring aspartame from the federal regulatory limbo in which it was stuck. He had put Robson on the case, hoping the former Washington official could work his connections to some advantage. Rumsfeld would wait and see.

Another setback, though, came in October 1980 when a group of independent advisers, convened by the FDA as a public board of inquiry, recommended additional research to address concerns that aspartame could cause brain tumors. Increasingly pessimistic about gaining FDA approval for aspartame, Rumsfeld reserved $21.3 million on Searle's books, writing off the seemingly moribund product.

Then came the election of Ronald Reagan in November 1980, which gave Searle a fortuitous break. A new FDA commissioner, Arthur Hull Hayes Jr., was appointed in the spring of 1981 and, as one of his first acts, overturned the public board of inquiry's decision and approved the use of aspartame in dry foods. In an effort to dispel the fears about brain tumors that had factored in the board's earlier ruling, Hayes cited a new study showing no connection between aspartame and rat tumors.

Critics were outraged. They noted that the study mentioned by the FDA commissioner had been sponsored by Ajinomoto, a Japanese food processor under contract to Searle to produce aspartame. Allegations also arose about undue industry influence. An investigative report by a United Press International journalist several years after the FDA's turnaround noted that Hayes and nine other federal officials who had played some role in reviewing aspartame had taken private-sector jobs linked to the pharmaceutical industry. Hayes himself had left the FDA to work as a consultant to Burston-Marsteller, then Searle's public relations agency.

Rumsfeld's own ties to the new Reagan administration also came under suspicion. He had campaigned for Reagan, and his name had appeared on Reagan's short list of potential vice presidential candidates. He had even attended the 1980 Republican National Convention in Detroit, expecting he might get the call. Reagan instead chose George H. W. Bush, but Rumsfeld continued as an adviser to the campaign on foreign policy and defense issues. Following the election, he served on Reagan's transition team.

Concerns about how the aspartame issue had been handled were serious enough to generate congressional hearings and other federal reviews. None of these, though, found anything improper about the FDA's action. The General Accounting Office concluded that the agency had adequately followed its approval process, and a federal appeals court rejected suits by consumer groups challenging the go-ahead for aspartame.

Where Searle did receive a break that aided the development of aspartame was in Congress. An obscure amendment late in 1982 to the Orphan Drug Act authorized an extension of patents to drug and food additives that had run into regulatory delays. The amendment was worded to make it appear to apply to a whole set of products, but it had been drafted with aspartame expressly in mind—a strategy conceived by Robson. Also helping to maneuver the measure through Congress was Rumsfeld's old friend and lobbyist, Bill Timmons. "The patent extension for aspartame was really crucial to the life of the company," Timmons acknowledged years later in an interview.

Several small companies that had been hoping to enter the sweetener market complained of a corporate giant benefiting from preferential treatment. But Searle officials argued that it was only fair their company not be made to suffer the loss of years from aspartame's original seventeen-year patent. Several key lawmakers in the Senate and House who had backed the measure—among them, Senators Howell Heflin (D-AL), Orrin Hatch (R-UT), and Robert Byrd (D-WV) and Representative Henry Waxman (D-CA)—received contributions from the Searle family or from soft-drink manufacturers.

The final hurdle for aspartame was cleared in 1983 when the FDA approved it for diet soft drinks. Once Searle received the expanded FDA approval, carbonated drink companies lined up to secure contracts. By the end of 1983, Coca-Cola, Pepsi, and other major bottlers had become Searle customers, and before long, the sweetener could be found in thousands of products, from chewing gum to nutritional bars.

Despite its widespread use, controversy about the risks of aspartame has persisted, kept alive by consumer groups that contend the sweetener poses a danger to public health. The scientific evidence appears to favor those insisting the product is safe, but skeptics point to some studies that suggest otherwise. In Rumsfeld's view, the debate over aspartame's potential health risks was settled long ago, and the product's longevity has provided adequate justification for him. He never seems to tire of lashing back at the critics. "It turns out that the people who were contending that NutraSweet is harmful to your health were wrong," he said in an interview. "This is the most studied food additive in the history of the world, and it is still on the market because the experts have deemed it appropriate for human consumption."

While Rumsfeld's mind was on managing Searle, his true passion remained with politics and government. He continued campaigning for Republican candidates when he could. He served on a couple of national panels, including a presidential advisory committee on arms control and an advisory commission on U.S.-Japanese relations. He kept abreast of national security and other public policy issues as chairman of the RAND Corporation, a prominent nonprofit research institute, from 1981 to 1986. Relying on such senior associates at Searle as Robson and Denny to run the company, he was also able to take on several other commitments that required him to absent himself for days or even, in one case, six months at a stretch.

One assignment he undertook was highly classified and emerged only years later. It involved a program, begun during the Reagan years, aimed at sustaining U.S. government operations during a possible nuclear war with the Soviet Union. Rumsfeld was one of a number of former high-level government officials who would gather at least once a year at Andrews Air Force Base in Washington and would then be surreptitiously ferried in the middle of the night to an underground bunker or some other remote location. There, the group, which included one current member of the cabinet and other representatives of key federal agencies, would simulate running the government and dealing with a protracted conflict.

Three different teams existed, each gathering at a different time, and Rumsfeld headed one of them, assigned in the war games his old role as

White House chief of staff. Dick Cheney, then a congressman from Wyoming, also served as a team leader. Through these continuity-in-government exercises, Rumsfeld, Cheney, and other participants were able to remain current on some of the thinking about plans and procedures for surviving a nuclear war and carrying on federal operations. They also stayed connected in what amounted to a kind of hidden U.S. national security structure.

The emergency plan for a shadow government was never triggered by an actual attack during the Cold War, but Rumsfeld and Cheney, back in power in 2001, found themselves in a real-life scramble to ensure continued government operations after the September 11 terrorist strikes. At that time, amid fears of follow-on attacks on Washington's power centers, Cheney was the most senior of a number of federal officials to be secreted to undisclosed locations.

In other, less hush-hush work for the Reagan administration, Rumsfeld served as an adviser on arms control issues. He also, at the president's request, embarked in 1982 on a trip to persuade world leaders to oppose ratification of the Law of the Sea Treaty, which sought to regulate deep-sea mining and to establish other rules governing ocean use. Embracing the mission enthusiastically, Rumsfeld argued in foreign meetings that the treaty worked against free-market interests and would create a bloated, expensive international bureaucracy with the power to control the oceans.

But his next assignment, as a special presidential envoy to the Middle East starting in November 1983, interested Rumsfeld even more. "Particularly as the years went by at Searle, once we got the thing righted and the stock was doing well and the prospects of the company were improving, you could kind of sense that Don was starting to wonder what he should do next," Denny recalled. "The fact that he went off as Reagan's ambassador to the Middle East was a telltale sign. He loved that assignment."

In the six months he served in the post, traveling extensively, Rumsfeld became deeply immersed in the conflicts and confounding tensions of the region. The experience impressed on him the enormous difficulty of ensuring peace and stability in the Middle East. It was a lesson he would learn again when, years later as defense secretary, he oversaw the U.S. war in Iraq.

George Shultz, Reagan's secretary of state and an old friend of Rumsfeld's from the Nixon years, had recommended Rumsfeld for the assignment, which called for facilitating a settlement of the civil war in Lebanon. In October 1983, a truck loaded with TNT had blown up a U.S. Marine camp in Beirut, killing 241 U.S. servicemen and gravely undercutting U.S. efforts to bring stability to the country. (The Marines had been sent in 1982 as part of a multinational peacekeeping force to help bolster the Lebanese military and buy time to arrange for the withdrawal of Iraqi and Syrian troops occupying Lebanon.)

Shultz was impressed by the way Rumsfeld, in preparing for the mission, adeptly plumbed the intelligence community for useful information. "Rumsfeld was plugged into Washington as a heavy hitter," Shultz wrote in his memoir. "The intelligence community provided him, as a former secretary of defense and a member of their club, with far more information than ever came my way."

Rumsfeld's Middle East assignment was complicated by serious rifts in the Reagan administration. The State Department and the National Security Council, both of which tended to favor military intervention overseas more often than did the Pentagon, wanted to support the Lebanese government and defend a U.S.-backed peace treaty between Lebanon and Israel signed in May 1983. But the Pentagon was wary of using U.S. military forces to shell Syrian positions in an attempt to influence developments. Instead, Rumsfeld concentrated on identifying alternate measures to strengthen U.S. diplomacy and increase pressure on Syria.

With limited knowledge of the Middle East, Rumsfeld soaked up what information he could before heading to the region in search of diplomatic openings. Visiting as many as three Middle East capitals a day, he attacked the mission with characteristic intensity, constantly pressing members of his traveling team for strategy papers and bombarding Washington with reports.

He quickly discovered for himself how frustrating the quest for peace in the Middle East could be. After stopping in Lebanon, reviewing the precarious presence there of U.S. Marines, and conferring with officials in six other countries in the region, he sent a cable to Shultz titled "The Swamp." Dated November 23, the classified eight-page memo revealed Rumsfeld's early pessimism about the prospects of resolving the conflict.

"I can't help but note some parallels in Lebanon with the U.S. role in Vietnam," he wrote. "Like Vietnam, few would honestly question our intentions. But the U.S. ability to bring about our desired outcome is limited." He cited poor coordination between U.S. and political efforts in Lebanon, noted the weakness of the Lebanese government, and expressed doubts that Syria, which had tended to treat Lebanon as one of its own provinces, would be willing to let it become an independent, sovereign country. "I wish we hadn't gone in," Rumsfeld wrote of the deployment of U.S. troops. "We need to be looking for a reasonably graceful way to get out."

He was especially worried about the prospect of Lebanon's growing reliance on the United States for political decisions as well as security. "I am struck," he wrote, "by the degree to which, by act or omission, we seem to have created or permitted to evolve a dependency on us by Lebanon. I've been told by some that we must pick the new GOL [Government of Lebanon] Cabinet. In my opinion, we risk being like an amateur brain surgeon."

Rumsfeld's concerns reflected a deep-seated skepticism about the exercise of American power abroad, especially in complex regions like the Middle East. In his view, the placement of U.S. troops anywhere in the world carried a significance that exceeded their specific actions on the ground. Once forces were deployed, he believed, America's superpower status inevitably complicated later decisions on when and how to withdraw them without creating security and power vacuums in host nations and without being perceived as acting out of weakness. Such considerations, which Rumsfeld confronted in the Lebanon case, came to the fore with greater consequences during the Bush administration in decisions over whether to order U.S. forces into Afghanistan and Iraq.

In the Lebanese conflict, as U.S. officials saw it, the key to a resolution lay with Syria. Rumsfeld urged the Reagan administration to bring more pressure to bear on the Syrians in the form of additional reconnaissance flights and shows of military power. But Pentagon officials were reluctant to undertake such missions, and in early 1984, Reagan called an end to the U.S. Marine presence in Lebanon. As much as Rumsfeld had favored pulling U.S. forces out, he considered Reagan's withdrawal premature, believing the Marines could still have played a role. Overall, the

Lebanon experience underscored for Rumsfeld the difficulties in a democracy of sustaining public backing for a costly fight against a shadowy enemy abroad.

It was as a special presidential envoy that Rumsfeld ended up shaking hands with Iraqi president Saddam Hussein. The visit was a breakthrough encounter at the time, part of an effort by the Reagan administration to reconcile with the Iraqi leader, who had broken off diplomatic relations with the United States in 1967 during the Arab-Israeli War. By the early 1980s, Saddam, finding himself in a prolonged war with Iran, was eager for U.S. assistance and had indicated a willingness to resume ties. While Rumsfeld at that time supported the return to more normal U.S.-Iraqi relations, his cordial session with the Iraqi leader became a source of some awkwardness for him twenty years later when, as defense secretary, he was helping make the case for invading Iraq.

Rumsfeld arrived in Baghdad on December 19, and after meeting more than two hours with Deputy Prime Minister Tariq Aziz, he was ushered in the next day to see Saddam. The Iraqi leader, greeting Rumsfeld in military dress with a pearl-handled pistol on his hip, was clearly pleased at the outset by a letter that the U.S. envoy delivered from Reagan expressing U.S. opposition to the continuation of the Iran-Iraq War. He also readily picked up on a point that Rumsfeld himself had made to Aziz, agreeing heartily that there were inherent dangers to having a generation of Americans and Iraqis growing up failing to understand one another. Saddam and Rumsfeld quickly found common ground in support of a stable Lebanon, limits on Syria's influence there, and curtailment of arms supplies to Iran.

Talking a little business, Rumsfeld raised the possibility of an oil pipeline that would stretch westward from Iraq to the Jordanian port of Aqaba and that could offer U.S. firms an alternative route for transporting oil. Part of the Trans-Arabian Pipeline, which ran from Saudi Arabia through Syria's Golan Heights and into Lebanon, had been seized by Israel in 1967 and shut down in 1976. Saddam had shown no interest in participating in a new pipeline project through Jordan, worried that Israel could disrupt that one as well. But he indicated to Rumsfeld a willingness to re-examine the option now that U.S. companies and the U.S. government were interested.

One topic that Rumsfeld steered clear of with Saddam was Iraq's use of chemical weapons. At the time, U.S. intelligence sources had con-firmed that Iraq had employed chemicals against Iranian forces and Kurdish fighters. But the Reagan administration had not yet decided to press the issue because of its interest in remaining neutral in the Iran-Iraq War and because of the limited probability that saying anything would achieve results.

During his meeting with Aziz, Rumsfeld had alluded to the matter, although largely in passing. According to Rumsfeld's own account of the meeting in a State Department cable, he told the Iraqi minister that while the United States wanted to help Iraq, one thing that "made it dif-ficult for us" was the use of chemical weapons.

In all, the meeting with Saddam lasted an hour and a half. Both men showed their genial sides, sensitive to the significance of the moment. At one point, underscoring his interest in expanding ties to the West, Sad-dam took Rumsfeld to a window and pointed to a tall building. "When the elevator doesn't work in that building, which way do you think I look?" the Iraqi leader asked. "I've got to look West. I need people who can help make this modern country of ours work."

Reflecting on the trip years later, after U.S. troops had stormed in and occupied Iraq, Rumsfeld sought to portray it simply as a practical strate-gic move that had to be viewed in the context of its time. "We were look-ing at it not from who do we want to be our new best friend, but from the standpoint of geostrategic circumstances in that part of the world," he said in an interview in October 2003.

Rumsfeld made a second visit to Baghdad in late March 1984, al-though he did not see Saddam that time, just Aziz. Earlier that month, the United States had publicly condemned Iraq's chemical weapons use. But the purpose of Rumsfeld's mission was to reassure the Iraqis of the likely availability of U.S. financing for construction of the proposed Aqaba pipeline.

Rumsfeld was also carrying a secret offer from Israeli prime minister Yitzhak Shamir. The Israeli leader was thinking that rather than building a pipeline to Jordan, Iraq should secretly open the Trans-Arabian Pipeline. Shamir was essentially looking to open a secret channel of communication aimed at strengthening Iraq in its war with Iran and reducing the prospects of a new Arab-Israeli war. When Rumsfeld raised the Israeli idea with Aziz in a private meeting, the Iraqi minister adamantly refused to convey it to Saddam. Aziz told Rumsfeld that were he even to suggest such a thing to his boss, Saddam would have him executed on the spot.

When Reagan ordered the U.S. Marines out of Lebanon in February 1984, Rumsfeld shifted focus from the eastern Mediterranean to the Persian Gulf, worried that America's defeat in Lebanon could erode America's already limited ability to defend vital interests in the gulf. To reinvigorate the confidence of gulf leaders in the United States, Rumsfeld conferred with the leaders of Saudi Arabia, Kuwait, Bahrain, Qatar, and the United Arab Emirates. His hope was to expand the scope of military planning to prepare for potential Iranian or Soviet aggression. But he made little headway on his proposals for joint planning.

Back in Washington on March 29, Rumsfeld warned Shultz about "a bigger disaster on the horizon" in the Middle East than Lebanon and complained that the Pentagon wasn't doing enough in the region. "He was disturbed by the timidity that had characterized Pentagon officials in Lebanon," Shultz later wrote. Calling Lebanon just a "sideshow" to what might come next, Rumsfeld spoke ominously of a potential implosion in the gulf if Iranian forces were to succeed against Iraq and then move against Kuwait and Saudi Arabia. He said the U.S. military was not prepared for such a contingency, even though the Carter administration had declared the Persian Gulf vital to U.S. interests. "The gulf is crucial, and we are neither organized nor ready to face a crisis there," Rumsfeld said.

By the end of his six-month stint as envoy, Rumsfeld had met with the head of state of every country in the Middle East with which the United States maintained diplomatic relations, and he had made an important breakthrough with Saddam Hussein. In November 1984, just eleven months after Rumsfeld's meeting with the Iraqi leader, the Reagan administration restored full diplomatic relations with Iraq. But Rumsfeld had been bedeviled by the region's problems and frustrated by his inability to effect much change. "He was deeply analytical about the whys and the prospects," Shultz recalled in an interview. "But he would also come back and shake his head saying, 'A just and lasting peace? You must be out of your mind!' Anybody who works on that issue gets frustrated."

In important ways, Rumsfeld's experience as envoy affected his thinking about the Middle East. It underscored the risks of deploying U.S. forces abroad and the difficulty especially of maintaining public backing for a U.S. military operation against an unconventional enemy. And it reinforced many of the concerns he had formed as defense secretary about the U.S. intelligence community's inadequacy. He was particularly frustrated by his inability to garner good intelligence from the CIA on the Middle East. He recognized that the agency had lost some valuable agents in the 1983 bombing of the U.S. embassy in Beirut. But even so, he found the shortage of useful information distressing.

"When I was Middle East envoy, and you saw what we didn't know about what was going on in the Middle East, it would break your heart," he told Pentagon historians in 1994. "Admittedly, we had a number of our assets killed in that one bombing in Beirut in the embassy there, but I think that there needs to be a much better connection between the gatherers and the users of intelligence."

Most significantly, Rumsfeld's time as envoy left him, as he said in an interview for this book, with "a healthy respect for the complexities" of the Middle East and "a healthy dose of humility as to what can be done about them." That, at least, was his retrospective assessment, although the remark suggested a level of hesitancy about venturing into the region that seemed less in evidence years later when, as a member of Bush's war cabinet, he supervised the invasion of Iraq.

While serving as an envoy, Rumsfeld had been on temporary leave from Searle. The company had continued to do well while he was away, a confirmation that in the seven years since he had taken over, he had succeeded in restoring viability and profitability. But on his return, Rumsfeld started looking at Searle's long-term strategic position, and he could see a problem. Much larger firms—Merck and Company, Eli Lilly and Company, some of the Swiss and German pharmaceutical giants—were outspending Searle's research budget many times over, leaving Searle in growing danger of slipping farther and farther behind the leaders in the field. The company's stock had climbed to over fifty dollars a share by the fall of 1984—a more than fourfold increase since Rumsfeld had been put in charge—so it seemed an opportune moment either to sell the firm or to look for a merger.

Denny, who had worked at Firestone before joining Searle, warned Rumsfeld about what had happened when the Firestone family, which owned 30 percent of their company, held on too long: They watched its stock go from a high of thirty-five dollars to a low of five dollars in the early 1980s. "I said, 'The Searle family shouldn't make the same mistake,'" Denny recalled. "That started the process of looking at what we should do."

But first, Rumsfeld wanted to examine every possible merger option. He asked his staff to generate scenario after scenario, and he pored over each one. It was typical of the way he tended to approach major decisions. Whether facing a pricing, product, or merger issue, Rumsfeld often pressed for more information in search of an additional clue or two that might point clearly to the way ahead. To some, the process could look like procrastination. And it did often result in decision delays. But Rumsfeld needed to feel certain that he had left no angle unchecked.

"It would haunt him if he decided to do something and, after the fact, discovered that he hadn't thought about a particular element thoroughly," said Jannotta, his friend and a frequent outside adviser. "I look at it as defensive. He doesn't want to come to a conclusion unless he's thought about all possibilities. The Searle case was quite incredible. I think we came to a very good conclusion, but we came to it after running a lot of traps that we found didn't work."

Initially, Rumsfeld looked for a single buyer for Searle; then he adopted a piecemeal approach. By March 1985, he was poised to sell each of the company's three divisions to a separate buyer. But he abandoned the approach in May after concluding it was too complicated. In July, Monsanto Company, which had initially hoped to purchase just Searle's prescription-drug division, came back with an offer for the whole company. A final agreement was reached within days.

During the time the company was up for sale, Searle's senior managers had been promised severance payments to keep them from leaving until a deal was struck. But nothing to this effect had been put in writing. As he was closing the deal with Monsanto, Rumsfeld asked the company to provide an open check to cover the payments. Monsanto officials hesitated.

It was less than an hour before the opening of Wall Street, and word of the sale was starting to leak. Unless the deal could be closed before stocks started trading, Rumsfeld said he would walk away. A Monsanto executive asked if Rumsfeld could at least estimate a cost for the severance payments. "I could if I'd thought about it but I have not thought about it and I'm not now going to start thinking about it with the clock ticking," he replied, according to Denny, who witnessed the scene.

The Monsanto executive urged him to just make up a large number, any number, that would leave plenty of room. Rumsfeld refused, reluctant to offer a figure off the cuff. "You have a choice: Either you have confidence I'll do what's right or we don't have a deal," he declared.

Finally, Monsanto agreed, trusting that Rumsfeld would not take advantage of the blank check he was being given to cover the promised employee payments. In the biggest financial transaction of his life, Rumsfeld had stood firm on a personal commitment and won. He also profited considerably. Under the terms of the sale, Monsanto paid sixty-five dollars a share, or about $2.7 billion, for Searle. A *Chicago Tribune* profile of Rumsfeld shortly afterward, citing "corporate insiders," reported his net worth at roughly ten million dollars.

Getting comfortable with having money had been a gradual process for Rumsfeld. He had kept his lifestyle relatively modest. He bought a rambling old house with a leaky roof in Winnetka. He drove a used Volvo. At the office, he made his own coffee, ate lunch at his desk or in the company cafeteria, and strolled about in his shirtsleeves. He walked around with a big hole in the sole of his right shoe.

Unlike many other executives living in the affluent communities of Chicago's North Shore, he had never gotten into the country-club life. Neither he nor Joyce liked the snobbery, the exclusiveness of the club scene. "We just hung out at home," Joyce recalled. "We're not country-club people. We did have a problem on that North Shore, the mentality. It really bothered us. Do you know how Don explained it to the children? This is an insight into him. He said, 'You know, as a result of the schools we attend and the places we live, we are thrown in with a certain group of people, and that's a given, but what you want to do in your free time, as you're able, is to branch out.'"

With more money in his pocket than he had ever enjoyed, Rumsfeld did allow himself one risky indulgence: He started investing through a partnership formed with Robson and Denny. Originally dubbed Three Blind Mice and later renamed Yellow Brick Road, the group focused first on real estate investments and then branched into venture capital deals. The sums weren't great—perhaps $25,000 to $50,000 in each investment. Some turned out well, some didn't. All in all, as Denny put it, the net results "never loomed very large on anyone's balance sheet."

Rumsfeld had also begun buying property in New Mexico, first a ranch with several others—including Jannotta, Denny, former school buddy Jim Otis, and CBS correspondent Dan Rather, a Washington friend—and then his own spread just outside Taos. Drawn to the area by his summer experience as a teenager at the Boy Scouts ranch, Rumsfeld eventually acquired considerable acreage and established a residence that became a favorite retreat.

———•———

With financial security, Rumsfeld could return to politics and attempt to fulfill his lifelong ambition of becoming president of the United States. He had made no secret of his desire to get back into politics full-time. "I expect that at some point the odds favor my being involved in government again," he said in *Fortune* in 1979. "One, I enjoyed it. Two, I think I did a good job. Three, I'm interested in our country and the world." Not long after taking the Searle job, Rumsfeld had given serious thought to running for president in the 1980 election. But he dropped the idea then because he was not yet financially independent, and he saw Ronald Reagan as too popular to beat.

Looking ahead now to the 1988 race, he was game. After selling the family's house in Winnetka and moving into an apartment on the Near

North Side, Rumsfeld took an office downtown at William Blair and Company, an investment-banking house run by his old friend Jannotta. There, above LaSalle Street, with an expansive view of Lake Michigan from the thirty-ninth floor, he began the first steps toward a presidential run. He formed a political action committee to raise money and started appearing on panels of potential Republican candidates. He talked to political reporters and editorial boards and delivered speeches around the country. He worked on defining what his campaign would be about.

He had lost little of the drive and energy of his youth, and his success in saving Searle had only enhanced his image as an effective operator. But his reputation in political circles had remained controversial, especially among those who had dealt with him. "To his admirers Rumsfeld is among the shrewdest and most talented leaders of his generation, a whiz kid who has lived up to his early promise," observed Steve Neal, a political reporter for the *Chicago Tribune*, in January 1986. "But to his critics Rumsfeld is a schemer and backroom manipulator, a fiercely ambitious man whose chief motivations are his own advancement and the destruction of potential rivals."

Moreover, Rumsfeld hadn't held public office for ten years or run for an elected position in nearly twenty years. And the history of corporate executives trying for the White House was hardly encouraging. As Neal pointed out in his article, not since Wendell L. Willkie in 1940 had a corporate man been nominated for the presidency, and not since 1928 had a former cabinet member, Herbert Hoover, made the cut.

As a stepping-stone to the presidency, Rumsfeld considered running for the Senate in 1986 against the Democratic incumbent, Alan Dixon. Even if he lost, he figured the campaign would thrust him back into the political spotlight. Among those Rumsfeld consulted about this option was Nixon, with whom he had rarely spoken since their time in government together. Nixon in 1962, under circumstances similar to those Rumsfeld was facing now, had made a bid for governor of California—and lost. The former president urged Rumsfeld to run directly for president.

Rumsfeld needed little arm-twisting to decide to skip the idea of trying to become a senator or governor before attempting a dash straight for the White House. He just couldn't see himself at that point in his life occupying an intermediate rung of the political ladder. He had already glimpsed the view from the White House. "He didn't want to go the other ways," Joyce recalled. "How can you run for senator if you don't want to be one? Can you imagine Don in the U.S. Senate today? And governor? His interest by then was more national security, global things."

Reagan, during his two terms as president, had left a strong imprint on the nation's political agenda through his advocacy of a strong military, a firm stance toward the Soviet Union, liberal domestic economic policies, and lower taxes. Toward the end of his time in office, tensions between the superpowers had decreased dramatically, and the U.S. economy was prospering. But Reagan had also run up huge budget deficits, and he and his administration had become embroiled in 1986 in a political scandal surrounding the use of proceeds from covert arms sales to Iran to fund the Contras in Nicaragua.

While Reagan had unified Republican conservatives under him, the party's right wing was showing signs of fragmenting as leading figures began jockeying to take Reagan's place. Bush had an inside edge as vice president. But also showing significant support was Representative Jack Kemp of New York, a chief advocate of supply-side economics, and Reverend Pat Robertson, a favorite of social conservatives. Other possible hopefuls included Senate Majority Leader Robert Dole of Kansas, former Senate majority leader Howard Baker of Tennessee, former secretary of state Alexander Haig, former governor Pierre du Pont of Delaware, and Senator Paul Laxalt of Nevada.

It was a crowded field. Acknowledging the heavy odds against him, Rumsfeld chose the image of a dark horse as the emblem of his campaign. Nonetheless, as a hawk on defense issues and a confirmed conservative, he considered himself well positioned to pick up where Reagan was leaving off.

He viewed the front-runners, Bush and Kemp, as weaker than generally assumed, and he looked for signs that the Iran arms scandal that was buffeting the administration might especially undercut Bush's chances. He calculated that the lack of a strong front-runner could play to his advantage, allowing him to emerge as a leading contender in early free-for-all GOP primaries. Never short of self-confidence, he figured that his background and breadth of experience made him the best qualified— and that he would be recognized by voters as such.

All through 1986, Rumsfeld continued to do what he could to get noticed and to build up a network among Republican activists. He made over two hundred speeches. His political action committee, Citizens for American Values, came to rank among the biggest. He even enjoyed the quiet backing of some senior members of the Reagan administration.

His old friend George Shultz, then secretary of state, had been a longtime Rumsfeld supporter. So had Frank Carlucci, who was serving as national security adviser. "If Republican presidential nominees had been selected by the National Security Council, Rumsfeld might well have won," observed the author James Mann writing about the 1988 campaign years later.

Kissinger, too, out of government more than a decade by then, had grown more mellow about his former Pentagon adversary and considered that Rumsfeld, if he ever reached the presidency, "might be a more comfortable chief executive than Cabinet colleague" and, indeed, had "the makings of a strong president."

But Rumsfeld's candidacy never managed to gain broader traction. He had been out of elective office too long. He suffered from a lack of name recognition and defining themes. His public speaking also left something to be desired. "His campaign style is about as colorful as a CEO's wardrobe," observed one reporter.

Additionally, Rumsfeld had relied heavily on a core group of old friends and associates to mount the campaign, failing to tap into a deeper network of political operatives around the country. "Elected officials keep their cadre intact. But Rummy never had that," said Somers Steelman, a Princeton roommate who helped organize support for Rumsfeld in New Jersey. "He never had a national organization that he could pull together."

Steelman vividly recalled a booster-group meeting in his state organized by another Princeton classmate, John McGillicuddy, the chairman of American Cyanamid Company. "There must have been about one hundred people there, the cream of the crop," Steelman said. "Rummy got up and spoke. It was a blockbuster presentation. After that, one of these muckety-mucks rose and said, 'Mr. Rumsfeld, I firmly believe you are the most qualified person to run for the presidency in the United States as a Republican. Having said that, could you please tell me what your organization is?' You know, it died right there. Rumsfeld replied that even though it may appear that he's divorced from his political contacts, he could reconstruct them with no hardship. But the push Rummy thing in New Jersey died in that room. Which was a shame."

National polls in the early months of 1987 were showing Rumsfeld barely garnering a percentage point or two. Struggling at the tail end of the pack, Rumsfeld had trouble raising money. He was particularly stunned when his old friend Cheney, whose political career Rumsfeld had done more to nurture than anyone else, declined to support him. "That was a big surprise," Joyce said years later. "We didn't understand it."

Cheney had jumped back into politics shortly after the end of the Ford administration. Elected to Congress from Wyoming in 1978, he had established a reputation as a committed conservative. Popular enough to have a future as a party leader, he had made his way to chairman of the House Republican Conference. With his eye eventually on becoming speaker of the House, he planned to try for Republican whip, the second-ranking party leadership position, when the job opened up after the 1988 election.

In his first public comment about his refusal to back Rumsfeld's presidential bid, Cheney explained in an interview for this book that he had felt constrained by his own efforts to win the whip job in the House. He had no criticism of Rumsfeld at the time. He just didn't want to get involved in the presidential campaign and risk offending other candidates. "The last thing I needed to do was to become identified as a partisan of one of the candidates when I was focused on my own race," he said. "If I went out and became a crusader for a Rumsfeld or a Kemp or a Bush, I was asking for grief I didn't need." The strategy paid off. No one challenged Cheney for the whip post. But his relationship with Rumsfeld was badly strained and remained so for some years.

Rumsfeld pulled out of the presidential race in April 1987. In a letter to contributors, supporters, and friends announcing his decision, he said his political action committee had raised over one million dollars. But he could not see attracting a sufficient amount of money soon enough to avoid a deficit in what would surely be an expensive campaign. "I am unwilling to proceed on a deficit basis," he said.

Among those he had consulted before ending his bid was Democratic senator John Glenn of Ohio, who shared with Rumsfeld his own horror story of running up a debt of three million dollars in his 1984 presidential campaign, a debt he was still struggling to pay off. Glenn told Rumsfeld that he deeply regretted not being able to pay back many supporters more quickly. "I never lost a night's sleep when I was a test pilot, I never lost a night's sleep before the orbit, and this is killing me," Glenn said to Rumsfeld. Recounting the conversation to his wife, Rumsfeld told her, "It would also kill me."

Even so, Rumsfeld agonized over what to do. Joyce urged him to stay in and at least help "elevate the conversation." Ending the campaign meant not just the close of a chapter of his life but very likely the final dissolution of a lifelong dream. For his part, though, he just couldn't see an affordable way forward. Withdrawal was the financially sensible, and the only real, alternative.

Afterward, Rumsfeld didn't appear to friends to dwell on the profound disappointment he must have been feeling. Joyce insists that she and her husband simply moved on. "Everyone was emotional, everyone was just kind of crushed at that moment," she said about the decision. "And then the next day we all got up and did something else."

CHAPTER 6

A Friendly Hawkish Guy

In August 1990, Ted Forstmann, one of Wall Street's more colorful and bombastic characters, made a bold purchase, paying $1.6 billion for General Instrument Corporation (GI), a disparate conglomerate that had been adrift for some time. A master of the leveraged buyout, Forstmann financed the deal largely with bank loans and subordinated debt. His plan was to refocus GI on its profitable core of cable- and satellite-television equipment divisions and to sell off other parts of the company that were struggling. But Forstmann needed a new CEO to manage the transformation—someone with a record of success at a technology-oriented company, experienced in corporate change, and skilled in the regulatory ways of Washington. Rumsfeld seemed made to order.

Rumsfeld's involvement in the political world had reached a low point. His presidential aspirations were dashed, and he had little to do in Washington with the administration of President George H. W. Bush. He had entered into several ventures after leaving Searle, but they were advisory roles or board-of-director positions rather than management, leaving him available for a major new business challenge.

Rumsfeld already had a connection to Forstmann, serving on the blue-chip—but largely symbolic—advisory board of the financier's New York–based firm, Forstmann Little and Company. Other board members included Colin Powell, George Shultz, and Henry Kissinger. In several respects, the situation with GI resembled the situation Rumsfeld had faced when he started at Searle: an opportunity to take a lackluster, bloated company, pursue a new focus, and restore energy and profitability. Similar also to the aspartame story, GI had a potential golden egg in incubation: the world's first all-digital, high-definition television technology.

But in contrast with the Searle experience, where it was Rumsfeld who had to conceive the rescue plan, in the GI case he was not being asked to come up with the blueprint. The strategy for restructuring the company had already been devised by Forstmann Little. Rumsfeld's job was essentially to execute it and, in the process, pull together the powerful—but previously feuding—heads of GI's cable and satellite divisions. "Don had a reputation as a good overall organizer and general manager," said Steve Klinsky, the Forstmann Little partner who had conceived the strategy and was principally responsible for day-to-day oversight of the investment. "We wanted a new, top-quality CEO at the helm to give GI structure and management discipline."

During Rumsfeld's first months on the job, GI's financial staff, working with Forstmann Little, concentrated on selling off the unwanted, unsuccessful businesses in such disparate product fields as defense electronics, lottery equipment, and racetrack tote boards. Rumsfeld declined to participate in this process, presumably to keep himself free of any conflicts in the event he returned to government and the defense establishment at a later date. He turned his full attention to the remaining part of GI, which involved broadcast gear. The company ranked as the world's leading supplier of cable-television equipment. It made the converter boxes that rested on top of TVs for cable subscribers. And it controlled the market for scramblers of satellite-TV signals.

Rumsfeld also presided over a sharp reduction in GI's corporate staff and began planning to shift the company's headquarters from New York to Chicago, where he had continued to keep a house, commuting back and forth weekly. By the time of the move in October 1991, the headquarters staff had shrunk from 165 to 17. A separate financial operation, which had been located in New Jersey, was also closed, and its jobs were transferred into GI's manufacturing divisions.

Under the original game plan, the sell-off of noncore businesses and the streamlining of the remaining part of GI were supposed to generate revenue that would allow Forstmann Little to cover the large debt it had incurred to acquire GI and then take the firm public again. But the plan suffered a serious setback in Rumsfeld's first year at GI when the company's cable-industry customers experienced a severe credit crunch—the result of a government decision to clamp down on bank lending in high-debt situations.

Cable firms were accustomed to borrowing heavily to finance rapid expansion. Now they couldn't. Skittish also about congressional efforts to reregulate cable, operators withheld orders for new equipment. GI never missed a bank covenant or had a debt problem, but its sales dropped more than 14 percent in the first ten months of 1991 compared to the same period the year before.

Strict cost control became more necessary than ever, and Rumsfeld bore down on GI's division managers, holding them more accountable for business plans. He instituted extensive reporting requirements to track performance. At meetings, he insisted that briefers adhere strictly to the agendas they had submitted beforehand and not wander off topic.

Company officials grumbled that Rumsfeld seemed to prefer form over substance. But anyone who bridled risked drawing Rumsfeld's unforgiving ire. Once, in a pique of dissatisfaction, Rumsfeld walked out of a presentation by the head of GI's satellite division. The division chief flew back to his office in San Diego and faxed a resignation letter. Rumsfeld scribbled on it, "I accept," and told his secretary to fax it back. When the executive phoned a little later to say he hadn't really meant to quit, Rumsfeld said it didn't matter, *he* had meant to fire him.

On occasion, Rumsfeld showed a softer side. He displayed a capacity for sympathy and support, for instance, in the case of an executive with an alcohol problem. Rumsfeld helped him through treatment, and the executive eventually recovered and proved an exceptionally valuable employee.

At times, too, Rumsfeld could be downright genial, particularly around longtime associate Bernard Windon, a former Searle executive who had managed Rumsfeld's exploratory presidential bid and then joined Rumsfeld at GI. Open and friendly by nature, Windon had an easygoing relationship with Rumsfeld and knew how to maneuver around Rumsfeld's rough edges. "You could see, in the relationship that existed between Don and Bernie, that Don wasn't this aloof monster he was often held out to be," observed Rick Friedland, GI's top financial officer and one of the few senior executives who stayed on the corporate staff after the purchase by Forstmann Little. "When Bernie was in the room for a staff meeting or other discussion, it just eased the conversation."

As he had with the Searle family when he ran their firm, Rumsfeld took special care to keep Klinsky, his day-to-day contact at Forstmann Little, informed of decisions and actions. "For almost three years, he would send me a copy of every memo that he wrote, which may be typical in government but is unusual for the way most executives work," Klinsky recalled.

Still, Klinsky sensed a certain distance interacting with Rumsfeld. There seemed something of the former NATO ambassador about Rumsfeld, a kind of standing-on-ceremony quality. He also could be highly structured in his approach to things. "He's not a folksy, back-slapping type guy," Klinsky remarked. "There's a great level of formality in dealing with Don, even in day-to-day matters. I've seen Don do some very kind and ethical things for other people, but he has this formal mask he puts out there."

———— · ————

Rumsfeld's first year at GI was dominated by revamping the company and putting new procedures and processes in place. His second focused more on managing the company's efforts to develop high-definition television (HDTV), which had the potential to revolutionize the broadcast business. In much the same way that aspartame had helped spur the growth of Searle, the new digital system promised to breathe new financial life into GI.

But as with Searle's innovative sweetener, GI's invention would be dependent on action by the federal government. The system was in contention with proposals by several other firms in a winner-take-all sweepstakes being run by the Federal Communications Commission (FCC) to determine a new television standard for HDTV in the United States. GI had been the first company in the world to propose a workable all-digital technology for the HDTV standard, but soon other firms had developed competing proposals.

Rumsfeld didn't know much about broadcasting technologies, but he did know about playing to the Washington crowd. He worked closely with a GI task force to devise a winning HDTV strategy. One of the first steps was to team with a competitor, the Massachusetts Institute of Technology (MIT), to narrow the field and to prepare a strong joint proposal under the name American TeleVision Alliance. The name was intended to highlight the strategic importance to the U.S. government of choosing American technology over that of foreign competitors.

To promote the GI/MIT technology, Rumsfeld staged a demonstration at the U.S. Capitol in March 1992—the first public showing of a TV system that transmits signals in the digital language of computers. A company brochure billed the occasion as "an historic event in broadcasting history," in the same league as Samuel Morse's demonstration of the telegraph in 1844, the arrival of the telephone in 1876, and television's big coming out at the 1939 World's Fair. While clearly hyped, the event did succeed in generating some excitement and filling a meeting room in the U.S. Capitol building.

Shortly after noon on a Tuesday, WETA Channel 26, Washington's public broadcasting station, stopped its regular programming for eleven minutes to send the compressed high-definition signals. Two RadioShack antennas temporarily placed on the Capitol roof picked them up. The first image to fill the screen was an American flag, followed by other U.S. scenes, of the Grand Canyon, Navy fighter jets, racing cars, blooming flowers, the Statue of Liberty, and cowboys in rodeo competition. The pictures definitely appeared sharper than conventional TV pictures—400 percent sharper, according to GI's figures.

GI's ability to showcase its system in such a high-profile setting to a lineup of elected officials and other influential guests was a public relations coup in a game with exceedingly high stakes. Once again, Rumsfeld was back in the headlines, championing change and appearing to move easily between the worlds of business and politics.

But the contest over HDTV dragged on. The FCC put off a decision on an industry standard, seeking more testing. Frustrated by the delay, Rumsfeld kept looking for a way to give GI an important stake in the future of HDTV. He spent some time pursuing a plan for a kind of "grand alliance," in which GI and MIT would join forces with three competing firms to present the FCC with a single, unified proposal. Eventually, new entrants entered from the computer industry and sought to alter the selection process.

Years would pass—and Rumsfeld would be long gone from GI—before the commission finally settled not on a single digital video format for HDTV but on several formats intended to be compatible with computer monitors as well as televisions. Still, in the nearer term, GI's breakthroughs in digital compression would give birth to a host of other important products, including digital satellite systems, "1,000 channel" cable systems, and digital set-top boxes. And for Rumsfeld, who was approaching the end of his second year heading GI, just having GI in the running for what promised to be an exciting new dimension of television was proving more than enough to spur investor interest in the company. The corporate restructuring efforts also were by then paying off in improved performance.

In June 1992, Forstmann Little began taking the company public with an initial offering of stock priced at fifteen dollars a share, about five times the original purchase price. By the time of a third stock offering in September 1993, the share price had shot up to fifty-one dollars. In the process, Forstmann Little was able to pay off or refinance the $750 million in bank loans and $600 million in subordinated debt used to finance the 1990 purchase. The impressive return on its original risky investment drew glowing news coverage featuring GI as one of the most successful leveraged buy-outs and corporate turnarounds ever. Along with other company insiders, Rumsfeld cashed in on the public stock offerings, personally gaining an estimated pretax profit of about $23 million.

But despite the success, Rumsfeld after three years was ready to move on. His heart had never really been in the business, and his departure was announced in August 1993. While it was clear that his influence on GI had been significant, the company had remained for Rumsfeld a project, not a career, and he had other projects either already under way or in mind for the future.

His waning interest in GI had become evident in his final year as he traveled to promote GI's public stock offerings with potential investors. His stature and reputation for integrity provided a reassuring presence at these meetings, but Rumsfeld hadn't enjoyed the process of having to sell himself in front of rooms full of stock market analysts and moneymen. Often at these presentations, after making a brief introductory speech, he would turn the proceedings over to other GI officers and essentially check out, opening his briefcase and attending to other matters. "There was some feedback from investors who felt that Don wasn't as interested in their participation as he should have been," Friedland recalled. "He did what he needed to do, but he got very tired of the process very quickly."

One evening in Denver, after his brief initial presentation to a group of analysts and prospective investors, Rumsfeld disappeared from the room. The Chicago Bulls basketball team was playing, and Rumsfeld, a Bulls fan, wanted to watch the game on TV. "I wouldn't say he had a particular passion for this industry," Klinsky said. "I think he took it on as a professional manager. He did what a skilled professional manager should do, and it worked out well."

Rumsfeld's assertive, probing style wasn't limited to the companies he ran. He exhibited the same characteristics as a corporate director. In 1992, when the Tribune Company in Chicago considered putting Rumsfeld on its board, senior officers consulted the heads of other companies on whose boards he had served. For all the value Rumsfeld brought, they were warned, he could also be very high maintenance. "I remember the response," said John Madigan, the Tribune executive—and childhood friend—who had recommended Rumsfeld for the position. "It was, quote, Don is a great board member, but you can only have one Rumsfeld on your board."

Rumsfeld ended up joining Tribune's board, where he lived up to his reputation. "He questioned almost everything we did," Madigan said. As a matter of fact, Rumsfeld wouldn't simply wait for board meetings to make his views known. In between meetings, he dispatched memo after memo containing his reflections on board sessions, his views on Tribune's strategic plans, his thoughts on company speeches he liked or disliked.

Correspondence from board members was filed away in drawers in Madigan's office. The amount of file space devoted to messages from Rumsfeld clearly dominated. "It was half Rumsfeld and half the other eleven or twelve directors," Madigan said. "The amount of correspondence back and forth between Rumsfeld and me was equivalent to all the rest of the directors combined."

At Tribune, Rumsfeld chaired the technology subcommittee, taking an active interest in new media technologies. Another focus of his was the compensation of executives. He disdained stock options, extensive perks, and excessive pay for executives. Whenever new compensation packages were presented to the board for approval, they would be very difficult to get by him.

He raised a number of ethical considerations, too, pressing the question, for instance, of whether the *Tribune* should continue carrying tobacco advertising. "He had a lot of thoughts on doing things the right way, not simply the legal way," Madigan said. "If we used legality as an excuse for doing something, he would question it. He caused us to soul search in the way we ran our business."

While Rumsfeld's critiquing seemed incessant, he did have a tendency to bear down hardest not when things were going poorly with the company but when things were going well. He had a philosophy about that, which Madigan summed up as, "Kick 'em while they're up."

The flip side was, "Pull 'em up while they're down," which Madigan once experienced with Rumsfeld in a very touching way. It was March 2000, and Tribune Company had just announced the purchase of Times Mirror Company, an $8 billion deal ranked then as the biggest newspaper acquisition in history. But investors initially greeted the move with skepticism, and Tribune's stock fell more than 17 percent. Madigan was feeling about as low as he'd ever felt in his business career. One of the first phone calls he made after the announcement was to Rumsfeld, expecting to receive a scolding for going ahead with the deal. Rumsfeld's reaction was just the opposite. "His support for me at that point when I needed it was tremendous," Madigan recalled. "He said, 'You did what you believe in, and when you do what you think is right, in the end it'll be fine.' He picked my morale up more than I can tell you. What I thought would be the toughest part of the day turned out to be the best part."

As difficult and demanding as Rumsfeld could be as a corporate director, a number of companies wanted him. Among the major companies on whose boards he served were Sears, Roebuck and Company, Kellogg Company, Metricom Incorporated, Gulfstream Aerospace Corporation, Allstate Corporation, Salomon Smith Barney, and ABB AB (formerly Asea Brown Boveri). He also spent time in 1995 and 1996 as the chairman of the RAND Corporation, a position he had held in the early 1980s.

Two of his favorite board experiences, though, involved not big firms or established think tanks but start-up operations in the drug field: Gilead Sciences, which he joined in 1988, and a California company called Amylin Pharmaceuticals, where a cousin already on the board helped bring Rumsfeld on in 1991.

"I'd been around big companies and run big companies," Rumsfeld recalled in an interview. "But going on a board of, in effect, a start-up or near start-up is a totally different thing. It was a new experience, and so I learned a lot, and you had a chance to work with much younger people and smart people and interested people and energetic people, who weren't presiding over something that was already there but were creating something. It was a heckuva lot of fun."

Fun and, in the case of Gilead, exceedingly profitable. Rumsfeld had signed on with Gilead after being pursued—"pestered" is how he put it in the interview—by the company's founder, an entrepreneurial doctor named Michael Riordan. Specializing in antiviral drugs, Gilead went for nearly a decade before introducing its own drug in 1996. It survived in the interim through partnership with an established British drug conglomerate and on funds from investors betting on several new pharmaceuticals that Gilead had in development.

Rumsfeld succeeded Riordan as chairman of the board in 1997 just as the company was taking off. Over the next few years it gained prominence with treatments for HIV (the virus that causes AIDS), for fungal infections, and for the flu. In 1999, in a case of the little fish swallowing the big one, Gilead acquired NeXstar Pharmaceuticals, a company more than twice Gilead's size. John Martin, Gilead's president, credits Rumsfeld—and another board member and longtime Rumsfeld chum, George Shultz—with helping steer the firm through a two-year negotiation that resulted in the purchase.

Like Rumsfeld's other business associates, Martin found Rumsfeld an imposing force. "Don is a very high energy guy," Martin said in an interview. "When he became chairman, he was in constant contact with me. I'd get a fax from him pretty much on a continuous basis with things he would be thinking of." But Martin said he appreciated the frequent contact and benefited from Rumsfeld's advice.

One of the consequences of having started young in politics and having spent a substantial part of his life there was that Rumsfeld kept finding himself drawn back in. Sometimes it was by his own design. Other times, chance provided the impetus, which is what happened in the 1996 presidential election.

Rumsfeld had been sitting on the sidelines watching Robert Dole, the former Senate majority leader, emerge as the GOP's likely nominee. Rumsfeld knew Dole and liked him. The two had served together in Congress and had once had offices next door in the Cannon House Office Building.

So when Dole's wife Elizabeth came to Chicago in the spring of 1996 to give a speech, Rumsfeld and Joyce attended, then chatted together afterward with Elizabeth. Her husband's campaign, she told them, could use some help. Rumsfeld couldn't resist the opportunity to get back into the game, and he soon was conferring with Dole over what role he might play.

By June, Rumsfeld had signed on to the campaign, agreeing initially to serve as a two-day-a-week policy director. But his involvement quickly grew, and by August, he was putting in six days a week as national chairman. "At first, it was just going to be, 'I'll be in and out,'" Dole recalled in an interview. "Then it got to be every day."

Dole was excited to have Rumsfeld by his side in his underdog attempt to deny Bill Clinton a second presidential term. Rumsfeld brought more than fresh energy and political savvy to the struggling GOP campaign. He had lots of contacts in the private sector and in government. And he could relate to Dole as a peer, drawing the candidate's respect and attention, which was particularly important given Dole's famous tendency to share little about what was on his own mind and listen mostly to his own instincts when making decisions. Dole was comfortable with Rumsfeld and trusted him.

Working with the campaign staff, Rumsfeld lived up to his reputation as an aggressive, impatient, task-oriented manager. When he attended meetings, he generally ran them. In contrast with Dole, who had a more relaxed management style, Rumsfeld pushed for decisions and imposed deadlines. He helped organize what had been an unwieldy mass of advisers into three manageable groups dealing with foreign policy, domestic policy, and economic policy.

Rumsfeld also brought with him a group of other advisers, infusing the campaign with greater expertise and reinforcing its conservative cast. Among those he recruited to work on foreign policy was Paul Wolfowitz, who had risen to prominence during the Reagan and Bush administrations while Rumsfeld was out of Washington. The two had worked together briefly a decade earlier when, as an assistant secretary of state, Wolfowitz had managed a commission on U.S.-Japanese relations on which Rumsfeld served. When Rumsfeld asked him to come work for Dole, Wolfowitz tried to beg off, saying he had a full-time job as dean of the School of Advanced International Studies at Johns Hopkins. Replied Rumsfeld, "It's just a matter of time management."

With the advice of Rumsfeld and Wolfowitz, Dole took hard-line positions on a number of foreign and defense policy issues. He supported development of an antimissile system to shield the United States against attack. He advocated the expansion of NATO into eastern Europe. He spoke critically of the United Nations. He sounded hawkish toward China and firm about the defense of Taiwan. On North Korea, he argued that the United States should avoid contact until after the Pyongyang regime of Kim Jong Il had opened the way for direct talks with South Korea.

On economic policy, too, Rumsfeld emerged as an influential voice, encouraging Dole to embrace the idea of tax cuts as a way to achieve prosperity. This endorsement of supply-side economics represented a switch for Rumsfeld as well as for Dole, both of whom had been wary of the notion that tax cuts could generate enough economic growth to compensate for the lost revenue. But the notion appealed to Reaganite economic conservatives, and Dole's signature issue became a proposed economic package that called for reducing personal income tax rates by 15 percent and other breaks for families and investors, while balancing the budget by 2002 without major cuts in costly entitlements such as Social Security or other social services.

Rumsfeld's name turned up on a list of potential vice presidential running mates that was put together for Dole by Robert Ellsworth, Rumsfeld's former congressional and Pentagon associate. Rumsfeld had made such lists before. Ford had considered picking him. So had Reagan. Each time he was passed over in favor of someone else thought to have characteristics that would better balance the ticket. And so it was with Dole, who ended up reaching even farther to the right and picking Jack Kemp to be his running mate. "Our view was that Rummy had been out of politics for so long, and Illinois was such a tough state anyway, and his strength was in the area of defense where I also had some strength," Dole said. "He didn't seem to quite fit, although I think he would have taken it."

Still, Dole highly valued Rumsfeld's role in the campaign and tried to persuade him to assume even more responsibility. Rumsfeld was reluctant to go beyond the job of chairman and take over day-to-day operations, in part because he didn't want to be perceived as shouldering aside Dole's existing campaign manager, Scott Reed, and in part because he didn't care for some of the other senior campaign operatives.

"Scott Reed is the executive of this campaign, and every piece of it operationally reports to him," Rumsfeld told a journalist at the time. "I have no line operating functions." Rumsfeld referred to himself as "a nonexecutive chairman" and declared his chief value was bringing an outsider's perspective to a Washington campaign.

"I was ready to just give him a blank check and say, Here Don, whatever you think ought to be done in this campaign, because we knew we were climbing uphill," Dole recalled. "But I could never get him to the point where he would be the boss. He kept saying he was just here to help on certain issues."

The final vote was not very close—Clinton won by more than eight million votes. Looking back, Dole said that even if Rumsfeld had taken a more active role, "it probably wouldn't have made that much difference."

———————

As the 1990s wore on, Rumsfeld kept a hand in Republican politics as a participant in a group advising congressional Republican leaders on national security issues. The group united prominent former officials from the Nixon, Reagan, and first Bush administrations with members of such conservative think tanks as the American Enterprise Institute and the Heritage Foundation. It sought in the near term to define a GOP legislative agenda, casting the Republicans as wiser trustees of U.S. interests than the Clinton administration and what were portrayed as Clinton's overly conciliatory and accommodating policies. Longer term, the group began framing GOP issues for the 2000 presidential campaign and, in so doing, served as a kind of farm team for a number of leading GOP figures who, like Rumsfeld, would later occupy senior positions in the second Bush administration.

Rumsfeld proved an especially active participant not only in meetings but between sessions, when he regularly phoned congressional staff members. Marshall Billingslea, a staff member on the Senate Foreign Relations Committee in the 1990s, said Rumsfeld showed a particular interest in weapons-proliferation issues and helped Republican efforts to scuttle the chemical-weapons convention. Ash Carter, then an assistant secretary of defense in the Clinton administration, remembers Rumsfeld as the most inquisitive of all the former defense secretaries when from time to time they were called to receive Pentagon briefings on current events.

But for the most part, the aging Rumsfeld was a marginal figure on the Washington political scene. Once the future of the Republican Party, he had become an eminent graying representative of its past. An enduring image for Billingslea was the sight of Rumsfeld walking alone down a Dirksen Senate Office Building hallway wearing a gray suit and carrying a worn leather satchel that had been with him for years. "This is a guy who doesn't throw things away," Billingslea remembers thinking. "He's not a consumer."

Rumsfeld's name in that period showed up from time to time on significant political declarations, including a couple of letters criticizing the Clinton administration's Iraq policy, and occasionally in association with a political advocacy group or two. One such group was the Project for the New American Century led by William Kristol and Robert Kagan, both prominent neoconservatives. "We all thought of him as a friendly and sympathetic hawkish guy," Kristol recalled in an interview.

Although Rumsfeld's connection with the group involved little more than the use of his name, this affiliation, along with personal ties to such other big-name neoconservatives as Wolfowitz and Richard Perle, led some to regard Rumsfeld as a neoconservative as well. He was not. From the start of his political career, Rumsfeld had hewed more to a mainline brand of conservatism. In foreign and defense policy, this meant a certain geopolitical realism and a wariness of U.S. military interventions. While

Kristol and Kagan, for instance, strongly pressed for U.S. involvement in Bosnia and Kosovo, Rumsfeld did not. Nor did he join neoconservative calls for a major U.S. military buildup, favoring instead better use of existing resources and greater incorporation of advanced technologies.

But his views were not always easy to pigeonhole. Rumsfeld had little confidence, for instance, in the United Nations, a fact that tended to color him as a unilateralist. Yet he also had a record favoring other international alliances, notably, NATO and U.S. alliances in Asia. Perhaps because he had been positioned to the right of Henry Kissinger during their Ford administration battles over détente, Rumsfeld retained an aura as an archrealist. Yet he also sometimes showed a deep moral streak, particularly in his lifelong commitment to civil rights. "He sees a world where there is good and there is evil, it's not all gray," said Billingslea, who served in several Pentagon policy posts under Rumsfeld during the Bush administration. "But he doesn't see the world only in black and white. He understands gray."

On some issues, particularly Iraq, Rumsfeld and the neocons did find common cause in the late 1990s. "They were friends and he associated with them and there was a certain overlap of views," said Peter Rodman, a onetime NSC official who accompanied Rumsfeld on his Middle East trips in the early 1980s and later served under him at the Pentagon as a senior policy official.

In early 1998, for instance, the Project for the New American Century drafted a letter to Clinton about Iraq that Rumsfeld signed along with seventeen others, most of them former U.S. national security officials. The letter, dated January 26, declared that the "current American policy toward Iraq is not succeeding." At that point, the Clinton administration was supporting a U.N. containment strategy for Iraq that rested on economic sanctions and weapons inspections. But Saddam Hussein appeared to be wearing down the resolve of the United Nations and the world at large, and critics of the containment strategy insisted it was unraveling.

The letter observed that containment of the Iraqi leader "has been steadily eroding over the past several months," and with it the ability to guard against Iraq's production of weapons of mass destruction. "Even if full inspections were eventually to resume, which now seems highly unlikely, experience has shown that it is difficult if not impossible to monitor Iraq's chemical and biological weapons production," the letter said. "The only acceptable strategy is one that eliminates the possibility that Iraq will be able to use or threaten to use weapons of mass destruction. In the near term, this means a willingness to undertake military action as diplomacy is clearly failing. In the long term, it means removing Saddam Hussein and his regime from power."

A number of signers of this letter were, like Rumsfeld, not neocons. Indeed, opposition to existing U.S. policy on Iraq crossed political lines. A few weeks after the January letter, Rumsfeld and many of the other signers joined a total of forty people—liberal Democrats as well as conservative Republicans—in another open letter to Clinton. Sponsored by a bipartisan group called the Committee for Peace and Security in the Gulf, this letter reiterated the call for "a determined program to change the regime in Baghdad."

———————

It was the issue of missile defense that ultimately gave Rumsfeld a fresh opening to make a significant political difference and again play a noteworthy role on the Washington stage. Republican lawmakers, after taking control of Congress in 1994, had been pushing to accelerate work on a national antimissile system. But they had a major problem: U.S. intelligence agencies saw little urgency in the kind of threat the system would be designed against—long-range missiles from rogue states such as North Korea and Iran—and said so in a 1995 National Intelligence Estimate.

The 1995 estimate concluded that no country outside the five major nuclear powers—the United States, Russia, China, Britain, and France— "will develop or otherwise acquire a ballistic missile in the next 15 years that could threaten the contiguous 48 states or Canada." It also asserted confidently that the United States could count on detecting any homegrown Third-World program aimed at building an intercontinental-range ballistic missile (ICBM). It predicted that at least five years would have to pass between the time a country started testing and the time it could actually deploy an ICBM, thus providing significant warning of the deployment.

Republicans were stupefied not only by the projection that the threat was as long as fifteen years away but also by the certainty with which the intelligence estimate was stated. They charged that the findings conflicted with the views of experts inside and outside the intelligence community. They accused the administration of distorting the intelligence process and soft-pedaling the threat to help justify its resistance to a national missile-defense system.

An outside commission was chartered by Congress to make an independent assessment of the ballistic missile threat. The initiative recalled the Team B study of Soviet military power in the 1970s. Then, too, a group of outside experts had looked at the available intelligence and ended up challenging the CIA's view of Soviet intentions as too benign. Rumsfeld, as secretary of defense at the time, had found support in Team B's conclusions for his own efforts to throttle Kissinger's détente policies.

A leading proponent of the new commission was Newt Gingrich, then speaker of the House. He enlisted Rumsfeld to head the group, seeing in him someone with the experience, drive, and flair to make the commission effective. It made a difference, too, that Rumsfeld had never retired entirely from the Washington scene but had sought to stay in the picture, especially on national security matters. "I liked Rumsfeld," Gingrich recalled in an interview. "He had the right characteristics. He had always kept his hand in on national security."

Getting down to work in January 1998, the nine-member commission consisted of three Democratic and six Republican choices, all with high-powered backgrounds. In addition to Rumsfeld, who was a former defense secretary and White House chief of staff, there was a former CIA director and two retired four-star generals. The remaining five all had Ph.D.'s and experience in handling state secrets in sensitive government jobs they had once held. Among the Republican picks was Paul Wolfowitz, then a university dean, and years earlier, an adviser to the Team B study.

Serving as staff director was Steve Cambone, a tall, lanky specialist in strategic studies, who, since earning a doctorate in political science in the early 1980s, had held various positions in government and in Washington think tanks. Cambone had been recommended for the job by a congressional staff member, and Rumsfeld was quickly impressed by Cambone's appetite for hard work, his efficiency, and his ability to get things done. Their association on the commission marked the beginning of a close working partnership that would carry over into Rumsfeld's return as defense secretary and have a significant impact on Pentagon policies and management.

Such blue-ribbon panels were notorious in Washington for leaving much of the work to staff members. But from the start, Rumsfeld made it clear that his commission would be different. He set a brisk pace, scheduling two or more all-day sessions a week through the winter and spring of 1998. He pressed relentlessly for information and placed much of the responsibility for drafting a final report on the panel members themselves.

It quickly became apparent from Rumsfeld's direction that what was on trial was not simply the CIA's assessment of the missile threat but the agency's whole apparatus for collecting and analyzing intelligence. Indeed, the commission's work ended up reinforcing the highly critical views of the CIA that Rumsfeld had acquired in his time as defense secretary under Ford and as Middle East envoy under Reagan. As he and the other commissioners dug for information on the missile threat, they soon concluded that the government's intelligence agencies were poorly staffed, inefficiently structured, and ill-equipped to assess the threat.

The commission brought Rumsfeld into contact with George Tenet, the CIA director. The two ended up serving together closely under President George W. Bush, but their initial dealings over the missile-threat study were strained. Rumsfeld and other panel members were dissatisfied with the access they were being given by the intelligence community. The first round of briefings had been superficial, providing little more than what was already available in the open press. The congressional statute establishing the commission had stipulated that the executive branch would allow access to whatever information the group required to do its job. That was not happening.

The commissioners confronted Tenet at a meeting in January 1998. The CIA chief promised to lift the veil. Later that afternoon, he summoned senior aides to his office and ordered changes in the intelligence community's approach to the commission. Panel members saw an immediate improvement.

Still, the deeper they delved into the evidence of missile-development programs in North Korea, Iran, Iraq, and other countries, the more troubled they grew about the adequacy of the U.S. government's own assessments. Among the most striking—and in the commission's view, handicapping—aspects of the intelligence process was the elaborate compartmentalization of information. Time and again, analysts briefing the commission on one topic would have to leave the room before other analysts could speak.

This led to some absurd situations. At the end of one two-hour briefing, for instance, a midlevel manager informed the commissioners, once the briefers themselves had left, that most of what the group had just heard was incorrect. He said that this was because the briefers did not have access to the information that was about to be provided to the commissioners. In another case, the commission summoned analysts monitoring North Korea, Iraq, and several other countries with the hope of doing a comparative analysis, only to find that the analysts lacked clearances to know what the others knew and so could not conduct a comparative look across countries.

Because the commissioners themselves were able to move between intelligence compartments, they came to know more than many of the analysts addressing them. They also found that those CIA analysts specifically assigned to monitor missile trade among countries tended to approach the matter more as a law enforcement problem than as a strategic one. These analysts focused on trying to determine who was supplying what to whom rather than on assessing the scope, pace, and direction of individual national missile-development programs, the motivations behind them, and their potential growth paths. Additionally, the commission identified substantial shortfalls in the education and experience of the analysts. Many analysts were trained in nonscientific and nontechnical disciplines and appeared to lack the technical, cultural, and language skills that would benefit their assignments.

But what most disturbed the panel were the methodologies employed. There was, it appeared, a seemingly pervasive reluctance to extrapolate beyond known, proven facts. A case in point came during a session about Iran. One of the commissioners, William Graham, who had been the White House science and technology director under Reagan and now headed a national security research firm, wanted to know what Iran might be doing with the Russian RD-214 engine, which Iran was reported to have acquired. The engine had powered a medium-range Soviet ballistic missile, the SS-4, and served as the first stage of the SL-7 space-launch vehicle.

"The answer I got back was, 'We haven't seen the Iranians do anything with it,'" Graham recalled. "And so I asked, 'What do you think their interest might be?' And they said, 'We haven't seen them do anything with it.' And I asked, 'Have you done any analysis about what they might do with it?' And they said, 'Until we see them do something with it, we're not going to consider it.'"

This exchange reinforced a view of the intelligence community as too narrow-minded. It was what Graham one day described to his fellow commissioners as a disturbing tendency by too many analysts to interpret the absence of evidence as evidence of absence. "It was part of the intelligence community's culture that before they would say something is being done, they wanted to have all kinds of evidence," Graham said months later. "If they didn't have such evidence, they would say there's no indication that it's happening, which is true. The trouble is, there's also no indication that it's not happening."

On a list he was compiling of memorable phrases that arose during the commission's work, Rumsfeld jotted down the words, "absence of evidence is not evidence of absence." The list, which ended up running several pages, eventually got incorporated as a section of Rumsfeld's Rules dubbed "Brilliant Pebbles," the name of a system of space-based interceptors proposed during the first Bush administration.

Also memorialized on the list, under the subheading "Thoughts from and on the Intelligence Community," was a phrase attempting to describe various categories of information as being either known or unknown, and then further subdividing them according to whether they had yet to be discovered or not. Plus a category of things that were thought to be known but ended up not being so at all. It went like this: "There are knowns, known unknowns and unknown unknowns. There may also be unknown knowns—that is to say, those things we think we know but we find out later we didn't know."

This wording would gain prominence later after Rumsfeld became defense secretary and drew on it in news conferences trying to explain the challenges of gathering intelligence on such secrets as Saddam Hussein's efforts to develop weapons of mass destruction. While the basic notion about things knowable and unknowable made sense, Rumsfeld had a tendency to stretch his distinctions into a lengthy riff that bordered on gibberish and was easy to mock.

To get at just how well the intelligence community had detected key events in North Korean and Iranian missile development, Rumsfeld's commission asked for timeline charts showing when certain events had occurred and when U.S. analysts became aware of them. The result was a series of large, multicolored charts, each stretching several feet across. The presentations, covering four or five incidents in all, amounted to a kind of audit of U.S. intelligence assessments. They showed a startling pattern of lagging estimates, the delays ranging from a few years to more than a decade.

The presentations reinforced for panel members the idea that U.S. officials would probably learn of some missile advances by rogue states only years after the fact. To drive home this point, Rumsfeld brought in a copy of Roberta Wohlstetter's book about Japan's attack on Pearl Harbor and passed out copies of the foreword by the economist Thomas C. Schelling, one of the major contributors to Cold War deterrence theory. The foreword says in part:

> It is not true that we were caught napping at the time of Pearl Harbor. Rarely has a government been more expectant. We just expected wrong. And it was not our warning that was most at fault, but our strategic analysis. . . . There is a tendency in our planning to confuse the unfamiliar with the improbable. The contingency we have not considered seriously looks strange; what looks strange is thought improbable; what is improbable need not be considered seriously. . . . The danger is not that we shall read the signals and indicators with too little skill; the danger is in a poverty of expectations—a routine obsession with a few dangers that may be familiar rather than likely. Alliance diplomacy, inter-service bargaining, appropriations hearings, and public discussion all seem to need to focus on a few vivid and oversimplified dangers. The planner should think in subtler and more variegated terms and allow for a wider range of contingencies.

Rumsfeld thought so highly of this cautionary passage that he continued for years, through his time as defense secretary under Bush, to distribute it to others. Even so, he and the rest of the Bush administration ended up falling victim to the same "poverty of expectations" that

Schelling had warned about, neglecting to give sufficient consideration to the possibility, however improbable, that there really were no stockpiles of weapons of mass destruction in Iraq or that an insurgency would take root after the U.S. invasion. This shortcoming was especially surprising on Rumsfeld's part, given his particular sensitivity to the risks of inadequate anticipation.

In the case of missile defense, a central focus of the commission's assessment was what could be done using Soviet Scud missile technology. North Korea had built a family of Scud and Nodong missiles based on Scud technology. The question for the commission was whether North Korea could expand further on the Nodong and develop the advanced propulsion, guidance, and multistage separation system necessary for long-range flight.

U.S. intelligence analysts tended to doubt that the relatively primitive missile technology embodied in the single-stage, four-decade-old Soviet Scud—slender steel cylinder, fixed fins, liquid fuel—could serve as much of a stepping-stone to a missile capable of reaching the U.S. mainland from North Korea. But North Korea had already proven itself quite resourceful, and there was evidence that the country had a multistage missile, the Taepodong, under development. Besides, enough once-sensitive technical information about how to build a missile had become available on the open market to teach the North Koreans whatever they did not know. And unlike the government's analysts, aerospace engineers in private industry thought that Scuds could serve as building blocks for long-range missile development.

At a briefing on May 7, 1998, Lockheed Martin engineers who had studied the matter and whose company had a long-standing interest in missile defense made this point. During the presentation, Rumsfeld scribbled a sentence on a piece of paper. He often wrote out propositions for the rest of the commission to discuss along the way, laying the foundation for the final report.

"Let me read something to you and see if this is what you're saying," he said to Lockheed's briefers. "Using Scud technology, a country could test-fly a long-range missile within about five years. Is that what you're saying?" The Lockheed experts concurred, and after some revising by Rumsfeld and other commissioners, the group ended with a sentence that became one of the commission's central conclusions: "With the external help now readily available, a nation with a well-developed, Scud-based ballistic missile infrastructure would be able to achieve first flight of a long-range missile, up to and including intercontinental ballistic missile range, within about five years of deciding to do so."

The statement conveyed the urgency of the threat. It also flew in the face of the intelligence community's earlier assertion that the United States was unlikely to face a new long-range missile threat in the next fifteen years.

———•———

In July 1998, the panel, known formally as the Commission to Assess the Ballistic Missile Threat to the United States, released its findings and recommendations to Congress. Challenging official U.S. intelligence estimates, the commission said that North Korea and Iran could—with little or no warning—develop weapons capable of striking U.S. territory within five years. "The threat to the United States posed by these emerging capabilities is broader, more mature and evolving more rapidly than has been reported in estimates and reports by the Intelligence Community," the commissioners concluded.

The report went on to highlight what it called the eroding ability of intelligence agencies to assess U.S. vulnerability to ballistic missiles. It cited shortcomings in the way analysts assessed information as well as a shortage of satellites and spies to track missile proliferation. And it said that various tactics—launching missiles from ships, for instance, or basing them in other countries—could further reduce warning times for U.S. officials.

At a news conference on Capitol Hill, Rumsfeld attributed his group's contrasting assessment of the threat to the fact that the commissioners had gained broader access to highly classified information than was available to most analysts in the compartmentalized intelligence world. He also said that the commission had taken "a somewhat different approach" from that of the intelligence community, weighing information "as senior decisionmakers would." By that he meant they had connected facts more freely, drawn inferences, and applied a more sweeping view.

In particular, the commissioners had placed greater weight on the likelihood that rogue states would receive outside technical assistance from other countries, notably, Russia and China. They had also taken the view that rogue states should not be expected to follow the same missile-development patterns evident in earlier U.S. and Soviet programs. Instead of running new missile models through extensive testing in order to ensure accuracy and safety, rogue states were prepared to test once or twice and then deploy.

The final drafting of the report had involved days and days of debate among commissioners as they struggled to accommodate potential objections from any one member. In the end, the findings of the bipartisan commission were issued without a single dissenting footnote. As chairman, Rumsfeld had been determined that the commission's final report be unanimous. Washington experience had taught him that the greater the consensus, the greater the commission's impact would be and the more its findings could rise above the partisan bickering that had marked discussions of the government's own threat assessments.

He had succeeded in winning the endorsement of the three Democratic appointees on the commission—including a leading opponent of missile defense, Richard Garwin—by staying focused on the issue of a missile threat and avoiding the question of whether the United States should respond by erecting a national missile-defense system. Significantly, too, the report's consensus had come at some cost in specificity. Its conclusions dealt essentially with what could happen, not with what was most likely to happen. The commissioners shied away from placing probabilities on their threat scenarios. If they had gone down that road, chances are their judgments would indeed have diverged, and unanimity would have been lost.

Nevertheless, the commission's report was seized upon by congressional Republicans as further justification for building an antimissile weapon. House speaker Newt Gingrich hailed the panel's study as "the most important warning about our national security since the end of the Cold War." And as if on cue, North Korea a month later, on August 31, launched a three-stage Taepodong missile over Japan in an effort to put a satellite into orbit. The effort failed—the missile disintegrated in flight—but the realization that North Korea had managed to fly the missile as far as it did on its first try shocked U.S. specialists. North Korea had essentially leapfrogged several developmental levels. The launch reinforced North Korea's reputation as a resourceful, daring builder of missiles—and drove home the warnings of Rumsfeld's commission.

———•———

In October 1998, three months after the commission delivered its report amid much fanfare, it quietly sent a "side letter" to Congress and to Tenet, laying out more specific concerns about how the intelligence agencies were going about the business of making assessments. The letter presented a searing portrait, describing an intelligence community buffeted by budget cuts, spy scandals, and excessive turnover. It also cited a decline in scientific and engineering competence, a highly charged political atmosphere, and overcompartmentalization of functions and information.

The letter reported that the amount of intelligence resources devoted specifically to monitoring ballistic missile development, and generally to weapons of mass destruction, had "declined significantly" in the previous five years despite the prominence of the proliferation issue. Exacerbating matters, the letter said, was the emphasis on intelligence to support real-time military, diplomatic, and counterdrug operations. This left less time and fewer resources for longer-term strategic issues such as missile proliferation. "Treating the threat as one of a hundred or more high-priority issues, all of which are placed on a back burner with each crisis and contingency that comes along, will not improve the capability of the IC [intelligence community] to provide actionable warning," the letter said.

The letter also criticized the intelligence community for focusing on proliferation more as a law enforcement issue than as a strategic puzzle. It urged that analysts be given broader access to information "wherever it may be held" in the intelligence community. And it called on analysts to consider not only what they knew but what they did not know in venturing beyond the hard evidence in their assessments. For many of the commissioners, this critique of the intelligence community carried greater lasting significance than the commission's final position on the missile threat. While the threat assessments remained open to argument, the deterioration of U.S. intelligence was irrefutable.

On the outside, the intelligence community chose to swallow its pride and assume a public stance of general deference toward the Rumsfeld commission's findings. In a letter to Congress, Tenet attempted some defense of the government's earlier threat estimates, saying that they had been "supported by available evidence" and "well tested" in debate. But for the most part, the CIA director decided not to dispute the Rumsfeld report in public.

In private, it was a different story. Intelligence officials were deeply offended by the report. They expressed indignation at the commission's general assertion that analysts were too narrow in their approaches and were missing the basic picture. "I take issue with the accusation that we take absence of evidence as evidence of absence," one senior intelligence officer said later. "The commissioners must recognize that when you're briefing a panel like theirs, you're going to stick to your evidence and talk about what you know. When we write reports, we do go out on speculation branches and sort these issues out."

Some government analysts also belittled the commission's report as simplistic, an indulgence in all the "what coulds." They said the report lacked any sophisticated attempt to assign probabilities to the various possible foreign missile threats. Almost anything *could* happen. For an assessment to be of value to policy makers, however, it should make some judgment about what was *likely* to happen, they said.

Most preposterous in this regard, one senior analyst said, was the commission's assertion that a country with a "well-developed, Scud-based ballistic missile infrastructure" could, if it set its mind to it, get to the point of flight-testing a long-range missile within five years. "Take Congo or Fiji, just grab a country," said the analyst. "Even if they had Scud technology, they lack the economic and scientific support for a missile program. So the first point is, you really need to go country by country; you just can't make blanket statements but must consider technology base, financing, and so on."

Years later, John E. McLaughlin, who served as Tenet's deputy, reflected that Rumsfeld and his commissioners had in effect created a new sort of ethic in the intelligence business. By faulting analysts for being too tied to the evidence—too tied to what they could confidently describe as facts—they had opened the door to the kind of leap of analysis that led the intelligence community to conclude, prior to the U.S. invasion of Iraq in 2003, that Saddam Hussein must have weapons of mass destruction.

"I'm not making any excuses for Iraq WMD [weapons of mass destruction]," McLaughlin said in an interview. "But by the time we were writing estimates on Iraq, the prevailing thinking—the way we thought about issues—was the absence of evidence is not evidence of absence. No one said it that way, but people leaned toward caution in ruling things out because we didn't have hard evidence."

While the commission was doing its work, McLaughlin said, analysts returned from having testified before it with complaints of merciless and unfair grillings. One of McLaughlin's great regrets, he confessed, is that he did not intervene personally in that period to combat that kind of treatment, but he had trusted the system to produce "a reasonable outcome."

In the wake of the embarrassment of Iraq, the pendulum in intelligence community assessments has swung back toward a position of greater caution in concluding anything that cannot be established as ironclad. "So now everything is highly caveated, and we're back to where we were in 1995," McLaughlin remarked. As for the 1995 intelligence assessment on the ballistic missile threat, its predictions, so heavily criticized initially, have been largely borne out over time.

———•———

In 2000, Rumsfeld was picked to chair another national commission, this one on management of space operations. The assignment drew Rumsfeld back to an issue that had occupied him as a young congressman. And while the U.S.-Soviet competition that had so dominated the discussion in those earlier days had long since disappeared, Rumsfeld was still seized by concerns that the United States could lose its edge in space.

Rumsfeld had to drop off the commission at the end of 2000 after he was nominated to become defense secretary in the new administration, but much of the panel's work had been completed by then, and it included the conclusion that the United States must improve its ability to defend its satellites and other critical space systems in order to avoid a surprise attack with the potential to become a "space Pearl Harbor."

The report, released on Capitol Hill on the day that the Senate Armed Services Committee was holding hearings on Rumsfeld's nomination, warned of the threat to U.S. space operations from hostile nations and called for an increased emphasis on the military's role in space to deter possible attacks on satellites. It said the potential for attacks that could damage U.S. ability to maintain military communications and spy on its enemies was likely to increase.

To deal with such threats, the panel urged a reorganization of the way the government, and the military in particular, managed the security elements of America's space operations. That shouldn't necessarily mean placing offensive weapons in space, the commission said. Suggested were such measures as hardened satellites capable of withstanding antisatellite attacks.

The commission also stopped short of calling for a new branch of the armed forces devoted to the military uses of space. But to highlight the military importance of space, it recommended the reestablishment of a Presidential Space Advisory Group at the White House and the creation of a senior interagency group on space within the NSC structure. It also proposed naming a new Air Force undersecretary of space to oversee the National Reconnaissance Office, which builds and runs defense satellites.

Rumsfeld's leading roles on both the space and missile threat commissions placed him out front in the national debate over new strategic concerns to the United States and burnished his credentials as a prominent national security player. The timing couldn't have been more propitious for him. Talk of new forms of twenty-first-century warfare and the need to better prepare the U.S. military for that new warfare was becoming a central theme of George W. Bush's bid for the presidency. Rumsfeld had important expertise to contribute. Despite being well into his sixties by then, he had found ways of staying relevant and in demand. And he was about to embark on the biggest challenge of his life.

CHAPTER 7

Operating from the Outbox

As the 2000 presidential campaign was getting under way, Rumsfeld received a call from his friend Ned Jannotta, who had been approached about supporting the Republican governor of Texas, George W. Bush, and wanted to learn more about him.

"What about George W.?" Jannotta asked, inviting Rumsfeld's opinion.

"I don't know him," Rumsfeld replied.

Indeed, Rumsfeld had been far from close to the Bush family. He and George W.'s dad had been keen GOP rivals in the 1970s, jockeying for political position. Both in prominent posts under Ford, they each had held a critical view of the other. Bush considered Rumsfeld arrogant and manipulative; Rumsfeld viewed Bush as dilettantish and weak in assessing the Soviet threat. Rumsfeld's brief bid for the presidency in 1986 and 1987 was prompted in part by his perception of Bush as a lightweight front-runner.

But the passage of time had dissipated much of the tension. Rumsfeld had come to regard the senior Bush as having been an able president, particularly in his management of the 1991 Persian Gulf War. And while the senior Bush was still wary of Rumsfeld, the bitterness with which they had regarded one another in earlier years was no longer apparent to such close associates of Bush's as Brent Scowcroft.

In May 1999, Rumsfeld traveled to the Texas governor's mansion in Austin to brief the younger Bush on the global ballistic missile threat, drawing on the work of the commission that Rumsfeld had led the previous year. To flesh out ways of accelerating Pentagon design and testing for a national missile-defense system, Rumsfeld organized a small study group and served as an occasional campaign consultant. He never became a part of Bush's principal team of national security advisers, which was led by Condoleezza Rice. But he readily joined the bench of former high-level officials from previous Republican administrations who appeared with Bush in public to bolster the candidate's image. At the National Press Club in May 2000, when Bush outlined the main planks of his defense policy—including deployment of an antimissile system and a reduction in nuclear weapons—he was flanked by Rumsfeld as well as by Scowcroft, Colin Powell, Henry Kissinger, and George Shultz.

Some of the younger group counseling Bush regarded Rumsfeld as a faded political star from a distant era. John Hillen, who subsequently served in the Bush administration as an assistant secretary of state for political-military affairs, recalled Rumsfeld then as "just a nice old guy— a missile-defense and space expert, a tireless campaign representative who would get up and do an early-morning interview when no one else would, but someone who was basically out of the loop."

Behind the scenes, though, the prospect of a top administration job for Rumsfeld was already under consideration. Overseeing the search for a vice presidential candidate, Dick Cheney included Rumsfeld on a list of possible choices. In a number of ways, Rumsfeld satisfied the criteria that Cheney had set forward for choosing a running mate for Bush—someone with congressional and White House experience, a background in elective office, a record managing a large federal executive department, and successful performance in the business world. Rumsfeld could bring widespread experience and veteran standing to offset Bush's relative youth and lack of exposure to international affairs.

Cheney, who met the same criteria, ended up filling the vice presidential slot himself. But Rumsfeld's name remained in circulation for an administration job after the election. Speculation centered on the possibility that he would become director of the CIA, where he could tackle the intelligence shortcomings highlighted in his missile-threat commission's report. A different opportunity opened, though, when the search for a defense secretary ran into a hitch.

Bush had nearly decided to give the Pentagon job to Dan Coats, a former senator from Indiana who had served on the Armed Services Committee before leaving Congress in 1998 and who had strong credentials among Republican conservatives. But an interview with Bush and Cheney went poorly for Coats, who was deemed not forceful enough to stand up to the generals and not enthusiastic enough about missile defense. With Colin Powell already slated to become secretary of state, there was also concern about whether Coats had the stature to match the charisma and authority of the former Joint Chiefs chairman. Since Rice, a much younger and less commanding figure, would be serving as national security adviser, it seemed all the more important to place a formidable counterweight to Powell at the Pentagon.

Rumsfeld emerged as a favored choice. His aggressive personality, bureaucratic savvy, and experience as a former defense secretary promised to make him a challenging match for the secretary of state. George Shultz lobbied for him, emphasizing Rumsfeld's record managing large organizations, his familiarity with Congress, and his toughness. Even Scowcroft, who knew firsthand how adversarial Rumsfeld could be, mustered a favorable comment. "He's capable and smart," Scowcroft told Cheney, who had called seeking opinions about several candidates for the job. But Scowcroft also cautioned that Rumsfeld could be a problem, noting, "He's a difficult person to work with."

Cheney, excited about the idea of bringing his longtime friend back with him into government and reviving their old partnership, enthusiastically recommended Rumsfeld for the job. More than a dozen years had passed since Cheney had declined to support Rumsfeld's bid for the presidency. A deep chill in relations between the two men had followed. Rumsfeld had watched in 1989 as Cheney, free of Rumsfeld's shadow and an increasingly prominent politician in his own right, had suddenly been plucked by George H. W. Bush to be defense secretary after the Senate rejected the nomination of John Tower amid allegations of personal misconduct. But the Cheney/Rumsfeld relationship had begun to thaw in the 1990s, and by 1999, when the Cheneys sent the Rumsfelds an invitation to their thirty-fifth wedding anniversary in Wyoming, Don and Joyce were happy to attend.

The younger Bush had not had much contact with Rumsfeld during the 2000 campaign and wanted to satisfy himself that their chemistry would be right. During a meeting in Austin, the two men talked about what the job would require and some of the important issues the next secretary would confront, particularly the need to transform the U.S. military for twenty-first-century challenges.

Bush had run for president on a platform promising a Pentagon overhaul that would involve shedding weapons conceived during the Cold War and fashioning a more agile, more quickly deployable U.S. military. Apart from his role championing the idea of missile defense, Rumsfeld hadn't said or written much on the subject of remaking the armed forces. But he was eager to take on the challenge and could point to his own lengthy record as an agent of change, from his shake-up of OEO to his makeovers of Searle and General Instrument.

Bush left the meeting impressed with Rumsfeld's zest, knowledge, and engaging personality. "They clicked and hit it off," said Cheney, who was present at the meeting.

Others were less enthusiastic about the return of Rumsfeld and told Bush so.

"All I'm going to say to you is, you know what he did to your daddy," James Baker, who had served as the senior Bush's White House chief of staff, told the younger Bush.

Andrew Card, who had been asked to serve as Bush's White House chief of staff, raised the matter as well. As a former deputy to Baker and transportation secretary under George H. W. Bush, Card knew the history with Rumsfeld and wondered whether the younger Bush would feel comfortable with someone known to be so headstrong and domineering, someone with a history of strained relations with Bush's own father. The president-elect made it clear to Card that he was not going to let whatever had happened between his father and Rumsfeld stand in the way of giving Rumsfeld a prominent position in the new administration.

Rumsfeld was at his house in Taos when Cheney phoned with the news he would be getting a second chance to run the Pentagon. "He's going to be a great secretary of defense, again," Bush told a news conference on December 28, announcing Rumsfeld's selection. It was the first time in history that someone who had been defense secretary before was called back to the post.

But the circumstances surrounding Rumsfeld's return were far different than in his previous tenure. He would be coming in at the start of a full presidential term, not the last year of an abbreviated one. The appointment had not occurred under the shadow of any unexpected cabinet shake-up or amid speculation that Rumsfeld had schemed for the position. And Rumsfeld would have the chance to put together his own management team.

At sixty-eight, Rumsfeld had once again been catapulted to the upper ranks of Washington's political scene. But he was at a very different position in his life than he had been the first time he held the top Pentagon post. No longer was he a young, up-and-coming Republican star, looked on as the future of the party. He now had much more past than future. Liberated from concerns about doing anything that might jeopardize a possible run for the presidency—or any other political office, for that matter—he could speak and act more freely. Having made a fortune in business and having earned a reputation as an effective, no-nonsense CEO, he was more confident than ever of his management skills and personal judgments.

In reaching into the ranks of corporate executives to find a defense secretary, Bush had ample precedent. More than a third of U.S. defense secretaries since the creation of the position in 1947 had come from the business world. It was tempting to assume that the skills required to run a large corporation would be applicable to managing the Pentagon.

But the record on CEOs-turned-defense-secretary was mixed, with Robert McNamara serving as the most cautionary example of the risks. McNamara's arrogant attitude and his efforts to apply systems analysis, using complex technical formulas to make key decisions about weapons and forces, had contributed to his unpopularity with military leaders, who viewed him as devaluing military advice. His coldly calculating management of the Vietnam War, with his emphasis on blunt force and enemy body counts, led to grave misjudgments about how to combat a well-entrenched, strongly backed insurgent force.

In general, though, the legacies of other defense secretaries who came to the job from nonbusiness backgrounds—including politics, law, and academia—suggested no particular pattern. A person's past career could not be used as a reliable predictor of success or failure in leading the Pentagon. As Stuart Rochester, deputy director of the Pentagon's historical office, noted in an interview, "Performance has tended to have more to do with personal characteristics of each secretary and the challenges that were presented."

With the appointment of Rumsfeld, Bush completed his national security team. The new president seemed mindful that he had created a group filled with sizable egos, although he viewed them as complementary, not clashing. "General Powell's a strong figure, and Dick Cheney's no shrinking violet, but neither is Don Rumsfeld, nor Condi Rice," he said. "I view the four as being able to complement one another."

Initially, Powell did not regard Rumsfeld as a potential problem for him. The two had met many years earlier when Rumsfeld, then defense secretary under Ford, visited Fort Campbell in Kentucky, where Powell was a brigade commander in the 101st Airborne Division. A photo of them together appears in Powell's autobiography. At that time, Powell had distributed copies of Rumsfeld's Rules to his battalion commanders. Since then, he had run into Rumsfeld only occasionally but still had great respect for him.

Bush declared that Rumsfeld's main task would be to carry forward a banner of military transformation and "challenge the status quo inside the Pentagon." Rumsfeld appeared eager to proceed boldly. "It is clearly not a time at the Pentagon for presiding or calibrating modestly," he said.

———•———

Before taking charge at the Pentagon, Rumsfeld met with his predecessor, Bill Cohen, on New Year's Day, 2001. The two men, both Washington veterans whose service extended back to the Nixon era, had not had much interaction with each other. It was a very private get-together, with each man accompanied by one aide, all seated around a rectangular table in Cohen's office.

Cohen had only just begun to outline the issues he planned to discuss when Rumsfeld reminded everyone that this was not his first time as secretary of defense. He'd done this job before, he said, and while he was interested in what Cohen had to impart, he also did not want to spend much time hearing things he already knew.

What was uppermost on Rumsfeld's mind—the item he mentioned first on his own list of discussion points—was how best to control the

Pentagon's generals and admirals. The Bush team had made it clear during the presidential campaign that they thought the military had grown too assertive and had gained too much of a say in running the Pentagon during the Clinton years. Rumsfeld intended to reassert civilian control of the armed forces.

Cohen did not buy the premise that the military was dominating the Pentagon, and he was somewhat surprised that Rumsfeld had opened with this issue. Cohen had expected Rumsfeld's first question might be about North Korea or Iraq, not about the Pentagon top brass. While the notion of an overly assertive military may have been useful as a campaign issue, Cohen told Rumsfeld, the reality was different.

He stressed the importance of trying to get along with the military rather than trying to dominate them. The challenges confronted by any secretary were hard enough, he emphasized, so the more help, the better. In his view, a defense secretary's ability to make something happen depended on his ability to build consensus with other key players—the military, the Congress, and other governmental agencies.

But Cohen didn't belabor the point with Rumsfeld. His intention was to be helpful to his successor, not to get into a protracted debate with him. Rumsfeld, too, had other issues he wanted to cover.

------·------

Army general Hugh Shelton, the chairman of the Joint Chiefs of Staff, was also concerned about Rumsfeld's attitude toward the military. Shelton had already had some dealings with Rumsfeld that had given him pause. In August 1998, he had written Congress expressing confidence that U.S. intelligence agencies would provide adequate warning of long-range missile deployment by a rogue state such as North Korea or Iran. The statement, which Shelton had drafted after consulting with CIA director George Tenet, contradicted a key finding of Rumsfeld's missile-threat commission. Rumsfeld hadn't appreciated the general's remarks and told him so afterward. Shelton, interviewed by the commission, had found Rumsfeld and some of the other panel members smug, arrogant, and disdainful of the military's view.

Eager to clear the air and get off to a good start with the new secretary, Shelton used the occasion of their first meeting on January 27,

2001, the day after Rumsfeld's swearing-in, to affirm his willingness to be a team player. "Mr. Secretary, I'd like for you to consider me to be one of the first members to join your team and not a holdover from the last team that was in office," Shelton offered.

"Well, how do you define your duties?" Rumsfeld shot back, responding so quickly as to seem rehearsed.

"I define my duties right out of Title 10 of the U.S. Code, and it says I am the principal military adviser to you, the president, and the National Security Council," Shelton replied.

"Oh, no, you're not the principal adviser to the NSC," Rumsfeld said.

"Mr. Secretary, unless Title 10 has been changed in the last twenty-four hours, I am," Shelton noted.

Rumsfeld, evidently realizing Shelton was correct, shifted the focus. "But not the NSC staff," the secretary said.

"I don't deal with the staff; I deal with the principals only, and I am the principal military adviser to the members of the NSC," Shelton reaffirmed.

Rather than belabor the point, Rumsfeld tossed out a compliment. He told Shelton that the chairman's staff—known as the Joint Staff—had the reputation of being the best in Washington.

"I've certainly got a great staff," Shelton agreed. "They've all got advanced degrees." Rumsfeld looked quizzical. "Some of them from northeastern universities, and almost all of them in warfighting. They're good; they're really good." Trying once again to express a cooperative spirit, Shelton added, "But they're your staff, too. Although I'll direct them, you're the guy they're really working for because we all work for you."

The two men bantered back and forth for a bit before the subject turned to a sweeping assessment of military strategy and programs that Congress had mandated be conducted every four years. The assessment, known as the Quadrennial Defense Review, was intended to examine essentially how big the military should be, what sort of weaponry to buy, and the rough size of the defense budget. The next review was due by the fall. The Joint Staff and military services had prepared volumes of briefing charts and position papers for Rumsfeld and the new administration in hopes of winning fresh backing for favorite projects. Shelton assured the secretary that the Joint Staff was standing by to provide all the help necessary to produce a report in the limited time remaining.

But Rumsfeld made it clear that he had no intention of being pushed into decisions too quickly and did not want the review to become a rubber-stamp process. "We really want to put some thought into this and think outside the box," Rumsfeld said.

"We've tried to do a lot of thinking out of the box, and whatever you want, you've got," Shelton sought to assure him.

Rumsfeld remained noncommittal, and Shelton left the meeting with a sense that the new secretary did not regard the uniformed military as being on the same team with him. "There did not seem to be any trust and confidence that I could detect in that first meeting, which was very worrisome, because I've always been a big team player," Shelton recalled in a later interview. "I've always believed that you can accomplish a helluva lot more when you've got everyone pulling together than you can by yourself. It's called synergy."

Days earlier, Shelton had received a letter from a retired officer who had served as a senior aide to General George Brown, the Joint Chiefs chairman during Rumsfeld's previous stint as defense secretary. Highly disparaging of Rumsfeld's earlier performance, the letter warned that Rumsfeld could not be trusted. Shelton thought it was strange that someone who had served so long ago under Rumsfeld would have taken the time to write such a letter.

———•———

The arrival of the Bush team initially buoyed hopes in U.S. military ranks that a time of bigger defense budgets and fresh attention to festering problems was at hand. Worries about tighter civilian control were more than offset by the prospect of more money and greater sensitivity to military concerns. During the campaign, Bush had accused the Clinton administration of shortchanging the military and sending U.S. forces on too many peacekeeping missions. At 2.8 percent of the gross domestic product, U.S. spending on defense was at a historical low. Cheney's promise that "help is on the way," made in September 2000 during an appearance at Valley Forge Military Academy in Pennsylvania, had become a campaign catchphrase.

But the kind of help the new administration had in mind extended well beyond simply patching up an underfunded and overused military.

Bush had called for a bold restructuring and modernization of the armed forces, away from the "industrial age operations" of the Cold War and toward the "information age battles" of the twenty-first century. His vision, laid out originally in a speech at The Citadel in South Carolina in September 1999, had outlined a need for less cumbersome and more easily deployable ground forces, stealthy ships loaded with longer-range missiles, and new aircraft capable of striking with pinpoint accuracy from great distances. Bush had pledged "to move beyond marginal improvements" and "skip a generation of technology," leaping ahead to a thorough "transformation of our military."

Such transformational thinking had been inspired by the work of a community of defense experts who argued that the demise of the Soviet Union and the absence of a military peer afforded the Pentagon an opportunity to carry out major change without worrying for the moment about facing down another superpower. It was an enticing notion that offered the promise of continued U.S. military dominance. But it wasn't without risk, and it was far easier said than done.

While the Citadel speech became a mission statement for Rumsfeld, it had provided few specifics for implementation. Even the ultimate goal was vague. One provision of the speech, for instance, had stipulated that 20 percent of the Pentagon's procurement budget would be assigned to advanced-technology programs not by the services, which traditionally did the allocating, but by the defense secretary. The 20 percent figure had been conceived somewhat arbitrarily by John Hillen, one of the speechwriters. "While Rumsfeld knew what the president had said in the Citadel speech, there was not a specific agenda on what transformation really meant beyond that," said Andy Hoehn, who became one of Rumsfeld's senior Pentagon strategists.

Among the first orders Bush signed as president was National Security Presidential Directive 3, which made the military-reform mission official. "The secretary of defense is hereby given a broad mandate to challenge the status quo and establish new and innovative practices and processes for acquiring U.S. defense capabilities for decades to come," the classified directive stated. The order was Rumsfeld's license to shake up the Pentagon. To what end, though, remained unclear.

As Rumsfeld knew, small gestures go a long way in a big bureaucracy, which is why early on he held a very public lunch with Andrew Marshall, the Pentagon's chief iconoclast. A veteran champion of military innovation who had been heading the Defense Department's internal think tank since before Rumsfeld was secretary the first time, Marshall, then seventy-nine, was looked on warily by the military services. Over the years, he had often questioned the continued significance of some of the military's most valued Cold War systems—among them, Army tanks, Navy aircraft carriers, and Air Force short-range fighter planes.

But Marshall had gotten along well with Rumsfeld during the Ford administration, regarding the young secretary as a quick learner and a strategic thinker. Eager to work with him again, he made a point of greeting Rumsfeld in the reception line following the secretary's welcoming ceremony and requesting an appointment. When an invitation to lunch arrived shortly afterward, Marshall had expected a private session in the secretary's office. Instead, they dined in the Gold Room, a more public setting, which Marshall interpreted as an attempt by Rumsfeld to advertise the meeting. During the meal, Rumsfeld asked Marshall to write a strategy piece within a month. "He didn't give me any particular guidance—just write a strategy piece," Marshall recounted.

———•———

The Marshall lunch disquieted many in the Pentagon who were searching for clues to the new secretary's thinking. Rumsfeld further unnerved the military services by setting up a series of review panels staffed with outsiders—mainly retired officers, industry executives, and think-tank experts. The panels, which grew in number to more than twenty, were given broad charters to challenge the conventional wisdom and come forward with bold new ideas. They covered a wide range of topics—strategy and force planning, military structure, capabilities and systems, personnel and readiness, information and intelligence, infrastructure and space.

"Rumsfeld was sort of casting around, trying to grab some ideas," said Paul Gebhard, who had been an assistant chief of staff to former defense secretary Bill Cohen and who stayed on for several months to assist Rumsfeld. "He was just trying to get something going."

But the panels troubled the military service leaders, who felt shut out of the process and worried that they would have little say in choices about their future. Lacking representation in many of the groups, service officials had difficulty even tracking the deliberations. "There was no cohesion to the thing, and it was really unsettling," recalled retired general James Jones, who at the time was commandant of the Marine Corps. "You just didn't know what was really going on or why it was going on."

Rumsfeld was not entirely without cause in turning to the panels. The services had not shown themselves particularly inclined to critical self-examination or willing to part with costly plans for new weapons systems conceived in an earlier era to fight the now-defunct Soviet Union. The Air Force, already dominant in the skies against any existing adversary, insisted on proceeding with development of a new dogfight jet, the F-22. The Navy hoped to build a new aircraft carrier. And the Army had in the works an exceptionally weighty artillery system called Crusader and an armed, stealthy reconnaissance helicopter called Comanche, both of which seemed more suited to large land warfare than to the kind of smaller conflicts considered more likely in the years ahead.

Efforts to encourage more cooperation among the four military services, both in the new weapons they developed and in the way they fought on the battlefield, had been frustrated by a deep parochialism and a fierce protectiveness of existing budget shares. With a total budget of $291 billion, the United States was already spending more on defense than were the next eight biggest-spending nations combined. But the military chiefs had identified more than $50 billion in additional requirements.

So Rumsfeld had reason to seek outside assessments free of service-centric biases. But he added to the natural resentment this engendered in military ranks by declining to say much to the military chiefs while the studies were under way. Until he could get a better sense of where he intended to lead the department, he appeared reluctant even to meet with the service leaders. "He did not want to talk to the chiefs," Gebhard recalled. "We worked on him very hard, saying he had to do so. He would say, 'I don't have anything to tell them.' And our response was, 'Sir, this isn't about telling them, this is about hearing them.' He wanted a message, and he didn't have a message, so he didn't want to get boxed in by what they were going to tell him."

Such behavior simply reinforced a feeling among the military chiefs that Rumsfeld regarded them as anachronistic and antichange, interested in keeping the Defense Department organized more or less as it had been since its creation in 1947, with little more than perhaps some adjustments around the margin.

"Most of the senior military there thought it was a stick in the eye for them that he didn't trust them to give him their best advice or the best information," Shelton remarked. Retired admiral Vernon E. Clark, who was the chief of naval operations at the time, also remembers a very difficult start with the new secretary. "He came in with certain prejudices and biases about the services being out of control," Clark said in an interview.

———•———

Rumsfeld arrived with a coterie of former associates and longtime friends to assist while he assembled a permanent staff. The group included several who had served with Rumsfeld during his earlier stint as defense secretary: Martin Hoffmann, a Princeton classmate who had been Army secretary and owned a place near Rumsfeld's in Taos; Steve Herbits, a management expert who had worked as Rumsfeld's special assistant; Staser Holcomb, a retired three-star admiral and former military assistant to Rumsfeld; and Ray DuBois, a business consultant. Having less of a past with Rumsfeld, but soon to emerge as his most trusted aide, was Steve Cambone, who had been staff director on both the missile-threat and space commissions. Smart, serious, and unfailingly loyal, Cambone had a reputation as an effective administrator.

Rumsfeld's reliance on this kitchen cabinet at the outset was only natural given their histories of working together and the initial absence of a new team of Senate-confirmed officials in the department's senior positions. But it also signaled what would become a feature of his management approach: heavy dependence on a small, tight circle of associates. Another early bellwether of how the department would be run and of the tone that would be set came in the critical selection of a deputy secretary.

Traditionally, defense secretaries had chosen to run the Pentagon much like chief executive officers run large corporations, reserving major matters of policy for themselves and handing off responsibility for day-to-day operations to a deputy. The deputy secretary was usually someone with a defense-industry or management background, who focused on budget, acquisition, personnel, and management tasks rather than on national security policy.

Had Coats become defense secretary, the plan had been to support him with a strong deputy, most likely Richard Armitage, Bush's leading campaign adviser on defense issues and a principal author of Bush's Citadel speech on military transformation. A former naval officer and assistant secretary of defense under Reagan, Armitage had held a variety of troubleshooting positions at both the Pentagon and the State Department.

White House officials recommended that Rumsfeld consider picking Armitage as his deputy. But Rumsfeld was wary of Armitage's close friendship with Powell and had no interest in making him his number two, as he conveyed when Armitage interviewed for the job. Instead, he turned to the other candidate suggested by the White House: Paul Wolfowitz, who was another of Bush's senior campaign advisers and someone with whom Rumsfeld had worked comfortably before.

Wolfowitz was known not for his management ability but for his intellect and capacity for hard work. While he had headed sizable bureaucracies—as assistant secretary of state for East Asian and Pacific affairs, ambassador running the large U.S. embassy in Indonesia, undersecretary of defense for policy, and university dean—he preferred policy making to administering.

A job under Rumsfeld at the Defense Department wasn't Wolfowitz's first choice. Having served in both the diplomatic and military worlds, he saw himself better suited for the State Department than for the Pentagon and was hoping this time to get the job of deputy secretary of state under Powell. But the most Powell would offer him was ambassador to the United Nations. As he was being pressed by Powell and Cheney to accept the post, Wolfowitz interviewed with Rumsfeld for the deputy's job at the Pentagon. He let Rumsfeld know that he was under some pressure to make a decision about the U.N. offer. "Somewhat to my surprise," Wolfowitz recalled, "Rumsfeld then said right away he'd like me to be his deputy."

At the outset, Wolfowitz sought to avoid setting up a clear division of responsibilities in his working relationship with Rumsfeld. He had seen the division model operate up close when he had served in the Pentagon before and witnessed Cheney's deputy, Don Atwood, largely cut out of such major policy issues as the 1991 Persian Gulf War, the drafting of a new post–Cold War defense strategy, and U.S. relations with Russia and the newly independent countries of the former Soviet Union. As the Defense Department's top civilian policy official at the time, Wolfowitz had found himself in the uncomfortable position of informing Atwood about discussions that had excluded him. He did not want to end up feeling similarly marginalized as Rumsfeld's deputy.

Rumsfeld was agreeable to treating Wolfowitz more as an alter ego and policy maven than as his top operations officer, particularly since he intended to act as his own chief of operations. The arrangement played to Rumsfeld's experience as a manager and to his deep interest in organization. In fact, Rumsfeld's attention to organizational structure sometimes trumped his attention to policy, as Douglas Feith discovered when he came to interview for the job of undersecretary of policy. Expecting to be grilled about policy matters, Feith was caught off guard when Rumsfeld asked instead about how the policy branch should be reorganized.

"Normally, the deputy secretary is the manager, but here you had a reversal of roles," remarked Dov Zakheim, another senior Bush campaign adviser who joined Rumsfeld at the Pentagon, taking the job of comptroller. "Rumsfeld was prepared to accept that because he saw himself as the one who was going to take charge and change the way this huge Leviathan was operating."

Indeed, early on Rumsfeld seemed to want to use Wolfowitz more for specific tasks than for general management functions. At morning staff meetings, when Rumsfeld handed out tasking orders, Wolfowitz would get his share as well from the secretary. "Rumsfeld didn't treat Wolfowitz as a deputy," said an aide to the deputy secretary at the time. "He likes action officers, and that's how he treated Wolfowitz."

So long as Rumsfeld's main mission was military transformation, it made some sense for him to plan on playing a more active administrative role. But eventually, when the wars in Afghanistan and Iraq came to dominate, Rumsfeld could not devote the time he had intended, and Wolfowitz found himself struggling between the policy issues he loved and the additional administrative tasks that were falling on his shoulders.

Rumsfeld's choice of Wolfowitz also ended up lending an ideological cast to the Pentagon's policy positions due to his reputation as a leading neoconservative. Wolfowitz himself has tended to shun the neoconservative label, disputing the clear existence of a large common set of notions

that bind him with such other prominent neoconservatives as Richard
Perle, Bill Kristol, and Bob Kagan. But they shared a democratic idealism
and a belief in the use of American power to confront totalitarianism and
oppression, as well as a particular eagerness to see the removal of Iraqi
leader Saddam Hussein.

Never much of an ideologue himself, Rumsfeld had his differences
with Wolfowitz. He was, for instance, more of a cautious pragmatist in
how far he believed democracy would work in some countries, although,
as a general matter, he did believe strongly in supporting democratic governments. In some nuanced ways, too, he differed with Wolfowitz over
U.S. policy toward Israel. But Rumsfeld ended up populating the Pentagon's policy department with other neoconservatives who came with
Wolfowitz's backing, and his appointment of Perle to head the Defense
Policy Board further ensured that neoconservative views would have
strong sway in the department.

Wolfowitz's presence by Rumsfeld's side served in addition to
strengthen the bond between the department and the White House. The
deputy secretary had his own personal tie to Cheney, having worked under him at the Pentagon during the administration of Bush's father. At
that time, Wolfowitz had supervised several officials who, in the new
Bush administration, now held key White House positions—among
them, I. Lewis "Scooter" Libby, Cheney's chief of staff; Steve Hadley, the
deputy national security adviser; and Zalmay Khalilzad, the NSC official
responsible for policy on Iraq and Afghanistan.

While Powell had served with this group, he was of a different, more
pragmatic mind-set. This exacerbated the contrast in visions and style
between his department and Rumsfeld's. When Armitage, shunned by
Rumsfeld, ended up as deputy to his close friend Powell, even less room
was left to work out tensions between the principals. Armitage tended to
reinforce Powell just as Wolfowitz did Rumsfeld.

———————

The few political holdovers from the Clinton administration who had
stayed on to help with the transition were, like the military chiefs, struck
by the sharp change in tone at the top. Rumsfeld had blown into the Pen-

tagon with great intensity and frenetic activity. He seemed intent on asserting his authority and questioning everything that had gone on before.
"There was a lot of resistance to just accepting that things were a certain
way," said Robert Soule, a twenty-year career civil servant who was the
Pentagon's chief program analyst at the time. "Rumsfeld thought he
could change everything, and he didn't have to start with any assumptions that other people might have had."

Subordinates quickly learned that one of the worst ways to justify the
continued existence of something was to argue that it had always been
thus. Rumsfeld hated being advised that circumstances required him to do
anything before he had taken the time to study a situation. He bristled, for
instance, when told he had to file an emergency request to Congress for a
supplemental appropriation to cover expanded health benefits for military veterans. The Clinton administration had approved the added benefits before leaving office, leaving the Bush administration to pay the bill.

Rumsfeld wanted time to sort through concerns he had about the
move. He questioned whether buying more health care had been the
right thing to do. More generally, he was critical of the whole process
that the Pentagon had fallen into of sending Congress ad hoc requests
for additional funding throughout the year. In Rumsfeld's mind, this
kind of patchwork budgeting was just another sign that the department
had not been run properly.

"Reserve the right to get into anything, and exercise it," one of Rumsfeld's Rules declares. He was without hesitation thrusting himself into
everyone's business. Intent on interacting with the organization he was
leading, Rumsfeld didn't want decisions served up just for approval. He
wanted to influence what was being served up. To his personal secretary,
Delonnie Henry, Rumsfeld seemed to want to "grab hold of this building
and make a difference." Indefatigable and supercharged, he reminded
Henry of the Energizer bunny.

Employing his penchant for memo writing that dated back to the
Nixon years, he let loose a blizzard of notes that were widely dubbed
"snowflakes," falling throughout the Pentagon and not letting up for six
years. Informal and printed economically on plain white paper, the
memos varied in length and purpose. Some were essentially administrative; others addressed policy. A short and trivial one might complain about

some fix needed in his office; a longer and more substantive one might inquire about a response to Russia. A number were personal thoughts or notes for his historical files, but most were aimed at someone—and that person could be well down the bureaucratic chain.

In one sense, the snowflakes reflected Rumsfeld's voracious appetite for information. But in another, they were a management tool for cutting through layers of bureaucratic hierarchy and reaching the people who could answer questions directly. In this way the memos served to give lower-ranking officials a more direct window into the secretary's thinking than they might otherwise have had. But they could also be a major distraction, creating havoc in the building as recipients dropped whatever else they were doing to respond to the secretary's queries.

Rumsfeld dictated his snowflakes into a tape recorder, then left the tapes in his outbox. His administrative assistants would empty the box, type up the memos, then send them back to him to review and sign. He didn't like stuff piling up in his outbox—or his inbox, for that matter. "You'd put stuff in his inbox and come back a couple of minutes later and it was in his outbox," Henry remembered.

For Rumsfeld, the snowflakes were part of being on the offensive, on the attack. "I want to run this department from my outbox, not my inbox," he had told his kitchen cabinet at the end of their first planning session. It was a phrase he would use often. In his view, someone who spent all day working out of his inbox instead of fashioning an outbox was bound to be reactive, defensive, distracted.

Rumsfeld knew that not everything he requested would get done, but he figured it was better to ask for more. "He had a philosophy about this," Steve Herbits recalled. "If you push people on everything, some of the things will get done and get done right."

At times, though, Herbits felt Rumsfeld was pushing too hard and risked losing credibility by spewing out more memos than could be acted on. To make this point, Herbits over the course of several days delayed distributing a large batch of snowflakes, then confronted Rumsfeld with the stack. "I walked into his office with them and said, 'Who do you think is going to answer these? We haven't got a single person but Wolfowitz confirmed here. What are you doing?'"

"Well, I want to get everyone thinking about these things," Rumsfeld said.

"They can think about them, but they can't run the building," Herbits responded. "No one can get any work done."

But the snowflakes continued to fall. After dispatching one, Rumsfeld would file a copy in the folder of the aide receiving it. He kept many folders neatly arranged on the top of a huge, hand-carved desk in the center of his office—a desk with no chair because the secretary preferred to work at an adjacent stand-up desk. Some folders were colored, others not. Some were labeled with the names of key aides; some were organized by subject.

Often when a top aide came in to talk about something, Rumsfeld pulled out the aide's folder and asked about the status of a particular snowflake. At the end of every day, all the folders were removed by an assistant, who noted the precise location of each on the desk before storing them in a safe. The next day before Rumsfeld arrived, the folders would be set out on the desk exactly as they had been.

It was hardly an efficient system for ensuring follow-up to Rumsfeld's many memos. A computerized tracking system would be set up eventually. But for now, this more antiquated approach would have to do.

———•———

Intensely focused on the internal mission of repairing all he considered wrong with the Defense Department, Rumsfeld at first wanted to skip certain external duties. He waved off early meetings with foreign counterparts and tried holding off taking foreign trips. "He said, 'That's the secretary of state's job, let them handle that stuff,'" Gebhard recalled.

Initially, he resisted attending an annual security conference in Munich in February that affords senior officials and defense experts from Europe and the United States a chance to confer. U.S. defense secretaries typically participated in the conference, but Rumsfeld argued that he could not afford to loosen his grip on the Pentagon even for a weekend. His predecessor, Cohen, urged him to attend and to use the occasion to introduce U.S. allies to the new administration's defense plans. "You know, you have a plane, so you don't have to be gone that long," Cohen told him.

The former secretary considered it somewhat odd for Rumsfeld to insist on having to remain in the Pentagon in order to manage it. If Rumsfeld really was reluctant to leave for fear the generals were going to run everything, Cohen thought, then he was doomed to stay stuck there. Cohen believed that an important aspect of being defense secretary involved diplomacy—getting out and meeting with foreign counterparts, showing the flag in a personal way.

Eventually, Rumsfeld relented and went to Munich, where he delivered a speech on missile defense and expressed disbelief that European allies weren't more supportive of the initiative. Then he rushed back, less worried about relations with the allies than with waging his Pentagon battle.

The first significant military action by the new administration—air strikes on February 16 against about twenty military targets at five sites inside Iraq—came less than a month after Rumsfeld had taken office and occurred without word reaching him in advance. The strikes, part of the decade-old effort to enforce no-fly zones over Iraq, constituted the largest attack on the country's air-defense system in two years and was designed to disrupt moves to link some command-and-control sites with underground fiber-optic cable. The action reflected a new set of "response options" recently approved by Bush, which gave pilots greater leeway to target radar, antiaircraft, and command-and-control centers beyond the no-fly zones, including sites around Baghdad.

While the White House had been advised in advance of the strikes by the Pentagon's Joint Staff, Rumsfeld himself hadn't been informed. Moreover, part of the action ended up hitting closer to Baghdad than Washington officials had expected, setting off air-raid sirens in the Iraqi capital and generating reports that the city was under attack. The episode coincided with a trip by Bush to the private ranch of the newly elected Mexican president, Vicente Fox, threatening to upstage an important diplomatic meeting meant to showcase the administration's early start at improving hemispheric relations.

U.S. officials struggled to portray the strikes as a routine response to continued Iraqi defiance of the no-fly zones, but behind the scenes, Rumsfeld was livid at having been left out of the loop. He fumed at Shelton, declaring that the military was out of control and that the chain of command had been subverted. In fact, the glitch had occurred on Rumsfeld's own staff; an aide had simply neglected to inform him. The miscommunication was indicative of the disarray and confusion that existed at the time as Rumsfeld sought to put together a staff. But the secretary's reaction only deepened Shelton's sense that his new boss lacked trust and confidence in the military structure serving him.

In those early months of the administration, if U.S. troops were to do any shooting, it was most likely going to be in Iraq. But Rumsfeld wanted more done quickly to anticipate other potential attack scenarios elsewhere in the world. He believed the Pentagon had been far too constrained in anticipating situations when U.S. force might be used, limiting much of the planning to major regional wars. In his view, one of the Pentagon's primary responsibilities was to be ready to provide such options to the president when various threats arose. "His point was that it's our job not to constrain options but to create them for the president," Hoehn said.

Of particular concern to Rumsfeld was how the United States might strike Iran if Iranian authorities were linked to a deadly terrorist attack on U.S. forces in the Middle East or elsewhere. In a meeting with Shelton, he had asked the chairman to report on existing options and was displeased with the response. "Shelton came back and gave a very cursory overview of the existing plan for Iran, which dated back to the early 1990s—500,000 troops going over the mountains into Iran and literally occupying the country," recalled Chris Williams, who was serving as a special assistant to Rumsfeld. "Rumsfeld said, 'You've got to be kidding. This is it? What else do we have?' Shelton essentially said, 'Nothing; that's it.'"

Rumsfeld gave Shelton a few more days to come up with what he called "more-nuanced options." But the result wasn't any more satisfying for the Pentagon leader. Seated at a table in the secretary's office with Rumsfeld and Shelton, Vice Admiral Scott Fry, the director of the Joint Staff, presented only a short list of alternatives. He said military planners had been unable to come up with anything more extensive and sounded somewhat exasperated at the secretary's desire to press the matter, according to Williams, who also was present.

"Well, that's interesting, admiral," Rumsfeld said, his temper rising. "You're telling me you're either not willing or not able to provide options to me and the president." The secretary turned to Shelton, saying, "Hugh, this is just totally unacceptable."

By April, Rumsfeld's frustration with the Joint Staff—and his pique with Fry in particular—had come to a head. Expecting an urgent cable from the head of Pacific Command, he erupted when he learned it had been held in Fry's office because it was addressed to Shelton, not to Rumsfeld. In Rumsfeld's view, Fry appeared to be too slow in responding to snowflakes and largely uncommunicative at staff meetings, where the admiral tended to rely on Shelton to report significant Joint Staff items.

Tipped off by a Rumsfeld aide that Fry was about to be fired, Shelton charged into Rumsfeld's office and confronted the secretary, threatening to quit if Fry was let go. "Because Fry works for me, if you're not happy with Fry's work, you're not happy with mine," Shelton told him. "So you can get two for the price of one." By Shelton's account, Rumsfeld immediately backed off, professing never to have intended to dump Fry. Shelton, for his part, left Rumsfeld's office even more wary about the defense secretary.

———•———

The administration's first full-fledged foreign policy crisis had flared earlier that month and had involved a military aircraft. A Chinese F-8 fighter jet and a U.S. Navy EP-3E reconnaissance aircraft had collided April 1 off the Chinese coast, sending the smaller Chinese plane and its pilot crashing into the South China Sea. When the damaged American plane landed on the Chinese island of Hainan, its twenty-four-member crew was taken hostage.

The State Department, not the Pentagon, took the lead in negotiating a solution, and with the help of Saudi Arabia, which had ties with China through oil and arms deals, an agreement was reached after a week and a half. The United States expressed regret for entering Chinese airspace for the emergency landing, but not for conducting what U.S. officials considered a legitimate intelligence-gathering mission. The Chinese, in turn, released the U.S. crew. At that point, the Pentagon stepped forward to handle the recovery of the EP-3E from the Chinese. Months later, after Beijing rejected the Pentagon's insistence that Americans be allowed to repair the plane and fly it home, U.S. technicians dismantled it and sent it to the United States in boxes.

Military-to-military contacts with the Chinese had been suspended in the midst of the tense diplomatic standoff, and the Pentagon's position was that future approval for such contacts would be granted on a case-by-case basis. Rumsfeld took a personal hand in the reviews. He appeared intent on pulling U.S. military personnel out of any training or education programs around the world in which the Chinese also participated.

A year before becoming secretary, Rumsfeld had visited China as part of a delegation organized by the American Foreign Policy Council. A tour of an exhibition hall in Beijing containing a commemoration of fifty years of Communist Party rule left a particularly strong impression on him. One display of a model of an island being invaded by Chinese troops caught his attention. "It was obviously meant to represent an invasion of Taiwan," recalled Dov Zakheim, who was also on the tour. "And I remember Rumsfeld just staring at it and staring at it. You could see he was processing this."

Rumsfeld took a pragmatic view of China, Zakheim explained. "He saw the Chinese as potentially a problem for us, but not inevitably one. They were folks who you couldn't give ground to because they'd fill any vacuum, but they were people with whom you could establish a relationship. He had no illusions about them. He was not—to use that horrible phrase—a panda hugger. But he was somebody who felt that as long as we both understand each other, we can deal with each other."

Now, in the wake of the spy-plane incident, Rumsfeld wanted to demonstrate that there would be a price if China played games with U.S. personnel and military equipment. He received a computer printout from Shelton of all the programs under way in which both U.S. and Chinese military personnel participated. Then, in what became a daily ritual, Rumsfeld met with the Joint Chiefs chairman each morning to review the next two weeks' worth of planned courses and decide whether to let this sergeant or that captain attend if the Chinese attended.

"It was laborious," Shelton recalled. "I thought to myself at the time, if we're going to try to run the Pentagon by micromanaging to that level of detail, there won't be enough hours in a day." The review meetings went on for several weeks, with Rumsfeld determined to make his point.

The EP-3E episode also prompted Rumsfeld to order a thorough reassessment of such U.S. intelligence-gathering missions—their risks, gains, and operating procedures. And it drove the new secretary to take the first steps toward a restructuring of the military intelligence apparatus.

One of Rumsfeld's main frustrations throughout the EP-3E drama had been a dearth of intelligence available to top U.S. officials about what their Chinese counterparts were up to. Was the air encounter an accident or a deliberate action? Were China's leaders dealing with an accurate picture of what had occurred, or had the information passed up the chain of command been distorted to protect those involved in the incident?

Rumsfeld could not get good answers from the U.S. intelligence community. U.S. officials on the ground in China, including the U.S. ambassador, appeared to have a much better sense of the situation there. "Their input about what happened and why, what to do and why, was more prescient and valuable than anything happening in D.C.," recalled Rich Haver, who was Rumsfeld's special assistant for intelligence.

In May, when the crew of the EP-3E visited Washington for an awards ceremony, Rumsfeld rode out to Andrews Air Force Base to pin on the medals and give a short address. The ceremony had particular meaning for the secretary. A close friend in flight school, James Deane, had died on a Cold War spy mission in August 1956 when his plane was shot down by the Chinese, and his remains had never been recovered. In his speech, Rumsfeld referred to the returning crew as the lucky ones who came back, noting that a number of their squadron mates in years past had not. Choked with emotion, he cut the speech short.

Back in the car afterward, Joyce Rumsfeld, who had accompanied her husband, noted that he hadn't finished his remarks. "I couldn't get Jim Deane's twenty-four-year-old face out of my mind," Rumsfeld explained. "I made that statement and I realized that my good friend never got any older, and he was just about the same age as most of these kids that I was looking at. And I figured I needed to stay composed in front of this audience, so I stopped."

Something else was on Rumsfeld's mind during the drive back. He had become increasingly frustrated with the way the department's various intelligence operations were being managed. In his previous stint as defense secretary, he had paid particular attention to intelligence issues, naming a second deputy secretary of defense, Robert Ellsworth, to focus on them. In later years, civilian oversight of the Pentagon's intelligence apparatus had been relegated down the ranks to an assistant secretary of defense who also had responsibility for communications, computers, and command-and-control issues.

Now, in the wake of the EP-3E incident, Rumsfeld wanted something done to give new focus to the department's intelligence-gathering apparatus. It was a mammoth task encompassing several sizable agencies, and it shouldn't be left to the part-time attention of an assistant secretary. "Haver, you've got to do something about intelligence," Rumsfeld told his special assistant, riding in the car from Andrews. "When a problem like this plane in China arises, I want one dog to kick, not a whole kennel."

"I understand, sir," Haver replied.

"Get me somebody in charge of DoD [Department of Defense] intelligence," the secretary continued with mounting conviction. "The way it is now is unmanageable. All these people report directly to me. I don't have time to run the intelligence community."

The conventional wisdom was that Rumsfeld, having served as defense secretary before and having taken on occasional national security assignments in the intervening period, would hit the ground running, knowing his way around the Pentagon and around Washington. The reality was something different. A number of department officials who had contact with him during his early weeks in the job found him unfamiliar with how much things had changed since his time leading the Pentagon in the mid-1970s. A more powerful chairman of the Joint Chiefs of Staff, expanded Joint Staff authorities, and greater congressional demands had all contributed to a different environment. Through the spring and into the summer of 2001, Rumsfeld struggled to understand how the Defense Department operated and to figure out where to go for answers, whom to hold accountable, and how to effect change in the Pentagon.

Andy Hoehn, who was heading the Pentagon's strategy office, remembers Rumsfeld acknowledging having a steep learning curve. "He was saying early on, 'People think that because I was once secretary of defense, I know exactly what was going on, but I don't. I've been doing other things for the last twenty-five years, and there are many things I need to become reacquainted with,'" Hoehn said.

Rumsfeld worried about inertia—about programs and budgets that had been set in motion years earlier and that had gained a momentum of their own. If he was ever going to bring about real change in the military, he would have to get a better handle on the department and avoid being run over by things already moving. He often invoked the analogy of coal cars, which get loaded up the track and then are sent off and go roaring by. His challenge was to figure out how to affect the loading, release, and routing of the cars without getting hit.

Rumsfeld wanted the main levers of control over the Pentagon identified for him, the main mechanisms through which to effect change in the department. He asked for someone to explain the key processes, the documents, on which to focus transformation.

The answers came in a classified briefing on April 7, 2001, titled "SecDef Levers for Implementing Decisions," prepared by several senior officials. It recommended that Rumsfeld concentrate on three areas: first, the selection of key military and civilian personnel; second, the drafting of broad policy directives, like the *Defense Planning Guidance* and fiscal guidance memos, that shaped the department's budget; and third, the preparation of contingency plans for war that set requirements for the weapons and troops considered necessary by commanders. "We basically just showed Rumsfeld the places where he could intervene, and the theme of it was, strike early to have the most impact, whether it be acquisition requirements or resource guidance," recalled Soule, one of the briefers.

The levers briefing occurred on a Saturday in a large conference room at the Pentagon. Rumsfeld had taken to meeting regularly on Saturdays, extending the work week for himself and his senior staff to six days. And the days could be long. Following the discussion about levers, Rumsfeld received an extensive presentation on how to begin converting his transformation vision into real program decisions. Titled "Strategy to Programs," the briefing laid on the table virtually all the prized weapons systems of the military services, suggesting which might be declared antiquated, and therefore eliminated or trimmed, and which might be labeled the promise of tomorrow, and therefore expanded or accelerated. Nothing was spared from consideration.

The Air Force saw its futuristic F-22 and F-35 Joint Strike Fighter jets on the list of potential cuts as well as its venerable B-52 and B-1 bombers and C-130 transport aircraft. The vulnerable Navy programs included the DD-21 destroyer and a next-generation aircraft carrier. The Army stood to lose its long-awaited Crusader artillery system, new Comanche helicopter, and planned upgrades of Abrams tanks and Bradley fighting vehicles.

On the other side, programs tagged as being transformational included sea-based missile defense, the Space-Based Radar constellation of satellites, the high-flying Global Hawk drone aircraft, the Army's fiber-optic–guided missile, the Navy's missile-firing arsenal ship, and plans to convert nuclear-armed SSGN submarines to conventional weaponry.

"This was an attempt to say to the secretary, 'Okay, this is the most aggressive course of action you could possibly take; this is the one that would give the services aneurisms,'" said a defense official who worked on strategy issues at the time.

Soule, who presented the briefing, thought that if nothing else, Rumsfeld would make a decision to eliminate the Crusader howitzer. If any big-ticket item represented the Cold War legacy that Rumsfeld and his team talked about shedding, it was this giant Army artillery unit—clunky, cumbersome, and expensive. Army officials would undoubtedly object to its cancellation, but even they had come to expect Crusader's demise. At that point, the Army's main interest was in being allowed at least to keep the money that had been budgeted for Crusader and to reinvest the funds in other Army programs rather than see the dollars go elsewhere in the Pentagon budget.

Rumsfeld, though, made no move to cancel Crusader or any other weapons system that day or in the immediate weeks that followed. His delay contrasted with the bold rhetoric of his transformational message and with the take-charge, man-in-command aura he sought to project.

"Rumsfeld had this reputation coming in as a really decisive guy, but he wasn't at all," Soule said later. "Basically, he said he didn't have enough of a basis to make any decisions yet. And I thought to myself, 'Oh my God, what is he going to need?' The brutal fact in all this decision stuff is, there's some analysis, but basically all you get are insights and you have to go from there. Something like killing Crusader, which was an expensive new artillery piece that wasn't very transformational, seemed a no-brainer."

Several officials who were in briefings with Rumsfeld have a lasting image of him in those early months as constantly asking questions and wanting more information. He never seemed to feel he had enough. He appeared to want not just more data but a more comprehensive analysis of whatever issue was being presented. Cambone, who became Rumsfeld's point man for much of the review of weapons and systems, was the same way.

To Mike Gilmore, a deputy in the programs analysis office, Rumsfeld and his new team seemed to be searching for a big theory that would explain the whole defense business, just as the big bang theory attempts to explain the origin of the universe—some overarching concept that would trace everything back and, in the process, illuminate a way to address every program issue. They appeared to want a comprehensive analysis that would give them *the* answer—an answer that would take everything into account and relate everything to everything else.

Looking back at that period, Cambone disputed this characterization. He said Rumsfeld was not trying to find a unified field theory but was simply intent on understanding more clearly why things were being done the way they were. Even so, the secretary came across at times as though he were hunting for a magic formula.

In trying to determine, for instance, an appropriate defense budget to present to Congress, Rumsfeld wondered whether there was a right way to calculate numbers for troop strength or for the operations and maintenance accounts once the overall military requirements were set. He sought a means of constructing a defense budget in a way that would allow him to come before Congress and present a kind of intrinsic, formulaic logic to the level of spending being requested.

"I tried to explain to him that you'll never get a black-and-white answer to something like that because, in the process of putting together a budget, you have to make lots of assumptions about how good is good enough," Soule said. "Depending on the assumptions you make, the resulting budget numbers can vary widely."

Borrowing from his experience in the corporate world, Rumsfeld also strove to come up with clearly defined departmental objectives and a set of measures for assessing progress toward those ends. In one of his morning meetings with aides, he explained that in a well-run business, a CEO ought to be able to ask any employee, whether in a vice president's office or a hallway, to recite the company's goals and get the same answer. The point was that everyone in an organization should know what the aims are and what the metrics are for gauging movement toward those aims. "He gave us sort of a Business 101 philosophy lecture," Soule recalled. "And then he asked what are our metrics."

In response, Rudy DeLeon, who had been Cohen's deputy and stayed on for three months under Rumsfeld until Wolfowitz could be confirmed, suggested gathering ideas from around the department. But as recommendations poured in, they formed an incoherent jumble. Soule, as one of his final acts before leaving the department in May, tried to consolidate them all into a readable package that he forwarded to Rumsfeld, if only to give the secretary a further sense of the issues on the staff's mind. The result was a fat, unfocused collection that Rumsfeld hated.

"I've seen this with other people who have come from the business world to the Defense Department," Soule said. "They're used to a handful of metrics that captures everything important—market share, profitability, or whatever it might be. Defense is much more complicated. You're never going to have a handful of metrics that represents the essence."

Until Rumsfeld had things all figured out, he appeared reluctant to move ahead with any major decisions on weapons programs. For all his bluster, Rumsfeld was at the same time strikingly averse to risk, even though the cancellation of a major program could have underscored the seriousness of his transformation agenda.

Several of Rumsfeld's associates saw the secretary's inclination to put off big cuts early on as a direct result of his own financial situation. Rumsfeld had taken steps to sell interests he had in firms that did business with the Pentagon so as to avoid any appearance of a conflict of interest. During his Senate confirmation hearing in January 2001, Rumsfeld had said he owned "a large number of investments and activities that would have to be characterized as 'conflicts' were they to be maintained during service as secretary of defense" and had promised to divest them.

But the divesture process was going slowly because a considerable amount of Rumsfeld's wealth was in private partnerships and closely held corporations that were difficult to sell. Under the circumstances, Rumsfeld told associates he was hesitant to take significant action on defense acquisition programs.

By the end of the 1990s, Rumsfeld had accumulated assets of at least $50 million and perhaps as much as $210 million, according to a financial report he submitted after becoming secretary. Compiling the report proved a major effort that Rumsfeld did not complete until almost a year and a half into his term. In a cover letter to Amy Comstock, the director of the government ethics office, he sounded fed up with the process. "I find it excessively complex and confusing," he said of the report. "To be able to attest to every word, or the checks in every box, would take me days and probably weeks of reviewing mountains of records. I do not have the time."

He went on: "Instead, I have hired an accountant to prepare the disclosure report for me. He and his firm spent some 490 man-hours to prepare the 54-page document, at a personal cost to me of more than $60,000. . . . We have done the best we can. If there are questions or problems, please contact my accountant." He concluded with a strong expression of doubt that the document's value equaled the burden it imposed and recommended it be slashed to about a third its length and rewritten to make it more understandable.

While Rumsfeld's personal financial situation may indeed have contributed to his hesitation about making decisions on major weapons systems, other factors also probably played a part, according to officials close to him then. Rumsfeld was a strong believer in letting processes run their course and thought that the appropriate place for sorting out which weapons systems to keep or cut was in the Quadrennial Defense Review, the results of which were not due until September. Further, most of Rumsfeld's senior civilian political appointees had not yet been confirmed. He was still having to rely on carryovers from the Clinton administration for advice and information.

In an internal memo that Rumsfeld wrote in May, he signaled plans to act on some big-ticket defense projects but indicated that he wanted to wait for the rest of his team to come onboard. "Make major weapon systems decisions in '02 and '03 budgets after the necessary key senior officials are confirmed (Service Secretaries, General Counsel, etc.)," he wrote.

In general, too, Rumsfeld throughout his life had shown a tendency not to rush ahead with major decisions. He preferred exercising caution and showing restraint, whether in cutting a weapons program or committing U.S. forces. "He's a guy who intellectually challenges the status quo constantly and, at the same time, he's a guy who's inherently conservative and doesn't make knee-jerk decisions," said a former official who dealt with him repeatedly.

———•———

It wasn't just Rumsfeld's intent to shake up the Pentagon that triggered the backlash against him during his initial months in office. It was his manner. The brusqueness and brashness that had been his style since his early management days now seemed so much a part of him that he couldn't stop himself from taking a briefer or a senior aide or even a cabinet colleague to task.

Tales quickly spread of the new defense secretary's subjecting senior generals to harsh questioning and dressing them down sternly in full view of others during meetings in his office. He would interrupt, berate, and nitpick. The outbursts could seem arbitrary at times, but there was also some method to his approach, making it possible to discern certain pet peeves that would set him off.

He had little tolerance for acronyms, for instance, and would come down hard on those who resorted to military speak. He demanded that each page in a package of briefing slides be numbered. And pity the briefer who tried to fake an answer to a question. Not knowing the answer could be excused, but pretending to know would open the way to a wrathful lashing by Rumsfeld.

Systematic in his own thinking, he demanded that presentations begin with a full exposition of all the assumptions underlying the points that were going to be made. Then he would pick the assumptions apart. All too often a briefer never got beyond the first page of a presentation because Rumsfeld, dissatisfied with a stated premise, would send him back to recast it.

"I am often briefed by folks who begin without addressing, or seemingly having considered, understood, let alone explained, the assumptions they have made which underlie their briefing, their conclusions and their recommendations," he wrote in a previously unpublicized memo on the subject during his second year in office. "It is a truth that you can proceed from outdated or inappropriate assumptions, perfectly logically to outdated and inappropriate conclusions. Staff folks need to be trained to develop and state assumptions at the outset of a briefing so that those being briefed know first that there are assumptions and what they are. I think that, generally, 25 to 50 percent of a briefing should be on the assumptions. If we get the assumptions right, the strategy, tactics and details follow logically."

In other instances, it was not always clear what might set Rumsfeld off. A bad mood? A desire simply to assert he was boss? His harsh treatment could extend even to very senior military officers, as it did during one early meeting about the Quadrennial Defense Review when Rumsfeld lashed out at Air Force general Richard Myers, then vice chairman of the Joint Chiefs of Staff. Myers had been chatting with someone seated beside him as the secretary was trying to talk.

One brigadier general on the Joint Staff was convinced that he had discerned a particular tic in Rumsfeld's gestures that revealed the secretary's mood. According to this officer, if Rumsfeld started pulling up the zipper on the green vest he frequently wore, it was a sign to keep talking; but if he started drawing the zipper down, it was time to change course. The officer felt he had broken Rumsfeld's code, much like identifying a poker player's tell. The zipper rule seemed to work about 80 percent of the time, the general claimed.

For all Rumsfeld's evident bluster and bullying, officers and civilian officials who met with him frequently found there was a purpose behind his gruff, abrasive style. The toughness, they concluded, was his way of taking the measure of people and testing their mettle. He wanted to see if they could speak in complete sentences and clear thoughts, if they knew their stuff and had confidence enough to stand up for their positions when challenged.

"I didn't know anything about him, and I thought he was going to be a kindly, old grandfatherly sort of guy," said John Abizaid, then a three-star Army general serving on the Joint Staff, recalling his first briefing with Rumsfeld. "I very quickly understood that he was a tough, bare-knuckled fighter and that you really had to know your subject or have people in there with you who knew the subject so that you could answer all his questions. He educated himself at your expense to a certain extent, so you had to have pretty good knowledge of the subject."

Abizaid found that Rumsfeld often had his mind made up about broad strategic issues at the start, although he could be persuaded by a good argument. In fact, he claimed he wanted people who were not yes-men, people who would push back. And some who ended up getting along most successfully with Rumsfeld attest that this approach worked for them.

One such case involved Stan Szemborski, who in the summer of 2001 was a two-star Navy officer on the Joint Staff when he found himself sitting on the edge of a meeting with Rumsfeld about a Pentagon budget plan. At the end of the briefing, Rumsfeld looked around the room and got one of those twinkles in his eyes suggesting he was looking for trouble, as Szemborski recalled. "I understand that you're the brains of this outfit. Is that right?" Rumsfeld said, peering at the admiral who had helped assemble the briefing.

"Sir, I'm just doing what my boss tells me," Szemborski replied, trying to back away.

"Well, let me tell you something. I've never been in a company where I couldn't save 15 percent," Rumsfeld boasted.

"Well, Mr. Secretary, let me get this straight. You've got about a $300 billion budget, so 15 percent would be $45 billion. If you think you're going to save $45 billion a year, I'm not sure you're going to be able to do that," the admiral remarked.

Recalling the conversation years later, Szemborski still wasn't sure what had compelled him to speak out that way with Rumsfeld. There was dead silence in the room for a few moments. Then Rumsfeld resumed. "There's so much waste in this department. I saw a guy who had two copying machines," he said.

"Mr. Secretary, you could get rid of a heckuva lot of copying machines and not save $45 billion," Szemborski countered.

"Well, here are some of my ideas on how we need to become more efficient. What are some of yours?" Rumsfeld asked.

The admiral listed some, and he and the secretary went back and forth for about ten minutes on potential cost-saving measures. Then Rumsfeld stood up, walked over to Szemborski, and said, "Don't you ever come into my office again unless you have your act together." And he walked out.

"He likes you!" exclaimed Dov Zakheim, the Pentagon comptroller, triggering laughter in the room. In time, Szemborski would receive a third star and serve as deputy director of the Office of Program Analysis and Evaluation.

Occasionally, too, Rumsfeld would show some of his gracious side, what several former subordinates described as his old-fashioned sensibilities. Soule, for all his frustration, actually liked Rumsfeld, noting that the secretary could be very engaging and personable. Years after leaving the Pentagon, he recalled a parting gesture by the secretary. "He came down to my office when I left to say goodbye, and at a dinner we both attended for another departing colleague, Rumsfeld was personable in talking to my wife," Soule said. "He didn't have to do that; he didn't have to come down to my office to wish me farewell."

But expressions of appreciation from Rumsfeld were for the most part few and far between. "He used to joke—and may have believed—that thanks, when given routinely, would 'ruin' subordinates," Feith, Rumsfeld's policy chief, wrote in a memoir. Said Gebhard, "His management style was sort of locker room, old school, which was, 'Well, you didn't screw up today, so I guess we'll keep you until tomorrow.' That was high praise."

As hard as he was on others, Rumsfeld was also hard on himself. He worked long days and long weeks. He took few vacations. And he edited his own prose with the same precision he brought to the picky wordsmithing of the briefing slides he was presented.

He often thought through issues by writing, which produced a series of concept papers. He would compose a draft, circulate it among some senior officials, incorporate revisions, then circulate the document again, frequently going through multiple drafts. "He was very much a paper person," said Delonnie Henry.

Rumsfeld's pickiness in editing caused his staff to joke about his tendency to "change 'happies' to 'glads'" and other seemingly insignificant edits. Sometimes he made so many changes in a text that by the end, the text read more or less as it had when he started.

He also tended to be strict about keeping any paper he wrote limited to one topic at a time. If there was a second topic he wanted to address, he would draft a second paper. He wouldn't ask someone in a single memo to tell him about the troops in Iraq and, say, the troops in Afghanistan. "He was very single-subject," Henry said. "You could only have one subject on one piece of paper. You couldn't mix things. It's like people who have to have their mashed potatoes and their meat separated." Similarly, he did not like people to mix subjects in memos and briefings to him. He demanded focus.

And he preferred simple forms over complicated ones. When he started as defense secretary, for instance, the office staff was in the habit of preparing a three-ring binder containing schedules, documents he needed to sign, and related backup materials, all extensively tabbed. He rejected the binder and instead asked his staff to give him just a folder for whatever meeting was coming up or whatever paper needed signing.

He also objected to the standard format of many of the action papers being sent to his office by subordinates—too many coordination lines on them, too bureaucratic in appearance. He wanted plainer forms— just white sheets of paper would do. But memos and other documents from others in the department should, he instructed, clearly show the name of the sender, not just the title, and any signatures on them should have the names clearly typed out so he could read them.

In addition to being a man of certain particulars, Rumsfeld had a strong streak of frugality. He insisted that the labeling for the manila folders stacked on his desk be done with Post-its or in pencil, not pen, so the folders could be reused. And rather than purchase new pencils and pens for the office, he wanted refills. He would shower his chief of protocol with snowflakes about things he considered unnecessary extravagances, like lemon wedges on water glasses or the number of glasses on the table for a luncheon meeting. He wanted the table dressed down. And when he traveled, he wanted his entourage small. Too many people holding doors bothered him.

While some of these measures could seem obsessively small, he also applied his economizing instincts in other ways that resulted in substantial savings for the department. In the summer of 2001, he wrote a memo listing the cost-cutting measures taken since becoming secretary. Under his tenure, he had:

1. Discontinued personal security inside the Pentagon for the secretary and deputy secretary. "If other DoD employees can walk about without protection, so can SecDef," the memo said.

2. Discontinued the military aide who met the secretary every time he came in or out of the Pentagon.

3. Switched from a Cadillac to a four-wheel-drive vehicle. Rumsfeld had "declined to purchase a new car as urged by security," the memo added.

4. Declined to repaint or redecorate the secretary's office.

5. Discontinued the display cases and other items that had existed in the secretary's mess and reorganized the dining room into a staff mess.

6. Stopped having a doctor travel with the secretary or deputy secretary.

7. Advised protocol not to purchase expensive personal representational gifts after, the memo noted, "finding there were thousands of dollars of unused gifts with the predecessors' names on them."

8. Instructed legal, protocol, and administrative staff not to do any "favors." The memo noted that Rumsfeld had been "deadly serious" about this. The staff members were instructed "to make certain that SecDef and everyone in OSD [Office of Secretary of Defense] are billed for every nickel that is personal" and not do any favors "by fudging."

9. Instructed staff to be sure that any use of office phone, postage, and fax machines for the secretary's personal business is paid for by him.

10. Made it clear that when the secretary was required to use military aircraft on personal trips, he reimbursed the government and did so at the private charter fee (which was higher than a first-class fare) because as a wealthy private citizen he had been accustomed to chartering for such trips.

11. Declined to have a special facility for handling classified material—known as a SCIF—put in his residence.

12. Discouraged the giving and exchanging of gifts. "If a foreign visitor visits, we can't stop them—we need to give something in return," the memo said. "But our gifts ought to be modest."

13. Terminated the use of a security chase car for the secretary when traveling in the United States.

14. Cut the size of the overseas traveling party by 30 percent.

15. Assumed the cost of his own meal when he had representational events involving Pentagon or U.S. official guests.

To avoid any possibility that a personal expense might even inadvertently have ended up paid for by the government, Rumsfeld also began writing a check each year to the U.S. government for $5,000. He delivered the check to the Pentagon's general counsel, William J. "Jim" Haynes II, who then passed it on to the Treasury Department.

Haynes initially tried to talk Rumsfeld out of the action. "I wanted to make sure he didn't feel he was buying $5,000 worth of graft," Haynes recalled. "Besides, such a check is not a simple thing for the bureaucracy to deal with. And third, there'll be other SecDefs in the future, and this would set some kind of precedent, but not all future secretaries of defense will be as wealthy as Rumsfeld. When I made that argument, he would say, 'Look, the last time I was here, I wasn't wealthy.' Anyway, we'd send the checks to Treasury, and they'd be deposited under miscellaneous receipts."

CHAPTER 8

Lots of Battlefronts

Any defense secretary intent on challenging the status quo at the Pentagon is likely to find the going tough. Bureaucratic by nature and beholden to tradition, the U.S. military doesn't change easily, and lots of groups—the military services, defense-industry contractors, politicians representing affected districts—have vested interests in ensuring things stay the way they are. So a case can be made for taking a cold, hard approach in trying to overhaul military structure and programs. But Rumsfeld made matters more difficult for himself with a management style seen as needlessly impolite and unforgiving.

Less easy to justify—and more dangerous from the standpoint of a Pentagon leader's political survival—is letting relations with Congress go bad. Yet here, too, tensions for Rumsfeld flared early, not just with Democrats on Capitol Hill, which could be expected, but with Republicans as well. And again, Rumsfeld's style was a factor—he could be as abrupt and dismissive toward lawmakers as he was toward generals and admirals.

The problem went beyond manners and wasn't entirely Rumsfeld's fault. For in his way, Rumsfeld initially tried to reach out to the Hill. He hoped to engage Congress in substantive discussion about how the Pentagon could better address new threats. Instead, he found parochialism and indifference, which merely confirmed a view he harbored of the legislative branch as not up to its responsibilities of thinking big or exercising proper oversight of federal agencies.

GOP lawmakers considered themselves the ones who had done the most when the White House was in Clinton's hands to carry the banner for such Republican causes as national missile defense, improved military readiness, and greater defense spending. After George W. Bush took office, they expected these issues to be addressed quickly, correcting the wrongs of the Clinton years.

Rumsfeld shared those concerns but didn't appear as definite about how to proceed. He sought time to study the issues and to proceed methodically. "While the Hill group was saying, 'This is what you need to be doing,' Rumsfeld was saying, 'Let's take a step back; let's elevate the debate; let's deconstruct things,'" said Robert Rangel, who was then the senior Republican staff member for the House Armed Services Committee and later became Rumsfeld's senior civilian assistant.

Rangel remembers Rumsfeld trying to get lawmakers to think about the big picture but finding most of them not particularly interested. Only a small group of members tended to regard themselves as real defense specialists and paid attention to the subject. The rest had more parochial concerns about facilities in their districts or defense contracts for constituents.

"He kept sending up some of the think pieces that folks were bringing to him or that he was writing himself and asking, 'What do you think?'" Rangel recalled. "He was wrestling with these issues at the fifty-thousand-foot level, saying come up and play, but the members didn't know how to deal with that. I can remember as a staffer trying to figure out how to seize on this opportunity because in many respects it was something brand new and different. Rumsfeld just operated differently. He was not a Bill Cohen, who tended to curry the favor of Hill members. Rumsfeld really wanted to open up and bring members along with his thinking. But it just never worked. There was just no connection there."

Victoria "Torie" Clarke, who had joined Rumsfeld's staff as his chief spokesperson, also has a recollection of Rumsfeld and senior lawmakers talking past each other. On visits to the Hill, Rumsfeld spoke of needing to revamp the U.S. military in the face of new threats posed by weapons of mass destruction, terrorism, cyberwarfare, and space warfare. "And I swear, members would practically reach over and pat him on the head and say, 'Now, how many ships are you going to build in my backyard?'" Clarke said in an interview. "They could not change their frame of reference."

But it wasn't just this in-my-own-backyard myopia on the part of lawmakers that bothered Rumsfeld. He regarded members of Congress as intrusive and overreaching. In his view, since his first stint as defense secretary, too many laws governing military activities had been passed, too many reports had been mandated by Congress, too many requests for information had been issued. The growth in the size of the annual Defense Authorization Act—from sixteen pages in the Ford era to more than five hundred pages now—said it all.

Rumsfeld started jotting down his concerns in a paper titled "The DoD Challenge." It began with the assertion that the "Defense establishment is tangled in its anchor chain." Commonly referred to now as "the anchor chain memo," Rumsfeld showed an early version of it in March 2001 to Senator John W. Warner (R-VA), the chairman of the Armed Services Committee. Within a couple of months, it had expanded to five pages and listed twenty-eight ways in which the Pentagon was hampered by congressional requirements or antiquated internal policies and processes.

"This situation has undoubtedly evolved over the past decades as a result of a series of instances that caused distrust between the Congress and the Department," Rumsfeld wrote. "Unfortunately, the result has not been improved oversight. Quite the contrary, each new layer of control and micromanagement has compounded the problem of accountability. From a practical standpoint, DoD no longer has the authority to conduct the business of the Department, and, as a result, its performance is deteriorating. . . . The regulations and requirements that have been laid on are so onerous that, over time, they are smothering incentive, innovation and risk taking."

The memo led to a "freedom-to-manage" initiative by Rumsfeld aimed at drafting legislation to remove some of the crippling regulations and requirements from running the Pentagon. The idea was to use the same approach as that taken in deciding military base closures—that is, to establish an independent commission charged with submitting recommendations that Congress could then only vote up or down, not amend. But the freedom-to-manage plan didn't sit well with some on the Hill, and nothing ever came of it.

Actions by Rumsfeld that either inadvertently or intentionally offended members of Congress didn't help his cause. The senior Republican on the House Armed Services Committee, Representative Duncan Hunter of California, was angered when he found himself assigned to a seat in the rear of a Pentagon plane ferrying officials to South Carolina for the funeral of a longtime congressman, Floyd Spence. In another instance, Rumsfeld went against the advice of his legislative affairs director and sent a harsh letter to the senior Democrat on the committee, Representative Ike Skelton of Missouri, in response to Skelton's remarks about a shortage of troops.

"A lot of people would have said, 'Okay, Ike, you and I have a disagreement, why don't you come out here for breakfast and let's talk about it,'" recounted Powell Moore, who handled legislative affairs for the Pentagon at the time. Moore saw the letter before it was sent and tried, without success, to persuade Rumsfeld to tone it down, noting that Skelton was popular on the Hill and the congressman's colleagues would not appreciate seeing him treated unkindly by the new secretary.

Even more irksome to GOP congressional leaders was Rumsfeld's reluctance to hire congressional staff for political appointee positions at the Pentagon. Historically, a number of these posts were filled by Hill aides, who brought with them a useful knowledge of the inner workings of government and helpful congressional connections. But Rumsfeld tended to see Hill staffers as lacking managerial experience and as beholden to congressional influence.

Some congressional aides who interviewed for Pentagon positions in the new Bush administration complained afterward of having been treated cavalierly and made to feel that their Hill background had little relevance to Defense Department employment. "They'd be asked something like, 'You know, in the executive branch you have to manage things, in the executive branch you have to make decisions, while on the Hill you don't have to manage anything or make decisions, so do you think you can make that adjustment?'" Moore said.

Some of the most influential members of Congress weighed in to try to give their aides a boost—among them, Senate majority leader Trent

Lott of Mississippi, who promoted Sam Adcock, and Republican senator Ted Stevens of Alaska, the chairman of the Appropriations Committee, who sought a position for Jay Kimmitt. But even these powerful law-makers were rebuffed. Frustrated and angry, Lott summoned Rumsfeld to a blunt meeting with a group of senior Republicans, where the de-fense secretary heard complaints about the perceived mistreatment of job applicants and other grievances.

After the meeting, Lott pulled Moore aside to register his own com-plaint about one of Rumsfeld's aides, Steve Herbits, a former staffer from the Ford era who was again assisting Rumsfeld as a senior adviser. Lott was opposed to Herbits for his openly gay sexual orientation and for his record of contributions to Democratic causes. Lott said he would exercise his senatorial prerogative to place a hold on all pending Defense Department nominees, delaying their confirmation by the Senate, until Herbits was gone.

Moore passed on the message to Rumsfeld as the two men rode back to the Pentagon. "Hell, I'm not going to cave in and let go of Herbits; I don't care if nobody ever gets confirmed," Rumsfeld said.

Moore agreed, worried about setting a precedent by conceding to Lott.

Herbits left in May when his transition stint had been scheduled to end, although he returned periodically over the next three years to ad-vise Rumsfeld and to carry out various projects. Moore then asked whether Rumsfeld wanted Lott informed of the departure of Herbits so that the hold on Pentagon nominations could be lifted. "Hell, no!" the secretary asserted. But Lott did find out, and the nominations were al-lowed to proceed.

Inside the Pentagon, Rumsfeld's tensions with the service chiefs bub-bled over in late May during an emotional session in the Tank, the chiefs' conference room. The secretary opened the meeting with a defense of his actions since coming to the Pentagon, emphasizing that he was de-termined to take a fresh look and so had gone outside the military for help. He added that it had never been his intention to be exclusionary.

The chiefs responded that they felt they had been excluded for months from his deliberations about those changes.

Admiral Vern Clark complained that he still hadn't been given a copy of the latest version of the overall strategy paper being written for Rumsfeld by Andrew Marshall. The service leaders were worried about that paper because it appeared to prescribe major shifts in the military, with new emphases on Asia and on long-range precision weaponry and less on large ground forces.

The meeting ended with new resolve by Rumsfeld to start holding intensive discussions with senior military as well as civilian officials in the weeks ahead in connection with the Quadrennial Defense Review. By then, the study panels that Rumsfeld had set up in his initial weeks had proven to be a largely useless exercise, yielding no clear way forward. With little direction from the top and riven by the conflicting views of members, the panels had produced a great hodgepodge of recommendations. "No one knew what transformation was about, so you had in these study groups an awful lot of rehashed diagnoses of the problem as opposed to coherent solutions for how to fix them," said Paul Gebhard, one of Rumsfeld's special assistants.

Over the next few weeks, Rumsfeld and his team conducted an intensive series of almost daily meetings with the service chiefs that eventually yielded general agreement on the need for a new strategy for sizing and shaping U.S. forces. During the Cold War, U.S. strategy was based on the possibility of global war with the Soviet Union. That had given way at the start of the Clinton administration to the notion that the U.S. military needed to prepare instead for the possibility of two major regional conflicts being fought almost at the same time—most probably one in the Middle East and the other on the Korean peninsula.

But this two-war construct had not held up particularly well in the 1990s as U.S. troops found themselves stretched thin not by major regional conflicts but by smaller fights in such places as the Balkans and by multiple peacekeeping missions. Moreover, a new array of dangers made military planning more problematic. Increasingly, planners had to worry about the possibility of terrorists coming across U.S. borders, missiles reaching U.S. territory, hackers attacking U.S. information systems, and enemies of one sort or another using chemical, biological, or nuclear weapons. The Pentagon thus required a more flexible, more realistic strategy, one that placed a greater emphasis on homeland defense and on smaller-scale contingencies.

"The current strategy isn't working," Rumsfeld declared on June 21, 2001, in his first public appearance before Congress since his January confirmation. The testimony provided an important marker for the evolution of Rumsfeld's thinking to that point. In back-to-back hearings before the Armed Services committees in both the Senate and the House, the secretary outlined a more layered strategy that he said would be tested further as the Quadrennial Defense Review wore on.

The new strategy had several parts. First, it softened the old requirement that the military be ready to win two regional wars at once, calling instead for U.S. forces to be able to swiftly defeat one enemy while at least holding a second enemy at bay. Second, it included a provision for a limited number of small-scale contingencies. And third, it added a specific requirement that the U.S. homeland be defended, although just what that should mean remained vague even to Rumsfeld and the rest of the Pentagon leadership.

Evident, too, in Rumsfeld's remarks to Congress were emerging signs of a more aggressive U.S. military posture. To the old concept of simply deterring enemies, Rumsfeld added a new emphasis on dissuading them from even thinking of developing certain weapons or taking menacing action. And he mentioned doing more to reassure friends and allies of America's ability to respond.

The secretary spoke as well of the need to base future procurement decisions less strictly on shaky predictions about specific threats. In a world of greater uncertainty, he argued, such decisions should rest more on projections of new capabilities that would give the United States a clear edge against all adversaries. This notion of "capabilities-based planning," as opposed to the "threat-based planning" of the past, was a controversial one. While it promised greater flexibility, it ran the risk of making some questionable new weapons easier to justify.

But Rumsfeld was clearly attempting to set the basis for what he hoped would be a profound shift toward a significantly restructured armed forces and toward new weapons choices, a shift that favored investment in such high-tech areas as space, information systems, and intelligence gathering. His statement showed him focused sharply on a set of threats very different from the single, overwhelming Soviet menace that he had confronted as secretary of defense before. As much as he had appeared in his first months in office as a kind of Rip Van Winkle character, awakening to new realities of Pentagon management after a quarter century away, his strategic view was very current.

This was not some Cold Warrior. Rumsfeld saw new dangers on the horizon, even if he failed to grasp just how imminent one of them would prove to be.

The new strategic guidance represented progress toward defining Rumsfeld's transformation mantra, but it was only a first step. What followed over the summer were extensive discussions between Rumsfeld and the Pentagon's senior leadership on how to translate the guidance into decisions about force structure and weapons systems. The discussions often turned heated.

Eager to free up money to fund futuristic systems like missile defense, unmanned and robotic vehicles, precision munitions, and space satellites, Rumsfeld and his team appeared intent on making cuts in force size. Proposals circulated to eliminate two Army divisions, three Air Force wings, an aircraft-carrier battle group, and more. The chiefs complained that such reductions were being conceived before the actual missions that the military might have to carry out had been adequately defined.

Compounding matters were budgetary pressures. Bush's decision to go with a $1.35 trillion tax cut meant that less money would be available for the rise in defense spending that the military services had expected. In June 2001, the White House announced an $18.4 billion increase in military spending, raising the total to $329 billion, but that was only about half the increase that Rumsfeld had requested and that the military chiefs had deemed necessary.

The smaller-than-desired increase was explained as a stopgap measure meant to stabilize the military budget while Rumsfeld devised far-reaching changes in strategy, weapons, and troop structure. But the decision suggested that Rumsfeld's reshaping would have to proceed more slowly. After paying for additional essentials such as spare parts, training, and fuel for ships and aircraft, the proposed budget hike left little for transformation initiatives. If money for these was to come from anywhere, it would have to be from troop cuts.

A central question in Rumsfeld's discussions with the chiefs thus became how much risk to take in the short term by reducing troop levels and lowering the readiness of military units in the interest of the long-term restructuring of forces and investments in new systems. "Here's the problem that the Joint Chiefs faced," retired general Hugh Shelton recalled years later. "We all understood that we had to look out twenty years, but we also were concerned about reaching a balance. You just can't be interested in who you're going to have to fight years from now. You have to preserve your force in the meantime."

Shelton and the other chiefs were concerned that Rumsfeld was so focused on buying new technologies that he wasn't fully accepting the near-term risks involved. "He wanted it both ways," Shelton said, meaning the benefits of long-term investment without the danger of short-term vulnerability.

Military planners surveying the world at the time saw a number of potential hot spots that could draw the United States into a conflict in the near term. What if the North Korean regime fell apart violently? If China tried to bully Taiwan? If the nuclear face-off between India and Pakistan worsened? If the Middle East plunged into war? Not to mention the possibility of Iraq's Saddam Hussein acquiring weapons of mass destruction.

But Rumsfeld and his aides argued that no one was likely to challenge the U.S. military directly in the short term. In this they were supported by Andy Marshall, whose strategy paper, written at Rumsfeld's request after taking office, had essentially concluded that the world looked relatively safe for the moment, so the United States could afford to concentrate on the longer term. Marshall contended that the United States had entered a period of global hegemony, giving it time and opportunity not only to extend its power but also to prepare for future military competitions.

Outside the Pentagon, proponents of change grew impatient with the lack of decision. Ken Adelman, a longtime Rumsfeld friend and former aide, published a piece in the *Wall Street Journal* titled "Stop Reviewing; Start Reforming" in which he accused the administration of "tiptoeing" around sweeping changes at the Pentagon. "So far, there's been more storm than reform," Adelman wrote. "Enough 'reviews.' It's clear what needs be done."

Rumsfeld was not pleased. "He came up to me afterwards at someone's house," Adelman recalled, "and, typical Rumsfeld, said, 'Joyce was really steamed by your column.' He told me I was a friend, and how could I do that to him. He poked his finger in my chest. I did feel badly."

By summer, tensions were so high that Rumsfeld, in a meeting with senior civilian and military officials, issued what sounded like a threat simply to quit. "The president has asked me to do a hard job, and we're going to have to do this together," he said, according to notes taken by a participant. "And if we can't, then I'm going to go back to New Mexico because I have better things to do with my time. I need you guys to work with me; I don't need you guys working against me."

Adding to the strain was a concern among the chiefs that the minutes of some of their sessions with Rumsfeld, drafted by the secretary's staff, did not reflect what had been said or decided. Repeatedly, Shelton tried to set the record of a meeting straight, telling Rumsfeld the minutes were incorrect. "It happened a number of times," Shelton recalled. "A lot of frustration developed out of that."

Rumsfeld never got comfortable meeting with the military chiefs alone in the Tank. As the Quadrennial Defense Review discussions intensified, he stopped going to the inner sanctum of the chiefs altogether. He had been livid when he read a newspaper story with details of one of his supposedly secret Tank sessions, believing the leak had come from the military side. "The Tank leaks," he complained to Shelton.

"He was very upset about it, and he came into the Tank and basically said something that I never thought I'd hear a secretary say, and that was that he didn't have much use for us as a body," recalled retired general Jim Jones, the former Marine commandant. General Eric Shinseki, the Army's chief of staff, thought the leak had come from Rumsfeld's office and told him so. "The secretary didn't stay long," Jones said. "It's clear he wasn't there to smoke the peace pipe."

Asked years later about his decision to shun the Tank, Rumsfeld said that when he tried to engage the four-star officers as a group, he found them reticent and overly inclined to back one another. "There was a reluctance to speak out on anything other than their own service," he said in an interview for this book. "It varied from individual to individual, but there apparently had evolved or developed within the department a pattern whereby if a broad subject came up that involved one service, then the other three services would not opine on that too much—at least not opine in any way that was anything other than very agreeable to whatever it was that that service chief was proposing."

Instead of conferring with the chiefs on their turf, Rumsfeld set up a different forum that became known as the Senior Level Review Group. It met in the secretary's conference room and included not just the uniformed service leaders but the department's senior civilian leadership. While initially established to work on the Quadrennial Defense Review, the group—abbreviated SLRG and pronounced "slurg" in Pentagon acronym parlance—became a fixture of Rumsfeld's tenure. Never really a decision-making body, it was used more by Rumsfeld as a sounding board, where a wide range of issues would be briefed and debated. The assumption of those who attended SLRG meetings was that the decisions would be made elsewhere—or already had been.

"It was very Socratic," said one regular civilian participant. "Rumsfeld used the session a lot to watch how people debated each other, how they answered his questions. Occasionally he'd throw a little bomblet on the table to see what would happen. Then as the debate progressed, he would try his 'What-I-think-I-hear-you-saying-is.' And then he would lay out, 'Here's-the-way-I'm-going-to-talk-about-it, how-do-you-all-feel-about-that?'"

The chiefs never really accepted SLRG sessions as a substitute for Tank meetings with the secretary and frequently wished they could return to talking with the secretary alone, without a larger chorus of civilian officials.

Rumsfeld came to learn that before some of the SLRG meetings in the summer of 2001, the chiefs would confer among themselves in the Tank. In fact, this would sometimes delay the start of the secretary's meetings. "It just frustrated him no end," said Andy Hoehn, one of Rumsfeld's senior strategists. "He'd say, 'Why are they down there? Why can't they just have this conversation in front of me?' I could never be sure, but I often wondered whether the intense pace of the secretary's meetings that summer—every day for several hours—was in part intended to avoid the chiefs precooking stuff."

In a memo later in the year to several of his top civilian staff members, Rumsfeld expressed his satisfaction with the pattern that had been established of mixing the chiefs and senior civilians together. "It worked," he wrote. "We were able to hear their individual views."

He drew a distinction between these individual views and the "collective views" of the chiefs that emerged from their separate meetings in the Tank. While sounding receptive still to the collective view, he encouraged each of his civilian aides to consider ways of drawing out the individual opinions of the military leaders. "Sometimes a collective view is a compromise, and that is understandable and fine," Rumsfeld said. "Finding ways to build them into the process and for each of you to learn their perspectives first-hand is a helpful thing to do."

———————

By August 2001, Rumsfeld was in retreat, under fire from all sides. Not only were the chiefs proving resistant to his direction, but members of Congress were signaling their opposition to suggested cuts in troops and traditional weapons systems. And conservatives were complaining that the Pentagon had not received the money needed for the renewed buildup they had expected. Indicative of the anger on the right, William Kristol, editor of the conservative *Weekly Standard*, called on Rumsfeld and Wolfowitz to resign to highlight "the impending evisceration of the American military."

"This is one of the most interesting situations I've ever seen in a long time," Representative Norm Dicks, a promilitary Democrat from Washington State, told *Time* magazine. Rumsfeld "says he wants the military to stop saying they can fight two wars on two fronts simultaneously. But he has opened more fronts in Washington than any defense secretary in memory."

Speculation that Rumsfeld would be the first member of the Bush cabinet to go was widespread and openly reported in news publications. Mindful of his early stumbles, Rumsfeld confessed to a reporter, "I was not in the rhythm of the place." He also said he had learned a lesson, which he summed up as, "It would be foolhardy to try to micromanage from the top . . . every aspect of everything that is going on."

Having taken office with such promise, how had the savvy Rumsfeld gotten into such trouble so soon? Part of the problem could be blamed on unrealistically high expectations for a quick, radical Pentagon overhaul—expectations that had been set not by Rumsfeld but by Bush during the campaign. Further, there was some question as to whether the time was even right for a dramatic transformation. Historically, reform had come easier in the wake of a major military defeat or in the face of a looming crisis, none of which was the case in 2001.

Then, too, Rumsfeld faced tighter fiscal constraints than expected. And he was still having to operate with only a few handpicked aides because of lengthy delays in filling the Pentagon's forty-eight slots for political appointees. Also missing was a political constituency in Congress for painful changes in the military. As Cheney remarked in defense of his old friend Rumsfeld, anyone would have had trouble reforming the U.S. military after "years of neglect." Or, as Rumsfeld and his aides frequently could be heard saying, "Change is hard."

But Rumsfeld bore some of the blame. Although his goal—to redesign an outmoded military—was commendably ambitious and important, he disregarded some of his earliest Washington lessons. Most notably, he neglected to engage the very people whose support he needed most to achieve the transformation he sought. Rather than draw the military brass into feeling personally invested in the process of change, Rumsfeld engendered attitudes of distrust, suspicion, resentment, and downright hostility. He had tried to change course in June, launching into an unprecedented series of intense meetings with the chiefs on an almost-daily basis. But by then the damage had been done. Relations remained strained.

The picture with Congress wasn't any more encouraging. His refusal to consider some senior Hill aides for Pentagon jobs had been only the start of a larger pattern of what members came to see as Rumsfeld's seeming disregard for them. He had been slow to share his thinking about his strategic review and had delayed presenting proposed changes to the defense budget. Lawmakers, like the chiefs, had felt excluded from the process.

Rumsfeld did make renewed efforts to reach out to Congress about the time he engaged the chiefs, but then defense conservatives on the Hill were riled afresh by a surprise decision in June to end training at a bombing range on the Puerto Rican island of Vieques by May 2003. Before the reverberations from that decision faded, congressional antagonism was deepened by a Pentagon move to mothball a third of the ninety-three-plane B-1 bomber force and consolidate the remaining fleet by shifting planes from Georgia and Kansas to Texas and California. "I am discouraged, I am frustrated and I am angry," Senator Pat Roberts, a hawkish Republican from Kansas, told Rumsfeld at a hearing.

The bomber decision sparked strong opposition not just from lawmakers in states with B-1 bases but from businessmen and Air National Guard officers as well. Privately, Rumsfeld blamed Air Force officials for mishandling the plan. But publicly, the controversy emerged as the first major test of Rumsfeld's ability to bring sweeping change to the military. If he could not cut back on the troubled B-1 force, how could he ever tackle an Army division or a carrier battle group?

Expectations of a new Pentagon era began to fade. Instead, the revised conventional wisdom held that Rumsfeld's review would fall short of the bold rhetoric of Bush's Citadel speech. Still, the White House showed little sign of easing him out. Indeed, Cheney told the *Washington Post* that Rumsfeld was well suited to carry on the fight. "It is going to be tough, and he's going to have to break some china," Cheney said. "But he's just the guy to do it."

Rumsfeld appeared to shrug off much of the criticism. A friend who dined with him and Joyce that summer in New Mexico asked about all the attacks in the press. The Rumsfelds didn't flinch. "Good grief," Joyce said, laughing it off. "It's nothing. It isn't ten percent of what garbage we got dumped on us the last time we were down there."

Rumsfeld went on the offensive. To make the case that he was engaging with Congress and with the chiefs, he had his staff tally the numbers of meetings and then boasted about them. He put out word that he had held 361 meetings with "200 or 300" members of Congress and had conferred with the military leaders 320 times. He also spoke of "93 events with the press of various types." That was quantity, of course, not quality. But for Rumsfeld, an incurable counter, the metrics mattered.

———————

Rumsfeld's relations with Shelton, which had started chilly, grew frostier. In various ways, Rumsfeld kept making it clear that he considered the chairman's position somewhere off to the side, not in the straight chain of command that ran from the president to the secretary to the regional combatant commanders. Although the chairman is a key military adviser, he does not, by law, have direct command over any forces.

Shelton thought Rumsfeld was handicapping himself by failing to recognize how helpful a chairman could be in coordinating various military activities. But Rumsfeld insisted on dealing with his regional commanders directly and hearing their suggestions and recommendations unfiltered through the chairman's office.

Nor did Rumsfeld make a secret of his view that the 1986 Department of Defense Reorganization Act, enacted since he had last served as defense secretary, placed too much power in the hands of the chairman. Known as the Goldwater-Nichols Act, the legislation sought to diminish the rivalry among the military services by enhancing the chairman's role. What irked Rumsfeld about it was its designation of the chairman, without the service chiefs, as the principal military adviser to the president, the National Security Council, and the secretary of defense.

"He felt that the chairman's position had been elevated higher than it should have been," Shelton said. "As the top civilian in the Pentagon, he felt perfectly capable of going over to the White House without having the chairman tailing along. I got the feeling he'd just as soon go to NSC meetings without having the chairman present because he really didn't feel that he needed the chairman."

Rumsfeld wanted the Pentagon to speak with one voice and insisted his staff and the Joint Staff coordinate views inside the building before engaging with the State Department and other agencies. Previously, Joint Staff officers had been accustomed to dealing directly in interagency discussions, coordinating positions and then bringing them to the secretarial level for a decision. Rumsfeld sought to put a stop to that, showing little tolerance for close collaboration with the State Department. He also did not like interagency working groups at lower levels, preferring issues to be hashed out among senior officials.

"He was very, very closed about his willingness to share things with the other agencies," remarked John Abizaid, then a three-star Army general in charge of the Joint Staff's policy branch. This side of Rumsfeld had surprised Abizaid. "I had this idea that because Rumsfeld had so much experience in government, he'd be very collaborative with the other agencies," the general said. "But he wasn't."

The chiefs as a group customarily issued letters to Congress on topics of particular concern. Called "twenty-four-star letters" because they were signed by all six four-star members of the Joint Chiefs—the four service leaders plus the chairman and vice chairman—they carried unusual authority. But Rumsfeld objected to the chiefs giving strategic advice outside channels. "It just drove him nutty," Abizaid said.

As the senior military officer with the secretary on a trip to Russia in 2001, Abizaid caught an earful from Rumsfeld about the Joint Staff. More than six years later, the general still recalled Rumsfeld, during the plane ride back from Moscow, describing Joint Staff officers as arrogant and unsupportive of him. Abizaid sought to assure him that the officers did respect their oaths to the Constitution and the chain of command. "You tell us what you want us to do, and we'll do it, but we can't guess," Abizaid said. "And we're not trying to tell you what to do."

"Well, sometimes I think you are trying to tell me what to do," Rumsfeld said. After letting the subject drop for a bit, Rumsfeld came back to it again during the plane ride. "I just feel like there's too much resistance to change," he said.

"There won't be resistance to change if you articulate the change you want," the general replied.

Persistently troubled by the power of the Joint Staff, Rumsfeld explored the possibility of trimming it by merging its protocol, legislative liaison, and legal functions into the Office of the Secretary of Defense. He presented this as an efficiency move, but Shelton considered it an obvious power play.

Shelton argued the importance of the chairman having his own group of specialists. He noted that under Title 10, the chairman is supposed to render independent advice, so it is critical for him to have his own set of lawyers. The chairman has many contacts with Congress, so it helps to have his own legislative office. And the chairman entertains many visiting foreign counterparts and other dignitaries, so he needs his own protocol office. "We've done a lot to try to pare these offices down," Shelton told Rumsfeld. He couldn't resist observing that the secretary's staff was much bigger than his own, and he suggested that Rumsfeld look there for economy measures.

Unable to get anywhere with Shelton or later chairmen, Rumsfeld continued looking for allies in the department. In 2002, he asked the department's historian, Alfred Goldberg, for an opinion on the merger idea. Goldberg wrote back warning that such a move would be perceived as diminishing the role of the Joint Chiefs and could well stir up a political storm. He also cautioned Rumsfeld against thinking the reorganization could be achieved simply on his own authority as secretary. "Congress may want the last word," Goldberg said.

Nowhere was the strain more pronounced between Rumsfeld and the chiefs than in the secretary's relationship with General Eric Shinseki. In style alone, the two men had difficulty relating. Shinseki's natural reticence contrasted with Rumsfeld's loquaciousness. The secretary liked to engage, to ask questions, and to get answers. Shinseki tended to keep his replies short and avoid extended conversation. "I would watch Rumsfeld try to draw him out, but Shinseki was not easily brought into a discussion," Hoehn said.

Shinseki tended not to put himself forward. He preferred to work in groups and build consensus. A well-mannered officer, he resented Rumsfeld's often harsh, abrasive treatment of subordinates and what he perceived as arrogance and, at times, overbearing infringement on the prerogatives of military leaders.

On the issue of military transformation, the two men actually shared a commitment. In fact, Shinseki, who had taken charge of the Army two and a half years before Rumsfeld arrived, had launched a program of change months earlier. Shinseki's initiative was aimed at the same goals that interested Rumsfeld—the creation of a lighter, more agile force. "If you don't like transformation, you are going to like irrelevance a lot less," Shinseki had told his soldiers, pushing to overcome stiff resistance in Army ranks to some of the changes. Rumsfeld liked that statement so much that he later added it to his published collection of rules.

Shinseki wasn't a natural reformer. He had to be pushed by Shelton and Cohen into coming up with a plan for change. Nonetheless, he had conceived a plan and was going forward with it before transformation was made fashionable by Rumsfeld. "He felt that he was doing the right things," said Staser Holcomb, one of Rumsfeld's senior assistants who tried to mediate between the secretary and the general. "He didn't really believe he needed the secretary's help in transforming the Army."

Rumsfeld found Shinseki's program insufficiently aggressive and somewhat unintelligible. The program envisioned not one but in effect three armies existing side by side, each representing a separate stage of development. There was a "legacy force" consisting of the Army essentially as it was before the Soviet Union's demise, an "interim force" featuring more agile combat-brigade teams built around a new wheeled, armored vehicle called the Stryker, and an "objective force" of the future. Questions existed even within the Army about exactly what Shinseki's transformation program was trying to fix and where it would lead. Although Rumsfeld hadn't figured out yet what kind of new Army he wanted, he knew Shinseki's notion wasn't it.

Army officials tended to regard Rumsfeld as simply biased against their service. Ground forces did not factor into the types of future systems he seemed to favor, systems that emphasized airpower, space operations, and intelligence gathering. His senior military assistant was a Navy officer, and the civilians he had picked as other special assistants tended, like Rumsfeld himself, to be ex-Navy. And he had been heard making little digs at the Army. "You just got this clear feeling that the Army wasn't high on his priority list, that he saw it as anachronistic, that the new way ahead was going to be high-tech weapons in space," Shelton said.

Rumsfeld's closest aides from that period insist he was not anti-Army. But they also note that the Army did little to help its case with the new secretary. Just the briefing style of senior Army officials tended to reinforce the service's image as plodding and uncreative. The contrast was greatest with the Navy, whose military leader, Admiral Vern Clark, seemed to figure out early how best to communicate with Rumsfeld.

"Clark would come in for a forty-five-minute meeting with three slides," said Steve Bucci, then an Army colonel serving as one of Rumsfeld's military assistants. "On those slides there might be three bullets each, none even a complete sentence. He'd lay them in front of the secretary but would hardly refer to them. He'd just start chatting with the secretary, and they'd have a dialogue. The secretary would ask questions, Clark would respond, and generally by the end of the session, Clark got whatever he wanted.

"The Army would come in for a forty-five-minute meeting with fifty-two slides dense with words. They'd start speaking, and the secretary would interrupt to ask a question. They would answer as directly and succinctly as possible, then get back to the slides. Then he'd ask another question, and they'd answer that one. And frequently there wasn't a third because by that point he was so frustrated at not getting the dialogue he wanted. Most of the time the Army guys didn't get what they wanted because they never got their point across."

The first clash between Rumsfeld and Shinseki had occurred in the early days of the administration. It involved a decision by Shinseki in late 2000 to issue black berets to all soldiers instead of just to Army Rangers, an elite, highly trained combat group. Shinseki had intended the move to symbolize his larger transformation effort by erasing one of the lines between the Army's heavy and light forces. But it set off a storm of controversy in the Ranger community, where the wearing of a black beret had been considered a hard-won right and the exclusive mark of their unit.

With members of Congress and officials in the new Bush White House sympathetic to the Rangers' protests, Rumsfeld urged Shinseki to reconsider. But the Army chief refused to budge. Finally, in mid-March 2001, Rumsfeld ordered Shinseki to appear with Wolfowitz at a news conference and announce what amounted to a retreat by the Army general. To regain a sign of their distinctive status, the Rangers were given new tan berets in place of the old black ones.

"I don't think Rick ever recovered with Rumsfeld, in terms of Rumsfeld's confidence," said retired general Jack Keane, who was vice chief of the Army at the time under Shinseki. "I think Rumsfeld lost confidence in his judgment."

The beret episode suggested that while Rumsfeld often held out for his way, Shinseki at times could be equally stubborn and poorly attuned to Washington politics. But the most crucial showdown between the two men in 2001, which involved the future size of the Army, ended in Shinseki's favor.

The Army had come down in size significantly during the 1990s, dropping from 710,000 to 482,000 active-duty troops, organized principally into ten divisions. The Army Reserve and National Guard also had shrunk, from 756,000 to 560,000. Even so, one of Rumsfeld's early study panels challenged the continuing need for so many ground forces, suggesting the era of major tank battles was over, and as the Quadrennial Defense Review got under way in earnest in late spring, proposals emanated from Rumsfeld's office to cut Army forces by another hundred thousand active-duty soldiers and another hundred thousand National Guardsmen.

"That's what we thought their agenda was," recalled retired general Kevin Byrnes, who was the Army's representative to a Quadrennial Defense Review working group. "In order to pay for missile defense, in order to pay for over-the-horizon attack and precision weapons, we thought the Army's bill was going to be about 20 percent of its active-duty manpower and about a third of the manpower out of the National Guard. And we could see some of their analysis being manipulated in that direction."

Army representatives argued that the demands of peacekeeping operations in the Balkans and elsewhere were already stretching the force too thin and limiting progress on transformational initiatives. If troop levels were going to be reduced, Army officials contended, expectations of what the Army could deliver in war and in peace-enforcement operations would need to be scaled back. Rumsfeld's aides pointed to war-gaming scenarios suggesting that trade-offs were possible—more airpower, for instance, in place of ground troops. But Army officials regarded the scenarios as rigged against them.

"One day a war game would be run that showed five Army divisions would be needed for the fight, but the next day, the game would show only two divisions," Byrnes recalled. "Why was that? Because the game would suddenly assume that enemy forces had decided to line up neatly along roads where airpower could take them all out. Now, do you think an enemy would ever do that—continue to line up fifty meters apart on roads even after their first brigade gets wiped out?"

The Army pushed its case hard, attempting to explain in great detail not only the troop requirements for major wars and for forward deployments in Europe and Korea but also the intricacies of its system for rotating forces. A decisive moment came in mid-August when, ahead of a senior-level meeting with Rumsfeld, a draft of a planning-guidance document was sent to service chiefs and service secretaries calling for the elimination of two Army divisions and four National Guard divisions. Shinseki, in Hawaii at the time, fired off a strongly worded letter to Rumsfeld and flew back ahead of schedule to attend the meeting, expecting a confrontation. But the future size of the Army never came up in the session with Rumsfeld, and the idea of cuts was dropped. Wolfowitz had come around to agreeing with the Army and had persuaded Rumsfeld to leave troop levels where they were.

While the Army had managed to avoid the ax for the time being, no one thought Rumsfeld had ceased his campaign. The *Armed Forces Journal International*'s September issue carried a picture of Rumsfeld on the cover with the headline "Why does this man hate the United States Army?"

Shortly after the September 11 attacks, when it was clear that the United States would be embarking on war in Afghanistan and probably elsewhere, Wolfowitz felt a certain vindication about having spared the Army. "Aren't you glad now that you didn't try to downsize the Army?" he asked Rumsfeld. The secretary emphatically agreed.

———•———

It took months to assemble but midway through Rumsfeld's first year as secretary, his top civilian leadership team was finally confirmed by Congress and in place. The group represented a mix of some who had dealt with Rumsfeld before and some entirely new to him. The more familiar faces ended up in some of the more nuts-and-bolts positions—Edward C. "Pete" Aldridge, an aerospace-industry executive who had headed the Pentagon's planning and evaluation unit when Rumsfeld first served as defense secretary, returned this time to be the undersecretary for acquisition, and Dov Zakheim, a budgeting and programs specialist who had dealt with Rumsfeld on earlier projects, took over as comptroller.

But in two of the most sensitive high-level jobs—the undersecretary for policy and the Pentagon's general counsel—Rumsfeld chose people previously unknown to him who would prove the most controversial on his staff. During his previous stints in government, Rumsfeld had tended to surround himself with aides who knew him well—Cheney foremost among them. Similarly, at Searle and General Instrument, Rumsfeld had leaned heavily on one or two close friends.

For the key job of undersecretary of defense for policy, Rumsfeld had hoped to pick someone he knew and respected—William Schneider Jr., the conservative arms control specialist who had served on the missile-threat commission. But Schneider, who operated a consulting business, declined the job for financial and family reasons, agreeing instead to serve as head of the Defense Science Board. The policy job was also discussed with Richard Perle, a prominent national security expert who, like Rumsfeld, had been a tough Cold Warrior decades earlier and who, like Wolfowitz, was closely identified with the neoconservative community. But Perle also preferred to continue with various business interests and settled instead to chair the Defense Policy Board.

In the end, Rumsfeld selected Douglas Feith, an attorney with strong neoconservative views and experience on the NSC and in the Pentagon under Reagan but no history with Rumsfeld. Some people who knew Feith questioned whether he had developed sufficient gravitas and perspective for the job and whether he had the management talent to handle the giant policy branch, with its staff of 1,800 employees. Feith himself hesitated, wondering if he was up to the task. But he came enthusiastically recommended by Wolfowitz, Perle, and several other prominent figures on the right who considered him very able, intelligent, and assertive.

The selection of Feith reinforced the neoconservative tilt of the Pentagon's policy branch already signaled by Rumsfeld's decision to accept Wolfowitz as his deputy. "Ultimately, Doug was Paul's decision, and Rumsfeld sort of went along with it," said Steve Herbits, who was involved in the candidate search.

Similarly, Rumsfeld went more on the recommendations of others than on firsthand experience in selecting Jim Haynes as general counsel. A former general counsel of the Army when Cheney was defense secretary, Haynes had not only a connection with the vice president but an even closer connection with Cheney's counsel, David Addington. It was Addington who had hired Haynes as his own special assistant in the Cheney Pentagon and had then promoted him to the Army job, and it was Addington and Cheney who were now backing him with Rumsfeld.

Unlike Feith, Haynes wasn't a particularly ideological thinker. But with Cheney and Addington as his patrons, he came to be seen by others in the Pentagon as doing the bidding of the vice president's office in his management of the Pentagon's legal processes and in the legal advice he provided

Rumsfeld on a range of critical issues involving, among other things, the treatment of detainees, interrogation techniques, and intelligence-gathering authorities.

Ken Adelman, a longtime friend who had served as an assistant to Rumsfeld at the Pentagon during the Ford years, recalls being puzzled by the choice of Haynes. Adelman had been visiting at Rumsfeld's house shortly before Rumsfeld was to interview Haynes for the job.

"He always cared deeply about his general counsel," Adelman said in an interview. "But when I was at his house that time, he said, 'Hey, do you know this guy Jim Haynes?' I said, 'Yeah, he was in the Army, a lawyer.' He said, 'That's right. I'm going to see him tomorrow about being general counsel.' I asked, 'Do you know him?' He said, 'Very little but I may end up with him.' I thought, Isn't that peculiar, because here was a guy who had worked in Washington and had hung around Washington where there are thousands of lawyers you know who are competent. Why would he go with this guy who he'd spent ten minutes with? I couldn't understand that."

To manage his inner office, Rumsfeld had relied initially on his old friend Steve Herbits as well as on Steve Cambone. But with Herbits no longer involved full-time by late spring, Rumsfeld turned to a newcomer, Lawrence Di Rita, a onetime Navy officer and former chief of staff to Republican senator Kay Bailey Hutchison of Texas. Di Rita had joined the Pentagon staff early in the new administration to work on congressional relations. Boyish and engaging, Di Rita quickly developed a rapport with Rumsfeld, taking over the role of senior special assistant. (The role was really chief of staff, but much like Ford, who had avoided the use of that term when Rumsfeld worked for him in the White House, Rumsfeld now preferred simply to designate Di Rita a special assistant.)

As is common with defense secretaries, Rumsfeld also had a staff of military assistants. Customarily, the senior military aide was a three-star officer. Thinking he could make do with someone more junior, Rumsfeld at first picked a one-star officer, Rear Admiral J. J. Quinn. But it quickly became evident that a single-star admiral, even as the secretary's representative, could not be as effective as a more senior officer in a Pentagon bureaucracy exceedingly mindful of rank. So by May, Quinn was gone, replaced by Vice Admiral Ed Giambastiani.

Still, Cambone emerged early as, and remained, the most influential figure around Rumsfeld. He held several titles during Rumsfeld's time in office—in policy, program analysis, and intelligence—but essentially Rumsfeld used him as the ultimate Mr. Fix-it, having great confidence in his loyalty and a high regard for his intelligence and effectiveness.

Cambone also had a brash, smug side that could be alienating. In his first major assignment spearheading a senior-level working group for the Quadrennial Defense Review, Cambone came off as contemptuous of the uniformed military, often lecturing them or dismissing their notions as outmoded. This compounded the resentment and frustration that many felt toward the new secretary, and it was enough to worry some of Rumsfeld's longtime associates.

Staser Holcomb, for one, saw in Cambone the same arrogant streak that he recalled in the systems analysts who had served under Robert McNamara in the 1960s. Holcomb tried counseling Cambone to ease up on his penchant to criticize the services.

"Cambone exhibited a lot of the characteristics of someone who didn't understand the military culture," Holcomb said in an interview. "I would talk to Steve about that and say, 'We're trying to make this work; we're trying to get the service chiefs to talk to the secretary of defense, and if you adopt an attitude that says it's hopeless, then you're not helping the secretary.' He sort of acknowledged that."

Holcomb, joined by Herbits, urged Rumsfeld to rein Cambone in. "The secretary didn't like us telling him that, but we were persistent," Holcomb recalled. In time, Cambone did become more adept in his dealings.

Asked once in an interview about his close working relationship with Rumsfeld, Cambone was hard-pressed to explain it. Other members of Rumsfeld's inner circle, notably, Di Rita and the head of public affairs, Torie Clarke, often charmed the secretary with humor and upbeat chatter. Di Rita, too, served as a regular squash partner for the secretary, who was an avid player. Cambone didn't play squash and wasn't known for having a sunny disposition; in fact, his pessimistic tendencies had earned him the office nickname "Eeyore." But he was not easily unsettled by Rumsfeld and showed a strong no-nonsense, down-to-business determination that clearly appealed to the secretary.

"We reflected different sides of Rumsfeld," Feith observed about himself and Cambone. Feith, the strategist, liked to think of himself as Rumsfeld's big-picture half. Cambone, the technocrat, represented the administrative side. "For instance, in the event of an international crisis, my first reaction would be to try to identify what U.S. interests were involved and then think about how they could be protected," Feith explained in an interview. "Cambone's mind, by contrast, would go immediately to organizational issues like which regional commanders would take charge, what ambassadors needed to be included, and what should be done from the Pentagon."

Feith also considered himself to be Rumsfeld's conservative soul mate in a way that Cambone wasn't. But Rumsfeld paired the two in the fall of 2001, designating Cambone the principal deputy to Feith, even though each man didn't particularly care for the other. Shortly afterward, on a flight back to Washington, Rumsfeld asked Feith how he and Cambone were getting along. Relations were strained, Feith told Rumsfeld. The secretary urged him to try harder to make the relationship work.

———

Rumsfeld made a point soon after taking office of arranging for weekly private meetings with Bush. From his previous experience in government, he knew how important it was for a cabinet member to have face time with the president. And he did not have with Bush the close relationship he had enjoyed with Ford. He would have to build one while in office.

The meetings were kept small and lasted less than an hour. Bush usually had his chief of staff and national security adviser present, and Rumsfeld nearly always brought the Joint Chiefs chairman. The agendas ranged widely, and Rumsfeld put considerable time each week into figuring out how best to use the opportunity. Frequently, Rumsfeld would try to flag Bush about an issue that was months away from requiring a decision but for which he would begin to lay the groundwork. According to several aides who helped Rumsfeld prepare for the meetings, he wanted, first, to avoid surprising the president later and, second, to receive guidance that would help him decide how to position himself and the department.

"He would ask, 'What is it that the president needs to hear,'" recalled Ryan Henry, who served as deputy head of policy later in Rumsfeld's tenure. "He really tried to become a student of how the president thought, what he needed." Rumsfeld's approach reminded Henry of a key lesson in management that someone once told him: "You've got to understand your own job and your boss's job and your boss's boss's job, and what you do in life is, you give your boss things that will make him look good to his boss."

Henry said most people who go in to see their boss are interested in how to make themselves look good. "I didn't see Rumsfeld think about that at all," Henry remarked. "It was, 'What is it that the president needs?' That's what he was focused on."

Shelton, a close observer of the interaction between Rumsfeld and Bush in the first months, saw a strong bond forming. "Bush had a great deal of respect for Rumsfeld, a great deal of confidence in him," Shelton said years later. "He would defer to him quite frequently. He would ask his opinion on a number of subjects frequently in the meetings. I got the feeling very early on that the secretary was very comfortable making recommendations to the president that had not been vetted with very many people in the room at the time, which is always a dicey thing to do."

The sessions not only offered Rumsfeld a chance to talk to the president out of earshot of other NSC members but also afforded him a certain bureaucratic cachet as a result. It was no secret at the upper reaches of the Pentagon that the secretary was seeing Bush on a regular basis, enhancing the perception that Rumsfeld had clout at the White House and was elevating defense issues in the president's mind.

On the NSC staff, the private Bush/Rumsfeld link was viewed more apprehensively since it sometimes complicated efforts to gain the secretary's compliance with guidance issued by the staff in the president's name. Resistant by nature to accepting direction from lower-level officials, Rumsfeld more than once was heard by his own aides rejecting some directive sent over by NSC staff. "I don't take guidance from staff," Gebhard remembered him saying. "If the president wants me to do something, he'll tell me."

In time, when Powell learned of the Bush/Rumsfeld meetings, he requested and received the same access. Only one other cabinet official, the Treasury secretary, was granted such regular private sessions during Bush's period in office.

It hadn't taken long after the formation of the new administration for the expected clashes to start between Rumsfeld's Pentagon and Powell's State Department. A number of decisions in its early months in office signaled the Bush administration's intention to take a harder line or more unilateralist approach in international affairs. The moves often came over the arguments of State Department officials for greater emphasis on diplomacy or allied cooperation. These actions included a tougher posture toward North Korea, abandonment of the Kyoto Protocol, withdrawal of support for the World Court, and the announcement, with no allied consultation, that the United States was ready to move "beyond" the Anti-Ballistic Missile (ABM) Treaty to deploy missile defenses. The administration also declared its opposition to internationally drafted enforcement mechanisms for a biological-weapons treaty and to a ban on nuclear testing. And Rumsfeld declared an intention to pull U.S. forces out of NATO peacekeeping operations in Bosnia.

In public, Rumsfeld and Powell minimized their disagreements, despite the background leaks by subordinates telling a different story. And even in private, the interactions between them were largely cordial. They kept in frequent contact, speaking nearly every morning in an early conference call with Condoleezza Rice, Bush's national security adviser. But the two men were not close, and it became evident early on that an alliance had taken shape between Rumsfeld and Cheney and their staffs, often in opposition to Powell and the State Department.

This antipathy between the two sides went beyond specific policy disagreements into a general clash of philosophies and style. Powell, noting the prominent roles of Wolfowitz and Feith in Pentagon policy making and the presence of Perle at the head of the Defense Policy Board, regarded Rumsfeld's group of senior civilians as motivated largely by neoconservative ideology. He saw his own staff, on the other hand, as an appropriate mix of nonpartisan professionals and political appointees.

On a more personal level, Powell was bothered by Rumsfeld's behavior at times. Stories of Rumsfeld's harsh treatment of subordinates at the Pentagon filtered back to Powell through his many military contacts. And in his own dealings, Powell sometimes found Rumsfeld's cutting humor nettlesome and was frustrated by Rumsfeld's proclivity during interagency meetings to stall or obstruct when issues weren't going his way.

For their part, Rumsfeld and his senior aides tended to pride themselves on having more talent and generating more creative ideas than officials at the State Department. They often suspected Powell of pursuing an agenda more in his own interest than in the president's. And they frequently surmised that Powell and his deputy, Richard Armitage, were behind press accounts describing sharp policy divisions within the administration.

Although leaking to the media to advance a particular interest in an internal government debate was a time-honored Washington practice, Rumsfeld declared he wanted no part in such dealings. And he ordered his aides not to talk to reporters about interagency battles. In early September 2001, Rumsfeld drafted a memo for his files on the subject. "I want to talk to the senior staff about not knocking the NSC, the State Department or individuals or anyone in the Executive Branch of the federal government," he wrote. "If you've got a problem, come and see me."

Aides who later recalled the gag order portrayed it as a sign of Rumsfeld's fierce loyalty to the president. But it also served Rumsfeld's purposes in interagency battles to see Bush and declare that the Pentagon staff had nothing to do with this or that article exposing administration rifts. He could blame the State Department or NSC staff instead.

Rice had principal responsibility for refereeing the growing strain between the secretaries of defense and state. But nearly a generation younger than Rumsfeld, Powell, and Cheney and less forceful by nature, Rice had never aspired to be a domineering figure in the mold of Henry Kissinger or Zbigniew Brzezinski, President Jimmy Carter's adviser. Scowcroft had been her mentor when Rice served under George H. W. Bush as director of Soviet and Eastern European affairs on the NSC staff, and Scowcroft's low-key approach was more her style. While close to George W. Bush, she was more coordinator than director and was not one to knock heads to get something done.

At the same time, Rice was reluctant to pass along the differing views of the principals in the form of "options papers" to the president. She was more inclined to try to devise what she called a "bridging proposal" among contrasting opinions. This was supposed to mollify all the principals and relieve Bush of having to choose one department's position over another. But the approach bothered Rumsfeld, who thought the president should receive options papers.

Already by the summer of 2001, Rumsfeld was growing impatient with Rice's management. He complained about endless White House meetings called by the NSC adviser. He also griped that detailed agendas were all too often not provided for the meetings in advance, so that he could not be sure what was going to be discussed. At a small lunch in his office on June 25, Rumsfeld told the State Department's John Bolton, "We have all of these meetings which never seem to decide anything, they just get scheduled one after the other, and, my goodness, the president's never there."

As a case in point, differences remained unresolved throughout the spring and summer of 2001 over what to do about Iraq. State Department officials had pressed for a narrowing and tightening of economic sanctions, while Pentagon officials had advocated developing a strategy to aid an anti–Saddam Hussein resistance.

Frustrated in his dealings with Rice, Rumsfeld would at times simply bypass her and go directly to Andy Card, the president's chief of staff. As a former White House chief of staff himself, Rumsfeld felt a certain kinship with Card. In fact, from time to time he offered Card advice on how to do the job. "He would call me up and say, 'You know, when I was chief of staff, I would question this or that or whatever,'" Card recalled in an interview. "Sometimes he would say, 'I would never have let that happen.' And I would say, 'It's a different time,' or whatever."

For the most part, Card said, he appreciated the advice, generally viewing it as an expression of empathy on Rumsfeld's part rather than a critique. But there were occasions as well when Card felt Rumsfeld was talking down a bit to a subordinate.

In his first months, the top diplomatic priority for Rumsfeld was to put a stake through the heart of the ABM Treaty. The defense secretary was in wholehearted agreement with Bush's own pledge to move aggressively in constructing a system for protecting the United States against ballistic missile attack, and the three-decade-old treaty with the Soviet Union represented a major obstacle to the kind of flight testing the Pentagon was eager to undertake.

Bush had no intention of building a system as ambitious as Reagan's proposed Strategic Defense Initiative, which had envisioned a comprehensive umbrella of space-based weapons aimed at blocking a massive Soviet attack. Instead, he wanted to create a defense against strikes by handfuls, not hundreds, of missiles—the levels of forces that Iran or North Korea might acquire in the future.

Still, the program that Rumsfeld quickly launched in his first months was considerably more expansive than what had existed during the Clinton years. He sought to shift the focus from a single-site system to a broad-based research, development, and testing effort aimed at the deployment of layered antimissile systems. The intention was to examine a number of previously untested technologies with the potential to create defenses able to intercept missiles at various ranges and phases of flight. This kind of network of defenses—which might include sea-based and airborne systems as well as land-launched interceptor missiles—would clearly breach the constraints of the ABM Treaty.

As the administration set its sights on removing the treaty impediments, divergent camps labeled the attempt either a bold move befitting the world's sole superpower or arrogant unilateralism that would offend traditional and potential allies. With Bush's first U.S.-Russian summit meeting coming up in June 2001 in Ljubljana, Slovenia, Bush and his top advisers met to hammer out an approach. Powell argued against delivering an ultimatum at the outset and gratuitously offending Moscow. In his view, the Pentagon had not progressed far enough operationally on missile defense to require ending the treaty, so there was still time for a deal. Rumsfeld and Cheney disagreed and were eager to get out of the treaty, determined not to risk obstacles that could prevent the country from making progress on a missile-defense system.

No progress was made on missile defense at the Ljubljana meeting between Bush and Russian president Vladimir V. Putin, and during the summer top administration officials continued to debate what to do. Powell proposed either withdrawal or negotiation to modify or replace the treaty. The NSC staff developed a third option: to "set aside" the treaty and allow for testing and development. But none of the principals appeared to favor this one.

For the administration, what to do about the treaty represented part of a larger diplomatic challenge, which was how to recast the U.S. relationship with Russia in view of lessened concern about nuclear arsenals and more about threats from rogue states seeking to acquire weapons of mass destruction and ballistic missiles. Administration officials spoke of the need for "a new strategic framework." In tandem with addressing the ABM Treaty, Bush and his team wanted to reduce U.S. offensive nuclear forces, either in agreement with Russia or unilaterally.

To this end, while deliberations on what to do about the treaty were under way, Rumsfeld undertook a "nuclear posture review" to recommend a new level of offensive nuclear forces given current global circumstances. Rumsfeld also spent a considerable amount of time with Wolfowitz and Feith on the question of how U.S. officials could persuade the Russians to cooperate. One approach was to work out what Rumsfeld called "alternative futures"—contrasting visions of the worlds the Russians could choose to inhabit, defining a choice between the world of the advanced economies and the world of the rogue regimes.

The prospect of tampering with the ABM Treaty was a politically divisive issue on Capitol Hill, where treaty-preserving Democrats and treaty-busting Republicans had long been split on the issue. Appearing before Congress in June in his first public testimony since confirmation, Rumsfeld ran into sharp opposition to nullifying the treaty and tough questioning about the high cost and unproven effectiveness of the national missile-defense system.

Nonetheless, at a meeting of principals in July ahead of a gathering of the Group of Eight leaders in Genoa, Italy, Rumsfeld made clear his eagerness to get out of the treaty as soon as possible, saying its provisions were already restricting what the United States could do. He suggested that Bush at Genoa raise the issue one-on-one with Putin and in effect warn the Russians that formal notice of U.S. withdrawal from the treaty would be coming. On July 22, Bush did tell Putin that the United States was proceeding with missile-defense preparations, so an understanding needed to be reached on what would happen to the ABM Treaty. Later in the summer, Rumsfeld made the same point with Putin in Moscow. Putin, in turn, pressed for a successor treaty and a new treaty on offensive nuclear weapons.

Meanwhile, inside the Pentagon, the Office of Program Analysis and Evaluation issued unpublicized warnings that the expanded missile-defense program being devised by the new administration would prove unaffordable. "We told them basically, 'You're making the problem we already have worse,'" Soule said. "The problem we had before was too many programs and not enough money for the ones we're doing, and you're adding a lot more program than you're adding money."

But rather than cut back, Rumsfeld created a special, separate process for monitoring the missile-defense program, a process that had a less formal structure than other major defense-acquisition programs. Gone were the detailed operational requirements and specific milestones normally applied by Pentagon officials to new weapons systems under development. Gone, too, was even a stipulation that the system be built to a specific, identified threat. Instead, the department's missile-defense organization was essentially instructed to pursue a more general set of capabilities and produce a set of land-based, sea-going, and airborne antimissile systems that could be knit together into some kind of overarching, yet-to-be-defined architecture.

Rumsfeld knew the power of a good narrative. In 1976, when he had last been secretary of defense, he had put together a scary briefing on the Soviet threat to help sell a military budget increase to Congress. He had had a master storyteller—Defense Intelligence Agency analyst John Hughes—deliver it to lawmakers during invitation-only sessions held for them at the White House. Looking back, Rumsfeld considered it one of the most successful tactics he had employed—so successful, in fact, that he wanted to try something like it as secretary the second time. "I want a story, and you're a good storyteller, Haver," Rumsfeld said to Rich Haver, his special assistant for intelligence, one day in April. "You're going to give this brief."

This time Rumsfeld envisioned a briefing focused on the threats presented by terrorism, weapons proliferation, and rogue nations. He wanted it delivered, as the previous one had been, at the White House to small groups of lawmakers, Republicans and Democrats. He had a wider audience in mind, too—Pentagon officials, outside defense analysts, members of the national security establishment, maybe even some leaders of industry, academia, and the media. The idea was to educate opinion leaders on how the world had changed and to build a constituency on Capitol Hill and elsewhere for the increased spending and shifts in programs and weapons that Rumsfeld hoped would mark his transformation initiative.

He brought in Newt Gingrich to work with Haver. A former speaker of the House who had resigned from Congress in 1998, Gingrich had remained an influential voice in the powerful neoconservative wing of the Republican Party. He had known Rumsfeld for years, and after Rumsfeld became secretary, Gingrich, a prolific memo writer—rivaling even Rumsfeld in that category—would often deliver advice on a range of subjects. Of all the outside advisers that Rumsfeld would hear from, Gingrich topped the list as most frequent contributor.

Rumsfeld proposed that the threat briefing address five subjects: the proliferation of weapons of mass destruction, the delivery means for those weapons, terrorism, information warfare, and the technology revolution. Russia and China were to be assiduously avoided so as not to suggest the specter of a new cold war. Instead, the focus was set on North Korea, Iraq, Iran, Pakistan, and Latin America. Also to be highlighted were al Qaeda, the USS *Cole*, Khobar Towers, and other examples of global terrorism.

"This was supposed to be one story," Haver recalled. "It would start with the enemy, meaning the proliferators and the means of delivery, then it would move to the central concern, which was terrorism—Osama bin Laden and all, and remember, this was before 9/11—then it would deal with the idea that these people could move into cyberspace where they could do egregious damage. Finally, there would be a discussion of the technology backdrop, with all this change being projected to happen in the first twenty-five years of the twenty-first century, raising the question of what this will do to determining who's a superpower and who isn't, what it will do to our economic position, our Defense Department. We drew this up on the back deck of Newt's house. We sketched it out over a number of afternoons."

After a few months, Rumsfeld wanted a dry run of the briefing. "Don't make it too long," the secretary had advised. Gingrich shot back, "Don, length isn't your enemy, boredom is—don't get the two confused!" Rumsfeld remembered that, and during the dry run, he let Haver know when the presentation was boring him.

Rumsfeld offered more guidance. The briefing should never be the same from week to week. He wanted it to "breathe," to be constantly renewed to take account of the latest developments. He also wanted it tailored to specific audiences. The point was to create buzz in Washington. "I want congressmen and senators talking to their buddies down in the cloakroom and in the athletic center and over in the cafeteria—'Gee, did you hear that brief yesterday?'" Haver recalled Rumsfeld saying. "I want the media asking, 'Can we see this?'"

Not everyone would like the briefing, Rumsfeld figured. "He told me, 'The Army is going to hate this because this isn't about the clash of Russia's Third Shock Army and the American 82nd Airborne south of the Fulda Gap,'" Haver said. "He knew where the resistance was going to come from, and that's why he had Gingrich there, because Newt knows almost everybody in the Army."

With this briefing, Rumsfeld was looking not just for something that would sum up where the Bush administration wanted to go with transformation. This wasn't supposed to be a sales pitch in the classic sense of "Please buy this or that high-priced program." It had a grander purpose. "He was looking for the next Mr. X article," Haver said, referring to the seminal *Foreign Affairs* article written in 1947 by George F. Kennan that laid out what became the policy of containing the Soviet Union.

The first briefing was slated for September 17. Rumsfeld had reserved the Roosevelt Room at the White House and had arranged for the White House mess to handle the catering. He did not want Bush or Cheney to attend, but he did want them to pass through the room, to make cameo appearances. It was all masterful stagecraft.

The first group was to be made up of friends of the administration in Congress, lawmakers who could be counted on to give a sympathetic hearing and provide constructive feedback. Rumsfeld intended to meet with them individually over the following month to gather their views on how the briefing had gone. Already he had invitation lists in mind for the next five or six briefings.

"He had it thought all the way out through the end of 2001 and into the middle of 2002," Haver said. "He wanted to run the briefings about every two or three weeks. He had the congressional calendar in front of him so that he could stage them around the time when members would actually have time to come listen. He never wanted more than twelve people in the room because, he told me, 'I want you to have eye contact with everybody; I want everyone to feel as though you're briefing them, you're not briefing an audience, and if you have twenty people in a room, it's an audience.' He said twelve is the maximum number you could have to enable them all to think they've had a personal experience. He wanted Wolfowitz or himself there to chime in from the sidelines, to observe what we were doing. But he told me, after it gets rolling, 'I don't want to be there for everyone, this isn't the Don Rumsfeld show.'"

He was also thinking about having the briefing converted into a book, like the Pentagon-issued *Soviet Military Power* books of the 1980s describing the buildup of Soviet forces. "We put together a helluva brief," Gingrich recalled.

But it never got delivered. The September 11 attacks forced postponement of the inaugural presentation. And although Haver and Gingrich kept tinkering with the material, Rumsfeld never could decide on an appropriate time to unveil it. Besides, after September 11, the briefing seemed somewhat superfluous. Its point had been made.

———·—·———

The head of U.S. Strategic Command, Admiral Richard Mies, was the keeper of perhaps the deadliest war plan in the Pentagon's files—the SIOP, or Single Integrated Operating Plan, a benign-sounding title for the list of nuclear targets that the United States might strike in the event of war. The plan had been routinely updated every two years, so right on schedule, Mies showed up one day in Rumsfeld's office to do a review with the secretary. No sooner had Mies begun his briefing than Rumsfeld interrupted. "Why am I reviewing this plan right now?" the secretary asked, according to a participant in the meeting. "You started this during the previous administration, and nobody came back to see what had changed. I need to give you new guidance before you spend all this time working on the plan."

Rumsfeld was frustrated. Here was yet another case of planning going on in the department, very important planning, that seemed to have a momentum all its own. He'd been told in the levers briefing that the war plans, devised by the regional and functional commanders, were one of the keys to controlling change in the department. From these plans came the requirements for weapons and troops on which the military services then built their budget requests.

"He understood that war plans drove force levels, they drove capabilities and the rest of it," said Ed Giambastiani, at the time a three-star admiral who was serving as Rumsfeld's senior military assistant. "So he knew that if you didn't get those right, then you'd unnecessarily plus up some area or provide too much impetus."

Rumsfeld was bothered to discover that the assumptions had gone unexamined for years, that the war plans no longer reflected new realities. What were the assumptions inherent in those plans about whether a particular country, say, North Korea, had nuclear weapons or might be close to acquiring them? What had happened to a potential adversary's military capabilities over time? All that had to be taken into account. So did the Pentagon's move under the Bush administration toward a new defense strategy that would be putting greater emphasis on winning battles speedily and employing more agile, more capable, and perhaps smaller numbers of forces.

On one of his working Saturdays in August, Rumsfeld arranged to meet in his conference room with Shelton and the director of operational plans on the Joint Staff and all the section chiefs overseeing war plans. Up to that point, the process for assembling a war plan had been very stylized, very prescriptive. It normally began with the secretary of defense issuing guidance to a regional commander on what assumptions to make about the enemy and about U.S. objectives, although the guidance was usually something that a colonel on the Joint Staff had drafted and then passed for approval to the undersecretary for policy. After that, planners spent months detailing how the war would be fought—what troops would be necessary, how they would be equipped, and what logistical support would be needed. Intricate timetables were developed for deploying the forces in very specific order.

For the major cases—involving war against North Korea or Iraq, or defense of Taiwan, for instance—the approach was essentially the same: mobilize a large portion of the U.S. military; deploy them over many months to the region in question with lots of food, fuel, and spare parts and long supply chains; then fight to the finish. The plans had little room for partial measures. They were designed to assume conditions of either world peace or World War III.

Sitting in his large conference room with the Joint Staff officers, Rumsfeld intended to go through each plan. He wanted first to focus on just the assumptions that had gone into the planning, assumptions about such factors as the size, weaponry, and tactics of the enemy force in question. "If you get the assumptions right, a trained ape can do the rest," Rumsfeld used to assert with a laugh.

By "right assumptions," though, Rumsfeld did not mean precise predictions. "He didn't believe anyone could predict the future, no matter how much intelligence was available," Feith recounted in his memoir. "The point of his skepticism was to make sure that the planning accounted for the possibility that important things might happen that no one had predicted. Commanders should therefore plan to be surprised. That meant planning to maintain broad capabilities, flexible tactics and an open mind ready to adapt to events as they develop. He wanted his commanders to talk adaptability and agility, not predictions."

The August session, initially intended to last several hours, took much of the day as colonel after colonel presented a war plan and Rumsfeld pressed each about the assumptions, often making it clear how outdated they had become and how necessary it would be to start incorporating the new thinking of the Bush administration. "They were just briefing what was on the shelf," Rumsfeld said, recalling the experience a couple of years later.

One of the plans with which he took particular issue that day detailed a U.S. invasion of Iraq. "He almost laughed at the force structure in it," Shelton recalled. "It was for four hundred thousand troops or more, and he said, 'You know, that's nothing more than what was left over from Desert Storm,'" referring to the 1991 Persian Gulf War. "He said, 'You guys need to go back and take another look. We can do this a lot faster and with less force.' I think his mind-set was, Iraq had a broken, tired army with very little capability left, and we needed to have our urine tested if we thought we were going to need as many forces as before to take out Saddam Hussein."

The long day of briefings confirmed for Rumsfeld his worry that the war plans were woefully outdated. In fact, the entire process for keeping them current needed to be changed, he concluded. Regarding the previous two-year cycle for revising and reviewing plans as much too long, he was determined to compress the time dramatically, wanting it cut to months, even weeks.

In late August 2001, Bush announced that Air Force general Richard Myers would step up from vice chairman of the Joint Chiefs of Staff and replace Shelton, whose four-year stint as chairman was expiring at the end of September. It seemed a logical choice, widely interpreted as a further sign of Rumsfeld's fondness for airpower. Myers was the first non-Army general in more than a decade to hold the military's top job and was the first Air Force general to have it in almost two decades. Myers more than Shelton had appeared to embrace the transformation slogan, and his earlier post as head of U.S. Space Command only reinforced the expectation that the Bush administration would pursue an expanded U.S. military role in space. Myers had also served in Asia and the Pacific—as a commander of U.S. forces in Japan and Hawaii—a fact that was taken as an indication of Rumsfeld's own view that China would be the next great military threat.

But what may have mattered most for Rumsfeld in picking Myers was the secretary's comfort level with the general. Low-key, down-to-earth, and self-effacing in spite of his size—he stood six feet, four inches tall—Myers was not the type likely to provide a powerful counterweight to the sometimes overbearing defense secretary. Though considered a straight shooter, Myers also had a reputation for being unfailingly loyal, so any differences he might have with Rumsfeld's leadership could be expected to stay behind closed doors. He was the kind of troubleshooter who could be counted on to avoid self-promotion and the limelight. "He's not a pound-on-the-table guy," General Michael Ryan, the Air Force chief of staff at the time, told a reporter. "He works these issues with his intellect, not necessarily his brawn, even though he is a big guy."

Shelton liked Myers, but his personal pick had been Admiral Vern Clark, who could be very outspoken and animated. Rumsfeld had also looked hard at Clark, who in fact had been a finalist for the job along with Myers. The admiral, though, was somewhat ambivalent about taking the position. While he would eventually learn how to get along with

Rumsfeld, becoming one of the secretary's favorite chiefs, he felt no particular rapport with him at the time. Nor did he think the secretary trusted him or the other chiefs.

"My position was, I would do this if they wanted me to do it, but it wasn't something that I wanted," he recalled years later. Still, at Rumsfeld's urging, Clark had interviewed with Bush and Cheney, then was invited back for another round. He told the president of his ambivalence.

When Clark met with Rumsfeld again, he bluntly expressed his concern that the two of them hadn't developed the kind of relationship he thought was important between a secretary and chairman—the kind that had existed, for instance, between Cheney and Powell. He felt unsure of just what Rumsfeld believed, given all the studies on transformation that had been generated, some of which Clark found silly. He was critical of Rumsfeld as well for taking a negative view of the Joint Staff.

After the meeting, Clark stopped in Shelton's office and recounted the conversation. "Well, I'm not going to be the chairman," the admiral told Shelton, adding that it was evident from the look in the secretary's eyes.

Clark's willingness to be so frank, even at the risk of forfeiting the top military job in the department, didn't surprise Shelton. Clark's forthrightness was the main reason that Shelton favored him as his successor; Clark would tell Rumsfeld what he thought. It was no surprise to Shelton when Rumsfeld settled on Myers. "I knew that Rumsfeld would view Dick as a more pliable, moldable personality than he would Vern Clark," Shelton said later.

To replace Myers as vice chairman, Rumsfeld chose another consummate team player, Marine general Peter Pace. The appointment marked the first time a Marine had attained the post of vice chairman.

————•————

Rumsfeld's interest in the selection of military leaders extended well beyond the choice of chairman. In late spring, he had put the services on notice that he intended to become personally involved in the promotion of all three- and four-star officers. While the secretary had always been the one to sign off on such appointments in the past, the actual decisions had tended in most cases to rest with the service chiefs.

But Rumsfeld was never one to accept rubber-stamp status. If he was going to be approving promotions, then he wanted to be sure he knew the people he was approving. He also understood, again recalling the levers briefing, that the senior military officers he chose would be key to effecting change in the department.

The task of informing the chiefs and service secretaries of the new selection procedures fell to Staser Holcomb, the retired three-star admiral who had served as Rumsfeld's military assistant during the Ford years. Rumsfeld had put Holcomb in charge of regularly culling through the candidates recommended by the services. From now on, Rumsfeld wanted at least two candidates for each job and intended to do his own extensive interviewing.

All the services resented the move to some extent, since the assignment of general officers constituted one of the most important powers of a service secretary and his chief. The loudest objection came from Shinseki. It was one thing for Rumsfeld to play a prominent role in deciding who would head the regional commands or occupy senior Joint Staff positions, Shinseki argued. It was another for him to take a greater say in other positions that were not joint and that Shinseki saw as internal to the Army.

"He just didn't see why that was any of the secretary's business," Holcomb said. "I'd say, 'Come on, Rick, in our system, you can't stick the secretary of defense. If he wants to be involved, he will be involved.'"

A main worry in military ranks was that Rumsfeld's increased involvement in the selection process risked making military officers more sensitive to the views of outsiders who could influence the secretary's judgment, particularly the secretary's personal advisers or the civilian political appointees on his staff. The services believed they already had an effective system for assessing officers moving up through the ranks. By the time someone was ready to be considered for a top job, an extensive record existed. For someone on the outside to step in and begin recommending other candidates seemed to open the system to questionable influence.

An additional concern among Army officers in particular was how Rumsfeld's perceived bias against their service might play in the selection process. Word quickly emerged of Army candidates receiving what seemed especially tough grilling by the secretary in interviews. "We had to prepare people for the way Rumsfeld liked to humiliate them when he interviewed," recalled Montgomery Meigs, a retired four-star Army general. Once, after confronting Rumsfeld over the treatment of Army candidates, Shinseki returned to a group of fellow four-star officers and told them that the secretary had thrown him out of the office for objecting so strongly. Over time, Army officers noted that fewer regional-command and high-level Joint Staff jobs were going to their service.

————•————

In a speech to Defense Department employees on September 10, 2001, Rumsfeld declared that the main threat to a more efficient and innovative defense structure was not outside the Pentagon but inside. "The topic today is an adversary that poses a threat, a serious threat, to the security of the United States of America," Rumsfeld began. "From a single capital, it attempts to impose its demands across time zones, continents, oceans and beyond. With brutal inconsistency, it stifles free thought and crushes new ideas. It disrupts the defense of the United States and places the lives of men and women in uniform at risk. . . . You may think I'm describing one of the last decrepit dictators of the world. But their day, too, is almost past, and they cannot match the strength and size of this adversary. The adversary's closer to home. It's the Pentagon bureaucracy."

The speech, titled "Bureaucracy to Battlefield," was billed as the kickoff to the department's Acquisition and Logistics Excellence Week. But it was really Rumsfeld's declaration of war on the department, and it revealed his level of frustration after trying to grapple with all the inefficiencies he had cataloged since his arrival. He complained of innovation being stifled "not by ill intent but by institutional inertia." The challenge, he asserted, was "to transform not just the way we deter and defend, but the way we conduct our daily business." Wasteful spending and redundant tasking were robbing the military of money and personnel that could be better applied to the battlefield, Rumsfeld went on. "I have no desire to attack the Pentagon," he said. "I want to liberate it. We need to save it from itself."

Echoing his anchor chain memo, he listed a string of deadweights on the department: "Our financial systems are decades old. According to some estimates, we cannot track $2.3 trillion in transactions. We cannot share information from floor to floor in this building because it's stored on dozens of technological systems that are inaccessible or incompatible. We maintain 20 to 25 percent more base infrastructure than we need to support our forces, at an annual waste to taxpayers of some $3 billion to $4 billion. Fully half of our resources go to infrastructure and overhead, and in addition to draining resources from warfighting, these costly and outdated systems, procedures and programs stifle innovation as well. A new idea must often survive the gauntlet of some 17 levels of bureaucracy to make it from a line officer's to my desk."

To his previous calls for new weapons and forces to counter new threats, Rumsfeld added another transformation goal: a revolution in Pentagon management and business practices. At the same time, he recognized that the forces of the business world that separate the strong from the weak don't apply in government. "Business enterprises die if they fail to adapt, and the fact that they can fail and die is what provides the incentive to survive," he said. "But governments can't die, so we need to find other incentives for bureaucracy to adapt and improve."

The rest of his lengthy remarks that day contained a blueprint of initiatives for revamping Pentagon business practices—"to shift our focus and our resources from bureaucracy to battlefield," as Rumsfeld put it. They included closing some bases, eliminating some advisory boards, revising acquisition processes, modernizing financial systems, cutting headquarter staffs, reducing duplication of effort among the services, and overhauling the department's forty-year-old system for planning, programming, and budgeting, to name a few.

Rumsfeld intended to vest responsibility for leading this business revolution with a newly created group to be called the Senior Executive Council, consisting of the service secretaries and the undersecretary for acquisition. The group, he said, would "scour the department for functions that could be performed better and more cheaply through commercial outsourcing." It would launch a review of the Pentagon agencies responsible for logistics, information services, and accounting systems. It would ask and, he hoped, answer such tough questions as, Why is the Defense Department one of the last organizations around that still cuts its own checks? When an entire industry exists to run warehouses efficiently, why does the Pentagon own and operate many of its own? At bases around the world, why does the military pick up its own garbage and mop its own floors rather than contracting services out, as many businesses do?

"The battle against a stifling bureaucracy is also a personal priority for me and for the service secretaries, one that will, through the Senior Executive Council, receive the sustained attention at the highest levels of this department," Rumsfeld pledged.

The idea for the council had been the brainchild of Steve Herbits, who was himself a student of organizational decision making. Rumsfeld had entrusted Herbits with much of the initial search for candidates to fill the service secretary posts and other key positions. The resulting cast consisted of Navy secretary Gordon England, a former executive vice president of General Dynamics Corporation; Air Force secretary James Roche, a former executive with Northrop Grumman Corporation; and Army secretary Thomas White, a former senior executive at Enron Corporation.

In the interest of fostering a sense of teamwork among the three nominees, the men were briefed together for their confirmation hearings, and the staffing for each was provided by a service other than the one each was to lead. The aim was to counter the traditional parochialism that tended to capture the secretaries as they went to work representing their services. Rumsfeld even went so far as to hire a business executive—Ken Krieg, a vice president at the International Paper Company—to serve as executive secretary for the group.

"He was looking for a council of seniors," Krieg recalled. "The plan was to take the senior-most appointees and give them a forum where they could lean on each other to talk about the forces of change, as opposed to letting the natural centrifugal forces of the department pull them apart."

But the council never really got off the ground. Pressing demands from other events, particularly after the September 11 attacks, Wolfowitz's own disinterest in business management, and Rumsfeld's own reluctance to use the group doomed it. During the Quadrennial Defense Review process, Rumsfeld became accustomed to doing business through the SLRG, which included not only the service secretaries but the military chiefs, and he stuck with that forum. "He never showed up to a single meeting" of the Senior Executive Council, Roche said several years later.

"I think there are a thousand and one reasons, and I'm not even sure I understand them all," Krieg said, reflecting on the council's failure to gel. "There probably was not a common set of expectations. There was a lack of time as the secretaries got engaged in the press of events. And the centrifugal force of the place captured them all."

CHAPTER 9

A Defining Moment

Uncertainty in the modern world was on Rumsfeld's mind as he convened an 8 a.m. breakfast with lawmakers in his Pentagon office on September 11, 2001. Rumsfeld had touted the theme for months, making his case for transformation, arguing the need to anticipate surprise attacks, prepare better against unconventional threats, and develop more flexible, agile military responses. His Quadrennial Defense Review had addressed this, and with the review's results due for public release soon, Rumsfeld found himself in a spirited discussion with the lawmakers over what was knowable, what was not, and what implications such unpredictability had for the U.S. military.

Even as the meeting wore on that morning, al Qaeda terrorists were in the process of delivering a devastating lesson in surprise attack and U.S. vulnerability. Intelligence officials had urgently warned over the summer of a possible terrorist strike, although the warnings had lacked specificity about place and time. NSC officials had issued instructions to update Pentagon contingency plans, but the attention of Rumsfeld and his top aides had been focused elsewhere. Their priorities were about to be dramatically reordered by a series of devastating attacks that would bring home the threat of terrorism and overshadow the rest of Rumsfeld's time in office.

As breakfast was ending, Rumsfeld received word that a plane had struck one of the World Trade Center towers in New York. Within minutes, another plane slammed into the second tower, leaving little question that the United States was under attack. While several of Rumsfeld's aides moved immediately to a command center on the building's third floor used to coordinate military operations during national emergencies, the secretary remained in his office for a daily intelligence briefing due to start at 9:30 a.m.

At 9:37 a.m., Rumsfeld felt the Pentagon shudder. Darting to a window, he tried to figure out what had happened. He ran to an aide's office next door, asked if anyone knew anything, then took off down the hall after being told by one of his security detail that an aircraft had hit the building.

Accompanied by several security officers and a communications aide, Rumsfeld went partway around the Pentagon to the Mall entrance side, where he'd been advised the crash had occurred, then learned it was farther away on the heliport side. Heading in that direction and dropping down two flights of stairs into darkened hallways and clouds of smoke, he bounded through an open door into daylight and massive carnage.

American Airlines flight 77 had rammed into the Pentagon's west side, leaving a blackened horror of debris, burning rubble, an overwhelming smell of jet fuel, and hordes of frightened defense employees, some badly injured, streaming out of the building. Looking for some way to assist, Rumsfeld helped an injured person onto a gurney. When an emergency worker advised him of the need for more equipment and medical supplies, Rumsfeld directed him to his communications aide.

The secretary remained at the site only minutes before reentering the Pentagon. He stopped briefly in his office to talk by phone with Bush, who was out of town when the attacks occurred, then moved to the Executive Support Center, where officials had gathered to manage military actions. According to the 9/11 Commission Report, Rumsfeld joined a conference call shortly before 10:30. About fifty minutes had elapsed since the plane had struck the Pentagon.

In the time that Rumsfeld had taken to go outside, he was out of the national command loop, out of touch with other high-level government officials who were trying frantically to figure out the nation's response, ordering military jets into the air and attempting to make sense of the unfolding crisis. He played no part in the urgent initial efforts to determine whether any additional air threats remained or in the decision to authorize military pilots to shoot down any menacing aircraft that refused to divert.

Critics later considered his impulsive move to the crash site as a desertion of his post and abandonment of command responsibilities. But for many others, Rumsfeld's instinctive response was a gutsy move that showed a basic humanity, and his involvement, however brief, in the rescue effort was a selfless act that won him a measure of appreciation and respect.

His spokesperson, Torie Clarke, recalled him entering the command center with his suit jacket over his shoulder, his face and clothes smeared with ashes, dirt, and sweat. As Clarke recounted the scene, Rumsfeld "was quiet, deadly serious, completely cool." By then, the Air Force was in the process of establishing a combat air patrol over Washington. In a phone call, Cheney advised Rumsfeld that the shoot-down order had been issued. Concerned about whether the pilots had a clear understanding of their rules of engagement, Rumsfeld asked who had received the order. Cheney said he had passed it through the operations center and confirmed that the directive had been transmitted to two fighter aircraft then patrolling over Washington.

Because the Executive Support Center was cramped, with a limited number of phones, desks, and screens, Rumsfeld moved to the nearby National Military Command Center, the main watch area. Taking a seat at the head of a conference table, he began organizing his thoughts, as he often did, by writing them down. Pulling out a yellow legal pad and proceeding methodically, he divided items into categories—what was known, what people were trying to find out, what needed to be done immediately, what options existed for a military response.

At the top of his list was the immediate need to raise the state of alert of the entire U.S. military. Five alert levels exist, the highest being Defense Condition (DefCon) 1, reserved for all-out war. Rumsfeld opted for DefCon 3, which had not been declared since the 1973 Arab-Israeli war. Cheney asked him to hold off until Bush, who was airborne at the time, could be consulted. But Rumsfeld, having checked Pentagon directives, concluded he had the authority to issue the order and did so. He advised Bush of the decision about half an hour later, at 11:15 a.m., and informed the president that the department was working on refining the rules of engagement so pilots would have a better understanding of the circumstances under which an aircraft could be shot down.

Uncomfortable with how broad the rules were, Rumsfeld kept returning to them throughout the day in conversations with other senior national security officials. He worried about the enormous responsibility being placed on someone's shoulders in making a shoot-down decision and tried to firm up the rules. The department did not circulate a set of written instructions until sometime in the afternoon.

Quarters in the command center at the Pentagon were crowded. The area—a rabbit warren of cubicles surrounding the main conference room—was packed with senior military and civilian leaders and at least a dozen communications technicians. With the air-conditioning off, the room was stuffy. Exhaust fans were not working, so smoke from the crash area was permeating the building. Rumsfeld and his team moved back to the Executive Support Center in search of better air.

General Hugh Shelton, the chairman of the Joint Chiefs, had been en route to Europe when the attacks occurred. While his plane headed back to Washington, Dick Myers, still vice chairman, was the senior uniformed military officer in the room and stayed close to the secretary throughout much of the day.

At about 12:45 p.m., Myers reported that a Korean Airlines flight was inbound from Asia squawking the hijack code, a covert signal to air traffic controllers that the plane had been commandeered. It turned out to be a false alarm—the flight was headed to Anchorage, Alaska, to refuel. "I want to tie up the rules of engagement," Rumsfeld said, asking again about the orders for pilots who might have to shoot down hijacked planes. "This is not simple for a pilot, especially if he knows he's shooting down a plane over a civilian area like Washington."

Looking past the demands of the moment, Rumsfeld began thinking about the kind of military response that the United States might mount in response to the attacks on the World Trade Center towers and the Pentagon.

"We're going to need to think big," he told Myers.

"You bet," Myers replied.

In considering various responses, Rumsfeld as early as that first day entertained the possibility of Saddam Hussein's involvement in the 9/11 attacks. According to contemporaneous notes taken by Steve Cambone, the secretary told Myers in the afternoon that he was not interested simply in striking empty training sites belonging to the al Qaeda terrorist network, which had already been identified as probably behind the attacks. He thought the U.S. response should consider a wide range of options and possibilities. His instinct, he advised Myers, was to hit Iraq and al Qaeda simultaneously. Rumsfeld later explained in an interview with the 9/11 Commission that at the time, he had been considering either of the two, or perhaps a third, as the responsible party.

With Bush due to return to Washington and a meeting of the president's top national security advisers expected later in the day, Rumsfeld wanted to be clear on what advice to offer. He focused on working the problem. "This is the defining moment," he told his top aides, asking for thoughts from everyone.

Whenever Rumsfeld confronted a large new challenge, he would begin by identifying the major thoughts—the strategic ideas—that should govern the approach to it. A discussion of goals had to precede talk of tactics. The question of how to think about something needed to come before the question of how to do it.

One aspect was already set in Rumsfeld's mind: The United States would not be playing just defense in combating future terrorism. Giambastiani recalled Rumsfeld insisting on the need to think offensively, to devise strategies that would keep terrorist networks under constant pressure. It was just not possible to defend everywhere, Rumsfeld argued. The attacker always had the advantage, so the fight had to be taken to the enemy. "We were talking about that from minute one," Giambastiani recounted. After several hours of animated discussion, Rumsfeld had his talking points summarized on a single sheet of paper to take that night to a meeting of the National Security Council at the White House.

Later in the afternoon, Rumsfeld returned to the crash site and walked around it, accompanied by the leaders of the Senate Armed Services Committee, Democrat Carl Levin of Michigan and Republican John Warner of Virginia. Countless pieces of wreckage, much of it

unidentifiable, were everywhere. But, oddly, a few items survived unscathed. "A desk sat alone in an office whose walls had been sheared off,"
Torie Clarke recalled. "A clock hung above what had been a door jamb,
the door blown away." Over on the grass away from the damaged building, uniformed personnel stood quietly over bodies covered in white
sheets. All 64 people on the hijacked jet and 125 people who had been
in the Pentagon—70 civilians and 55 military service members—died in
the crash. Another 106 people were seriously injured.

Despite the devastating impact of the attack on Defense Department
employees and the crippled condition of the Pentagon itself, Rumsfeld
was determined the building remain up and running. There would be no
ground given to the enemy. To underscore that fact, he held a news conference that evening. "The Pentagon's functioning," Rumsfeld declared.
"It will be in business tomorrow." A few days later, Barbara Starr, a CNN
correspondent, ran into Rumsfeld on a stairway. It was early morning,
and the Pentagon was still largely quiet. Rumsfeld spoke briefly about the
attack. "The fire went through here so fast," he said. "Those people—they
had no chance." His eyes watered as he spoke.

———•———

In the months before the September 11 attacks, Rumsfeld had talked a lot
about terrorism. In congressional testimony, news conferences, and other
forums, he had regularly cited it as one of the new threats that the Defense
Department wasn't adequately organized or prepared to deal with.

And yet he hadn't made counterterrorism operations a priority, even
in the face of warnings by top CIA officials that al Qaeda might be about
to launch a damaging attack. Just how persuasive a case the U.S. intelligence community had assembled remains subject to dispute. Clearly, the
level of reporting on terrorist threats and possible attacks increased dramatically in the spring of 2001 and surged further over the summer. But
while the reports warned of imminent attacks of catastrophic proportions, they struck Rumsfeld and senior aides as vague and focused on targets abroad—specifically, in the Middle East and Europe—rather than in
the United States. Some senior Pentagon officials questioned whether al
Qaeda's actions could be an elaborate ruse or deception to test U.S. responses, a speculation that CIA director George Tenet firmly rejected.

Acting on the warnings, the U.S. military raised the force protection for troops in six countries in the Middle East to the highest level, Delta. The U.S. Fifth Fleet moved out of its port in Bahrain, and a U.S. Marine exercise in Jordan was halted. Beyond that, though, Pentagon authorities were uncertain about what more to do. "It was not a case of not thinking there was a problem out there," said Cambone, recalling discussions at the time with Tenet and other senior intelligence officials. "It was a case of not being able to identify it in a way that would have given you some sense of what we ought to go do."

Nonetheless, the 9/11 Commission concluded that few in the administration had considered terrorism an urgent threat before September 11. In his first months in office, Rumsfeld had been consumed by other issues— getting new officials in place, completing the Quadrennial Defense Review, revising war plans. In an interview with the 9/11 Commission several years later, Rumsfeld could not recall any particular counterterrorism matter that had engaged his attention before 9/11, other than the possible arming of an unmanned Predator aircraft to strike al Qaeda targets.

Discussions about converting the Predator from a spy drone into an attack aircraft that could go after Osama bin Laden had been the focus of some interagency meetings in August 2001. Other covert action options were also reviewed at that time to pressure Afghanistan's Taliban government to cut off support for al Qaeda. But the talks lacked urgency. Moreover, the idea of a Predator attack on bin Laden raised a slew of questions, some major (What are the legal authorities? What rules of engagement should apply? Should the finger on the trigger be military or CIA?) and some minor (Which agency should pay for the operation?). These would take time to work out.

Despite his interest in revamping major war plans, Rumsfeld hadn't examined the limited options drawn up by the Pentagon in the late 1990s to strike targets associated with al Qaeda. The Clinton administration effectively relied on the CIA to take the lead in preparing long-term offensive plans against an enemy sanctuary, and the Bush administration had essentially adopted this approach.

As part of an emerging new counterterrorism strategy, NSC officials had envisioned some further military role in addressing the problem and thought they had put the Pentagon on notice over the summer to produce new military plans. They had circulated a draft presidential directive in

June 2001 that contained a section directing Rumsfeld to "develop contingency plans" to attack both al Qaeda and Taliban targets in Afghanistan. But the military didn't particularly want this mission, given the big challenge and small-bore focus involved, and with the directive still awaiting Bush's signature, Rumsfeld had not ordered preparation of any new military plans against al Qaeda or the Taliban before the September 11 attacks.

So when Bush and his national security team convened on the evening of September 11, Rumsfeld's focus was on going after not al Qaeda but the countries that provided support for the network, countries such as Iraq, Afghanistan, Libya, Sudan, and Iran. During the NSC meeting, he urged the president to think broadly about which nations might have harbored the attackers. He wondered aloud how much evidence the United States would need in order to take action against these countries. He questioned how soon to act, cautioning that because the military had no plan or forces in Afghanistan, major strikes there could take up to sixty days to organize.

He wasn't advocating action at that point, just raising questions, trying to direct the discussion and frame the issues without taking a position himself. It was a practiced technique of his, ideal for playing for time, which he needed since his department lacked a plan to go after al Qaeda or even much of any program for going after terrorists.

In the days that followed, Rumsfeld continued to warn in NSC meetings and internal Pentagon discussions against limiting the U.S. response to actions against al Qaeda and the Taliban in Afghanistan. He worried about getting too focused on a single threat and urged a broad view of the enemy. To him, the problem was not just al Qaeda but other countries that supported terrorism.

He feared that pressure on Bush to take some kind of retaliatory action would prompt an ineffective strike. Afghanistan, as a haven for al Qaeda training camps, was a logical target, but he fretted that Afghanistan's spare infrastructure offered very little for U.S. forces to do. Again and again he advocated planning for going after multiple terrorist targets around the world and not just aiming at al Qaeda.

The possibility of hitting Iraq, which he had mentioned to Cambone in the first hours after the September 11 attacks, remained very much on Rumsfeld's mind. His deputy, Paul Wolfowitz, strongly favored making

Iraq a principal target in the first round of what administration officials were starting to conceive of as a "war on terrorism." Wolfowitz had long been an advocate of destroying Saddam Hussein and his regime, believing that the Iraqi leader posed a great menace to U.S. security. And while no evidence had surfaced firmly tying Iraq to the September 11 attacks, he figured chances were good that Saddam's agents had played some role.

But Colin Powell, for his part, opposed striking Iraq. He and his State Department team argued that the U.S. response to 9/11 should focus on Afghanistan and al Qaeda. A narrowly scoped campaign of punishment against the perpetrators of 9/11 would, in their view, be more acceptable to allies and friends abroad. They were eager to incorporate as many other countries as possible into whatever military operations were undertaken.

Rumsfeld favored organizing a coalition as well, but not at the expense of an effective response. Building a coalition shouldn't be an end in itself, he maintained. Allied participation often came with political conditions, and he didn't want conditions that would limit Bush's freedom of action to protect the United States. Besides, for Rumsfeld, as for Wolfowitz and Feith, the principal aim of military action should not simply be retributive. They wanted action that would affect terrorist networks as extensively as possible and, of greatest concern, prevent a biological, chemical, or nuclear attack.

Nonetheless, Bush was focused on the Taliban and al Qaeda and pressed Rumsfeld from September 11 onward for what the military could do immediately in response to al Qaeda's attacks. The military options were disappointing. The Pentagon did not have an off-the-shelf plan for Afghanistan, the sanctuary of bin Laden and his network.

But the CIA did. The agency's paramilitary teams had been in contact for several years with leaders of Afghan militia groups loosely united against the Taliban under the Northern Alliance. The CIA plan, which was quickly conceived, called for inserting teams inside Afghanistan with each opposition warlord while military Special Operations units infiltrated the country to direct a bombing effort. By making arrangements with the Afghan militia commanders, the CIA operatives could smooth the way for the U.S. military teams to embed with the local militias. The combination of special agency and military groups providing support on the ground as U.S. aircraft strike from overhead could give the Northern

Alliance, as well as other tribes in the southern part of the country, the necessary edge to defeat the Taliban.

The contrast between the extent of Pentagon and CIA readiness became clear at a meeting of Bush's war council at the Camp David presidential retreat over the weekend of September 15–16. There, the set of limited military options presented by Shelton, including cruise-missile strikes against al Qaeda training camps and some manned bomber attacks, seemed unimaginative and hardly promising, particularly when compared to the bold CIA plan for inserting agency teams and Special Operations groups. The air attacks outlined by the Pentagon were the kind of limited actions that the Clinton administration had launched in 1998 on the al Qaeda camps in Afghanistan, with little effect. While another option would be for the U.S. military to couple an air assault with a ground assault, any substantial deployment of U.S. troops would take months and require hard-to-get access through neighboring countries.

A Defense Department paper prepared for the Camp David briefing book had again raised the prospect of hitting Iraq. Outlining a strategic concept for the war on terrorism, the paper proposed that "the immediate priority targets for initial action" should be al Qaeda, the Taliban, and Iraq. It argued that of the three, al Qaeda and Iraq posed a strategic threat to the United States. Iraq's long-standing involvement in terrorism was cited, along with its interest in weapons of mass destruction.

Although uniformed U.S. military leaders were far from eager about action against Iraq, combat operations there did at least appear to be a much more straightforward proposition, offering lots of targets that could be hit with precision weapons, while Afghanistan had little infrastructure and few high-value targets. Iraq, a state known to support terrorism, provided an opportunity to wage the type of war that the U.S. military was comfortable waging. It also would afford the Pentagon a chance to spearhead a complementary effort to what was shaping up as an unconventional war in Afghanistan led by the CIA.

Wolfowitz, with Rumsfeld's encouragement, took the lead at the Camp David sessions in arguing for action against Iraq. Rumsfeld, according to Wolfowitz, also favored the idea, but he may have left it to his deputy to present the case because Wolfowitz was exceptionally emotional about it. "Paul had a passion for a lot of what he was advocating," observed John McLaughlin, who was deputy CIA director at the time. "I never saw Don display the kind of passion that I saw with Paul."

Still, there was little support among the president's other top advisers for attacking Iraq at the same time as Afghanistan, particularly in the absence of evidence linking the Iraqis to the September 11 attacks. Powell pointedly warned that going beyond Afghanistan would upset Arab states and hamper efforts under way to build an international coalition against al Qaeda.

Rumsfeld countered that a coalition unwilling to take on Iraq wasn't a coalition worth having. But even he never offered a formal recommendation at the Camp David meeting to go after Iraq—no doubt mindful that Shelton, as well, opposed such military action. Bush, eager to get a read on the group, had asked each to express an opinion on the afternoon of September 14. Powell went first, backing the CIA plan and urging that the focus remain initially on al Qaeda. Cheney, Tenet, and Card also spoke up opposing action on Iraq. Rumsfeld skirted the matter, talking mostly instead about girding for what would likely be a long struggle against terrorism.

Bush ended up shelving the Iraq option for the time being and, concentrating on Afghanistan, decided to go with the novel CIA plan. He ordered preparations for it should the Taliban reject an ultimatum to end al Qaeda's presence in Afghanistan.

———•———

Although Bush rebuffed the initial urgings from Rumsfeld and Wolfowitz, the Pentagon proceeded to draft a plan to seize Iraq's southern oil fields. The order for the plan, sent just before the Camp David meeting, went to Lieutenant General Paul Mikolashek, head of the Third Army, an Atlanta-based headquarters that served as the major command for land warfare in the Middle East.

The plan was conceived less as an invasion operation than as a preemptive strike should there be any indication that Iraq was considering an attack on Kuwait or Saudi Arabia. It called for several brigades plus artillery, Patriot antimissile batteries, and support units—a force totaling seventy-five thousand to a hundred thousand troops and requiring a month or two to deploy. Although it turned out to be little more than a contingency plan, it energized Third Army headquarters and the Army's V Corps, which would later carry out the main attack on Iraq.

Rumsfeld, meanwhile, kept pressing to enlarge the aperture through which Bush and other senior advisers viewed possible military action. In a message to regional commanders on September 19, he requested worldwide targets for the budding counterterrorism campaign to indicate early on that the field of action should be considered much wider than Afghanistan.

In another memo drafted that day, Rumsfeld put down some thoughts about fighting terrorism. He anticipated that the campaign would be "a marathon, not a sprint" and that terrorist networks could not be dealt with simply by using bombers or cruise missiles. He wrote about the role that foreign partners might play, predicting (with what turned out to be considerable accuracy) that the interests of the United States and its allies would not always mesh on all aspects of the war. "The coalitions that are being fashioned will not be fixed; rather, they will change and evolve," he wrote. Moreover, he added, America's "relationships and alliances will likely be rearranged over the coming years" as a result of the impact of U.S. activities.

Reinforcing Rumsfeld's worries about focusing on Afghanistan was a disappointing briefing he received from Army general Tommy Franks, the head of U.S. Central Command (CENTCOM), on September 30. Rumsfeld recognized that Franks was handicapped by a dearth of intelligence about legitimate enemy targets in the country. But the defense secretary wanted a broader plan than the one Franks outlined—a plan that would better address the larger task of dealing with international terrorism.

The more Rumsfeld thought about it, the more arguments he mustered for why any military action prompted by the September 11 attacks should go beyond striking the perpetrators. He worried that the targets were too meager in Afghanistan, and the intelligence there too inadequate. The goal should be aimed at preventing further terrorist attacks. To that end, Rumsfeld wanted to show that the war was global and find ways of disrupting terrorist operations and generating pressure on terrorism's state supporters.

Rumsfeld was also concerned that singling out bin Laden would elevate the terrorist leader and potentially narrow the base of support for the antiterrorist campaign, robbing the United States of its ability to frame a larger war. Rumsfeld argued that the objective had to be stated correctly. It would not be effective to succeed in removing or killing bin Laden or Taliban leader Mohammad Omar without trying to address more comprehensively the basic problem of terrorism.

Some of Rumsfeld's concerns were outlined in a September 20 draft of a memo intended for Bush and composed by Feith in consultation with Rumsfeld. "If the initial U.S. military action is not confidence-inspiring, it could undermine our entire effort," the memo warned. U.S. strikes should be designed to produce "impressive results." Expressing doubts about the quality of available information and analysis for Afghanistan, the memo suggested targeting al Qaeda forces and assets "in more than one country, including some outside the Middle East." It also advised hitting "at least one non–al Qaeda target." Iraq was mentioned as an example.

"The president has stressed that we are not defining our fight narrowly and are not focused only on those directly responsible for the September 11 attacks," the memo said. "It would drive this point home if the initial military strikes hit [targets] in addition to al Qaeda. That is one of the reasons why I still favor an early focus on Iraq as well."

Rumsfeld also presented his arguments for a broader war in several NSC meetings. A couple of times in late September, he even raised the idea of deferring military strikes in Afghanistan until better intelligence was available. His notion was that U.S. troops could take time to build up outside of Afghanistan while efforts were made to engage opposition forces there initially with train-and-equip activities, humanitarian aid, and intense information operations.

Some of the president's other senior national security advisers regarded Rumsfeld's repeated advocacy of wider military action as a reflection of his desire to see U.S. troops in the lead someplace rather than playing a supporting role to the CIA in Afghanistan. But accounts of internal Pentagon discussions and memos written at the time suggest that Rumsfeld was motivated by an aggressive view of how to proceed. He and his top aides saw in the events of September 11 an opportunity to create a new perspective about the challenges from terrorist extremists—the geographic scope of terrorism, the definition of enemy networks, the significance of state supporters of terrorism, and the special dangers of weapons of mass destruction. While Powell and Armitage continued to argue for keeping the focus narrow, stressing the importance of respecting the views of allies and friends abroad, defense officials encouraged Bush to act to shape those views.

In the end, Bush preferred to take the narrower approach. He did not favor starting with U.S. strikes outside Afghanistan or deferring U.S. military strikes to build up troops in the Middle East. He wanted the world to see that the United States was taking military action against those responsible for 9/11. He remained focused on Afghanistan, figuring the chances of success would be greater if the degree of difficulty were limited.

———————

For all Rumsfeld's emphasis on the worldwide nature of the conflict and his interest in conducting a broader campaign, he was having trouble coming up with practical options beyond the Taliban, al Qaeda, and Afghanistan. The initial proposals from regional commanders for other possible action were disappointing. So was Rumsfeld's first effort to employ Special Operations forces, the military's most-skilled, best-equipped fighters.

Responsibility for Special Operations forces fell to a command at MacDill Air Force Base in Tampa, Florida, that belied the hard-charging image such forces like to project. Known for its easy, rather happy-go-lucky ways, Special Operations Command, or SOCOM, had been dubbed "Happy Command," in contrast with Central Command, which also was located at MacDill and whose reputation for long hours and hard work had earned it the nickname "Sad Command." At the time of 9/11, SOCOM was headed not by a door-busting commando but by a pilot who had flown lumbering AC-130 gunships. Colleagues described Air Force general Charles Holland as courtly, polite, and soft-spoken. He was a compromiser, not a bureaucratic infighter like his boss, Rumsfeld.

Eager to strike back at al Qaeda, Rumsfeld turned to Holland immediately after the terrorist attacks and asked for ideas for hitting the terrorist group around the world. The request marked the start of what eventually became a major effort by Rumsfeld to transform SOCOM into a sort of global command post for leading the fight against international terrorism. If he could not get his regional combatant commands—those with geographic areas of responsibility—to adopt a global view of the war, Rumsfeld figured, SOCOM could be used for worldwide planning and operating.

On September 25, Holland reported back to Rumsfeld. Aside from the obvious targets, like Afghanistan, the general mentioned several other potential areas for going after al Qaeda operatives and their support network—among them, terrorist training camps in the West African nation of Mauritania, a transshipment point on the beaches near the Somali capital Mogadishu, the bases of the Abu Sayyaf rebel group in the Philippines, and the triborder area in South America of Paraguay, Brazil, and Argentina. The list of potential operations suggested that the United States could launch a series of attacks throughout the world to make al Qaeda think U.S. forces were coming at them from everywhere. This idea excited Rumsfeld.

"Well, when can we get these guys?" the secretary wanted to know.

The answer he got back was deflating. Holland told him there wasn't sufficient "actionable intelligence" to target the terrorists reliably. He explained that going after al Qaeda involved not going after individuals here and there but targeting a whole network. The process was akin to penetrating organized crime, which required a different kind of intelligence, a different mode of operation, from what the military was accustomed to.

Rumsfeld, frustrated by the constraints and disappointed by Holland's caution, would in time reinvigorate sleepy SOCOM with an expanded mission and much fatter budget. He would also attack the intelligence problem by broadening the kind of intelligence gathering done by military operatives, encroaching on domains once reserved for the CIA.

The other surprise for Rumsfeld at the late-September meeting with Holland was the answer to a question on when the Special Forces groups would make it into Afghanistan. "When CIA gives us the go-ahead," Holland replied.

Rumsfeld's face showed stark astonishment, according to Robert Andrews, who had recently joined the department as a senior civilian official overseeing Special Operations. The secretary was deeply troubled by the notion of U.S. military forces being dependent on the CIA to act. Disdainfully, in a comment repeated to his staff, he compared the Defense Department to baby birds sitting in a nest waiting for the CIA to bring them the worms. The remark was an expression not of Rumsfeld's regard for the CIA but of his growing frustration with the inadequacy of U.S. military forces to take the kind of action he deemed necessary. In his view, what was needed was an organization capable of targeting individuals around the world, not specific countries. "This is a global war," Rumsfeld told Holland. "The regional commanders won't be able to fight it. I need a global commander."

———•———

Formal release of the results of the Quadrennial Defense Review came at the end of September. Although the review had largely been completed before the September 11 attacks, the terrorist strikes confirmed the strategic direction and planning principles in the assessment. Its emphasis on homeland defense, on surprise, on preparing for asymmetric threats, and on the need to develop new concepts of deterrence all had greater resonance in the wake of the deadly tragedy. "However," Rumsfeld wrote in the preface to the review report, "the attack on the United States on September 11, 2001 will require us to move forward more rapidly in these directions, even while we are engaged in the war against terrorism."

The report contained no call for any of the force reductions or major weapons cuts that had been feared in the first months of the new administration. But it did set the stage for a number of changes to follow. It signaled an intention to restructure U.S. forces abroad, moving away from the Cold War concentration of troops in western Europe and northeastern Asia and toward the development of other bases or temporary stations in other regions. It called for strengthening cooperation among the services through a more integrated command-and-control structure, including "standing joint task force headquarters" in each regional command. It stressed the need for greater investment in intelligence-gathering platforms, including satellites and unmanned aircraft, in human spying, and in methods for fusing intelligence information, making it more responsive to commanders and civilian leaders. It put a premium on precision weapons and on improved communications.

On the question of how to size the force, the report was similarly a mix of old and new. It preserved the basic two-war strategy that had been adopted by the Clinton administration after the demise of the Soviet Union. But at the same time, it broadened the planning to aim for a wider spectrum of possible conflicts, seeking to take into account the larger number of tasks actually assigned to the U.S. military through peacekeeping operations and homeland defense.

The result was a force-sizing concept known by a numerical label, "1–4–2–1." The "1" called for maintaining enough forces to protect the U.S. homeland. The "4" meant the United States needed to be ready to deter hostilities and conduct smaller-scale peacetime operations in as many as four critical areas of the world. The "2–1" stood for the requirement that U.S. forces be shaped sufficiently to "swiftly defeat" aggression in two near-simultaneous major combat operations while preserving the option to achieve "decisive victory" in one through regime change or occupation.

The report also spoke of a fundamental shift in the basis of defense planning. In the past, it noted, decisions about forces and weapons had rested on assessments of specific threats such as large conventional wars in distant theaters. But in an uncertain world, identifying precise scenarios had become more difficult. Consequently, the report argued, planning should focus more on the development of a portfolio of capabilities to enable the United States to address a broader array of requirements, both functional and geographic. This kind of "capabilities-based" approach, in contrast with the previous "threat-based" model, promised to favor such systems as remote-sending technologies, long-range precision strikes, and expeditionary forces and did not bode well for some of the military's pet projects carried over from the Cold War.

Now Rumsfeld had the beginnings of a road map for change. Pursuing it, though, while also waging war would present some challenges all their own.

Months before the September 11 attacks, Rumsfeld had given some thought to the circumstances in which he would recommend the use of force. He had raised the issue with Bush before his own confirmation as secretary, wanting to ensure that the new president would be ready to take military action if the United States were provoked. In the past, Rumsfeld thought, U.S. military responses, most notably, to terrorist attacks, had been too limited. U.S. action should be commensurate with its talk, he stressed.

As early as March 2001, Rumsfeld had begun drafting his own set of guidelines for the use of force, which he walked the president through. To an extent, Rumsfeld's guidelines echoed those of Caspar Weinberger, who had been the last defense secretary to set forth rules for employing combat forces. In a November 1984 speech, Weinberger had stipulated three conditions: A vital national interest must be at stake, a wholehearted commitment to win must be made, and support from Congress and the public must be reasonably assured. Weinberger's list was purposefully restrictive and meant to answer arguments advanced at the time by Secretary of State George Shultz that the threat of military force needed to be available to support diplomacy in a broader range of cases. Elaborating on the doctrine later, Colin Powell, when he was chairman of the Joint Chiefs of Staff, added the notion that "overwhelming" force should be applied once a determination is made that military action is needed to meet a clear national interest.

"If people could be killed, ours or others, the U.S. must have a darn good reason," Rumsfeld wrote in typically blunt language in a two-page memorandum setting out his updated guidelines. Military action must be "in the U.S. national interest," and the nation's leadership must be sure to have marshaled public support.

But he was less restrictive than Weinberger and Powell, stating that military action need not be limited to protecting "vital" interests. Any action should be "achievable—at acceptable risk," with clear goals and an acknowledgment of the risks of casualties, he wrote. He also stressed that all required resources must be committed for the duration of combat.

"Just as the risks of taking action must be carefully considered, so, too, the risk of inaction needs to be weighed," he went on. He also emphasized the importance of taking international opinion into account.

"Before committing to an engagement," he wrote, "consider the implications of the decision for the U.S. in other parts of the world—if we prevail, if we fail, or if we decide not to act. U.S. actions or inactions in one region are read around the world and contribute favorably or unfavorably to the U.S. deterrent and influence. Think through the precedent that a proposed action, or inaction, would establish."

If there is to be action, he added, it is important to act early. He did not specifically endorse preventive war or preemptive action, as Bush would later do, but he stressed the importance of being quick off the mark. "If it is worth doing, U.S. leadership should make a judgment as to when diplomacy has failed and act forcefully, early, during the pre-crisis period, to try to alter the behavior of others and to prevent the conflict," he said. "If that fails, be willing and prepared to act decisively to use whatever force is necessary to prevail, plus some."

Art Cebrowski, an admiral picked by Rumsfeld as an adviser on transformation, had developed a chart underscoring the advantages of the early use of force in a conflict. It was purely a theoretical exercise, but Cebrowski's point was that force applied early could in some situations keep the conflict contained and avoid a much larger military commitment later. The diagram had caught Rumsfeld's attention.

In his paper, Rumsfeld also warned that while the United States should expect to fight most often in the company of a coalition, it should avoid operating with collective command structures "where a committee makes decisions" or accepting restrictions on U.S. military options. "In working to fashion a coalition or trying to persuade Congress, the public, the U.N. or other countries to support an action," Rumsfeld said, "the National Command Authorities should not dumb down what is needed by promising not to do things (i.e., not to use ground forces, not to bomb below 15,000 feet, not to risk lives, not to permit collateral damage, etc.). That may simplify the task for the enemy and make the task more difficult. Leadership should not set arbitrary deadlines as to when the U.S. will disengage, or the enemy can simply wait us out."

He also included a paragraph near the end about honesty. "U.S. leadership must be brutally honest with itself, the Congress, the public and coalition partners. Do not make the effort sound even marginally easier or less costly than it could become. Preserving U.S. credibility requires that we promise less, or no more, than we are sure we can deliver." Inserting one of the long-standing axioms from his list of Rumsfeld's Rules, he added, "It is a great deal easier to get into something than it is to get out of it!"

———•———

As planning for military operations in Afghanistan intensified, Rumsfeld continued to fret over what he considered an inadequate target list. Most proposed targets were Taliban military—early-warning radar, communications centers, storage depots, a few aircraft. The al Qaeda camps were mostly empty. Further, a great many of the targets were fixed sites, not movable ones like troops and equipment deployed for battle.

The absence of base rights in neighboring Uzbekistan also remained a worry. The bases were needed for stationing search-and-rescue teams, which would pick up any pilots forced down during the bombing campaign, and for launching U.S. Special Forces teams into northern Afghanistan to link up with the anti-Taliban militia there. In the south, the issue was reversed—basing wasn't a problem since search-and-rescue planes could fly out of Oman and Special Forces could stage from aircraft carriers, but identifying local forces with which U.S. teams could partner was difficult.

On a trip to the Middle East and South Asia in early October, Rumsfeld stopped in Uzbekistan and won agreement for U.S. use of the country's airspace and of an airfield. The first CIA team had already moved into place in Afghanistan in late September, and on October 7, after the Taliban refused a final ultimatum to turn over bin Laden and eject al Qaeda, U.S. cruise missiles and aircraft began to strike targets in Afghanistan.

But the problem of too-few targets that Rumsfeld had feared surfaced quickly. The day after the initial wave of strikes, U.S. aircraft did not know what to hit. Planes loitered, waiting for targets to emerge. The vast military capability of the United States appeared helpless in the absence of targets that could be considered of much value and clearly identified.

Further, the bombing wasn't spurring the Afghan militias to engage the Taliban and al Qaeda decisively. Three days into the campaign, Rumsfeld asked Franks, who was commanding the war, how closely the air strikes were being coordinated with the Northern Alliance and the anti-Taliban southern tribes. "Not too well yet," Franks replied.

Coordination was not going to improve until U.S. Special Forces could get on the ground and serve as forward air controllers, managing the timing and laser targeting for the bombers overhead. But those forces were being held up while CIA teams smoothed the way, making contact with militia leaders, distributing cash, and establishing communications links. Rumsfeld was anxious about the United States losing credibility through ineffectual action in Afghanistan.

At an NSC meeting on October 9, Rumsfeld returned to the question of expanding U.S. action beyond Afghanistan. He still thought that if the anti-terrorism campaign stalled in Afghanistan, U.S. forces could and should do something elsewhere. Countries at the top of his list included the Philippines, Yemen, and Indonesia. (In the Philippines, Muslim insurgents, most notably, the terrorist group Abu Sayyaf, had rooted in the south. Yemen, which had been the site of the October 2000 attack on the USS *Cole*, harbored a sizable al Qaeda presence and was home to representatives of Hamas, Palestinian Islamic Jihad, and other terrorist organizations. In Indonesia, militant Muslim groups abounded.) But Rumsfeld could not generate interest in mounting early operations outside Afghanistan.

Rumsfeld's frustration at the dearth of alternative attack options elsewhere came through the next day when he complained to Myers and General Peter Pace, the vice chairman of the Joint Chiefs of Staff, about the lack of "actionable" proposals for pursuing terrorists other than through the use of cruise missiles and aerial bombs. In a snowflake to them that was copied to Wolfowitz and Feith and titled "What Will Be the Military Role in the War on Terrorism," Rumsfeld asserted that something was "fundamentally wrong" in a department that was getting a third of a trillion dollars a year but could not produce a proposal for action. He wondered whether the defense establishment had become too risk averse and made it clear that he didn't want any bold ideas dismissed just because they might seem too risky.

Several days later, Rumsfeld ordered Feith to reassess the approach in Afghanistan, which had assumed that a small number of U.S. forces would support an aggressive Northern Alliance. He suggested the possibility of placing Special Forces with the southern tribes and taking over that responsibility from the CIA, and he questioned whether larger numbers of U.S. ground forces should be sent in.

At the start of an NSC meeting on October 16, the CIA's deputy director, John McLaughlin, reported that a second CIA team would arrive in Afghanistan that night. But no military Special Forces teams had yet entered the country, hampered by various obstacles. The delay only intensified Rumsfeld's frustration with the military's inability to act as nimbly and rapidly as the CIA. During the NSC meeting, his irritation boiled over.

"This is the CIA's strategy," he said. "They developed the strategy. We're just executing the strategy."

McLaughlin disagreed. "Our guys work with the CINC," he said, using the acronym for Commander-in-Chief, referring to a regional U.S. military commander. "We're supporting the CINC. The CINC is in charge."

"No, you guys are in charge," Rumsfeld said. "You guys have the contacts. We're just following you in. We're going where you tell us to go."

Armitage, observing the exchange, could see the dysfunction. "I think what I'm hearing is FUBAR," he said, using an old military acronym for "fucked up beyond all repair."

Rumsfeld had reason to be edgy. The bombing campaign should have induced the Afghan fighters to take territory from the Taliban but had so far failed to do so. Northern Alliance commanders complained to the press that U.S. air strikes were unimpressive. Franks expected improvement once U.S. Special Forces teams could link up with their Afghan partners, but the insertion of those teams was being delayed until the CIA could connect with the Northern Alliance commanders. For their part, the CIA operatives were facing logistical problems entering Afghanistan.

Still, Rumsfeld's outburst was puzzling for someone so inclined to assume command. Perhaps it was a calculated attempt to shift blame to the CIA. Perhaps it was a veiled strategy to get the CIA to defer to military command, although as McLaughlin had said, CIA officials were already operating on the understanding that their teams worked for the CINC.

In any case, Rice told Rumsfeld after the meeting that he would have to take charge of the operation. Powell and Steve Hadley, the deputy national security adviser, also weighed in several days later, encouraging

Rumsfeld to develop a coordinated strategy incorporating military and CIA functions.

———•———

Another interagency debate flared around this time over the pacing of the war. CIA officials were arguing against rushing to seize Afghanistan's capital, Kabul, for fear of alienating the Pashtun, Afghanistan's largest ethnic group, and triggering a civil war in the aftermath of overthrowing the Taliban. State Department officials also liked the idea of having more time to train and equip the Northern Alliance. But Rumsfeld, along with Cheney, argued against a prolonged campaign. In the strategy paper that Feith prepared, it was stressed that an early defeat of the Taliban and al Qaeda would make additional terrorist operations more difficult and would increase leverage against other state supporters of terrorism. Success in Afghanistan, the paper asserted, would build U.S. public confidence for action in other theaters.

Meanwhile, Rumsfeld's dissatisfaction with the course of the war had left him unusually testy with Franks. For days, the secretary had been pressing the general about when the Special Forces teams would be inserted. "I do not see any movement, General Franks," he would say. "Can you predict when something is going to happen?" The strain between the two of them had reached the point that Franks felt Rumsfeld had lost confidence in him, and he suggested the secretary find another commander. But Rumsfeld reassured the general that he had his "complete confidence."

Rumsfeld was also intent on formalizing the chain-of-command relationship between the Pentagon and the CIA rather than continuing to operate, as Tenet preferred, on the basis of informal understandings and handshake agreements. Franks felt squeezed. "He felt like he was caught between Rumsfeld and Tenet," recalled retired Air Force lieutenant general John Campbell, the associate CIA director who served as liaison between the agency and the Pentagon at the time.

At a meeting at CIA headquarters, Franks suggested the CIA draft a memo of understanding that would stipulate who worked for whom. Campbell prepared a paper specifying that in peacetime, the CIA station chief in a country was the senior intelligence representative through which the military should coordinate intelligence activities, while in wartime, the CIA representative would answer to the regional military commander. But the document never went anywhere. Tenet shelved it, and CENTCOM dropped the matter. The memo did not break new ground, but neither side was ready to put the terms on paper.

————•••————

Finally, on October 19, twenty-three days after the first CIA team had entered Afghanistan, U.S. Special Forces from Operational Detachment 555 infiltrated Afghanistan on two MH-53J Pave Low helicopters and linked up with the Northern Alliance's Uzbek commander, Abdul Rashid Dostum. A couple of other teams followed over the next two days. In the south, meanwhile, units of Special Forces and Army Rangers launched assaults on an airfield and a compound near Kandahar—largely demonstration raids orchestrated to show capability and to gather intelligence.

U.S. ground troops were at last in the fight, but two more weeks passed with seemingly little progress on the ground. Even with the Special Forces teams in position to relay targeting information for the air campaign, U.S. bombs were making little apparent dent in the Taliban's strength, falling instead on more-conventional sites such as airfields and antiaircraft facilities. The Northern Alliance was reluctant to risk its troops in attacks on well-defended Taliban positions unless the United States provided more air support.

Rumsfeld kept pushing Franks hard to move additional Special Forces target spotters to the front lines of the Northern Alliance on the Shamali Plain, north of Kabul, where the Taliban's military units were arrayed. But getting more U.S. military teams into northern Afghanistan remained problematic. Bad weather interfered, and Uzbekistan was also causing delays. In at least one instance, too, a Northern Alliance warlord raised objections to joining with a U.S. team.

In the meantime, the administration's war plan was drawing increased fire in the news for appearing timid and ineffective. Even conservative columnists were taking the Bush team to task. In an op-ed piece for the *Washington Post* on October 30, Bill Kristol said too many self-imposed constraints had produced "a flawed plan," and Charles Krauthammer said the war was being fought with "half-measures." The next day in the *New York Times*, R. W. Apple Jr., one of the paper's most prominent correspondents, published an analysis asking whether Afghanistan could become another "military quagmire" like Vietnam.

In private, Bush was pressing top Pentagon officials about where they thought things in Afghanistan were headed. On October 24, he shot a barrage of questions at Rumsfeld and Myers during an NSC meeting. He asked whether CENTCOM had a "winter scenario," how the United States could surge its aircraft to help the Afghan opposition forces, and how airpower could be used against cave hideouts. Rice suggested to the president the possibility of changing the strategy and Americanizing the Afghan effort by adding large numbers of U.S. ground forces. But at an NSC meeting on October 26, Bush appeared determined to stay the course, reminding his national security team of the need for patience.

In public, Rumsfeld was also putting up a confident front. He made the Sunday talk-show rounds on October 28, expressing satisfaction with the campaign. And in a November 1 news conference, he recalled several historical analogies, noting that it had taken four months after the attack on Pearl Harbor in December 1941 for the United States to initiate military action, three and a half years of bombing before Japan surrendered, and five years on the European front before Germany was defeated.

Behind the scenes, though, Rumsfeld was considering the possibility that things might take a turn for the worse. Some of the strategic brainstorming in his office took place in what were called "roundtable" meetings that included the deputy secretary, chairman, vice chairman, and policy undersecretary. At one such session on October 29, Rumsfeld pressed for ways to achieve an important result in Afghanistan before much more time had passed. He thought aloud about combat operations, humanitarian supplies, and diplomatic missions. He reiterated that the war on terrorism should extend far beyond Afghanistan and appealed for "visible military action that demonstrates the breadth of the war."

At another roundtable meeting two days later, Rumsfeld ordered Pace and Feith to produce a new strategy paper to address Bush's questions. He wanted ways to put U.S. troops into the south quickly to support the tribal leader Hamid Karzai, the CIA's only substantial contact there. And he sought a list of revised objectives. Some of the ideas tossed around then included deploying a major ground force, undertaking a Berlin-airlift-scale humanitarian aid effort, and establishing a provisional government, either in exile or in a portion of the country.

———•———

By early November, the focus of the air campaign finally shifted from going after fixed assets to targeting Taliban and al Qaeda forces in the field. The turning point came as Special Operations target spotters began calling in precise and devastating B-52 raids on the Taliban front lines. Key Afghan towns started to fall to coalition forces—first Mazar-e-Sharif, a northern city not far from the Uzbek border, on November 9, then Herat, in the west, on November 11. The speed of the unfolding victory was stunning and overtook a debate under way within the Bush administration over how fast to proceed—particularly over whether to enter Kabul or hold on the outskirts for a broader political structure to take shape. Kabul fell on November 13.

In the south, more than a thousand U.S. Marines established a base of operations, while Special Forces teams worked closely with Pashtun tribes to tighten the noose around Kandahar, which finally fell on December 7. The Taliban no longer held power, cities, or transportation routes. They had been crushed by an impressive display of military force. The Northern Alliance, its Pashtun allies, and U.S. forces were in charge of the country.

All told, the U.S. plan had achieved a rapid triumph: The air campaign was launched within twenty-six days of the September 11 attacks, U.S. forces were on the ground in Afghanistan within thirty-eight days, and the Taliban were overthrown within sixty-three days. In that period, the size of the U.S. force in Afghanistan never exceeded four thousand troops.

At a November 27 briefing to the news media, Rumsfeld took the position that this successful outcome had been certain all along. "I think that what was taking place in the earlier phases was exactly as planned," he asserted. With evident delight he recalled earlier pessimistic press reports, suggesting they had been uninformed. "It looked like nothing was happening. Indeed, it looked like we were in a"—and he asked the press to join in—"all together now, quagmire." Reporters chuckled.

In truth, Rumsfeld and the rest of the administration had launched the war with very little notion of how it would unfold. At first, the execution of the war plan had proved clumsy. A cumbersome process of approving targets initially resulted in some lost opportunities to fire on leaders of al Qaeda and the Taliban. Complicating matters, rules had to be worked out to coordinate military air strikes with CIA-operated Predator drone aircraft outfitted with Hellfire missiles. U.S. Special Forces had run into days of delay as they attempted to enter the country. Then, as the war quickly turned in favor of U.S. and allied Afghan forces, and it appeared that the Taliban and al Qaeda would soon be defeated, there was little clarity in Washington about what to do next.

But many of those shortcomings and much of the behind-the-scenes disagreement, confusion, and uncertainty ended up overshadowed by the victory achieved and particularly by the unusual way in which it came about. As Bush had promised at the beginning, the campaign had demonstrated "a different kind of war." It had borne out Rumsfeld's declaration that the way to fight terrorists was not with conventional capabilities but with unconventional ones.

Undeniably, U.S. forces had innovatively defeated their enemy. One of Rumsfeld's favorite photos from the war showed U.S. troops on horseback in Afghanistan using global positioning devices to call in air strikes. The carrier USS *Kitty Hawk*, its deck normally crowded with attack jets, had been converted into a floating base for some Army units. As the combination of Army Special Forces and airpower helped sweep the Taliban from power, the Afghanistan campaign appeared to validate Rumsfeld's vision of twenty-first-century warfare.

Up to a point. A cautionary note about the risks of trying to do more with less came in the waning days of the offensive. In late November and early December, as many as 1,500 Arab and Chechen fighters from the al Qaeda network took shelter in cave complexes at Tora Bora, high in the mountains of eastern Afghanistan. The area was not far from the border with Pakistan, across which lay the Pashtun tribal areas of the North-West Frontier Province, whose inhabitants were sympathetic to the Taliban and were largely beyond the control of Pakistan's central government in Islamabad.

A few days into the fighting, the Americans intercepted a radio communication out of Tora Bora from bin Laden himself. American warplanes pounded the region from the air, Afghan units attacked on the ground, and on December 16, the remaining al Qaeda fighters abandoned Tora Bora. But by then bin Laden had already slipped away into the nearby mountains, with no U.S. conventional forces to block his escape.

Franks had rejected the urging of the senior CIA operative in the region and others to move a substantial contingent of Marines from Kandahar to Tora Bora to help seal off escape routes into Pakistan. He feared losing the momentum of the battle by waiting for additional troops to arrive, and there was concern the Marines could get mired in the snowy mountains. Moreover, the head of the Afghan forces in the area had opposed having uniformed U.S. troops in the fight.

Rumsfeld, viewing the decision as largely an operational matter, had left it up to Franks. Nonetheless, bin Laden's escape from Tora Bora represented a failure for him as well as the U.S. military and was a disappointing reminder of the risks of being too sparing in the use of U.S. troops. While the bulk of the enemy's forces had been killed or captured by year's end, those who had fled into the rugged mountains along the Afghanistan-Pakistan border would regroup and eventually pose a new challenge to U.S. efforts to secure Afghanistan. In the meantime, the United Nations organized a conference of non-Taliban Afghan tribal leaders, and on December 22, Hamid Karzai, an Indian-educated, ethnic Pashtun from southern Afghanistan, was installed in Kabul as president.

———•———

Seen overall as a stunning success, the Afghan War remade Rumsfeld. Having spent his first months at the Pentagon struggling to transform the U.S. military, he was himself suddenly transformed into an unexpected secretary of war. His combat before had been largely of the bureaucratic kind over turf, policies, and budgets against rival players in Washington. He had never overseen a military campaign. But he quickly understood the importance of projecting his own authority. Although the particular nature of the Afghan conflict had initially limited the role the U.S. military could play, Rumsfeld assumed a leading role with the public, becoming the face and voice of the U.S. military at war.

Much of what was known about the fighting came from the televised press briefings that Rumsfeld conducted as often as once a day. Occupying Washington's spotlight, he put on display his virtuoso skills as a spokesman—quick-witted, blunt, knowledgeable, evasive, cutting, amusing, and entertaining. Virtually overnight, the pre-9/11 talk of Rumsfeld being on his way out vanished as he turned into a media star and an exceedingly popular administration figure.

The decision to have Rumsfeld brief the media so frequently had been a controversial one. It went against the previously accepted practice of leaving detailed talk about military operations to military officers, and it appeared to accentuate Rumsfeld's dominance, particularly over the military chiefs. During the 1991 Persian Gulf War, it had been Powell, then chairman of the Joint Chiefs, who had overshadowed Cheney. Now, Rumsfeld was the feature attraction at news conferences, with Myers standing alongside or slightly back, commenting only sparingly.

Rumsfeld's tough-guy image seemed made-to-order for a Pentagon at war. Dispensing with the arcana and acronyms that normally clutter Pentagon parlance, he showed a startling willingness to talk bluntly about war, skipping such euphemisms and sanitized phrases as "collateral damage." In one meeting with the press, for instance, Rumsfeld used the word "kill" nine times. He justified the use of cluster bombs, which spray bomblets, saying that the munitions were being dropped on front lines against al Qaeda and Taliban troops "to try to kill them." And he saw striking enemy troops who were in retreat as "perfectly legitimate."

Rumsfeld could be antagonistic and amusing all at once, but his performances, delivered with eyes squinting through wireless glasses and arms chopping and waving through the air, were invariably theatrical. They reflected both an undisguised enthusiasm for the job and a love for the jugular. He was anything but the conventional bureaucrat.

If he didn't want to answer a certain question, he would say so. Other times he would reply with a quirky expression or colorful metaphor. When asked on Fox News one Sunday whether the United States was close to apprehending bin Laden, he replied, "If you're chasing a chicken around the barnyard, are you close or are you not close until you get him?"

He could also use fractured syntax to suddenly cloud an issue. Referring, for instance, to the idea of a possible international stabilization force in Afghanistan, he commented, "There's been a good deal of discussion about that. And at the present time it has not been felt that it was necessarily necessary, nor has—if it were to become necessary, which it conceivably could—nor has it been decided exactly what the composition and make-up of that might be."

He drew on folksy terms from his native Midwest, frequently injecting a "gosh" or "by golly" or "goodness gracious" or "you bet!" His performances made him seem a more charming and entertaining figure than his earlier image as an arrogant, gruff, and overcontrolling Pentagon boss had suggested. Indeed, the remarks, which aides said were unscripted, seemed to reveal more of Rumsfeld's personality.

Smitten with this new, plucky character on TV, Americans tuned in by the millions. Torie Clarke, Rumsfeld's spokesperson, received calls, faxes, and e-mails asking when Rumsfeld was due to appear. His lexicon was widely parodied, got converted into a collection of quotations on a British Broadcasting Corporation Web site, and became the centerpiece for an online fan club.

Bush nicknamed him "Rumstud" and declared his star defense secretary a "matinee idol." *U.S. News & World Report* dubbed his style "Rum Punch" in a cover article on Rumsfeld in December 2001. *People* magazine included Rumsfeld in its list of the world's sexiest men. A famous *Saturday Night Live* skit showed him intimidating reporters to the point where they were rendered incapable of posing any further questions.

Among those skeptical enough to question out loud whether such adoring treatment of the once disparaged defense secretary would last was Rumsfeld's own wife. She had been around Washington—and her husband—long enough to know how fleeting such adulation could be. In a speech titled "The Rock Star and the Goat" to a group of wives of senior officers, Joyce Rumsfeld asserted that the same person could end up as both the star and the goat, the only difference being one of public perceptions.

———— • ————

Rumsfeld's surge in popularity helped strengthen his own primacy within the Pentagon. Although he often appeared at the Pentagon podium with Myers at his side, he consistently outshone the chairman, seemingly relegating him to the role of military assistant rather than principal military adviser. Behind the scenes, too, Rumsfeld involved himself to an extraordinary degree in the war. He not only exercised a broad supervisory role but also immersed himself in everyday details. Some of the great interest he showed in tactical information reflected a need to prepare for his own many news conferences. But much of it derived from a driving desire to control.

During the war in Afghanistan, he talked with Franks two or three times daily. For those calls, Franks and his staff gathered in the Trophy Room at Central Command headquarters to field the secretary's many questions. "They were pretty painful meetings," recalled Abizaid, who by then had become director of the Joint Staff and participated in the conferences. "It wasn't that the secretary was trying to be disrespectful. It's that he had this huge capacity to ask questions and try to gain knowledge."

Many CENTCOM staffers spent much of their day preparing for the conferences and then chasing down answers afterward to Rumsfeld's many queries. "Those daily video conferences could be debilitating," Jim Robb, then a two-star admiral heading CENTCOM's policy branch, remembered. "We'd get up at 4 a.m. to prepare for the 7 a.m. conference, then we'd get a whole bunch of taskers that had to be answered by the next conference in the afternoon. So finally at 16:30 we'd be able to sit down at our desks and start work."

Tied up with meeting Rumsfeld's requests, CENTCOM officers were sometimes unavailable to commanders seeking help in the field. "When the SecDef started having a briefing every day, it meant that for hours of the day you could not talk to the CENTCOM staff," recounted Army major general Warren Edwards, the deputy commander for operations involving Central Command's ground forces. "It didn't matter what was going on. For hours of the day you were unable to get to a senior person to make a decision at CENTCOM because they were tied up prepping themselves for the SecDef's briefing."

Rumsfeld could be so particular about the information he received that officers, fearful of sending forward incorrect data, would go out of their way to avoid acknowledging a mistake that might require the secretary to issue a correction. "Numbers became so important that if the SecDef went to a briefing, and we had reported that we had captured 14 al Qaeda, and it really turned out to be 12 or 16, then it would be easier to let two go or go back and capture two more than to go back and try to change the OSD [Office of Secretary of Defense] number," Edwards said.

Even with the successful outcome of the U.S. invasion, Rumsfeld could not get over his initial frustration with how long it had taken for the Pentagon to get military forces into Afghanistan. In early January 2002, Rumsfeld asked Albert M. "Bert" Calland, a Navy SEAL admiral who had commanded U.S. Special Operations units in Afghanistan, to come by his office to review the operation. "He said to me, 'You must have thought I was a maniac about trying to get your guys on the ground quicker,'" Calland recalled. "I said, 'Well yes, I did.' Because he was just obsessed with that."

Rumsfeld told Calland that he still didn't fully understand why the Special Forces couldn't have acted faster. Calland explained that it had made sense for the CIA teams to arrive first because the agency had relationships with the Afghan warlords extending back to the 1980s when the Russians were occupying the country. The military's teams had no such contacts and lacked the language skills. While some spoke Russian or Farsi, few had any knowledge of Urdu or Pashtun, making communication with local militia leaders problematic at best.

In addition to needing CIA operatives on the ground to make introductions and help converse, Calland told Rumsfeld, the military teams relied on their CIA partners to distribute cash for the purchase of guns and ammunition. The Special Forces units could be given their own cash to spread around, Rumsfeld asserted. True, Calland explained, but not in the large amounts that were necessary and not for weapons, given U.S. laws prohibiting military troops from providing "lethal aid" to foreign militias such as the Northern Alliance. The CIA had the requisite spending authority—and knowledge about what things actually cost in a place like Afghanistan.

It seemed to Calland that Rumsfeld was hearing for the first time about what could and couldn't be done by an A-team, the basic twelve-man unit used by Army Special Forces. "The impression I got was, this was new information for him," Calland later recalled. "I think he appreciated the frankness of the conversation and the explanation."

That didn't mean, however, that Rumsfeld was satisfied with what he heard—to the contrary. He remained determined to expand the skills and authorities of Special Forces, enabling them to be less dependent on the CIA in future situations. "He just didn't like having to rely on another agency that he didn't control, that he couldn't beat over the head to make something happen," Calland said.

———•———

In shaping the international force that remained in Afghanistan to help rebuild and chase after remnants of the Taliban and al Qaeda, Rumsfeld pushed hard to keep U.S. troop numbers as low as possible. While the fighting had been under way in the fall, he had made clear his aversion to seeing U.S. forces bogged down in nation building. Skeptical of America's ability to help form a new political system in a nation like Afghanistan, he told a Pentagon news conference in October that he didn't think throwing out the existing Afghan government "leaves us with a responsibility to figure out what kind of government that country ought to have." He allowed that the United States would have "a humanitarian interest" in the people of the country, but added that he didn't see it as America's job to tell Afghans how to run their country.

Rumsfeld wanted to avoid the examples of Bosnia and Kosovo, where U.S. and allied military actions in the 1990s had led to those countries becoming essentially long-term wards of the international community, with large numbers of U.S. and other outside troops still there. Years after the U.S. military had helped save victimized Muslims in those regions, a functioning government still had not been established in either place. Reconstruction was slow, inadequate, and directed largely by foreigners rather than by locals. When Rumsfeld had sounded out European allies about reducing the U.S. presence there, they warned that such a move could bring about wholesale collapse. Rumsfeld didn't want the Afghans to think the United States intended to take the same approach to their country.

In early 2002, State Department officials proposed that U.S. troops join the small international peacekeeping force patrolling Kabul and help Karzai extend his influence beyond the capital. At an NSC meeting in February 2002, Powell cited as a model the 1989 invasion of Panama, in which U.S. troops spread out across the country after ousting Manuel

Noriega's government. In the case of Afghanistan, informal talks with European officials had led Powell's staff to believe that a force of twenty thousand to forty thousand peacekeepers could be recruited, half from Europe, half from the United States.

But Rumsfeld, doubting the willingness of the Europeans to contribute, worried that if the United States began sending peacekeepers, it would be left without real partners. He warned that an expanded U.S. role in Afghan peacekeeping would actually lessen the pressure on other countries to contribute and to pull their weight in a truly multilateral effort. "We were by no means mindless opponents of multilateralism," Feith wrote in his book, describing Rumsfeld's position at the time. "But we did not support mindless multilateralism either."

In April 2002, a test case emerged of how far the United States might be willing to go in backing Karzai. The Afghan leader faced his first armed challenge from a warlord—a fellow Pashtun named Pacha Khan Zadran. Originally appointed by Karzai as governor of Gardez, a region south of Kabul, Pacha Khan was opposed by a council of elders and religious leaders, prompting Karzai to rescind the appointment. Pacha Khan's militia responded by setting up roadblocks and firing artillery at the town of Gardez.

Worries that the confrontation could spiral out of control and topple Karzai prompted Powell, Rice, and Cheney to urge that U.S. forces come to the Afghan leader's aid. But Rumsfeld opposed entangling U.S. and coalition forces in fights among Afghan clans. In Rumsfeld's view, propping up Karzai would compromise him if it made him appear to need U.S. forces to remain in power. "I didn't think it was right for us to give a foreign leader the ability to pull our trigger," Rumsfeld recalled in an interview. "If we told him we'd back him up, then he could do whatever he wanted with a warlord and call us up to go beat him up, kill him, destroy him. I said, 'That's the president's decision; it is not a decision for a foreign leader, and therefore I'm not going to do it.'"

Rumsfeld told Karzai directly not to expect U.S. forces to do his bidding but instead to rely on patronage, the distribution of foreign assistance funds, and other political tactics to win over his warlord adversaries. "You're going to have to figure out how to be a politician," he said he advised the Afghan leader. Ultimately, Karzai did manage to resolve the Pacha Khan issue without major fighting and without involving U.S. troops.

That same month, Bush delivered a speech on Afghanistan that recalled America's hand in the rebuilding of postwar Europe under the Marshall Plan, fueling expectations of an enlarged U.S. assistance effort. Mindful of Afghan concerns about being abandoned—as Afghans felt they had been by his father's administration after the Soviets left in 1989—Bush vowed to avoid the syndrome of "initial success, followed by long years of floundering and ultimate failure."

But at a Pentagon news conference a few days later, Rumsfeld sounded a considerably less generous note, indicating that the Afghans would have to rely largely on themselves. "The last thing you're going to hear from this podium is someone thinking they know how Afghanistan ought to organize itself," he said. "They're going to have to figure it out. They're going to have to grab ahold of that thing and do something. And we're there to help."

In the end, the United States deployed eight thousand troops to Afghanistan in 2002, with orders to hunt Taliban and al Qaeda members and not to engage in peacekeeping or reconstruction. A four-thousand-member international peacekeeping force took up positions in Kabul, but it did not venture beyond the Afghan capital. The country's main requirements were divided into categories, and each was assigned to a "lead nation." The United States took on responsibility for training a seventy-thousand-member army; Japan for financing a program to disarm some hundred thousand militia fighters; Britain for mounting an antinarcotics program; Italy for organizing the country's judicial system; and Germany for training a sixty-two-thousand-member police force.

The result was that no single power assumed overall command, and no effective strategic plan for Afghanistan's recovery emerged within the Bush administration. The challenges facing Afghanistan were immense. A poor country to begin with, it had suffered even more through years of Soviet invasion and occupation, civil disorder, and Taliban oppression. Lacking roads and other basic infrastructure, its most thriving economic activity was a narcotics trade that threatened to corrupt the entire nation. Months would pass—and more opportunities for an Afghan recovery would be lost—before Rumsfeld came to recognize the need for greater U.S. involvement.

As the Afghan invasion and other operations got under way and the number of detainees began to mount, the Bush administration faced the question of what to do with prisoners captured in the war on terrorism. Much of the initial sorting of legal issues was largely handled by a small working group led by White House counsel Alberto Gonzales and including legal counsels to Cheney and Rumsfeld, as well as officials from the Justice Department. But it was then Cheney who spearheaded the effort to draft a presidential directive that established military commissions for dealing with detainees, essentially barring the captives from federal courts, affording them no constitutional guarantees, and empowering the military to imprison and interrogate them indefinitely. On November 10, at a small White House meeting on the subject chaired by Cheney, the draft directive was approved for Bush's signature. After a lunchtime discussion with Cheney on November 13, Bush signed and released the order.

The next issue was where the detainees would be imprisoned and interrogated. A growing number of captured enemy soldiers were already being temporarily held in makeshift prisons controlled by U.S. forces in and around Afghanistan. But these facilities were quickly becoming inadequate. Human rights groups had begun to complain about the prison conditions, and U.S. authorities were worried about security. In late November 2001, Taliban fighters being held captive at a nineteenth-century fortress known as Qala-i-Jangi rioted, killing CIA agent Johnny Spann and others, and seizing control of the facility for a week before being subdued in vicious battles involving U.S., British, and Afghan forces. Other prisons remained vulnerable to sniper fire and breakout attempts. Clearly, the fanatical Islamist fighters that U.S. forces were facing would not stop fighting even after capture.

An interagency group in Washington looked at options for more-permanent prisoner placement, trying to find a place within U.S. jurisdiction that still would not subject detainees to provisions of U.S. law. Rumsfeld was deeply reluctant to accept responsibility for jailing the detainees. He thought the mission belonged elsewhere in the government, with the Justice Department, perhaps, or the CIA, or even the State Department, which had experience handling mass refugee situations. But as a consensus built around using a military base for housing prisoners, the Pentagon appeared destined to get stuck with the task.

Bases inside the United States and on Guam were considered, but they were deemed relatively easy targets for terrorists to attack, and there were concerns that detainees held there could more easily be subject to legal challenges, since they were on U.S. soil. By contrast, the U.S. military facility at Guantánamo Bay on the southeastern tip of Cuba was isolated and well defended, bordered by water and already fenced and mined. And because it was technically not a part of U.S. sovereign soil, it offered the prospect of keeping enemy prisoners away from U.S. courts.

A strong objection against turning the facility at Guantánamo into a prison camp was registered by the Pentagon official responsible for Latin America, Roger Pardo-Maurer. He predicted the move would prove controversial and would afford Cuban leader Fidel Castro a fresh opening for political attacks on the United States. Further, Pardo-Maurer disputed the notion that Guantánamo would shield detainees from the U.S. legal system. Rather, he contended, the proximity of the site to U.S. shores would make it convenient for American lawyers to represent detainees there. Instead, he recommended holding detainees on "some radioactive rock in the Pacific that takes thirty-six hours of flight time to get there— a place where no one would want to go, a place out of sight, out of mind."

Justice Department lawyers also warned that use of Guantánamo could not guarantee exemption from judicial review. In a memorandum to Jim Haynes, the Pentagon's general counsel, on December 28, Patrick Philbin and John Yoo, both deputy assistants to the attorney general, concluded that a U.S. court probably could not "properly entertain an application for a writ of habeas corpus by an enemy alien detained" at Guantánamo. But they added that because "the issue has not yet been definitively resolved by the courts . . . we caution that there is some possibility that a district court would entertain such an application." Nonetheless, senior administration officials figured that the war would not last very long and that by the time the legal challenges had exhausted themselves, the military situation would be resolved.

Rumsfeld knew the choice of Guantánamo was far from perfect. At a Pentagon news conference on December 27, he called the facility "the least worst place" available but added that its disadvantages "seem to be modest relative to the alternatives." Afterward, aware of how passionately opposed Pardo-Maurer had been to the use of Guantánamo, Rumsfeld personally met with him to explain the decision. "He went out of his way," Pardo-Maurer recalled. "He invited me to his office and said, 'Listen, this is why we have to do it, this is the least bad option.' I was very surprised, because I had been overruled before on things and he'd never tried to unruffle my feathers. But this was one where he did. I still don't know why."

Rumsfeld was concerned that the detention mission could easily become too big and that if he wasn't careful, the Defense Department would end up retaining responsibility for many more people than he thought appropriate. In the early planning for Guantánamo operations, military officers produced plans envisioning a facility that could accommodate more than two thousand inmates. Rumsfeld asked for something much smaller, complaining that he didn't want to become the "world's jailer." If faced with a limited capacity prison, Rumsfeld argued, commanders would feel pressure to release all but those they had true reason to retain. "He basically thought, whatever number we build, we will fill," said Matthew Waxman, a young Yale Law School graduate who was on the NSC staff at the time and who became the Pentagon's point man for detainee affairs in the summer of 2004. Ultimately, Rumsfeld approved a Guantánamo plan to house about four hundred detainees.

Still to be decided was whether federal or international law had any jurisdiction over how the captives were treated during their detainment and interrogation. The military was particularly concerned about the Geneva Conventions, the international treaties last revised after World War II that govern the wartime treatment of noncombatants and captured enemy soldiers. In keeping with U.S. values and traditions, the conventions had been respected by all U.S. administrations since 1949. They had been incorporated into domestic U.S. law with the 1996 War Crimes Act, making American officials liable at home for violating provisions of the conventions abroad.

In early January 2002, the Pentagon queried the Justice Department for an opinion on whether the conventions or the War Crimes Act applied to treatment of al Qaeda or Taliban fighters. A forty-two-page draft memorandum circulated on January 9 by Deputy Assistant Attorney General John Yoo and Special Counsel Robert J. Delahunty concluded that neither group was entitled to prisoner-of-war (POW) status or any protection under Geneva. It justified excluding al Qaeda because of the terrorist group's status as a "non-state actor" and because of the nature of the conflict. It disqualified the Taliban, saying that Afghanistan was a failed state, not a normal sovereign country, and that the Taliban were so dominated by al Qaeda and complicit in its actions that one group couldn't be distinguished from the other.

By the time this Justice Department opinion appeared, international criticism of the handling of prisoners by U.S. forces had already erupted in response to photographs of the initial group of captives—chained, clad in orange suits, their eyes and ears covered—arriving at Guantánamo. Asked by reporters about the treatment of prisoners, Rumsfeld suggested at a January 11 Pentagon news briefing that they would be "handled not as prisoners of war, because they're not, but as unlawful combatants." He said that while they were not entitled to the protections of the Geneva Conventions, they would "for the most part" be treated in a manner "reasonably consistent" with the conventions.

Privately, Bush had accepted the Justice Department opinion, which also reflected the views of White House lawyers. Without any formal administration announcement, Rumsfeld issued written instructions to the military on January 19 that effectively nullified half a century of U.S. military adherence to the conventions. He said there would be no prisoner-of-war designation, and although he directed that al Qaeda and Taliban captives should still be treated "humanely" and "in a manner consistent with the principles" of Geneva, he added a broad limiting clause saying that such treatment would be undertaken "to the extent appropriate and consistent with military necessity."

The president's decision had come without any consultation with Myers or Powell, both of whom strongly objected to its terms. Powell and his legal adviser, William Howard Taft IV, pressed White House officials to reconsider. Angered, Myers went to see Rumsfeld, insisting the matter be reviewed at an NSC meeting where he could offer his military advice. The general argued that adherence to the conventions was a cornerstone for the U.S. military and that any departure from its provisions could invite mistreatment of U.S. troops taken captive in the future.

Rumsfeld didn't argue for or against the conventions, according to Feith, who also attended the meeting. But not wanting to be put on the defensive himself, the secretary began firing questions at the general.

Feith had dealt with Geneva issues as far back as the 1980s, when, as a midlevel Pentagon official in the Reagan administration, he had opposed international efforts to extend protection to anti-Israel terrorists. Seeing Myers struggle with some of Rumsfeld's questions, Feith jumped in with what sounded like a compromise. He agreed that al Qaeda did not qualify for the conventions but contended that Afghanistan, which had signed the conventions, was different. In his view, the United States should recognize that Geneva applied there.

In a legalistic twist, though, he said that accepting the applicability of the conventions wasn't the same as granting Taliban captives prisoner-of-war status. In fact, he argued, Taliban combatants weren't conventional fighters and so did not qualify as prisoners of war under Geneva. Feith was trying to have it both ways: reaffirming Geneva but simultaneously declaring that Taliban fighters didn't qualify for the POW provision. Rumsfeld liked the argument so much he asked Feith to come to an NSC meeting that Bush had agreed to convene to reconsider the matter.

In the end, an executive order that Bush issued February 7 tried to walk this line and give the appearance of a balance being struck. It said the president had determined that none of the provisions of Geneva applied to al Qaeda, but the conventions would continue to apply to the conflict with the Taliban. At the same time, the order declared that Taliban fighters did not qualify for POW status because they were "unlawful combatants." Even so, the order went on, echoing Rumsfeld's original directive, the U.S. military would "continue to treat detainees humanely and, to the extent appropriate and consistent with military necessity, in a manner consistent with the principles of Geneva."

Myers saw the president's new order as a partial victory for the case he had made in support of the conventions, and Feith continued to insist for years afterward that a vital principle had been sustained in affirming that the conventions applied at least to the conflict with the Taliban if not to that with al Qaeda. But in practice, there was little distinction in the treatment stipulated for Taliban captives, who were said to be under Geneva, and al Qaeda prisoners, who were placed outside. Bush was promising humane treatment "as a matter of policy," not law. And the caveat about "military necessity" appeared exceedingly flexible and open to broad interpretation by the troops charged with the actual handling of detainees.

From the start, most of the administration's top officials, Rumsfeld included, appeared intent on treating detainee-related issues essentially as a technical legal matter. In so doing, they ended up undervaluing the political repercussions of departing from America's traditional adherence to the conventions. And they failed to anticipate the full impact on military behavior of the move—and the difficulty of devising and executing a new set of rules. The decision to sweep away POW status left a serious gap in standards for treating detainees.

Shortly after Bush's November 2001 order, lawyers representing the Justice and Defense departments and the White House began a series of secret deliberations on methods of prisoner interrogation and on interpretation of a different treaty—the international Convention against Torture and Other Cruel, Inhuman, or Degrading Treatment or Punishment. This would prove another source of major internal division within the Pentagon and the administration and would take years to resolve.

Although the Pentagon ended up with the detainee mission, Rumsfeld continued to regard his department as simply the implementer, not the originator, of a policy that belonged to the whole U.S. government. As Waxman later explained, this mind-set allowed Rumsfeld a degree of remove. "The implication of that being that if you've got a concern, if you've got a problem with the idea of enemy combatants and holding people outside of the strict standards of the Geneva Conventions, don't look at me as though it's a Rumsfeld policy," Waxman said.

At the same time, Rumsfeld himself tended to resist changing the policy after it was set. As problems arose, his inclination was to see them as matters of inadequate implementation, poor oversight, or miscommunication, not of unsound policy. "Whenever it came time to reexamine the policy and consider alternatives or revisions to it, he was not generally among the more enthusiastic reexaminers," Waxman said.

With the passage of time, Rumsfeld has come to recognize that he made a mistake, although he sees the error as one of process, not basic judgment. He faults himself for taking too legalistic an approach initially, saying it would have been better if senior Pentagon officials responsible for policy and management matters had been brought in earlier to play more of a role and provide a broader perspective. As he explained in an interview in late 2008, policies were developing so fast in the weeks after the September 11 attacks that he did not follow his own normal procedures. "All of a sudden, it was just all happening, and the general counsel's office in the Pentagon had the lead," he said. "It never registered in my mind in this particular instance—it did in almost every other case—that these issues ought to be in a policy development or management posture. Looking back at it now, I have a feeling that was a mistake. In retrospect, it would have been better to take all of those issues and put them in the hands of policy or management."

Further, Rumsfeld conceded, more should have been done to engage Congress in drafting the new policies on detainees—something he said that White House officials had opposed. Although Congress did eventually get involved, he noted that this occurred "in duress" after the Supreme Court ruled in 2006 against the administration's original approach.

Donald Rumsfeld (left) wrestles Kent Marlin at the Rainbow Arena in Chicago in 1950 in the finals of an Amateur Athletic Union tournament.
AUTHOR'S COLLECTION

Rumsfeld and his Princeton Roommates, 1954. Front row, left to right: Somers Steelman, Peter Gall, Michael Weatherly. Back row, left to right: Richard Stevens, Joseph Castle, Sidney Wentz, Derek Price, Rumsfeld, Prewitt Turner. AUTHOR'S COLLECTION

Rumsfeld is kissed by his wife Joyce after being sworn in on May 26, 1969, as director of the Office of Economic Opportunity. President Nixon holds their two-year-old son, Nicholas. CORBIS

A Japanese Geisha entertains Rumsfeld, then President Ford's chief of staff, in Kyoto, Japan, in 1974. DAVID HUME KENNERLY/GETTY

Rumsfeld fingers his "stand-up" desk in the White House as he talks with his successor as chief of staff, Richard B. Cheney. BETTMAN/CORBIS

President Ford confers with Rumsfeld, then his defense secretary, at the start of a cabinet meeting in April 1976. AP PHOTO

Rumsfeld describes a flight he made in the B-1 bomber in April 1976 to dramatize the Ford administration's bid for approval of the plane. BETTMAN/CORBIS

President Reagan meets with Rumsfeld who, in November 1983, was beginning a six-month mission as presidential envoy to the Middle East. RON SACHS/CNP/CORBIS

Rumsfeld and General Richard Myers, chairman of the Joint Chiefs of Staff, discuss the start of airstrikes against Taliban and al Qaeda targets in Afghanistan during a Pentagon news conference on October 7, 2001. CORBIS

Rumsfeld engages Secretary of State Colin Powell in discussion in the Oval Office in February 2003. CHARLES OMMANNEY/CONTACT PRESS IMAGES

Rumsfeld and Deputy Secretary of Defense Paul Wolfowitz confer in Rumsfeld's office at the Pentagon in November 2003. DAVID HUME KENNERLY/GETTY

Cheney and Rumsfeld chat during a relaxed moment near their country houses in St. Michaels, Maryland, in March 2006. DAVID HUME KENNERLY/GETTY

In May 2003, General Tommy Franks, head of U.S. Central Command, gestures during a Pentagon news conference as Rumsfeld looks on. CHARLES DHARAPAK/AP PHOTO

In June 2003, Rumsfeld briefs the press at the Pentagon on the situation in Iraq. CHARLES DHARAPAK/AP PHOTO

Rumsfeld flashes a grin during a meeting with L. Paul
Bremer III in Mosul, Iraq, on September 5, 2003.
GURSEL ESER/ANATOLIA/AP PHOTO

Rumsfeld visits Abu Ghraib prison on May 13, 2004, accompanied by Major General Geoffrey D. Miller (third from left), who had charge of U.S. military detainee operations in Iraq.
DAVID HUME KENNERLY/POOL/REUTERS/CORBIS

A master of expressive hand gestures, Rumsfeld displays
a variety during appearances before Congress.

DENNIS COOK/AP PHOTO

J. SCOTT APPLEWHITE/AP PHOTO

Ron Edmonds/AP Photo

J. Scott Applewhite/AP Photo

Rumsfeld is surrounded by U.S. troops after an address at a town hall-style meeting in Fallujah, Iraq, on December 23, 2005. JIM YOUNG-POOL/GETTY IMAGES

Rumsfeld is joined by General George Casey at the Baghdad International Airport during a visit to Iraq in April 2006. JIM WATSON/POOL/EPA/CORBIS

Rumsfeld addresses reporters during a Pentagon briefing on August, 21, 2003, as General John Abizaid, head of the U.S. Central Command, looks on. KEVIN LAMARQUE/REUTERS/ CORBIS

Rumsfeld and General Peter Pace, vice chairman of the Joint Chiefs of Staff, speak during a briefing at the Pentagon on August 20, 2002. Pace also later served as chairman under Rumsfeld. REUTERS/CORBIS

Rumsfeld and his wife Joyce arrive for an official White House dinner on July 19, 2005.
MATTHEW CAVANAUGH/EPA/CORBIS

In the Oval Office on November 8, 2006, just after the announcement of his resignation, Rumsfeld glances down as President Bush looks on. KEVIN LAMARQUE/REUTERS/ CORBIS

Rumsfeld waves to the audience during his farewell ceremony at the Pentagon on December 15, 2006. ATLAS PRESS

CHAPTER 10

Iterative Planning

While the war in Afghanistan demonstrated new possibilities for the use of U.S. military forces, it left Rumsfeld still groping for clarity in what he wanted to achieve under his slogan of transformation. In the immediate aftermath of the September 11 attacks, he had seemed to indicate in some public statements that the drive for change would have to slow. Many had assumed that the plan to make over the armed forces would need to give way, at least in part, to the demands of waging war.

But behind the scenes, Rumsfeld had not let up. Determined to press ahead, he began a series of meetings with his senior civilian and military staffs aimed at defining just what transformation should mean and how it should accomplish its ends. He knew that if the campaign was to take hold in the vast Pentagon bureaucracy, the military chiefs and service secretaries would have to buy into it themselves. He recognized the need for senior management to have a common view of what they were working toward.

Responsibility for coordinating this exercise in reaching a consensus definition fell to Ken Krieg, the former paper-industry executive initially hired to coordinate a senior management council made up principally of the service secretaries. Krieg hadn't really given much thought to military transformation. But assigned in the fall to put together a briefing for the Senior Level Review Group—Rumsfeld's forum of top civilian officials and the Joint Chiefs—Krieg assembled some charts and videos, hoping that the presentation would at least come across as high-tech and visually appealing.

Rumsfeld was thoroughly unimpressed. He told Krieg to get rid of the vapid slogans and marketing photos and to develop something instead that would spark staff dialogue about the elements of military transformation. More meetings followed through the winter and into the spring of 2002, with the Defense Department's senior leadership seated around a conference table trying to hammer out a common set of terms that would define transformation.

"Rumsfeld didn't care what the group came up with," recalled Art Cebrowski, a retired three-star admiral hired by Rumsfeld to set up and head an office of transformation. "Regardless of who offered a definition, he kept pulling the words apart, drawing out the implications of them, asking why this concept or that one lay behind them, what evidence was there that supported the definition and so on. He was relentless about it. In meeting after meeting, he'd go back to the last discussion of what we'd said transformation meant and then challenge the definition with something he'd thought about afterward. And we argued over every single word.

"After several of these sessions, I realized Rumsfeld was making three points. First, that whatever its definition, the senior leadership had to believe they had come up with it. It was theirs. They owned it. They were not to delegate their ownership down into the various staffs. Second, transformation was a top priority, worthy of the personal time and energy of the leaders. And third, that the secretary of defense was going to be relentless in its pursuit."

The group looked at historical examples of military change. They discussed risk taking in a traditionally conservative military culture. They considered the difficulty of delegating decision making in a place like the Pentagon with a rigid hierarchical structure, stovepiped functions, and a need-to-know mind-set. They pondered how to shift from a central-planning structure to one much more attuned to adaptive planning, from a closed architecture to an open one, from a Cold War world where the threat had been largely fixed and predictable to a contemporary world of shifting threats.

"Frankly, the debates about what they thought transformation was were far more important than the product," Krieg said in an interview. He likened the process to painting on a blank canvas, with the result being more like an impressionist portrait than a nineteenth-century landscape.

What began to emerge from the discussions was a sense not of any particular endpoint but of the journey itself. Nor was transformation something to be accomplished in a short period of time or something limited to particular weapons systems and programs. As always with Rumsfeld, it was about changing the mind-set and the culture. From that, everything else would flow.

"People were inclined just to say, You tell me what transformation means and I'll go do it," Krieg said. "But we were saying, We can't tell you what it means; you've got to go figure it out. We can give you directions, but if we say item X means transformation, you'll buy a lot of item X and nothing will necessarily change."

Rumsfeld and the group finally drafted a formal definition, although it hardly had the makings of a bumper sticker. Transformation, they agreed, was to be "a process that shapes the changing nature of military competition and cooperation through new combinations of concepts, capabilities, people, processes, and organizations that exploit our nation's advantages and protect against our asymmetric vulnerabilities to sustain our strategic position, contributing to peace and stability in the world."

The phrasing was nearly unintelligible, but the basic idea was that transformation should be assertive and should apply broadly to much of what the Pentagon does. A more helpful definition came in a list the group made saying what transformation wasn't. It wasn't, for instance, a silver-bullet solution to problems. Nor was it something to be done to all the force at once or in a short period of time. And it wasn't just about weapons systems or platforms.

Missing from these definitions was any indication of how quickly change should occur—or how it should be measured. But Rumsfeld at least had gotten the department's senior staff fully engaged in thinking about the process.

At the same time, he had secretly begun planning the invasion of Iraq and was stepping up efforts to hunt down al Qaeda operatives around the world. Skeptics doubted that he could transform the military and wage war. But Rumsfeld figured the very challenge of fighting a different kind of war would help transform the military.

By the time the defense secretary's 2002 annual report to the president and Congress was issued in August, Rumsfeld had stopped talking about how to balance the demands of winning the war on terrorism with the need to transform the military. He was focused instead on how to transform the military quickly enough to win wars. The campaign for change had taken on an even greater urgency.

The September 11 attacks, he wrote, had underscored the increased vulnerability of the United States to novel and surprising means of attack. "As a result, the United States faces a new imperative. It must both win the present war against terrorism and prepare now for future wars— wars notably different from those of the past century and even from the current conflict. Some believe that, with the U.S. in the midst of a difficult and dangerous war on terrorism, now is not the time to transform our Armed Forces. The opposite is true. Now is precisely the time to make changes."

For Rumsfeld, it was not either-or. It would have to be both.

Rumsfeld's effort to transform and fight simultaneously was fateful for the defense secretary. While there arguably was a certain synergy between the two, attempting both at the same time threatened to muddle the focus of military leaders and exhaust the energies of the Pentagon.

Still, Rumsfeld was hell-bent on making a go of it. The success of the Afghan experience had reinforced his notions of a new kind of warfare. It had demonstrated some of the principles of transformation—the effectiveness of a small number of forces when coupled with the right technology, for instance, and the ability of technology and tactical surprise to substitute for mass.

The Afghan War, though, had been small scale, and its unique characteristics left open the question of whether what had worked in Afghanistan could be applied elsewhere. U.S. military commanders, particularly in the Army, continued to hold to the doctrine of overwhelming force that Colin Powell had articulated as chairman and that had proven itself in the 1991 Persian Gulf War. They believed that war could not be fought on the cheap, that numbers and weight of fire still counted.

The Iraq War looming on the horizon presented Rumsfeld with another chance to employ new concepts. A rapid defeat of Iraq on Rumsfeld's terms would go further than had the Afghan case in eroding Army resistance to his goal of transformation. And while the Afghan War plan had been devised in a hurry and executed with much improvisation, Iraq would afford more opportunity for preparation.

On November 21, 2001, after Rumsfeld received the first order from Bush to start developing notions of what it would take to remove Saddam Hussein from power, he immediately directed General Tommy Franks to devise a concept of operations. It was the beginning of a war-planning process that would show Rumsfeld in full immersion.

Rumsfeld's interaction with Franks was complex, much more than a defense secretary dictating to a general. Rumsfeld wanted to be sure Franks took ownership of the war-planning effort. At the same time, the secretary had no intention of simply waiting to approve a finished plan. In typical Rumsfeld fashion, he involved himself deeply from the start, thinking through concepts, reviewing early proposals, and providing frequent feedback. He conferred often with Franks, on the phone, in person, and in writing, always questioning, challenging, nudging.

"Rather than issuing orders, Rumsfeld preferred to massage concepts," Feith explained in his memoir. "Rumsfeld worked on strategic analysis through a kind of Socratic method of question and answer. He had a way of getting people to offer him back his own ideas, as if they were their own. It was a tour de force of reason and education, not compulsion. But it could be discomfiting for those on the receiving end."

Rumsfeld and Franks called their war-planning process an "iterative approach," and there was no question that it involved a healthy give-and-take. But it was also clear that much of the pushing and prodding came from one direction.

During the Afghanistan campaign, Rumsfeld had forged a strong bond with Franks, a six-foot-three former artillery officer with a drill-sergeant manner and a Texas drawl. The general had nearly quit under the secretary's incessant pounding, but he had stood his ground. Rumsfeld appreciated subordinates who could push back respectfully. Skirting outright confrontation, the defense secretary and the CENTCOM chief had learned to work as a team.

The original plan for invading Iraq that CENTCOM had on its shelf, OPLAN 1003, was a relic of old-think. Massive, cumbersome, and inefficient, the plan essentially envisioned refighting the 1991 Persian Gulf War. It called for a force of at least 380,000 troops—and potentially well over 400,000 if the full complement of support units were sent—and required more than six months for a buildup before the start of offensive military action.

Rumsfeld told Franks he wanted the plan replaced with an entirely new concept that would use some of the tactics that had worked well in Afghanistan—heavy reliance on sophisticated, well-targeted precision weaponry and on Special Operations forces that would lessen the need for large numbers of combat ground troops. Rumsfeld was looking not to just rejigger the old plan but to convert to another model.

By the end of December 2001, when Franks first discussed the plan with Bush, the general had managed to shrink the projected force significantly and shorten deployment timelines considerably. His concept called for an initial invasion force of 145,000 to deploy and start fighting, with additional forces flowing until the troop level reached about 275,000. Still, Rumsfeld wasn't satisfied. As the war planning continued through the winter, the secretary repeatedly pressed Franks to come up with new iterations involving greater speed and lower force levels.

By early February 2002, Franks had refined his plan and dubbed the new version the "Generated Start." It allowed only ninety days for forces to build from the time the president decided to attack until the start of combat—half the time of the original plan—but it also envisioned continued reinforcements after the invasion began. The reduced preparation time was intended to catch the Iraqis by surprise. Near-simultaneous ground and air attacks, another departure from the past practice of holding back ground forces until after days of air strikes, were also under consideration.

Rumsfeld, though, urged more work be done on options with even less buildup time and even smaller numbers of forces. Over the next few months, Franks and his staff produced another approach, called the "Running Start," that provided for the possibility of launching a ground attack within just forty-five days and with as few as eighteen thousand troops. This came closer to satisfying Rumsfeld, but the risks of such a quick start made military planners uneasy. By August, a sort of middle option, referred to as the "Hybrid," was presented; it also had a short buildup time but took advantage of preparations already made in Kuwait to deploy forces there more quickly.

Eventually, commanders, worried about an advancing force finding itself stalled in southern Iraq while waiting for reinforcements to arrive, were able to increase the size of the invading force back up to the neighborhood of the Generated Start. The final invasion plan, known as Cobra II, wasn't as revolutionary as some of the earlier, more innovative versions, but it did mark an evolutionary advance over what Rumsfeld had found on the shelf when the planning began.

———•———

To help carry out his larger vision of military transformation, Rumsfeld was determined to bring a new group of leaders into top positions, leaders who shared his notions of change and his sense of urgency. What he wanted to avoid was another strained relationship like the one he had with General Eric Shinseki, the Army chief of staff. Shinseki had stopped coming to most transformation brainstorming sessions. The Army tended to be represented instead by the vice chief, General Jack Keane, an engaging, assertive New York City native who got along well with Rumsfeld.

Shinseki's term as Army chief wasn't up until the summer of 2003, but early in 2002 Rumsfeld was already looking at a successor. Custom called for the successor to be named a few months before the end of the departing chief's term. In this case, though, Rumsfeld didn't wait, and a full fourteen months before Shinseki's scheduled exit, the *Washington Post* reported that Keane had been designated the next chief. Rumsfeld never fired Shinseki, but the disclosure of the successor in April 2002 was widely perceived as an affront to the Army leader and a further sign of the deep rift between the general and the secretary.

The decision appears to have been an outgrowth, at least in part, of an effort by Rumsfeld to do some longer-range personnel planning about more than just the top Army job. Steve Herbits, one of Rumsfeld's kitchen cabinet members, had urged the secretary to depart from the past practice of considering vacancies only as they occurred and instead to start mapping out replacements for a whole set of senior officer positions as much as a year and a half in advance. Herbits argued that such advance planning would allow for better matchups between available candidates and open jobs.

To this end, Herbits put together a briefing for Rumsfeld in early 2002 with a giant chart showing the key openings that would need to be filled in the coming eighteen months or so. In the near term, the top NATO military job and the head of a newly established Northern Command, set up to focus on defense of the United States, required consideration. Later was a requirement for a new Army chief of staff to replace Shinseki.

At the time, Keane was expected to become head of Northern Command. But Herbits instead recommended making him Shinseki's successor, given Keane's reputation as an innovative thinker. Rumsfeld liked the idea; he was eager to bring some fresh thinking to the Army. But the worry was that if Keane didn't get the Northern Command job and wasn't assured of the Army chief's position, because that selection normally wouldn't come for another year or so, he might feel slighted. So the decision was made to let him know he was slated to succeed Shinseki and to pass the word to Bush and other officials.

Word also leaked to the *Washington Post*, although the article that appeared was not just about the choice of Keane. It reported a series of personnel changes that Rumsfeld had recommended. These included filling the top NATO job with a Marine for the first time and selecting an Air Force general to take over Northern Command. The choices were portrayed as an effort to establish a new generation of relatively nonconformist top officers deemed likely to be more supportive of the administration's goal of radical alterations in the armed forces.

Indeed, especially the choice of General Jim Jones, the Marine commandant, to become supreme allied commander in Europe represented a sharp break with tradition. No Marine had ever held the coveted European position, and no Marine commandant had ever moved on to another high-level post in the U.S. military. The Army traditionally had held the top slot in Europe and had hoped to regain it after the expiration of the term of General Joseph Ralston, an Air Force officer. By picking a general from the Marines—the service with a reputation for agility and versatility—Rumsfeld appeared to be sending another message of diminished confidence in the Army and to be seeking to shake up the U.S. military in Europe.

The Jones decision turned out to be the first of a series of moves Rumsfeld would make to break the traditional patterns of which officers occupied the regional commands and other high-level Pentagon positions. In time, he would send Navy admirals to jobs historically held by Air Force generals, Air Force generals to jobs previously held by the Army, and Marines to atypical positions as well.

But there was no denying that the disclosure in the spring of 2002 that a new Army chief had already been chosen was also a slap to Shinseki. Rumsfeld had considered simply firing him. But both Dick Myers, the chairman, and Pete Pace, the vice chairman, had strongly objected. Publicizing Rumsfeld's selection of Keane so far in advance effectively made an early lame duck of Shinseki, and Rumsfeld did nothing to minimize the impact of the report. Shinseki took great offense, and the move was interpreted in military ranks as the kind of harsh treatment other senior officers could expect if they crossed Rumsfeld. It cast an even darker pall over relations between the secretary's office and the Army.

———•———

Less than a month after the Shinseki/Keane disclosure, the Army received another blow in a decision by Rumsfeld to cancel plans to build the Crusader, a mobile, rapid-firing artillery system. The Army had argued that the Crusader, designed to deliver three times the firepower of the existing Paladin system and to do so farther and faster, was vital to its future needs. The new weapon also was strongly backed by influential lawmakers from Oklahoma, where it was to be assembled and where many of the new howitzers were to be based.

But the Crusader had drawn controversy for months. Critics contended that the forty-ton system was too heavy to be transported quickly to battle. Particularly after the war in Afghanistan had demonstrated the high accuracy of satellite- and laser-guided bombs, the Crusader looked even more like an anachronism of outdated Cold War thinking.

Pressed by some civilian aides to cut the $11 billion program, Rumsfeld had initially resisted. His budget plan for fiscal 2003 had already gone to Capitol Hill with funding for the Crusader still intact. But in early 2002, as an important planning document was being completed for the 2004 budget, the matter again came under review.

Several senior aides to Rumsfeld and Wolfowitz—among them Cambone; Barry Watts, the Pentagon's chief programs analyst; and Jaymie Durnan, Wolfowitz's chief of staff—pressed the case for termination of the program. More persuasive for Wolfowitz were the arguments of a retired general, Paul Gorman, who advised the money could be better invested in new, more accurate artillery systems. Accordingly, he asked the Army to look at funding such alternate technologies as the Excalibur, a precision-guided 155 mm artillery shell. Shortly afterward, he was informed that the Army, without telling him, had delayed completion of the Excalibur program. "That for me was the final straw, and I decided we really needed to bite the bullet and take all the money from Crusader and put it into other kinds of Army artillery," Wolfowitz recalled.

He recommended cancellation to Rumsfeld, who approved the move. Wolfowitz then informed Tom White, the secretary of the Army, triggering a brief battle on Capitol Hill to try to save the program. Army officials conferred with lawmakers and faxed to the Hill a set of talking points, which argued that terminating the Crusader program would endanger soldiers on the battlefield. The lobbying, and particularly the talking points, drew Rumsfeld's ire, and he ordered a probe by the Army inspector general into whether Army officials had behaved inappropriately. White claimed no responsibility for the talking points, blaming them on an overeager midlevel official. The inspector general eventually cleared White, but relations between the Army secretary and Rumsfeld never recovered.

By narrow margins, the relevant congressional committees agreed to the Crusader's demise. The fight over it marked a pivotal moment in Rumsfeld's effort to bend the individual armed services to his will by enforcing his priorities on weapons purchases. The Crusader was the most prominent Pentagon weapons program to face cancellation since 1991, when Dick Cheney killed the Navy's A-12 fighter jet program. Even so, the Crusader episode was more than a battle over a single weapon; it represented a clash of visions over how best to transform the military to prepare for future threats.

Although Rumsfeld succeeded in eliminating the weapon, the long-term value of the victory was questionable. The uproar over the decision—aggravated in part by the awkward timing, after the 2003 budget had already gone to the Hill, and in the face of fierce Army resistance—made the Bush administration skittish about going after other military programs in their sights. "We were basically told by the White House after Crusader, 'OK, you killed one. Don't try it again; it's too painful for us,'" recalled a senior Pentagon official who had pushed for termination. Moreover, the Army eventually ended up with a new artillery system called the Non-Line-of-Sight cannon—highly mobile and capable of launching multiple rounds like Crusader, although with a smaller gun.

The handling of Crusader also underscored Rumsfeld's own reduced role in the acquisition area. While the secretary did forcibly defend the decision before Congress and other critics, the initiative had come not from him but from his subordinates. As interested as he was in some nuts-and-bolts aspects of Pentagon management—notably, organizational and command-structure issues—the ins and outs of the procurement business never engaged him to the same degree. He just was not much of a hardware guy.

His lack of involvement extended to an absence of contact with defense-industry executives. Barry Blechman, a private consultant who had served with Rumsfeld on the missile-threat commission, discovered this early. Soon after Rumsfeld took office, Blechman, who was organizing a conference on procurement reform sponsored by the aerospace industry association, tried to get Rumsfeld to attend. The presidents of all the major defense contractors would be at the breakfast, providing Rumsfeld a great opportunity to meet and mix. But the secretary refused.

In fact, during Rumsfeld's entire time in office, he declined to meet with any executives about a defense contract. He told associates that he did not want industry representatives with business interests affecting his strategic judgments.

———•———

Recognizing how badly strained his relations with the Army had become, Rumsfeld sought to make at least a token gesture of reconciliation by picking an Army officer to be his senior military assistant when the spot opened in the fall of 2002. However, after asking the Army to recommend some candidates, he was disappointed with the list. It appeared to Rumsfeld that the Army wasn't offering up its best officers. So Vice Admiral Ed Giambastiani, Rumsfeld's departing military assistant, arranged to meet privately with Shinseki and White.

"I don't understand what you guys are doing," Giambastiani said to them when they got together. "The secretary and I would like to select an Army officer to be my relief as a senior military assistant. We asked for nominations, but the ones you gave us were not very good." Giambastiani appealed to the Army leaders to reconsider and forward the names of some of their most capable three-star generals for the job. The admiral just about guaranteed them that if they put forward some good candidates, the position would go to the Army.

Others were quickly nominated, and Rumsfeld picked Lieutenant General Bantz John Craddock, a onetime tank commander who had led the U.S. forces in Kosovo. After taking over as Rumsfeld's military assistant in the fall of 2002, Craddock did what he could to patch up the battered ties between the secretary and the Army. Trying, for instance, to facilitate Shinseki's appearance at meetings attended by the other chiefs and Rumsfeld, Craddock would check proposed meeting dates in advance with Shinseki's office. But he was successful only part of the time in ensuring the Army general's presence.

Craddock also sought to get the Army to tailor its briefings to the secretary by making them more succinct and by reducing the number of pages. But Army officials could not seem to limit themselves. Their briefing packages continued to contain dozens of complex PowerPoint slides. "I'd say to the Army, 'You've got forty-five minutes; you need to come in with five slides and talk,'" Craddock recalled. "They'd come in with thirty slides and would get through three because the secretary would lose patience."

———·———

The Navy had its own issues with Rumsfeld, but was helped in resolving them by the better relationship that existed between Rumsfeld and Admiral Vern Clark. A top priority for the Navy was to build a new aircraft carrier. Dubbed the CVNX-1 (the "X" was for experimental), the proposed ship was to usher in a new class of carriers to replace the Nimitz-class designed in the 1960s. Among the innovations would be a more powerful nuclear reactor, a new electrical distribution system, and an electromagnetic (instead of steam-powered) aircraft catapult system. The new ship would be a transitional model—more cutting-edge technology was planned for its successor, the CVNX-2. But that ship wasn't joining the fleet until 2018—which struck Rumsfeld and his aides as too long to wait. They wanted to skip the transitional carrier and go right to the CVNX-2. They also started looking at other options, such as smaller conventional carriers and an oversized amphibious assault vessel that could host more vertical-takeoff jets.

The problem for Navy officials with skipping the CVNX-1 was that it would reduce the number of carriers in the fleet from twelve to eleven, since aged carriers currently limping toward retirement would not be replaced in a timely fashion. Without at least a dozen carriers, Navy officials contended, they would not be able to meet military requirements.

To save the CVNX-1, Clark presented a briefing to Rumsfeld that included a map of the world with hockey pucks spread on it to represent the Navy's carrier fleet. Most of the pucks were located in home ports and in maintenance yards. At any given time, the map showed, only one out of every four carriers was deployed because of lengthy maintenance cycles and long transit times to theaters of operation. Clark also showed Rumsfeld a chart indicating the substantial number of carriers that had been deployed just since the September 11 attacks. That got the secretary's attention.

Given the lack of ships normally ready for sea duty, Clark argued, the Navy needed its full complement of a dozen carriers, particularly if it intended to support operations like an invasion of Iraq. At the same time, Clark acknowledged to Rumsfeld that something had to be done to make more ships available for deployment on short notice. The admiral also recognized that the Navy couldn't afford to wait for some of the new technology on its drawing boards. He proposed incorporating into the CVNX-1 some of the improvements that were planned for the succeeding model.

Impressed with the briefing, Rumsfeld virtually approved the new carrier at the meeting. "That was the first and maybe the only time we got a decision on the spot in a meeting with Rumsfeld," Clark recalled.

In time, the Navy developed ways to make considerably more efficient use of its entire fleet. This included swapping crews by flying them out to ships, rather than bringing the ships all the way back home and then all the way back out, and investing in more spare parts to reduce maintenance downtime. Further, the Navy adopted a new approach to turning ships around after they returned from deployments and making them ready to go back to sea. Previously, a returning ship would enter a maintenance period of two months, then begin four months of basic crew training. Under the new plan, training began almost immediately and was conducted more flexibly, so that ships were ready sooner to deploy again. The goal was to enable the Navy to be prepared, if necessary, to deploy six carriers within thirty days of notification and two more within ninety days—twice the number of ships available under the previous approach.

"The way to get Rumsfeld's attention was to show that you had challenged basic assumptions, to admit that you were wanting, and to demonstrate that you were going to do better," Clark said. "I believe that when he really started listening to me, he decided, 'Hey, this guy gets it.'"

———

As the Iraq War plan took shape, Rumsfeld conferred with his staff to define the precise goals for the operation. In the immediate aftermath of the September 11 attacks, he had been quick to consider military action against Iraq and now supported the major arguments the administration was putting forward to build its case for an invasion: Iraq was controlled by an evil regime that brutalized its own people; its role in sponsoring terrorism and harboring terrorists made it as guilty and liable for punishment as the terrorists themselves; it was thought to have weapons of mass destruction and to be pursuing more; and since its forces had been driven out of Kuwait in 1991, it had refused repeatedly to abide by a long list of U.N. resolutions.

Some in the administration were also driven by the powerful notion of implanting a democracy in Iraq to foster the spread of democracy throughout the Middle East. This idea had little appeal to Rumsfeld. He tended to be wary of countries installing government systems in other countries. He certainly believed in the exercise of U.S. power, but for the purpose of freeing people and creating the conditions enabling them to set up the kind of government they wanted. With Iraq, his foremost concern centered on the security threats it posed. Besides, he worried about getting bogged down in a prolonged occupation. If U.S. troops went in, he wanted them to get the job done quickly and then get out.

Feith recalled a number of discussions with Rumsfeld in the summer of 2002 about the idea of promoting democracy in the context of Iraq. He described the secretary as wanting to ensure that the internal memos and papers being drafted then to explain the administration's goals and objectives in Iraq did not come across as too ambitious or overly simplistic about implanting democracy. "His main point was that the U.S. government should not suggest that specific institutions or formulas suitable for the United States are necessarily imposable or suitable or workable elsewhere," Feith said in an interview. "I spent a lot of time with him coming up with words that he was comfortable with."

Rumsfeld argued against making the establishment of democracy the goal. Rather, he favored less direct wording that portrayed the United States as assisting in the creation of institutions for democracy. That was, in his mind, an important distinction. The first suggested imposing a system from outside; the second, building one up from inside. "It's not for us to create, it's for us to assist them to create," Rumsfeld argued, according to Feith. "People have to create their own democracies."

While not one to talk about exporting democracy, Rumsfeld nonetheless did like to speak pointedly about the differences between what freedom-loving countries could achieve and what dictatorships could. The most frequent example he cited was the case of the two Koreas, and to illustrate his argument, he often mentioned a satellite photograph of the Korean peninsula that he kept in his office under glass on a coffee table.

The photograph, which he referred to as his favorite picture, was a nighttime shot in which no lights are visible north of the Demilitarized Zone except for the area around the capital, Pyongyang. In the south, the land is ablaze. He liked it because of the visual image it provided of the stark contrast between the communist north and the democratic south. Same people, same resources, Rumsfeld would note. The difference was, the north has a repressive political regime and a command economy, and people there are starving and economic growth is stunted, whereas in the south, where a free political and economic system exists, an economic miracle had occurred.

———•———

In other ways, too, Rumsfeld appeared somewhat detached from controversial policy actions or positions on Iraq taken by his department. One particularly contentious undertaking involved a small two-person intelligence-analysis cell set up in Feith's policy office in late 2001. Called the Counter Terrorism Evaluation Group, its purpose was to sift through existing intelligence to find possible links between terror networks and governments.

Although intelligence analysis was normally the province of the CIA, some administration officials regarded the CIA as insufficiently aggressive on the subject of Iraq. By the summer of 2002, the group, whose membership had evolved over time, was aimed at identifying links between al Qaeda and Saddam Hussein's government.

The operation subsequently became the subject of considerable scrutiny by the media and Congress, where it was portrayed as an example of excessive Pentagon zeal and part of a larger effort to distort intelligence data to justify the invasion of Iraq. The CIA viewed the Pentagon group as a relatively amateurish operation inclined to cherry-pick existing bits of information and use them to support the case for war. An investigation by the Pentagon's inspector general, completed in 2007, found that the group did not violate any laws or mislead Congress but called its effort to provide "alternative intelligence assessments" from those given by the CIA and other intelligence agencies "inappropriate." Feith and other Pentagon officials insisted the group wasn't producing any formal assessments, just subjecting the conclusions of the intelligence community to a fresh look.

Rumsfeld authorized the group, but his own involvement remained largely tangential, limited to receiving a briefing or two from the group and recommending that its analyses be shared with senior officials at the White House. Much of the inspiration and direction for the effort came from Wolfowitz. "The role of Wolfowitz gets lost here," Peter Rodman, an assistant secretary who played a part in overseeing the operation, said in an interview. "He'd be calling us into his office every day, asking for stuff. That was the case with the intelligence group."

Feith, in his memoir, also credited Wolfowitz with being the driving force, noting the deputy secretary's long-standing criticism of intelligence work. "As a student of intelligence, a walking encyclopedia in some areas of the field, and a severe critic of poor intelligence tradecraft, Wolfowitz was not shy about challenging the quality of intelligence products," Feith wrote. "He had been doing it since at least the Ford Administration, from inside and outside the government."

Similarly, Wolfowitz and Feith took the Pentagon lead in a major interagency struggle over the composition of an interim government in Iraq after the fall of Saddam Hussein. The question was whether it should be filled with exiles who had lived outside Iraq or with people who had remained inside the country and endured Saddam's rule. The Pentagon's policy staff, backed by outside conservatives such as Richard Perle, favored incorporating externals in the interest of turning power over to the Iraqis as quickly as possible. But State Department and CIA officials argued that an interim government composed solely of externals would lack domestic legitimacy. And they suspected the real motivation of the pro-externals crowd was to install a particularly prominent but controversial exiled activist, Ahmed Chalabi, as Iraq's next leader.

A Western businessman and secular Shiite who had left Iraq as a child and spent the 1990s rallying support for a U.S. effort to depose Saddam, Chalabi headed the Iraqi National Congress, a London-based umbrella group of anti-Saddam exiles. CIA officials considered him discredited following bank fraud charges against him in Jordan, and State Department officials viewed him suspiciously as a manipulative operator with little following inside Iraq. But he was popular with Wolfowitz, Perle, and officials in the vice president's office, who regarded him as a skillful, hardworking organizer, and Pentagon officials had treated him as an important source of intelligence about Iraq.

Wolfowitz and Feith have maintained that their position on Chalabi was grossly distorted by State Department and CIA officials. They insist that they were not pushing to anoint Chalabi as the leader of Iraq after Saddam and contend that the animosity toward him at State and the CIA was much greater than the support for him elsewhere in the administration.

But Feith's own deputy, Ryan Henry, recalls a strong preference among the Pentagon's neoconservative contingent for Chalabi. Henry recounted how, in discussions soon after the invasion of Iraq about setting up an interim government there, he had suggested simply looking for the best Iraqis to work with. "But I was told by the neocons, 'You can't say that,'" Henry said. "They had a model, a view of the people they could trust, which included Chalabi and his crowd. They'd say, 'If we'd just embrace Chalabi, we'd be better off.'"

In any case, Rumsfeld tended to leave dealings with Chalabi and the rest of the Iraqi exile community to Wolfowitz. But the secretary did meet with some exiles on occasion at Wolfowitz's urging and, over time, came to see a role for them in postwar Iraq. "He was never really enamored with Chalabi," said Craddock, Rumsfeld's senior military assistant at the time. "He pretty much deferred to Wolfowitz, who would come in and say, 'You've got to talk to this guy, you've got to hear what he's got to say.' So he'd listen and be skeptical. But over time, I think, Wolfowitz wore him down. That may be a harsh judgment, but Paul was very persuasive and persistent."

Along with the rest of the Pentagon's leadership, Rumsfeld was fully supportive of the quick establishment of an interim Iraqi government after Saddam's fall. This interim authority would have drawn heavily from exile groups, including Chalabi's Iraqi National Congress. "Although he opposed trying to choose another country's leader, Rumsfeld favored helping to establish political principles for Iraq's reconstruction," Feith recalled. "He thought the U.S. government should organize a group of responsible Iraqis in the hope that, when the time came, they might steer Iraq toward creating a broad-based, representative government. Laying the groundwork for a political process would be crucial to a timely transfer of authority to Iraqis, to avoid a prolonged occupation government."

———·———

Wayne Downing, a retired four-star Army general and onetime head of Special Operations Command, found Rumsfeld both fascinating and infuriating as defense secretary. Downing joined the administration after the September 11 attacks, signing on to the NSC staff as the deputy adviser for combating terrorism. He got off to a rocky start with Rumsfeld, who initially objected to Downing's position. In a November 2001 memo to Condoleezza Rice, with copies to Cheney and Powell, Rumsfeld took issue with the charter for the new position, noting that it had been drafted and signed without his approval. He said it called for Downing to provide military advice to the president, which he observed pointedly was the responsibility of the chairman of the Joint Chiefs of Staff. And he said Downing's mandate "could be read as infringing on the chain of command from the president to the secretary of defense to the combatant commanders," warning that the suggestion of any additional layers is "exceedingly dangerous."

The charter had meant to define Downing's role only as a coordinator. But as Rumsfeld's memo made clear, the defense secretary wasn't going to abide any encroachment on his turf. Not long afterward, at a White House meeting that Downing was attending as a backbencher, Rumsfeld walked over to talk. The secretary was interested in Downing's military record. "I can remember him asking what I was doing in 1975," Downing recalled. "I told him I was the executive officer of a Ranger battalion. He said, 'What rank were you?' I said, 'Major.' He said, 'You know what I was doing then?' I said, 'Yeah, you were the secretary of defense.' He said, 'Yeah, that's interesting, isn't it?'"

Downing took the remark as just one of the mind games that Rumsfeld seemed to enjoy playing with other senior administration officials. The military tactician in Downing admired Rumsfeld's skills in maneuvering to gain a psychological edge in the administration's internal skirmishes. He especially enjoyed watching Rumsfeld in action at meetings with the president and other principals. "Rumsfeld would make a statement or ask a question, and I'd be thinking at the time, Why did he make that point? That's not really germane, or that's not a good point," Downing remarked. "Then three weeks later I'd find out why. There'd be a string of four or five things that he'd done, and they'd all tie together somehow. It was brilliant."

Seeing Rumsfeld deal with Colin Powell was particularly intriguing for Downing. Before a meeting, for instance, Rumsfeld might say or do something to get Powell rattled or angry. "He'd talk about something that he knew was a hot button for Colin," Downing recounted. "It might be about voting rights or immigration or education or abortion—just something to get Colin pissed off. Then the meeting would start, and Colin, who is usually a cool head, would lose his cool. And I'd think to myself, Wow, Rumsfeld is screwing with his head. That's when I decided he was a very dangerous man."

Not that Powell himself was unaware. He knew Rumsfeld would not miss an opportunity to try to throw him off guard. Often Rumsfeld's tactics would take the form of needling, as when he chided Powell for mispronouncing the capital of Afghanistan. It's not KA-bul, Rumsfeld told him more than once, it's Ka-BUL, with the accent on the second syllable. (In fact, Rumsfeld himself was mistaken; Afghans put even emphasis on both syllables.)

Powell looked for ways of punching back, giving Rumsfeld grief, for instance, about his old clothes. "Why don't you buy a new suit," he would tell Rumsfeld. "The damn knees are getting pretty worn."

While there was humor between the two veteran Washington infighters, many times the taunting wasn't really funny and heightened the tensions between them and their staffs over policy disputes. To some extent, the disagreements reflected the traditionally different institutional biases of the departments they represented. But the strains were compounded by a tendency on the part of both secretaries to get into the other's business.

"It was most obvious from Powell, who would say, 'I was at DoD for such a long time, I know how they think and I'm not going to second guess it, but I have my sources—you all know I have my sources,'" Andy Card recalled. "So he was a little more transparent about it. Rumsfeld's position tended to be, 'I've got a job to do; I'm sticking within the Defense Department; I'm not going to worry about the State Department.' But he was always peeking over the wall."

This intrusiveness was even more pronounced at the level of their deputies. "Wolfowitz had wanted to be at State and Armitage at Defense, and since they both had great antennae into the other departments, they frequently were on that frequency rather than the frequency of their own departments," Card said. "That was a source of great strain because almost everybody knew it. It wasn't a secret. It wasn't anything they talked about but we all knew it. It would frustrate the process, although it wouldn't really interrupt the result. And I think Secretary Powell liked it, and I don't think Secretary Rumsfeld did."

While previous administrations had suffered internal clashes over foreign and defense policy, there was more of an ideological tone this time to the disagreements—or at least that was the view from State, where they felt locked in battle with the neoconservative hawks around Rumsfeld. From the Pentagon's vantage point, the arguments weren't so much ideological as fiducial, with Rumsfeld and his group often seeing State as a rogue agency insufficiently committed to the president's policies and overly solicitous of foreign sensibilities.

Moreover, the disputes, which in previous administrations might have been worked out at lower levels, were in this group magnified down the ranks. "The lineup of Powell versus Cheney and Rumsfeld was duplicated among their deputies and undersecretaries," observed Karen DeYoung in her biography of Powell. Armitage faced off against Wolfowitz and Scooter Libby, while Marc Grossman, the undersecretary of state for political affairs, wrestled with Feith and John Hannah or another member of Cheney's office.

Particularly frustrating for Powell was the nagging sense that he was not accepted or appreciated by the other side. No matter how much he delivered, whether managing the demise of the ABM Treaty in late 2001 without rupturing relations with the Russians or, in early 2003, making the case for war with Iraq at the United Nations, he was never admitted as a card-carrying member of the Rumsfeld/Cheney club. And conversely, no matter what Rumsfeld did, the Pentagon leader was never, in Powell's view, held to account by Bush.

In interagency dealings, officials at State were constantly irritated by what they saw as a host of stalling tactics by Rumsfeld and his team. Defense officials appeared intransigent at meetings. Minutes that circulated after interagency sessions sometimes included new positions not stated in the discussions or summaries not reflecting the overall balance of debate. And Pentagon authorities would refuse to follow through on certain tasks once agreements were reached.

"I was constantly having to call Powell to say, 'Remember the decision that you told me had been made in the Principals Committee that would permit a certain cable to go out? Rumsfeld won't sign it out. Can you call him?'" recounted Beth Jones, who served under Powell as the assistant secretary of state for European and Eurasian affairs. "I was constantly on the phone with my NSC colleague and my Pentagon colleague, saying, 'How's the separate government going over there at the Pentagon?'"

Jones kept a running list of issues that needed Pentagon action, and she called her Pentagon counterpart daily to check on progress. Frequently, she found Pentagon officials restrained from acting without explicit approval from Rumsfeld, which often took time to obtain. By contrast, Powell vested his subordinates with authority.

Andy Card saw the same problem. "I don't think that Rumsfeld empowered his deputies to be as engaged as they needed to be," the former White House chief of staff said. "They came to meetings with no authority, and lacking direction from the secretary, they were afraid to offer direction in the meetings. This contributed to the dysfunction and also to the strain between Defense and State."

Card, who says he likes Rumsfeld, observed a fundamental irony about him: Although a complex person, Rumsfeld believed in simple rules. "His expectations of others were simple: Follow my rules," Card remarked. "He tended not to accept the complications that other people brought to their lives and responsibilities." And when his rules weren't met, he could be especially troublesome, absenting himself from meetings or putting up roadblocks to action. "If something didn't fit his expectations sometimes, he didn't want to play," Card said.

As an example, Card cited Rumsfeld's lack of participation in meetings to establish the Department of Homeland Security and the Homeland Security Council. "He didn't like that organization, and it was hard to get him to participate with other council members," Card recalled. "Rumsfeld would send a deputy or sometimes not even anybody. Other cabinet members would come, and they'd say, 'Where's the secretary of defense?' It was a management challenge for me when I had to explain why he wasn't there or why he didn't send the right level person or why the person who came said I can't speak for the secretary of defense."

Instead of reaching out and appearing cooperative, Rumsfeld came across as a naysayer. "Rather than say, 'I understand your problem, let's try to solve it,' he would say, 'I don't like the solution you've proposed, so don't propose it.' He wouldn't say, 'Let me help you through it,'" Card explained.

Card recognized that Rumsfeld was very smart. But Card had known many smart people, a number of whom would not make an issue of their intelligence and would, in fact, work to raise the level of discourse of everyone else in the room with them. Rumsfeld was not always that way. "Sometimes Don would fall into the trap of saying, 'I'm smart, you're not,'" Card said.

Downing offered a similar view. "He was toxic to the interagency process because there was little cooperation," Downing observed. "It was Rumsfeld's way or no way."

———•———

One thing on which both Defense and State could agree: The inter-agency process was poorly managed by Rice and her NSC staff. Although a poised and articulate defender of Bush's policies, Rice was widely criti-cized for failing to coordinate and enforce the presidential decision-making process. She and other NSC officials seemed either unable or unwilling to play the council staff's traditional role of resolving the in-ternecine squabbling between Defense and State.

Time and again, State Department officials would complain to the NSC staff of Pentagon foot-dragging on decisions that had been taken in interagency meetings. But the staff members declined to intervene. When Beth Jones, for instance, groused to one of Rice's deputies, he told her it wasn't his problem. "He would say to me, 'My job is to make nice to the Pentagon; your job is to fight with them,'" Jones recalled.

Rumsfeld, in turn, had grown increasingly frustrated over what he re-garded as Rice's lax management of interagency meetings, which would be convened on short notice, without agendas, and with little informa-tion forthcoming from Rice's assistants. Finally, in August 2002, he cre-ated a new position in his office devoted solely to staffing Wolfowitz, Feith, and himself for White House meetings. Advising Rice of the move, Rumsfeld told her it was meant to "try to help us deal with the many changes in dates, times, agendas, materials, attendees and the like." At the same time, Rumsfeld sent Rice a lengthy list of suggestions for managing interagency meetings that reflected how fed up he had become.

He recommended, for instance, shortening the length of the meet-ings and allowing officials to participate in them by video teleconference to save travel time to and from the White House. He also urged more consistent scheduling. "Changing the time or date of scheduled meetings has major ripple effects on the schedules of officials throughout all departments," he wrote. "Last minute changes are especially disruptive, particularly when the meeting time is moved up. Shifting from afternoon to morning cuts into preparation time." He told Rice that NSC members should be asked in advance whether the rescheduling of a meeting is "workable" for them. And he said a rule should be established giving at least forty-eight hours' notice before changing the date, time, or subject of a meeting.

He went on to make a number of general points about how meetings should be structured and run. He advised that principals ought to be allowed to bring a second person to most meetings, noting that Rice always had someone accompanying her. And he said that meetings ought to be concluded with a summation by the official whose department had the lead on the subject in discussion. But he stressed that the summations needed to be accurate. "It sometimes happens that a matter mentioned at a meeting is said to have been 'decided' because it elicited no objection," Rumsfeld wrote. "That is not a good practice. Nothing should be deemed decided unless we expressly agree to decide it."

Additionally, Rumsfeld included a number of thoughts about how papers for principals ought to be prepared and presented. He said they should be only two or three pages long, "bulletized, thoroughly formatted and well-edited." They should also "let the reader know up-front what the issue is, set out the basic facts and concepts, specify agency positions, highlight differences, provide pros and cons for the options."

Lengthy documents or more discursive papers, he counseled, should be worked at lower-level meetings first, then their points should be condensed into shorter papers "suitable for principals." He noted approvingly that the NSC staff had made an effort to distribute papers forty-eight to seventy-two hours in advance of meetings. "There are still many times, however, when this rule is observed in the breach, a problem for which, I suspect, every agency is, at one time or another, responsible," he observed. "Except for honest to goodness time-critical issues, a meeting should automatically be postponed if the materials are not distributed at least 48 hours in advance or if the time or agenda have to be changed."

Distribution of papers, too, he complained, had been a problem on occasion. "When the NSC staff wants to distribute an especially sensitive paper by courier rather than by fax, it would help to get a phone call and have the option to send over a trusted agent to pick it up so that hours are not lost," he wrote. "A paper recently was sent around by courier with the result that DoD got it last, hours after it was sent out and long after the addressee had departed for the night."

It is easy to see how such didactic memos, however well-intentioned, could get on the nerves of Rumsfeld's colleagues. But Rumsfeld had a general and deep-seated preoccupation with how processes should work. Eventually, to save himself travel time between the Pentagon and the White House, Rumsfeld got permission to participate in meetings of principals by a video link from a room in the Defense Department. Still, the NSC meeting process remained a constant source of frustration for him and was a repeated cause for more memos.

On October 30, 2003, for instance, Rumsfeld wrote Rice to complain that an upcoming NSC meeting had been scheduled with no subject. "I like to be prepared for meetings," he stated, "but if we don't have the subject of the meeting a working day ahead of time, then there is no way for us to be prepared. If we cannot get a schedule the preceding Thursday so we can prep it on Friday, why don't we move the NSC meetings to Tuesday, Wednesday, or Thursday, instead of having the meeting on Monday?"

Less than a week later, on November 5, he sent another memo to Rice noting that the schedules for NSC and Principals Committee meetings changed frequently. "There must be a way to inject some stability into the process," he wrote. He objected in particular to a situation the day before in which Pete Pace, arriving for a meeting in the White House Situation Room, had unexpectedly been asked to provide an update on Iraqi security operations, even though the NSC staff had been listed to do the briefing. "If you want people from DoD to do something, please tell us that, not in the meeting, but the day before—and we will do our best," Rumsfeld wrote. "We need to find a way to get the schedules to settle down and be issued early enough so papers can be distributed the day before."

In April 2004, he presented a lengthy argument for shifting from Rice's insistence on always trying to form a consensus view among principals.

The consensus approach, he complained, was too time-consuming and also sometimes resulted in important issues not being brought up to the president. Instead, Rumsfeld contended, the NSC should serve more as an "honest broker," meaning that if the principals differed on a subject, the president should be given various options papers reflecting the conflicting points of view. "My view is that, even if the president ended up selecting the same option that might have been arrived at by consensus, it would be far better for him to have had an options paper and been able to consider the pros and cons of the different recommendations," Rumsfeld wrote. "This approach would save time in getting decisions made, and the President would know that he had seen the best arguments, pro and con, that his key advisers could offer."

After raising the issue directly with Bush and seeing no change, Rumsfeld concluded that the president himself did not want options papers.

———•———

One of the Bush administration's major failings in its handling of the Iraq War was the lack of an adequate plan for the postwar phase. It is not that no planning occurred—in fact, many in the U.S. government identified postwar challenges and proposed strategies for dealing with them before combat began. But the overall effort, as RAND and other well-documented studies have concluded, was disjointed and poorly coordinated. It reflected the general optimism in the White House and in the Pentagon about Iraq's future as well as a profound ambivalence toward nation building. Rumsfeld's own expectation was that U.S. forces would be able to get in and get out within a matter of months, avoiding a prolonged occupation.

Most of the initial planning fell on CENTCOM, but the staff devoted much of its effort to planning the invasion itself. Historically, the U.S. military had tended to put more focus on preparations for the combat phase—or "phase three," in military parlance—than on the postwar period, or "phase four." That traditional tendency was reinforced in this case by Franks's own view that postwar Iraq was not his long-term responsibility. He later wrote in his memoir that he had expected a huge infusion of civilian experts and other resources to come from the U.S. government after Saddam was removed. His message to the defense secretary's staff and the Joint Chiefs was "You pay attention to the day after, and I'll pay attention to the day of." Observed Lieutenant General William Scott Wallace, who commanded V Corps during the invasion and went on to head the Army's Training and Doctrine Command, "I give no credit to the politicians for detailed phase-four planning, but I don't think that we, the military, did a very good job of anticipating either."

The military's most detailed postwar planning was done by a group belonging to CENTCOM's ground operations staff in Kuwait. The group went so far as to carry out some specific troop-to-task calculations on how many forces would be necessary to handle the occupation of Iraq, estimating about three hundred thousand troops. But the colonel in charge, Colonel Kevin C. M. Benson, had trouble getting his commanding general, Lieutenant General David D. McKiernan, to pay much attention. And by the time the group's plan was formally distributed to the troops in April 2003, the ground invasion was already under way. "We were extraordinarily focused on phase three," Benson told Army historians in an extensive study published in 2008. "There should have been more than just one Army colonel, me, really worrying about the details of phase four."

At the prodding of Rumsfeld and Myers, who recognized that CENTCOM was concentrating on the combat phase, the Joint Staff took steps to assist. It created a task force headed by a one-star general to lead a planning effort and to prepare a headquarters to take over operations after the removal of the Baghdad regime. But the group's relationship to CENTCOM remained unspecified, and it ended up having little influence, ultimately disbanding in early April 2003.

Most significantly, much of the postwar planning was based on assumptions that proved wrong—for instance, that U.S. forces would continue to flow in after major combat operations ceased, that the bulk of the Iraqi army would be recalled to duty at some point, and that Iraq's ministries and institutions would continue to function after Saddam's government was toppled. A number of these assumptions were derived from what turned out to be faulty CIA predictions—that many Iraqi soldiers and police would remain at their posts, that much of Iraq's infrastructure was in adequate working order, and that Saddam's Baathist Party had little capacity to organize an insurgency. "We had the wrong assumptions and therefore we had the wrong plan to put into play," Wallace told Army historians.

That Rumsfeld did not do more to challenge assumptions is especially ironic given his own practice of cautioning others to avoid what Thomas C. Schelling, in one of Rumsfeld's favorite essays, called a "poverty of expectations," obsessing over familiar dangers while ignoring others. In the case of Iraq, Rumsfeld's thinking may have been clouded by his aversion to the idea of getting involved in a nation-building operation and by a desire to demonstrate the new principles of warfare touted by his transformation campaign. He and his leadership team reached a point where their minds were made up, and they did not welcome arguments by others who warned that Iraq after the invasion could be messier than anticipated and might require more military troops and police than expected.

Lowell E. "Jake" Jacoby, who as a three-star admiral headed the Defense Intelligence Agency at the time, recalled a lengthy afternoon session in late 2002 in his office during which he and two intelligence specialists cautioned Rich Haver, Rumsfeld's special assistant for intelligence, that Iraq was going to be more problematic than was being assumed. "I told him it was going to be a helluva mess because they were going to get into tribal fighting, and it was going to be just like the Brits experienced when they were in Iraq," Jacoby said in an interview. But the warnings were dismissed, reflecting what the former intelligence chief called a tendency by Rumsfeld and some senior aides then for "selective listening."

Jacoby did not go directly to Rumsfeld with his concerns. Asked why not, he said he figured it would have been a waste of his time given the "bullying, dismissive" climate engendered by Rumsfeld's management style. "But in retrospect I'm kicking myself because I should have gone around the adviser in a more forceful way," he added.

Initially, military planners had counted on a relatively quick drawdown of U.S. forces from Iraq. "The secretary's notion—and I believe it was in oral guidance that he gave to Franks—was don't plan on a big occupation afterwards," recalled John Abizaid, then a three-star Army general and director of the Joint Staff. "It was go in there, unseat the government, and turn it over to civilian control. Everybody was concentrating on the problem at hand—winning the combat phase of the war. The problem of the occupation was a second thought, not the first thought."

At the root of this thinking was the expectation that U.S. and allied forces would find postwar Iraq a benign environment, that the situation would be analogous to what had happened after the Allies reached France in World War II, where they were greeted as liberators. This analogy had been advanced in an influential paper written by Peter Rodman, one of Rumsfeld's top policy advisers, during the summer of 2002. The paper argued against the idea of establishing a prolonged occupation in Iraq as had occurred in Germany and Japan after World War II. A better model, Rodman suggested, was France.

Rodman noted that U.S. and British authorities had planned to set up an Allied military government in France on the theory that the French Resistance movement under Charles de Gaulle, the exiled French general, did not truly represent the French people. In retrospect, Rodman said, it was fortunate that de Gaulle succeeded in assuming power and that the Allied plan failed, because had an occupation government been established, it would probably have fostered resentment among the French and fueled a communist-dominated resistance in the countryside. Drawing on Rodman's work, Rumsfeld sent a memo on July 1, 2002, to Cheney, Powell, Tenet, and Rice urging that all the friendly, democratic Iraqi opposition groups be organized into a cooperative body that could help establish an interim government after the invasion.

But the French liberation analogy had its critics in the Pentagon, who argued that one of the main elements missing among the Iraqis was a leading figure like de Gaulle. Further, the tensions in Iraq among Kurds, Shia, and Sunnis made for a much more complex environment than had existed in France.

Abizaid, a Lebanese-American who speaks Arabic, remembers taking issue with the French analogy at a meeting with the military service chiefs and several senior Rumsfeld aides in late summer. He said that the civilian aides had claimed that the Iraqis, like the French, were very nationalistic—more nationalistic than other Arabs. "They're not more nationalistic, they're tribal," Abizaid declared. "This will not be like the liberation of France. In that case you had two things that were important—a Free

French army and a Free French government. In the case of Iraq, there is no free Iraqi army and no free Iraqi government."

In an interview later, Abizaid concluded that the use of such faulty World War II models had contributed significantly to the failure to do sufficient postwar planning. "I think because we went in there with a liberation mentality as opposed to a destruction mentality, our phase-four planning was inadequate," he said.

Two U.S. intelligence assessments, issued in January 2003 and widely circulated in the Bush administration before the war, also warned about the dangers of a U.S. invasion. Authored by the National Intelligence Council under the direction of a career CIA intelligence analyst named Paul R. Pillar, the administration's top Middle East analyst, the reports predicted that an invasion would be likely to spark violent sectarian divides and provide al Qaeda with new opportunities in Iraq and Afghanistan. "Iraq would be unlikely to split apart, but a post-Saddam authority would face a deeply divided society with a significant chance that domestic groups would engage in violent conflict with each other unless an occupying force prevented them from doing so," one assessment said. It warned of "score-settling" and "heightened competition for power among the different groups."

Rumsfeld was not without some sense of caution. He put himself on record in October 2002 as warning Bush and other NSC members of what could go wrong with an invasion of Iraq. At the time, Congress had recently voted to give Bush complete authority to invade Iraq and topple Saddam Hussein, and a White House spokesman had just confirmed that invasion plans were on Bush's desk.

In a memo that he began drafting in August and reviewed with the president in October, Rumsfeld listed twenty-nine pitfalls to consider before invading Iraq. The list, written in typical Rumsfeld style as a series of crisp bullet points, included dire scenarios that did not happen, such as chemical warfare and close combat with Saddam's troops in Baghdad. But some of the things it anticipated did come to pass—most significantly, the possibility of not finding any weapons of mass destruction. It also correctly foresaw the potential for strife among Iraq's religious factions and for the successful exploitation of the war as a public relations vehicle by the enemies of the United States.

Still other critical possibilities were overlooked entirely in the memo. Most notably, Rumsfeld failed to imagine a protracted conflict against an entrenched insurgency. Asked how he could have been blind to that, aides have cited several factors: bad intelligence predicting a warm Shia welcome and underestimating any post-Saddam Sunni threat; the lack of attention by military planners to the issue; and Rumsfeld's own preoccupation with the details of the invasion, which were themselves overwhelming.

Rumsfeld certainly had expert company in underestimating the threat of an insurgency. Planners on McKiernan's land-war command staff, who ended up giving the most extensive thought within CENTCOM to postwar scenarios, did consider the likelihood of an insurgency, but even they did not regard the chances as high enough to prompt a change in war plans. War games run by McKiernan's command in early 2003 further anticipated that a precipitous end to the war could result in some form of unrest or lawlessness or in a rise in acts of terrorism, raising the risk that U.S. and coalition forces would not be in a position to address the immediate security challenges brought about by the collapse of the Iraqi government. But the planners chose not to press McKiernan to reshape the conduct of combat operations, figuring it was better to accept greater risk in the postwar phase than in the combat phase.

Even the assessment by the National Intelligence Council played down the prospect of an insurgency, leaving mention of it to the final paragraph of its January report and then providing only an understated preview. "Rogue ex-regime elements could forge an alliance with existing terrorist organizations or act independently to wage guerrilla warfare against the new government or coalition forces," it said.

In the years after the invasion, Rumsfeld cited his October 2002 memo a number of times in interviews, as if to suggest he did not dash, heedless and underprepared, into Iraq. He kept a copy of the memo close at hand, in the top drawer of his stand-up desk. But just what was the memo's significance? Did it mean to show that he had doubts? Was he implying that he didn't fully support the effort? By highlighting all the things that could go wrong, had he been trying to dissuade Bush and Cheney?

It is doubtful that Rumsfeld wrote the memo because he was hesitant about going into Iraq and hoped to stay Bush's hand. "There's no question in anyone's mind but I agreed with the president's approach and his decision," he told Bob Woodward in an interview. Even though Bush never explicitly asked whether his defense secretary favored the invasion, the written record shows where Rumsfeld stood on the question. "If you look at the mass of memos that we wrote, Rumsfeld reviewed and sent over—or that he wrote himself—they make a very strong case that Saddam Hussein was a serious threat, that the threat was going to worsen over time, and that we had effectively exhausted all reasonable means to contain or counter the threat," Feith said.

Rather than being a sign of Rumsfeld's reluctance for war, the memo most probably reflected just the opposite—his methodical preparation. It was typical of a process often used by Rumsfeld to work through an issue. "It's an example of how his mind works," Feith said. "He is the kind of guy who, when he develops a conviction that we should do something as big and important and dangerous as going to war, he checks himself."

But if his purpose was to spur adequate thinking and preparation for the complexity of the Iraq mission, Rumsfeld failed dismally. Even his own advisory think tank, the Defense Science Board, concluded after examining the issue in 2004 that the architects of the Iraq War—led by Rumsfeld—lacked necessary knowledge of Iraq and its people, and that they neglected to factor in well-known lessons of history. "It is clear that Americans who waged the war and who have attempted to mold the aftermath have had no clear idea of the framework that has molded the personalities and attitudes of Iraqis," the board declared. "It might help if Americans and their leaders were to show less arrogance and more understanding of themselves and their place in history. Perhaps more than any other people, Americans display a consistent amnesia concerning their own past, as well as the history of those around them."

———•———

Apart from the Pentagon, several other government agencies put time and effort into looking at the potential aftermath of war in Iraq. Starting in August 2002, the NSC set up the Executive Steering Group to coordinate both combat and postwar planning with representatives from the Pentagon, the State Department, and other agencies. Throughout 2002, the State Department compiled what would become the broadest assessment of postwar requirements within the U.S. government. Called the Future of Iraq Project, it was not so much a plan for postwar management as a collection of papers, assembled in thirteen volumes, that identified a broad range of reconstruction and government challenges ahead. Many of the predictions proved accurate.

But Pentagon officials remained wary of State's work and ignored much of the information and insights of the study. They regarded Powell and his staff as intent on undermining support for the war. Such suspicions only deepened in August when Powell persuaded Bush that a renewed diplomatic effort through the United Nations was a necessary precondition for building international support for possible military operations against Iraq. Rumsfeld, along with Cheney, had doubted the effectiveness of another diplomatic push.

NSC officials complained, in turn, that efforts at interagency coordination were hampered by inconsistent Pentagon participation. The Defense Department sent different representatives—or none at all—to interagency meetings, and all too often guidance papers drafted by the Pentagon were not reviewed with other agencies before being presented at meetings, giving rise to a sense that Rumsfeld's team was trying to dictate policy. Defense officials involved in the process insist they were team players and lacked the authority to impose anything. Clearly, though, they were regarded as the first among equals, and in October 2002, Rumsfeld formally asked Bush to designate the Pentagon as the lead agency for postwar planning.

Rumsfeld himself could appear overly controlling. After briefings at the White House on his war plans, for instance, he would retrieve the slides and take them back to the Pentagon. He once instructed Frank Miller, the NSC official overseeing the steering group on Iraq and a veteran of highly sensitive government assignments over more than two decades, not to take notes during a briefing on the war plan.

To get around Rumsfeld's tight hold on information, Miller dispatched a military aide, Marine colonel Tom Greenwood, to the Pentagon to obtain useful material through contacts on the Joint Staff. Then, widening the loop to top State Department officials, Miller and Greenwood quietly shared their information about the war plan in a briefing to Powell and Armitage in December 2002. Such surreptitious tactics to ensure that senior officials remained up-to-date on important planning elements reflected the dysfunctional nature of the interagency process—both Rumsfeld's wariness of sharing and Rice's inability to enforce greater cooperation and information flow.

Within the Pentagon, too, Rumsfeld was known to limit the contributions of others to the war-planning effort. He kept much of the planning channeled narrowly between himself and Franks, which left the military chiefs in particular feeling sidelined. His close tie with Franks represented the epitome of Rumsfeld's notion of how the chain of command is supposed to work: At the request of the president, the defense secretary confers with his regional commander to produce a war plan that the president can order into action.

In Rumsfeld's view, the responsibility for talking to the service chiefs about the war plan rested with Franks. But Franks himself made no secret of his low tolerance for working with the chiefs. He had expressed frustration when they offered advice during the Afghanistan War, and he didn't want them meddling in his preparations for Iraq. His memoir recalling the planning process includes a number of unflattering references to the four-star service leaders, whom he saw as "narrow-minded," hopelessly parochial "bean-counters" preoccupied with "fighting for turf" to maintain their troop levels and weapons systems.

In fairness, it is far from clear that the war plan would have turned out much differently had the chiefs been more directly involved in the planning process. Although they expressed some early misgivings about the urgency of invading Iraq and about the demands such an operation would place on already stretched U.S. forces, little has emerged to suggest they would have altered the plans considerably. Even on the controversial question of U.S. troop numbers, which flared publicly a few weeks before the invasion, the chiefs privately had not pressed the point, figuring the war would go quickly.

But they did feel that with decades of varied military experience behind them, they had some advice to offer Rumsfeld and Franks on how to battle Iraq. The Air Force chief of staff, General John Jumper, had overseen air operations in Europe during the Kosovo campaign. General Eric Shinseki, the Army chief, had lost part of a foot in Vietnam and had run operations in Bosnia. And General Jim Jones, the Marine commandant, had led the initial relief effort in Iraqi Kurdistan after the 1991 Persian Gulf War.

As a group, too, they had shown an ability to work together in ways they thought belied Rumsfeld's notion of them as squabbling parochial rivals interested only in their own prerogatives. The Air Force and Navy, for instance, had closely coordinated air patrols over Iraq for more than a decade. They had also traded programs involving maritime patrol planes and Global Hawk reconnaissance aircraft. But Rumsfeld gave them little credit for their efforts, lecturing instead on the need to be more transformational.

"His presumption was—he said this to me several times—that you guys are so hidebound you only know how to describe things in terms of your own service," Jumper recalled in an interview. "During meetings, he would reemphasize that this military is a relic of the Cold War, that we've got to find new ways of thinking, that you guys don't know new ways of thinking, you've got to really think transformationally. Meanwhile, we were already out there doing all this transformational work."

Even Rumsfeld's view of how the chiefs lived and what they could afford seemed to Jumper distorted at times. Interviewing Jumper for the job of Air Force chief in late 2001, Rumsfeld mentioned his custom of writing a check for thousands of dollars each year to the U.S. government to cover any personal expenses that might inadvertently have been charged on the official budget. Jumper took the remark as a suggestion that the chiefs consider doing the same. At home later, Jumper related the remark to his wife, who mused about how impossible it would be, on their income, to follow Rumsfeld's example.

Jumper got the impression that Rumsfeld regarded the chiefs, who occupy large houses with large staffs, as enjoying an excessively grand lifestyle. The general joked with a colleague once that he and his wife would be more than happy to give up the four aides in their house if Rumsfeld would excuse him from all the protocol duties that the chief's job entails, including entertaining dozens of foreign Air Force chiefs when they visit Washington. "He presumed that we rode around in these large convoys, and I sort of smiled at that because I actually drove myself most places when I was the chief. I didn't have a roomful of drivers and security guards," Jumper said.

Rumsfeld's needling about the lifestyle of the chiefs reflected a more general pattern of behavior by the secretary, what Jumper called Rumsfeld's "baiting style." "You never knew whether he was saying something because he actually believed it or because he was trying just to gauge your reaction to it," Jumper said. "But when you have someone treating you that way, it's very hard to be trusting. Now I will say he treated everyone the same way, so I don't think I was singled out."

For Admiral Vern Clark, the chief of naval operations, adjusting to Rumsfeld and the new administration team had been the most difficult challenge of his career. "I'd never worked for someone who hadn't believed in me," Clark said in an interview. This was from someone considered one of Rumsfeld's favorite chiefs. So raw were feelings that even seemingly small matters of protocol could be perceived as major affronts. Clark recalled an instance in 2002 when Cheney visited the Pentagon and the chiefs were invited to a meeting in a small conference room but ended up being seated in the back, behind the secretary's civilian staff. "It was a statement of what they thought of us," the Navy chief said.

The chiefs weren't the only ones feeling left out of the tight connection between Rumsfeld and Franks. Feith and his policy shop did, too. Their civilian planning effort for Iraq was concentrated in the Office of Northern Gulf Affairs, which in August was expanded from two to more than a dozen people and renamed the Office of Special Plans to avoid drawing attention to its stepped-up war planning and undercutting diplomatic efforts to gain international support.

But Franks had a low regard for Feith and, given his open door to Rumsfeld, felt no need or obligation to coordinate his efforts with Feith's own enlarged planning operation. "You had the marginalization of the policy shop on Iraq," said Marshall Billingslea, who was an assistant secretary for Special Operations in 2002. "They were trying to think through Iraq in ways broader than CENTCOM was looking at it. But Rumsfeld gave CENTCOM too much latitude."

Feith found that if he wanted to talk to Rumsfeld about an operational issue involving Iraq, he could rarely do so in front of Franks because the general would get upset. Instead, Feith would wait and raise his issue with the secretary separately, although even then Feith tended to make little headway. "Rumsfeld did not want my organization screwing around with military operational things," Feith said.

The exceptionally close working relationship that Rumsfeld had with Franks was forged by the wars they planned and directed together. But it also reflected a more general effort by Rumsfeld to strengthen the link between himself and the four-star regional commanders. In October 2002, he formally changed the title of those officers from commanders in chief of their respective regions to combatant commanders—a move meant to make it clear that there was only one U.S. commander in chief, the president. But he left little doubt that those regional chiefs, because of their position directly after the secretary in the chain of command running up to the president, held exalted positions. "He attached great importance to the chain of command, and he didn't want anybody interfering with the purity of the chain," Feith recalled. "He didn't like the idea that his underlings might be giving orders to people who should get orders only from him."

Aware of the secretary's preference for working directly with them, many of the regional commanders, like Franks, tended to limit their communication and coordination with Feith's policy office. Feith, in his memoir, said that Rumsfeld "properly guarded the chain of command," but he noted that an unfortunate consequence was a lack of staff-level contact between the commands and his policy office. When Feith proposed assigning civilians from his office to work full-time at the regional headquarters, the commanders balked.

While the chiefs considered themselves largely out of the loop on war planning and other matters, Myers, the chairman of the Joint Chiefs of Staff, was tethered tightly to the secretary. The Air Force general had a much closer, more trusting relationship with Rumsfeld than had his predecessor, Hugh Shelton. This was due in part to personality and in part to circumstance. The pressures of waging war in the aftermath of the September 11 attacks helped forge a close bond between the secretary and the chairman and also made each more careful about showing any public display of differences.

The two men spent much of every day conferring together in meetings, although time spent did not necessarily translate into influence exerted. Exactly how much impact Myers had on Rumsfeld's thinking was difficult to discern, even by those who were frequently in the same room with them. The general tended to keep his most bitter confrontations with Rumsfeld private, and he was not one to boast about the times he prevailed over the secretary.

Outside the Pentagon, in interagency meetings, Myers often deferred to Rumsfeld, letting him present the Defense Department's view. Card, who regularly attended NSC meetings and gatherings of principals, found himself noticing several times how silent the chairman had been and wondering what the silence meant, whether it could be interpreted as disagreement or not. When Myers did speak, Card was struck by how much he echoed Rumsfeld. In an interview a year after he left office in 2006, Card could not recall an instance in which the chairman appeared to challenge Rumsfeld or was responsible for a major shift in Pentagon direction.

At the Pentagon, in small-group meetings with Rumsfeld, Myers spoke up more than he did in the White House Situation Room. Often, the general sought less to change Rumsfeld's mind about something than to moderate his perspective. "The secretary would think something was totally screwed up, and Myers would then walk him through the facts and show it wasn't unsalvageable, it wasn't irrevocable," Craddock said.

Sometimes, though, Myers took sharp issue with the secretary. Rumsfeld's disparaging treatment of and remarks about the Joint Staff was one thing almost sure to set the general off. "The secretary always felt the Joint Staff was too ponderous, too slow and was never responsive," Craddock said. "He would start beating up on the Joint Staff in front of Myers, and Myers would be incensed. He'd say, 'Okay, I need a few minutes to talk to you after this meeting.'"

Abizaid recalled that the general "tried very hard to be collaborative and to understand the secretary." By nature, Myers was someone more inclined to attempt to make things work than to look for problems. "But once every two weeks or so," Abizaid said, "there'd be an issue that would cause him to lose his temper, and he would express his difference in very sharp terms with the secretary, and then they'd talk about it privately and figure out a different way."

Because Rumsfeld took a more assertive role in deciding on appointments for all three- and four-star officers, Myers had difficulty preserving the chairman's traditional prerogative of picking the Joint Staff. One proposed hire that Rumsfeld blocked in 2002 reinforced a perception of Myers as unable to withstand the secretary's pressure.

The case involved a three-star Air Force general, Ronald Keys, whom Myers had wanted to name director of operations on the Joint Staff. Rumsfeld resisted, but Myers was insistent. After several weeks of this standoff, during an informal moment on an escalator in the Pentagon, Rumsfeld pressed Myers again. "Dick, I know you really want Ron," Rumsfeld said. "I really feel he would not be the best one for the job, and I wish you'd go along with me." Myers finally agreed. He dropped Keys and recommended Air Force lieutenant general Norton Schwartz instead.

Asked about the Keys case several years later, Myers said it was the only instance out of several hundred officer selections in which he conceded to Rumsfeld. He voiced some exasperation about it being cited repeatedly as an example of his inability or unwillingness to stand up to the secretary.

The close involvement between Myers and the secretary often worked against the general in his relations with the chiefs. Because of his frequent meetings with Rumsfeld, Myers had difficulty making some sessions with the chiefs. "It was sort of a joke, that whenever a Tank meeting started, he'd get called upstairs," Jumper, the Air Force chief, said. Myers denies that he was summoned from Tank meetings more than once or twice. But Jumper recalled things differently. "It happened enough times it was obvious," Jumper said. "He would have to pull out of a Tank meeting and go upstairs, or we'd cut a Tank meeting off because he was told he had to be up there at a certain time." Clark, the Navy leader, also reported that Rumsfeld kept both Myers and Pace so "tied up" that "they didn't have time to spend any quality time with the chiefs."

Additionally, both Clark and Jumper recalled unhappiness over how little information Myers passed to them about the war planning. And Clark said he was never sure that his concerns about matters, when expressed to

Myers, were adequately presented to Rumsfeld. "By law, the chairman is required to represent our negative views," Clark said. "You know how many times I got a report that my negative views had been represented to the secretary of defense or president?" Clark indicated zero. "I'm not telling you they didn't represent my view," the retired admiral continued. "All I'm telling you is that I was never told that they did. I don't know what went on in their private meetings."

For his part, Myers said he kept track of the attendance of service chiefs at Tank meetings, "and probably the ones who are now most critical were there the least."

Few things Rumsfeld did before the invasion more riled the military than his personal rejiggering of an extensive plan carefully devised to sequence the deployment of troops to the war zone. During his first year in office, Rumsfeld had sought to impose more control generally over where and when U.S. forces were sent. Instead of simply signing deployment orders that were presented to him after review by the Joint Staff, he requested briefings on each one and established regular weekly sessions to go over all the new orders in detail before granting his approval. "He didn't like the way the previous system had worked," Larry Di Rita explained. "He thought it was haphazard. And he regarded it as an example of the Joint Staff presenting decisions rather than the secretary making decisions."

Approaching the Iraq War, Rumsfeld ran into a new challenge with the deployment system that involved trying to balance the need to get troops in place against the desire to avoid the appearance that war was a foregone conclusion. By the autumn of 2002, some U.S. forces had already arrived in the Middle East in anticipation of the invasion, but Rumsfeld had kept the military buildup relatively modest and undramatic. Iraq had agreed to new weapons inspections starting in late November, and there was still some hope of a peaceful solution.

Franks and his commanders, though, were eager to get the Pentagon to commit to sending the rest of the forces that would be necessary for the invasion. So on November 26, Franks sent Rumsfeld a deployment request to start mobilizing about three hundred thousand troops. It was dubbed the "Mother of All Deployment Orders," or MOAD, given the enormous number of troops involved. Military planners had worked out the projected force flow in minute detail, relying on a computerized deployment system known as the Time-Phased Force Deployment (TPFD) list. The list automatically determined which logistical and auxiliary units should be sent to support which combat forces and in what order. Field commanders considered the system an essential element of the war plan.

But for Rumsfeld, with his businessman's interest in efficiency, the deployment system represented yet another opportunity for major reform. It appeared prone to excessive inventory and wasted effort. Many of the forces sent to the Middle East for the 1991 Persian Gulf War, he recalled, ended up never being used. He didn't want the same to happen this time.

Moreover, he was particularly concerned that the buildup of forces not be so large and rapid as to disrupt ongoing diplomatic efforts to avert war. But the deployment system also seemed to have just two speeds—on or off—and once sent in motion, it took on a life of its own. Rumsfeld wanted more control over the flow. He wanted a gradation of speeds, a system of brakes and acceleration pedals that would allow him to slow deployments while the diplomacy continued, rush them if war came, then cut off reinforcements deemed unnecessary once victory was in sight.

He was not pleased to receive the MOAD and declined to approve it. He balked at its large scale and also at its proposed schedule. While the plan called for forces to flow in phases, sizable numbers would have to start getting ready even before the holidays. Rumsfeld wanted most deployments delayed until after Christmas.

In complaining about the way major deployments had been handled, Rumsfeld had a point. As some Army generals acknowledged, at least in private, the TPFD was rigid and anachronistic. But Rumsfeld's intervention marked the first time that a defense secretary had managed the deployment process with such scrutiny. He was taking a hand in deciding not only which units should go but also which should be alerted that they might possibly end up deploying. Once he and his aides started fiddling with the plan, a difficult situation was made worse. The second-guessing in Washington led to enormous disruptions in the field and to much grumbling by Army officers.

Many of the units affected were reserve components, whose call-up schedules had been intricately synchronized with active-duty components to allow for sufficient alert, mobilization, and training time. The delay in their activation led to rushed deployment orders later, with some re-servists receiving notice only a few days before they were to report for duty and having barely time enough to advise employers they were leaving. The resulting chaos in force flows meant that reservists who were supposed to run port and airfield facilities were not fully in place as the troops and equipment started to arrive; nor were many of the military police.

"It turned into an absolute nightmare," said Peter Chiarelli, then a two-star general in the Army's operations center. "Abandoning the TPFD created issues that were just unbelievable. There were second- and third-order events that we didn't even understand. We got to a point to-ward the end where the chairman of the Joint Chiefs of Staff was leading video teleconferences on how we were going to get the flow right."

Tom Reilly, an Army lieutenant colonel who worked in CENTCOM's ground command headquarters, told Army historians after the war that the civilians in the Pentagon simply did not understand how dependent the military was on reservists, especially for logistics. "We often joked that we would like to be able to invite Mr. Rumsfeld down here and say to him, 'Mr. Secretary, meet Isaac Newton. We live in a Newtonian world. We cannot change the size of the ocean or the distance between CONUS [the continental United States] and Iraq. With no maintenance problems it takes 21 days to sail from Beaumont, Texas, to the port of Ash Shuaiba, Kuwait.' Some say that the secretary of defense is not sup-posed to worry about those details, and that it is the Joint Staff that is supposed to inform him about those issues and how they impact on the desires of the senior civilian officials. If that is the case, then it appears that the Joint Staff failed to do its job."

After the war, Rumsfeld maintained that he had not intended to dis-assemble the whole TPFD, just to make some adjustments in it. He told a conference of disbelieving Army generals in the spring of 2003 that he had proceeded to sign some individual deployment orders without real-izing the impact on the overall flow.

Craddock, Rumsfeld's senior military assistant, provided a similar account in an interview for this book, saying it came as a sudden revela-tion to the secretary when he was advised that his troop-flow changes had resulted in the total collapse of the Army's intricate deployment plan. "No one had told the secretary that if he signed this or that individual order, he'd be breaking the TPFD," Craddock recalled. "It was like disassembling the carburetor without knowing it and then being told the car won't run because you just took the carburetor apart."

Chiarelli, for one, finds it hard to accept that Rumsfeld had been unaware of the impact of his actions. "I don't know how he could have been surprised," Chiarelli said. But senior Army leaders may not have been entirely blameless either. Chiarelli, whose own life in the Army's operations center was made miserable for weeks because he had to manage the broken-down deployment process, recalls urging his superiors to advise Rumsfeld of the havoc being caused and holds them responsible for evidently not standing up to him sufficiently. "If they did push him, they didn't push him hard enough," he said.

To wage the war on terrorism more effectively, Rumsfeld figured he needed at least two things: better intelligence on terrorist networks and Special Operations forces to conduct manhunts around the world. He set his sights in 2002 on achieving both.

His plan for improving intelligence involved the creation of a new civilian post to manage the military's intelligence apparatus. This was a major bureaucratic restructuring aimed at tightening control over the Pentagon's array of giant spy agencies—the Defense Intelligence Agency, the National Security Agency, the National Reconnaissance Office, and the National Geospatial-Intelligence Agency—which account for nearly 80 percent of the government's overall intelligence budget. With a firmer grip on these Pentagon assets, Rumsfeld hoped to be able to boost collection and analysis of intelligence and also to tailor it more closely to what the military needs to mount operations.

The move was eyed suspiciously at the CIA as an empire-building power play by Rumsfeld and a competitive bid for Pentagon dominance over the U.S. intelligence community. Rumsfeld's frustration during the Afghan invasion at having to watch U.S. forces initially yield the lead to CIA operatives was no secret. Nor had Rumsfeld hidden his dim view of the quality of both military and CIA intelligence.

Further, Rumsfeld's initiative ran counter to a proposal by a presidential commission led by Brent Scowcroft that called, in late 2001, for giving the director of central intelligence broader budget authority over the intelligence community, including over at least some of the military agencies.

When Scowcroft had briefed Rumsfeld about the commission's recommendation for a stronger director of central intelligence, Rumsfeld had told him it would never happen. "And if it did," Rumsfeld quipped, "I'd have to run it because the Defense equities are so powerful." Rumsfeld saw the Pentagon's intelligence operations as so integral to the Defense Department that if they were ripped out and shifted elsewhere, the department would just end up having to re-create them.

Scowcroft replied that if the positions were reversed and Rumsfeld had been chairman of the commission, "you'd be making exactly the same recommendation—and you know it." In Scowcroft's view, the director of central intelligence, not the defense secretary, should be the principal intelligence coordinator, even though a preponderance of intelligence assets lay in the Defense Department. Scowcroft argued that those assets had been placed on the Pentagon's books largely as a budgetary sleight of hand to conceal how much money was actually being spent on intelligence. They weren't there because they belonged to the military or were principally a military interest, Scowcroft contended.

Within the Pentagon, too, the idea of setting up a new intelligence office was opposed by the assistant secretary responsible at the time for intelligence, John Stenbit. His duties encompassed more than just intelligence. He also had charge of what the Pentagon called "C4," lumping together communications, computers, and command-and-control issues. Stenbit contended that the C4 activities belonged with intelligence in a natural symbiosis. The intelligence agencies, he noted, were among the biggest users of the electronic and information systems.

But Rumsfeld worried that under this arrangement, issues relating to the more costly and visible C4 systems had dominated the assistant secretary's time and crowded out consideration of intelligence concerns. By separating out the intelligence area and assigning it to a new high-level official, Rumsfeld figured, it could get more attention and end up with a stronger advocate in Pentagon deliberations and in interagency discussions.

Rumsfeld received crucial backing for this change from George Tenet, the CIA director, whose initial reservations melted away under the heat of Rumsfeld's urging. The defense secretary assiduously courted Tenet's endorsement of the plan in the spring of 2002. "George, I don't want your acquiescence, I want your support," Rumsfeld told him at one lunch, according to a participant. "I can't sell this on the Hill. You can. If you go up there and advocate this, it will get done. If you're passive or neutral, it won't happen."

Particularly persuasive for Tenet was the argument that the reorganization would give him and other senior CIA officials a single point of contact and thus facilitate cooperation on a range of policy and resource matters. Going to bat for the measure in Congress, Tenet told lawmakers of situations in which he had been confounded by multiple layers of Pentagon bureaucracy. He said he would welcome having a principal intelligence official at the Pentagon to call to get something done.

Initially, the plan envisioned giving the new official the rank of assistant secretary of defense. But Rumsfeld reconsidered and raised it to the level of undersecretary, placing it on a par with only four others in the Defense Department—the undersecretaries of policy, personnel, and acquisition and the comptroller—all of whom fall one step down from the deputy secretary of defense.

Haver recalled the meeting in which Rumsfeld made the decision to elevate the office. "I've been thinking about this," the secretary said, speaking to Haver and Wolfowitz at the time. "If you get on that escalator outside my office and see ten people on it, the chances are good that one of them is an assistant something." Haver agreed.

"And let me ask you this," Rumsfeld went on. "When you get a phone call from an assistant, do you return it immediately?"

"If I can," Haver said.

"If you get a phone call from an under, what do you do with it?" Rumsfeld asked.

"I drop everything," Haver replied.

"Then make it an under," Rumsfeld ordered.

Wolfowitz, raising a reservation, noted that the intelligence function didn't really carry the same importance as the other major areas at the undersecretary level. He called it more of a subspecialty, along the lines of public affairs, which was overseen by an assistant secretary. Rumsfeld acknowledged that that may have been true in the past, but the war on terrorism, he argued, would be won or lost more on the intelligence the United States could gather about the enemy than on the strength of U.S. military power.

Congress approved the new undersecretary position in December 2002 as part of the Defense Authorization Act, and in early 2003, Rumsfeld named his most trusted aide, Steve Cambone, to fill it.

———•———

While strengthening control over the military intelligence community, Rumsfeld was keen to ensure he had forces focused on hunting down terrorists. Historically, though, the Pentagon had preferred to stay out of the manhunt business. That was considered a CIA or FBI job. Even Rumsfeld, publicly at least, had sought to play down talk of the military making the capture particularly of Osama bin Laden a top priority, concerned that it would be turned into a measure of the success or failure of the administration's war on terrorism. But privately, Rumsfeld was intent on developing a hit squad mentality and capability. On July 1, 2002, he sent a memo to Feith asking how to organize the Department of Defense for manhunts.

The answer he got back came from Robert Andrews, a former Special Forces soldier and CIA operative who was a senior official on the Pentagon's policy staff dealing with Special Operations. Andrews offered several bits of advice to Rumsfeld: Be willing to take greater risks; stop "overplanning" for every contingency; let the Special Operations teams do their jobs; keep the action elements small and agile and enable them to operate clandestinely, moving in and out of countries surreptitiously.

Like many associated with the Special Operations community, Andrews had felt that the Pentagon's elite forces—the Army's Delta Force and the Navy's SEAL Team 6—had not been used to their full potential. He was particularly frustrated that they had never been employed to chase terrorists—not after the World Trade Center bombing in 1993 or the bombing of two U.S. embassies in East Africa in 1998 or the attack on the USS *Cole* in Yemen in 2000. Operations were planned to capture or kill bin Laden and his lieutenants, but each time the missions were blocked.

Prior to the September 11 attacks, Andrews had been discussing this issue with a friend, Richard Shultz, a professor at Tufts University's Fletcher School of Law and Diplomacy and an expert on Special Operations. Andrews asked Shultz to study the matter. After September, the study moved into high gear. Shultz conducted interviews with a range of civilian and military officials, serving and retired, at the center of U.S. counterterrorism policy and operational planning in the late 1980s and 1990s. He found that as terrorist attacks had escalated in the 1990s, President Clinton had issued an increasingly tough series of directives ordering offensive actions, which led to the planning of several operations. But none was ever executed, in large part, Shultz concluded, because of military reluctance and subsequent political considerations.

From his interviews, Shultz distilled nine "mutually reinforcing, self-imposed constraints" that had kept the missions sidelined. He called them "showstoppers." They included a U.S. government view of terrorism as a crime, not a military threat, which had led to the fight against terrorism being seen as more of a law enforcement mission than a military one. In addition, past attempts at hunting down terrorist leaders, like the 1993 effort in Mogadishu, in Somalia, to capture the warlord Mohammed Aidid, had gone badly, reinforcing a wariness about using Special Operations forces for such activities. There also were legal concerns: Pentagon lawyers and some officials in the intelligence community had argued that the Defense Department lacked the authority to undertake covert missions, which were more the province of the CIA. Senior military officers had themselves grown wary of using Special Operations for counterterrorism activity, and when they did plan such operations, they tended to make them too big to be practical.

For Rumsfeld, there would be no showstoppers. Special Operations units were to be his weapon of choice. He had come to doubt that he could get his regional combatant commands—those with geographic areas of responsibility—to adopt the kind of global view necessary to go after terrorist networks. Special Operations Command, by contrast, did not have to be tied to specific operational theaters. It could take on a global counterterrorism role.

Shortly after the September 11 attacks, Rumsfeld reportedly set up a highly compartmentalized special-access program to go after high-value terrorist targets. Commando teams operating outside the Pentagon's regular structure were provided with aliases, dead mail drops, and unmarked clothing and given advance legal authorization to use lethal force. At a moment's notice, this rapid deployment force was ready to cross borders without visas, using its own aircraft.

But General Charles R. Holland, the SOCOM commander, still appeared somewhat reluctant to embrace the expanded mission. The military traditionally ran wars with regional commanders, not global ones.

"Why aren't your guys going somewhere and doing things?" Rumsfeld asked Holland, with some impatience, when they met for an update discussion on July 15, 2002.

Holland, according to another official present, responded that he lacked the authority to do so.

"General," Rumsfeld said pointedly, "I don't recall you ever asking me for the authority to do anything."

A week later, Rumsfeld directed Myers to order Holland "to develop a plan to find and deal with members of terrorist organizations." The objective of the plan, Rumsfeld wrote, "is to capture terrorists for interrogation or, if necessary, to kill them, not simply to arrest them in a law enforcement exercise." It should "identify the authorities needed for global operations and the steps necessary to acquire such authorities in advance."

Holland, Rumsfeld added, would be responsible for "operational preparation of the battlespace" for such operations, and SOCOM would screen the civilian and military personnel who had the "languages, ethnic connections and other attributes needed for clandestine or covert activities." Rumsfeld gave Holland a week to come up with an initial "30 percent solution" and to be ready to brief it to him.

Nearly six more months passed but finally, in January 2003, Rumsfeld formally announced new powers for SOCOM, handing it the lead role in hunting down terrorists around the world. No longer would the command be considered just a supporting player, responsible for providing elite units to regional commanders for them to do with as they saw fit. Now, SOCOM would have charge of its own operations. It would, in military jargon, become a "supported" command, with the tables turned and regional headquarters providing assistance to it. Rumsfeld had his manhunting force.

The move opened the door for a series of unconventional activities that would press the legal limits of what military troops had previously been authorized to do. Actions by newly empowered and expanded Special Operations teams abroad would trigger concerns at the CIA about encroachment on agency operations. The State Department would grouse that its ambassadors were being left in the dark about sensitive military operations in some countries. Lawmakers filed similar complaints. Even the Pentagon's regional commanders took exception to the idea that they should allow SOCOM's teams to plan and conduct military operations in their regions without their knowing about it. Rumsfeld's fight had only just begun—and it wasn't going to be limited to terrorist networks.

Of all the decisions he made in office, the one that haunted Rumsfeld the most came at the end of 2002, when he approved a set of harsh interrogation techniques for prisoners at the Guantánamo detention facility. Although Rumsfeld rescinded the measures a few weeks later after being confronted with strong objections from lawyers for the military services, his initial action subsequently contributed to a blurring in the minds of military interrogators down the ranks and a world away in Afghanistan and Iraq about what was and was not allowed in the treatment of prisoners.

From the time the prison facility at Guantánamo was established, Rumsfeld had a nervous feeling about the place. He hadn't wanted the mission of caring over the long term for the detainees in the war on terrorism. Having the responsibility created a certain foreboding in the secretary.

Indeed, Rumsfeld had made time soon after Guantánamo was set up to meet in his office with the officer chosen to supervise interrogations there, Major General Michael Dunlavey, an Army reservist who in civilian life served as a state trial judge in Pennsylvania. The secretary questioned him closely, then issued an unusual request. "General, I want you to call me every morning," Rumsfeld told Dunlavey.

For a two-star officer in the field to report directly and frequently to the secretary of defense would be highly out of the ordinary. It would mean circumventing the normal chain of command, since Dunlavey served under the four-star general in charge of Southern Command.

Pace, the vice chairman and a former head of Southern Command himself, was at the meeting and immediately saw the problem the secretary would be creating. So did Robert Andrews, who was in the room as well; he glanced at Pace as soon as Rumsfeld had spoken. The vice chairman had the look of someone trying to think fast about how to correct a very awkward situation.

Pace suggested to the secretary that there might be another way to keep him informed of what was going on at Guantánamo, a way that would not circumvent Southern Command. He assured Rumsfeld that he need not worry, that something would be worked out to provide the secretary with timely information.

After the meeting, as the others filed out of Rumsfeld's office, Andrews stopped to ask the secretary if he had really intended to have Dunlavey call him every morning. Rumsfeld smiled. He didn't say yes or no. "I've found," Rumsfeld told him, "that when you take on something so sensitive it could come back and bite you, it's best to keep it firmly in hand yourself until you gain confidence and can delegate it to somebody else."

As much as Rumsfeld wished to be rid of the detainee mission, other administration officials working on detainee issues found him and his representatives resistant and unhelpful whenever the matter came up in interagency meetings. In her book *The Dark Side*, Jane Mayer reported several such examples. Rumsfeld was reluctant, for instance, to allow trips to Guantánamo by foreign allies to see detainees from their own countries. He ultimately agreed to the visits, but only for intelligence, not consular, purposes. When John Bellinger, the NSC's legal adviser, suggested to Rumsfeld that the detainees be given something to read, preferably books portraying more-positive views of America to "reeducate" them, Rumsfeld retorted, "If you want to reeducate people, get the Department of Education!" Eventually, Rumsfeld reportedly avoided high-level interagency meetings about Guantánamo altogether.

For his part, Rumsfeld was wary of other administration officials who had wanted to assign the detainee mission to the Pentagon and then sought to dictate conditions. He viewed some at State and on the NSC staff as often trying to reopen the issue of the applicability of the Geneva Conventions, though Bush had decided the matter in February 2002. And he generally preferred to leave detainee matters to Wolfowitz and other subordinates to handle, given the complex, time-consuming nature of the issues. "It was one of those areas that he knew could consume a lot of time, so either you dedicate yourself to it or you delegate," Di Rita said. "He had confidence in the people to whom he delegated these issues."

The initial intelligence haul from the prison population at Guantánamo was disappointing, and there were early indications that a substantial percentage of the six hundred captives had no connection to terrorism. But by the summer of 2002, Pentagon officials were focused less on thinning the prison ranks than on developing more-aggressive interrogation techniques out of a concern that at least some of the detainees knew of coming terrorist attacks. Particular urgency was attached to breaking Mohammed al-Qahtani, a Saudi who U.S. authorities suspect would have taken part in the September 11 attacks had he not been denied entry to the United States shortly before.

On October 11, the military officials at Guantánamo asked Rumsfeld for permission to use eighteen harsher interrogation techniques, including stress positions, exploitation of detainee fears (such as fear of dogs), removal of clothing, hooding, deprivation of light and sound, and a simulated drowning treatment known as waterboarding. In compiling the list, officials had researched U.S. military programs that teach survival training. These programs employ aggressive questioning techniques to replicate what U.S. troops might experience if captured. Used this way, the techniques are considered legitimate and important training tools. But some of them ended up on the Guantánamo list for offensive use against detainees—a reversal of purpose.

Lieutenant Colonel Diane Beaver, then the top legal adviser at Guantánamo, wrote a memo to superiors arguing that the more aggressive approaches were necessary and legal if appropriately reviewed, controlled, and monitored. To get around what were normally considered criminal acts, she presented an inventive legal theory, suggesting that immunity be obtained from command authorities in advance, before any crime had been committed. In later testimony before Congress, Beaver admitted how ill prepared she had felt in drafting the opinion and said that she had expected it would be carefully reviewed by legal and policy experts at much higher levels before any decision was reached. "Perhaps I was somewhat naïve that I did not expect to be the only lawyer issuing a written opinion on this monumentally important issue," she said.

But Beaver's memo was sent to General James Hill, the head of Southern Command, who pushed it up the chain of command, saying in a note to Myers that he wasn't certain himself whether the most aggressive measures on the list were legal. When the request reached Jim Haynes, the Pentagon's general counsel, he did little additional research, relying on endorsements of Beaver's memo by Dunlavey and Hill.

Beaver was shocked when she later realized that her opinion had become the basis for action with little elaboration by other lawyers. "In hindsight, I cannot help but conclude that others chose not to write on this issue to avoid being linked to it," she told Congress. "That was not an option for me."

The lack of oversight, particularly by Rumsfeld's top lawyer, underscored one of the dangers inherent in the secretary's decision to pick as his general counsel someone known more for his close association with Cheney's office than for his independence and legal rigor. Lawyers from several military services issued memos in November 2002 expressing serious legal concerns about the Guantánamo request. And the chief legal adviser to the Pentagon's criminal investigative task force, which had responsibility for preparing military cases against the detainees, cautioned that some of the measures might subject service members to punitive action under military law.

Jane Dalton, then a Navy captain serving as legal adviser to the chairman of the Joint Chiefs of Staff, did initiate what she intended to be a legal and policy review with the services and other agencies of the proposed techniques. But Haynes intervened, requesting the review be stopped in order to keep the matter confined to a smaller circle of people.

Despite the concerns raised by the military lawyers, Haynes sent a memo to Rumsfeld on November 27 recommending the secretary approve all but three of the eighteen techniques in the Guantánamo request. There is nothing in the memo reflecting other Pentagon views that the recommended course might be inhumane and unlawful. Five days later, on December 2, Rumsfeld signed the recommendation.

Rumsfeld was ill served here by Haynes. "When Rumsfeld appointed Haynes, it was a mistake," Steve Herbits said in an interview. "Haynes tended to take the White House position over the Defense Department's, which meant the department didn't have a real advocate for its view.

This, I think, contributed to the whole slide into issues of civil liberties." (The nomination of Haynes in 2003 to the Fourth Circuit U.S. Court of Appeals—which went nowhere in Congress—reinforced this view of him as a White House favorite.)

Myers, too, for all his earlier interest in ensuring the application of the Geneva Conventions, appears to have raised no objections. Dalton has testified that leading up to approval of the Guantánamo request, Myers participated in a number of meetings with Rumsfeld, Haynes, and her over the various techniques and the safeguards that would be applied. "And my understanding and my recollection is that General Myers was satisfied with the techniques that the secretary approved," Dalton said.

Rumsfeld's decision was in line with his own keen interest in extracting as much intelligence as possible from the inmates at Guantánamo and in pressing al-Qahtani in particular. Rumsfeld was "personally involved" in al-Qahtani's interrogation, according to Lieutenant General Randall M. Schmidt, an Air Force officer who interviewed the secretary twice in connection with a 2005 Army inspector general's investigation into abuse at Guantánamo.

In signing the memo, Rumsfeld made matters more difficult for himself later, when the document became public, by adding a flippant handwritten note in the margins. "I stand for 8–10 hours a day," he scribbled. "Why is standing limited to 4 hours?"

Following Rumsfeld's authorization, Pentagon criminal investigators and FBI personnel at Guantánamo raised additional red flags about the measures. The Navy's general counsel, Alberto Mora, bluntly warned Haynes that the policies could threaten Rumsfeld's tenure and could damage the presidency. Made aware of these objections, Rumsfeld rescinded his authorization orally on January 12 and in writing on January 15 and ordered the establishment of a "working group" to review interrogation techniques.

But when the group completed its work in April 2003, its recommended list of thirty-five interrogation methods included a number that the military lawyers had opposed. Mora and others who had objected found themselves shut out of the process and were not even informed that the final report had been submitted. On April 16, Rumsfeld authorized twenty-four of the techniques for use at Guantánamo.

CHAPTER 11

Too Many Hands on the Wheel

At the beginning of 2003, the Defense Department received from Bush formal authority for all postcombat operations in Iraq. It was a responsibility that Rumsfeld had requested in October and one even Powell agreed the Pentagon should have. It also represented a marked departure from the way the United States had tended to handle postwar efforts.

In the Balkans in the 1990s, the State Department had taken the postwar lead, while more recently in Afghanistan, responsibility for reconstruction and stabilization had been divided among several nations. Both approaches, though, had led to serious problems. In the Balkans, U.S. forces had been compelled to remain after their mission was complete because of a lag in civil reconstruction over which they had little control. In Afghanistan, the multinational model had proven largely ineffective.

With the Pentagon in charge, Rumsfeld figured civil authority could be reestablished promptly after the invasion, allowing for the near-term withdrawal of U.S. troops. But while the idea made theoretical sense, it overlooked a basic practical point: The Pentagon was woefully out of practice doing this kind of work. The U.S. military hadn't directly managed an occupied country since World War II.

One perceived advantage of vesting control in the Pentagon was that it would ensure unity of command in Iraq after Saddam Hussein and his

Baath Party were swept from power and before a new Iraqi government was established. In keeping with this principle of single leadership—a basic tenet of military operations—the Joint Staff had drafted a plan in the fall of 2002 for postwar Iraq to be administered by a new military headquarters, with a three-star general in charge of a staff of experts drawn from various U.S. government agencies. The thought was that, much as General Douglas MacArthur had controlled postwar Japan, a senior general would administer Iraq during the transition back to sovereignty.

But such a dominant military hand in postwar Iraq could prove politically problematic for the United States. Instead of opting for a single military-run command, Rumsfeld chose a split civilian-military approach. He ordered two distinct authorities: a civilian administrator to oversee the reconstruction and governance of the country, and a U.S. military commander responsible for security and for retraining the Iraqi military. This provided a civilian face on at least a major part of the postwar activity. But it had a serious downside. It would mean a system with divided command, and this, as things turned out, led to conflict and poor coordination between the civilian and military branches.

Further, the civilian element in this postwar planning structure got a late start. Rumsfeld had considered establishing something in October, but he was constrained by Bush, who worried that too many signs of U.S. war preparations could disturb efforts to achieve a diplomatic solution. Not until early January did Rumsfeld move to set up what became the Office of Reconstruction and Humanitarian Assistance, or ORHA. To run it initially, he hired Jay Garner, a retired three-star general who had earned high marks in an earlier postwar operation overseeing relief efforts in Kurdistan after the 1991 Persian Gulf War. Garner had also served on the space policy commission that Rumsfeld had chaired during the Clinton years.

Plans called for Garner to set up the office and eventually be succeeded by a more prominent political figure. Feith, who phoned Garner to pitch the job, told him his role wasn't so much to generate his own plans as to coordinate and integrate previous efforts and to be ready to form the core of an organization that would administer Iraq after conflict ended.

Rumsfeld related to Garner's enterprising spirit. "He immediately felt like they were simpatico," John Craddock recalled. "Garner was talking the language that Rumsfeld wanted to hear, which is can-do—'I've been over there before, and did it after the Gulf War with the Kurds, I'll need this and that, we can pull it off.' That was music to his ears because it was action."

But Garner had little time to accomplish what proved to be a massive assignment. Two months after the announcement of ORHA's creation, the war started. Garner's orders had called for him to draft plans to deliver food and other emergency assistance and to restore electricity and other basic services. His office was also supposed to be ready to help reshape the Iraqi military, safeguard Iraq's infrastructure, and dismantle whatever stashes of weapons of mass destruction might be found. And Garner was to coordinate his activities with the United Nations, nongovernmental relief groups, and Iraqi exiles.

Complicating matters, the staff of ORHA became a source of serious friction between the Pentagon and the State Department, with Garner initially prohibited from accepting the participation of some diplomats offered by State. When Garner sought Rumsfeld's approval of a proposed list of senior U.S. advisers to key Iraqi ministries, the secretary crossed off eight or nine names that had been sent over from State and asked that several candidates be recommended for each position so that he could choose. Powell, incensed, threatened to hold back all State Department personnel from the effort. Rumsfeld relented, allowing participation by a significant number of State Department officials in ORHA. Years later, though, Powell told Army historians that the planning effort "would have been better served" if the Pentagon "had asked for more help from people outside."

Tom Warrick, who had directed the State Department's Future of Iraq Project, was notably kept off the team. Cheney's office blacklisted Warrick because he had criticized the Pentagon during a meeting with Iraqi exiles in Michigan, warning them against working with Wolfowitz. Rumsfeld told Powell that work on postwar planning had to be done by those who were truly committed to the effort and not those who had written or said things that were not supportive.

The Army's study of the postwar planning effort, published in 2008, concluded that ORHA's work "appears to have suffered from this lack of interagency support." In any case, neither ORHA's mission nor its relationship with CENTCOM was ever well defined, nor was ORHA given resources adequate for the planning and oversight it was asked to do. ORHA deployed 151 staff members to Kuwait on March 16, only half the number Garner had estimated the organization needed. Its planning had focused on preparing for the four potential crises it considered most likely: oil field fires, large numbers of refugees, food shortages, and outbreaks of epidemics. None of these problems emerged once the fighting started.

————————

Weeks before the war began, James Schlesinger, who had remained a prominent figure in national security circles after being removed by Ford as defense secretary and replaced by Rumsfeld, warned Rumsfeld that planning for the postwar period had not been given its due. Schlesinger served on the Defense Policy Board, which afforded him a window on Pentagon developments. In a private conversation with Rumsfeld, Schlesinger advised that Iraqi society, with its rival groups of Shiites, Sunnis, and Kurds, could prove very difficult to manage, yet many U.S. troops seemed clueless about what they were getting into. Afterward, Schlesinger wasn't sure how much of an impression his warning had made, although Rumsfeld did ask him to raise his concerns with Tommy Franks and then phoned Franks to say Schlesinger was coming. When Schlesinger met in Tampa with the general and the CENTCOM staff, he received assurances that everything had been thought through.

Others also pointed to serious planning gaps. Numerous studies both inside and outside the government raised concerns about the potential for postwar difficulties and about the need to keep significant numbers of troops in Iraq during the crucial stabilization period. The conclusions of the State Department's Future of Iraq Project, handed over to the Pentagon at the end of 2002, included the possibility of widespread looting and lawlessness and emphasized the need to quickly repair Iraq's infrastructure. In December, a joint study by the Council on Foreign Relations and the James A. Baker III Institute for Public Policy at Rice University warned of possible anarchy and of the need for the U.S. military to quickly turn to humanitarian efforts and law enforcement.

The Center for Strategic and International Studies issued a report in January 2003 noting that the success of any war with Iraq "will be judged more by the commitment to rebuilding Iraq after a conflict than by the military phase of the war itself." The report argued that postwar planning efforts conducted to that point had been incomplete and insufficient. And a paper by the U.S. Army War College in February cautioned that "the possibility of the United States winning the war and losing the peace in Iraq is real and serious."

Civilian officials in the Pentagon who were focused on postwar peace-keeping considerations were increasingly anxious about what might un-fold in Iraq. Joseph Collins, a retired Army colonel who headed the Pentagon's Office of Peacekeeping and Humanitarian Affairs, feared that too few troops were being sent to adequately maintain supply lines for an invading force, and he also foresaw a more costly and problematic occupa-tion than CENTCOM had anticipated. Chris Lamb, another official in the policy branch with experience in constabulary forces in Bosnia, warned that the U.S. military could undermine a war victory in Iraq if it failed to take care of law and order after the invasion. A fourteen-page memo that he wrote with Feith expressed concern that CENTCOM had not given high enough priority to providing an adequate policing force.

Others, like Robert Perito, an expert on peacekeeping operations at the United States Institute for Peace, a government-financed research center, and David Kay, a deputy to Garner, were urging a sizable interna-tional constabulary force. But their calls went unheeded. To the extent that CENTCOM planners had addressed the issue, they assumed that elements of the Iraqi army could be enlisted after the war to help restore order and alleviate some of the burden on U.S. troops.

According to John Craddock, Rumsfeld eventually recognized that CENTCOM "was behind the power curve" in preparing a postwar plan, having been focused on the combat phase and having been unable to work well with Feith's policy shop. In the final weeks of planning, Rums-feld began asking more questions about the state of postwar prepara-tions. "I'll say to Rumsfeld's credit that he did push to get postwar planning done," recalled George Casey Jr., then a three-star general di-recting the Joint Staff. "It was very hard to get anybody to focus on the postwar part of it. Rumsfeld used to say, 'I've had twenty-seven briefings on the war but I've had one on the postwar. What's going on?'"

But Rumsfeld and his senior staff continued to operate on the as-sumption that U.S. forces could avoid a prolonged occupation. Their guiding notion was that American troops would help Iraqis get back on their feet, not bring the country back to normal themselves. The term most often used to describe this approach was "enabling."

In a speech on February 14 titled "Beyond Nation-Building," Rumsfeld drove this point home. At a black-tie gala in New York honoring the armed forces, he offered the Balkans as a model of a postwar policy gone wrong. The Clinton administration's intervention in Kosovo and the lengthy deployment of U.S. and allied peacekeeping forces there had led, Rumsfeld said, to a "culture of dependence" that had made it hard for the Kosovars to stand on their own feet. By contrast, in Afghanistan the Bush administration had resisted the temptation to mount a major nation-building effort or to deploy a large peacekeeping force; instead, it was helping the Afghans rebuild their own country.

Iraq, Rumsfeld said, might be easier to restore than Afghanistan in several respects. Iraq was rich in oil, and the Bush administration had more time to prepare the postwar plan. He touted the services of Garner's postwar planning office, which he said had been established "to think through problems and coordinate the efforts of coalition countries and U.S. government agencies." Franks, he added, had also "been working hard on this for many months" in an interagency process.

Rumsfeld's references to Garner and Franks both were misleading. Garner's operation had only just begun, and Franks had paid insufficient attention to postwar planning. But the thrust of Rumsfeld's speech made clear his view that it would be possible to invade Iraq and then manage the aftermath in a way that would allow Iraq to put itself back together while the United States avoided a long, expensive, difficult nation-building effort like the one the Clinton administration had taken on in the Balkans.

The war strategy that CENTCOM devised and Rumsfeld approved at the end of 2002 envisioned that the invasion would begin before all forces had arrived in the region, so it depended on the remaining forces continuing to flow. That would be critical to ensure the protection of vulnerable supply lines and to sustain combat forces as the fight advanced to Baghdad.

But Rumsfeld's relentless scrutiny of the Army's troop deployment list continued into 2003 and raised worries among commanders that they would be denied adequate forces to conduct the fight. Rumsfeld, anticipating the possibility that Saddam's regime could collapse quickly, asked Franks to identify points at which the flow of reinforcements could be stopped—"off-ramping" them, in Pentagon parlance. David McKiernan, the land commander, was reluctant to see planned reinforcements canceled even if the regime collapsed, figuring all the troops called for in the plan could be necessary for the postwar period.

Eric Shinseki was increasingly concerned as well. He had worried for months that the leaner invasion strategy being assembled by CENTCOM did not adequately provide for the considerable logistical demands of pushing to Baghdad. In late January, called to the White House with the other chiefs to convey their views on the war plan, Shinseki offered a qualified assessment. He expressed some reservation about the number of forces that would be in place at the start of the invasion, and he stressed the need to keep reinforcements coming and the logistics lines protected. But he did not press his points and, seeking to give Bush a balanced assessment, declared the plan executable.

"It was the opinion of the chiefs, especially Shinseki, that we were very short on land power," recalled John Jumper, the Air Force chief. "The worry was, we were setting up the situation, as the land forces progressed, they would be leaving black holes behind them because we didn't have the people to stay behind and stabilize."

The chiefs did tend to subscribe to the belief that the war would go quickly, Jumper said. But they, like others, worried that inadequate attention had been paid to managing the aftermath. "We had long talks with Tommy Franks about phase four," Jumper recalled, using the military term for the period after combat operations. "The chiefs thought that we should be working very hard right after the major combat operation on engineering things—getting the water flowing, getting the electricity, getting the schools and hospitals open—those things that would make the Iraqis think their lives were better. Franks assured us he had this well in hand, but in fact what we saw was that we really didn't pursue that as an objective after the major combat operation."

Aside from Shinseki, though, the chiefs did not voice such concerns in the meeting with Bush in January because, Jumper said, the discussion centered on the invasion, not the occupation afterward. "When we got asked our advice and whether we were comfortable with the war plan, it was almost entirely about the major combat operation part."

The question of the extent to which the chiefs were consulted, and whether Rumsfeld was open to hearing them, would later dog the secretary. He insisted publicly that their views had been solicited, and in memos he wrote for his files, he maintained that the service leaders had put forward no objections. In one memo, for instance, dated September 29, 2004—a year and a half after the invasion—he noted that he and Myers had "met repeatedly during that period with the Chiefs and the Combatant Commander." Neither he nor Myers, he wrote, could recall Myers "ever raising any differences of views of any of the Chiefs with POTUS [the acronym for president of the United States] on Iraq. The reason no differences were raised is, very simply, because no differences existed. Therefore, any suggestion that the President overrode his military advice is not correct."

———•———

On February 25, Shinseki and his fellow chiefs appeared before the Senate Armed Services Committee, which was examining the administration's movements toward war. During the hearing, Senator Carl Levin, the senior Democrat on the panel, asked Shinseki how many troops would be needed to control Iraq after Saddam was ousted. Shinseki estimated "something on the order of several hundred thousand soldiers," adding, "We're talking about post-hostilities control over a piece of geography that's fairly significant, with the kinds of ethnic tensions that could lead to other problems. And so it takes a significant ground-force presence to maintain a safe and secure environment, to ensure that people are fed, that water is distributed, all the normal responsibilities that go along with administering a situation like this."

His estimate drew in large part on his experience as a commander in postwar Bosnia, where the United States had sent fifty thousand troops to quiet five million people, a population one-fifth that of Iraq. The suggestion that the Pentagon was underestimating the difficulty of the task ahead in Iraq and providing an insufficient number of forces made headlines. The next day, Army secretary Tom White received an early-morning phone call from Wolfowitz, who complained that Shinseki was wrong and had no business offering an estimate, since the Army chief was not leading the operation. White argued that Shinseki, in providing his professional assessment, had simply done what Congress had asked him to do.

Two days after Shinseki's testimony, Wolfowitz, in congressional testimony of his own, called the general's estimate of several hundred thousand troops "wildly off the mark." He said he knew of no historical reason to believe that free Iraqis would fight against one another or the United States. "I am reasonably certain that they will greet us as liberators, and that will help us to keep requirements down," he said.

Moreover, Wolfowitz added, the Pentagon anticipated that many countries then objecting to the use of force would be eager to help once Saddam was gone. "There is simply no reason to assume that the United States will or should supply" the bulk of the military forces needed for postwar stabilization, he said. "I would expect that even countries like France will have a strong interest in assisting Iraq's reconstruction."

Rumsfeld also weighed in, making it clear at a Pentagon news conference on February 28 that he disagreed with Shinseki's estimate, although because Wolfowitz had been so blunt, the secretary could afford to sound less so. "My personal view is that it will prove to be high," he said of the Army's chief's number.

In fact, Shinseki's figure was only a little above the total number of forces in CENTCOM's own plan, once all the reinforcements had arrived in the war zone. Indeed, in giving his estimate, Shinseki referred to "what's been mobilized to this point" and equated that to what in his view would be required. The CENTCOM plan projected that while the attack would begin with only a portion of the force, as many as 250,000 troops would be in Iraq by the time Saddam was defeated and the United States began to stabilize Iraq.

Nonetheless, the sharp official rebuke dealt Shinseki had an intimidating effect on the rest of the military's officer corps. It sent a chilling signal to the uniformed leadership about how that kind of military judgment was going to be valued, and it served to silence critics just at a moment when it would have been helpful to have them. "Anecdotal evidence," a RAND study in 2008 concluded, "suggests that other Army general officers shared

General Shinseki's main concern, namely, that more troops would be needed immediately following combat with Iraqi forces than would be required to defeat those same forces; however, none spoke up publicly before the war."

———•———

With war fast approaching, the Bush administration was still trying to rally as much international support as possible for an invasion force. Yet at times Rumsfeld managed instead to rile U.S. allies. Responding to a Dutch reporter's question on January 22 about European opposition to the use of force against Iraq, Rumsfeld said the resistance had been centered in Germany and France, which he called "old Europe" and contrasted with the "new members" of "NATO Europe," new members made up in large part of the formerly communist nations of eastern Europe. "They're not with France and Germany on this; they're with the United States," he said.

The remark generated a flurry of news stories that cast Rumsfeld as the antidiplomat. In later explanations, Rumsfeld said that he had been thinking at the time about how NATO had grown from fifteen members to twenty-six with the addition of the eastern European nations, and that he had meant to say old and new NATO. He never repeated the quip, nor did he ever apologize for it.

The White House claimed that forty-nine countries were part of a "coalition of the willing" in support of military action, but most had promised little more than permission to put their names on the list. Rumsfeld seemed intent on making it clear that the United States could still go it alone if necessary. A week before the invasion, he suggested that even assistance from Britain—the ally that had provided the most support—was superfluous, telling a Pentagon news conference that Britain's role was "unclear" and that the invasion plan could proceed without British troops.

The defense secretary's offhand remark, made as Prime Minister Tony Blair was insisting to his own Parliament that Britain's support was crucial to the effort, sent London reeling and demanding an explanation. The Pentagon quickly issued a "clarification"; Rumsfeld said he had "no doubt" of Britain's "full support" for the effort to disarm Saddam Hussein. But the incident reinforced a widespread impression that the Pentagon simply was not interested in coalition warfare.

The most sensitive alliance issue involved Turkey. While the bulk of the U.S. invasion force expected to enter Iraq from the south through Kuwait, the war plan also called for the U.S. 4th Infantry Division to sweep in from the north, which would require passage through Turkey. By attacking from both the north and the south, U.S. commanders hoped to compel Saddam's regime to divide its attention and resources. A northern entry would, moreover, speed the arrival of U.S. forces to safeguard the oil fields near Kirkuk and to prevent ethnic fighting between the Kurds and the Arabs.

Turkey had allowed the United States to conduct air strikes from its bases during the 1991 Persian Gulf War, but the economic consequences of that war for Turkey had been severe, and subsequent U.S. assistance had fallen short of what the country had anticipated. The Turkish public was overwhelmingly opposed to another war with Iraq, fearing that it would facilitate the breakup of Iraq and lead to the establishment of an independent Kurdish state, which could fan secessionist tendencies among Turkish Kurds.

Negotiations for arranging the U.S. use of Turkish territory, begun in the summer of 2002, had been difficult, with the Turks placing conditions on the number of U.S. troops and on how they could be transported across Turkish soil and demanding compensation, financial and otherwise. It didn't help matters that the Pentagon's precise needs kept changing.

Turkey eventually joined the long list of internal issues dividing the administration. State Department officials worried that defense officials were oblivious to the challenges they were posing to Turkey's fragile democracy. Rumsfeld, along with Cheney, suspected that the State Department wasn't trying hard enough to win Turkey's agreement. Powell was later criticized for not having made a personal trip to Ankara. Rumsfeld never went either, but that was by design. "I remember one of the senior guys at State saying to me several times, 'God, we can't send Rumsfeld there, he'll scare the heck out of the Turks,'" recalled Eric Edelman, a career diplomat then on Cheney's staff.

On March 1, the Turkish parliament rejected a measure that would have permitted U.S. troops to establish a northern front, forcing a major change in the war plan. To maintain the impression that a northern attack might still occur, Franks kept the 4th Infantry Division floating off the coast of Turkey for a while longer, then brought it around to Kuwait, enabling it to enter Iraq from the south.

Rumsfeld has repeatedly cited the absence of a northern front as his major regret about how the invasion plan played out. He has argued that the delay in getting U.S. troops into Sunni strongholds north of Baghdad, including such cities as Tikrit, Saddam's hometown, hampered efforts to root out Baathists. Certainly, the loss of that part of the plan cost the U.S. operation something in terms of surprise and perhaps spared some Iraqi forces. But just how many more Saddam loyalists would have been killed or captured and what difference it would have made to the subsequent rise of an insurgency in Iraq remains questionable. The U.S. forces surging up from the south did not stop to do much rooting out there either. Their essential objective was to get to Baghdad and topple the regime, even if it meant bypassing southern cities and towns in the process.

In any case, Rumsfeld's comments about the refusal of the Turks to open the way for the 4th Infantry Division angered Turkish authorities. Edelman, who subsequently left Cheney's staff to become the U.S. ambassador to Turkey in mid-2003, tried unsuccessfully to persuade Rumsfeld to stop complaining about the absence of a northern front.

"The Turks say that's just the Americans blaming us for their multitude of failures," Edelman said in an interview. "Truth be known, had the division gone in, Saddam's regime might have crumbled a little quicker than it did, but it did crumble in three weeks anyway. I suppose we might have killed more of the people in the Republican Guard divisions, some of whom instead may have gone on to become insurgents. But no one will ever be able to establish frankly what contributed more to all this. I think it's a not very productive line of discussion."

—————

In early March, Rumsfeld met with some of his senior subordinates—Wolfowitz, Myers, Pace, Di Rita, Craddock, Feith, and Ryan Henry—to survey their views on how long the war was likely to last. Several declined to answer at first because Rumsfeld had drilled his staff never to forecast about such operations, often describing the future as essentially unknowable. All remembered how Army general John Shalikashvili, as chairman of the Joint Chiefs of Staff under Clinton, had predicted just ahead of the Bosnia conflict that U.S. forces would be out within a year. As the U.S. presence there persisted for years, Shalikashvili was ridiculed for having misjudged so badly.

Nudged by Rumsfeld to hazard guesses this time, his aides offered estimates ranging from seven to thirty days, reflecting a good deal of optimism about the plan. But Rumsfeld refused to play himself. He told the others that they should be open to the possibility that the war could drag on, noting that the enemy also had a big say in the outcome.

In the early morning, Iraq time, of March 20, four bunker-busting bombs dropped from two U.S. Air Force F-117s and a volley of more than three dozen Navy cruise missiles struck Dora Farms, a compound in a palm grove on the Tigris River outside Baghdad where Saddam and his two sons were thought to be hiding. The Iraqi leader and his family were not there, but the war had begun.

At dawn the next day, U.S. ground forces moved into Iraq, crossing twenty-four hours earlier than planned out of concern that the Iraqis would be sabotaging the oil fields. The total U.S.-led invasion force consisted of fewer than three Army divisions plus a large Marine division and a British division—in all numbering about 145,000 troops. Hours later, U.S. and coalition aircraft and ships launched a furious barrage of bombs and missiles, blasting air-defense sites, command centers, communication links, Baath Party headquarters, Republican Guard facilities, and other sites. The aim, officials said, was to achieve "shock and awe" and deliver a crippling blow to Saddam's regime.

Iraq's regular forces proved little problem for U.S. troops, with a majority of the Iraqi army abandoning positions and seeming to dissolve. But to the surprise of American commanders, thousands of irregular fighters called fedayeen put up determined resistance, launching guerrilla-style attacks on rear supply convoys of the advancing U.S. and British forces. While forecast as a threat, the fedayeen had not been expected to be so ferocious and tenacious.

Sandstorms and mud rains enveloped Iraq on March 24 and lasted three days. The foul weather grounded helicopters and stopped many of the invading troops in their tracks. Momentarily stalled, U.S. officers expressed some frustration. "The enemy we're fighting is a bit different than the one we war-gamed against because of these paramilitary forces," Lieutenant General William Scott Wallace, who was leading the advancing Army forces, observed at the end of the first week. "We knew they were here, but we did not know how they would fight." At the Pentagon, Rumsfeld was not pleased with Wallace's remarks and the doubts raised about the strategy.

With the invasion appearing to falter, a chorus of critics grew louder. They included some prominent former Army commanders from the last war with Iraq. Their critique centered on the size of the invading force, which they said was not large enough to guard ever-lengthening supply lines, cope with the paramilitary units in the south, establish control throughout Iraq, and prepare for an assault on Baghdad.

"Their assumptions were wrong," said retired general Barry M. McCaffrey, who led the 24th Mechanized Division in the 1991 war and had become a frequent television commentator. "There is a view that the nature of warfare has fundamentally changed, that numbers don't count, that armor and artillery don't count. They went into battle with a plan that put a huge air and sea force into action with an unbalanced ground combat force."

Retired general Ronald Griffith, the commander of the 1st Armored Division during the 1991 war, declared that if it had been up to him, he would have deployed additional armored divisions and more artillery. Others said the war plan had taken significant risks by leaving key units in the United States and Germany at the start. That resulted in an invasion force that was too small and too strung out, underprotected, and undersupplied.

Criticism of the war plan, particularly from the retired military community, angered Rumsfeld. He and his aides tended to perceive much of it as part of a larger fight over the future direction of the military. "It was playing internal politics out in the press during the war when American lives were at stake," said Ryan Henry.

Henry recalled a small staff meeting during which Rumsfeld grew enraged over some of the remarks that had come from retired officers.

"He just couldn't hold it in any more, and he stood up and said to Myers, 'It's your guys, it's your community, those retired people. This isn't fair to the country; it isn't fair to the boys fighting over there. What are we going to do about it?'"

Henry couldn't believe Rumsfeld's intensity. "It was Mr. Cool losing control," he recalled. "Nobody was talking."

Myers did not remember that meeting several years later when asked about it. But according to Henry, it sparked an unusual public outburst by Myers shortly afterward. During an April 1 Pentagon news conference, the general suddenly appeared uncharacteristically fierce in responding to the attacks on Rumsfeld and the war plan.

A journalist had asked about criticism that the number of U.S. forces in Iraq were insufficient. As Rumsfeld started to comment, Myers stepped forward. He called the complaints "bogus," said that those who were spreading them were misinformed, and warned that such talk during combat seriously undermined the war effort.

"I've been in this process every step of the way," Myers asserted. He said that Franks had gotten everything he wanted, and he defended the plan as designed to coordinate with sensitive U.N. diplomacy and also maintain a certain element of "tactical surprise." He said that all the chiefs and all the component commanders under Franks had endorsed the plan. Rapping on the lectern with a clenched fist, he angrily mocked the armchair analysis on television as "a great sport here inside the Beltway."

He was as emphatic and demonstrative as the normally unflappable Myers had ever been at a news conference during a year and a half of briefings on terrorism and war. Asked about his performance several years later, Myers said he considered it one of his most important and described his remarks as "premeditated." "I couldn't take it any longer," Myers said, recalling his feelings at the time. "Because it's not the secretary's plan, it's the military's plan, and the military ought to speak out."

———•———

Rumsfeld also weighed in against his critics, insisting to the Pentagon press and several television interviewers that he was not the author of the war strategy. Everyone had agreed that the old plan for invading Iraq had been flawed, Rumsfeld argued. The new plan, he declared, had been produced by Franks. "I keep getting credit for it in the press, but the truth is, I would be happy to take credit for it but I can't," Rumsfeld said. "It was not my plan. It was General Franks's plan, and it was a plan that evolved over a sustained period of time."

He seemed irritated when it was suggested that in saying it was Franks's plan, he was distancing himself from it. "Goodness gracious!" Rumsfeld exclaimed. But the downplaying of his involvement was certainly belied by the facts. Politically, he may have felt reason to do so, seeing some advantage for the administration's civilian leadership to be able to say that they were just implementing the military's plan. Personally, such posturing afforded him a way of avoiding responsibility and placing it fully on his commanders should that become expedient. More probably, Rumsfeld, who genuinely seemed to view his role in the planning as more contributor than architect, was simply trying to ensure that Franks received sufficient credit.

For the record, Rumsfeld sent Myers a private memo later that day that sought to spell out his view of the war-planning process and also to address criticism of his handling of the deployments. "There has been no small number of articles and stories in the media over the past week alleging that I have imposed an unworkable, 'high tech' war plan on the military, destroyed the 'carefully crafted' time phased force deployment plan (TPFD), disapproved and 'delayed proposals' from Gen. Franks for forces to flow, and cut in half the forces Franks requested, with the result that U.S. and coalition forces are being killed unnecessarily and the U.S. is losing the war—all of this after 10 or 12 days of war," Rumsfeld wrote in the memo. "The articles and breathless statements on television by retired Army generals suggest that the TPFD was a brilliant piece of work and that Gen. Shinseki 'wisely' advised the president that the plan was bad because the forces were inadequate and not heavy enough and that he and they are now being proven correct. I don't remember the past several months quite that way."

Discussing the lengthy process that led to development of the war plan, he insisted the responsibility for it rested with Franks. "Gen. Franks received a lot of advice, some of which he took, some of which, properly, he did not," Rumsfeld wrote. "Press reports have repeatedly said it was

'Rumsfeld's war plan.' As much as I would be delighted to take credit for the war plan, because I believe it is excellent, the fact is I don't remember imposing any of my opinions on Gen. Franks with respect to the plan. We talked many, many times, to be sure. I raised many questions, and I energetically offered my views. Sometimes I suggested thoughts on particular aspects of the plan. I helped connect Tom's work to the goal of having a plan that complemented and did not compete with the President's diplomacy in the UN."

Moving on to the controversy over the TPFD, Rumsfeld recalled cautioning against preparing a single, giant deployment order—the MOAD—in the fall of 2002 in light of then-ongoing diplomatic efforts. "Instead, we sought a steady flow of forces over the period," he wrote. "That decision was made early enough to preclude any adverse delay on the total forces that arrived by D-day. As to my dismembering the TPFD, my recollection is that it was Gen. Franks who decided he wanted to accelerate the flow of some TPFD forces, not me. He recommended that certain elements be pulled forward and deployed in advance of the TPFD flow."

Rumsfeld noted that he had refused to sign only two deployment orders: One was the MOAD, and the other involved a Puerto Rican National Guard unit slated to go to Germany for protection of U.S. forces there. "I suggested we ask the Germans to provide the force protection," Rumsfeld wrote. "We did so, and the Germans agreed."

The secretary told of being presented with deployment orders with as few as five days between notification and activation. He had been surprised by the orders coming to him so late and said Myers and Pace had also been surprised. The Joint Staff's senior operations officer was instructed to avoid such minimal notification for reservists. "I had never been told that was going on until I attended an Army generals conference and was told that the Army average was five days," Rumsfeld wrote. "I was shocked. I should have been told the system was that screwed up."

He also noted a meeting in the Tank in the fall of 2002 at which a plan for reserve mobilization was discussed. The plan, he said, would have led to as many or more reserves being called up as were activated for the 1991 Persian Gulf War. The proposal had concerned him, as well as Wolfowitz, Myers, and Pace, all of whom, Rumsfeld said, saw it as providing too little flexibility and as being likely to end up unnecessarily disrupting the lives of many reservists right before the holiday.

"Further, we routinely asked Gen. Franks if he had all that he needed," Rumsfeld wrote. "In every instance, Gen. Franks said he had what he needed." Additionally, on three or four occasions Bush asked Myers, Pace, and the chiefs whether they agreed with the plan, and each said he did, Rumsfeld said. And, he noted, in a meeting with Myers, Pace, Franks, and each of CENTCOM's component commanders just before the invasion, Bush asked whether they had everything they needed to win, and each said yes.

Rumsfeld concluded with a paragraph saying he found the second-guessing by Army generals revealing. The seeming pervasiveness of anonymous negative comments about the plan did not augur well for future U.S. Army leadership, he said, adding that general officer promotions would have to be examined closely to ensure higher-quality leadership.

That last comment was a stark expression of the conflict in which Rumsfeld found himself with the Army. He did not elaborate on how he thought those senior officers who were critical of his own leadership could be weeded out in the selection process. But his thought of using the process to create a more supportive and amenable group of Army commanders is evident.

———•———

In the end, Iraqi forces proved no match for the U.S. military juggernaut marching toward Baghdad, and after several days of battles with Saddam's tougher Republican Guard forces on the outskirts of the capital, American troops reached the city center on April 9, nearly three weeks after they had crossed the Kuwaiti border. Saddam himself managed to escape into hiding, and scattered fighting continued around the country, but on April 15, coalition forces secured Tikrit, bringing Iraq effectively under U.S. control. American casualties had been relatively light, with 139 dead and 542 wounded. Although ground troops went into battle with special suits to protect them from Iraqi biological and chemical attacks, no weapons of mass destruction were deployed.

On April 16, Franks visited Baghdad. He sent a message to Rumsfeld recommending that the United States declare a military victory in Iraq and announce that it was transitioning to postwar operations. He also instructed his officers to be prepared to reduce forces rapidly. In line with the prewar planning and the general euphoria at the rapid crumbling of the Saddam regime, Franks expected a very limited role for U.S. ground forces in Iraq.

But the situation on the ground was hardly calm. After several days of euphoria following the arrival of U.S. troops in Baghdad, the Iraqi capital erupted in a frenzy of crime and looting. American soldiers, without orders, manpower, or a plan to intervene, stood by while government facilities were stripped of everything from furniture and fine art to plumbing and electrical wiring. Because of the speed of the American victory, fewer Army divisions than planned were on hand in Iraq to help stabilize the situation. And the 3rd Infantry Division that had led the U.S. Army's charge into Baghdad was equipped not with the military police and civil affairs units useful in policing but with tanks and armored fighting vehicles meant for combat.

"Never, from the first day that we ever started planning this until we got to Baghdad, in all the processes, rehearsals—nobody ever mentioned the word 'looter,'" Major General Buford "Buff" Blount III, the division's commander, told a journalist later. "I mean, it was just never, ever, ever mentioned. Our focus was on fighting the war."

Moreover, Blount and other commanders were reluctant to issue shoot-to-kill orders to quell the looting, seeing the mayhem as probably a short-term indulgence in vengeance after years of mistreatment under Saddam. Similarly, White House and Pentagon officials in Washington, fending off rising criticism of inadequate postwar planning, described the destruction as a normal turn of events that would play itself out quickly. In a news conference on April 11, Rumsfeld minimized the images of looting that were being shown on television.

"It's the same picture of some person walking out of some building with a vase, and you see it twenty times, and you think, 'My goodness, were there that many vases?'" The press corps laughed. "Stuff happens! But in terms of what's going on in that country, it is a fundamental misunderstanding to see those images over, and over, and over again of some boy walking out with a vase and say, 'Oh, my goodness, you didn't have a plan.' That's nonsense. They know what they're doing, and they're doing a terrific job. And it's untidy, and freedom's untidy, and free people are free to make mistakes and commit crimes and do bad things. They're also free to live their lives and do wonderful things, and that's what's going to happen here."

But the scale of the destruction that followed the fall of Baghdad went far beyond what the term "looting" normally conveys. Whereas the war itself had caused little damage to infrastructure because U.S. forces had relied heavily on precision weaponry, the looting destroyed almost three-quarters of the government ministries and many other structures and facilities.

When Garner and his team arrived in late April, they found that seventeen of twenty-three government ministries had been completely destroyed. Also damaged were most of the city's hotels, department stores, museums, schools, universities, and hospitals, as well as Saddam's palaces. A notable exception was the Ministry of Oil, which was heavily guarded by a company of U.S. Marines. In neighborhoods where U.S. forces were positioned, looters were deterred, but there were far too few American soldiers to make a notable difference.

Rumsfeld's failure to grasp the scale of the destruction and its significance was compounded by his public effort to play it down. In the process, he not only undercut U.S. military efforts to deal with the violence but conveyed an image of U.S. insensitivity. "Some senior officials in Washington chuckled about a 'new spirit of freedom' that had suddenly sprouted . . . among 'grateful,' liberated Iraqis," wrote Fred Ikle, who served as the Pentagon's policy chief during the Reagan administration and who still had high standing in conservative circles. "America lost most of its prestige and respect in that episode. To pacify a conquered country, the victory's prestige and dignity is absolutely critical."

The violence grew worse, transforming from initially unorganized, individual activity into increasingly systematic, large-scale crime. McKiernan considered declaring martial law and issuing orders to shoot looters on sight. He told Pentagon investigators later that he hadn't been able to bring himself to issue a shoot-to-kill order out of concern that innocent women and children might be harmed. But other accounts have portrayed the general as having also been dissuaded by top Washington officials.

Major General William Webster, the deputy ground commander, fielded queries from Iraqi leaders about the possibility that martial law might be declared. In an interview with Army historians, he remembered McKiernan responding, "The president and the secretary of defense have said that we will not declare martial law. We are not going to put our military in a position of enforcing Iraqi laws."

Despite the unsettled situation in Iraq and evident shortfall in U.S. forces, Rumsfeld approved a recommendation from Franks to cancel the planned deployment of the 1st Cavalry Division, which had been scheduled to go as part of a reinforcement flow that also included the 1st Armored Division. In the weeks leading up to the war, Rumsfeld had indicated a desire to off-ramp some Army units if Iraqi forces were quickly defeated, and after the fall of Baghdad, he had questioned Franks as to whether both the 1st Cavalry and 1st Armored needed to deploy.

Initially, Franks wanted both divisions in Iraq to help extend the military's reach into northern and western parts of the country and to start the process of reconstituting the Iraqi army. But after discussing the matter for several days with Rumsfeld as well as with Myers, Pace, and his own staff, Franks changed his mind and recommended fewer reinforcements. The 1st Armored Division was sent, but the deployment of the 1st Cavalry Division was officially canceled on April 21. General Jack Keane, the Army's vice chief of staff, supported the decision.

Back in Washington, strains between the Pentagon and the State Department flared anew—this time in plain view. The spark was remarks by former House leader Newt Gingrich, a Rumsfeld ally.

Speaking to the American Enterprise Institute, where he was a resident scholar, and also to the *Washington Post*, Gingrich assailed the State Department as "ineffective and incoherent" and a "broken instrument of diplomacy." He blamed the department for a list of U.S. diplomatic defeats, among them the inability to win a U.N. resolution authorizing force in Iraq, the failure to win Turkey's acceptance of U.S. troops, and the ineffectual effort to stymie France's campaign against the war. He criticized State Department officials for undue deference to the United Nations and for tolerance of terrorism in Syrian-occupied Lebanon. Contrasting State's "pattern of diplomatic failure" with what he described as the successes of the Defense Department under Rumsfeld, Gingrich said the Pentagon had "delivered diplomatically and then the military delivered militarily."

Gingrich's remarks reflected deep frustration among conservatives with Powell's State Department, which they saw as not sympathetic to the president's policies. Because of Gingrich's association with Rumsfeld, his assault was interpreted as reflecting an intensified struggle between the Pentagon and the State Department over the direction of U.S. foreign policy. Conservatives, suspicious of Powell from the start, had viewed him and his subordinates at State as repeatedly undercutting the president's policies.

In response to Gingrich's broadside, State Department officials defended their record. They cited the department's efforts before the invasion of Iraq to secure foreign basing rights for U.S. troops, enlist allies in the military campaign, and find financial backing for rebuilding Iraq. They also let loose a biting quip about the former House leader, a quip that Powell and Armitage had drafted together. "It's clear that Mr. Gingrich is off his meds and out of therapy," Armitage declared.

———•———

In the immediate aftermath of the fall of Baghdad, U.S. authorities were on track to set up some kind of Iraqi interim government. Garner and his team organized a political conference in Nasiriyah with indigenous civilian leaders on April 15, and Ryan Crocker, a senior diplomat, and Zalmay Khalilzad, an NSC official designated as a presidential envoy, were dispatched to help find individuals interested in joining a new government.

On April 23, the Bush administration announced plans to have an appointed interim authority in place by early June and pledged to continue meeting with emerging Iraqi leaders and political organizations. ORHA began calling weekly meetings of Iraqi leaders and coalition forces. News reports described plans for the creation of a "transitional government" with power over "nonsensitive" government ministries such as education and health care, to be followed by the formation of a "provisional government" within six months to two years after the establishment of an interim authority.

But on the evening of April 24, only three days after Garner had reached Baghdad, Rumsfeld called him to say Bush planned to appoint L. Paul "Jerry" Bremer III, a terrorism expert and former career diplomat, as his permanent envoy to Iraq. For Rumsfeld, the move was all part of the original plan. He had expected before the war to put in place a civilian administrator with a political or diplomatic background and, by late April, had judged that the effort in Iraq required a diplomatic dimension outside Garner's experience. Before settling on Bremer, Rumsfeld even mused in a meeting with top aides that he himself should be the one to take over in Iraq. "It was a recognition of how important he considered the next phase could be," Steve Cambone recounted.

In some ways, Bremer was an odd choice. Although an acknowledged expert on terrorism and a career foreign service officer, he had little previous experience with Muslim society except for a stint in Afghanistan in the 1960s. He had never served in the military, spoke no Arabic, and had never worked in the Middle East or in a postwar occupation or reconstruction effort. Nor had he ever managed any large budget or organization.

Weighing heavily in his favor, though, at least in Rumsfeld's mind, was his State Department experience. Rumsfeld told Feith that picking Bremer would make it easier for Defense and State officials to work together on Iraq. When Powell and Armitage were informed of Bremer's selection, they were relieved. They considered Bremer, who had retired from the Foreign Service in 1989 after twenty-three years, someone they could talk to.

There had been complaints about Garner's operation. State Department officials worried that Garner, who had been organizing meetings with Iraqi political figures even before he and his staff had shifted their headquarters from Kuwait to Baghdad, was moving too quickly to hold local elections and establish a new government amid the unanticipated chaos. At the Pentagon, some groused that Garner was not an effective manager and that ORHA was floundering. They were also critical of a number of State Department recruits on Garner's staff. "The neocons were saying that the people the State Department had offered up were their B team, that they weren't putting their very best out there, so that the effort would not succeed and they could then come in with their A team and say, 'We're the ones to be able to run it,'" Ryan Henry recounted. "That was a school of thought, and they were part of a chorus that was influencing the secretary, persuading him that things weren't working out with Garner."

When Bremer's appointment was formally announced by Bush in early May, it was considered a hasty decision, made quickly after Bush and his advisers decided that both the perception and the reality of reconstruction efforts were deteriorating. Rumsfeld did not regard Bremer's appointment as a rejection of Garner, and he had hoped that Garner would stay and work under Bremer, who was being given broader responsibilities as head of an occupation administration being called the Coalition Provisional Authority (CPA). But Garner, who thought he was on the verge of a political breakthrough in setting up an interim government, was frustrated by the timing of Bremer's appointment and left.

———•———

Over the next few months, Bremer's actions produced a major shift in the approach to the governing of postwar Iraq from the Bush administration's original plans. ORHA had been conceived as a temporary organization designed to assist a new Iraqi government during a short transitional period. By contrast, the CPA possessed all the powers of an occupation authority, and Bremer exercised those powers to establish a longer-term and more complicated reconstruction effort than U.S. policy makers had anticipated.

Bremer's moves have become a source of lingering dispute between his team and Rumsfeld's. The Rumsfeld group contends that the envoy, without fully consulting Pentagon officials, abandoned the original plan to set up an Iraqi interim government and quickly pass sovereignty back to the Iraqis. Bremer, for his part, insists he was just carrying out Bush's wishes.

Determining even the basic facts is complicated by an evident lack of communication and coordination among top officials in Washington during that period. A number of decisions appear to have been taken without the full involvement of principals. "The interagency process in Washington was not working, which explains a lot of the confusion," Bremer said in an interview.

This breakdown in the process was evident at the outset of Bremer's mission when, even before departing Washington, the new envoy managed to establish his own primacy over U.S. efforts in Iraq during a direct conversation with Bush, without discussion in any interagency meeting. Plans had called for Bremer to share responsibilities with Khalilzad, who on the ground in Iraq was still spearheading political arrangements for a new government. But in a meeting with Bush, Bremer insisted that Khalilzad be removed from the Iraq account, telling the president that he needed "full authority." In Bremer's view, it made simple sense that there be only one presidential envoy in a country. Bush agreed.

Khalilzad learned his mission had been canceled just minutes before Bremer's appointment was announced on May 6. Powell was stunned when he was advised of the cancellation and called Rice, noting how damaging it would be to lose Khalilzad's involvement. Powell described Khalilzad as "the only one there who knows what's going on or can relate to those people in Iraq." Rice replied that Bremer had made his own preeminence a condition for taking the job. Rumsfeld, too, professes not to have known that Khalilzad's assignment was going to be canceled.

Arriving in Baghdad in mid-May, Bremer quickly dashed expectations raised by Garner and Khalilzad for an early transfer of authority when he informed Iraqi leaders that the creation of a new Iraqi government would have to wait. His first two decrees—one banning members of Saddam's Baath Party from official positions, the other disbanding the Iraqi army—were meant to signal a clean break from the past, make it clear that the Baathists were not coming back, and begin the process of reestablishing political and military institutions with a fresh slate.

But the exclusionary nature of the decrees reversed initial plans that had counted on retaining some elements of the old order to get Iraq rapidly back up on its feet. With thousands of Baath Party members banned, many government institutions were immediately left without their top several levels of management, and in time, lower bureaucratic levels were also depleted of such critical personnel as engineers, physicians, and schoolteachers. With the Iraqi army disbanded, U.S. forces lacked a potential source for local security and reconstruction assistance while hundreds of thousands of unemployed men roamed the chaotic and dangerous streets. Most significantly, the decrees, which became Bremer's most controversial actions, have since been blamed for creating a pool of disaffected and unemployed Sunni Arabs that later served to fuel the insurgency.

Bremer insists that the measures were coordinated with Rumsfeld and other Pentagon officials, and the record shows that the senior civilians at the Defense Department as well as Franks were advised. Feith has acknowledged backing both actions. Indeed, his office drafted the de-Baathification order, which defense officials regarded as a limited measure meant to target only the top slice of the party's leadership and only about 1 percent of the party's members. The problem, they say, came when the order was implemented too widely and aggressively by a committee of Iraqis chaired by Ahmed Chalabi. But the decree was issued over the strong objections of Garner and the CIA station chief in Baghdad, who warned the move would needlessly fuel anti-American sentiment and undercut national reconciliation efforts.

As for the disbanding of the army, Bremer argued that the action merely reflected facts on the ground, since Iraqi forces had essentially dissolved during the invasion. Senior officers close to Saddam had gone underground, conscripts had abandoned their units, and the military's facilities had been ransacked and dismantled. It would better serve U.S. interests, the argument went, to create an entirely new Iraqi army because calling back the old Sunni-dominated army, first, might not succeed, and second, would certainly risk political problems with the Shia and the Kurds.

Bremer sent a draft of the disbanding order to Rumsfeld on May 9 and to Wolfowitz, Haynes, Feith, Franks, and Garner the next day. Walter Slocombe, the CPA's director of security and defense, discussed the proposed order with Feith, and Bremer briefed Rumsfeld on it several times, forwarding a final draft to him for his approval on May 19. That same day, Rumsfeld sent Bremer a classified set of planning instructions on how to establish what was to be called the New Iraqi Corps, envisioned to grow to three divisions and forty thousand troops.

But while Rumsfeld and other senior Pentagon civilians had been consulted in advance about the disbanding of the old army, some key players were blindsided by the edict. Myers, Pace, and the military service chiefs have said they did not know it was coming. The decrees weren't discussed in interagency meetings by deputies. And McKiernan as well as

John Abizaid, who had served as deputy CENTCOM commander during the war and was preparing to replace Franks, considered the decision an abrupt and unwelcome departure from their previous planning.

McKiernan and the CIA had been working on reviving the Iraqi army, meeting with former commanders on ways to reconstitute some units. Garner's team, too, was engaged in an effort to use the former army as a source of labor and had arranged for contractors to retrain some troops. His staff had collected the names of fifty thousand to seventy thousand military and police personnel who might be drawn back. Bremer and Slocombe were aware of U.S. military contacts with former officers, but did not view these officers as the nucleus of a new Iraqi command, merely as holdovers from the old force.

The poor coordination between the civilian and military commands in Baghdad was symptomatic of the problem created by the earlier decision to separate the two. The rushed move to disband the Iraqi military also reflected a failure to think through how postwar events might unfold. By eliminating the prospect of a ready pool of Iraqi troops to help restore order, Bremer exacerbated the security vacuum already created by Rumsfeld's decision to reduce the flow of scheduled reinforcements. Now, not only was the number of outside troops coming into Iraq limited, but the number of Iraqi forces immediately available had dried up.

According to Abizaid, Rumsfeld recognized quickly that a mistake had been made in bringing the number of Iraqi military forces down to zero. "I told him, and he agreed with me," Abizaid recalled in an interview.

At the time, Abizaid was sharply critical of the relatively small size of the new army being planned. He persuaded Rumsfeld of the need to create an Iraqi Civil Defense Corps, consisting of ad hoc paramilitary units, that would complement the army and assist U.S. and allied forces in dealing with local security problems. These units gave U.S. operations an "Iraqi face" and soaked up unemployed young men to keep them out of the insurgency, but they proved of widely inconsistent abilities and never amounted to a national force capable of filling the security gap in Iraq. Eventually, the corps was converted into a national guard before it was finally folded into the regular army.

Over the next few months, Bremer moved farther away from the idea of arranging for the transitional Iraqi authority that Garner and Khalilzad had pursued and that Rumsfeld and his staff thought was still a main objective. Bush had endorsed the plan for an Iraqi Interim Authority at an NSC meeting shortly before the invasion on March 10. But Bremer contends that by the time he was asked to take the CPA job in late April, fresh doubts had arisen—at least among some top U.S. officials—about trying for a rapid transfer of sovereignty.

While senior Pentagon officials still favored ceding authority early to a small group of Iraqi exiles, State Department and CIA officials were arguing again for a longer-term effort to manage the deep divisions in Iraqi society. Bremer understood from his discussions with Bush and from NSC meetings that the president had tilted toward the take-your-time advocates and had come to favor a longer-term process to build support for democracy in Iraq.

"Sometime after March 10—I've been told by various participants it was early April—Bush decided the idea of a short occupation and a quick handover wasn't going to work," Bremer said. "But the problem was, I don't think it was ever documented. No one ever put a piece of paper in front of him and said, 'Here's the new guidance,' and so there was a lot of confusion."

Rumsfeld himself appeared somewhat ambivalent. Although he believed a sooner transfer was better than a later one, he was not as eager as Wolfowitz, Feith, or some conservatives outside the Pentagon, such as Richard Perle, to see an immediate handover. Rumsfeld's initial focus was on ensuring U.S. forces were free to root out terrorist elements and locate suspected stockpiles of weapons of mass destruction. He worried that establishing a new Iraqi governing entity too soon could interfere with these efforts.

Rumsfeld also anticipated a lengthy new political process ahead in Iraq. In memos in May to the NSC and to Feith, he cautioned that the transition to democracy in Iraq would not happen fast or easily and urged that elections not be rushed. Feith recalls Rumsfeld expressing concern to him about the Iraqis pressing for power before they had expanded their leadership council. Noting reports of a lack of discipline among Iraq's emerging leaders, Rumsfeld cautioned as well against creating an Iraqi governing entity that might undermine Bremer's ability to do his job.

Nonetheless, Rumsfeld expected a relatively early turnover of sovereignty to the Iraqis and assumed that Bush's approval of the plan to establish an Iraqi Interim Authority as soon as possible after liberation remained in force. Bremer, for his part, has pointed to a paper trail indicating that he kept Rumsfeld apprised of the shift in approach and that Rumsfeld raised no objection.

On May 22, for instance, Bremer outlined to Rumsfeld a plan to move first to a constitution and then to elections. Bremer wrote several more memos to Rumsfeld and the Pentagon through the rest of the spring and summer and into the fall, reporting on talks with Iraqi officials and repeating plans for drafting a new constitution first, estimating that elections couldn't be held for at least a year. He also spoke publicly about these plans—in a June 22 address to the World Economic Forum in Amman, Jordan, for instance, and in a July 23 appearance at the National Press Club in Washington.

But evidently neither Rumsfeld nor his senior staff realized that Bremer's talk of putting off full sovereignty until after the elections meant there would be no sovereign control in the meantime. In an interview for this book, Rumsfeld said he has no recollection of Bremer giving indications in the summer of 2003 of an intention to put aside the Interim Iraqi Authority plan. Instead, he said he understood the creation in July 2003 of the Iraqi Governing Council, consisting of twenty-five Iraqis selected by the CPA through a nationwide search, to be the first phase toward establishing the interim authority. Bremer even called it an "interim administration," although it was given far less power than the Interim Iraqi Authority had been intended to have.

Rumsfeld does allow for the possibility that Bremer, in separate discussions with the president, State Department officials, and NSC staff, may have received guidance, or what he interpreted to be guidance, in pursuing an approach for a longer occupation—or at a minimum to use his own judgment. But Rumsfeld asserts that Bremer did not receive such guidance from him.

Bremer described himself as "flabbergasted" by the claims that Pentagon officials were unaware of his plan. Citing his voluminous reports to Washington, he said not once did Bush, Rumsfeld, or any other U.S. official object to the CPA's course. "If Rumsfeld says he doesn't remember giving guidance, I guess silence is some of kind of guidance," Bremer remarked. "It's simply not credible. There is simply no case to be made that they didn't know what I was doing."

Even so, Rumsfeld and Feith maintain that only when an op-ed article by Bremer was published in the *Washington Post* on September 8 did they realize that the CPA leader was taking a different route and was not ready to hand over responsibility for governance of Iraq to an Iraqi leadership. In the article, Bremer outlined seven steps that he called Iraq's "path to sovereignty." They included such formidable and uncertain goals as a ratified constitution and nationwide general elections. The article also asserted that the CPA would stay in existence until the country had achieved all seven steps—which CPA officials had estimated privately could take two years.

Rumsfeld said the article had not been reviewed by Pentagon officials beforehand, nor had Bremer told him that he envisioned a two-year process before the CPA could be dissolved. In the weeks that followed, Rumsfeld, along with other administration officials, pressed for an earlier termination of the CPA, and Bremer ultimately concurred. Agreement was reached in November for the CPA's term to end in June 2004.

Feith, Perle, and other conservatives have pointed to this turn toward an imposing, lengthy rule by the CPA as perhaps the most ill-fated decision of the postwar period. They blame it for the failure to achieve the early postwar peace they had envisioned under an exile-led government. In their view, the decision dashed any chance that the coalition forces would be received as liberators rather than as occupiers, and it hobbled the coalition's response to the widening insurgency.

This rationale for what went wrong in Iraq is too simplistic an explanation—and suspect, coming from those who had so aggressively pushed for the invasion in the first place. Events in Iraq have provided no compelling evidence that a provisional government, quickly installed, would have thwarted the rise of an insurgency or, once confronted with one, would have taken more-effective action against it earlier. Bremer has continued to defend his approach as correct, saying that what it sacrificed in immediate Iraqi sovereignty was more than made up for by giving the

Iraqis time to put in place an interim constitution and political structures and to organize politically to build a new democracy.

Rumsfeld, for his part, places much of the blame for veering off into a prolonged occupation authority on the deep split in views in Washington and on a lack of firm coordination over how best to proceed. "If you have six or eight hands on the steering wheel, no one's got their hands on the steering wheel," he said in an interview.

He described an ongoing "tension" between essentially "two groups of thinking" among those advising Bush. One group, he said, favored going into Iraq, removing Saddam, ensuring the country did not return to making weapons of mass destruction and engaging in terrorism, and then leaving. "That way of thinking argued for a relatively light footprint, a relatively short period of being involved, and a sensitivity to not being seen as too much of an occupying force," Rumsfeld said.

The other view, Rumsfeld noted, basically argued, "We've got to make darn sure this thing works out, we've got to make darn sure that they end up with a democratic government and a government that is at peace with its neighbors." Such thinking, he added, can lead to a prolonged occupation with a "very American" face. "You start making a lot of decisions for them and you start having a larger group doing it and you run the risk of creating a dependency and anger and opposition."

"There's no roadmap, there's no guidebook that says this is what you should do," Rumsfeld observed. He personally favored the smaller-footprint, lighter-handed, shorter-duration approach. But he hinted at some doubt in his own mind about whether this would have worked any better than what resulted with the CPA.

"In retrospect, who knows?" he remarked. "We didn't go down that road."

———•———

Two weeks after Baghdad fell, Tom White, the Army secretary, was told to report to Rumsfeld's office for a late-afternoon meeting. When White walked in, Rumsfeld came right to the point. "I want to make a change," he said.

"Fine, that is your choice," White replied curtly.

White's earlier resistance to terminating the Crusader program and some of his other views on the Army's future had become an unpardonable offense for the defense secretary, who continued to believe the service was too enamored of large forces and slow change. White told Rumsfeld he would write a short resignation letter that day. The Army secretary had planned to stay through the end of Shinseki's term, but a week later Wolfowitz called to say that was no longer acceptable, and White left on May 9.

White was the only Pentagon official Rumsfeld ever fired during his time as defense secretary under Bush. Rumsfeld lost confidence in others and came close to dismissing them but settled for simply freezing them out in hopes they would leave of their own accord. At the same time, in deciding promotions to coveted joint command positions, he showed little hesitancy about blocking those uniformed officers who got on his bad side. That was the case with two senior Army commanders who had helped lead U.S. forces into Iraq: David McKiernan, who had responsibility for all ground troops, and William Scott Wallace, who headed the Army's V Corps.

Wallace had upset Rumsfeld with his remarks to reporters, one week into the war, about the unpreparedness of U.S. forces to deal with the attacks they were facing from the Saddam fedayeen. McKiernan, in turn, had rubbed the secretary the wrong way during a visit Rumsfeld made to Baghdad shortly after firing White. Rumsfeld thought McKiernan was keeping his distance from him. On plane rides into and out of Iraq from Kuwait, the general chose not to sit near the secretary and talk about any issues, and in Baghdad, McKiernan shunned a request from Rumsfeld's military assistant to introduce the secretary at a town hall meeting with troops, passing the task off to Wallace. As the secretary spoke, McKiernan stood on stage looking stern, his arms folded across his chest. Rumsfeld was angered by McKiernan's behavior and complained to Craddock and others.

"Rumsfeld never forgot that, and it was a long time—a couple of years—before McKiernan recovered and received his fourth star," recalled Staser Holcomb, the retired admiral who assisted in the selection of senior officers. "Rumsfeld does make some fairly quick judgments about people, and he made a judgment about McKiernan—that Mc-

Kiernan was a grouch and resisting the secretary of defense and resisting civilian control." Wallace, too, had to wait two years before receiving his fourth star. In Rumsfeld's eyes, according to Holcomb, both Wallace and McKiernan were seen as loyalists to White and Shinseki, which was a big strike against them.

Army leaders had presumed that McKiernan, then the senior officer in Baghdad, would be picked to stay on and head the task force being set up in the Iraqi capital to oversee military occupation forces. But in May, Franks instructed McKiernan to leave Iraq along with the staff of his land-war command, which had helped plan and direct the invasion. Like other senior U.S. military and civilian authorities, Franks assumed the major fighting was over, and he wanted McKiernan's command staff out of Iraq and returned to their normal role of support of land operations throughout the CENTCOM region.

A new headquarters was established to command the military forces in Iraq, and Lieutenant General Ricardo S. Sanchez was named to head it. Sanchez had led the 1st Armored Division into Iraq before being promoted and picked to succeed Wallace as the head of V Corps. It was this corps headquarters that was to serve as the nucleus of the newly established command known as Combined Joint Task Force 7, or CJTF-7. But the group had never expected to run a massive peacekeeping and reconstruction effort and was hampered from the start by personnel shortages and by a poorly coordinated transfer of responsibilities.

The belated decision to allow not only McKiernan but his whole headquarters of senior, seasoned officers to leave and to replace them with an ill-prepared team led by the Army's newest three-star general was another of the major mistakes of the postwar period. "The lateness of this decision suggests the degree to which senior civilian and military leaders within DoD underestimated the challenges that would confront coalition military forces after the defeat of Iraqi forces," RAND's study of the war concluded.

Explaining the move several years later, Franks told military historians that he acted so quickly to redeploy McKiernan's headquarters as a way of spurring the Pentagon to send another task force to work with ORHA. He said he had told top Pentagon officials what was needed and, further, that it was their responsibility to ensure the new headquarters was rapidly installed. "I thought it was sufficient to tell Don Rumsfeld and Dick Myers, 'Here is what we are going to do in Iraq. Here is what we need in Iraq. We need a joint headquarters, a CJTF. You figure it out,'" he said. "So that is a task that John Abizaid and I very simply laid on Washington and said, 'Figure it out. Do it fast.'"

But the effort didn't quite work as planned, and Franks decided to make V Corps the senior headquarters in Iraq. That decision was taken over the objections of Keane, the Army's vice chief, who had assumed that McKiernan's headquarters would oversee the occupation in Iraq. Learning of the switch to Sanchez, Keane raised his concerns with Abizaid, who had been picked to succeed Franks as the head of Central Command. "I said, 'Jesus Christ, John, this is a recipe for disaster,'" Keane told Army historians. "I was upset about it to say the least, but the decision had been made and it was a done deal."

Rumsfeld had approved the promotion of Sanchez to lieutenant general, but he has denied responsibility for the decisions to remove McKiernan's headquarters in the summer of 2003 and to make Sanchez the senior U.S. commander in Iraq. The changes, he insists, were never brought to his attention at the time.

In his memoir, Sanchez writes of two meetings in which Rumsfeld professed his noninvolvement. Hearing the claim the first time, in September 2004 shortly after Sanchez had left Baghdad, the general was incredulous. Rumsfeld also asserted he was never told that Sanchez's headquarters had remained at less than half its stipulated manning levels during the year it was in operation.

"Why didn't you tell somebody?" Rumsfeld asked. Sanchez replied that he not only frequently argued for more support but appealed to every leader who visited Iraq, and he said that "every senior leader in the Pentagon knew the status of CJTF-7." When Sanchez later told Army leaders of this exchange with Rumsfeld, they contended that Rumsfeld had himself been the problem behind the staffing shortage.

Sanchez recounted another meeting with Rumsfeld, nineteen months later, in which the secretary again insisted he had been in the dark. Rumsfeld showed Sanchez a two-page memo he had written asserting he had not taken part in the decision to move McKiernan's headquarters out and put Sanchez in charge of the entire mission. When Sanchez expressed his disbelief that Rumsfeld hadn't known, the secretary grew agitated.

Sanchez concluded that this was a pattern on the secretary's part of trying to deny involvement, assign responsibility to others, and put it all down in writing. "In essence, Rumsfeld was covering his rear," Sanchez wrote. "He was setting up his chain of denials should his actions ever be questioned. And worse yet, in my mind, he was attempting to level all the blame on his generals."

Given Rumsfeld's reputation for hands-on management, it is indeed difficult to believe that he had no role in the selection of the general who would be commanding postwar operations in Iraq and the composition of his headquarters staff. Myers himself said in an interview that it was "possible but not likely" that Rumsfeld was not involved "because all those key personnel decisions we worked pretty carefully." If the decision did somehow occur without Rumsfeld's involvement, it would at least suggest a grave breakdown in communication and oversight.

———•———

A month after White's departure, Shinseki retired. In his June 11 farewell address, the general got in a few last jabs at Rumsfeld. "You must love those you lead before you can be an effective leader," he said in a parade-ground speech delivered on a humid morning. "You can certainly command without that sense of commitment, but you cannot lead without it. And without leadership, command is a hollow experience, a vacuum often filled with mistrust and arrogance."

Shinseki did not refer directly to his clashes with Rumsfeld and Wolfowitz over the number of U.S. troops in Iraq, the Crusader, or the selection process for senior military officers. But he alluded to his tensions with the department's civilian leadership. "The Army has always understood the primacy of civilian control," he said. "In fact, we are the ones who reinforce that principle with those other armies with whom we train all around the world. So to muddy the waters when important issues are at stake—issues of life and death—is a disservice to all those in and out of uniform who serve and lead so well."

The general also sided solidly with White. "When they call the roll of principled, loyal, tough guys, you will be at the top of the list," he said to the former Army secretary. Further, with an eye toward Rumsfeld's continued interest in reorganizing the Army and perhaps trimming its ranks,

Shinseki warned against cuts in the fighting force. "Beware the twelve-division strategy for a ten-division Army," he said. "Our soldiers and families bear the risk and the hardship of carrying a mission load that exceeds what force capabilities we can sustain."

Rumsfeld, who was traveling in Europe en route to a NATO meeting, wasn't in attendance. Nor was Wolfowitz. Their absence was interpreted by many as a snub, but Shinseki had not invited either of them.

After leaving office, Shinseki kept a strict public silence, telling associates that he didn't want to criticize while soldiers were still fighting and dying in Iraq. In 2008, however, a copy emerged of a memo he had written to Rumsfeld just before leaving. In it, Shinseki offered what he called some "closing thoughts" on several of the controversies that had so roiled relations between the two men. "While our disagreements have been well-chronicled, and sometimes exaggerated, these professional disagreements were never personal, never disrespectful, and never challenged the foundational principle of civilian control of the military in our form of government," the general wrote. "When the discussions were about the national security, I felt it was my duty to provide my best professional military advice."

He said his February 2003 testimony estimating the forces required to stabilize postwar Iraq had been misinterpreted. "I didn't believe there was a 'right' answer on the number of forces required to stabilize Iraq until the commander on the ground had the chance to conduct both his mission analysis and a troop to task assessment," Shinseki wrote. He explained that he had deliberately chosen a high number in an effort to avoid imposing a "force cap" and foreclose options for Rumsfeld and Franks. It was unfortunate, he added, that he hadn't had the opportunity to explain the rationale before the matter blew up into a public issue, although he noted that neither Rumsfeld nor Wolfowitz had ever discussed the issue with him "despite all the commentary in the press."

He also wrote that his actions on the cancellation of the Crusader system were misinterpreted or misconstrued by Rumsfeld and the secretary's aides. Noting the decision to eliminate the weapon had come "without any consultation or forewarning," Shinseki said his subsequent testimony was meant to defend not the Crusader specifically but simply the Army's continuing need for some kind of cannon artillery fire.

In a discussion of the direction that U.S. military change should take, he stressed the importance of developing human leadership over new technologies. He noted that Rumsfeld had repeatedly questioned the need for multiple echelons of Army command and had pressed to eliminate layers and headquarters, and he suggested the secretary think twice before doing so. "I would recommend that we 'make haste slowly' here and that technology theorists not be allowed to hold sway over practical analysis and operational experience," he wrote.

Shinseki observed that the Army's multiple command levels had proven useful in Iraq in executing a constantly changing plan. "Again, it's about leadership, not fixed organizational designs," he wrote. He also cautioned against trading "current capabilities" for "future possibilities," urging Rumsfeld and the secretary's aides to base their decisions on analysis and to "listen to commanders with combat experience." Further, he advised Rumsfeld to keep in mind the many contributions the Army makes to other forces, whether fuel deliveries to the Air Force, artillery support to the Marines, or logistical help to Special Operations forces. "They are consistently overlooked," he wrote, "which skews the perception" of the Army as a service staffed by too many support troops.

He warned against cutting back on troop strength, saying, "It is near impossible to undo the effects of bad end strength or force structure decisions." And while he did acknowledge that "the Army is still slower to deploy than we would like," he said the problem is an insufficient number of aircraft to transport troops, not too many troops.

But he reserved his sharpest criticisms for some of the ad hoc processes that Rumsfeld had instituted at the expense of long-established conventional ones. In the absence of Tank sessions with the secretary, he said members of the Joint Chiefs of Staff "are not given the opportunity to express their best military judgment as often as they should." He also complained about "a lack of strategic review to frame our day-to-day issues" and "a lack of explicit discussion on risk in most decisions." Additionally, he objected to "a tendency to compartmentalize analysis" and to senior-level meetings that lacked "structured agendas, objectives, pending decisions and other traditional means of time management."

With the Army's top military and civilian leaders gone, Rumsfeld was finally free to install the kind of people he wanted to carry out the transformation he hoped to see in the Pentagon's oldest and largest armed service. For secretary of the Army, he recommended James Roche, the Air Force secretary, whom Rumsfeld regarded as an innovator, although that nomination ran into trouble over Roche's fierce advocacy of a controversial deal to lease tanker aircraft rather than buying them outright. For chief of staff, Rumsfeld had wanted Keane, who declined the offer and retired because his wife, Terry, was ill with Parkinson's disease. The secretary then tried unsuccessfully to recruit Franks and Abizaid before settling on Peter Schoomaker, a retired general who had headed the Special Operations Command from 1997 to 2000.

The selection of Schoomaker, who had spent much of his military career in Special Operations and once led the elite Delta Force, underscored Rumsfeld's interest in reshaping the Army into a more agile, rapidly deployable organization. The decision to skip over the ranks of three- and four-star generals still on active duty caused some grousing and was taken as a further sign of Rumsfeld's low opinion of the Army's military leadership. But it was difficult to quarrel with Schoomaker's credentials as a commanding presence and unconventional warrior.

The same day the choice of Schoomaker was announced, Rumsfeld recommended that Myers and Pace be nominated for second terms. "The secretary feels this team has been terrific," a senior Defense Department official said, citing the work by Myers and Pace and the senior civilian leadership in redrafting military strategy, reshaping the forces, and redrawing regional commands.

———•———

Shortly after the invasion of Iraq, Newt Gingrich, in an effort to persuade Rumsfeld to pace himself, reminded him that General George C. Marshall had carefully managed his days during World War II to avoid exhaustion. Rumsfeld could relate to Marshall. On March 30—within days of the war's start—Rumsfeld had surpassed the record set by Marshall as the oldest serving secretary of defense. Marshall had left office at the age of seventy years, nine months, and twenty-one days. Rumsfeld, approaching seventy-one, was still fit and vigorous but was beginning to question how much longer he could sustain the six- and seven-day weeks he had been working since taking over at the Pentagon.

To get her husband to ease up a bit, Joyce Rumsfeld had started hunting for a house outside Washington that could serve as a weekend retreat. She found one in the neatly maintained waterside village of St. Michaels on the Eastern Shore of Maryland, an hour-and-a-half drive from the nation's capital.

The Rumsfelds paid $1.5 million for the brick Georgian. Located on four acres at the end of a gravel drive, the five-bedroom, four-bathroom, five-fireplace house is named Mount Misery. Legend attributes the name to the gloomy temperament of the Englishman who originally built the house in 1804. By 1833, Mount Misery's owner was Edward Covey, a farmer notorious for breaking unruly slaves for other farmers.

CHAPTER 12

Long, Hard Slog

One curious case that occupied Rumsfeld's attention for several years involved four U.S. Air Force F-15 fighter jets that were regularly rotated through Iceland. The arrangement, which grew out of a 1951 treaty between the two countries designating the planes for Iceland's air defense, had made sense in the context of the Soviet threat. But Rumsfeld started pushing for removal of the jets soon after taking office, regarding their presence in Iceland as a dispensable remnant of the Cold War—a prime example of the kind of outdated, needless practices that his military transformation initiative was intended to correct.

Iceland, a NATO member, wanted to keep the planes on its territory as a sign of the continued U.S. commitment to protect the country. The presence of the aircraft was popular among Icelanders, and their removal would cause political problems for the center-right government at the time. Iceland's prime minister David Oddsson appealed directly to Bush not to withdraw the jets.

State Department and NSC officials were sympathetic to Iceland's wishes. Their view was that the detrimental effects on bilateral relations outweighed the desire to pull out the planes. The Bush administration needed all the allies it could get in Europe, they argued, and Oddsson's government was proving to be a particularly strong friend.

In 2001, it supported the war in Afghanistan and the administration's decision to pull out of the ABM Treaty; later, in 2003, it backed the invasion of Iraq.

In meetings with his national security advisers, Bush expressed reluctance to support withdrawal of the aircraft until a way could be found to mollify the Icelanders. But Rumsfeld persisted. For him the issue was largely a matter of limited resources. The United States was spending several hundred million dollars a year for the maintenance of the planes at Keflavik air base and for a support operation that included search-and-rescue capabilities. There were other, less costly ways of continuing to meet America's commitment to Iceland's security, Rumsfeld argued. He reminded Bush of the promise to U.S. voters to streamline the military, and one way to do so was to reduce the number of U.S. military aircraft permanently deployed abroad.

The controversy, which received little coverage in the U.S. media, mushroomed into one of the biggest interagency battles of Rumsfeld's tenure, involving hours of discussions and multiple high-level White House meetings. "It's amazing how much interagency resources, how much time and commitment, were devoted to such a relatively small issue," recalled Ian Brzezinski, who handled NATO affairs for the Pentagon at the time.

Beth Jones, who was in charge of European affairs at the State Department, said that she and colleagues wondered, as the arguments lasted over several years amid the wars in Iraq and Afghanistan and other much larger concerns, why the secretary of defense was devoting such time and attention to four planes in Iceland.

For the State Department, Iceland became a symbol of an excessive intrusion by Rumsfeld's Pentagon into traditional diplomatic areas. At the NSC, officials were skeptical of the urgency that Rumsfeld attached to the proposed withdrawal of the jets. Top NATO authorities also got involved in the dispute. George Robertson, NATO's secretary general, raised the Iceland case with Bush at least three times and complained about Rumsfeld's insistent push to remove the planes. Robertson couldn't understand Rumsfeld's fixation on the matter, particularly given the defense secretary's own past experience as a U.S. ambassador to NATO.

But Rumsfeld would not let up. The conflicts in Iraq and Afghanistan fueled his case for pulling the planes out of Iceland, as he argued the need to reduce the stress on the U.S. armed forces resulting from the wars and counterterrorism operations. Although the commitment of crews and support staff for four planes might seem of little consequence to the U.S. military's overall burden, Rumsfeld considered it significant enough and also emblematic of his larger campaign to relieve pressure on the force. He frequently pinged his Pentagon staff with snowflakes asking about the status of the discussions, and in early 2003, he decided to force the matter by ordering that the funds for the Iceland operation be cut off. But termination was delayed as Defense and State hammered out a negotiating position and entered into talks with Iceland later in 2003.

The Bush administration offered the Icelanders a variety of mutually beneficial options. U.S. officials proposed making aircraft immediately available should an emergency arise. They also stressed that an end to the permanent presence of U.S. jets in Iceland did not mean an end to the U.S. commitment to defend the country. To underscore that, U.S. officials said regular military training exercises could be held there. NATO authorities, seeking to be helpful in striking some kind of arrangement, looked at a plan for rotating other alliance aircraft in and out of Iceland to supplant the U.S. effort.

But the Icelanders, for their part, showed little flexibility, even walking out of the talks at one point. State Department officials became increasingly frustrated with what they regarded as Iceland's unnecessarily acrimonious stance in the negotiations. Finally, in 2006, the United States simply pulled the planes—along with several helicopters, 1,200 military personnel, and about a hundred Defense Department employees—while promising to honor treaty obligations by defending Iceland and training Icelandic forces.

By then, Rumsfeld had managed a much larger repositioning of U.S. forces around the world, scaling back the long-standing presence of American troops principally in Germany, South Korea, and Japan. The realignment—the most significant rearrangement of the U.S. military around the world since the beginning of the Cold War—was intended to move away from large, full-service bases abroad toward a network of skeletal outposts closer to potential trouble spots in the Middle East, in the Caucasus, and along the Pacific Rim. Potential threats had changed since the end of the Cold War, and the U.S. military needed greater flexibility in sending forces to fight beyond Europe and Asia.

Against that backdrop, the departure of four Air Force jets from Iceland was a relatively minor adjustment. Rumsfeld could use the global repositioning initiative as a strategic context for shifting the F-15s, noting that Iceland was far from alone in losing U.S. forces. He could contend that if much bigger allies in Europe and Asia understood the need for a revised U.S. basing blueprint, Iceland should as well.

But the Iceland case had begun months before Rumsfeld had unveiled the global rebasing plan, a fact that Doug Feith, the Pentagon's top policy official at the time, came to regard as a political blunder by the secretary. Rumsfeld could have made a stronger case at the outset, Feith thought, had he framed the withdrawal of the jets from Iceland as a logical part of the worldwide realignment.

In fact, Rumsfeld himself had often urged subordinates to cast their proposals in the broadest conceptual terms possible. "Normally, Rumsfeld would take a strategic approach," Feith said. "He would always advise us to figure out first at the broadest level what you want to do, what you want to accomplish. Once you get your principles formulated and written down, he would say, you can then logically apply them and come to a conclusion."

Iceland, however, was initially treated as a separate initiative, probably because the planes seemed an easy target. "The president had the kind of reaction to the Iceland project that Rumsfeld had to people who came to him with a disconnected thing that wasn't part of a strategic big picture," Feith said. "I believe the Iceland matter would have been handled differently and come out much more to Rumsfeld's satisfaction had it been brought up initially in the context of the whole defense posture realignment. It's an interesting example of Rumsfeld kind of jumping the gun on himself."

———•———

As the summer of 2003 wore on, Iraq entered a vicious spiral of increasing violence that impeded both political and economic reconstruction. A mix of outside terrorists, Iraqi Islamic extremists, and what Rumsfeld called Saddam-allied "dead-enders" mounted attacks on infrastructure facilities and U.S. troops. At the same time, a lack of jobs, services, and any form of self-rule left growing numbers of Iraqis receptive to religious and ethnic incitements to rise up against the U.S. occupiers and against one another.

One big break came in July when a tipster betrayed the hideout in Mosul of Saddam's sons, Uday and Qusay, who resisted capture and were killed in a firefight with U.S. troops. Elsewhere, though, setbacks arose. Pentagon officials had hoped U.S. forces would be supplemented by Iraqi and foreign troops. But such additional security help was proving hard to come by. Assembling, vetting, and training new Iraqi forces from scratch would take time, and few countries were showing a willingness to commit peacekeepers to what was clearly a war zone. Concern at the United Nations with the situation escalated sharply when a truck bomb exploded outside the U.N. headquarters in Baghdad on August 19, killing the chief U.N. representative in the country, Sergio Vieira de Mello, and nearly two dozen others.

Given the absence of other forces, the U.S. troop level in Iraq appeared increasingly inadequate. The planned flow of forces out of Iraq was halted, and a new policy was issued stating that units would not leave until their replacements were in place. In July, the Army, recognizing the long-term nature of the mission, announced that rotations to Iraq would last a year—double the deployment time that had been used in Bosnia. The evident need to sustain a substantial level of forces in Iraq provoked fresh tension in the Army.

Although senior U.S. commanders in Iraq continued to insist they had sufficient forces on hand to accomplish their missions, they began very rapidly to make trade-offs in assigning forces, shifting troops from less immediately troubled areas to ones requiring more urgent attention. In addition to dealing with the mounting insurgency, other military tasks emerged, including the need to secure the borders, destroy massive numbers of ammunition dumps, and guard key Iraqi infrastructure facilities.

Paul Bremer himself had been concerned about the number of U.S. military forces in Iraq. Before taking up his post, he had read a forthcoming RAND study on nation-building exercises from World War II through Afghanistan, which underscored the advantages of sending in bigger rather than smaller peacekeeping forces. Smaller forces were more tempting targets for adversaries, and peacekeepers, when in smaller numbers, were more likely to rely on firepower to protect themselves. Bremer sent an executive summary of the study to Rumsfeld but never received a response.

Several other reports that indicated things weren't going as well as they should came to Rumsfeld's attention. An interim assessment from a military team sent over by Joint Forces Command to conduct a thorough "lessons-learned" study of the operation concluded in June that the U.S. military lacked the right forces and the right capabilities to transition to the postwar management phase. It noted that Jay Garner's ORHA had been unprepared and that the people and structure for exercising firm control of U.S. activities in Iraq were missing. "Basically we were telling them, 'The challenges run much deeper than just changing ORHA out for the CPA, and we don't think they are fixed yet,'" recalled an Army officer who was involved with assembling the briefing.

Also in June, Rumsfeld asked John Hamre, a former deputy secretary of defense in the Clinton administration, to travel to Iraq for an assessment. Hamre, head of the nonpartisan Center for Strategic and International Studies in Washington, was hesitant. He thought it might be a political trap—a way to get a onetime senior Clinton official to say that things were not as bad in Iraq as critics were alleging.

So Hamre sent Rumsfeld a one-page list of conditions for agreeing to undertake the mission, among them, that he be allowed to talk to a number of other senior administration officials, including those at the State Department. When he received the list back, a line had been drawn through the request to talk to State, and in the margins had been written, "Not applicable." "It wasn't no; it was like they don't matter," Hamre recalled. "Everything else that we asked for they were very supportive of."

Ultimately Hamre spent four days in Iraq, and his team stayed another ten days and interviewed a total of eighty people. In a confidential nine-page report to Rumsfeld and Bremer afterward, Hamre warned that while Bremer's CPA was making progress, "the security situation is difficult and getting more so." He said that the lack of security was allowing Saddam loyalists and criminal elements to plunder both the electric system and the oil industry. "In short, if the security situation is not fixed, the entire rebuilding process will fail," Hamre wrote.

Hamre said more forces were needed. While the troop levels appeared adequate to engage enemy fighters, Hamre said, it was insufficient to protect critical infrastructure and support U.S. civilian activities. With development of a new Iraqi army likely to take two years or more, Hamre pointed to a critical short-term gap not likely to be filled by contributions from coalition partners. Hamre also expressed concern about the "fatigue" he saw in U.S. forces. "You need to seriously address rotation policy and R&R policy quickly," he advised.

Acknowledging Rumsfeld's reluctance to add more U.S. forces in Iraq, and the political advantage that Democrats in Washington would take if the administration did so, Hamre promised not to press the issue in public. If asked, he said, he would talk about the need to make other sources of troops the top priority—expanding Iraqi forces, seeking coalition contributions, or hiring contract forces for low-risk installations.

"But I honestly believe we need to bring in more forces," Hamre confided. "You don't have enough forces to undertake patrols today and support the high-value missions that the CPA needs to undertake, plus defend fixed installations. For the next six months the most reliable source of augmented security will be U.S. forces. The next 6–9 months are crucial."

Additionally, Hamre cited a shortage of funds, warning that the operation would "run out of money" in less than a year if not addressed soon. He described the CPA as hamstrung by constraints in obtaining funds and arranging contracts, and he urged much greater flexibility for CPA operations rather than the existing "business as usual" approach. "This isn't adequate for the urgency of the situation," he declared.

Rumsfeld never spoke to Hamre about the memo, although he did send a brief thank-you note. And he passed the memo on to Bush, who in turn showed it to Powell. It was Powell who then asked to see Hamre. "Because I had known that Rumsfeld had read the memo and had shared it with the president, I interpreted it to mean that it had served its purpose and it was sufficiently clear that he didn't need a meeting, although I was surprised that he didn't want a meeting," Hamre said. "There were lots of things that they could have done early on that would have made a difference."

———•———

General Jack Keane, who had become the Army's acting chief in the summer of 2003 following Shinseki's departure, believes he was the first to raise with the service chiefs in the Tank the matter of a budding insurgency in Iraq. He had just returned from a visit to Iraq and remembers telling the other military leaders that the attacks on U.S. troops appeared to involve a measure of complexity and some level of organization. "It probably means a protracted war," he predicted at the time.

That wasn't what the senior Pentagon leadership wanted to hear. Myers in particular cautioned Keane to avoid such talk "on the third deck," meaning in Rumsfeld's office on the Pentagon's third floor. "Dick, you as well as I know the most important thing we have to do in fighting a war is define the kind of war we're fighting," Keane told him. "If we don't get that right, we have real trouble."

Wolfowitz also viewed what was happening in Iraq as more than the untidy impulses of a newly free people. He had been influenced by Gary Anderson, a retired Marine colonel and defense consultant, who had written an op-ed piece in the *Washington Post* in April saying Saddam's loyalists had never expected to win a conventional battle against the United States and so had planned to resort to guerrilla warfare. The next month, on a visit to Romania, Wolfowitz heard how, after the revolution there, deposed Romanian leader Nicolae Ceauşescu's secret police had started an urban guerrilla campaign against the new regime. In that case, though, Ceauşescu's quick capture and execution stopped the counter-revolution abruptly.

In testimony before the House Armed Services Committee on June 18, two months after the fall of Baghdad, Wolfowitz acknowledged, "There's a guerrilla war there." But even he hedged, insisting the enemy did not have broad popular support and suggesting victory could come in short order. Three weeks later, Franks weighed in, saying that "guerrilla and insurgency operations are supported by the people, and I've demonstrated to my own satisfaction that the people of Iraq do not support the violence that we're seeing right now."

Rumsfeld was especially resistant to using the terms "insurgency" or "guerrilla war" to describe what was happening in Iraq. His primary concern, as he and several senior aides recall, was that the use of such terms would somehow dignify the enemy as freedom fighters and imbue them with a sense of political legitimacy. "My issue was, Do we want to use a word that gives credence to the enemy, a word that has positive connotations as opposed to negative," Rumsfeld said in an interview. "I didn't think we did. That was my only issue."

But publicly, Rumsfeld gave the impression that he did not yet accept the existence of an insurgency. Indeed, he had been stating for weeks that the United States was merely conducting mopping-up operations against "dead-enders." At a Pentagon briefing on June 30, a reporter asked Rumsfeld why he was so averse to calling what was going on in Iraq a "guerrilla war." "I guess the reason I don't use the phrase 'guerrilla war' is because there isn't one," Rumsfeld replied bluntly, then advised, "and it would be a misunderstanding and a miscommunication to you and to the people of the country and the world."

He explained that the disturbances in Iraq were being caused by looters, criminals, remnants of the regime, foreign terrorists, and Iranian agents. "Doesn't make it anything like a guerrilla war or an organized resistance. It makes it like five different things going on that are functioning much more like terrorists."

The reporter then proceeded to provide the official Defense Department definition of "guerrilla war." "Military and paramilitary operations conducted in enemy-held or hostile territory by irregular, predominantly indigenous forces," the reporter read from a Pentagon document, adding, "This seems to fit a lot of what's going on in Iraq."

Two weeks later, Abizaid, who had recently taken over as head of Central Command, weighed in to the definitional fray. One of his first acts after succeeding Franks was to put a halt to plans for a further drawdown in U.S. forces because of concerns about the growing conflict. At a Pentagon news conference on July 16, he contradicted Rumsfeld, declaring that U.S. forces in Iraq were under attack from "a classical guerrilla-type campaign." He noted that the insurgents were mostly midlevel Baathists, members of Saddam's Republican Guard and security services, and that they had organized regionally into cells.

The description was the first time that a senior officer had openly stated that the United States confronted an insurgency. Although Abizaid was a Rumsfeld favorite, the secretary was unhappy with the general's contrary comments and with the appearance they created that he had been wrong. A week later, he sent Abizaid a snowflake. "Attached are the definitions of 'guerrilla warfare,' 'insurgent' and 'unconventional warfare,'" he wrote. "They came from the Pentagon dictionary. I thought you might like to see them."

Other memos on the subject followed. "He sent me a series of four or five snowflakes that would tell me the definition of insurgency—you know, according to this or according to that," Abizaid recalled years later. "So I kept sending him countersnowflakes to prove that my position was right. He wanted me to conform to his way of thinking, and I wasn't going to conform to his way of thinking. I wasn't going to get out there and say, 'I've looked at it and I've determined it's not a guerrilla campaign, it's not an insurgency.'"

On November 11, for instance, Abizaid dispatched a memo to Rumsfeld in which he provided a definition of "counter-insurgency" taken from the Pentagon's own dictionary of military terms and attached a one-page primer called "Elements of Successful Counterinsurgency," which included the advice to "develop a coordinated, *integrated* plan based on an accurate assessment of the insurgency's goals, techniques, and strategies."

That same day, Rumsfeld also took issue with the CIA on the matter. Rob Richer, who had been heading the CIA's Near East Division for a year, started an intelligence briefing at an NSC meeting saying, "We are seeing the establishment of an insurgency in Iraq." Rumsfeld interrupted him, asking for a definition of insurgency. Richer, citing the Defense Department's own publications, cited three defining characteristics: popular support, sustained armed attacks or sabotage, and the ability to act at will and move independently.

Well into the winter, Rumsfeld was still harping on the use of the term and had expanded his concerns to other words. In a January 7, 2004, memo with the subject line "Terminology," sent not only to Abizaid but to Wolfowitz, Myers, Bremer, and Feith, the secretary wrote:

> As we discussed, the terminology we use is enormously important. The fact that so many of our folks are talking about the situation in Iraq as a "guerrilla war," with the word "guerrilla" having a positive connotation in some people's minds, is unfortunate. So too, the use of the phrase "former regime loyalist" is unfortunate in that "loyalist" has a positive connotation. The use of the phrase "Sunni Triangle" in a negative sense is harmful to our efforts with the Sunnis.

We have to do a better job of using words that are well thought through and calculated to express exactly what we mean. The word "fanatic" has a negative connotation. The word "terrorist" has a negative connotation in most cases.

I hope you will continue thinking through what words we ought to use to describe the people who are causing us the difficulties in Iraq and come back with some suggestions that we can all then use.

For Rumsfeld to have concurred that an insurgency had taken root in Iraq would have led him to acknowledge the enemy as an organized and durable force. That, in turn, would have pointed to a much longer struggle ahead for U.S. forces, since historically insurgencies were not quickly defeated. By resisting the labeling of the resistance in Iraq as an insurgency, Rumsfeld contributed to a delay in the crafting of an effective counterinsurgency campaign. And for Abizaid to have had to engage in such wordplay with his boss while settling into the top CENTCOM job seemed a needless diversion from the mounting challenges at hand in Iraq.

Rumsfeld took time out on September 3 to start a list of the precedents he had set as defense secretary. In a memo titled "Firsts" and addressed to Larry Di Rita, his special assistant, he compiled eleven examples and suggested that other people add to the roster. The secretary tended to take stock regularly of his progress in revamping the department and making good on his plan to transform it. By the fall of 2003, with his management of the war under increasing fire, it was not surprising to see him standing back and jotting down what he considered to be some of his greatest successes thus far.

A couple of items on the list involved significant new staff positions that he had established—notably, an undersecretary for intelligence and an assistant secretary for homeland defense. Also cited were changes in the lineup of the military commands, including the creation of a Northern Command to focus on homeland defense, the combining of the Strategic Command and Space Command, and the designation of a Joint Forces Command as the lead headquarters for transformation. The decision to put Special Operations Command in charge of the war on terrorism and to make it a "supported" command also received mention.

The rest of the list consisted of personnel actions. Rumsfeld had named the first Marine, Pete Pace, to serve as vice chairman of the Joint Chiefs of Staff. He had, for the first time, promoted a Navy SEAL, Eric Olson, to three-star rank. He had chosen a former Special Operations officer, Pete Schoomaker, to command major conventional forces. And in choosing Jim Jones to be NATO's top military commander, he had set two firsts—the first Marine to take over the NATO job and the first Marine commandant to go on to serve as a combatant commander.

Rumsfeld had clearly shaken things up, shattered some old conventions, and made some strides in reshaping the U.S. military. But as the situation in Iraq began showing signs of a protracted struggle, it increasingly threatened to overshadow Rumsfeld's change agenda.

In early September, the team from Joint Forces Command responsible for compiling lessons learned from the Iraq War returned to Washington for another briefing, this one focused on occupation operations. Their presentation noted a number of problems that had worsened for U.S. troops since the preceding report in June.

Still missing, the team advised, was a clear campaign plan to coordinate U.S. military efforts in a common direction. Division commanders reported receiving no long-range guidance. There were massive three-ring binders filled with orders from Sanchez's CJTF-7 headquarters. And there were hundreds of pages of slides and briefing charts laying out the operations being pursued, many of them named after Civil War generals, like Operation Chamberlain, aimed at securing the borders. "But they did not have an overarching plan that spelled out conditions, for instance, for when an interim Iraqi government might take over," said an Army officer who participated in the report.

To address this serious gap, Abizaid had recently decided to send several senior planners from Central Command to Baghdad to work with CJTF-7. The Baghdad headquarters eventually published a campaign plan in January 2004, but even then it consisted of only a broad framework, providing little specific direction to field commanders, and it retained an emphasis on offensive combat operations rather than ordering a shift to counterinsurgency tactics.

The lessons-learned team cited other problems as well. They found the U.S. command in Baghdad woefully undermanned for all the tasks assigned to it, with only about half the troops it should have. And conditions at the CPA weren't much better, with people coming and going on ninety-day contracts. The short tours prevented continuity of planning and action and severely constrained the alignment and integration of activities among the various ministries, the CPA regions, and the military divisions in Iraq.

Intelligence support, too, was lacking, with assets and personnel focused on searching for weapons of mass destruction, not on tracking or penetrating insurgent networks. Without good human intelligence about the enemy, U.S. troops were often engaging in large roundup operations, cordoning off neighborhoods and conducting door-to-door searches. "It was creating a lot of hostility with the Iraqis," recalled Ed Giambastiani, who by then had received a fourth star and had been switched from being Rumsfeld's senior military assistant to heading Joint Forces Command, where he oversaw the lessons-learned review.

Even communications among various U.S. military units was poor, complicating efforts to put together a common operating picture for commanders. The troops who had carried out the invasion had much better command-and-control capabilities and intelligence networking than did those managing the occupation, the review group found. "So here we are in the transition phase and we don't have anything that even comes close to approaching what we had during the warfight," Giambastiani recalled telling Rumsfeld.

U.S. military efforts to inform Iraqis were also failing. "We are losing the information war to Iranian radio and TV, Al Jazeera, et cetera," Giambastiani reported. Media sponsored by the CPA were being dismissed by the Iraqis as amateurish. "They would rather watch, or listen to Iranian- and Lebanese-sponsored media that are rife with anti-American and anti-coalition propaganda and misinformation," Giambastiani said.

Of all the recommendations, the one that Rumsfeld acted on most quickly involved the depletion of funds that field commanders were using for local reconstruction projects. Known as the Commander's Emergency Response Program, or CERP, the money initially had come from captured Iraqi cash as well as from Saddam-regime funds frozen in the United States. Rumsfeld ordered his staff to work with Congress urgently for a special appropriation to sustain the program, which had been enacted in the fall of 2003. "Rumsfeld understood the importance of CERP," Giambastiani said. "He went after it, and he got the money. He knew it was ammunition."

Rumsfeld took notes furiously during much of the briefing, and afterward he issued fourteen snowflakes related to various aspects of the report. By his own account, he had never written so many snowflakes out of a single briefing.

On September 5, Representative David R. Obey, a Wisconsin Democrat who was the ranking minority member on the House Appropriations Committee, became the first congressman to call for Rumsfeld's resignation. Obey, who had first entered Congress as Rumsfeld was leaving in 1969, had regarded Rumsfeld as a smart and reasonably progressive individual. But he saw him differently as defense secretary, put off by Rumsfeld's arrogance and by what he considered condescending, belligerent behavior toward Congress. Obey had been offended in meetings by Rumsfeld's bullying treatment of the secretary's own assistants.

"What I found really stunning was that we'd be sitting there for lunch in a meeting and he'd have one of his assistants walk through an issue, and if the assistant didn't do it exactly the way he wanted, he'd respond in a way that was absolutely belittling," the congressman recalled. "The problem was, that same attitude permeated everything he dealt with. He had very little regard for people who differed with him in any way."

Six months into the occupation of Iraq, Obey had had enough. He wrote a letter to Bush recommending the removal of both Rumsfeld and Wolfowitz, saying their mistakes had cost U.S. lives and incurred a financial expense that threatened the nation's fiscal health. "It is impossible to review the record of the past year and not conclude that they have made repeated and serious miscalculations," Obey wrote. He added that the unilateral conduct of the war and the planning for postwar occupation could not be seen as "anything other than a disaster."

His remarks reflected a growing anger among congressional Democrats about the handling of the occupation and the realization that vast sums would be required to rebuild Iraq at a time of record-setting budget deficits in the United States. News reports anticipated that the administration would be submitting a supplemental spending bill for more than $40 billion to keep tens of thousands of troops in Iraq and to rebuild the country.

Later that month, when Rumsfeld started to deliver a speech before a large audience attending the Eisenhower National Security Conference in Washington, a few protestors broke out in chants. They were quickly silenced, but the show of opposition underscored the extent to which public opinion had begun to turn against the defense secretary, who only the year before had been celebrated as the administration's most popular media star.

Rumsfeld gave the appearance of being unfazed by the criticism. As the heckling subsided at the conference, he couldn't resist recalling the protests of an earlier era, just after the Vietnam War during his first time running the Pentagon. He had experienced such antics before and had survived.

"Twenty-five years ago when I was secretary of defense," he said, "we would have the Berrigan brothers come in and dig graves in our front yard. So I guess everything changes and nothing changes." (The comment referred to an incident in August 1976 in which three people were arrested for attempting to dig holes, representing the mass graves of warmongers, in Rumsfeld's front lawn in Bethesda, Maryland. Among those arrested was Philip F. Berrigan, a former priest who with his brother, Daniel Berrigan, helped galvanize opposition to the Vietnam War in the late 1960s.)

Resuming his prepared remarks for the evening, he recalled all the nay-saying by armchair generals early in the war about how flawed the Iraq War plan had been, how insufficient the number of U.S. troops, how underestimated the level of Iraqi resistance. Notwithstanding all the criticism, he noted, U.S. and allied forces ended up taking Baghdad in twenty-one days. "Today we're again hearing suggestions, this time declaring that the postwar effort is on the brink of failure—that it will take longer than 21 days," he said. "But I believe that when all is said and done, the Iraq plan to win the peace will in fact succeed, just as the war plan to win the war succeeded."

Rumsfeld attributed the early predictions of failure to the novelty of the invasion plan—a plan, he said, that "was unfamiliar to the people who were commenting." Similarly, he went on, the postwar effort is different and unfamiliar to many people. He said the United States was pursuing the same strategy in Iraq as it had in Afghanistan, one that involved avoiding a massive U.S. occupation force and focusing on the development of indigenous forces and the establishment of national governing authorities. "And we've made solid progress," he asserted.

As a standard of comparison for judging the pace of Iraqi recovery, Rumsfeld harkened back to the aftermath of World War II. He drew on a memo that Bremer had sent him showing that the establishment of the Governing Council, local municipal councils, a central bank, a new army, and a police force had all occurred much faster in postwar Iraq than in postwar Germany. "All this and more has taken place in Iraq in less than five months," Rumsfeld said. "I know of no comparable experience in history—whether postwar Germany, postwar Japan, Kosovo, Bosnia—I know of no example where things have moved as rapidly."

Returning to a favorite theme, Rumsfeld emphasized that U.S. forces had no intention of rebuilding Iraq for the Iraqis; rather, the objective was to enable them to do so themselves. He compared the military occupation of a country to a doctor resetting a bone: It must be done properly to remove as much evidence of the original break as possible, or else it becomes all that much harder to repair later.

He also underscored his eagerness to bring down the level of U.S. forces in Iraq. "Long-term stability will come not from the presence of foreign forces—ours or any other country's—but from the development of functioning local institutions, and the sooner the Iraqis can take responsibility for their own affairs, the sooner U.S. and coalition forces can leave," he said. "The goal is not for the U.S. to rebuild Iraq; rather, it is to help the Iraqis get on the track where they can pay to rebuild their own country."

Iraq was not the only country proving more problematic than anticipated. The situation in Afghanistan was posing new concerns as well. Despite the presence of 8,500 U.S. combat troops in the country and a multinational peacekeeping force in Kabul, small groups of Taliban fighters had slipped back over the border from Pakistan and killed aid workers, stalling reconstruction in the south.

Additionally, the American-led training of a new Afghan army was more challenging than officials in Washington had expected. Plagued by high desertion rates, the new force had only six thousand trained soldiers by September 2003, out of a projected total of seventy thousand troops. Germany's effort to train police officers was off to an even slower start, and the British-led counternarcotics effort was dwarfed by an explosion in the poppy crop. U.S. officials had come to acknowledge that putting different countries in charge of different operations had been a mistake.

Hoped-for progress on other critical initiatives, from reforming the country's defense forces to establishing a government presence in rural areas, was also lagging. A program to disarm and demobilize private armies was stalled, and several powerful regional militia bosses were showing determined resistance to central authority. Momentum for change appeared to be slipping away from the U.S.-backed government of President Hamid Karzai.

Rumsfeld's own thinking about how to approach Afghanistan had evolved. Initially averse to an expanded U.S. military presence and to activities that could be construed as nation building, the defense secretary had turned his attention increasingly to other matters through 2002 and all but took his eyes off Afghanistan during the late war planning for Iraq and the first weeks of the invasion. U.S. military resources, too—including Special Operations units and new Predator surveillance aircraft—shifted away from Afghanistan toward the effort to oust Saddam Hussein. So preoccupied was the Pentagon's leadership with Iraq that in the fall of 2002, Rumsfeld had to tap the Pentagon's comptroller, Dov Zakheim, to serve as the reconstruction coordinator in Afghanistan—an unusual role for someone charged primarily with overseeing the Defense Department budget. "They needed somebody, given that the top tier was covering Iraq," Zakheim later told a journalist.

But in December 2002, Rumsfeld received a briefing on Afghanistan that suggested the United States should start doing more there than just chasing terrorists and training a new national army. It argued that, contrary to the cliché that seemed prevalent in the U.S. government and elsewhere at the time, Afghanistan was not a hopeless, ungovernable place of warlords and mayhem and could be turned into a moderate Muslim force in the region.

The briefing was delivered by Marin Strmecki, an Afghanistan expert at the Smith Richardson Foundation, on whose advisory board Rumsfeld had served before becoming defense secretary. His objective was to counter what he saw as a poverty of imagination in the U.S. government about what could be achieved in Afghanistan.

Strmecki reminded Rumsfeld that Afghanistan had not always been so volatile. Before the Soviets invaded in 1979, he recalled, it was a fairly stable, functioning country with a positive export balance. After the Soviet withdrawal in 1989, the warlords who had fought as mujahideen against the Soviet army fell to fighting among themselves. Such instability provoked popular resentment, which the Islamist extremists of the Taliban movement exploited to seize power in 1996.

But Strmecki contended that if new political structures could be assembled in Afghanistan, structures free of narrow ideologies and rooted in traditional groups, then a modernizing leadership could emerge. He recommended that the United States do more to help the Afghans create effective, broad-based national institutions, advising a smaller role for some Northern Alliance factions and greater prominence for the Pashtun.

Strmecki could not tell exactly how much of an impact he was having on Rumsfeld. "He's not someone who, when you brief him, he briefs you back on how he thinks," Strmecki later observed. But Rumsfeld was moved, and quickly arranged to hire Strmecki as Afghanistan policy coordinator under Feith. The job didn't have a particularly high status, but Strmecki had the kind of easy access to Rumsfeld and other senior administration officials that allowed for an influential role.

Initially, Strmecki tried to win acceptance from other government agencies for a more ambitious Afghan plan but made little headway. "I found the interagency completely status quo oriented," he said. "If you brought any idea forward, they'd say, 'No money for that.' So I quickly concluded that as a deliberative, creative process, the interagency wasn't going to work."

On a trip in early May to Iraq for his first postinvasion inspection, Rumsfeld also stopped in Afghanistan. The visit got the secretary focused again on Afghanistan, according to Strmecki, who accompanied Rumsfeld and who, afterward, received a snowflake asking for a briefing on the way forward. The resulting presentation two weeks later laid out an ambitious agenda with provisions for beefing up the new Afghan army, weakening the warlords, and assisting economic development. This kind of extended commitment looked like nation building, although Strmecki preferred the term "state building." Rumsfeld asked him to explain the distinction. Stremecki noted that nation building is aimed at creating a national identity. It is a term that emerged from a period of decolonization, when artificial states encompassing different ethnic groups were forming. Afghanistan, Stremecki said, is a different case because the Afghans already have a powerful sense of who they are.

Stremecki's proposal eventually found its way to the White House and served as a basis for an NSC action plan dubbed "Accelerating Success" and for Bush's approval of a major boost in funding for Afghanistan. In some ways, it was the approach that Rumsfeld had rejected right after the invasion. Central to the revised approach was a melding of U.S. military and political efforts into a more coherent strategy. Bombing raids and troop sweeps through Taliban-infiltrated areas would not be enough. U.S. forces would need to launch longer-range strategies against the growing terrorist threat by setting up regional reconstruction centers, building roads and schools, and engaging in other assistance efforts.

As a sign of this shift, Army lieutenant general David W. Barno, who took command of U.S. forces in Afghanistan in October 2003, had orders to work closely with the new U.S. ambassador there, Zalmay Khalilzad, the Bush administration's highest-ranking Muslim official and an American of Afghan descent. The general set up headquarters in the U.S. embassy in Kabul and adopted as his main mission the establishment of conditions for a successful Afghan presidential election in 2004. It was not a traditional military task, but the strong partnership that developed between Barno and Khalilzad proved very effective and became a model of what military-civilian collaboration can accomplish.

———•———

By the autumn of 2003, Bremer had essentially become his own operator in Iraq. Although Rumsfeld had recruited Bremer, and Bush's appointment letter had instructed Bremer to work under the "authority, direction and control of the secretary of defense," the CPA leader appeared to operate increasingly independently of the Pentagon. Told by Rumsfeld that he could feel free to talk with other principals whenever he deemed it useful, Bremer took full advantage of the open invitation. His frequent contacts with Rice, for instance, evolved at Rice's request into daily telephone calls, and he met privately with Bush on trips back to Washington.

Wolfowitz, Feith, and other senior Pentagon officials around Rumsfeld grew increasingly frustrated with Bremer's seeming disregard for them. But Rumsfeld initially defended the CPA leader. "He commented favorably on Bremer's energy," Feith recalled. "He talked of the hardships of life in Baghdad—the multiplicity of demands on Bremer and his team, the lack of respite and amenities. He admired Bremer's take-charge demeanor. Bremer was spared the kind of grillings and rebukes that Rumsfeld routinely visited on his other subordinates."

Rumsfeld's reluctance to reassert his authority over Bremer puzzled some of his oldest associates. Staser Holcomb, who had been Rumsfeld's military assistant during the Ford years and who had returned to manage the process of selecting senior officers, saw a contrast between then and now, believing the old Rumsfeld would have taken a more hands-on approach with Bremer and with postwar developments. "It was uncharacteristic of him not to try to manage that important process," the retired admiral noted.

To some extent, Rumsfeld's hands were tied by the way Garner had been treated. Because of a widespread perception that Garner had been fired, any effort to remove or even tightly restrain Bremer might be taken as a further sign of disarray in the administration's postwar management of Iraq.

Besides, Bremer's independent image served a certain purpose for Rumsfeld. Holcomb remembered asking Rumsfeld why he wasn't intervening more aggressively with Bremer. "He said, 'Well, that's the State Department; they're doing that,'" Holcomb recalled, suggesting that Bremer was more State's responsibility than his.

Indeed, Rumsfeld considered the rebuilding of Iraq as essentially a State Department function, not a Pentagon one. Although he had requested and received the mission before the war, he had expected to hold responsibility for only a short time before handing it off to the State Department. Several months into the occupation, Rumsfeld was eager to lose the mantle of the one in charge of what he regarded as essentially nonmilitary activities. U.S. troops could still address security issues and handle the training of Iraqi security forces, but in his view, issues involving Iraqi governance and economics weren't his concern. Deferring to Bremer afforded him a way out. "He never liked nation building as a mission for the Pentagon," said Peter Rodman, assistant secretary of defense for international security affairs. "Bremer solved that problem for him, or so he thought."

Steve Herbits, one of the secretary's outside advisers, suspects that Rumsfeld's acquiescence involved an element of political calculation. Worried about the negative turn of events in Iraq, Rumsfeld may have figured that he could distance himself from a bad outcome and make Bremer the fall guy. "That's a very classic Rumsfeld kind of thing to do," Herbits said. "It's the rubber gloves image"—meaning a tendency to avoid leaving his fingerprints on decisions.

Another factor may also explain Rumsfeld's reluctance to rein Bremer in. As short a leash as Rumsfeld sought to maintain on people around him in the Pentagon, he was often averse to taking responsibility for field operations, uneasy about second-guessing those closest to the action. "I think he had a deep view that you do not pretend in Washington to have the kind of detailed knowledge of operations that you need to have to be making field decisions," Feith said.

Rumsfeld wanted the chain of command linking him to Bremer to resemble what he had with his own regional commanders. He treated Bremer much like a field commander, giving him authority and extraordinary freedom of action.

More than once Feith suggested that Bremer be required to talk to him, Pace, and their staffs several times a week to discuss matters in greater details. But Rumsfeld rejected the idea, saying it would impose too much of a time demand on the CPA leader. "Rumsfeld spoke protectively of Bremer's time and status," Feith wrote in his memoir. "Rumsfeld did not want Bremer to think he had to report to any defense official other than himself. Once Bremer understood Rumsfeld's view, he largely stopped communicating with anyone at the Pentagon other than the Secretary."

Bremer had his own frustrations initially with having to report through Rumsfeld. On his first trip back to Washington in July 2003, Bremer discovered that his cables to the defense secretary, sent through military channels, had not been disseminated to others on the NSC. The oversight could be explained by a mechanical feature of the Pentagon's routing system, which distributes cables only to those specifically named as recipients. But Bremer was never sure whether the lack of distribution had also been intentional.

Bremer had always found Rumsfeld courteous in their personal dealings. But he knew the secretary could be very wearing, always peppering people with questions, insisting on answers and intimidating his own staff. "Don terrifies his civilian subordinates, so that I can rarely get any decisions out of anyone but him," the envoy told Bush during a visit to Washington in late October.

Ultimately, Rumsfeld may simply have regarded himself as somewhat powerless to affect Bremer's other relationships in Washington. Although technically Bremer was supposed to report to Rumsfeld, the CPA leader saw himself as essentially the president's man. This, too, was how Rumsfeld came to regard him. "I think there were things that he felt were too hard for him to take control of," Holcomb observed, noting that as solid a relationship as Rumsfeld had with Bush, it didn't approach the connection he had had with Ford during his previous stint as defense secretary.

Asked in an interview to explain why he appeared so resigned to Bremer's independent operating style, Rumsfeld said that by the time he realized what was going on, Bush had given Bremer "a very long leash" and "the cow was out of the barn. So my attitude was, fine, let him report to the president or Condi or Colin. Doesn't bother me."

In early October, Bush decided to give Rice new authority and responsibility for coordinating the task of stabilizing and rebuilding Iraq. The move inserted a new layer of supervision over CPA operations by establishing an NSC-based Iraq Stabilization Group. A *New York Times* article announcing the creation of the group portrayed it as a reflection of concern about postwar management and a direct effort to diminish Rumsfeld's authority in the next phase of the Iraq occupation.

Rumsfeld was displeased both by the existence of the new group and by the way it was announced. He worried that the heightened involvement of Rice's office would lead to confusion about the military chain of command. He also objected to the suggestion, which had appeared in the news article, that he had been thoroughly consulted on the shift. He testily told European reporters that the first he had heard of the move was in a memorandum from Rice dated October 2, a few days before the *Times* story. In a seeming criticism of the White House, he suggested that the NSC staff was finally focusing on doing what they should have been doing all along—coordinating the work of the many government agencies dealing with Iraq.

Privately, Rumsfeld sent a blustery memo to Andy Card, Bush's chief of staff, on the day the article appeared. "I was not consulted—only advised," Rumsfeld wrote, seeking to set the record straight. In view of the announcement, Rumsfeld recommended in the memo that Bremer's "reporting relationship" be transferred from Defense to State rather than to Rice's office, which he said was not staffed for, organized for, or capable of handling the task. Rumsfeld had a long-standing concern that the NSC staff not take on executive authority but, rather, assign responsibilities to the cabinet departments and hold them responsible.

He reminded Card in the memo that everyone had agreed earlier that stabilization responsibilities would eventually move out of the Pentagon, and he noted that Bremer had already been reporting directly to Rice, Powell, and Card, "so the effect of the change should not be major." He also pointed out that Bremer's responsibilities were increasingly political and economic rather than military in nature, and he recalled telling Bremer earlier that he would be happy to have the reporting chain switched anytime the CPA leader "felt his work was such the transfer would be appropriate and desireable."

Not only did Rumsfeld consider the State Department better suited than the NSC staff to oversee Bremer's activities, but he also observed in his memo that many State officials "adamantly felt" that Bremer should report to their department, so a transfer might "calm them down and stop them from complaining to the press."

Rumsfeld and his top aides suspected that a recent series of news stories sharply critical of the Pentagon's handling of postwar Iraq had been generated by State Department officials. At a meeting with Bush, Cheney, and Card in early October, Rumsfeld asserted that the news stories stemmed from a meeting that Richard Armitage had held in his office in which he had instructed State Department staff to lay blame for problems in Iraq on the Pentagon. According to Pentagon notes of the White House meeting, Rumsfeld said he had told his own staff not to fight back with their own leaks to the press.

Bush, sounding surprised by the matter, asked what the basic issue was. Rumsfeld said it was the State Department's contention that the Pentagon was doing a poor job managing postwar Iraq and that the State Department could have done better had it been placed in charge. Rumsfeld pointed out the ludicrousness of the claim, given that 70 percent of Bremer's staff were State Department people.

Card expressed his intention to confer with Powell, Armitage, and Andrew Natsios, the administrator of the U.S. Agency for International Development, and instruct them to plug the leaks. There was also talk at the meeting of the need for Rumsfeld to do some TV interviews and clarify matters.

———◆———

The growing difficulty that Iraq was presenting, particularly the rise in violence, heightened Rumsfeld's concerns about U.S. progress in battling terrorist networks around the world. On October 16, Rumsfeld wrote to Myers, Wolfowitz, Pace, and Feith asking whether the U.S. government was "winning or losing" the global war on terror.

It was a typical Rumsfeld musing, but when the memo ended up on the front page of *USA Today* a week later, it caused a minor sensation for revealing the defense secretary's doubts. It also disclosed a more mixed internal assessment of the counterterrorism campaign than Rumsfeld or other senior administration officials had publicly acknowledged. It spoke of "mixed results" with al Qaeda members, noting that "a great many remain at large," and cited even "slower progress" in tracking down the Taliban. "Have we fashioned the right mix of rewards, amnesty, protection and confidence in the US?" Rumsfeld asked. "Does DoD need to think through new ways to organize, train, equip and focus to deal with the global war on terror? Are the changes we have and are making too modest and incremental?"

Rumsfeld went on to say that it was his impression that the United States had "not yet made truly bold moves," and he complained about a lack of "metrics to know if we are winning or losing the global war on terror," adding: "Are we capturing, killing or deterring and dissuading more terrorists every day than the madrassas and the radical clerics are recruiting, training and deploying against us? Does the US need to fashion a broad, integrated plan to stop the next generation of terrorists?"

The memo was more a collection of disparate thoughts than a carefully reasoned argument. Rumsfeld was throwing out questions: "Do we need a new organization? How do we stop those who are financing the radical madrassa schools? Is our current situation such that 'the harder we work, the behinder we get'?" He ended by expressing himself confident of victory in Afghanistan and Iraq "one way or another," then added, "but it will be a long, hard slog."

———•———

In the autumn, tensions built between Rumsfeld and Bremer over how long to wait before turning over control of Iraq to the Iraqis. The go-slow approach that Bremer had outlined in his September op-ed article had taken Rumsfeld and his staff by surprise and clashed with the Pentagon's interest in a much quicker transfer of sovereignty. Defense officials favored establishing an appointed government rather than waiting for an elected one. Belatedly recognizing that Bremer's plan would stretch out the process, they began pushing harder for the earliest possible divestment of power to an Iraqi government, arguing that this would remove the stigma of "occupier" from the coalition forces.

Feith's office drafted a paper in late September suggesting that sovereignty be given to the twenty-five-man Governing Council of Iraqis that

Bremer had created and that the council be renamed a "provisional government." In a meeting with Bremer in Washington, Wolfowitz pressed the envoy to expand the council and to then just hand over sovereignty to it.

Bremer understood the reasons for urgency. In view of mounting violence and rising U.S. casualties, there was growing pressure on Rumsfeld and the rest of the administration to show progress in Iraq. Moreover, the original rationale for going into Iraq had been dealt a serious blow with the inability of investigators to find any stockpiles of weapons of mass destruction. In an interim report to Congress on October 2, David Kay, who was supervising the search as head of the Iraq Survey Group, declared that Saddam, at the war's start, had almost certainly not possessed the poison gas, biological warfare agents, delivery warheads, or industrial system and fissile material needed to produce nuclear weapons that the intelligence services of all major Western countries had judged he had.

Although Kay's team had discovered "dozens" of what Kay called "WMD-related program activities" along with evidence of Saddam's "intent . . . to continue production at some time," the absence of stockpiles was a disastrous setback for the administration and personally embarrassing for Rumsfeld. The defense secretary, dropping his usual tendency to hedge about the future, had allowed himself to get pinned in an on-the-record assertion ten days after the invasion about where Saddam's stockpiles would be found. "We know where they are," he told ABC's George Stephanopoulos on March 30. "They're in the area around Tikrit and Baghdad and east, west, south and north somewhat." Even amid early signs that no stockpiles might be found, Rumsfeld had rejected suggestions that the prewar assessment of the Iraqi threat might have been wrong, surmising that Saddam might have destroyed incriminating weaponry as U.S. troops advanced or might have spirited it into neighboring Syria.

The disappointing news for Rumsfeld did not stop with the lack of stockpiles. At around the same time, the CIA was refining its view of the enemy confronting U.S. forces in Iraq and affirming that an increasingly strong insurgency had taken root there.

Bremer, while mindful of the need to demonstrate movement on the political front, continued to argue for more time to lay a foundation for

Iraqi self-rule and to cultivate new leadership. He maintained that handing over authority to the Governing Council was inadvisable because the group was not representative and lacked credibility in large sectors of the population. Further, the group had not been effective or shown much ability to organize anything, Bremer said.

Any new government the CPA would appoint, he warned, risked being condemned as a creature of the U.S. government. Further complicating matters was an order issued in June by Grand Ayatollah Ali al-Sistani, the most influential Shia religious leader in Iraq, demanding national elections to select the country's political leaders and the body responsible for drafting Iraq's new constitution.

Rumsfeld saw risks in both a quick handover and a delayed approach. In a memo written on October 28 titled "Risk in the Way Ahead in Iraq," he seemed determined to show he was aware of all the arguments pro and con in the debate.

"There is a tension with respect to the pace at which sovereignty is moved to the Iraqis," Rumsfeld wrote. On the one hand, he observed, moving too quickly risked preparing inadequately for the switch, which could result in conditions in Iraq degenerating into civil war or sliding back into dictatorship. On the other hand, moving too slowly, he reasoned, risked turning Iraqis against the coalition and also could lead to a deterioration in the security situation and a loss in support from the American public, Congress, and the international community.

Personally convinced, though, of the need to accelerate the transfer of authority, Rumsfeld weighed in directly with Bremer. In a lengthy set of Pentagon meetings in late October, the secretary walked the CPA leader through the results of an internal Pentagon strategy review in hopes Bremer would recognize the need for early sovereignty. According to Feith's account of the briefings, Rumsfeld sought to avoid an outright confrontation. Instead, he pushed and prodded, raised questions, examined assumptions—in short, he applied his usual tactics of persuasion.

During the talks, Pentagon officials suggested the Governing Council simply appoint an "interim legislature" that would receive sovereignty by April 2004. Bremer argued it wouldn't be responsible to turn over sovereignty to a nonelected Iraqi body without a constitution in place. Absent an established system of political checks and balances, he cautioned, Iraq could fall into chaos. Bremer was still hopeful that a constitution could be in place first to help protect individual and minority rights and to establish a governmental structure, although with an accelerated timetable, he now was estimating the transfer could occur by the end of 2004.

Rumsfeld's role in Bremer's dropping the seven-step plan he had outlined in his *Washington Post* article and agreeing to a quicker transfer of sovereignty is portrayed differently by each side. In his memoir, Feith credits Rumsfeld with securing Bremer's agreement. Bremer, in his account, says it was his own idea to abandon the seven steps after realizing they simply would take too long, given al-Sistani's demand for elections and U.N. assertions that elections would not be possible for many months.

The truth probably lies somewhere in between. Rumsfeld's push for an accelerated timetable was not lost on Bremer. But internal considerations in Iraq were also causing the CPA leader to adjust his notions of what made the most sense. In early October, several weeks before his intensive meetings with Rumsfeld at the Pentagon, Bremer ordered CPA officials to begin looking at alternative approaches. "It may be that pressure from Washington made him more open to alternative strategies," said Meghan O'Sullivan, a senior aide to Bremer at the time who was working political issues. "But the impetus for the early transfer of sovereignty was, from where I sat, largely Iraqi."

By early November, Bremer and his staff had devised an alternative plan calling for the Governing Council to write an interim constitution by the spring, followed by summer elections for a transitional government, or by caucuses if timely elections did not prove feasible. Members of the Governing Council accepted the idea, and Bush approved it. The agreement set a deadline of June 30 for ending the CPA and transferring sovereignty, although it proved impossible to organize either elections or caucuses by then. Instead, when the CPA ceased, Bremer handed power over to an appointed interim government headed by Prime Minister Ayad Allawi. The main task of that government was to organize national elections by January 2005.

Underlying the debate over when to hand over sovereignty was a deeper tension among those setting policy on Iraq. The argument centered on which would have to come first in Iraq: a safe and secure environment to allow political and economic reconstruction, or progress on the political front.

Pentagon officials stressed the need to accelerate the governance track, contending that no amount of military force could ensure a stable Iraq unless the governance and reconstruction pieces fell into place. While military action would be required to suppress the violence, defense officials said, it was equally important to move forward on political reconciliation, the transfer of governmental authority to Iraqis, and visible improvement in the Iraqis' standard of living. A Pentagon review in late October had reaffirmed this point.

A counterargument was advanced by State Department and CPA officials. While Powell had supported Rumsfeld in the push for an accelerated transfer, he sided with Bremer in believing the real problem in Iraq remained the lack of security. No political progress was possible, this argument went, until the military established security.

The differences in view led to constant finger-pointing between the diplomats and the military over who was letting down the effort and who needed to do more. Bremer and his CPA team considered the Pentagon in too much of a hurry, not just in transferring sovereignty but in developing Iraqi security forces.

During a visit to Iraq in early September 2003, Rumsfeld pushed Bremer, then in charge of the training of Iraqi security forces, to move as fast as possible in preparing them for duty. The following week, Rumsfeld wrote Bremer and Abizaid instructing that reporting on security issues should include not just U.S. forces but also international and Iraqi forces—an evident attempt to counter criticism that the number of U.S. troops was insufficient by showing the whole picture. "We need to array them all, because they are now what comprise the security forces for Iraq," Rumsfeld stated.

Bremer appreciated the pressures that Rumsfeld was under. But the CPA leader worried that the Pentagon's timetable for growing the new forces was overly optimistic and that Rumsfeld was trying to make more of existing Iraqi force numbers than was warranted. He told Wolfowitz at a late-September meeting in Washington that the training was going as fast as possible and that it would be unrealistic to think that either the army or the police would have substantial capabilities by the spring, when a major rotation of U.S. forces was scheduled.

Beyond the focus on Iraqi force numbers, Bremer was also concerned about a shortage of good intelligence on the insurgency and an evident lack of an overall military strategy for defeating the enemy. U.S. troops, in Bremer's view, had gone into a passive or reactive mode since late August after attacks by roadside and car bombs began to escalate.

In early November, Bremer complained to Cheney in a secure phone call about the absence of a military strategy for victory in Iraq. "I've been asking the same question," Cheney said. "What's our strategy to win? My impression is that the Pentagon's mind-set is that the war's over and they're now in the 'mopping-up' phase. They fail to see that we're in a major battle against terrorists in Iraq and elsewhere." He promised to raise the issues on his own at the White House.

———•———

Struggling with notions of insurgency, frustrated by the absence of weapons of mass destruction, and facing a rise in terrorist attacks, Rumsfeld moved to shed some responsibility for Iraq. On December 6, during a visit to Iraq, the secretary pulled Bremer aside in the VIP room at the Baghdad airport for a private conversation.

"I told him that it was clear to me that he is now reporting to the President and to Condi," Rumsfeld said in a memo he wrote for his files after the meeting. "I said I would keep my hand in on security and would try to be as helpful to him as I could, but I did not want four hands on the steering wheel." Rumsfeld added that he was happy to be rid of the responsibility. At the same time, he didn't think the NSC was doing its job well, and he was concerned about the risks of having it take on this operational task, recalling that the last time the NSC took on an operational role, it resulted in the Iran-Contra scandal during the Reagan administration. Rumsfeld wished Bremer well.

Bremer, who recalled the conversation in his memoir, described it as "friendly" but added that "Rumsfeld was clearly unhappy that Rice had stepped in and taken control of policy. I guessed he was also reacting to those saccharine press stories about my close relationship with the president. And probably Rumsfeld was just fed up with bureaucracy."

At around this time, coming out of the White House Situation Room one day, Rice asked Rumsfeld to call Bremer to handle some routine matters. Rumsfeld declined, saying Bremer didn't work for him, he worked for her. Standing nearby, Powell and Cheney witnessed this exchange. Dumbfounded by Rumsfeld's surrender of responsibility, Powell phoned Rice later in the day. "Do you know what you just heard?" he asked. "Rumsfeld has left. Have you reported this?" Rice seemed to shrug off the incident. To Powell, though, it was another sign of Bush's willingness to let Rumsfeld do what he wanted, to just give him free rein.

A week later, the beleaguered Bush administration received a much-needed boost when U.S. troops pulled a bearded, disheveled Saddam Hussein out of a makeshift underground hiding place on a farm near Tikrit. The next day, December 14, when Rumsfeld and Joyce hosted a holiday reception at their house, the discovery was still a secret. U.S. military authorities were swiftly attempting to confirm that the man they had captured was indeed the former Iraqi leader.

At the party, Rumsfeld took his old friend, Larry Silberman, aside to share the news. He could barely contain himself. "He was really ecstatic," Silberman said, recalling that night as the happiest he saw Rumsfeld during his time as defense secretary.

With news of the capture scheduled to be disclosed in Baghdad, Rumsfeld phoned Sanchez to say he wanted him, not Bremer, to make the announcement. Sanchez advised Bremer of this, and Abizaid reinforced the point later. Nonetheless, Bremer delivered the announcement himself, intent on trying to give the moment a political context and to encourage Iraqis to step up efforts toward national reconciliation.

When Sanchez and Abizaid met with Rumsfeld in Bahrain the next month, the secretary angrily asked Sanchez why he had let Bremer take the lead in announcing Saddam's capture. Sanchez said he didn't control Bremer, and Abizaid affirmed that the ambassador would not relent. "Well, dammit, you guys ought to listen to my guidance," Rumsfeld declared.

CHAPTER 13

The Thought of Resigning

Through much of 2003, pressure built on Rumsfeld to increase the size of the U.S. armed forces in order to better accommodate U.S. commitments in Iraq, Afghanistan, and elsewhere. The mounting strain on U.S. troops because of the rise in overseas operations reverberated throughout the system. Recruiting numbers were down, training exercises were cut back, and shortages were experienced in such key skill areas as military police and civil affairs. As bipartisan support for a troop increase grew on Capitol Hill, some senior military officers, particularly in the Army, predicted that a larger force would inevitably prove necessary in the absence of any significant reduction in overseas missions.

But Rumsfeld firmly resisted an expansion of the Army. In his view, adding soldiers would drain away funds that could be better invested in technology. He also figured that the strain on the Army would ease once conditions in Iraq improved and the U.S. troop level there came down. To lock in an increase, only to be faced with pulling out of Iraq in a year or two, would risk the bloating that had plagued the Army in the 1970s.

Rumsfeld outlined his thinking in late September 2003 in a nine-page confidential "working paper" titled "Stress on the Force," one of the longest personal memos he composed as secretary. The question he immediately raised in the subject line was, "Are current U.S. military forces sufficient for the challenges facing our country?"

Citing an analysis by the Joint Chiefs that indicated U.S. forces were sufficient, Rumsfeld warned that an increase could be "an expensive mistake." He made it clear that he considered the existing pressure to enlarge the force temporary. "The current stress on the force is very likely a 'spike,' and we hope it will not be permanent," he wrote. To help ease the burden on U.S. troops, he pointed to three factors: the development of Iraqi forces, increased participation by foreign allies, and more-effective action against enemy fighters.

The rest of the paper consisted largely of a roster of efficiency measures and restructuring moves, under way or under examination, intended to reduce the general demand for ground troops in U.S. military operations. The forty-seven items in it constituted a catalog of the reforms that Rumsfeld had pushed under his transformation slogan.

Some of the initiatives involved general undertakings, such as the revision of contingency war plans to favor speed, agility, and precision weapons over concentrations of troops; the fostering of greater "jointness" among the services; and the streamlining of the troop-deployment process. Other efforts were more specific—among them, the development of standing joint task force headquarters, ready-to-go command units intended to avoid the traditional helter-skelter assembly process.

Some of the proposals focused on manpower, including plans to rely more on contract employees and to replace uniformed troops in noncombat jobs with civilians. Others dealt with technology, notably, new ships that would run with smaller crews, drone aircraft to substitute for piloted planes, and security sensors to replace armed guards. Still others sought efficiency through the restructuring of units, the thinning of headquarters staffs, and the smarter allocation of forces. In a section titled simply "Policy," Rumsfeld listed paring down long-standing U.S. commitments in the Sinai, Bosnia, Kosovo, and Iceland, as well as plans to reduce the presence of U.S. forces in Europe and Asia. "During a crisis, when there is an understandable spike in demand on U.S. forces, DoD cannot behave as though it is 'business as usual,'" Rumsfeld concluded. "It isn't."

The sheer number and scope of the measures cited in the memo illustrated the extent to which Rumsfeld had shaken things up in the Defense

Department, but there was no telling how the changes would play out and when they might begin to relieve the stress on U.S. forces. For its part, the Army, under new leadership, was moving to take matters into its own hands. General Pete Schoomaker, who succeeded Eric Shinseki as the Army's chief of staff in August, recognized that a plea for more troops for the same Army was out of the question. But there was a chance Rumsfeld would agree to grow the force if he saw the Army transforming itself.

Within a few months, Schoomaker had drafted a plan for the most significant reshaping of Army units since World War II. It called for a shift in focus away from the Army's large, cumbersome divisions—organizations of more than ten thousand troops containing all the elements considered necessary to fight. The new focus would be on the next unit down, the brigade, which consists of about three to four thousand troops.

While the Army had thirty-three active-duty deployable combat brigades, sending them overseas individually had presented problems. Key headquarters and support elements had to be stripped from the rest of a parent division to support the brigade being sent. Under the new plan, the brigades would be restructured into more mobile, self-contained units that could be deployed more easily but with enough of their own firepower, armor, logistics, and administrative assets to protect and sustain themselves over time.

Additionally, the total number of brigades would grow to forty-three or possibly more. Staffing for this expanded brigade system would come from reorganizing and rebalancing skills and positions, shifting troops from the "institutional Army"—the "tail" that trains, supports, and administers the force—to the "operational Army" that deploys and fights. Traditional functions that were less in demand, such as air defense and artillery, would decrease, while high-demand fields such as military police and civil affairs would surge. More civilians would be hired to replace soldiers in noncombat jobs, thereby freeing up troops for the newly restructured brigades.

Similar notions for revamping the Army into a more brigade-oriented structure had been kicking around for years but hadn't made headway in the face of deep institutional resistance. Schoomaker didn't bother to work his plan through the ranks first. He went straight to the top, taking advantage of the quick rapport he had established with Rumsfeld.

"Schoomaker worked his relationship with Rumsfeld very hard," re-called General George Casey Jr., then vice chief of the Army. "The way he operates is, he starts at the top, so his idea was to get Rumsfeld satis-fied with what he was going to do, then use that as a vehicle to force the plan down through the rest of the department."

Rumsfeld was excited about the proposal. As much as he had spoken of the need for a new Army, he had lacked a clear idea of how it should be restructured. Schoomaker's brigade modularity approach offered a vision and a pragmatic way forward, promising a more flexible but still very lethal ground force.

Attempting to remake an Army structure that had remained largely unchanged for decades was challenging enough in peacetime. In wartime, it could prove reckless and damaging. By the start of 2004, the Army had embarked on the largest troop rotation since World War II, moving about 250,000 troops in and out of Iraq and Afghanistan. The rotation involved eight of the Army's ten active-duty divisions. In addition, nearly 165,000 Army National Guard and Reserve members found themselves serving tours far longer than what they had expected as part-time soldiers.

But Rumsfeld and Schoomaker saw more opportunity than danger in the urgency of the moment. "We should take advantage of this movement that we currently have to reset and transform during this emergency," Schoomaker told the House Armed Services Committee in January 2004. "And that's what gives me the encouragement that in fact we can do this."

At the time, Pentagon authorities did not envision the war commit-ments continuing to consume troops in the same large numbers for more than another year or two. Even so, the flux of deployments meant there was little slack in the system for the restructuring.

To provide some cushion, Schoomaker requested that the Army be allowed to grow 30,000 troops above its congressionally approved limit of 482,000. The increase at that point was presented as only a temporary move, subject to review in a few years. Shedding his earlier opposition to expanding the ranks, Rumsfeld agreed to the rise in the interest of facili-tating the Army makeover. Implicitly, his approval acknowledged the in-ability of his other reform efforts to provide more forces, at least in the near term.

Meanwhile, in Iraq, the effort to reconstitute Iraq's military and police was faltering badly. Unity of command did not exist. Resources were badly managed. At least half a dozen security services were operating, but none had a well-defined role or mission. Development was uneven. And new capacity was not being built fast enough. Those were the findings of a secret report by a Pentagon team sent by Rumsfeld in January 2004 to assess Iraq's new security forces. More than half a year into the occupation, the report concluded, "an overarching security strategy" for Iraq was still lacking.

The drive to establish new Iraqi security services had been hobbled from the start by insufficient staffing and equipment and by conflicting visions between the U.S. military command and the CPA. The U.S. officer initially chosen to lead the mission, Army major general Paul Eaton, hadn't received word of his assignment until early May and had started with a staff of just six people and a budget of $173 million. Plans had called for him to recruit and train three infantry divisions by September 2006, about three years away. The idea was that the new army would be built in a benign environment with a focus on external defense and with time to incubate. Internal security was to be handled by separate forces, including police, a civil defense corps, border patrol, and infrastructure protection guards.

But Eaton and his team found themselves having to rebuild bases and barracks that had been stripped bare in the postinvasion looting and having to scrounge for such basic equipment as boots, rucksacks, belts, beds, and blankets. Recruitment and training of the new force was further complicated by the decision by Paul Bremer and Pentagon officials to dissolve the old Iraqi army and not to preserve or recall any complete Iraqi units.

As the insurgency worsened, the need for Iraqi units to help with the fight took on greater urgency. In a September 5 briefing in Baghdad for Rumsfeld, Eaton proposed accelerating the creation of new forces by sending former Iraqi army officers for training at a base in Jordan and establishing a separate academy in Iraq for training noncommissioned officers. Rumsfeld approved the plan, moving the deadline for fielding the first three divisions up by two years to September 2004.

Overwhelmed by an increasing number of security tasks and hard-pressed to wait for the new Iraqi troops to emerge, U.S. commanders started creating ad hoc paramilitary units to assist American troops. Nearly every U.S. division stood up its own Iraqi units, which came to be known collectively as the Iraqi Civil Defense Corps. Bremer, whose CPA had jurisdiction over the development of Iraqi forces, was wary of this improvisation, worried about how the officially sponsored militia would be integrated later into Iraq's regular chain of command. But Abizaid and Sanchez defended the initiative as complementary to the establishment of a professional army. At the same time, the commanders began pressing to have responsibility for building up all Iraqi security forces, including the police, transferred from the CPA to the U.S. military.

This jumbled state of affairs was evident to Wolfowitz during a visit to Iraq in November. Frustrated with what he considered a lack of sufficient high-level Pentagon attention, Wolfowitz reported to Rumsfeld that Iraqi forces were poorly equipped and minimally trained at best. New forces were being created too slowly, and the scope of the force was inadequate to the task, Wolfowitz observed. He also cited little coordination among U.S. divisions in how Iraqi forces were being used, with each division having its own pay scale and benefits package. Wolfowitz urged that more money be dedicated to the effort and that greater coordination and standardization of forces be established nationwide.

It was at Wolfowitz's suggestion that Rumsfeld sent the assessment team in January. Led by Major General Karl Eikenberry, who had just completed more than a year in Afghanistan overseeing the creation of a new Afghan army, the team not only confirmed the program's many shortcomings but relayed warnings from U.S. commanders in the field that the insurgency was growing much faster than were the Iraqi security forces.

In its most significant recommendation, Eikenberry's team sided with Abizaid and Sanchez and said all training and employment of Iraqi security forces should be consolidated under U.S. military command. Rumsfeld concurred and, in February, authorized the switch. He designated that the training effort receive the "highest priority" from the Baghdad command and, in a memo to Abizaid and Bremer, made it clear that he wanted "the most rapid development" of Iraqi security forces.

At the same time, Rumsfeld continued to hope that other nations could be persuaded to send more troops and relieve some of the burden on U.S. forces, not just in Iraq but in Afghanistan, Kosovo, and Bosnia. In a memo to Wolfowitz, Myers, and Feith on February 20, he suggested ways of making the contribution of forces more attractive to foreign countries. "If people are looking for easier or less politically sensitive assignments, we can put them in the Kurdish area, put them in Kuwait, use them as force protection in the United States or in other countries, where we have forces to protect, or use them to help protect the UN when they go back into Iraq," he wrote. "We can find things that are less offensive or less sensitive from their standpoints."

Rumsfeld continued, "We need to have a person working this full-time, the way Dov has been tin-cupping the world for money," referring to Dov Zakheim, the Pentagon comptroller, who had been tasked to raise funds for Afghanistan among U.S. allies. "Please come back with a proposal. If we leave DoD to its own devices, we will end up dipping into the taxpayers' money and using DoD military personnel because it is easier, they are there and it seems to be a bottomless pit—but it isn't, it can't be, and it shouldn't be."

———— · ————

In the weeks after he had pulled Bremer aside to inform the CPA chief that he was washing his hands of much responsibility for Iraq, Rumsfeld appeared—at least to some people around him—to be less engaged in the war. In early 2004, Wolfowitz confided his own concerns about Rumsfeld's evident withdrawal to Jack Keane, who had stepped down as Army vice chief of staff and retired from military service. The subject came up when the two men met in New York for a Sunday brunch at an apartment belonging to a friend of Wolfowitz's. Wolfowitz was sounding out Keane's interest in coming out of retirement and taking over command of U.S. military operations in Iraq.

"He told me that Rumsfeld seemed detached," Keane recalled. "Rumsfeld had been involved for a part of every day while we were getting ready to go to war in Iraq and while the war was being prosecuted, but not anymore, Wolfowitz said. He told me that he was having difficulty getting Rumsfeld involved. He was very frustrated by it, very frustrated that Rumsfeld wasn't intellectually engaged."

At the White House, too, officials began to sense that Iraq was no longer the top priority it had been for the defense secretary, that Rumsfeld saw his larger calling as transformation of the Defense Department and was devoting more time and attention to it. This wasn't always the case, and over the rest of his term, Rumsfeld certainly continued to invest considerable hours and energy in Iraq. But a preoccupation with other matters would be evident even in meetings with the president when, instead of briefing further on Iraq, Rumsfeld would want to talk about something else.

Andy Card, who attended many of the meetings, was surprised at times by some of Rumsfeld's choice of subjects. "He was drifting more toward his passion for transformation than his responsibility for executing the war," the former White House chief of staff said in an interview.

Dan Bartlett, the president's communications director, was also struck by where Rumsfeld was focusing his attention. "I don't think it was so much a loss of interest in Iraq as it was more of an interest in other things," he recounted. "I would just be surprised at times with the issues he'd be choosing to discuss. I'm not saying that he shouldn't be focused on these other issues and that these weren't of presidential importance. They were. But it seemed at times tilted too much away from the war."

Having seen Rice's NSC staff take more of an oversight role and believing that the State Department should assume greater responsibility over postwar Iraq, Rumsfeld may simply have figured he could afford to turn his attention to other things. Bartlett recalled that Rumsfeld had bought into the notion being advanced by Abizaid that the broader war on terrorism would take decades, and this also could have influenced the secretary's desire to focus on reordering the Pentagon. "Given how his mind works, he may have thought that what he personally could do to help win the war over the long haul was to make sure that the Pentagon is structured right, that it was in position to sustain this conflict," Bartlett surmised.

At the time, Rumsfeld did express concerns that change wasn't coming fast enough at the Pentagon. In mid-March, he wrote a memo to his senior staff listing some of the problems addressed to that point. He cited the start of a process to update war plans on a more regular basis and the streamlining of decisions on troop deployments to Iraq. He noted the better balance being achieved in Army ranks between active-duty and reserve units, and he mentioned the speeding up of once-sluggish procedures for assigning aircraft and satellites to high-priority strategic reconnaissance operations.

But he was troubled by an article highlighting that U.S. reservists in Iraq weren't being adequately compensated, and he wanted the matter fixed. He also wanted the Pentagon's senior staff on guard for any other problems that might pop up. "I am concerned about what we'll discover next that is broken," he wrote in the memo. "We've made lots of progress on the operational side, but please review the systems, procedures and business practices that you use and/or are responsible for, and advise me of those that you believe we need to fix now, before we need them and before we discover they are not suited to the 21st century. I'd like to try to get ahead of the curve."

Beyond the Pentagon, Rumsfeld was frustrated by what he saw as the failure of U.S. government agencies to pull together in Iraq and Afghanistan and against terror networks worldwide. It was a theme he came back to repeatedly in discussions with NSC colleagues and in memos to them, often to their great annoyance, since they naturally didn't appreciate being accused of shirking responsibility. But Rumsfeld saw a disproportionate share of the burden falling on the military and contributing to the stress on American forces. In his view, the situation called for legislation that would do to the various agencies of the U.S. government what the Goldwater-Nichols Act of 1986 had sought to do to the military services—improve coordination and cooperation among them.

"To get where we are, each of those Services had to give up something—some authorities, some notoriety, some fame—to achieve a greater good," Rumsfeld wrote in a memo in early February 2004. "The US Government is now where DoD was in the pre-Goldwater-Nichols days."

For better interagency coordination, he recommended establishing "country teams" made up of representatives from the Pentagon, the State Department, and other agencies. He envisioned the teams being led not by senior foreign service officers but by more-prominent individuals.

"We need to have competent people who are the equivalent of our combatant commanders," he wrote, citing as examples two former Senate majority leaders (Republican Howard Baker of Tennessee and Democrat Michael Mansfield of Montana), a former House speaker (Democrat Tom Foley of Washington), and a Democratic power broker (superlawyer Robert Strauss).

In a further attempt to reduce the use of U.S. forces, Rumsfeld in late March outlined his thoughts on just what role the U.S. military should play in various kinds of domestic and international emergencies. He was particularly irked by what he considered an often knee-jerk impulse to send the Marines or other U.S. troops when a crisis suddenly arose.

In principle, he favored rapid action by U.S. troops if no other country had forces available. But he thought there should be a framework for such deployments. And he especially wanted to avoid U.S. forces getting stuck in a prolonged operation. He wrote:

> The United States has one of the few militaries, if not the only military, in the world that can move fast to deal with a serious, immediate military problem. The difficulty is that when the US does move rapidly, it fills the vacuum and, after a vacuum is filled, it relieves the pressure on other countries to step forward, leaving the US stuck with the responsibility.
>
> In the Defense Department, I have adopted an approach whereby, when it is necessary to act fast to fill vacuums that cannot be filled by others, we will do so, but we will avoid unnecessarily filling vacuums for sustained periods by making sure that that is well understood up front and we have a follow on plan.

He cited the dispatch of forces to U.S. airports in the immediate aftermath of the September 11 attacks, when Army secretary Tom White sent troops without advising him. Rumsfeld reversed the order and insisted that Transportation Department officials sign a memorandum agreeing to replace the troops with trained civilians within a specified period of time. "Had I not done that," Rumsfeld wrote, "DoD would still be in the airports."

More recently, in 2003, there had been pressure inside and outside the U.S. government to rush U.S. troops into Liberia after an escalation in its civil war. Although a small U.S. Marine contingent was eventually sent, Rumsfeld noted that arrangements were made "up front" to prepare the United Nations and the Economic Community of West African States to replace the U.S. troops with another international peacekeeping force "in an agreed period of time."

Similarly, in early 2004, the Pentagon had been urged to act quickly to deploy U.S. forces to Haiti. But Rumsfeld had held back until he received an agreement that several other countries would join in the mission and that U.N. forces would follow the American troops there. "The key," he noted, "is to not fill a vacuum unnecessarily." At the same time, he cautioned against waiting so long that the problem becomes "much worse while the US is trying to get other countries to commit to following us in."

Whatever lingering hopes Rumsfeld may have had for a further reduction in U.S. forces in Iraq were dashed in the spring of 2004 when the country experienced its most intensive fighting since the U.S.-led invasion. During the course of the battles, which involved attacks by Shiite as well as Sunni groups around much of Iraq, Rumsfeld was pressed to extend the deployment of a U.S. division that had been scheduled to leave.

The initial trigger came on March 31 in the western city of Fallujah, then a center of Sunni resistance. Two sports utility vehicles carrying four Blackwater USA security contractors ran into an ambush near the center of town. In a grisly assault, a mob grabbed the four men out of their cars, beat and killed them, then hung two of the mutilated corpses from the girders of a bridge over the Euphrates River as crowds of cheering Iraqis watched. The atrocity highlighted the brutality of the conflict and the seeming impotence of the United States. To avenge the deaths and find the perpetrators, U.S. Marines began an assault on the city.

As the battle was joined in Fallujah, U.S. authorities also moved against Moqtada al-Sadr, a young anti-American Shiite cleric. Al-Sadr and his populist strain of Shiism had been a worry from the start of the occupation, but U.S. military and civilian leaders had argued over how to deal with the rebellious cleric, and Rumsfeld had hesitated to order action against him.

In his memoir, Bremer writes that he was twice prevented from executing a plan to arrest al-Sadr for his suspected involvement in the April 2003 assassination of a moderate cleric, Abdul Majid al-Khoei. Once, in August 2003, Bremer says Rumsfeld blocked the move by raising questions about it and allowing an opportune moment for the operation to pass; then Wolfowitz in October expressed reservations and effectively stymied another potential move. An internal Pentagon review in 2006 disputed Bremer's accounts and concluded that there was no indication anyone in the Defense Department had denied a request from the CPA leader to go after al-Sadr. In any case, the cleric had remained a problem into 2004, with his weekly newspaper, *al-Hawza*, criticizing the U.S. occupation and his militia, the Mahdi Army, clashing with U.S. forces.

Finally, in late March, Bremer took action. He closed down al-Sadr's newspaper and, a few days later on April 3, ordered the arrest of al-Sadr's top deputy, Mustafa Yaqoubi. The next day, the capture of al-Sadr himself was sought. In response, the cleric's supporters staged street demonstrations and invaded television and radio facilities, police stations, and other civil installations around the country. In Sadr City, the slum that occupies the eastern third of Baghdad, fierce fighting broke out between U.S. troops and al-Sadr's loyalists. The cleric himself took refuge in Najaf, where his militia maintained control of the city, and battles erupted in several other Shia-dominated cities, including Kufa, Al Kut, and Karbala.

The decision to try to break al-Sadr's power rather than wait until after the transfer of sovereignty scheduled for June 30 reflected the belief that Shiite grand ayatollah Ali al-Sistani would quietly back the action and that most Iraqis would welcome the crackdown. But attacking al-Sadr's militia the same week that U.S. forces were pounding the Sunni resistance in Fallujah backfired. Rather than enhancing the rule of law, the al-Sadr crackdown added to Iraq's chaos. Confronted by the new surge in violence, U.S. commanders clamored for more troops. Thousands of soldiers from the 1st Armored Division, who had served their twelve months and were preparing to leave, were suddenly ordered to stay for another ninety days to help suppress the uprisings.

According to Abizaid, who had made the request to extend the division's tour in Iraq, Rumsfeld initially resisted. The secretary had promised to limit the length of any soldier's deployment to Iraq to one year and didn't want to go back on his word. But Abizaid stressed the need to keep the division in the fight, and the secretary relented. The division proved instrumental in quelling al-Sadr's forces. Rumsfeld never publicly acknowledged the opposition he had put up to the requested extension, although his irritation flashed at a news conference when asked why the twenty thousand troops had to stay longer. "Oh, come on. People are fungible," he replied. "You can have them here or there."

Rumsfeld persistently maintained that force levels in Iraq were based on the judgments of top U.S. commanders. He portrayed himself as always willing to increase the number of U.S. troops if needed. But the situation with the 1st Armored Division illustrated a more complicated reality. While Rumsfeld could be persuaded to provide more troops, his strong predilection was for fewer forces. To change his mind required much persuasive argument. Sometimes Abizaid and other commanders felt the push was worth it, sometimes not.

"Fighting him was not quite the way you probably imagine it," Abizaid said. "I would have discussions with him and tell him what I thought. He'd tell me what he thought. And it would be clear we had a difference of views. But I was fairly persistent, and when I was persistent, he would come around. Did he ever deny us any major reinforcement? No. But he would slow things down by questions. In the case of the 1st Armored Division, though, it was an emergency, and he agreed."

To his credit, Rumsfeld made it clear to his top commanders that he expected them to be frank and to come to him if something was on their minds. In April 2004, apparently concerned about perhaps not getting enough straight talk from two of his most important generals, he reminded them of their obligation. "I told Myers and Abizaid today that they owed me their best military advice and that I expected them to give it to me without my asking for it every five minutes," Rumsfeld wrote in an April 26 memo for his files. "I said that I also expect them, as they do, to do what the President wants them to do and to report back as to how that is going. But they ought not to then case their brains and then stop giving me their best military advice, because I have to have that."

Eventually, the major city battles in the spring of 2004 subsided. In Fallujah, where the fighting had started, the U.S. Marine offensive was halted after about a week. Members of the Iraqi Governing Council, eager to avoid seeming acquiescent to a major American assault on an Iraqi city, argued for obtaining custody of the murderers of the U.S. contractors through negotiation with city leaders. Bremer had become worried that the battle was threatening to fracture Iraqi support for the American presence in Iraq and could endanger the U.S. plan to transfer power to an interim government in June.

At an NSC meeting on April 9, Bremer proposed a cease-fire in Fallujah, and Rumsfeld went along. Abizaid was ambivalent, swinging between concern over the safety of the Marines who were exposed and worries that a full-out attack could spark an Arab revolt beyond Iraq. The attack was halted. The next day, at another NSC meeting, Abizaid proposed easing up on de-Baathification as a way of mollifying the Sunnis. He had been pushing efforts to reach out to the Sunnis, arguing that CPA's declared policy of purging Baathists had cut too deeply and that resentment in the Sunni community was fueling the insurgency.

According to Abizaid, Cheney had resisted the idea that more effort needed to be put into drawing the Sunnis back into the political process, but Rumsfeld came around to accepting it. At the April 10 NSC meeting, the secretary echoed Abizaid's concerns that the CPA had been too harsh toward the Sunnis and that the de-Baathification policy was perceived as too strict. He wrote Bremer two days later urging the CPA leader to reenergize the process of reconciliation with the Sunnis.

Ultimately, the Marines were kept from resuming the fight for Fallujah in the spring, and the city was entrusted instead to a new Iraqi organization called the Fallujah Brigade, conceived as a fig leaf for U.S. withdrawal. Made up of former Iraqi soldiers and headed by a renegade Baathist two-star general who had served in the Republican Guard, the unit proved ineffectual. It dissolved within weeks, many of its soldiers joining the ranks of insurgents that swelled anew over the summer.

The botched handling of Fallujah proved a critical strategic failure. The hesitant assault broadcast a weakness of American will and became an international rallying point for anti-American forces. Further, it highlighted the fundamental tension in the U.S. mission between needing to maintain order and control and having to protect the fragile incubating political structure that was being prepared to accept the transfer of sovereignty.

The Fallujah episode also revealed continuing serious problems with Iraq's nascent security forces. A 620-man battalion of the new Iraqi army refused to proceed after being called to the city to fight alongside allied forces, and as fighting spread to other major cities in Iraq in April, Iraqi forces collapsed elsewhere as well. The unreliability of the Iraqi units called into question the U.S. approach, which hinged on developing new Iraqi security troops who could take over the fight.

In early May, David Petraeus, then a two-star Army general who had commanded the 101st Airborne Division during the invasion and early occupation, was sent to conduct a fresh assessment of the Iraqi force buildup. He found that the quality of Iraqi troops was very uneven and that no true national force existed. Troop training, carried out by different U.S. and allied divisions with little direction from Sanchez's headquarters, varied widely. Facilities and basic equipment were still in very short supply. And as bad as the situation was within Iraqi military units, Petraeus concluded that the Iraqi police force was worse off.

Recognizing the need for a vastly expanded train-and-equip effort, Rumsfeld approved the establishment of a new command to focus on development of the Iraqi forces. Petraeus, promoted to three-star rank, was dispatched to head it up.

In the intensified battle against an increasingly entrenched insurgency, prison facilities in Iraq run by the U.S. military had swelled with detainees. The rising numbers of inmates overwhelmed the ill-prepared units of military police charged with caring for them and the crews of military interrogators under pressure to gather intelligence. Such conditions, coupled with lax oversight and uncertainty even at senior officer levels about just what rules applied to the handling of detainees, were a disaster waiting to happen. And it did.

On the evening of April 28, CBS News broadcast shocking photographs of mistreatment of Iraqi prisoners at the hands of U.S. guards. In the pictures, naked Iraqis were shown piled on top of one another in sexually suggestive positions. Some inmates were shackled to prison bars; others wore leashes or cowered before snarling dogs. In one iconic image, a hooded man was pictured draped in a large crude cloth and standing atop a box with arms outstretched and wires trailing from his hands. In most of the photos, U.S. soldiers were featured smiling, pointing, or giving thumbs-up signs.

The photographs had been taken by guards on duty at the Abu Ghraib prison outside Baghdad. Once a torture palace under Saddam Hussein, the prison had become a U.S. military installation where thousands of Iraqis, from common criminals to "high-value" suspected terrorists, were held. The graphic scenes of such inhumane treatment triggered outrage and revulsion around the world. Editorial pages lamented the erosion of U.S. moral standing, Congress demanded to know how U.S. troops could have sunk to such despicable behavior, and the White House and the Pentagon appeared as shocked as everyone else.

The discovery of the scandal at Abu Ghraib had begun on January 13, 2004, when a U.S. military policeman, Specialist Joseph Darby, gave a CD containing the photos to the Army's Criminal Investigation Division. Assigned to investigate, Major General Antonio Taguba concluded within several weeks that U.S. military personnel had committed numerous acts of "sadistic, blatant, and wanton criminal abuse" at the prison in 2003.

With the public disclosure of the photos several months later, questions quickly arose about how much Rumsfeld had known about the case, and when. Records show that two days after criminal investigators received the photos, Lieutenant General John Craddock, Rumsfeld's senior military assistant, and Vice Admiral Timothy Keating, the director of the Joint Staff, were e-mailed a summary of the alleged abuses. Five days after that, CENTCOM's chief of staff e-mailed Keating, copying Craddock and Sanchez, to report that four confessions had been obtained implicating "perhaps 10 soldiers" and to confirm that criminal investigators had about a hundred photos and a video.

In an interview in 2007, Craddock said that neither he nor Keating could recall receiving either e-mail. But in a separate interview, Abizaid acknowledged seeing the photos within days of their receipt by criminal investigators and said he informed both Rumsfeld and Myers. At the time, Abizaid worried that the photos would become public in an eventual court-martial and would trigger further violence in Iraq. According to Abizaid, Rumsfeld also fretted about how the photos would be handled.

In later testimony before Congress, Myers affirmed that information about the photos was given to Rumsfeld and him as early as January. He said "the general nature of the photos—about nudity, some mock sexual acts and other abuse—was described" at that time.

But Rumsfeld maintained that he was surprised by the graphic content when the photos appeared in the media. He first saw them on May 6, the day before he testified in Congress about the scandal. Asked at the hearing when he had been made aware of the photographs, Rumsfeld replied, "There were rumors of photographs in a criminal prosecution chain back sometime after January 13th. . . . I don't remember precisely when, but sometime in that period of January, February, March."

In the military, commanders and civilian officials are conditioned to steer clear of matters under investigation to avoid accusations of command influence, and it is possible this kept Rumsfeld from asking more questions initially. Still, his lack of action to learn more about the photos in an effort to contain the scandal surprised some associates.

Staser Holcomb, the retired vice admiral who had been Rumsfeld's military assistant in the mid-1970s, took it as another sign that his old friend had changed since his first stint as defense secretary. Holcomb considered it uncustomary of Rumsfeld not to have inquired further when first apprised of the investigation. "I suspect that he wakes up in the middle of the night and asks himself, 'Why didn't I ask more questions about what was going on at Abu Ghraib?'" Holcomb remarked. "I saw half a dozen things in this most recent time around that surprised me, key issues on which he didn't show the same degree of involvement that I would have expected him to show."

Steve Herbits, another carryover from Rumsfeld's first tour as defense secretary and an expert on organizational structures and processes, saw the Pentagon leader as poorly served by a senior civilian staff inclined to insulate Rumsfeld from the rest of the bureaucracy. As a result, Herbits argued, Rumsfeld lacked the kind of fluid, informal channels that would have helped bad news surface to him faster. "It's my hypothesis that had people around Rumsfeld been more capable, Abu Ghraib would never have happened," Herbits said. "Someone in the field would have called, which would have resulted in early action in the fall of 2003. It became a devastating issue because Rumsfeld heard about it too late."

When the photos were publicized, Craddock said he and other aides had trouble getting copies to show the secretary. "I had to call the Army three times and finally order them to send me a CD," the general said. When the photos arrived, Craddock and another assistant hurriedly organized them to show Rumsfeld on a laptop. "He was just devastated, as we all were," Craddock recalled. Ryan Henry, the deputy policy chief, remembers the moment as one of the few times he had seen Rumsfeld shaken. "He told a small group of five or six of us in his office, 'It feels like someone hit me in the stomach with a baseball bat.'" Rumsfeld had many questions. "What would go through people's minds to do this? And who are these people that this is being done to? Are they under interrogation or are they just regular inmates?"

At the White House, the president was upset about having been left largely uninformed. Rumsfeld had said something to Bush about the case months earlier, but apparently not enough to prepare the president for the extent of the abuse shown in the photos. On May 5, White House officials, speaking to journalists anonymously, reported that the president had expressed his displeasure to Rumsfeld in an Oval Office meeting for having failed to inform him adequately in advance about the graphic details.

The disclosure, clearly authorized by Bush, was an extraordinary slap by a president who put a high premium on order and loyalty. And Rumsfeld was not happy about the public reprimand, which made him the scapegoat in the scandal at a particularly vulnerable moment during an ongoing foreign war. But Bush's senior aides were concerned about protecting the president's image and thought Rumsfeld should take the hit. "Cabinet secretaries and staff are there for a reason—they take bullets; presidents don't take bullets," Dan Bartlett, Bush's communications director at the time, said later.

Testifying before Congress on May 7, Rumsfeld offered an unambiguous apology to Iraqis abused by their American military jailers and accepted full responsibility for the misdeeds of the soldiers on his watch. "It was inconsistent with the values of our nation, it was inconsistent with the teachings of the military to the men and women of the armed forces, and it was certainly fundamentally un-American," he declared.

He promised to investigate thoroughly, and faced with suggestions that he step down, he admitted to having "given a lot of thought to" the possibility since the photos had become public. But he said he would not leave office simply to quiet critics. "Needless to say, if I felt I could not be effective, I'd resign in a minute," he said. "I would not resign simply because people try to make a political issue out of it."

Bartlett worried that Rumsfeld had left open the question of resignation. The communications director knew that Bush had no intention of making a change in his defense secretary so close to the presidential election in November. He phoned Larry Di Rita, a senior Rumsfeld aide, to express concern about what Bartlett regarded as posturing by Rumsfeld and to nip in the bud talk of the secretary's removal.

Privately, Rumsfeld submitted two letters of resignation to Bush several days apart in the interest, Di Rita said later, of getting the president himself to make clear just where he stood on the matter. Bush rejected both letters, and a few days after Rumsfeld's appearance on the Hill, he went to the Pentagon to deliver an unqualified endorsement of his defense secretary. "You are courageously leading our nation in the war against terror," he declared to Rumsfeld in front of reporters and television cameras. "You are doing a superb job. You are a strong secretary of defense, and our nation owes you a debt of gratitude."

A poll showed that two-thirds of those interviewed believed Rumsfeld should not lose his job over Abu Ghraib. And in affirming his support for Rumsfeld, Bush surrounded himself with Powell and Myers to create a united image of the national security team as it dealt with the repercussions of the scandal. Nonetheless, one adviser confided at the time that White House officials were well aware that Rumsfeld might still have trouble hanging on to his job, especially if further revelations of abuse surfaced. Bush's support was a calculated risk. "The question now is whether the drip, drip, drip will kill Rumsfeld," the anonymous adviser told the *New York Times*.

The day of Bush's visit to the Pentagon, Rumsfeld wrote a memo to himself with the subject line "Nightmare." For all the shock of Abu Ghraib and its grave impact on public perceptions of U.S. policy and actions, what Rumsfeld dreaded most at that moment had little to do with the prospect of more appalling behavior by U.S. soldiers being disclosed. "My worst nightmare is not that there will be another prison abuse problem," he wrote. "The US military is so sensitive to that now that it is unlikely. My concern is that we will find another process, or procedure, or habit we are engaged in that is 20th century industrial age and is inappropriate to the 21st century. We need to find them." Even in the midst of the most disturbing events of his tenure as defense secretary, Rumsfeld's mind was on his transformation mission—on those outmoded, uncorrected aspects of the Pentagon structure and operations that had yet to come to his attention.

In the months that followed, Rumsfeld mentioned in private the resignation letters he had submitted, even letting some journalists in on the secret during an off-the-record session in November 2004 while traveling in South America. The Pentagon leader often used such sessions to test the reaction of journalists before deciding to go public with something. Sure enough, in early February 2005, Rumsfeld announced the news that his traveling press contingent had been forced to hold in confidence, disclosing on CNN's *Larry King Live* that he had twice offered to resign in the wake of the Abu Ghraib revelations.

By then, Bush had been reelected, and Rumsfeld had been carried over into a second term. With congressional Democrats and other critics still calling for him to leave, Rumsfeld made a point of letting the public know of his prior willingness to go.

———•———

To deal with the congressional and media clamor for information about detainee practices that followed the Abu Ghraib disclosures, Rumsfeld established a special task force inside the Pentagon headed by Pete Geren, a former Democratic House member from Texas who had come onboard as a special assistant to the secretary, and Army major general Michael Maples, then vice director of management of the Joint Staff. He also launched an assortment of investigations, assessments, and reviews with the stated purpose of exposing those responsible for the misdeeds and preventing recurrences. Some, like a panel headed by James Schlesinger, were broad; others were limited to the events at Abu Ghraib. One examined detainee operations only in Afghanistan; another looked at just Special Operations forces. In all, a dozen senior-level reports were issued between 2004 and 2006. But none offered an in-depth, all-encompassing review that could yield a complete picture of what had gone wrong with the handling of detainees, not just at Abu Ghraib but at a number of other prison facilities run by the U.S. military in Iraq and Afghanistan, as well as at Guantánamo.

Pentagon officials promised that all trails would be pursued wherever they led and that the guilty would be held accountable. But some military lawyers, lawmakers, and defense experts pointed to what they saw as fundamental shortcomings in the investigations. In most of the probes, the Army was investigating itself, and each investigation was focused on only one aspect or another of the burgeoning scandal—the role, for instance, of military intelligence personnel who served as interrogators, or the adequacy of training of reservists, or the need for revisions in Army training and doctrine. Not a single investigating authority was given the specific task of assessing the roles of top authorities either in the U.S. Central Command or at the Pentagon.

In Congress, too, the investigative effort failed to match the comprehensiveness of past probes. Republican leaders resisted calls from Democratic lawmakers to establish a special panel of inquiry, as had been done in the Iran-Contra scandal of the 1980s, or to authorize a blue-ribbon commission, like the one that had investigated government mistakes related to the September 11 attacks. Instead, congressional action was kept within regular committee channels. Only the Senate Armed Services Committee, under Virginia Republican John W. Warner, showed any investigative rigor, convening a series of hearings on the handling of detainees. House Republicans complained that such hearings served only to give more political ammunition to critics of the Bush administration.

"Frankly, I think one of the big errors from the very beginning was the way we did those investigations sequentially," Geren acknowledged in an interview several years later. "Somebody early on within the Army should have gathered the whole thing up and said we're going to do detention operations and intelligence operations together—do the whole thing as one great, big deal. But unfortunately you ended up having one doing this piece and another doing that piece and so on. We were our own worst enemy as far as the way we gathered the information and rolled it out."

The closest the Pentagon came to initiating an overarching independent review of detainee treatment was the appointment of the Schlesinger panel, which also included Harold Brown, who like Schlesinger had served as defense secretary; Charles Horner, a retired Air Force general; and Tillie Fowler, a former Republican congresswoman from Florida.

In its August 2004 report, the panel said it had found no U.S. "policy of abuse" or "approved procedures" that permitted the torture or inhumane treatment of detainees. But it contradicted administration claims that the scandal was largely the result of the actions of a few individuals at the Abu Ghraib prison. Examining problems throughout the system of U.S.-run prisons in Iraq, Afghanistan, and Guantánamo Bay, the panel disclosed up to three hundred cases of alleged abuse at other U.S. military-run detention facilities, a far higher number than previously reported and much more widespread. By the time the office of the Pentagon's inspector general issued its report in late 2006, the tally of criminal investigations into allegations of detainee abuse had reached 842.

The Abu Ghraib case remained the most notorious because of the photos and because of the extreme nature of the mistreatment. In some ways, it was also the easiest scandal to explain away as the result of outright criminal misconduct not sanctioned by any law or policy and clearly in violation of Army values. But investigators subsequently cited a larger systemic breakdown—involving inadequate training of guards and interrogators, personnel shortages, and lax oversight—in describing how the abuse was allowed to occur, not just at Abu Ghraib but at other detention centers in Iraq and Afghanistan. The extensive scope and severity of the problems pointed to a general failure in management.

The Schlesinger panel concluded that senior military commanders in the field bore some responsibility for the scandal. Sanchez and his deputy, Major General Walter Wojdakowski, were cited for failing to press for necessary resources to manage the burgeoning number of detainees, for neglecting to take stronger action to correct leadership problems at Abu Ghraib, and for overseeing "a series of tangled command relationships" that fostered confusion in ranks over the handling of prisoners. The Joint Chiefs of Staff and senior officers at U.S. Central Command were also faulted for underestimating the need for detention-facility personnel in postwar Iraq and for not moving fast enough to provide such troops once the demand became apparent. "The abuses were not just the failure of some individuals to follow known standards, and they are more than the failure of a few leaders to enforce proper discipline," the panel said in its

126-page report. "There is both institutional and personal responsibility at higher levels."

The Pentagon's civilian leadership, too, came in for blame for its failure to exercise adequate oversight and to clearly articulate a prison policy. But Rumsfeld's own role goes beyond simply not having been on top of the problem. It is tied up with his decision in December 2002 to approve a set of harsh interrogation techniques for prisoners at Guantánamo and his subsequent decisions to rescind those measures in January 2003 and to issue a revised set of methods in April 2003.

The Schlesinger panel asserted that the techniques Rumsfeld had authorized, while intended for use solely at Guantánamo under carefully controlled conditions, nonetheless "migrated to Afghanistan and Iraq where they were neither limited nor safeguarded." Rumsfeld might have avoided the policy confusion, the panel suggested, if he had encouraged a wider range of legal opinions and a more robust internal debate over detainee policies and operations in 2002, before the war started.

Other Pentagon investigations provided further confirmation that Rumsfeld's approval of the harsh techniques for Guantánamo contributed to the use of aggressive methods against prisoners in Afghanistan and Iraq. A copy of the secretary's initial December 2002 order, for instance, ended up with interrogators in Afghanistan and influenced the techniques employed there even after the order was rescinded in January. The procedures used in Afghanistan were picked up in Iraq by a special missions unit. A copy of that unit's practices eventually became a reference for the chief interrogation officer at Abu Ghraib. When lawyers for the Baghdad command drafted an interrogation policy for all U.S. forces in Iraq, they drew on the April 2003 revised instructions that Rumsfeld had issued for Guantánamo as well as on the experiences of interrogators in Afghanistan.

Anticipating the potential for spillover, Rumsfeld had specified in his April directive that the techniques he was authorizing applied only to interrogations at Guantánamo. But the stipulation ended up having little effect. And the line between Guantánamo and operations elsewhere was blurred in late August when the Pentagon dispatched Major General Geoffrey Miller, the Guantánamo commander, to Iraq to provide guidance and training in interrogation operations.

As the office of the Pentagon's inspector general observed in its report, the migration of techniques occurred because troops abroad believed that traditional methods were no longer effective. Moreover, in the absence of clearly stated policy on what was and was not permitted, commanders and their staffs improvised by relying on whatever official documents and field lessons they considered appropriate. By the time Sanchez and his Baghdad team sought in the fall of 2003 to draft detention and interrogation guidelines for troops in Iraq, they were so uncertain that they changed the interrogation rules three times in less than thirty days, according to an Army investigation conducted by Lieutenant General Anthony R. Jones and Major General George Fay.

In at least one instance, military officers tried to diagram the viral process from Guantánamo to Afghanistan to Iraq that had spread the use of harsher interrogation methods. The diagram made its way into a briefing shown to Rumsfeld on July 17, 2004, reporting on an investigation of detention operations in Afghanistan by Brigadier General Charles Jacoby.

Colonel David Lamm, the chief of staff at the U.S. command in Afghanistan, had meant to exclude the diagram from the briefing because it had not yet been reviewed by the Defense Department's policy office. But a copy turned up in the package of slides that Rumsfeld received before the briefing. As the presentation proceeded by video teleconference from Afghanistan, Rumsfeld, leafing through the pages of his briefing package, stopped at the diagram.

"Dave, I want to talk about slide 27," Rumsfeld said, addressing Lieutenant General David Barno, the senior U.S. commander in Afghanistan at the time. "I can look at this matrix and see exactly now what the problem is."

As Lamm recalled in an interview, Rumsfeld bore in on the links. He wanted to know how authorities that were granted for the treatment of detainees in one place could have been assumed in other places. Who had said the same methods could be adopted? Who was in charge?

But while Rumsfeld may have recognized that some degree of unintended migration had occurred, he never accepted the notion that his actions for Guantánamo contributed in any significant way to the abuses at Abu Ghraib or elsewhere. Nor did he accept the premise that fundamental systemic problems underlay the abuses, according to several senior aides who conferred with him on detainee issues. He was especially disappointed in the findings of the Schlesinger panel. "He thought that with two former defense secretaries on the panel, they should have understood the complexity of the situation," Ryan Henry said. "He thought they should have understood just how much control over forces in the field a secretary has."

In Rumsfeld's view, the basic cause of the detainee mess lay in the field, not in his own actions or in administration policy. He did not see much wrong with the policy. It was the bad behavior of individual troops and inadequate supervision by their superiors that explained the mistreatment. "He thought that the policy itself at macro level was generally sound but that we had significant implementation problems— poor oversight or individuals operating outside of guidance and so on," said Matthew Waxman, a lawyer and former NSC official who took over responsibility for detainee affairs in 2004 in a newly created deputy assistant secretary position.

Indeed, Schlesinger himself drew a distinction between what he called "direct" and "indirect" responsibility. He held commanders on the scene up to brigade level directly responsible for failure to supervise adequately what went on at Abu Ghraib. Rumsfeld and other high-level military and civilian officials were, in Schlesinger's view, only indirectly responsible for neglecting to take the corrective action that should have been taken sooner once the shortfalls in manning and training were apparent.

Schlesinger and members of his panel declined at the time they issued their report to call for the resignation of Rumsfeld or of senior commanders, saying the mistakes they made were not sufficient to warrant their removal. But years later in an interview, Schlesinger remained firm in his assessment that Rumsfeld's actions had been a contributing factor to what went wrong. "The secretary of defense probably should be a source of restraint in these things," he said, "and Rumsfeld had not been a source of restraint."

———•———

In the end, the harshest punishment for what happened at Abu Ghraib fell on the eleven low-ranking soldiers featured in the infamous photographs. Additionally, Brigadier General Janis Karpinski, who commanded the military police unit in charge of the prison, received an administrative punishment and was demoted for leadership failures not directly linked to the abuse. Colonel Thomas M. Pappas, a military intelligence officer who ran Abu Ghraib, accepted an administrative punishment and a fine for inappropriately authorizing the use of dogs. Lieutenant Colonel Steven L. Jordan, a civil affairs specialist who headed the debriefing center at the prison and the only officer to face trial in the scandal, was convicted on one count of disobeying an order and was handed a reprimand.

No top-level figure—civilian or military—was fired for what remains the darkest blemish on the record of the U.S. military's performance under Rumsfeld. He and senior aides contend that a complex leadership structure surrounding the operation of the prisons made it difficult to identify any single individual to dismiss.

On the civilian side, Rumsfeld could have sacrificed Steve Cambone, the Pentagon official in charge of intelligence activities, or Doug Feith, the undersecretary for policy, for failing to issue definitive guidance on interrogation techniques for U.S. forces in Iraq and Afghanistan. But both men were far removed from the abuses.

On the military side, John Abizaid, who as CENTCOM commander was responsible for issuing interrogation policy for U.S. forces in the region, and Dick Myers, who had sought to persuade CBS to delay broadcasting the story that revealed the photographs, could have been relieved of duty. But Rumsfeld relied heavily on both generals, and Myers in particular had argued against Bush's original decision to shift away from full adherence to the Geneva Conventions.

At the field level, it was easier to identify senior officers to hold to account—Ricardo Sanchez, for one, and others in the Baghdad command. But aides said Rumsfeld did not feel it was his position to reach three or four levels down to order a dismissal, and besides, Sanchez was already close to giving up his Baghdad post when the Abu Ghraib scandal broke.

Complicating matters was a dispute over which military command bore principal responsibility for many of the oversight failures—Central Command, which supervised military operations in Iraq, or the Army, whose duty it was to provide the necessary forces and ensure they were appropriately trained and equipped. "You had the Army saying it was Central Command that screwed up, while Central Command maintained it was the Army's fault for not organizing, training, and equipping properly," recalled Larry Di Rita. "The finger-pointing between the service and the combatant command frustrated Rumsfeld to no end."

Of all the military services, the Navy tends to take the firmest no-excuses stand on accountability in cases where responsibility might be blurred. If a ship runs aground, for instance, the captain as a general rule takes the hit, whether he was piloting at the time or not. That approach appealed to Rumsfeld, a former Navy officer. Even so, as Pentagon leader, he consistently avoided exercising his authority to remove somebody in the name of demonstrating accountability. "Rumsfeld spoke often about the admiration he had for the Navy system," Di Rita said. "But he didn't think it was his role as the secretary of defense to make decisions about accountability at lower echelons of leadership. He also recognized that very rarely was there such a circumstance that somebody, just by virtue of being the leader, should be terminated."

In his entire time in office, Rumsfeld dismissed only one senior official—Tom White—and even then he waited months as his relations with the Army secretary continued to sour. While he showed no hesitancy in making clear his dislike of certain other subordinates—or undercutting them, as he did with Eric Shinseki—Rumsfeld tended to stop short of letting people go.

His record in the corporate world had been different. At Searle and General Instrument, he had overseen dozens of firings. But in both positions, he had been driven by pressures to downsize and other economic imperatives. At the Pentagon, he had other considerations. "If he saw the essential competence and value-added in an individual, he tended to stick with him," Di Rita explained. "He's also very loyal to people who are loyal to him."

In the case of Abu Ghraib, Rumsfeld left judgments of accountability and punishment up to the Army instead of to Central Command, which he figured had its hands full with Iraq and Afghanistan. The secretary had hoped the Army would act quickly. Instead, the investigations and prosecutions dragged on for several years. "He was very frustrated with how slowly the wheels of justice turned, if they turned at all," Geren said. "He used to get so darn upset with the Army. He would ask things like, 'Why can't you get this darn thing done, make some decisions, show some leadership?' Yet because of his concern about command influence, he was very respectful of the process and let it work. He said, 'I can't do it but you all can do it. Why don't you do it?'"

A subsequent internal history of the Pentagon's detention practices, prepared for Rumsfeld but never made public, was critical of how long the judicial process lasted. "The length of time it has taken for the Army and the combatant commanders to establish accountability for abuses at Abu Ghraib and other places was greater than what should have been necessary," the report concluded, according to a copy dated November 29, 2006.

Ultimately, the multiple investigations and assessments ordered by Rumsfeld to examine the military's handling of detainees produced 492 recommendations, and in July 2004, Rumsfeld established a deputy assistant secretary of defense for detainee affairs to provide policy advice. Plans called for the new office to focus on the way ahead, while the Geren/Maples task force continued to look back and deal with the fallout from Abu Ghraib and other detainee abuse cases.

"Unfortunately, that division of responsibility couldn't hold," recalled Waxman, who served in the new post until the end of 2005. "We never put the retrospective matters behind us, we never reached closure, partly because the reviews and investigations were never perceived as sufficiently comprehensive and credible to convince the public, Congress, and others that everything had really been examined. There was always the sense that every stone had not really been turned over. The demands on my time to assist with retrospective work, in terms of doing research and responding to congressional requests, very much weighed down the ability of the office to look forward."

During his first three years as defense secretary under Bush, Rumsfeld had experienced remarkable highs and lows in media coverage. Early stories in the late summer of 2001 predicting his demise as the first cabinet casualty had given way after the September 11 attacks and the Afghan invasion to fawning portrayals of him as a tough-talking, confidently commanding war minister. But with the war in Iraq foundering, Rumsfeld's image darkened into that of an overbearing, stubborn, misguided Pentagon leader.

In public Rumsfeld tended to convey the impression that he paid little attention to much of what was written about him. But in private he brooded about the coverage, especially about what he considered inaccuracies and distortions. In his view, a mass of skewed reporting had given rise to a set of "myths" portraying him and other senior officials in a negative light and creating a distorted picture of the administration's deliberations and actions.

On May 18, 2004, he sent a message to Di Rita, who had become the acting head of the department's public affairs office, suggesting that a list be assembled "of all the myths that have gotten circulated over the last three years and what the real answers were" and that the department "try to demystify" them. For starters, he offered up thirty-one items.

The items ranged from a claim that the military could have prevented the September 11 attacks to allegations that the Bush administration intended to reinstate the military draft after Bush's reelection in 2004. The widespread impression that Shinseki had been fired from his post as Army chief of staff made the list. So did the notion that pre–Iraq War intelligence was based solely on Defense Department findings, not on CIA reports.

Several of Rumsfeld's points concerned criticisms leveled against the Pentagon's planning for postwar Iraq: that there was no plan for reconstruction, that the planning had been based primarily on the input of Iraqi exile groups, and that the Pentagon had intended to install Ahmed Chalabi as the president of postwar Iraq. Other items dealt with accusations that Rumsfeld had provided too few troops: that he had overruled requests for more forces from his military commanders, that more U.S. troops in Iraq could have prevented most of the postwar violence and terrorism, and that Osama bin Laden could have been captured at Tora Bora if only the United States had sent more forces.

A number of the assertions were indeed false. Shinseki, for instance, was never fired; he served out his full term, although Rumsfeld did undermine him by selecting a successor much earlier than was the custom and doing nothing to mitigate the affront to Shinseki when word of the decision was leaked. Other points, though, on Rumsfeld's list were less clear-cut. Questions of whether more troops could have prevented bin Laden's escape from Tora Bora or could have reduced postwar violence in Iraq were debatable. And while there was no evidence that Rumsfeld had actually overruled requests for more troops by commanders, his resistance to such requests had undoubtedly inhibited some senior officers from pressing for more.

Rumsfeld remained deeply frustrated by his inability to set the record straight on a number of what he considered falsehoods, exaggerations, or misimpressions. From time to time, he raised the matter with his staff, urging them to be more aggressive in rebutting something that had been said or printed. But he never felt able to get ahead of the tide of myths.

His sense of having been victimized by false media coverage may have contributed to a siege mentality that made Rumsfeld even more combative and intransigent. As much as he relished his frequent encounters with journalists at news conferences and elsewhere, he expressed downright hostility toward media criticism and seemed more intent on rebutting than on exploring whether any of the negative assessments had merit.

As early as 2002, he and his aides developed an aggressive operation to counter the criticism, cultivating a network of former senior officers who were regularly granted special briefings by Pentagon and other administration officials and who appeared on television as military analysts. Often echoing the administration's talking points, this small army of surrogate spokesmen tended to provide a more sympathetic view of Pentagon actions. (Not until 2008, when the *New York Times* wrote a lengthy article about the program, raising questions about the propriety of using former officers this way—and noting that some had undisclosed ties to military contractors—did the Pentagon halt the practice. A subsequent investigation by the Pentagon's inspector general found no wrongdoing in the program.)

In attacking much of the negative coverage of Iraq, Rumsfeld frequently lambasted the media for focusing on what wasn't working and ignoring what was. If only the American public heard and read more about the hospitals being built, the clinics being opened, the schools being staffed, and the economic progress being made, their view of the war would be much more positive, Rumsfeld argued. Instead, the reporting was dominated by images of violence, death, and detainee abuses.

This charge of unbalanced coverage wasn't simply a tactic by Rumsfeld. He seemed genuinely to believe in a different reality about Iraq. This was evident in a five-page paper he sent Bush on June 8, 2004. Titled "Some Thoughts on Iraq and How to Think About It," the paper noted two sharply contrasting views on Iraq, one portraying progress and encouraging optimism, the other fixated on the difficulties and sowing despair. Rumsfeld argued that the positive perspective was the correct one and so should be informing military policy.

The negative view, he wrote, arose from wrongly judging Iraq "against a false standard of countries that have already succeeded in their struggle for freedom, countries that today enjoy relative tranquility." Better, he contended, to compare Iraq to countries that went through difficult wars to toss off undemocratic rule. "What is taking place in Iraq is not unusual," he stated, citing postwar struggles experienced by the United States, Japan, Germany, and Italy. "In each case, it was hard, it took time, but they succeeded to the benefit of the civilized world."

Asserting that "we are on the right course," Rumsfeld warned that the risk of defeat came not from the struggle on the ground in Iraq but from the battle over public perception. "This struggle is being waged during an era of 24-hour news, seven days a week—for the first time in history," he wrote. "And it is being waged during a Presidential election year, when there seems to be a suspension of civil discourse. So, we are in for a rough period of months."

A few days later, on June 10, Peter Rodman, one of Rumsfeld's senior policy advisers, sent the secretary a note commenting on the memo. He cautioned that blaming the media for misrepresenting Iraq's reality was a potentially explosive tactic. "You would need to prepare the ground well," he added. For his part, Bush scribbled back a note to Rumsfeld saying the June 8 memo was the work of a great defense secretary.

—•—

With the end of Bush's first term approaching, and nearly three years into the administration's counterterrorism campaign, Rumsfeld sent the president a memo on June 18 titled "What Are We Fighting? Is It a Global War on Terror?" The three-page, single-spaced paper suggested that the administration may have defined the challenge it was facing too narrowly by calling it a war on terrorism and by viewing it essentially as a struggle between extremists and moderates in the Muslim religion.

Rumsfeld proposed thinking more broadly in terms of an ideological challenge by a minority of radical Muslims against not only Islamic moderates but also much of the rest of the civilized world. Their aim, he noted, was not just to drive the United States out of Iraq and the Middle East but to restore a "Caliphate" over large portions of the globe and to reestablish an Islamic superpower. "I do believe that how we characterize it, how we set it up, directly affects what we do about it and what our coalition does about it," Rumsfeld wrote in his cover letter.

Rumsfeld pointed to the lack of a common perception of the threat. "Europe, it seems, does not understand the problem," he stated, chiding "some Europeans" (notably, the Spanish, who had just announced their withdrawal from Iraq) for thinking they could make a "separate peace." He added that the "UN Secretariat does not seem to get it either." In time, Rumsfeld predicted that Europe would be more threatened than the United States. "Israel, of course, represents the ultimate target in the Middle East—and is seen as an outpost of democracy, progress and Western values," Rumsfeld stated.

If the terrorists were posing an ideological challenge, he argued, then the United States and its allies needed to consider preemptive action "to keep the radicals off balance." That would require more measures in support of moderate Muslims. He also advocated pressing for political reforms to make Middle Eastern governments more representative—particularly in recognition of women's rights—and he urged moves to encourage oil-producing Muslim states to diversify their economies away from a heavy dependence on oil. "Too often, oil-rich Muslims are against physical labor, so they bring in Koreans and Pakistanis to do the labor, while their young people remain idle," Rumsfeld wrote. "An idle population is vulnerable to radicalism, particularly when they conclude it is prudent to pay off the extremists so they can maintain their preferred positions."

Further, he advised making the failure of the Iranian regime a strategic goal of the United States, contending that such a development would be a blow to radical Islam in the way that the Soviet Union's collapse discredited Marxist-Leninist parties nearly everywhere. "So if what is occurring is not a war against terrorism, we need to consider changing how we describe it and seek to get others to see the problem in a new way, because it will affect their attitudes and how they and we approach the critical problem of this decade," Rumsfeld concluded.

Abizaid, given a copy of the memo, wrote Rumsfeld concurring with the notion that the United States confronted an ideologically based challenge. But he disagreed with Rumsfeld's contention that Israel represented the ultimate target in the Middle East, pointing instead to Mecca and Medina, "the heart of Islam," as the end objectives. The main fight, he asserted, would be fought within Islam. "Our problem is to figure out how to aid the moderates without inadvertently undermining their stature and credibility," Abizaid cautioned.

The general took issue as well with Rumsfeld's focus on Iran, noting that its Shia population, along with Shia elsewhere, were on the target list of Sunni extremists. "This is not a struggle about nation states, but rather one of ideology," he stated. "It is Salafist extremism vs. mainstream Islam."

———•———

With the demands of Iraq escalating, Abizaid had been urging that a four-star officer be appointed to replace the three-star Sanchez in overseeing all U.S. forces in Iraq. Such a move would not only have the advantage of freeing Abizaid to spend more time on other pressing matters in the CENTCOM region but would also allow for the consolidation under a single command of all U.S. military operations in Iraq—including Special Operations forces and the Iraq Survey Group, which had been hunting for weapons of mass destruction. Rumsfeld accepted the idea and considered naming his military assistant, John Craddock, to the new position. But he decided against it after concluding that Craddock's close association with him would probably prove a liability in trying to win Senate confirmation.

Rumsfeld settled instead on General George Casey Jr., a mild-mannered, quick-witted officer who had recently become the Army's vice chief of staff. Casey had no previous combat experience, and aside from a stint as a U.N. military observer in Cairo in 1981, he had spent little time in the Middle East. But he was held in high regard by many active and retired officers for his thoughtfulness and calm temperament, and he had shown considerable skill in dealing with international bureaucracies during a tour commanding U.S. forces in the Balkans. Rumsfeld had seen Casey in action during more recent assignments on the Pentagon's Joint Staff as the senior policy officer and, later, as staff director. Casey had appeared very comfortable working at the national level and had demonstrated a good understanding of how to coordinate matters between the Pentagon and the State Department.

Casey's household goods had just been moved into the renovated residence of the vice chief of staff of the Army in late May 2004 when word arrived that he was probably headed to command all U.S. forces in Iraq. At a congressional hearing on his nomination a few weeks later, Casey deferred answers to a number of central questions about the Iraq mission. Would there be enough U.S. troops to deal with the surging violence? How would he coordinate with Iraqi authorities after the transfer of limited authority? What role would private security contractors continue to play? Casey promised to get back to Congress once he'd been out in the field.

Casey was a respected figure on Capitol Hill, and senators appeared willing to cut him some slack until he took up his new post. "I don't know of a tougher job in regards to our national security than the one you're assuming," Senator Pat Roberts, a Republican from Kansas, remarked. Citing the increasing sophistication of the insurgency in Iraq and the inability up to that point of U.S. and Iraqi forces to secure the country's borders, Senator John McCain, the senior Republican from Arizona, impressed on Casey that the situation had reached "a very, very critical" moment.

Casey received little specific guidance from Rumsfeld—or anyone else in the Bush administration—about determining the way ahead in Iraq. The general and the secretary met to discuss Iraq for less than half an hour before Casey headed to Baghdad. Years later, what stood out in Casey's mind about the session was what Rumsfeld had said about the U.S. military's tendency to want to do everything when undertaking activities in other countries. "Our guys are trying to do too much," Rumsfeld told him. "You need to work to change that attitude. We have to figure out how to do less so that the Iraqis can do more."

The message resonated with Casey, who had seen the same thing as a one-star general assigned to the Balkans during the 1990s. Sorting out the international jumble in Bosnia and Kosovo had reinforced in him the risk of an overbearing U.S. military presence.

Beyond that, Rumsfeld left the framing of the strategy for Iraq largely up to Casey and the newly appointed U.S. ambassador, John Negroponte. Casey considered the lack of high-level civilian direction for the high-stakes military mission in Iraq symptomatic of a larger problem in Washington. In his view, while political appointees would stress the importance of civilian control of the military, all too often they failed to provide adequate strategic guidance, instead allowing operations to be driven by short-term events. It was a serious abdication of civilian responsibility. In the case of Iraq, the burden was falling on the new military commander to fill the policy void.

Shortly after being selected, Casey phoned Negroponte, then U.S. ambassador to the United Nations. Most of Negroponte's forty-year career had been spent in the Third World. He had been U.S. ambassador to Honduras, Mexico, and the Philippines. A consummate diplomat, he was accustomed to dealing with poorly run and ineffective governments.

Casey wanted to get off to a cooperative start with the senior diplomat. The two men had met only once, several years earlier. They arranged to get together at the Pentagon, where they began to put their goals and plans in writing. The strong working tie that formed between the four-star general and the veteran diplomat would contrast sharply with the strained relations that had existed between their predecessors, Sanchez and Bremer, and the lack of communication and coordination between CJTF-7 and the Coalition Provisional Authority.

———•———

At the start of the summer, Rumsfeld received word that his longtime secretary, Arlene Nestel, was resigning to take a job as special assistant to the chief executive of General Dynamics. Nestel had first come to work for Rumsfeld in Chicago in the late 1990s and had moved to Washington to continue working for him in the Bush administration. Unfamiliar with the federal government and the military, she had found life in the Pentagon difficult.

The long hours in the job were wearing her out, and Rumsfeld was a tougher and more distant boss as defense secretary. He had a way, in her view, of keeping even those employees with whom he had regular contact off balance. Just when someone might start to feel comfortable with him, she observed, he would do something to rattle the person.

When Nestel approached Rumsfeld to tell him she was contemplating leaving, he went cold, making little attempt to change her mind. He assumed she had already decided to go. He told her he respected her decision and asked when she expected to start her new position. She told him she would start in a month. The next week, she took a previously scheduled trip to Chicago. When she returned, she found that all her tasks had been reassigned to others in the office. Stunned and angry, she went to see Rumsfeld. "Your job as you knew it is gone, done; it's not that way anymore," he told her.

The office staff organized a small farewell ceremony with wine, cheese, crackers, and a cake on Nestel's final Friday in July. When Rumsfeld entered the room with Joyce, everyone fell silent, expecting him to deliver some parting remarks. "It won't be like this at General Dynamics," he quipped before walking over to the food table.

Nestel, who had long been devoted to Rumsfeld, was hurt by the abrupt send-off. All she could figure was that he regarded her departure as an act of disloyalty. Nestel knew all ties were severed when she found her name had been dropped from Rumsfeld's annual Christmas card list.

Years later, the memory of how things had ended with her former boss was still painful for Nestel. But she remained grateful to him for having hired her in Chicago, having given her some tremendous job opportunities, and having challenged her to perform well.

About that same time, Steve Herbits took leave of Rumsfeld as well. He felt the secretary had stopped listening to much of his advice, particularly on personnel issues, and he had grown frustrated with Rumsfeld's performance since the invasion of Iraq. "His behavior from the summer of 2003 was unusual for him," Herbits later observed. "All of his worst instincts were coming to the fore."

As a parting shot, Herbits typed a seven-page report listing problems with the postwar management of Iraq. He questioned why Rumsfeld hadn't handled Bremer as firmly as he had handled Franks, how the decision had been made to disband the Iraqi army, why no one had anticipated the importance of a postwar stabilization effort, and why the de-Baathification edict had cut so widely and deeply.

He likened "Rumsfeld's style of operation" to the arrogant manner of Nixon's White House chief of staff, H. R. "Bob" Haldeman. "Indecisive, contrary to popular image," Herbits wrote of Rumsfeld. "Would not accept that some people in some areas were smarter than he. . . . Trusts very few people. Very, very cautious. Rubber glove syndrome." Rumsfeld was "often abusive" in meetings, diminishing important people in front of others, Herbits went on. "He had a prosecutor's interrogation style. While he was trying to improve product—and his questioning almost always did—his style became counterproductive."

But for all his personal criticism of Rumsfeld, Herbits also saw him as having been poorly served by the small, tight circle of civilian aides. For the most part, they were people Rumsfeld had not known long—or at all—before becoming secretary, people like Steve Cambone, Larry Di Rita, Ken Krieg, and Torie Clarke. Herbits considered them a different kind of team from the one Rumsfeld had surrounded himself with during his first tour as defense secretary. In Herbits's view, they were more political, more out for themselves, more interested in the game of power than the game of policy.

Herbits had written memos to Rumsfeld suggesting some members of this inner circle should go. But Rumsfeld trusted them. "This is a guy who is very cautious," Herbits explained in an interview several years later. "He was never an instinctively trusting person—you had to earn his trust. And it was black or white. If he trusted you, he was too trusting; if he didn't trust you, he was too untrusting."

Indeed, Rumsfeld ended up promoting several of his favored aides to ever-more-senior Pentagon positions. Cambone went from special assistant to the number two position in the policy branch to chief programs analyst to undersecretary for intelligence. Krieg moved from executive secretary of a senior committee to chief programs analyst to undersecretary for acquisition. Moreover, as Rumsfeld shifted them around, he continued to turn to these same aides for advice or action on matters unrelated to the jobs in which they were serving.

Rumsfeld's general preference, too, for small meetings contributed to a view of him as insular. Feith, in his memoir, observed that Rumsfeld's closed style reflected, at least in part, a concern for secrecy. "He worked with his military and civilian inner circle by thinking out loud and inviting comments and challenges," Feith wrote. "He did not like to think out loud in large meetings or in front of people he did not know, respect and trust. He usually insisted on keeping his meetings small, even if this meant barring top-level personnel who had strong arguments for participating."

But while it allowed a degree of confidentiality, Rumsfeld's reliance on a small circle complicated follow-through on projects because members of the circle spent much of their time in meetings with Rumsfeld and were overwhelmed with tasks. John Hamre, a former deputy defense secretary under Clinton, observed as much after briefing the secretary three times on work done by the Center for Strategic and International Studies, which Hamre ran. Each time, Rumsfeld seemed excited about some of the center's recommendations and directed his staff to move on them. But little got done.

"He didn't use people as much as he could," remarked John Young, who headed the Navy's acquisition office during much of Rumsfeld's time. "He had this small coterie of people around him who thought they could run the whole Pentagon. They failed to recognize what a great reach the secretary could have if he used the people willing to do what he wanted done."

CHAPTER 14

Framework for Iraq

When CNN correspondent Barbara Starr sat down for an interview with Rumsfeld in June 2004, in the wake of Ronald Reagan's death, the subject was supposed to be Rumsfeld's reminiscences about the former president. Starr was surprised when the defense secretary shared that his father had died of Alzheimer's, the disease that had afflicted Reagan for some years.

The camera was not yet rolling, and Starr asked if Rumsfeld would be willing to talk about his father on TV. He agreed. Rumsfeld started to recount the pain of watching his dad decay, noting how Alzheimer's is the one illness that is worse on the family than on the victim. During his dad's final year and a half, Rumsfeld was ambassador to NATO, and when he would return to visit, his dad no longer recognized him.

The memory was too much. Only a sentence or two into the interview, Rumsfeld lost his composure. He waved his hand, motioning for the camera to be turned off. "His eyes filled up, his voice broke, he started to cry a bit," Starr recalled. "You could see him physically trying to pull himself together."

The sight of Rumsfeld fighting back tears was sharply at odds with his public image as a tough-talking Pentagon boss, insensitive to the feelings of subordinates and stoic in the face of mounting U.S. casualties in Iraq.

"Suddenly, I wasn't looking at Donald Rumsfeld," Starr recounted. "I was looking at an old man weeping for his father."

Larry Di Rita, in the room at the time, quickly asked Starr not to broadcast the segment, and it was never aired. Starr says the camera had captured very little of Rumsfeld's tearful reaction anyway.

Long after her emotional encounter with the secretary, Starr wondered whether his intensity, obsessive traits, and continued immersion in a fast-paced life—even at his advancing age—was somehow driven by a fear of someday falling victim himself to Alzheimer's. "I've thought at times," Starr said, "that everything about Rumsfeld may just be an effort to keep his mind active and moving because he's afraid what might happen to him if he stops."

———————

With the scheduled transfer of Iraqi sovereignty approaching in June 2004, the Pentagon and the State Department engaged in often argumentative negotiations during the spring over a revised division of responsibilities. The planned opening of a U.S. embassy in Iraq and the assignment of a new U.S. ambassador to the country led Powell to expect the State Department would assume primary charge over American activities. But with about 140,000 troops in Iraq, Rumsfeld maintained that the Pentagon should continue to have a substantial say. While he and other defense officials were quite willing to see the State Department take responsibility for Iraq's political developments, they resisted ceding control over billions of U.S. reconstruction dollars provided by Congress.

Bush ultimately sided with Powell and, on May 11, signed National Security Presidential Directive 36 superseding the prewar order that had given total control over Iraq to the Pentagon. Upon termination of the CPA by June 30, the State Department would take charge of all U.S. activities in Iraq, except for military operations and the development of Iraq's security forces, which would naturally remain under the Pentagon's jurisdiction.

Freed from formal responsibility, Rumsfeld became very proprietary about what missions U.S. forces would and would not perform in Iraq. The extent to which, for instance, the military would provide security and logistical support for embassy and other State Department personnel was painstakingly negotiated in a forty-page document signed by Armitage and Wolfowitz on the eve of transition to Iraqi sovereignty. But Rumsfeld continued for the remainder of his term to quarrel with State Department and NSC officials when proposals arose involving use of U.S. forces for missions he thought should be handled by others, whether protecting diplomats or guarding Iraqi oil pipelines.

Moreover, with the Pentagon's job now narrowed to ensuring security, Rumsfeld appeared even more determined to hold others to account for their roles in Iraq's recovery. He complained repeatedly about the acute focus in high-level administration meetings on what the military was or was not doing in Iraq while little attention was paid to the efforts of other departments. On June 26, he sent a brief snowflake to a handful of senior Pentagon officials grousing that when the subject of Iraq came up at Principals Committee and NSC meetings, Pentagon briefings generally dominated the discussion. He wrote:

> We regularly have PCs and NSCs on Iraq, where the Pentagon always briefs. There is a great deal more going on in Iraq beyond security, including governance, essential services, the economy, the diplomatic side of keeping our coalition partners in the game, getting additional partners, solving the MEK issue [a reference to the Iranian dissident group, the Mujahedin-e-Khalq], progress in developing the ministries, plans for the elections, solving the Kurd displacement issues, etc.
>
> We ought to suggest to the NSC when they try to schedule Iraq briefings with DoD briefing that other departments should put together briefings on other subjects of interest. We need to make it clear that Iraq is not simply a security issue.

Months went by with little change. So in November, Rumsfeld wrote Bush directly, outlining how the agendas of NSC and Principals Committee meetings could be broadened. On the subject of Iraq, he suggested that the State Department be asked to brief on the strategy for elections, economic reconstruction, and "efforts to widen the coalition." He listed a similar set of topics for State regarding Afghanistan. And on the global war on terrorism, he proposed that the Treasury Department report on the "strategy to stop financing of terrorists," that the CIA provide "regular intel assessments," and that State, the CIA, and the NSC staff report on the "strategy to counter global propaganda put out by al Jazeera and other hostile news services."

Given the importance of these issues, Rumsfeld wrote, "I believe it would be helpful for the NSC to be regularly updated on what the various USG [U.S. government] departments and agencies are doing, and whether progress is being achieved. These important threads need to be pulled through the eye of a single needle if we are to achieve success. Knowing who has the lead responsibility and having the lead agencies provide plans and regular reports should provide the high level focus these tough issues will need."

When the curtain came down on the CPA at the end of June, Bremer handed power to an appointed interim government. Taking command in Baghdad at about the same time, Casey, working with Negroponte, put the finishing touches on a new strategic plan that provided the definition and direction previously lacking for the U.S. military mission in Iraq.

The plan recognized that the coalition was no longer an occupying power but would be serving as a support system to the interim government. Labeled a counterinsurgency campaign, the plan made clear that the enemy in Iraq was unconventional and that the nature of the war had shifted since U.S. forces entered Iraq. Success would require a different set of tactics, no longer focused primarily on offensive operations but involving a more sophisticated mix of activities. Several "lines of operations" were stipulated, only one of which involved security. There was a governance segment with the goal of establishing "a legitimate Iraqi government," an economic development piece to ensure that "basic needs" were met, and a communications part to work on tarnishing the image of the insurgents and improving public regard for U.S. and coalition forces.

A main objective of the new plan was to suppress the insurgency sufficiently to allow for a series of elections in 2005. To do this, the military would focus on clearing safe havens where insurgent groups had found refuge. It would aim to secure Baghdad and fourteen other key cities as well as to strengthen Iraq's new security forces. The key to weakening the insurgency, the plan asserted, was to drive a wedge between enemy fighters and the Iraqi people by demonstrating the effectiveness of the new interim government.

While the enemy was seen as dominated by "former regime elements"—essentially former members of Saddam's military and security organizations—foreign terrorists, Iraqi Islamist extremists, and Sunni rejectionists were also part of the mix. This hodgepodge of opponents lacked an overarching ideology. Instead, enemy groups appeared to be bound more by "marriages of convenience," joined in a common desire to see the U.S.-led enterprise fail. Although some former regime elements were considered prone to being won over to the new order, many of the foreign and Islamic extremists were, in Casey and Negroponte's assessment, lost causes and would have to be either captured or killed.

As the plan was presented to Rumsfeld in a series of briefing charts, the secretary painstakingly scrutinized phrase after phrase. At a July 8 briefing, for instance, titled "Framework for Iraq," he fiddled with a page that sought to describe the general conditions in the country. One sentence characterized the economy as "faltering" and "leading" to poverty, unemployment, and some disillusionment. Rumsfeld suggested changing "faltering" to "slow" and "leading" to "exacerbating," according to Casey's notes at the time. Elsewhere, in language depicting the basic strategy as "isolating the insurgency," "ensuring popular support," and "applying military power" to protect Iraq, Rumsfeld wanted the words "help Iraqis" inserted ahead of each phrase. His point was to underscore that U.S. forces were in Iraq to assist, not do the tasks themselves.

Casey shared Rumsfeld's determination to have the U.S. military assume as much of a backseat role in Iraq as possible. But the general also cautioned the secretary that building up the capability of Iraqi forces and turning security responsibilities over to them would take time. According to the plan's timeline, by spring 2005 all Iraqi regular army troops and two-thirds of the police would be manned and trained. Except for in the far western reaches of the country, Iraqi forces were expected to be able to assure governance and security with little or no foreign coalition help by July 2005.

These efforts were to lead squarely to an "end state" defined in a single sentence. Drafted to encompass a range of objectives, the wording stopped short of declaring the establishment of democracy—or even military victory—as final goals. The statement set largely political goals: "Iraq at peace with its neighbors, with a representative government that respects the human rights of all Iraqis, and security forces sufficient to maintain domestic order and to deny safe haven to terrorists."

To Army colonel Will Grimsley, who in May 2004 had taken over as the Iraq policy chief on the Joint Staff, it was striking to see Casey and Negroponte essentially fill what had been a policy and strategy void with a defined course of action after arriving in Baghdad. "Nobody had really identified very specifically the strategic ends we were after," Grimsley recalled.

———

As the campaign plan was being drafted, Rumsfeld asked Casey to conduct a thorough reassessment of the training and equipping of the new Iraqi security forces. Although at least two other assessments had been completed earlier in the year, including those by Karl Eikenberry and David Petraeus, Rumsfeld continued to grope for a clearer view of how the Iraqi forces should be sized and shaped.

"He kept saying no one had ever laid out for him the rationale about why we have an Iraqi army that's this size, why we have an Iraqi police force that's that size," Casey recalled. "My impression was that nobody had ever sat down and said, for instance, 'Okay, Mr. Secretary, we think you need one thousand police in Babil Province because the historic ratio between police and people is 1 to 300 and the security situation in Babil Province is such that that makes sense.' Or explain why ten Iraqi army divisions were necessary. They just hadn't gone through that process."

Since the invasion of Iraq more than a year earlier, the basic assumptions for the types of forces that Iraq would need had changed significantly. Initially, under Bremer, the idea had been to design an Iraqi military oriented essentially toward defending the country's borders and deterring Iran. This approach called for a heavier, less mobile force than was required for domestic operations against an entrenched insurgency. Replacing Paul Eaton, Petraeus came with orders to reorient the program toward a lighter force focused on fighting a counterinsurgency campaign.

Arriving in Baghdad just ahead of Casey, Petraeus quickly drew fresh media attention, appearing on the cover of *Newsweek* under the question

"Can this man save Iraq?" Such prominent, favorable coverage only served to reinforce Petraeus's reputation for courting the press, and Rumsfeld was not pleased by the personalization of the mission in a single general. Moreover, he wanted the Iraqis to understand that they would have to save themselves, not rely on the U.S. military. One of the first phone calls that Casey received in Baghdad was from Myers, telling him to "get Petraeus off the net." Casey then passed word to Petraeus, advising him that he would need to maintain "a little lower profile" in Iraq.

With a new team of commanders in place in Baghdad, Rumsfeld himself seemed reenergized and intent on getting a grip on the conflict. He took particular interest in tracking the buildup of Iraq's new forces. "Rumsfeld was really pushing hard on us—the Joint Staff and his own staff—to get into the development of Iraqi forces," Grimsley recalled. "He'd say, 'I gave you a three-star, he's building a staff, what does he need out there, what do we need to do for him in Washington, and how do we know if we're doing it right.' He was very engaged and wanted to be told what more he could do to help. He would say, 'I can only fight a battle in Washington and help you do things if you tell me what decisions you need from me, what resources you need from me. Do we need to ask for more money? Do we need to spend more time educating Congress on something?' He'd take those on as tasks."

———•———

For U.S. troops in Iraq, the political change from occupying power to supporting partner was supposed to be accompanied by a major shift in military mission and tactics. U.S. commanders spoke at the time of their intention to reduce combat operations and concentrate instead on training and assisting Iraqi forces. But many of the 215,000 members of Iraq's fledgling forces were far from ready to take over much of the security burden. And the deadly insurgency continued to bring fresh waves of violence. While expressing a willingness to step back and let Iraqi forces take the lead, commanders were hedging their bets by keeping U.S. troop levels at around 140,000, although even that level continued to be questioned.

Shortly before leaving Iraq, Bremer had written Rumsfeld reiterating his own concern that the number of U.S. troops in the country was inadequate. Although Rumsfeld had been reviewing the troop level issue regularly with Abizaid, Bremer's letter prompted the secretary to order a more formal assessment by the Joint Staff and Central Command in May 2004.

In a secret memo to Myers and Wolfowitz, Rumsfeld asked for an estimate of "force levels appropriate to accomplish the mission in Iraq." He said that the estimate should include several considerations, including the protection of military supply lines, the CPA, selected U.N. and Iraqi civil officials, and critical infrastructure as well as support for the training and equipping of Iraqi security forces. In his response on July 13, Myers said he and Abizaid agreed that existing forces totaling eighteen U.S. brigades and five coalition brigades were "adequate to perform the current tasks." But he said that options had been developed for more troops "should the current environment change."

Joint Staff intelligence warned at the time that the potential existed for sectarian fighting in Baghdad, Karbala, Kirkuk, and Mosul and that the atmosphere remained unstable. Additionally, Islamic extremists and foreign terrorists were seen as a particular ongoing threat. In a worst-case scenario, the Joint Staff had advised that the total number of U.S. brigades required in Iraq could grow to as many as twenty-five.

"The number of brigades will be dependent upon the security situation, the need for increased security during the elections and whether or not Coalition forces will provide UN security," the Joint Staff said in a secret five-page assessment. "The Coalition is looking at numerous options to put Iraqis in charge as soon as possible, wherever possible. The current projection is that the Iraqi Security Forces will not be ready to take control of the country until April 2005 (at the earliest), but the Coalition may be able to hand over control of specific areas or cities based on the security situation and Iraqi Security Force proficiency. USCENTCOM assesses readiness to hand over local control to the Iraqis much quicker in the north and south than in other areas."

Myers, in his memo, noted that although the Pentagon was prepared to sustain U.S. forces through March 2006 at existing levels, CENTCOM was estimating optimistically that control could be shifted sufficiently to the Iraqis to allow for a reduction in U.S. troops to only seven brigades by January 2005.

Abizaid sent Casey a memo inviting the new commander to request whatever force level he wanted. By his own account, Abizaid would have approached Rumsfeld and pressed for additional troops if Casey had asked for them. But Casey did not see the need.

———•———

Just over a month after taking office, the interim Iraqi government of Prime Minister Ayad Allawi was confronted with its first crisis-management test when fighting again erupted in Najaf in early August. Moqtada al-Sadr's forces had launched fresh attacks on coalition forces, and U.S. and Iraqi troops responded by mounting an assault on Najaf to counter al-Sadr's attempts to gain control of the city. A cease-fire deal at the end of the month led to the withdrawal of al-Sadr's fighters, who had been holed up in Najaf's Imam Ali mosque, and bolstered the authority of Baghdad's political leadership, at least temporarily.

The Najaf battle marked the start of what became a series of U.S. military operations aimed at denying safe havens to insurgents and extending the control of the central government to key provinces. In early October, U.S. forces launched a rapid large-scale attack on Samarra, which had been cleared of insurgents earlier in the year only to see them return and reestablish control. This time the city was cleared in two days.

Next, U.S. commanders turned their attention to Fallujah, the scene of an aborted attempt in the spring to chase out enemy fighters. Since then, the city had become an even greater hub of insurgent activity. Rumsfeld wanted to avoid another situation in which Iraqi officials balked over concern about the political fallout and settled for a cease-fire. In an October 8 memo, he instructed Myers and Wolfowitz to work with Casey on detailing the "red lines" for talks with any groups that might come forward with offers for a negotiated outcome once operations began. At a minimum, he said, the United States in such a case should require the surrender of Abu Musab al-Zarqawi, the leading foreign terrorist in Iraq, and the restoration of an Iraqi government presence in the city. Rumsfeld insisted that there be agreement with Allawi's government that once the assault started, the operation would be carried through to completion.

As details of how U.S. and Iraqi forces would attempt to seize Fallujah took shape, Casey found Rumsfeld interested in a number of specifics, but not overly involved. Rumsfeld wanted to know enough about such things as troop numbers and attack scenarios so that he could brief

Congress and the media, but he left the details of the tactical planning to the military. Further, he didn't want others in Washington looking too closely over the shoulders of commanders. He preferred to shield the military planning from other senior administration and congressional officials. "Rumsfeld was actually pretty good in saying, 'Hey look, don't give the political guys the tactical details—they'll leak them,'" Casey recalled. "For him, less was better."

Rumsfeld also won high marks from Casey and other commanders for making the tough calls in combat and for backing up senior military officers when things went wrong. Under standing rules of engagement for U.S. forces in Iraq, Rumsfeld's approval was required for any air strikes that military planners anticipated could result in the killing of more than thirty noncombatants. Casey made about ten such calls over a period of two months for the assault on Fallujah, which was launched in November after the U.S. presidential election. In response to each request, Rumsfeld might ask a question or two, interested to know how confident Casey was about the intelligence on the insurgents being targeted or about the methods that had been used to identify them. After his questions were addressed, Rumsfeld never flinched. "He's a tough guy," Casey said. "He was the kind of guy you wanted on the other end of the phone."

Similarly, Abizaid regarded Rumsfeld's firmness in battle as one of the defense secretary's greatest strengths, describing him as "a great battle buddy." The general particularly appreciated Rumsfeld's backing when a U.S. air strike missed its target in Iraq or Afghanistan and civilians were inadvertently killed. "I'd call him up and say, 'Hey, we had a bad air strike and we killed some civilians,'" Abizaid recounted. "I would explain that there was either a technical error or an error in intelligence or whatever, and that we would certainly investigate. He never ever got in the way by freezing the action. Quite the contrary." On one occasion, when informed that U.S. forces intending to hit a suspected al Qaeda hideout had struck the wrong house, Rumsfeld told Abizaid, "Maybe next time you should target more houses."

Myers described Rumsfeld as more tolerant of troop mistakes in the field than he was. In 2002, for instance, after an American F-16 fighter jet dropped a 500-pound bomb on Canadian forces in Afghanistan, killing four soldiers and wounding eight, Myers said Rumsfeld expressed concern when he read that Air Force authorities planned to court-martial the U.S. Air National Guard pilots involved. As secretary, Rumsfeld had the authority to intercede and pull the case up to his level. Myers advised Rumsfeld not to do so. (The pilot who released the bomb, Major Harry Schmidt, was subsequently found guilty of dereliction of duty; his flight leader, Major William Umbach, was reprimanded for leadership failures and allowed to retire.)

Rumsfeld tended to grant very broad rules of engagement to military commanders, giving U.S. troops considerable freedom in deciding how much force to employ. "He was very aggressive about killing the enemy," Abizaid said. But Abizaid added that Rumsfeld was not trigger-happy, and was aware that civilian casualties could undercut U.S. military efforts by alienating the very populations American forces were seeking to protect. "He understood and believed that killing people unnecessarily would move us in precisely the wrong direction," the retired general said.

The U.S. military's second attempt to pacify Fallujah ran into none of the political roadblocks that had choked the first go. Nor were there any shortages of firepower. The force of 6,500 U.S. Marines, 1,500 U.S. Army soldiers, and 2,000 Iraqi troops involved in the assault was more than three times the size of the U.S. Marine contingent that had attacked in April. Under a massive barrage of ten thousand mortar shells, four thousand artillery rounds, and ten tons of bombs, much of the city was reduced to rubble. But by eliminating Fallujah as an insurgent stronghold, the battle achieved its main objective.

———•———

In the early fall, the Baghdad command produced a study that charted the violence in Iraq and that showed that many of the attacks were concentrated in just four of the country's eighteen provinces. As many as ten provinces were averaging fewer than one incident a day (an incident being any violent act against the U.S.-led coalition troops, Iraqi security forces, or civilians).

Always eager for statistics that indicated progress, Rumsfeld leaped on the numbers, citing them publicly. The figures also became a regular talking point for other administration officials. But the suggestion that most of Iraq was relatively quiet or stable troubled Wolfowitz. Overall, the violence level was escalating, reaching nearly three thousand attacks in November. "I went to Don and said, 'It may be true that the fourteen are stable relative to where the other four are, but they're not stable relative to where they were a year ago or even six months ago,'" he recalled. "There's been a general deterioration of security."

Wolfowitz thought U.S. military strategy should pay more attention to the fourteen tamer provinces, shoring them up to isolate the insurgents in the four other provinces and eventually extending the secure zone. Rumsfeld seemed open to the idea. For several months, Wolfowitz drafted plans for how to best pursue this strategy. He pushed the approach hard, preparing several versions of the idea for Rumsfeld. But it was never adopted. Underscoring Wolfowitz's waning influence, Bush reverted to the old talking points in a public question-and-answer session at the White House. "Listen, fourteen of the eighteen provinces appear to be relatively calm," the president said.

Privately, Rumsfeld wasn't comfortable relying on a count of violent enemy acts as a main barometer for measuring success. "He kept pushing us to try to find other ways to talk about success," Casey recalled. "We didn't like the violence metric either, but it was there." Other possible indicators of progress—growth in the number of Iraqi security forces or in the number of provinces transferred to Iraqi control—were cited, but they were developing slowly, and Washington was impatient for results.

In the fall of 2004, Newt Gingrich, who was an indefatigable provider of ideas to Rumsfeld, suggested dedicating a room in the Pentagon to showing the state of play in Iraq. He said information displays could be set up that would enable anyone entering the room to obtain a quick picture of progress in the war.

The Joint Staff went to work on the notion, modeling a room after a command center on a ship or an Army command post in the field, where charts and video screens provide commanders with up-to-the-minute views of a battle space—the positions of enemy and friendly forces, aerial surveillance pictures, and ground-camera images. To illustrate the Iraq War, a series of flat-panel video screens were programmed to represent the "lines of operation" of the campaign plan—security, governance, the economy, and strategic communications.

For each line, facts and figures were flashed on the screen and progress was ranked by color—green for good, yellow or orange for less good, and red for needing urgent attention. Initially, red dominated many screens. Only the screen representing the search for weapons of mass destruction was lit in green, indicating no weapons had been found.

Indeed, at the end of September 2004, Charles Duelfer, who had been leading the search in Iraq, submitted a final report that contradicted nearly every prewar assessment made by top administration officials. He told Congress that Saddam Hussein's stockpiles of weapons of mass destruction and production capability for them had been effectively destroyed in the 1991 Persian Gulf War and by U.N. inspectors during the 1990s. No evidence had emerged of "concerted efforts to restart" a nuclear weapons program. Although the Iraqi dictator had dreamed of reconstituting his arsenal of chemical and biological weapons, there was no indication that he had taken steps to do so. Duelfer's report echoed the interim findings of his predecessor, David Kay, who had abruptly left the job in January 2004, telling reporters that the weapons stockpiles cited as justification for the war did not exist.

Rumsfeld showed the metrics room off several times, bringing others from the State Department and the NSC staff to view it. The secretary hoped that it would be used extensively and that identical rooms would be constructed at the State Department, NSC, and CIA. But the idea never caught on in the rest of the government.

———•———

In the face of criticism that he and other senior officials had misjudged the cost and duration of the Iraq War, Rumsfeld took some solace in historical examples of great men who had grossly miscalculated in other wars. Churchill, for instance, had once speculated at the outset of World War II that the conflict would last two or three years. Rumsfeld recalled that and, in late August, asked his speechwriter, Matt Latimer, to find the exact quote. Latimer located it in an October 1, 1939, broadcast.

"Directions have been given by the government to prepare for a war of at least three years," Churchill said at the time, a month after Germany had invaded Poland. "That does not mean that victory may not be gained in a shorter time. How soon it will be gained depends on how long Herr Hitler and his group of wicked men, whose hands are stained with blood and soiled with corruption, can keep their grip upon the docile, unhappy German people."

Rumsfeld also looked at battles in World War II. It interested him that the D-day invasion of Europe, now commonly considered a great military achievement, had been hampered by significant mistakes. He asked Alfred Goldberg, the Pentagon historian, to provide a paper listing all the errors that had occurred. "He emphasized points like that because basically he was saying no military operation is going to be perfect," Latimer recalled.

The same went for postwar reconstruction efforts. As a cautionary tale to those critical of the administration's management of postwar Iraq, Rumsfeld distributed copies of a 1946 *Life* magazine article by the author John Dos Passos titled "Americans Are Losing the Victory in Europe." Touring the devastated cities of Europe six months after the end of the war, Dos Passos found people bitterly disappointed in the U.S.-led recovery effort. He cited European complaints of "ignorance and rowdyism" by U.S. troops, of fumbled U.S. negotiations with the Soviet Union, and of a misguided denazification policy in Germany. In time, of course, such negative perceptions would fade, and U.S. efforts to aid in the reconstruction of postwar Europe would be regarded as one of the great achievements of the twentieth century.

On Rumsfeld's personal reading list were a number of war histories. He had focused for a time on the Revolutionary War period and stories about George Washington, John Adams, and Thomas Jefferson before delving into the Civil War, particularly enjoying a book about Ulysses S. Grant but being disturbed by how much bloodshed had occurred in the War Between the States. Rumsfeld moved next to World War II, indulging a longtime interest in Churchill.

In his office, too, he surrounded himself with images of U.S. historical figures. There was a painting of Dwight D. Eisenhower, which Rumsfeld liked because it showed the former general-turned-president shorn of his usual grin. Another portrait captured a young Abraham Lincoln. A relief of Theodore Roosevelt, which Rumsfeld had obtained in a flea market, bore the inscription "Aggressive fighting for the right is the noblest sport the world affords." The paintings and books all were reminders of tough decisions made by tough men who had also suffered through their share of criticism in their day. Rumsfeld could identify.

But having gone into Iraq and taken on the fight of his life, he was certain of one thing: There was no alternative to seeing the war through. It frustrated him that not enough attention was being paid in the public debate about what it would mean if the United States simply pulled out and the insurgents were allowed to take over in Iraq. On September 28, he wrote Latimer suggesting "a page or two" be drafted "on what would happen if the extremists won" in Iraq.

———•———

While attending to the war in Iraq, Rumsfeld had paid less attention to the one in Afghanistan. Bremer had labored in Iraq under what he and other CPA officials jokingly referred to as "the eight-thousand-mile screwdriver," but senior military officers in Afghanistan experienced what one called Rumsfeld's "salutary neglect." Lieutenant General David Barno, the senior U.S. commander in Afghanistan, had a good working relationship with U.S. ambassador Zalmay Khalilzad, and together, without having to check everything with Washington, they managed to get a lot done.

But in the summer of 2004, Rumsfeld decided to initiate regular video teleconferences with Barno similar to the weekly video sessions he was holding on Iraq with Casey. Preparing the agenda and briefing slides for these forty-minute conferences required considerable effort, and Barno's staff, which was only a fraction the size of Casey's, suddenly found themselves hard-pressed to pull the information together each week.

Rumsfeld, who even on his good days could be overbearing, had a reputation for being exceptionally difficult in video teleconferences. "I'd frequently find myself having to police up the battlefield with my commanders, who all thought that their lives were over because the secretary had been so unhappy with some presentation or other," Abizaid said, recalling Rumsfeld's tendency for disrespectful treatment of briefers. "I'd explain to them that, well, actually, I hadn't read the interaction that way at all."

When Barno's chief of staff, Army colonel David Lamm, was advised by a couple of senior Rumsfeld subordinates to model the Afghan briefings after Casey's approach in Baghdad, Lamm asked for copies of the Iraq presentations. What he found were, in his words, "business charts" filled with statistics showing such things as how many Iraqi forces had been trained so far, how many more were going to be trained in the weeks ahead, and when they were projected to be able to undertake independent operations.

In Lamm's view, the briefings left out the most significant elements of a counterinsurgency campaign, including an assessment of the political climate and a sense of local opinion. Rejecting the business chart approach as inadequate for measuring progress in a counterinsurgency campaign, Lamm and Barno sought in drafting their initial briefing to Rumsfeld to convey some less tangible general impressions.

Rumsfeld was unimpressed. "When are you going to tell me how many guys are being trained?" the secretary wanted to know. "What are the measures of effectiveness? What's the glide slope so we can get guys out of here?" Barno had never made the personal connection with Rumsfeld that Casey had. But the general interpreted the beating he took as a reflection of the secretary's basic impatience to withdraw U.S. forces from Afghanistan. All that seemed to matter was how quickly the Afghan forces could be built up so that U.S. troops could leave.

Disappointed by how poorly the first briefing with the secretary had gone, Barno phoned General Pete Pace for advice. "Just be focused," the vice chairman of the Joint Chiefs told him. "And don't read off notes."

Barno's second briefing didn't go much better than the first. But when he returned to Washington in early September for consultations and met with the secretary in person, he acquired a better idea of the kind of information Rumsfeld wanted in the briefings. The secretary seemed most interested in three main points, Barno concluded: the rate at which new Afghan troops were being generated, the amount of customs fees being raised by the Afghan government (a chief source of federal revenues), and projections for drawing down U.S. force levels in Afghanistan.

For the next briefing that Barno delivered to the secretary by video teleconference from Kabul, the general and his staff prepared charts showing past and projected growth of the Afghan army, along with estimates of the funding and other resources needed to achieve various growth rates. As the briefing got under way, Rumsfeld zoomed in on charts and declared, "By God, Barno, you've got it!"

Lamm was astonished—and elated. They had finally figured out how to satisfy the secretary. Afterward, Barno's briefings tended to be dominated by status reports on the training of Afghan security forces. Only a few minutes tended to be devoted to an update on U.S. military operations. "It was all about how do you get the Afghan national army stood up and get U.S. forces drawn down," Barno recalled.

Similarly, on his occasional visits to Afghanistan, Rumsfeld focused on how quickly responsibility could be transferred to Afghan forces. Usually, his itinerary included a stop at one of the provincial reconstruction teams (PRT) set up around the country in an effort to combine U.S. security with local reconstruction assistance. "He would go to a PRT and essentially ask, 'What are the metrics that tell you that you're finished? How do you get this transitioned then to something that doesn't require U.S. military forces?'" Barno recounted.

As a general rule, U.S. military planners figured that for every three new Afghan army battalions created, one fewer U.S. battalion would be needed. The Afghan government's ability to finance this growing military depended in large part on customs fees collected at border-crossing points. So Rumsfeld took a particular interest in these financial figures as well.

"Rumsfeld wanted to look at security production and at revenue production as sort of a business model so he could figure out when to pull out troops," Lamm said. He pressed for answers to such questions as how many Afghan soldiers and police were considered necessary per thousand inhabitants of the country. "We built the whole campaign plan around very strict metrics for measuring success. Rumsfeld's view of winning the counterinsurgency campaign—his measure of effectiveness—was basically how quickly could we build the Afghan army."

Barno and Lamm worried, though, that Rumsfeld's narrow approach failed to take into account a number of critical factors in how to defeat an insurgent force. In Afghanistan, in particular, securing a stable government would be as much or more the result of negotiating warlord politics and curbing the booming narcotics trade than the result of enlarging Afghan forces. Rumsfeld's predilection for hard metrics left his commanders struggling to express in numbers a situation they believed could be better conveyed in words. "Our challenge," Lamm said, "was to figure out how to operate as an art form but then explain things to the secretary as a science so we wouldn't get into trouble."

———•———

It was often said by those who worked closely with Rumsfeld—and sometimes got their way with him—that he could be persuaded to change his mind. His arrogant attitude and demeaning treatment of subordinates, according to this description of him, were largely tactics, ways of testing people to see if they knew what they were talking about. Down deep, Rumsfeld actually desired pushback—even respected it in people who made the attempt—although he rarely made it easy for them. "He usually was convinced he knew what the right answer was, and if that wasn't the right answer, you had to work extraordinarily hard to disabuse him of that notion," Barno said.

Some approaches worked better than others. One particular lesson that Barno learned arguing against Rumsfeld was that the more analytical one could be, the better. Simply asserting one's personal judgment wasn't sufficient. "People like Rumsfeld who are very successful, they become utterly convinced of their own judgment, their own intuition, to the extent they're not terribly open to other ideas," Barno said. "We suffered to some degree with that with him."

But Rumsfeld was not entirely without an element of self-awareness, a recognition—at times at least—that he was coming across too aggressively, coming down too forcefully on someone. Barno even once discovered that Rumsfeld could be considerate enough to apologize. After one particularly rough session with the secretary during a visit to Washington, the general, who had been ill that day, received a phone call from Rumsfeld, who was riding in his car. Rumsfeld offered an apology for having been so gruff with him earlier. "He said he understood I'd been sick and asked if I was doing all right," Barno recalled. "I was shocked. I was really kind of taken aback."

Several other senior officials who worked closely with Rumsfeld also recalled instances when the secretary showed second thoughts about his harsh treatment of people during briefings. "It was very, very rare," said Feith, who attended countless sessions with Rumsfeld, "but there were two or three occasions when he asked me to stay behind after a meeting and asked whether I thought he'd been too hard on someone. I found that absolutely fascinating. Until he did that the first time, it wasn't clear to me that he even had the capability to ask a question of that kind. He was not oblivious to how people reacted to him. And by the way, every time he asked me, the answer was, 'Yes, you were,' and I recommended that he either send the person a note or call him. And he would do that."

By 2004, after several years of showering the Defense Department with snowflakes, Rumsfeld's memo writing had snowballed into an administrative avalanche. The ad hoc system initially established to track the destination of and responses to his memos was overwhelmed by the sheer number of memos, which reached well into the hundreds each week. Frustrated with the lack of follow-through, Rumsfeld told his new senior military assistant, Vice Admiral Jim Stavridis, that the snowflake system was broken and that a better tracking process needed to be developed.

Air Force colonel Greg Lengyel, another military assistant in Rumsfeld's office, had been waiting for just such an opening, having quietly developed a computerized system to track Rumsfeld's snowflakes. But confidentiality was a major sticking point. Rumsfeld was very particular that his snowflakes be read only by those to whom they were addressed. Pentagon technicians eventually managed to devise a Web-based system for storing snowflakes that was searchable and secure, and Lengyel won Rumsfeld's consent to give it a try.

With the system up and running, Lengyel was able to prepare weekly status reports showing who owed Rumsfeld answers to which memos. Bar graphs indicated how many snowflakes had been issued, how many had been answered, and how many were awaiting responses. The statistics were divided by departmental branch, revealing among other trends that Feith's policy office tended to lag in its responses while the Joint Staff was very efficient. Several officials close to Rumsfeld—notably, Cambone, Di Rita, and Stavridis—received an exceptionally high volume of memos because Rumsfeld was accustomed to tasking them.

Failure to respond promptly could lead to a stressful moment or two with Rumsfeld. "He used to play what I called 'snowflake roulette,'" recounted one senior official who received more of the secretary's memos than most. "You'd go into a senior staff meeting, and he'd have tons of snowflakes sitting there. First, he'd pull out some that you hadn't answered yet, and you'd say, 'Yeah, we're working on it,' and he'd say, 'I want an answer.' And then sometimes there'd be one that you had sent but you'd have no idea what it said because there were hundreds of these things. You wouldn't know which one he's got sitting in his hand, and he'd start talking about it, and you'd think, Oh heck, what was that one about?"

The snowflakes were not confined to Defense Department employees. Rumsfeld also regularly sprinkled some on senior colleagues elsewhere in the government. At the State Department, Powell had a policy of responding to each one, although his staff debated whether to do so. "The snowflakes were an issue—should we answer them or should we not," recalled Beth Jones, a former assistant secretary of state for European and Eurasian affairs. "There was a view that they should be ignored because they weren't worth the effort. But Secretary Powell was adamant that they deserved a response."

At the NSC, officials responded variously. When a memo contained a good idea that the staff intended to act on, Steve Hadley would phone Rumsfeld, acknowledge receipt, and let him know action would be taken, although he would also advise the secretary not to expect any answer back in writing. "You don't need to send back a memo to me on any of these," Rumsfeld would say. "If it's a good idea, just go do it."

When Hadley disagreed with Rumsfeld's characterization of something and wanted to clarify the record, he responded to snowflakes in writing. While Rumsfeld closely tracked responses in the Pentagon and pushed for answers, Hadley could not recall any occasion that the secretary had phoned him to ask why there had been no action on a snowflake.

———•———

In August 2004, Bush announced the most sweeping realignment of U.S. forces overseas since the end of the Cold War. Plans called for dozens of U.S. bases in Germany, Japan, and Korea to be closed, for up to seventy thousand troops and a hundred thousand family members and civilian employees to come home, and for a new network of skeletal sites to be established in eastern Europe, Asia, the Middle East, Africa, and Latin America to support rotational rather than permanently stationed forces.

The initiative represented a move by Rumsfeld to redraw the world map, erasing obsolete garrisons and placing U.S. forces in better position to surge rapidly to wherever crises might erupt. The number of U.S. troops abroad had already fallen by more than three hundred thousand since the Soviet Union's demise, but remaining overseas forces were still concentrated in the same regions that they had been at the end of World War II—Europe, which continued to host about 109,000 U.S. troops, and East Asia, which had about 93,000. Rumsfeld wanted not only steeper cuts in traditional locations but a rebalancing of forces worldwide.

The plan fit with Rumsfeld's vision of a much more expeditionary U.S. military. Early in his tenure, he had begun challenging the notion that certain troops were apportioned to each of the Pentagon's regional commanders. All forces, he argued, belonged to the Defense Department, and the military would be most productive if it were managed globally.

After giving some preliminary thought to the reposturing, Rumsfeld began pushing it in earnest with regional commanders in the spring of 2003, as the Iraq War was getting under way. "He wanted to move quickly," recalled Andy Hoehn, the Pentagon policy official who spearheaded much of the planning. "He said we're going to have an opportunity to make changes worldwide, and we need to do it with some speed."

One factor driving the timing was a plan to seek the biggest round yet of domestic military base closures. Many in Congress, fearful of losing home-district bases, had told the administration not to start that process until it had scrutinized the overseas basing system for possible savings. Rumsfeld asked the commanders to come back to him soon with detailed proposals. He instructed them to think globally, not regionally, and to look for ways of repositioning forces that would favor speedier, more flexible, and more agile military responses and greater cooperation among the military services.

"Some of this started with smaller discussions over whether we need one or two divisions in Europe and what we were going to do about U.S. forces in Okinawa," Hoehn recalled. "But Rumsfeld kept saying, 'We have to make it bigger.' If it hadn't been for him insisting that we look at everything, it wouldn't have happened the way it did."

By the fall, Rumsfeld had the outlines of a plan to present to other members of Bush's national security team. But entering a briefing at the White House in September 2003, the secretary was uncertain how Powell in particular would react. Clearly, a massive repositioning of U.S. forces abroad would have a profound impact on American relations around the world. Some State Department officials had expressed misgivings about disturbing the status quo, arguing that the presence of U.S. troops abroad was important not just to fight but to show political will and to demonstrate continued U.S. security guarantees. "There were indeed some in the State Department who wanted nothing more than for the initiative to go away and who feared damage to alliances if it went forward," recounted Lincoln Bloomfield, who headed State's bureau of political-military affairs at the time.

At the White House meeting, Rumsfeld laid out the plan's concepts, underscoring the enormity of the undertaking and the need for the administration to work together on it. He said that if there was going to be resistance, it wouldn't be worth doing.

Hoehn briefed on some details. Questions and comments followed. Finally, all eyes turned to Powell, who hadn't yet offered a view. He said he had a problem—a bad sign, some in the room thought, figuring Powell was about to try to stymie the plan. Deadpan, Powell said he disagreed with an assertion in the Pentagon's presentation that had described existing U.S. Army bases in Germany as a legacy of World War II. Citing personal experience, the former Joint Chiefs chairman said some of those bases didn't date from that war—they went all the way back to the Franco-Prussian War!

There were chuckles around the table, and relief among Pentagon officials. Powell was onboard—with one condition. The secretary of state said the initiative had to be conducted in full consultation with affected governments around the world.

Consultations soon began. Rumsfeld made it clear publicly that an important factor in determining where to position U.S. forces would be freedom of action. Countries that would impose nettlesome constraints on deploying U.S. troops should not expect to be significant hubs in a new U.S. defense posture. Still fresh in the minds of defense officials was Austria's refusal in 2003 to grant airspace- or ground-transit rights to

U.S. forces heading to Iraq. "We want to have our forces where people want them," Rumsfeld said in Singapore on June 5, 2004. "We have no desire to be where we're not wanted."

When announced, the final plan met with some sharp criticism. A *New York Times* editorial decried the redeployment for making "little long-term strategic sense" and warned it would "strain crucial alliances, increase overall costs and dangerously weaken deterrence on the Korean peninsula" without addressing the chronic strain on ground forces. Senator John Kerry, the Massachusetts Democrat running against Bush for the presidency, also attacked the initiative as dangerous and politically motivated, saying it would undermine America's relationship with NATO. But the countries most affected by the proposal were onboard with it, and a number of defense experts endorsed the changes.

Under the realignment, the majority of U.S. troop cuts were slated in Germany, where all U.S. heavy combat forces were to be replaced with a lighter, more easily deployable brigade of Stryker vehicles and a Special Operations group. In South Korea, the number of U.S. ground troops was due to drop from thirty-seven thousand to twenty-five thousand, and the remaining forces were to shift from congested Seoul into two major hubs in the central and southern sections of the country. In Japan, the U.S. Marine presence on Okinawa was to be thinned from eighteen thousand to ten thousand.

But offsetting these cuts and bolstering U.S. ability to respond in the region, the Pentagon planned to expand the number of Marines, aircraft, and submarines in Guam; increase the Army's presence in Alaska and Hawaii; and add more aircraft-carrier strike groups in the Pacific. Moreover, Rumsfeld and other Pentagon officials had taken a lead in strengthening U.S. military relationships with both South Korea and Japan. South Korean authorities had agreed to assume responsibility for the Demilitarized Zone and to reconsider plans to reduce their own forces. Japanese officials had committed to stepping up government investment in missile defense and other military projects and to hosting the first nuclear aircraft-carrier strike group based overseas.

"In Rumsfeld's view, the whole plan involved a rebalancing away from the European continent and toward Asia, and that's exactly how he described it to the president," Hoehn recalled. "It wasn't so much a matter of bringing forces home as it was of positioning them closer to deal with potential problems in Asia."

Rumsfeld's success in recasting U.S. security ties with South Korea and Japan, both vital Asian allies, contrasted with his management of the Iraq War. It helped, in part, that Iraq drew some of the glare away from the delicate Asian negotiations. But as defense analyst Robert Kaplan observed, Rumsfeld and other senior defense officials seemed more comfortable dealing with East Asia than they were confronting Islamic terrorists and Iraq's ethnic divisions.

Rumsfeld's own experience with Japan dated from his days in Congress, when he had cofounded a group that organized regular meetings between U.S. and Japanese lawmakers. Further, Rumsfeld's vision of a more agile U.S. military that could quickly respond to trouble around the world was, as Kaplan noted, better suited to the Pacific. The secretary appeared more passionate about preparing forces for future challenges there than he did about dealing with the difficulties of counterinsurgency and occupation in Iraq.

"I think, in his heart of hearts, he is a strategist and wanted to be one," said Hoehn, now a RAND vice president. "There's nothing he enjoyed more than thinking big and long term. But a lot of the demands of the job didn't let him do that. In many ways, the Rumsfeld I saw when he was at his best was when he was doing this, when he was trying to look at forces and capabilities and how we're going to line them up to meet future challenges."

As he was repositioning U.S. forces overseas, Rumsfeld reordered the Pentagon's system of regional and functional commands. In his mind, the ultimate aim was the same: to produce a much more effective global military.

Under the structure he had inherited, some parts of the world had never been assigned to one of the geographic commands. Rumsfeld took it upon himself to assign them. He created Northern Command for the defense of the continental United States plus Canada and Mexico. He gave European Command responsibility for Russia and extended Pacific Command's duties to Antarctica. In one of his last acts, he established a command for Africa, which had been treated as a kind of stepchild of European Command.

He also handed new duties, financing, and personnel to some of the functional commands. Transportation Command was given control of various air- and sealift operations to deliver matériel to battlefronts. Strategic Command took on such new missions as missile defense, cyberwarfare, global strike, and the hunt for weapons of mass destruction. And Special Operations Command received expanded authority and additional troops and equipment with which to pursue terrorists.

Further, Rumsfeld sought to break with tradition in selecting top commanders. Each command, run by a four-star officer, is supposed to represent all the services. But some of the services had tended to lay claim to one or another of the commands. An Army officer, for instance, had more often than not headed European Command, while the Navy had seemed to have a lock on Pacific Command. Rumsfeld sent a Marine to Europe and nominated an Air Force general to take charge of the Pacific.

———•———

Despite his business background, the weapons-buying side of the Pentagon never came close to interesting Rumsfeld as much as the strategy. While he had to make major decisions on weapons in preparing annual budgets and conducting Quadrennial Defense Reviews, he showed little enthusiasm for the process. With multiple wars to fight, he had even less time to get into the details of acquisition deals and less inclination to meet with defense contractors.

But early in Rumsfeld's tenure, John McCain had tried calling the secretary's attention to a particular deal taking shape that worried the Arizona senator. At issue was an Air Force plan to replace an aging fleet of refueling jets with aircraft leased from the Boeing Company. Initially, Rumsfeld failed to give the matter much attention. Over time, though, the case festered into a scandal that portrayed McCain as wisely prescient and Rumsfeld as oddly out of the loop.

Normally, the Pentagon prefers to buy rather than lease equipment, but Air Force officials, who laid the groundwork for the plan in the fall of 2001, argued that leasing would enable them to acquire new tanker aircraft more quickly and with lower costs on the Pentagon's near-term budget books. They said the growing demands on refueling aircraft resulting from a post-9/11 surge in military activity, coupled with the corroded condition of the existing fleet, made replacing the planes an urgent necessity.

For Boeing, the world's largest manufacturer of jets, the $23 billion proposal to lease one hundred aircraft promised new life for its 767 production line, which was struggling to survive in the face of declining commercial orders. The plan also had powerful backers on Capitol Hill, among them House speaker Dennis Hastert, an Illinois Republican whose state is home to Boeing headquarters.

But critics blasted the proposal as an extravagant sweetheart arrangement and a waste of taxpayer dollars. They challenged the need for such urgency, contending that the corrosion that Air Force officials claimed was eating away at existing KC-135 Stratotankers was manageable. They asserted that the planes could be upgraded at a much lower long-term cost than the lease plan. Opposition came not only from outside research groups and defense experts but from inside the government, including the White House budget office and the Pentagon's office of program analysis and evaluation.

Leading the charge in Congress as head of the Senate Committee on Commerce, Science, and Transportation, McCain began slamming the idea in late 2001 as a taxpayer "rip-off." But when he raised the issue with Rumsfeld, the secretary seemed somewhat dismissive. "We invited the senator over to lunch one day, and he was steaming because he had heard about this tanker lease deal," recalled Powell Moore, Rumsfeld's legislative affairs director at the time. "Well, the secretary doesn't focus on everything, and he had not focused on the tanker lease deal, and he didn't have the same sense of outrage that McCain had about it. So that touched off a standoff."

Never close to begin with, the relationship between the strong-willed defense secretary and the similarly hard-nosed Republican senator turned increasingly sour as the Pentagon proceeded to push the leasing arrangement. Pete Aldridge, the Pentagon's top procurement official, formally recommended the deal to Rumsfeld in May 2003 as one of his last actions before leaving the Defense Department, and Rumsfeld approved it. Two months later, Rumsfeld nominated James Roche, who as Air Force secretary had masterminded the leasing plan, to be the new Army secretary. McCain had no intention of allowing that nomination—or, for that matter, the nomination of other senior defense officials—to proceed until he got satisfaction on the tankers, and so he exercised his senatorial prerogative to block confirmation.

By early November 2003, the Pentagon had worked out a compromise with lawmakers and Boeing that called for the Air Force to lease twenty tankers and to buy up to eighty more. But shortly afterward, the deal fell apart when a Boeing investigation revealed that during negotiations a year earlier, the company's chief financial officer, Michael M. Sears, had spoken to the key Air Force official overseeing the project, Darleen Druyun, about a possible job for her at Boeing. Druyun had since gone to work for Boeing, and she and Sears had sought to cover up evidence of their improper contacts.

The disclosure turned the leasing arrangement, which had initially been portrayed by opponents as a poster child for wasteful government spending, into an outright corruption scandal. Druyun and Sears were fired, and investigations by the Justice Department and other agencies were initiated against them. Boeing's chief executive, Philip Condit, resigned.

Several reports in the spring of 2004—one by the Pentagon's inspector general, another by the National Defense University, and a third by the Defense Science Board—took the Air Force to task for bypassing normal Pentagon contracting procedures and for failing to do sufficient homework in drafting the deal. In late May, Rumsfeld deferred further action on the tanker program until more studies could be completed. And he sought to mollify McCain, who had been demanding documents, e-mails, and other internal government papers and who was continuing to hold up military nominations. As many as twenty appointments, including the selection of Casey to take command in Iraq, had run into delays.

"My plan is to be as cooperative as we can be," Rumsfeld wrote Alberto Gonzales, the White House counsel, on June 9. "Senator McCain is holding up a number of the President's DoD nominations. It is increasingly difficult to run the Department with so many key open positions, and particularly during a war. The only reason I would not be fully cooperative is if the President decided it was a matter of privilege. I am at the point where I believe the interests of the Department and, absent advice to the contrary, the interests of the administration are that we provide these materials to the Committee. Please let me know if you agree; and, if not, which documents the President wishes to withhold."

That summer, Rumsfeld arranged a private meeting with McCain in hopes of smoothing the waters. But the meeting turned into a turbulent exchange of views. The senator went public with copies of Pentagon e-mails showing that the Air Force and Boeing had worked as partners to promote the controversial agreement and that some Air Force officials continued to press for the contracts even against mounting opposition within the government.

In October 2004, Congress finally terminated the Air Force's authority to lease the tanker aircraft. The next month, Roche, who had remained Air Force secretary after his nomination to head the Army was blocked, and the official in charge of Air Force acquisition, Marvin R. Sambur, resigned.

Meanwhile, Druyun admitted in federal court proceedings that, as a favor to Boeing, she had agreed to a higher price for the tankers than she had thought appropriate. She also acknowledged favoring Boeing on three other Air Force contracts involving C-130 and C-17 cargo aircraft and a NATO airborne early-warning and control system. After pleading guilty to a conflict of interest charge, she was sentenced in October to nine months in prison. Sears, the Boeing official who hired her, entered a similar guilty plea and received a four-month jail term in February 2005. And in May 2006, Boeing agreed to pay $615 million to settle all liability for the tanker scandal and for an unrelated impropriety. It was the largest penalty ever paid by a defense contractor.

Despite his role in approving the deal, the scandal never tarnished Rumsfeld. A report by the Pentagon's inspector general in May 2005 placed principal blame on Aldridge, Roche, Sambur, and Druyun. It had no comment on Rumsfeld's involvement.

Establishing the full extent of Rumsfeld's involvement proved challenging for investigators. In an interview with two members from the office of the Pentagon's inspector general on April 1, 2005, Rumsfeld professed uncertainty over how his department had come to support the plan in the first place. Citing the demands of the aftermath of the September 11 attacks and of the wars in Afghanistan and Iraq, Rumsfeld noted how little of his attention had been devoted to weapons buying. "My time basically in the Department was focused on those things and certainly not on acquisition or—or what have you," he said.

His part in the tanker lease deal, he claimed, was "modest," and he added, "I don't remember approving it. But I certainly don't remember not approving it, if you will." At another point, he said, "I must have been sufficiently comfortable with the package or it wouldn't have happened. I obviously didn't run out with my hair on fire and say, 'Stop it! Don't do that!' Because it was done."

Pressed to explain his evident distance from such a major and unusual weapons contract, Rumsfeld said it was his custom to rely on senior acquisition officials who had authority to make many decisions themselves. "Basically, I spend an overwhelming portion of my time with the combatant commanders and functioning as the link between the president . . . and the combatant commanders conducting the wars," he explained.

He could not recall what initial guidance he had given Aldridge or Air Force officials or what he may have known at the time about the internal debate over cost, aircraft pricing, and other aspects of the proposed arrangement. He suggested that the sheer volume of issues that were presented to him had left him unable to remember details about many things. "I work in here, I am going to guess, twelve hours a day," he said. "I also know that people come in and out of this office all the time. Send me memos, half of which I—are appropriate for me to have, some of which aren't, which I don't read. And call or come in and say, I am going to do this, or, What do you think about that."

Rumsfeld asserted that he considered it his responsibility not to attend to the details of acquisition deals but to choose the right people to oversee such matters and to ensure the proper guidelines. "My task is not to pick tankers," he said. "My task is to see that we get people in here. My task is to see that the systems and procedures are changed and fixed so that the likelihood of something like this happening again are dramatically reduced."

His performance with the investigators was vintage Rumsfeld—factually correct as far as it went, but with a lot of bobbing and weaving, effectively distancing himself from a bureaucratic mess that had developed right under his nose. He may well have had little to do with conceiving the deal or promoting it, but he also wasn't doing much to help his own inspector general's office sort through the record.

The inspector general's report contains a couple of references indicating that Rumsfeld was briefed on the deal by Roche in January 2003 and held a meeting with senior officials from his staff and from the Air Force in March 2003 to consider whether to accept the lease proposal or proceed with a purchase. There is also evidence of Rumsfeld's eagerness to avoid involvement with the deal. In their meeting on January 31, 2003, for instance, Rumsfeld indicated to Roche that he wanted the decision on whether to lease delayed until after he had testified to Congress on the recently submitted defense budget plan that contained a provision to buy the planes. "Don asked that the decision be delayed until after he testified!!!" Roche reported in an e-mail to General John Jumper, the Air Force chief of staff, after the meeting. "Note: he doesn't want to touch it. But there is no doubt that he understands our position."

———•———

In a November 2 memo about the Druyun case addressed to the department's civilian and military leadership, Rumsfeld asked, "How could such major corruption happen, over such a long period, without those serving above and around her seeing her corruption and reporting it to the proper authorities?"

He answered by blaming the scandal largely on high turnover among other senior managers who, he suggested, might have questioned some of Druyun's decisions if they had been on the job longer. From the time Druyun became the Air Force's deputy acquisition chief in 1993 until she left to join Boeing in early 2003, there were five different secretaries or acting secretaries of the Air Force and four different people in the job overseeing all Pentagon acquisitions. The assistant secretary's post directly responsible for supervising Druyun lay vacant for four of the ten years she served, Rumsfeld noted, and in the other six years it was filled by four different people. Such "turbulence" in senior positions, Rumsfeld warned, contributes to "an environment that is hospitable to corruption. And corruption is what we got."

Rumsfeld did not in his memo explore all the causes of the employment turnover, but he did link the problem to one of his pet peeves about the federal job system: the difficulties posed by an elaborate—and slow—congressional confirmation process. It was an issue that Rumsfeld had started complaining about early in his tenure, and the problem, in his view, had only gotten worse.

Two days after writing on the Druyun case, he fired off an exasperated memo to Dina Powell, the White House personnel director. He noted that the "vacancy rate" in the four dozen or so politically appointed positions at the Pentagon had run at about 20 to 25 percent during the Bush administration's first term. The Army secretary post, he pointed out, had been vacant eighteen months "because of the refusal of the Senate to confirm a nominee." He added that the Army secretary was the Pentagon's "executive agent" for handling detainee issues.

"Something has to be done to fix this process," he declared. "There is only a modest veneer of civilian control in the Department of Defense." With so many top jobs unfilled, "a President's grip on the Executive Branch is even thinner. DoD is responsible for more than three million people, including the active force, the reserve components, civilians and contractors, and a budget of more than $400 billion. Operating at a 20–25 percent vacancy rate during a war is unacceptable. This process needs to be fixed."

Dan Stanley, who served in the Pentagon's legislative liaison office under Rumsfeld as deputy and later director, was sympathetic to the secretary's complaint. But he thought Rumsfeld was also part of the problem. The secretary was asking for trouble, for instance, when he tried to have Roche approved as the secretary of the Army given Roche's prominent role in promoting the tanker lease deal. A less controversial nominee would probably have stood an easier chance of confirmation. On other occasions, Rumsfeld had delayed the selection process by hemming and hawing over candidates. "If you look at the record, the fact of the matter is the long pole in the tent was the secretary actually making a decision about an individual," Stanley said. "It wasn't the Senate."

———————

In small ways as well as big, Rumsfeld took steps now and then that seemed to confirm his reputation for keeping his fingerprints away from where he didn't want them found. When he became aware in 2004, for instance, that all the papers passing through his office were being marked with a stamp that said, "Secdef has seen," he instructed his secretary, Delonnie Henry, to stop using the stamp, saying it gave a false impression. "Just because something has come into my office and touched my inbox and gone into my outbox, it doesn't mean I saw it, it doesn't mean I read it, it doesn't mean I processed it," he told her. "It means it moved from one box to the other, and that's all that anybody will ever know for sure. So you're never to do that again."

Henry discarded the stamp and adopted a different system for recording which documents had entered and exited Rumsfeld's office. She considered it important to have some way of documenting the paper flow. "I'd put a checkmark on each paper that moved, then my initials and the date," she recalled in an interview. "Otherwise, because there was so much paper, somebody could come back and give me something a week later, and unless I had read it and processed it the first time, I wouldn't have known if it had already been in to him or not."

Henry saw Rumsfeld's opposition to the use of the "Secdef has seen" stamp as an indication of his discomfort with being held accountable later for having looked at something that had crossed his desk. "He didn't like being pinned down," she said. "Even though he likes to think he bellied up to the bar and took responsibility for things, if you listen and read very carefully what he said, he had a way of passing the buck."

———•———

As the presidential election approached in November, speculation about a potential second Bush term centered on the likelihood of cabinet changes. With Iraq in chaos, some thought that Rumsfeld was sure to be let go. Others, recognizing that Rumsfeld's departure would be seen as a broader acknowledgment of the administration's failure in Iraq, were less certain. Powell, the most popular member of the administration, had made known his plan to leave, although reports were also circulating that the president might try to persuade him to stay. Some speculated that Powell would condition his answer on whether Rumsfeld would be going as well.

Since David Obey's call for the resignation of Rumsfeld and Wolfowitz in September 2003, a number of other members of Congress had appealed for a new defense secretary. Representatives Charles Rangel (D-NY), Mark Udall (D-CO), and Diana DeGette (D-CO) did so in May in the immediate aftermath of the Abu Ghraib disclosures. Joining in soon after were Democratic presidential candidate John Kerry and Representative Nancy Pelosi (D-CA), the House minority leader. Senators Joe Biden (D-DE), Jon Corzine (D-NJ), and Tom Harkin (D-IA) and Representative George Miller (D-CA) subsequently added their voices to the cry for new leadership. The Congressional Black Caucus issued a statement that Rumsfeld's time was up, as did such publications as the *New York Times* and the *Economist*.

Notwithstanding Rumsfeld's particular problems with McCain stemming from the tanker lease deal, there had not yet been a break in senior ranks on the Republican side. But in the president's inner circle, there was increasing desire for a change at the Pentagon. Powell certainly favored it. Rice and her deputy, Steve Hadley, considered it advisable under the right circumstances. And Andy Card had begun suggesting to Bush that he consider replacements.

Card had great regard for Rumsfeld's intelligence, breadth of experience, energy, and patriotism. But he recognized that Rumsfeld's usefulness as defense secretary may have run its course. In the weeks before the election, Card had urged the president to look hard at whether to keep Rumsfeld in a second term, and he raised the question again after the election when Bush took a long weekend at Camp David to mull his cabinet lineup.

But the president remained reluctant to do anything that might disrupt the management of the war and wasn't convinced that anyone else could easily take over from Rumsfeld. Besides, he valued Rumsfeld's efforts to shake up the Pentagon and to pursue a transformation agenda. Cheney, too, had warned that removing Rumsfeld risked being perceived as a sign of the president's own misgivings about the war. Moreover, naming a new defense secretary and trying to win Senate confirmation would invite fresh debate over the handling of the war.

In the end, it was Powell, not Rumsfeld, who was asked to resign. The move appeared at first to play to Rumsfeld's advantage. Without Powell's moderating influence, Rumsfeld's hawkish tendencies would presumably meet less resistance. Moreover, Bush had decided to make Rice the new secretary of state—a move viewed, at least at the Pentagon, as apt to bring the department more in step with administration policy. While Rumsfeld had chafed at Rice's management abilities as national security adviser, he viewed her as a team player, and with her at State, he wouldn't need to try as much to offset that department.

Indeed, there was a noticeable reduction in tensions and mutual suspicions between State and Defense in the months immediately following Powell's departure, with top officials in both departments working more easily together on shared initiatives such as expanded Pentagon authority for foreign security assistance and additional funds to build up State's new office for postconflict reconstruction activities.

Additionally, Rumsfeld was glad to see Hadley succeed Rice as national security adviser. Low-key, even-keeled, tireless in his attention to detail, Hadley had a knack for ensuring that no one felt excluded or blindsided in high-level administration deliberations. Rumsfeld viewed him as an honest broker who drew out the best ideas from the cabinet and presented them to the president. Further boosting Rumsfeld's confidence in the NSC was the arrival there of two people who had worked for him: J. D. Crouch, a former assistant secretary of defense, was picked to replace Hadley as deputy director, and William Luti, another Rumsfeld loyalist in the Pentagon's policy branch, was named as the new NSC director for defense policy.

Even with these personnel shifts, though, Rumsfeld's standing within the administration was eroding. He appeared less assertive in Middle East policy and other areas outside his Pentagon lane. And within months, he began to face more pointed challenges from Rice, Hadley, and some of their senior aides about the handling of the Iraq War, detainee policies, and other matters. While he had been able to lay claim to a greater affinity with Bush than Powell had, Rumsfeld could not presume any such edge over Rice and Hadley, both of whom had been with Bush since the start of his run for the presidency and had close, trusting relationships with him.

No sooner had Bush indicated that he would not be naming a new defense secretary than Rumsfeld ignited a new controversy. In early December, at a town hall meeting with National Guard troops in Kuwait, where units were preparing to deploy northward into Iraq, he was met with skeptical questions from soldiers, who complained they were being sent into combat with insufficient protection and equipment.

By then, the strains on the U.S. military as a result of the prolonged wars in Iraq and Afghanistan were impossible to ignore. The combined conflicts had occupied the bulk of America's frontline ground forces. More than half of the regular Army's fighting forces had served in Iraq or expected to be on their way there soon, along with a substantial percentage of the Marine Corps and historically high proportions of the Army National Guard and Reserves. Rotations were being accelerated, with units that had already served in Iraq returning for second tours.

Recruitment of new Army National Guardsmen had dropped almost 30 percent, and, despite enlistment bonuses, the regular Army was hurting, too. Shortages of armor and other equipment remained a chronic problem and underscored how ill-prepared the Army and Marine Corps had been for the demands placed on them.

At the town hall meeting in Kuwait, Specialist Thomas Wilson, a scout with a Tennessee National Guard unit, told Rumsfeld that troops had to dig through landfills for pieces of scrap metal and bulletproof glass to bolt onto their vehicles for protection against roadside bombs in Iraq. "Why don't we have those resources readily available to us?" Wilson asked, drawing cheers and applause from many of the 2,300 troops assembled in a cavernous hangar to meet the secretary.

Rumsfeld responded that the Army was producing extra armor for Humvees and trucks as fast as it could, sparing no expense. But he added that only so much was physically possible. "As you know, you go to war with the Army you have," he remarked. "They're not the Army you might want or wish to have at a later time." Noting that he had discussed the armor issue at length with people at the Pentagon, Rumsfeld further suggested that armor is not the guarantee of safety that some think it is. "You can have all the armor in the world on a tank and a tank can be blown up," he said. The same applied, he added, to the much smaller Humvee utility vehicle used extensively in U.S. convoys and patrols in Iraq.

A few minutes later, a soldier from the Idaho National Guard's 116th Armor Cavalry Brigade complained that active-duty troops seemed to be getting priority over Guard and Reserve units for the best equipment used in Iraq. Rumsfeld took his time to answer as a murmur spread through the crowd. "Now settle down, settle down," he said. "Hell, I'm an old man, it's early in the morning, and I'm gathering my thoughts here."

Rumsfeld explained that all organizations had equipment of different vintages, but he expressed confidence that Army leaders were assigning the newest and best equipment to the troops headed for combat, who were most in need. That said, he warned that equipment shortages would probably continue to bedevil some American forces entering combat zones like Iraq.

Another soldier asked how much longer the Army would use its "stop loss" power to prevent soldiers from leaving the service who were otherwise eligible to retire or return to civilian life at the end of their enlistment. Critics had pointed to this provision as a further sign that the Army had been stretched too thin. But Rumsfeld described it as simply a fact of life for soldiers in times of war. "My guess is it will continue to be used as little as possible, but that it will continue to be used," he said.

Rumsfeld's remarks, which made headlines, reinforced his image as insensitive and dismissive. Days before, in another seeming sign of disregard, news had emerged that the Pentagon had been using a signature machine to pen Rumsfeld's name to letters of condolence to the families of soldiers killed in Iraq. Relatives of the dead voiced anger and indignation at what they perceived as an unfeeling act by the secretary. Rumsfeld himself was surprised and upset by the disclosure. He had personally written each of the letters and had signed a number of them. But he had given Di Rita authority to approve use of the signature machine, and as a matter of expediency, Di Rita had routed some condolence letters through the machine. Rumsfeld never blamed Di Rita publicly, but he issued a statement promising to sign all condolence letters in the future with his own hand.

In the wake of further negative fallout from the Kuwait appearance, Rumsfeld argued that his remarks had been taken out of context and that he had sought to address the concerns of the soldiers. But his tone had clearly struck a chord. And the complaints of the soldiers reinvigorated protests that the Bush administration had failed to anticipate the kind of tenacious insurgency that troops were facing in Iraq.

That some soldiers would dare confront Rumsfeld directly on the readiness and equipment issue in such a public setting was surprising. In his town hall–style meetings with troops, Rumsfeld usually received questions about general policy or very specific complaints about pay or benefits. The group in Kuwait was made up largely of reservists, who may have felt bolder about challenging the secretary. In any case, interviews afterward revealed that the equipment issue resonated with many soldiers and commanders. Rumsfeld's handling of the issue also drew criticism from pundits, who saw the defense secretary as refusing to accept responsibility. William Kristol, editor of *Weekly Standard*, accused Rumsfeld of "arrogant buck-passing" by pushing off responsibility for the armor, as he had for troop levels, to the generals.

The episode gave rise as well to the first public expressions of eroded support by Republican members of Congress. McCain expressed "no confidence" in Rumsfeld, stopping just shy of calling for the secretary's resignation. Other Republican senators followed—among them, Trent Lott of Mississippi, Susan Collins of Maine, and Chuck Hagel of Nebraska—voicing diminished regard for Rumsfeld and criticism of his management of the war.

Back at the Pentagon after his visit to Iraq, Rumsfeld tried to get on top of the armor problem. He seemed uncertain where to place the blame—on the Army and Marine Corps for not doing enough to meet the requirements of the regional commanders, or on the regional commanders for setting too many requirements that the services just couldn't meet. On December 14, he fired off a memo to Myers demanding more be done:

> If this Department is not capable of meeting the AOR [area of responsibility] needs on armor and fixing the issue that has been raised about possible preference to active forces versus Guard and Reserve, given that they are the responsibilities of the Services to organize, train and equip, then I would think it is the responsibility of the Combatant Commanders to adjust their strategies and tactics to fit the capabilities of the Services to organize, train and equip. We can't have strategies devised by the Combatant Commanders that the Services have demonstrated they are not capable of meeting by way of training and equipment. My suggestion is this: until the Services can organize, train and equip the forces in a way that fits the tactics and strategies being used by the Combatant

Commanders, the Combatant Commanders need to call a halt to what they are doing, and revise their tactics temporarily until they can bring closure on seeing that the two separate responsibilities mesh properly.

A week later, he instructed Myers and Pace to provide written reports at least three times a week on what had been done to ensure troops weren't driving around in unprotected vehicles. In a memo to the two generals, he offered several suggestions for what commanders could do if they found themselves facing a shortage of armored vehicles. He recommended bolting armor on each vehicle that needed to be taken outside a protected compound, mounting a massive "Berlin airlift" to fly large quantities of reinforcing material forward, and hiring more contractors to bring in the necessary materials. Additionally, he advised consolidating the vehicles that needed armoring into fewer locations until more armored vehicles were on hand and, as a last resort, changing tactics to rely on fewer vehicles. "I need a date certain—soon—when no U.S. forces will be traveling in Iraq, outside of protected compounds, in vehicles without appropriate armor," he declared.

———•———

By December 2004, U.S. commanders in Iraq had concluded that the insurgency was so entrenched that it was unlikely to be defeated in a matter of months or even a few years. A briefing to Rumsfeld on December 15 titled "Post-Election Posture" reported that insurgents had "gotten better organized over the past year," while the Iraqi government still lacked the ministerial capacity to "manage a counterinsurgency campaign." Iraqi intelligence organizations had "not developed nor consistently produced meaningful intelligence on the insurgency." Iraqi forces, while progressing, could take years to develop the capacity for independent operations, the briefing said. Rumsfeld was advised that the insurgency would "continue at roughly the present level throughout 2005 in Sunni areas" and that the performance of Iraqi forces would "remain mixed."

The next day, Bush heard a similar assessment. Although the campaign plan was described as "broadly on track," he was told to expect that by the end of the following year, Iraq would still be facing "an insurgency, a dilapidated infrastructure, long-term development challenges and meddling from unsupportive neighbors."

History had shown that once insurgencies had taken hold, they took time to uproot—nearly a decade or more, according to a study ordered by Casey that looked at other counterinsurgency efforts in the twentieth century. The study was done by Kalev Sepp, a retired Special Forces officer with experience fighting in El Salvador and Panama and a doctorate in history from Harvard. Distilling the lessons of fifty-three counterinsurgencies, Sepp, who was then an assistant professor at the Naval Postgraduate School, drew up two lists of factors—one characterizing winning campaigns, and the other, losing ones.

It wasn't difficult to see that, during the first year of occupation at least, the U.S. military operation in Iraq had shown many traditional features of a losing counterinsurgency effort. Its intelligence operations were inadequate. The priority had been on killing or capturing the enemy rather than on engaging the population. There hadn't been much of a psychological operations campaign. U.S. military units had tended to remain concentrated on large bases for protection. U.S. Special Forces were focused on raiding. Efforts to place U.S. military advisers with Iraqi forces had received low priority. And the Iraqi military was being built and trained in the image of a foreign force, the U.S. Army.

Casey underscored with Rumsfeld that even successful counterinsurgency campaigns had tended to drag on, although it would be another nine or ten months before Casey would make this point in public. The notion that the United States was facing a protracted struggle in Iraq destined to last more than a decade conflicted with the administration's continued suggestion that the war, or at least the U.S. military presence in Iraq, could begin to start winding down within a year or so, when plans anticipated that Iraqi forces would reach a threshold and begin to carry out counterinsurgency operations independently. Testifying with Rumsfeld before the Senate Armed Services Committee on September 29, 2005, Casey interjected a sober note into such wishful thinking.

"The average counterinsurgency in the twentieth century has lasted nine years," Casey told the committee. "Fighting insurgencies is a long-term proposition, and there's no reason that we should believe that the insurgency in Iraq will take any less time to deal with." As he spoke,

Casey glanced out of the corner of his eye at Rumsfeld, who was seated beside him. "The secretary was just looking straight ahead," Casey later recalled. "Up to that point, no one had said publicly how long we should plan on this taking."

The counterinsurgency study had iterated the importance of developing strong indigenous troops to carry on the fight. No great power to date had succeeded against an insurgent force without a capable local partner. In Iraq, Casey concluded, it was time to step up efforts to shift the burden of the counterinsurgency fight to the Iraqi military and police.

The study also showed that in successful counterinsurgencies, foreign military advisers were present with indigenous forces. U.S. authorities had seen this demonstrated in the fighting in Najaf in August and in Fallujah in November, where the best-performing Iraqi units were those with U.S. advisers. Further, the United States was investing considerable amounts of equipment with the new Iraqi units but did not yet have U.S. military personnel to account for much of it at lower unit levels.

These considerations gave rise to an ambitious plan to embed many more U.S. trainers with Iraqi forces—nearly 150 military teams, totaling several thousand U.S. troops. When Casey and Abizaid first pitched this plan to Rumsfeld in late 2004, the secretary reacted coolly and had many questions. How would these embedded teams be protected, he wondered. What would be their rules of engagement? Who would provide the necessary interpreters? How would injured soldiers be evacuated? Could the U.S. military find several thousand soldiers sufficiently skilled to be trainers?

Rumsfeld worried particularly about the safety of the trainers. "He's one of the world's toughest guys, but the risk of casualties really bothered him," Abizaid recalled. "When a U.S. soldier was killed in combat, he took it personally. He always wanted to know what more we were doing to protect the troops. It was hugely important to him."

It would take several months and some contentious briefings for the military commanders to work through the secretary's questions and to persuade him to endorse the expanded training team program and the major shift in focus it represented for the U.S. mission in Iraq. But the generals, like others who worked closely with Rumsfeld, were accustomed by then to the often drawn-out process of introducing a new idea to the secretary and allowing time for him to warm to it. The best approach in such cases was to bring Rumsfeld in on a plan early and ensure he felt involved in its development. "One of the things I learned with him was never bring the cake in fully baked," recalled J. D. Crouch, who served as the assistant secretary for international security policy. "As a manager, he was a guy who liked to have cookie dough on his hands."

———•———

On the Thursday after Bush's reelection in November 2004, Rumsfeld used a meeting of the Senior Level Review Group—the undersecretaries, service secretaries, military chiefs, and other senior aides—to kick off work on the next Quadrennial Defense Review. The last review had been conducted during Rumsfeld's first months in office and, drafted in large part before September 11, 2001, essentially outlined a strategy for a long peace. By the end of 2004, it was evident that the United States had entered an enduring conflict, and major strategic shifts were necessary to ensure adequate troop levels and the right mix of weapons and equipment.

The 2001 review process had been largely ad hoc, lacking in deep analysis. At the time, Rumsfeld's team was just taking shape. This time, with a team already well-established and with its views largely set, a more orderly process could be expected. Rumsfeld himself, though, would not be able to devote as much time to the process in 2005 as he had in 2001. He defined the strategic course, making clear the questions he wanted addressed. But he would have to delegate a lot of the day-to-day management to his deputy and the vice chairman.

At the meeting in November, Rumsfeld said that in deciding how to focus the new review, he wanted to know what kept his senior civilian and military staff awake at night. "I don't want to know what your staffs think," he told them. "I want to know what you personally think." But within a few days, before everyone could draft their replies, a surprise order arrived from the White House requiring the Pentagon to cut $60 billion from the projected defense budget over the next six years. That triggered several weeks of intense internal review and forced Rumsfeld to confront the need for deep cuts in some costly weapons systems.

Although he had taken office in 2001 intent on going after those major weapons programs he considered Cold War relics, only the Army's

Crusader artillery system and a planned Army reconnaissance helicopter called Comanche had been canceled. The armed services had resisted more extensive cuts and were buoyed by big increases in military spending—up 41 percent since 2001, to about $420 billion.

But mounting deficits and the growing cost of keeping more than 150,000 American troops in Afghanistan and Iraq were driving the White House to look at reductions in federal spending across the board. Savings in troop cuts or current military operating expenses were out of the question given the stress already being felt by the Army and Marines. Instead, the Pentagon's budget for new weapons, then about $78 billion a year, became an immediate target.

Initially, Rumsfeld's senior civilian staff and the service chiefs were invited to nominate whatever projects they wanted as candidates for elimination. Virtually everything ended up on the table for consideration. Pros and cons were aired at three meetings of the Senior Level Review Group. The service chiefs tended to be wary of going after one another's projects. The civilians had fewer reservations. As for Rumsfeld, he mostly listened.

At the last of the meetings, the chiefs of the Navy, Marine Corps, and Air Force each spoke of the sacrifices his service was making in trimming their weapons-modernization programs. Only the Army appeared to be holding back. Indeed, General Pete Schoomaker, the Army chief, underscored the strain his service was under as a result of bearing the brunt of the wars in Iraq and Afghanistan and, at the same time, converting its structure to provide for more flexible combat brigades. Nevertheless, Gordon England, then the Navy secretary, complained that the Army could still afford to tighten its belt.

"The conversation got a little dicey at that point," recalled Ken Krieg, who as the Pentagon's chief program analyst helped shepherd the process. "England basically said, 'You Army guys are getting better at the expense of the fewer number of ships we're building.'"

Finally, on a Sunday in December, Rumsfeld met in the living room of his Washington house with top military and civilian subordinates to settle on a list. The Navy took some of the most prominent hits, in large part because of the increased efficiencies it had achieved through its revised ship deployment and crew-manning plans and other initiatives. Rumsfeld decided to retire one of the Navy's twelve aircraft carriers—the *John F. Kennedy*, one of the oldest carriers in the fleet, first deployed in 1968. And he ordered reductions in planned purchases of a next-generation destroyer and Virginia-class nuclear submarines. Plans to buy new LPD-17 amphibious landing ships to transport Marines were slashed as well.

In the Air Force, purchase orders were cut for the new F-22 fighter jet and C-130J transport aircraft. The reduction in F-22s—the Air Force's new pride and joy—was especially hard to take. But the plane—the most technologically advanced fighter jet ever—had been designed at the height of the Cold War to penetrate areas under Soviet radar coverage without detection, and critics questioned its necessity when U.S. troops were battling insurgents in Iraq, whose weapon of choice was a makeshift bomb detonated by a garage door remote control. Although the Air Force had enhanced the plane's ability to hit targets on the ground in an effort to make it more relevant in the post–September 11 world, a number of Rumsfeld's senior aides remained unconvinced.

As for the Army, Rumsfeld decided to delay development of its main new weapons program—the $120 billion Future Combat System—designed to link soldiers by computer with remotely piloted aircraft and combat vehicles. But the secretary also resolved to seek additional funds for the Army to finance its brigade-restructuring plan.

The final plan, detailed in a Pentagon document known as Program Budget Decision 753, constituted the farthest Rumsfeld attempted to go in cutting major weapons systems as secretary. In time, many of the reductions would be restored by Congress. But for the moment, Rumsfeld and his team could claim to have delivered on their talk of transformation by actually going after some of the military's sacred cows.

It had taken the intense pressure of a federal budget crunch and an order from the White House to compel the cuts. Still, Rumsfeld had demonstrated his willingness in the end to make difficult choices about weapons and to stand up to vested interests in the military, Congress, and the defense industry. And with another Quadrennial Defense Review on the horizon, the budget decision had signaled that everything would again be on the table, with more cuts seeming probable. "It was one of those moments when push really did come to shove," Krieg later observed.

CHAPTER 15

Second Thoughts

In early January 2005, Rumsfeld sent Myers and Pace a memo titled "Views from generals" to invite their thoughts and those of their subordinates on whether troop levels in Iraq were adequate. Rumsfeld noted that Abizaid and Casey held regular conferences with senior staff and asked that they use such sessions to pose several questions about troop strength. "I don't need to know the names," Rumsfeld wrote, "but it would be helpful for me to have a sense of what the commanders at various levels think on these issues. Please include minority opinions and their reasoning."

The question of troop levels had become an especially sore point for Rumsfeld. He had faced searing criticism for not sending enough troops for the invasion and for not having sufficient forces on hand to quickly establish security and deal with the looting after the fall of Saddam Hussein's regime. In the year and a half since, the secretary had come under repeated fire for providing too few forces to combat the insurgency.

Journalists, members of Congress, and other visitors who spent time with U.S. forces in the field often heard grumbling from officers about insufficient numbers of troops. The problem was most obvious in the inability to sustain security in areas that had been cleared of enemy fighters. No sooner would U.S. troops chase insurgents out of one town and move on, than the enemy would creep back to take root once more.

Rumsfeld was widely thought to have blinders on whenever the issue of adding forces came up. Yet here he was, reaching out for other opinions down the ranks. He asked whether senior officers involved with Iraq were convinced that U.S. and coalition forces were "doing about the right things overall" and operating with "about the right number" of troops in their areas.

If more troops were necessary, Rumsfeld wanted to know where they were most needed. At the same time, he questioned whether it would be helpful to have even fewer U.S. troops on the ground if they were deployed differently. Should more be assigned to mentoring Iraqi security forces? Should more be tasked to police Iraq's borders? Should there be fewer U.S.-only patrols and more combined patrols with U.S. and Iraqi troops?

Finally, Rumsfeld pondered the location of coalition ground forces, seeking feedback on whether more should go toward consolidating the relatively secure areas of northern and southern Iraq and fewer toward fighting in the unsettled Sunni Triangle in the central part of the country.

The memo came just as the number of U.S. troops in Iraq had surged to bolster security during legislative elections in January. Casey had requested two battalions from the 82nd Airborne Division and had delayed the departure of two brigades that had been due to leave Iraq, effectively raising the troop total in the country to more than 150,000.

Having cleared insurgents from Fallujah, Samarra, and other earlier safe havens in the fall, U.S. military planners hoped to maintain momentum after the elections and to chase enemy fighters from their remaining strongholds around the country. Additionally, Casey had given Rumsfeld a proposal at the end of 2004 seeking several thousand more trainers to embed with Iraqi forces in a major push to improve the performance of the new units. The move would constitute a significant shift in the focus of the U.S. military mission in Iraq, away from counterinsurgency operations and toward more-intensified mentoring activities. Rumsfeld was mulling the plan.

As interested as the secretary was in obtaining the opinion of senior officers, there was no question where his own bias lay. Although he would tolerate an increase in troop levels to bolster security for major events such as Iraqi elections, he considered these surges temporary and expected that force levels would promptly return to where they had been and would continue to decline.

Casey's staff had felt pressure to lower the level of U.S. forces from the time they had arrived in Baghdad in mid-2004. Colonel Bill Hix, Casey's chief strategist, recalled a request from Casey in September 2004 to examine ways of drawing down the force. Already at that point, southern Iraq had fewer U.S. and coalition troops, and the aim was to shrink the footprint of foreign forces elsewhere. "The question was, how could we do it and how long might it take," Hix recalled.

The Baghdad staff drafted a chart showing that as Iraqi forces formed, U.S. troops could withdraw. The chart, presented to Rumsfeld as part of a CENTCOM briefing, indicated an aggressive downward slope but lacked a timeline. "The feedback from CENTCOM was that the secretary had liked the slide quite a bit," Hix said.

Rumsfeld conveyed his sense of urgency about bringing down force levels in another briefing on January 27, 2005. Casey had flashed a chart during a video teleconference with the secretary that showed best, worst, and most likely rates of draw down.

"George, this line does not feel right to me," Rumsfeld remarked, referring to the best-case scenario, which projected only a slight decline in U.S. forces—from twenty to seventeen brigades—in the first half of the year, followed by a steeper decline in the second half down to nine brigades, or about sixty-six thousand troops.

"How's that, Mr. Secretary?" Casey asked.

"The slope is not steep enough," Rumsfeld asserted.

By the time Rumsfeld visited Iraq two weeks later and received an updated briefing, the chart had been amended. The best-case projection for bringing down troop levels showed a drop to thirteen brigades by June and to as few as six by December. "He was always pushing us to go faster with the transitions," Casey said of Rumsfeld. "There's no question that he thought faster reductions were better."

To help relieve some of the demands on the U.S. military in Iraq, Rumsfeld kept a constant lookout for substitute troops. He had written Myers and Feith in August 2004 asking about an idea that Abizaid had discussed with Arab leaders regarding the creation of a "bridge force" that would draw troops from Muslim countries. The plan proposed putting the Muslim units under a separate U.N. command and using them for peacekeeping-type activities rather than for direct operations. Rumsfeld wanted a status report on the initiative.

Myers responded that while some Muslim countries had indicated a willingness to contribute, it was unlikely that the numbers would reach the suggested thirty thousand. Besides, Myers noted, Iraqi prime minister Allawi was reportedly against any new chain of command for Muslim forces and disagreed with the notion that for every Muslim soldier in the new force, the United States could withdraw one of its own.

In October 2004, Rumsfeld had asked Casey to look at various possibilities for employing Kurdish fighters, the peshmerga. Although these forces were considered among the most capable in Iraq, their presence in Shia or Sunni neighborhoods risked igniting sectarian conflict. Mindful of that danger, Rumsfeld suggested that they be used to help protect U.N. representatives or NATO trainers working with new Iraqi troops, or to assist in guarding convoys, high-value sites, or Baghdad's Green Zone, the walled-off, heavily guarded section housing the interim Iraqi government and the U.S. embassy.

In addition to hunting for alternative manpower, Rumsfeld was eager to cut down on certain kinds of assignments, particularly noncombat missions such as protecting U.S. diplomats and other State Department officials. On February 14, 2005, he gave Abizaid and Casey several months to devise a plan to remove Special Operations troops from these personal security detachments. Casey proposed either having Iraqi teams take over the mission after undergoing a ninety-day training course or contracting with a private security firm to provide guards while the Iraqi teams trained for a longer period. He favored the second approach, and by summer of 2005, the transition to private security guards was under way.

———•———

Abizaid and Casey shared Rumsfeld's interest in keeping troop numbers as low as possible in Iraq, although each general came at the issue from a somewhat different angle. Rumsfeld's focus was on achieving Iraqi self-sufficiency. He wanted to get responsibility into the hands of Iraqis as soon as possible so that they would not develop a long-term dependence on the United States. Frequently he invoked a bicycle analogy: For the Iraqis to learn to pedal by themselves, Rumsfeld would say, the United States needed to take its hand off the seat.

Abizaid, in turn, was driven by concerns about a long war and a long U.S. commitment. He wanted to get the U.S. presence in Iraq down to a size that could more easily be sustained over a long period. At the same time, he hoped to avoid a precipitous reduction in the U.S. troop level and was intent on ensuring that enough U.S. trainers were available for Casey's proposal to step up the mentoring of Iraqi security forces. "We must avoid letting our strategy become a 'drawdown strategy' for U.S. forces," Abizaid advised in a January 9, 2005, memo to Rumsfeld and Myers. "George has a sophisticated view on how to proceed."

Casey's concerns, meanwhile, were mixed. Like Rumsfeld, he worried that the longer U.S. forces bore the brunt of the counterinsurgency fight, the more Iraq's forces would depend on them. And like Abizaid, he fretted about the potentially damaging impact on the U.S. military of large, prolonged deployments. He also believed that adding ground troops would give terrorists more targets and could engender further Iraqi resentment against the U.S. occupation.

When asked in an interview, Casey could recall receiving only a few appeals from subordinate commanders for additional forces. For the most part, he said, senior field officers were reluctant to seek more manpower because of what he described as an intrinsic make-do-with-what-you-have attitude. But no doubt many officers were also discouraged from making requests by a widespread recognition that the chances of winning approval were very low.

As firm as Rumsfeld was in keeping a lid on force numbers in Iraq, he was even firmer in the case of Afghanistan, according to Abizaid. Because the secretary hoped eventually to transfer responsibility for security there to NATO, he seemed to set a higher hurdle for approving any additional resources for the operation.

In Abizaid's view, at least some of Rumsfeld's tightfistedness derived from the secretary's deep-seated desire to be economical and save taxpayer money—an attribute the general admired. "You have to understand that part of Don Rumsfeld is being the world's cheapest man," Abizaid observed after retiring from military service. "If you said to him, 'This project is going to cost you a certain number of dollars,' he'd cut the number in half automatically."

This same tendency was often at work, Abizaid noted, in Rumsfeld's dealings with the Pentagon budget. The military services would prepare elaborate plans and cost estimates and present them to the secretary, only to have them summarily rejected. "He would automatically tell them whatever project they were working on was too expensive," Abizaid said.

But Rumsfeld's attempts at economizing would sometimes backfire and result in higher costs by allowing problems to fester and become even more expensive to fix. Abizaid observed, for instance, that the secretary's initial resistance to investing more troops and resources to build an Afghan national army ultimately contributed to a bigger bill for the United States.

Abizaid and Marine general Jim Jones, the top NATO commander, had cautioned Rumsfeld against assuming that a larger NATO role would mean a diminished U.S. presence. And in fact, even as NATO took on more responsibility, the number of U.S. forces in Afghanistan continued to creep up during Rumsfeld's term, from about 1,300 in late 2001 to more than 20,000 in 2006. It was a quiet, gradual buildup, without the public attention that force levels in Iraq were attracting, and the overall numbers were far fewer than in Iraq, but they were significant nonetheless.

———•———

One of Rumsfeld's recurring concerns, not just in Iraq but in the administration's larger war on terrorism, was that the U.S. government simply wasn't organized properly to confront the unconventional enemies that were waging these first conflicts of the twenty-first century. While presiding over a transformation at the Pentagon, Rumsfeld often argued that the U.S. government also needed its own transformative agenda to overhaul a national security structure that had essentially been set in the early years of the Cold War and that had changed little since.

Laying out his case, the Pentagon leader composed a paper in January 2005 explaining why the new counterterrorism struggle differed from previous wars the United States had fought and therefore required novel approaches. As he saw it, the global campaign was especially difficult and complex because of certain "new realities," which had little to do directly with the nature of the enemy and a lot to do with the nature of modern media (ubiquitous and always on), government (poorly organized and burdened by constraints), and public attitudes (not fully engaged in war and not very knowledgeable about unconventional war).

Presented largely as a series of thoughts loosely strung together in bullet paragraphs, the four-page paper attempted to frame the conflict as something much greater than purely a military matter. "It is a task not only for the Department of Defense," Rumsfeld wrote, "and not only for the USG [U.S. government], but for the entire civilized world."

The paper, which said next to nothing about the troops-and-weapons side of the struggle, mostly addressed the need for better organization and communication by the government. The nonmilitary focus made it an unusual document for a secretary of defense to be passing around to senior officials in the Pentagon. But the paper was indicative of Rumsfeld's ongoing frustration with challenges that in his mind should not have been left to him and his department to battle alone.

He wrote of a world in which the media had been transformed by multiple global satellite TV networks; twenty-four-hour TV news coverage; live coverage of terrorist attacks and combat operations; a global Internet with bloggers, hackers, and chat rooms; and digital cameras and camcorders. He noted that Congress had fewer members who had served in the U.S. military, while the number of congressional staff members had jumped from eight thousand to more than sixteen thousand since the Vietnam War era. He complained about the "near continuous hemorrhaging" of classified information and a Freedom of Information Act that was compelling the government to provide well over one million pages of documents a year to news organizations and others.

He also lamented that terrorists, "unburdened by bureaucracy and its constraints," seemed able to get their messages out more quickly than the U.S. government. He griped that they were held to a lower standard, citing "a pattern where our government is punished for prompt but less than perfect responses to fast-moving events, while competing against an enemy that goes unpunished for its lies and outrages."

All of which, Rumsfeld noted, had led to criticism from the press, Congress, and foreign governments about U.S. "incompetence" and "cover-up." But given the nature and magnitude of the new realities and their associated challenges, he went on, "it is impressive that the USG has been able to cope with these multidimensional problems as successfully as it has."

While intent on identifying the problems, Rumsfeld didn't offer any detailed fixes. He closed with a list of several broad and undeveloped proposals, more to suggest certain possibilities than to make a strong case for any one. The list included calls to "revamp the interagency process," "improve public education," and "develop better access to the non-mainstream media (talk radio, bloggers, etc), international and domestic."

"Understand," Rumsfeld wrote, "that our country (and our values) is in a campaign—a war to be sure, but a prolonged campaign—and to win it, we must organize to win it, and we must develop a new sense of urgency and sustain it for the long, hard slog ahead. Lives are at stake."

———•———

In the spring of 2005, Wolfowitz stepped down as deputy defense secretary to take over as head of the World Bank. He had a longtime interest in foreign assistance, dating back to his time as ambassador to Indonesia, and tended to enjoy thinking about economic development issues more than about military matters. The World Bank job offered him a chance to indulge this interest and also to run his own show.

His tenure as deputy defense secretary had been stormy, his role as a leading advocate for the invasion of Iraq having made him a lightning rod for criticism. Deeply involved in policy matters, he had struggled with administrative responsibilities. Papers piled up on his desk, decisions were deferred, and actions got delayed. It wasn't that Wolfowitz didn't attend to matters that were before him. It was more that he would dwell on them. "The amount of material that he would have to sign was incredible, and it would pile up day after day in his office," recalled a senior official in Wolfowitz's office. "But he felt he had to read every word. And he would agonize over the smallest decisions."

For a new deputy, Rumsfeld chose Navy secretary Gordon England, whose efficient management skills and affable manner had made him a favorite of the secretary's. A onetime executive vice president of General Dynamics, where he had helped develop the F-16 fighter, England had a reputation for being less ideological than Wolfowitz and more attuned to the business-operations side of the Pentagon's second-ranking civilian position. Importantly, he also had a knack for working with Congress.

Rumsfeld and England agreed to a more traditional division of responsibility. "We had an understanding that I would have some degree of autonomy," England recalled in an interview. "I would be able to work on things important in terms of managing the department, because our joint view was that this job was primarily a COO [chief operating officer] type function. So he made lists and I made lists and we got together a few times and we agreed on how we'd run the department."

For himself Rumsfeld reserved the wars—in Iraq and Afghanistan and globally—against terrorism. Contingency planning also remained in his basket, as did Special Operations, intelligence activities, and nuclear policy—the Pentagon's most secretive, most intriguing, and indubitably most controversial stuff. Additionally, the secretary held on to issues related to the structure and condition of the armed services, including the global repositioning of troops, the rebalancing between active-duty and reserve units, and efforts to relieve stress on the force.

England's tasks were more the nuts-and-bolts variety. He was given oversight of the department's financial and business management systems, the base-closure process, foreign weapons sales, medical affairs, and a number of issues related to facilities and infrastructure.

Rumsfeld also looked to England to help repair strained relations on Capitol Hill, which meant handling some of the more politically sensitive tasks—among them, implementation of the National Security Personnel System stipulating new hiring and firing procedures, mandated by Congress in 2003 for the Pentagon's civilian workers. Reflecting England's talent for problem solving, he assumed responsibility for a special task force desperately trying to figure out how to defend against the roadside bombs that accounted for the majority of U.S. military casualties in Iraq.

Oversight for about twenty other areas was designated "both," although lead responsibility was assigned to either Rumsfeld or England. In this joint category, Rumsfeld took primary charge of setting detainee policy, developing a national missile-defense system, managing public affairs, and selecting senior military and civilian personnel. England, in turn, assumed the lead role for developing the budget, managing the next Quadrennial Defense Review of Pentagon strategy and military structure, working through homeland-defense questions, and addressing troop quality-of-life concerns. Curiously, although it was a signature issue for Rumsfeld, the lead for "transformation" was assigned to England. A category called "accountability" also fell to the deputy.

As England settled into his new position, management of the department's business affairs improved. Under England, decisions were made with a speed and decisiveness that had often been lacking under Wolfowitz. "The frustration with Wolfowitz was that he would call meetings to address a certain problem, and there'd be a lot of hand-wringing and options discussed, but once the meeting was over, there'd be no clear indication of what he wanted to do," recalled one senior Pentagon official who dealt with him regularly. "England, on the other hand, wanted to fix problems and wasn't afraid to be the guy to make tough calls and sign on the dotted line. His attitude was, There's not necessarily going to be consensus about what to do, but bring me the issue, tell me the pros and cons, and I'll make a decision. Wolfowitz tended to intellectualize issues, whereas England saw them much more in operational terms."

England wasn't averse to an occasional act of bureaucratic daring. An attempt to revise policy for the handling of terror suspects was a case in point. It was one of the areas that the secretary and the deputy had agreed would be shared between them, with Rumsfeld supposedly having lead responsibility. But England, who as Navy secretary sought to improve processes at the Guantánamo prison, had some experience with the issues, and when an opportunity came along with several lawyers at Defense and State who were trying to push through a major course change for the administration, he seized it.

Despite the Abu Ghraib scandal, the administration had remained deadlocked internally for months over a range of detainee-related matters. Hard-liners in the vice president's office, the Justice Department, and the Pentagon insisted the president should retain wide power to decide who could be held and how they should be treated, while State Department officials, along with senior military lawyers and some Defense civilians, argued that U.S. detention policy should adhere more closely to international law to prevent further abuses. In their view, the existence of the Guantánamo facility and ongoing disputes over military interrogation procedures were causing irreparable damage to America's image abroad. Further, they contended, the controversies were undercutting U.S. ability to conduct cooperative intelligence operations overseas with partner governments that objected to the U.S. policies.

Philip Zelikow, the former executive director of the 9/11 Commission who was serving as a counselor to Rice, had been working secretly with Rice's legal adviser, John Bellinger, on a plan to reshape the legal landscape. They concluded that the piecemeal, incremental approach, addressing detainee and interrogation matters one by one and working methodically through an interagency process, was ineffective. In their minds, the best way to break the impasse would be to attempt something radical.

England was game to try something different. So was Matthew Waxman, a lawyer by training who had taken the newly created post of deputy assistant secretary of defense for detainee affairs in the summer of 2004. In dealings with foreign allies, Waxman saw ample evidence that U.S. standing in the war on terrorism had been eroded by rights abuses and by claims that the Geneva Conventions did not apply in the handling of many prisoners.

Over the weekend of June 11 and 12, Zelikow and Waxman huddled with England over a laptop in the deputy secretary's Pentagon office, drafting a memo that proposed a sweeping new approach to the detention, interrogation, and prosecution of terrorism suspects. (Bellinger was unable to attend.) Their hope was that if Rumsfeld and Rice signed on, they could push past likely resistance from Cheney and Attorney General Alberto Gonzales and persuade the president of the plan's merits. The plotters were betting that if Bush could see what a groundbreaking initiative might look like, he would be more easily enticed into endorsing it.

The document that emerged contained broad and dramatic recommendations. It called for the closure of the detention center at Guantánamo, the repatriation of some prisoners, and the transfer of others to a long-term detention facility in the United States. It also urged that all prisoners held by the CIA in secret cells abroad—the existence of which had not yet been publicly revealed—be tried before military commissions, whose rules should be revised. It appealed as well for full adherence to the minimum standards of treatment under the Geneva Conventions, including the ban on "humiliating and degrading treatment" contained in Common Article 3 of the Conventions. And it proposed seeking congressional legislation for the handling of detainees.

While forceful, the arguments in the memo were carefully couched to avoid sounding critical of past decisions. The memo asserted that existing rules had made sense in the immediate aftermath of September 11 but maintained that a refined approach was needed. Contending that change would inevitably be forced from outside if the administration continued to resist, the memo noted the political advantage of taking the initiative.

On the evening of Sunday, June 12, England's assistant dropped off a copy of the memo at Rumsfeld's house. Rice, who also received a copy, liked the results and forwarded the memo to senior officials on the National Security Council staff. But Rumsfeld was bothered by the whole process. He was angered that his new deputy had participated in drafting the memo without authorization and without circulating it among other key Pentagon officials with a role in detainee issues. "He didn't like this idea of something that was written and given to him that hadn't been vetted with the general counsel, the chairman of the Joint Chiefs of Staff, the undersecretary for intelligence, and the undersecretary for policy," a senior Pentagon official said later.

At a staff meeting on the morning of June 13, Rumsfeld complained about the memo and blocked plans for its distribution at a Principals Committee meeting the next day. England, who represented the Pentagon at interagency meetings of deputies, stopped attending sessions on detainee issues and was replaced in these instances by Steve Cambone.

But with the need for an updated Defense Department directive on prisoner treatment and for a revised Army manual on interrogations, England and Waxman soon made another attempt to restore the applicability of the Geneva Conventions. On August 26, England gathered three dozen Pentagon officials for a meeting where Waxman argued for incorporating Common Article 3 directly into the new military rules.

Common Article 3 sets out minimum standards for the treatment of captured fighters and others in "armed conflict not of an international character," such as a civil war. The reference to noninternational conflict had led Bush in February 2002 to determine that the article was irrelevant to the war against al Qaeda or the Taliban. But Waxman, while acknowledging the arguments against invoking the article as a matter of treaty law in such cases, contended it should be adhered to at least as a matter of Defense Department policy.

Two of Rumsfeld's closest aides—Steve Cambone and Jim Haynes—spoke out against the proposal. Haynes, the general counsel, warned that the change could have perilous consequences for intelligence gathering, while Cambone, the undersecretary for intelligence, argued that it was inappropriate to incorporate in the Pentagon's documents language from an international agreement that could be considered ambiguous and that presented another standard, apart from U.S. statutes, for judging the actions of troops engaged in armed conflict.

But others at the meeting, including the vice chief of each of the military services and every judge advocate general, supported the applicability of Common Article 3. The divided opinion left Rumsfeld, who did not participate in the meeting, inclined to keep the current policy. "I never felt like the secretary was actually hard against" formally applying the Conventions, England said. "It was just sort of the status quo because there were forces pro and con. I think he was just getting buffeted by different views."

Waxman, who met a number of times with Rumsfeld to discuss treatment standards, said the secretary saw the matter essentially as an implementation problem, not a policy one. "Aside from the legal merits," Waxman explained, "those of us advocating the change argued that so long as we're not using an internationally recognized standard of humane treatment, we're never going to get international legitimacy and credibility nor the ability to work effectively with our coalition partners. But others, including the secretary, were generally more comfortable with the unilateral approach of saying, 'We commit and promulgate orders to treat them humanely and that's good enough.'"

Those pushing for change later concluded that the attempt to reconsider the applicability of Common Article 3 had never stood a chance with Rumsfeld. Not only were two of the secretary's most trusted aides opposed, so too was Cheney and his senior staff. On significant issues involving detainees, Rumsfeld had tended to defer to the vice president.

After the Pentagon meeting in late August, Scooter Libby, the vice president's chief of staff, and David Addington, the vice president's legal counsel, assailed Waxman for having pushed to apply the article in the new Pentagon documents. Waxman left the Pentagon soon after this clash, taking a job at the State Department and then eventually a teaching position at Columbia Law School.

He was proud of some of the progress that had been achieved during his year in the job, though he was deeply frustrated that White House officials were unwilling to revisit some of their earliest legal and policy decisions about detainees. By the time of his departure, the U.S. military regularly registered detainees with the International Committee of the Red Cross. Care for prisoners had become more humane. Procedures for the initial screening of captives had been improved. So had efforts to negotiate with partner countries over the return of some Guantánamo detainees, although the prospect of closing Guantánamo in the foreseeable future appeared dim. "Rumsfeld's attitude," recalled Cambone later, "was that unless and until someone comes up with a better idea, we're stuck with it."

———————

Hearing rooms on Capitol Hill come in various sizes for various occasions. The smaller rooms, where most of the space is consumed by committee members and staff and where few chairs are provided for public audiences, serve as backdrop for more intimate sessions. The larger rooms, which can accommodate sizeable crowds, host the more celebrated and historic congressional spectacles. Room 325 of the Russell Senate Office Building, with its marble columns, French windows, and gilded ceiling, belongs to the grander variety. (Among its claims to fame, it was the site for hearings on the sinking of the *Titanic* and the Watergate scandal.) On June 23, 2005, Rumsfeld, Myers, Abizaid, and Casey were summoned to the room to discuss the situation in Iraq.

At a morning hearing there, then at another in the afternoon on the House of Representatives side, concern among lawmakers over the course of U.S. strategy in Iraq boiled over into a scalding attack on Rumsfeld and some of the toughest questioning of the Pentagon leader since the war began. Rumsfeld disputed assertions that the U.S. campaign was faltering and argued that the conflict remained worth its costs in lives and dollars. He rejected the idea, backed by a small bipartisan group of lawmakers, of setting a timetable for withdrawing U.S. troops, although he favored pressing Iraqi authorities to keep to their schedule for elections on a new constitution and government later in 2005. "Any who say we have lost or are losing are flat wrong," he declared in an opening statement, appealing for perseverance. "We are not."

But lawmakers in both parties, citing continued violence in Iraq and uncertainty about when the conflict would end, expressed growing misgivings about an open-ended U.S. involvement. The harshest criticism came in the Senate. In the day's most dramatic confrontation, Senator Edward M. Kennedy (D-MA), a leading critic of the Iraq campaign, told Rumsfeld that the war had become a "seeming intractable quagmire." He recited a long list of what he called "gross errors and mistakes" in the U.S. military campaign and concluded with a renewed appeal for Rumsfeld to step down. "In baseball, it's three strikes, you're out," Kennedy said before a standing-room-only session of the Armed Services Committee. "What is it for the secretary of defense? Isn't it time for you to resign?"

Rumsfeld paused, appearing to collect his thoughts and composure. "Well, that is quite a statement," he responded, adding that none of the four-star generals seated with him "agrees with you that we're in a quagmire and that there's no end in sight." Each of the officers—Myers, Abizaid, and Casey—later affirmed as much. Rumsfeld also noted that he had offered to resign twice and that Bush had decided not to accept the offers.

Nonetheless, Republicans as well as Democrats joined in calling Rumsfeld's attention to signs of declining public support for U.S. involvement in Iraq. "I'm here to tell you, sir, [that] in the most patriotic state that I can imagine, people are beginning to question," said Senator Lindsey O. Graham (R-SC). "And I don't think it's a blip on the radar screen. I think we have a chronic problem on our hands." Warned Senator Joseph I. Lieberman (D-CT), "I fear that American public opinion is tipping away from this effort."

Alluding to unfavorable news coverage and political commentary, Rumsfeld countered that if such a shift in opinion was occurring, people were "getting pushed," and he expressed confidence that support would rebound. Abizaid, in turn, voiced concern that U.S. troops, aware of the drop in public backing, were asking him "whether or not they've got support from the American people." Abizaid noted that while confidence among U.S. forces in the field had "never been higher," the political mood in Washington was strikingly different. "I've never seen the lack of confidence greater," he said.

Abizaid offered a sober assessment of the Iraqi insurgency, observing that the resistance remained about as strong as it had been six months earlier and acknowledging the possibility that enemy fighters had sufficient reserves to mount "a military surprise," such as a surge in coordinated attacks. At the same time, he, Rumsfeld, and the other military authorities attempted to present a picture of considerable progress in Iraq across military, political, and economic fronts. They noted that Iraqi security forces were becoming more capable and that Iraqi opinion polls showed more confidence in the forces and in the interim government. Additionally, Iraqi political authorities remained on track to draft a new constitution and to elect a new national government by the end of the year.

Privately, Casey delivered a fresh assessment to Rumsfeld that reaffirmed the existing strategy while reiterating the long duration and difficulty of the battle ahead. The general warned that "steady attacks" on U.S. allied forces, then averaging about four hundred to five hundred a week, would continue, adding that "the insurgency can sustain the current level of violence over the next six months." He pointed to some successes—no insurgent stronghold, an elected legislature, some Sunni participation in the government, and growth in the ranks of the Iraqi security forces to about 168,000. The insurgency, he noted, was not enlarging or spreading.

But it wasn't weakening either. Insurgents had sufficient popular support to sustain operations, and their operations were expected to remain concentrated in four provinces. Further, enemy groups still had the capacity to surge in number and to move about the country with some freedom. Aiding the insurgency were a strong recruiting effort inside Iraq and an influx of fighters and material support from Syria and Iran. Also, Casey said, there was little sign that the enemy's will to fight had been broken.

The emphasis in this briefing—and in a follow-up to service chiefs in their Tank conference room—was that the long-term solution in Iraq lay not in military action but in the political process and in economic development. And the military plan still envisioned a reduction in U.S. force levels in 2006. A chart shown to the chiefs on June 27 projected the number of U.S. brigades in Iraq dropping from seventeen to fifteen by January 2006, then to thirteen by spring and to ten by the end of 2006— a decline in troop numbers from 138,000 to about 90,000. In the process, the number of U.S. bases in Iraq was to shrink dramatically, from ninety-two to just four giant, heavily fortified ones.

———•———

That same summer, Rumsfeld and Myers started using new terminology for the global counterterrorism campaign, referring to it as a "struggle against violent extremism" rather than a "war on terrorism." While the change seemed subtle, it represented an important distinction, at least in the minds of the Pentagon leaders.

Rumsfeld had not liked the phrase "global war on terrorism." Adopted by the administration in the immediate aftermath of the September 11 attacks to apply to the pursuit of the al Qaeda network and other terrorist groups, it seemed to Rumsfeld to make the international campaign sound exclusively like a military fight rather than a broader effort requiring economic, diplomatic, and legal measures as well. He also worried that use of the term "war" suggested a conventional conflict and raised expectations of an early victory rather than what he figured was more likely to be a long, drawn-out struggle.

In developing a comprehensive plan for fighting terrorism, Feith's office had put together a briefing for the president and other top officials in early 2005 that formally raised the question of changing the name from GWOT (global war on terrorism) to GSAVE (global struggle against violent extremism). Rumsfeld insisted that the first page be devoted to explaining what was wrong with the old phrase. "He said the terminology is what drives what people think about this subject when they get up in the morning," Feith recalled. "If it's called the war on terrorism, they think differently about it than if it's called a struggle against violent extremism."

Opinion polls showed that the American public was increasingly pessimistic about the mission in Iraq and doubtful about the verity of a link between the costs and casualties of the war there and success in the global counterterrorism campaign. Some in uniform complained that only members of the armed forces were being asked to sacrifice for the effort. So Rumsfeld and Myers began testing the new phrase publicly in the summer of 2005 in speeches and news conferences, stressing the importance of employing all instruments of national power.

When Rumsfeld proposed going public with GSAVE, Feith warned him that he might run into resistance from Bush. After all, GWOT was the name the president had given to the war. And, in fact, once the secretary and Myers invoked the term publicly, Bush didn't wait long to make clear his preference for the old terminology. In a forty-seven-minute speech in Grapevine, Texas, on August 3, the president used the phrase "war on terror" no fewer than five times. Not once did he refer to the "global struggle against violent extremism."

Administration officials were concerned that the Pentagon's attempted change in language had been interpreted in some news reports as signaling a shift in policy away from military action and toward diplomacy and partnering with moderate Muslims in combating Islamic extremism. By insisting on the old formulation, Bush was continuing to frame the conflict primarily in military terms and appeared intent on emphasizing that there had been no policy change.

In a speech the previous day to the Dallas Chamber of Commerce, Rumsfeld himself had backed away from his proposed new language. "There has been comment in the press of late about whether or not we're even engaged in a 'war on terror' or whether our purpose might be better explained in a different manner," he said. "Let there be no mistake: . . . It is a war. The president properly determined after September 11th that the United States no longer could deal with terrorists . . . in the traditional law enforcement sense. Indeed, the only way to defeat terrorism is to go on the attack."

It was a rare occurrence for Rumsfeld to have gotten out in front of the president in public. It was also rare to see the headstrong secretary reversing himself.

———•———

In deciding when and where to commit U.S. troops, Rumsfeld was perhaps most wary of involving combat forces in domestic security operations. American law and custom set high barriers for the use of federal forces in such circumstances, preferring to rely on local law enforcement and civilian emergency-response units, and Rumsfeld heartily agreed. But when a domestic emergency is large enough to overwhelm civilian responders, U.S. troops may be the only force capable of stepping in to manage the consequences. Rumsfeld had been thinking about this challenge in the context of a potential terrorist attack when Hurricane Katrina struck late in the summer of 2005.

The hurricane's devastation resembled the effects of a major terrorist strike—many people dead, houses and businesses destroyed, thousands stranded, local and state authorities incapable of ensuring order or providing other necessary services. The Bush administration's slow, disjointed, and woefully inadequate response resulted largely from poor planning and inept coordination by the Department of Homeland Security (DHS) and its Federal Emergency Management Agency (FEMA). But Rumsfeld's own reluctance early on to send active-duty U.S. ground troops contributed to a delay in some federal military assistance.

When the hurricane slammed into the central Gulf Coast on Monday, August 29, Rumsfeld was in California to join Bush at a military event. England had been left in charge at the Pentagon to coordinate the U.S. military's initial response. Never one to let legal complexities get in the way of action, England was inclined to rush as much military assistance as possible to the disaster areas in Louisiana, Mississippi, Alabama, and Florida. He started issuing orders authorizing the dispatch of a hospital ship and other units.

But England's forward-leaning actions didn't sit well with Rumsfeld, who wanted time to consider the relevant laws governing the domestic use of federal troops. Paul McHale, then the Pentagon's assistant secretary for homeland defense, recalled the evident contrast between the reactions of the two Pentagon leaders.

"England knew instinctively that we had to provide a rapid, effective response, and he was not going to waste time with unnecessary detail," McHale said in an interview. "Lives were in the balance, property had been catastrophically destroyed, and England had a management style that reflected an immediate, intuitive grasp of the situation and a willingness to make a robust response. He was prepared to deal with the more complex and technical issues at a later point in time. Rumsfeld is a methodical manager. He demands a detailed understanding of an issue and a clear presentation of the relevant facts as a prerequisite for thoughtful decision making."

But the enormity of the disaster rapidly overwhelmed early efforts by local, state, and federal government agencies, confronting the Bush administration with the question of whether to take control, federalize National Guard forces, and even dispatch military combat troops to assist in evacuations and searches and to help restore calm. The sense of crisis was particularly acute in low-lying New Orleans, which was largely underwater and where thousands of people were either stranded in their houses or crammed into an unruly Convention Center or Superdome. By Wednesday, looting was rampant, and city authorities declared a state of emergency.

The prospect of sending combat forces to help ensure safety on the streets and in evacuation centers presented tough legal and political considerations—among them, how to coordinate with the thousands of National Guard units already on the scene or due to arrive later in the week. While White House officials pressed for action, Rumsfeld insisted on clarifying legal authority and command-and-control arrangements. "Certain folks at the White House just wanted basically to hit the button and have the 82nd Airborne drop out of the sky without these issues being sorted out," recounted Robert Rangel, Rumsfeld's senior civilian assistant at the time. "But Rumsfeld was not going to be stampeded into giving unwise advice to the president."

The difficulties of deciding on a course of action were compounded by tensions between federal and state authorities. When White House officials tried to persuade the governor of Louisiana, Kathleen Blanco, to issue an official request for the federal government to take control of the

Louisiana National Guard and the New Orleans police, she refused, whether out of pride or mistrust or a desire to maintain some degree of control. Bush had the authority, by way of the 1807 Insurrection Act, to federalize Louisiana guardsmen and to send in active-duty troops. But the Insurrection Act was a particularly touchy issue in the Deep South. Since World War II, it had been invoked only a few times.

Rumsfeld cautioned against sending in combat troops or federalizing National Guard forces. But not calling the National Guard into federal service gave rise to concerns that the reservists and active-duty military forces would be answering to separate chains of command—one state, the other national. To ensure unity of command, consideration was given to having a single officer serve in dual status as commander of both sets of troops. Louisiana's Blanco, though, again refused.

Ultimately, Bush decided to dispatch federal combat troops but designated their mission as humanitarian, thereby avoiding the issue of the Insurrection Act. When Andy Card phoned Rumsfeld to convey the decision, the secretary wanted to hear it directly from the president. "Look at the chain of command," Rumsfeld told Card. "Where's the chief of staff? I report to the president, I don't report to the chief of staff. If the president really wants me to do this, he'll tell me." Rumsfeld had his rules and was insisting on sticking to them. But Card couldn't avoid the thought that the secretary, unhappy with the decision, was merely trying to toss up some flak.

Ultimately, paratroopers of the Army's 82nd Airborne Division flew into New Orleans from their base in North Carolina. The division proved useful in facilitating a further evacuation and in conducting house-by-house searches to locate people in need of assistance. The paratroopers were joined by 1st Cavalry Division soldiers from Texas and by Marines from California and North Carolina.

Although the Army soldiers in New Orleans were not allowed on police duty, their presence freed up National Guardsmen and law enforcement officers for peacekeeping. By Saturday, five days after the hurricane had struck, New Orleans had been wrested from the chaos of the preceding week, and a kind of weary calm had settled over the streets.

England, for his part, regretted that more hadn't been done sooner. "I felt that was something we should have immediately stepped into, and we didn't immediately step into it," he said later. "We should have been leaning a lot farther. To this day, I think we could have done more than what we did."

He attributed the slower response to legal considerations. As a former corporate executive, he was struck by the "outsized influence" that legal considerations tended to play in Washington decision making. "I think people who've been here a long time tend to get overly sensitized to legal considerations," he said, seated in his Pentagon office. Asked whether his statement applied to Rumsfeld in the Katrina situation, England replied, "I think that's a characteristic of Washington, including the secretary."

He noted that Rumsfeld had a voracious appetite for gathering data, which sometimes kept him from making rapid decisions, although in England's view, this trait also enabled Rumsfeld to approach problems with exceptional thoroughness and knowledge. "He is a very analytically based decision maker, not sort of the broadest," England remarked. "His approach was more based on data, facts, and analysis, so decisions always involved a lot of hard work leading up to them. That's different than a lot of senior executives who sort of assimilate things, have a lot of sense about things and make broad-based decisions, but of course his were decisions of national importance. I think that's a personal characteristic not everybody understands about Don Rumsfeld. That's not a pro or con statement, it's just a factual statement, an insight into the personality."

———— • ————

The Katrina crisis underscored the U.S. government's lack of preparedness—even four years after the September 11 attacks—for dealing with a major domestic emergency. In the months leading up to the hurricane, Rumsfeld had been focusing on this fact, expressing growing concern privately about shortcomings in plans to handle a catastrophe.

"He became very uneasy in the late spring or early summer of 2005 that a catastrophic event like a terrorist attack would hit the United States and we would be ill prepared to respond," McHale said. "It frustrated him that the United States government had not yet clearly defined the relevant authorities, nor had the various departments of the federal government fully integrated and planned their responses. He communicated that concern in various memos to senior officials at the White House and in snowflakes circulated in our own building."

Rumsfeld's interest in limiting the involvement of federal troops in domestic emergency operations was evident in the immediate aftermath of the September 11 attacks. He complained, for instance, when the Army secretary, on his own authority, sent National Guardsmen to U.S. airports to help bolster security. Rumsfeld noted that important details about the deployment had not been clarified in advance and demanded that an agreement be drawn up to stipulate whether the troops were acting under state or federal authorities, who was funding them, and when their mission would end.

In the months that followed, the secretary was notably proprietary over military personnel assignments. He went so far as to order a steep reduction in the hundreds of U.S. officers who had been loaned to other federal agencies and congressional offices. These officers often facilitated dealings between the Pentagon and other government offices, but in calling them back, Rumsfeld argued the need to preserve military manpower for wars and other overseas operations.

By 2005, though, Rumsfeld and senior aides had recognized that the military would play a significant role in certain domestic emergencies and probably would even have to take the lead in managing the response to a domestic biological, chemical, or nuclear attack. Admiral Timothy Keating, the head of Northern Command, acknowledged as much in an interview with the *Washington Post* in August 2005. At the time, Keating's headquarters was drafting the U.S. military's first-ever war plans for guarding against and responding to attacks on U.S. soil.

The admiral's assertion about a lead Pentagon role drew a sharp objection from the secretary of homeland security, Michael Chertoff, who complained privately to Rumsfeld that the national response plan had designated the Department of Homeland Security, not the Pentagon, as the lead agency. But Keating had only been stating the obvious—that no matter what had been written on paper, the Pentagon would end up taking charge.

That same summer, Rumsfeld asked McHale to prepare a briefing showing the shortcomings in logistics, medical support, and other U.S. government capabilities for responding to a catastrophic event. The presentation, dubbed the "gaps and seams" briefing by defense officials, was to be given to Bush during the president's August stay at his ranch in Crawford, Texas. But Chertoff, who had received an advance copy, objected to parts of the briefing that portrayed his department in a poor light. According to McHale, the DHS secretary wanted time for his staff and Pentagon officials to make revisions. "DHS had some issues with the briefing because they saw it as sort of stepping on their toes," recalled another senior Pentagon official. "They wanted it to be a more consensus, government-wide view—meaning, they wanted to make sure that they agreed with everything we said in it."

Bush never received the briefing, but the Katrina experience proved a far more powerful catalyst for change, underscoring the unsettled policy issues, equipment shortages, and poor interagency coordination that Rumsfeld had wanted to highlight. Even so, many more months of argument passed before Rumsfeld and Chertoff were finally ordered, in 2006, to reach agreement on the conditions under which the Pentagon would take charge in a domestic emergency.

Rumsfeld wrote Chertoff on March 7, 2006, outlining a set of proposed criteria for a president to use in deciding to involve the military. Included were such considerations as the magnitude of the disaster, the capability and effectiveness of the initial local and state responses, and the adequacy of assistance by FEMA and its contractors. "To the extent that local, state and federal civilian responders cannot handle the disaster, there is clearly no institution in our nation other than DoD capable of promptly marshalling the necessary capabilities," Rumsfeld observed. "Further, it would make no sense for the U.S. Government to try to create a stand-by capability the size of the U.S. Military to be dedicated solely to catastrophic events—man-made or natural."

Three days later, Chertoff wrote back agreeing with the list of criteria and with the general notion that the Pentagon's involvement would have to be driven by particular circumstances. No test could be defined in advance for when the Defense Department would take over the lead in responding to a catastrophic event.

—•—

Eric Edelman took over as Rumsfeld's new policy chief in August, replacing Doug Feith. A career foreign service officer, Edelman had a reputation as a genial, able diplomat, with little of Feith's ideological bent, and he had proven himself adept at operating in government assignments outside the State Department. He had a particular history with Cheney, having worked for him in the vice president's office and, earlier, at the Pentagon when Cheney was secretary of defense.

Edelman's recent assignment as U.S. ambassador to Turkey had kept him up-to-date on many of the issues involving neighboring Iraq. As Rumsfeld's top civilian adviser, Edelman attended the secretary's weekly video teleconferences with Casey and had hoped those would enable him to stay abreast of developments in the war. But he found the sessions insufficient sources of detail on what was occurring in Iraq.

The briefings tended to be too general—too much outline and too little detail—to give Edelman the specifics he was looking for. Although Rumsfeld and Casey supplemented the briefings with phone calls during the week, those too, from what Edelman could tell, were more perfunctory than enlightening.

Edelman was frustrated by the sketchiness of the information and surprised by Rumsfeld's apparent satisfaction with the extent of information provided. The secretary just didn't appear as informed about Iraq as Edelman had expected.

To get a better handle on the Iraq strategy and its execution, Edelman started asking for copies of the "Battle Update Assessment" briefings that Casey received daily from his staff in Iraq. Largely overviews, the briefings contained more detail about specific field operations, intelligence findings, political developments, and reconstruction efforts than was often provided in the conferences with Rumsfeld, and they helped Edelman fill in some, though far from all, of the blanks in the Iraq picture.

The summer of 2005 was a time of growing doubt about the effectiveness of the U.S. strategy in Iraq. Continued car bombings and suicide attacks in Baghdad and elsewhere underscored the continued ability of the loose, elusive networks of Abu Musab al-Zarqawi, former Baathists, and other extremists to recruit discontented Iraqis and foreign fighters and to launch well-coordinated attacks. One senior CENTCOM officer was quoted as saying that al-Zarqawi's organization remained "a very robust network" despite the heavily touted capture and killing of numerous underlings in Mosul, Tal Afar, and other communities where the insurgents found refuge. A U.S. Marine officer in Anbar Province, a stronghold of the insurgency, said the military effort against the insurgency was like "punching a balloon in the fog."

U.S. forces, pursuing Casey's view that the insurgency's "center of gravity" was now in the bends and towns of the Euphrates River valley near the Syrian border, had started to squeeze enemy fighters in those areas, raiding hideaways, confiscating weapons, and killing scores of insurgents. Citing thousands of enemy fighters killed or captured, a drop in the number of "effective" attacks (measured by casualties and property damage), and significant gains in intelligence about the insurgency, U.S. authorities pointed to marked progress.

But many enemy fighters had shown a startling ability to disappear into the countryside, and areas that U.S. forces cleared continued to refill with insurgents as soon as the Americans moved out. Field commanders were counting on Iraq's new military and police forces to build up quickly and provide the manpower to keep cleared areas secure. But the training of the reconstructed security services was going more slowly than anticipated.

A number of independent analysts had begun underscoring the flaws in the U.S. approach. The unabated violence, they argued, suggested the military had focused too much on hunting down insurgents using search-and-destroy tactics and not enough on protecting major population centers and creating safe zones from which stability could then spread, as defense expert Andrew Krepinevich wrote, like "oil spots."

When critical articles and internal reports that called the U.S. strategy into question crossed Rumsfeld's desk, he sometimes sent them on to Casey and Abizaid for comment. In September, for instance, he dictated a memo to the two generals asking their thoughts on a *Time* magazine piece titled "Saddam's Revenge" that cataloged a series of U.S. missteps in Iraq. It reported that the U.S. intelligence community still lacked an adequate understanding of Iraq's terrorist networks and warned that the Pentagon was repeating the same mistakes it had made in Vietnam. The article pointed to a "hot debate" in the intelligence community over whether to stop the aggressive sweeps through insurgent-riddled areas and concentrate instead on improving security and living conditions in population centers like Baghdad.

Later that month, Rumsfeld sent Casey a CIA paper that said delayed follow-up in Iraqi cities after coalition military operations was allowing terrorists to return. "Please take a look at it and let me know what you think we can do about it," Rumsfeld wrote.

But Casey saw no need to change strategy. He had considered the arguments for an "oil spot" approach but had dismissed them as academic and not really applicable in Iraq—better suited, he thought, for a rural insurgency than for urban fighting. Besides, he contended, the plan that the United States was pursuing had the ultimate safety of the Iraqi population in mind. By targeting terrorist safe havens in places like Fallujah and Najaf and by attempting to choke off the flow of foreign fighters from Syria into Iraq, U.S. forces would, Casey believed, improve security for Iraqi civilians.

———•———

At the White House, there was still a strong tendency to give Rumsfeld and his commanders the benefit of the doubt. The success story of the early war in Afghanistan stood out in many minds. In the initial stages of that fight, when the U.S. strategy of backing Afghan rebels against the ruling Taliban had appeared to stall, newspaper articles about a pending quagmire and calls for a change in strategy had sounded quickly. But Rumsfeld and Bush had held firm, and the battle had turned in America's favor.

"That was in the back of a lot of our minds as we started entering into difficulties in Iraq—the thought that, Hey, critics are going to come out early and often, but we're committed to the strategy; look what happened in Afghanistan, how quickly things can turn," said Dan Bartlett, who oversaw White House communications from 2002 to 2007. "When it came specifically to Don Rumsfeld, and there was increasing scrutiny about why things weren't going well in Iraq, the thinking was, We've been down this road before and it had a positive outcome. So he had a longer leash."

But with criticism of the Iraq strategy growing, NSC officials recognized privately that the administration could at least be doing a better job publicly explaining and defending the plan. Staff members began drafting a paper intended to provide a clearer sense of what the strategy entailed and how it was expected to play out in the months ahead. "We started asking, What's the narrative, how's this going to evolve," recalled

Meghan O'Sullivan, who had taken over in the fall as the deputy national security advisor for Iraq.

O'Sullivan, though, couldn't obtain any sense from the Pentagon of the anticipated timeline. Steve Hadley, Bush's national security adviser, arranged a meeting at the Pentagon with Rumsfeld to explain what the NSC staff was trying to do and hopefully to draw the defense secretary into the process. NSC officials approached the session with some hesitation, not sure how receptive Rumsfeld would be. "We were all a little nervous about how it would go," recalled J. D. Crouch, Hadley's deputy at the time. "You know, the secretary was protective of the Defense Department's prerogatives on military policy, although the meeting proved very constructive."

Hadley knew getting Rumsfeld onboard was essential. But the idea had to be presented the right way. It couldn't look as if the NSC was attempting to preempt the Defense Department or do the department's work. When the project was presented to Rumsfeld, it was described as a public relations effort to better explain U.S. strategy to critics in Congress, the media, think tanks, and other groups. While true, there also was more to it. An unstated aim was to engage Rumsfeld and the Pentagon in greater depth about the strategy, its execution, and its future phases. "We were presenting this as a PR thing, essentially as potential building blocks for a presidential speech or something, when in fact it was really intended to try to elicit from the Pentagon what the strategic horizon was," O'Sullivan said.

Rumsfeld raised no objection to the NSC project, opening the way for a session in which Casey briefed Hadley in even greater detail about the campaign plan. Such direct contact between the senior U.S. commander in Iraq and the president's national security adviser was highly unusual. As a rule, Rumsfeld insisted that Casey talk to senior administration officials only in the context of NSC meetings when the president was present. The secretary did not want the general participating in interagency meetings below the NSC level.

Such limited access was intended partly to shield Casey from time-consuming Washington meetings. But it also reflected Rumsfeld's strict views about the chain of command. He didn't want the national security adviser or the secretary of state or their deputies going straight to the field commanders, bypassing the secretary of defense. He was particularly wary of anything that could lead to the NSC staff actually running military operations, recalling the policy disasters that such links had caused in the Iran-Contra scandal of the 1980s.

For other high-level administration officials, though, the restricted contact with military commanders in Baghdad meant they received a filtered view of the war, and it complicated their own efforts to obtain detailed information. "I think it would have been enormously helpful if the commander or his deputies could have participated in some of our deputies meetings," Crouch said later. "I think that the Pentagon was trying to insulate them, but what they ended up doing was isolating them, which hampered them, too. They weren't as connected to Washington."

Casey briefed Hadley by video link on September 16, reviewing the history of U.S. strategy in Iraq, from initial liberation to early occupation to the "partnership" that had followed the transfer of limited sovereignty in mid-2004. Now, in 2005, the general noted, the campaign was transitioning to a fourth and final phase—"self-reliance"—which involved shifting the U.S. military focus from fighting insurgents to enabling Iraqi forces to take the leading combat role. This was being accomplished by inserting teams of trainers into Iraqi units and by building up the Iraqi ministries of Interior and Defense and independent Iraqi command-and-control networks, Casey explained.

The briefing confirmed Casey's own sense that the campaign plan had never been completely understood by a number of officials in the upper reaches of the administration. Part of the problem, as he saw it, was that the administration's leadership had not provided much direction for the strategy. The plan had been devised in Baghdad by the military command and the embassy staff. Had it come from Washington, Casey believed, officials would have had to think it through, master the details, and grasp the nuances.

Casey also had the impression that some White House officials were concerned that the U.S. military mission had recently shifted emphasis too far and too fast toward transitioning responsibility to Iraqi forces at the expense of keeping U.S. troops focused on fighting insurgents. He had tried to impress on Bush and other White House officials that to win in Iraq, the United States had to do less and rely on the Iraqis to do more. He knew that a more conventional mind-set also held sway at the White House—one that assumed that as long as U.S. forces were taking aggressive military action, everything would eventually be okay. Casey didn't agree, but that view was proving hard for him to get past.

"There was a tension that we were all training and no fighting," Casey recalled. "You had a group of folks who I think didn't believe the transition strategy was the right way to go. They believed that if we simply went in there with American power and waxed everybody, things would be okay." Bush in particular, Casey thought, seemed to view the war in conventional terms, often inquiring about the number of enemy killed or captured and appearing more interested in the military gains than in the political and economic aspects of the struggle.

As the Bush administration struggled internally over finding a way to describe its military strategy in Iraq, Rice tried out a new bumper sticker in the fall of 2005. Testifying before the Senate Foreign Relations Committee in October, she summarized the U.S. approach as: "clear, hold and build." The phrase was meant to depict three main phases of operations: clearing areas of insurgent control, holding them securely, then building Iraqi institutions. But Rumsfeld hadn't been consulted, and the wording irritated him—especially the idea of "building," which he understood to suggest an expensive, long-term commitment and to shift the focus away from having the Iraqis do more for themselves.

"Anyone who takes those three words and thinks it means the United States should clear and the United States should hold and the United States should build doesn't understand the situation," Rumsfeld told a Pentagon news conference. "It is the Iraqis' country. They've got 28 million people there. They are clearing, they are holding, they are building. They're going to be the ones doing the reconstruction on that country."

For his part, Bush liked Rice's phrase, and despite Rumsfeld's objections, the president started using it himself in speeches. Within a few weeks, it was incorporated in a lengthy document on the war released by the White House titled "National Strategy for Victory in Iraq."

Casey had not liked the phrase either. He thought it missed the basic point of the U.S. strategy, which was to train and equip the Iraqi forces and focus on transitioning security responsibility to them. And he, like Rumsfeld, was miffed that no one had discussed the phrase with him ahead of Rice's testimony. (That lapse, it turned out, appeared to result from a miscommunication. Rice's staff had advised the senior liaison officer between the Pentagon and the State Department, Lieutenant General Ray Odierno, thinking he would relay the information, but he did not.)

Since taking the Baghdad job, Casey had tried to keep a low profile, in keeping with efforts to press the Iraqis to take on more overall responsibility. But, increasingly in his view, the Bush administration, and particularly Rumsfeld, had run out of credibility on the subject of Iraq. Casey concluded that if the U.S. strategy was going to be articulated properly to Congress and to the American public, he and other commanders would have to step forward more and play the role of spokesmen.

Even so, Rumsfeld took a controlling hand in the public appearances that both Casey and Abizaid made during their periodic visits to Washington. Before a trip by the generals in October 2005, the secretary asked to see their planned schedules. "I'm looking forward to having you both back here next week," he wrote Abizaid and Casey in a September 23 snowflake. "The schedule is fairly demanding, but it's important that we take maximum advantage of your presence here with the media and Congress."

After looking over their itineraries, Rumsfeld instructed the generals to do the Sunday TV talk shows separately in order to cover all five programs. But he advised Casey to forgo a meeting with the *Washington Post* editorial board, saying the time "might be better spent doing radio interviews."

The commanders did their part, and afterward, Rumsfeld sent a congratulatory note thanking them for their efforts in Washington and assuring them that the time they had put into talking to the media and giving congressional briefings made a difference. "It's always a bumpy road, but our obligation is to tell the story honestly to the American people," he told them. "Thank you for all you are doing each day in two of the most demanding jobs on the planet!"

About this time, Rumsfeld also spoke to Abizaid and Casey about the need for them to be direct and honest with him. "It was clear that people whose opinion he respected were telling him that we were on the wrong course," Abizaid recalled. "He challenged us to make sure that we were telling him what we believed. We were kind of incredulous. We said, 'What else would we be telling you other than what we believed?' But I knew what he meant."

CHAPTER 16

A Period of Continuous Change

Pete Pace took over from Dick Myers as chairman of the Joint Chiefs of Staff in the fall of 2005, a transition facilitated by the four years Pace had spent as vice chairman. Myers had faced criticism for failing to challenge Rumsfeld or to fully represent the concerns at times of other members of the Joint Chiefs. But there was little expectation that Pace would prove any more assertive in the top military post.

During his time as vice chairman, Pace had shown the same deference toward Rumsfeld as had Myers. Both generals, in public appearances with the secretary, usually in the Pentagon press room, had taken pains to avoid any sign of disagreement. Both believed as a matter of principle in the confidentiality of their discussions with the secretary. They also figured their chances of influencing Rumsfeld were greater if their private debates were not played out in the press.

But even behind closed doors, it was not evident that either military adviser had provided much resistance to the secretary. Rumsfeld frequently noted that he spent more time with his chairman and vice chairman than had his predecessors, and the secretary's aides contended that with all the give-and-take between the secretary and his top military advisers, it was difficult to identify who was influencing whom. Still, the perception was widespread that the generals had allowed the chairman's office and Joint Staff to lose some of their power and independence.

Because Rumsfeld was comfortable with him and because he was well known to other senior administration officials, Pace had long been considered the likely successor to Myers. Known in the Pentagon as "Perfect Pete" for his unflappable personality, straight bearing, and telegenic appearance, the senior Marine had a reputation as a good communicator and a skilled manager with a witty streak. He used his humor to handle Rumsfeld. Taken to task by the secretary at one meeting for not having his brief together, Pace showed up at the next session wearing a flak jacket. Although Rumsfeld considered several other candidates, Pace had no serious competitors for the chairman's job, according to Staser Holcomb, who participated in the deliberations. Noted Larry Di Rita, "With Rumsfeld during this period, continuity mattered a lot."

To replace Pace as vice chairman, Rumsfeld chose another familiar face—Admiral Ed Giambastiani, who had served as Rumsfeld's top military aide before taking over the military's Joint Forces Command in 2002. In that position, the admiral had overseen a number of Rumsfeld's initiatives aimed at transforming the U.S. military and revising NATO's Atlantic command structure.

The selections of Pace and Giambastiani signaled that Rumsfeld was opting for loyalists and proven team players in the Pentagon's uniformed leadership as he confronted continued criticism about his own management. So it was all the more surprising when Pace, at a news conference in late November 2005, less than two months after assuming the chairmanship, challenged Rumsfeld directly on a matter involving the treatment of detainees in Iraq, not by U.S. troops but by Iraqi forces.

Mounting evidence of abusive actions by Iraqi forces had prompted U.S. commanders to deliver warnings to Iraqi officials and instructions to U.S. troops to report mistreatment and, whenever possible, to step in to prevent it. Friction was evident between U.S. and Iraqi forces in the field, with Iraqis questioning demands for humane treatment of enemy fighters who themselves showed little respect for the laws of war.

U.S. officers cautioned the Iraqis that failure to curtail abusive behavior could tarnish the image of the new security services, risk a loss of Iraqi public support, and jeopardize other foreign assistance. Privately they also worried about U.S. troops getting drawn into an Iraqi dirty war.

At the Pentagon news conference in November, Rumsfeld and Pace were asked about the obligations of U.S. troops faced with misconduct by Iraqi forces. Pace asserted that American forces were responsible for intervening to prevent inhumane treatment. But Rumsfeld interjected with a correction. "I don't think you mean they have an obligation to physically stop it; it's to report it," he said. Pace insisted that he had meant what he said. "If they are physically present when inhumane treatment is taking place, sir, they have an obligation to try to stop it," the general reiterated.

Rumsfeld didn't appreciate being contradicted by Pace in public, and the incident left strained relations between the two men. As Pace recounted several years later in an interview, "That made the secretary and me uncomfortable for a while." Characteristically, the secretary also refused to drop the matter. "For several weeks after that," Pace recalled, "he had his folks looking at all the wording of all the documents to see whether or not there was some way to change what I had said in a way that would make it closer to what he had said."

In private, Pace continued to stand his ground, contending that the matter was, in his words, "very black and white" and explaining the importance of keeping it black and white so that U.S. forces would not be confused about their obligations. Pace had considered the point significant enough to depart from his usual rule about avoiding a public show of disagreement with Rumsfeld. But the episode remained a very rare example of the general taking issue with the secretary. For the rest of their service together, Pace was careful to appear to be in lockstep with Rumsfeld.

———◆———

Politically, Iraqi voters had passed an important milestone in October 2005, approving a new constitution by a large margin. The referendum had occurred with little violence, to Rumsfeld's great relief. The threat of a surge in terrorist attacks, similar to the Tet Offensive by communist insurgents in Vietnam in 1968, had been a serious concern for U.S. officials. The CIA, in a three-page secret assessment before the referendum, had concluded that while insurgents lacked the organization or military formations to carry out a Tet-like offensive in Iraq, they could create the perception of one with far fewer numbers. After the vote, Rumsfeld had sent Casey and Lieutenant General John Vines, the top U.S. operational commander in Iraq, a memo congratulating them for "excellent work" and citing a voter turnout rate of 60 percent and involvement by Iraqi security forces "at every level."

A few days later, on October 21, Casey presented Rumsfeld with options for reducing the number of U.S. combat forces in Iraq in early 2006. The general argued that a successful referendum and continued improvement in Iraq's security forces would provide a "strategic opportunity to demonstrate progress" by cutting U.S. troop levels. But Casey also warned that conditions feeding the insurgency would not be resolved in the coming year. He anticipated that Iraq was in for another protracted transition period and that insurgents would try to use violence to influence the process. Nonetheless, he recommended dropping from seventeen brigades, which had been the base level in 2005, to fifteen brigades—a reduction of about 12,000 troops from nearly 140,000—and keeping one brigade on reserve in Kuwait as a hedge against uncertainty. Iraqi security forces totaled 211,000 at that point and were projected to reach 270,000 by mid-2006 and 325,000 by mid-2007.

The proposed reduction in U.S. troops, Casey argued, could underscore the Bush administration's stated intention to "stand down" American forces as Iraqi forces "stood up." Moreover, it could lessen the exposure of U.S. forces. And it could send a strong signal that the campaign plan was on track. But Casey also worried that withdrawing too quickly might unhinge the development of Iraq's security forces and that it might diminish the effectiveness and flexibility of U.S. forces. Further, if it were misperceived as a U.S. retreat, the move could create expectations for continued reductions.

The speed and timing of a drawdown in U.S. force levels depended in large part on estimates about the development of Iraqi security units—estimates that were more art than science. A system of monthly reports that graded individual Iraqi units had been instituted in the spring. But the evaluations—known as Transition Readiness Assessments—were proving unreliable predictors of future performance.

In an embarrassing disclosure before the Senate Armed Services Committee on September 29, Casey testified that only a single Iraqi battalion was capable of independent operations—a significant step back from just several months earlier, when he had reported three battalions at the top rating. Military officials explained that the ratings were based on judgments by officers embedded with the Iraqi units, judgments that were highly subjective and that tended to fluctuate as the officers rotated in and out.

Such complications frustrated Rumsfeld. Although he never suggested to Casey that the system be junked, the secretary clearly appeared to Casey to be bothered that his own general was struggling to describe the assessment methodology to Congress.

———•———

In November, Rumsfeld received a twenty-seven-page report done by the U.S. command in Iraq assessing counterinsurgency operations in the country. Based on an extensive survey, the report measured the performance of U.S. and Iraqi forces against the list of historically proven counterinsurgency practices compiled by Kalev Sepp a year earlier when the campaign plan was drafted. It found that U.S. strategy and operations "generally align with the best practices of history's successful counterinsurgencies." But it also concluded that forces were falling short in a number of areas, with wide disparities in the practices of individual units.

U.S. troops, for instance, were having particular trouble establishing secure areas and isolating the insurgents from the population. "There are no 'white areas' in Iraq where the population is not subjected to intimidation," the study concluded. "Many areas remain 'safe' for insurgents due to the size of Iraq and resource limitations."

The report also expressed concern about the Iraqi police, who were regarded as crucial to achieving stability but who could not be developed effectively "under the pressure of insurgent violence and intimidation" and interference from the Ministry of Interior. Additionally, the study cited a lack of unity of effort among U.S., Iraqi government, and nonmilitary foreign agencies and a shortfall in money and manpower for commanders.

When Rumsfeld wrote Casey on November 15 after reviewing the paper, he expressed interest in a recommendation to establish a center on counterinsurgency, which Casey had already taken steps to set up in Iraq. The secretary also took note of a chart outlining successful counterinsurgency practices. "We clearly need to continue to shape our efforts in Iraq and Afghanistan along those lines," he wrote.

From the study it was evident that U.S. troops were struggling to understand the kind of conflict that Iraq had become. The lessons of counterinsurgency warfare, which American forces had learned during the Vietnam era, had never been taught to the ranks now fighting in Iraq. Casey himself had not realized how hard it was going to be to adjust the thinking and performance of his forces from a conventional war to an antiguerrilla campaign.

If the commanders and their troops were having trouble grasping the different tactics required, it was, in Casey's view, even more challenging for Rumsfeld and the rest of the senior civilian leadership in Washington. To the extent they had any familiarity with war, it was conventional, not guerrilla-style. They spoke in black-and-white terms of victory, exit strategies, and end states, not the less tangible, less quantifiable terms of negotiated solution, public opinion, and extended commitment more characteristic of counterinsurgency warfare.

Casey and Abizaid wrestled with how to articulate the nature of the Iraq War to Rumsfeld, particularly the demands that combating an insurgency placed on U.S. soldiers to go out on patrols and interact with local Iraqis. The commanders received snowflakes from the secretary questioning, in so many words, the need for U.S. soldiers to be driving around so much, given the risk of being blown up by roadside bombs. "I'd try to explain," Casey recalled. "I'd say, 'Look, this is a counterinsurgency environment, and to be successful you have to have contact with the population, and to have contact with the population, you have to be outside of your base.'"

Casey perceived that over time Rumsfeld's understanding of the special nature of the conflict deepened. But it was still a stretch for the secretary. "I don't mean this in a negative way," Casey reflected, "but I think the baseline that he was operating on was so different that it took more than I was able to muster to get him to understand it better."

To help inform Rumsfeld, Casey took advantage of the secretary's visit to Iraq in December 2005 to hand him a copy of *Learning to Eat Soup with a Knife*, a recently published book by Army lieutenant colonel John Nagl, a West Point graduate and Rhodes Scholar who had led a tank platoon in the 1991 Persian Gulf War and who had served as operations officer with a U.S. armored battalion in Iraq in 2003 and 2004. In his book,

Nagl compared the British military's successful counterinsurgency experience in Malaysia from 1948 to 1960 with the U.S. military's difficulty adapting and winning in Vietnam in the 1960s and early 1970s. Nagl himself had been working next door to Rumsfeld for months as a military assistant to the deputy secretary of defense, although Rumsfeld had never sought to discuss counterinsurgency warfare with him.

For all the effort Casey himself had put into understanding the strategies and tactics of fighting an insurgency, the general may have been slow to appreciate some of the fundamentals and therefore may have been less able to communicate them to Rumsfeld. Critics later faulted Casey for failing in particular to give high enough priority to ensuring the safety of Iraqi civilians in Baghdad and other major cities, concentrating instead on going after enemy fighters.

Casey knew the argument—that in conducting a counterinsurgency campaign, a central focus on protecting the local population was necessary to deny insurgents a critical base of support. But he considered it even more important to bolster the perception of the Iraqi government as a sovereign power. That was more likely, he thought, to bring the population around than anything U.S. forces could do.

Moreover, Casey tended to concentrate U.S. military activity on hunting down the enemy rather than on shielding the Iraqis, figuring that succeeding at the first would automatically result in the second. But other officers, including Casey's own chief strategist, Colonel Bill Hix, took issue with this judgment. "Early on, General Casey had a principal focus on the enemy," Hix said in an interview. "This focus was shared by many in Iraq. I think there was a feeling that if we were pressuring the enemy, killing him, we were taking care of the population. Others were less sanguine about that because no other agency was effectively addressing the Iraqi population. There were significant discussions within the senior leadership concerning this issue. My point in these discussions was that we should not be so complacent about the Iraqi population just being a tactical asset. We should be doing more to cultivate their support—in part by protecting them—because in counterinsurgency, the people are the prize."

All too often, Hix said, he found among U.S. field commanders a misguided expectation that if their troops took care of the enemy, other government entities would step forward to care for local Iraqis. But those other entities either didn't exist or weren't adequately resourced to provide government, economic, and reconstruction assistance. "When I talked to nearly every U.S. and coalition brigade commander over the summer of 2005, they all said, 'I don't have a partner out here to deliver on any of the expectations of the population, so even when I get security in an area, there's nobody to do anything else,'" Hix recalled. It was a crippling gap in the Rumsfeld/Casey approach.

———•———

Several times a year, Rumsfeld met with the Defense Policy Board, a group of outside advisers who served as a kind of sounding board for the Pentagon leader. Among the members were two former secretaries of defense (James Schlesinger and Harold Brown), a former secretary of state (Henry Kissinger), a former speaker of the House (Newt Gingrich), some retired four-star officers, and others with high-level experience in national security affairs.

The board meetings generally lasted two days, with much of the time devoted to briefings that ranged widely from updates on developments in North Korea or the Middle East to reviews of Defense Department personnel reform, Army troop rotations, or changes in the Pentagon's regional and functional command structure. Typically, at the end of the second day, Rumsfeld would arrive to discuss with members what they had covered. Always looking for facts, phrases, and arguments he could use in his battles elsewhere, he took extensive notes during the sessions, writing on yellow legal pads.

Iraq was noticeably absent from the board's agendas during the early months of the war. But requests from several frustrated board members eventually led to briefings on the war being added. One of the board's favorite briefers became Army colonel Derek Harvey, a foreign area officer specializing in the Middle East and working for the Defense Intelligence Agency.

Harvey had traveled extensively in Iraq, meeting with tribal leaders, observing U.S. interrogations of insurgents, and poring over uncovered Iraqi documents. He had concluded that the insurgency was much more robust, more extensively organized, and better financed than U.S. officials generally understood. In Harvey's view, the insurgency was driven largely by former beneficiaries of the Saddam Hussein regime aiming to regain influence and power and having the money, the weapons, and the will to carry on the fight for a long time.

An outspoken man with strong opinions, Harvey was a controversial figure in the intelligence community, and his detailed descriptions of an escalating threat contrasted with Rumsfeld's portrayal of the insurgents as dead-enders and thugs. But at the board's urging, Rumsfeld agreed to hear Harvey's analysis.

Seated around a conference table in his office with other senior Pentagon authorities in late 2004, a skeptical Rumsfeld peppered the colonel with questions about his take on the war. Harvey explained that his information had been developed from various sources, including interrogation data, intercepts, and documents. He didn't mind the push back from Rumsfeld. What struck him most was the seeming timidity of everyone else in the room. "The interesting thing is that no one else said much, no one stepped in," Harvey recalled in an interview. "I looked around occasionally, and people were looking at their feet. I realized I wasn't getting any help."

Rumsfeld considered Harvey's presentation significant enough to recommend it to Bush, who received the briefing in December 2004. But the colonel was never invited to return to update Rumsfeld. Harvey contended that the secretary and the military commanders in Iraq became focused on the wrong threat. In his view, they spent too much time on targeting al-Zarqawi and other foreign fighters and not enough on how best to deal with the old Sunni oligarchy that Harvey considered the heart, brains, and brawn of the insurgency. He argued that more should be done to address this group through engaging tribal leaders, offering economic incentives, and undertaking other initiatives. "There was an antipathy toward tribal leaders and dealing with legitimate leaders of communities who were viewed as tainted by the old regime," Harvey said later. "This ended up isolating them and contributing to their fears of a Shia government that would be sectarian."

A number of Defense Policy Board members were increasingly bothered by the discrepancies between the information they received from

Harvey and the much more sanguine view of Iraqi developments conveyed by Rumsfeld and other senior administration officials. They confronted the secretary about the differences and encouraged him to hear from other sources. The most vocal challenges at the board meetings came from Ken Adelman, Rumsfeld's old friend, who had been one of the biggest supporters of the invasion, predicting in the *Washington Post* that it would be a "cakewalk."

Disgusted with the management of the war and disillusioned with Rumsfeld, Adelman argued with the secretary during a session in December 2005 over the rotation of U.S. troops in and out of Iraq, contending that tours of a year or less undercut their ability to develop the kind of familiarity with Iraqi culture and local communities necessary in counterinsurgency warfare.

Several heavier hitters on the board weighed in as well. Jack Keane, the retired Army general who had been a Rumsfeld favorite, questioned the strategy. Eliot Cohen, a professor at the Johns Hopkins School of Advanced International Studies and an authority on civil-military relations, challenged discrepancies between Rumsfeld's optimistic accounts and the grim developments on the ground.

At one point Schlesinger told Rumsfeld bluntly, "Mr. Secretary, there's just too much happy talk coming out of this building. In the long run, that doesn't help you because when the happy talk doesn't materialize in a happy situation, you lose credibility.'" Rumsfeld appeared to make a note of Schlesinger's remark, although he did not respond.

Keane knew from his own contacts with Harvey that the intelligence analyst was periodically invited to brief Cheney and others in the vice president's office. Harvey was asked to craft questions that the vice president could then put to Rumsfeld about the situation in Iraq. Keane surmised that Cheney was also pressing the secretary. But Rumsfeld appears to have remained confident about the course that had been set in Iraq. There is nothing in the files of the message traffic between the secretary and Casey indicating that, with each other, they fundamentally questioned the strategy being pursued. To the contrary, they figured that if they could just get to the election of a new Iraqi government at the end of 2005 and see steady improvement in Iraq's security forces, they could turn the corner in the war.

Chris Williams, a former congressional staffer and onetime special assistant to Rumsfeld who chaired the Defense Policy Board from 2004 to 2006, saw the criticism from board members getting to the secretary. "I think towards the end he was really saddened and frustrated by the relative pessimism of the board on Iraq," Williams said in an interview. "He so wanted things to go well and wanted to see signs of improvement. When the board would challenge pretty strongly on the way things were going and what needed to be done, he would typically come back with individual items that he would cite as evidence that it wasn't going as badly. But I think it was a forest and trees sort of thing. He was concentrating on individual trees as opposed to the forest. You know, he handpicked every member of that board, knew many of them for years, decades in some instances. And to hear their sadness, pessimism, frustration—it was painful to him."

———•———

On November 30, the *Los Angeles Times* reported that as part of an information offensive in Iraq, the U.S. military had secretly paid Iraqi newspapers to publish stories that inflated the image of U.S. forces while negatively portraying insurgents. The articles were written by U.S. military "information operations" troops, translated into Arabic, and then placed in Baghdad newspapers with the help of a small Washington-based firm named the Lincoln Group.

Rumsfeld was surprised to learn of the propaganda effort. The day the story appeared, he sent a copy to Casey, Pace, Edelman, Abizaid, and Di Rita with a note of concern. "The attached article could be troubling," he wrote. "Please see if you can provide me the facts. It also would be helpful for me to understand how you are organized for communications: How well-connected to you are your public affairs people? How well-connected are your public affairs people to the people who may have been in a position to make such decisions? If what is described in this article is accurate, we may have public affairs concerns across the board that could make everything we do harder."

Doing battle on the information front had posed a dilemma for Rumsfeld for months. Early in the administration's war on terrorism, the secretary had recognized that the fight would be much more than physical battle. He had spoken of a "war of ideas" that had to be waged against Islamic extremists in schools and mosques throughout the Muslim world. But the U.S. government, in his view, was inadequately set up to explain its policies abroad and desperately needed a coordinated "strategic communications" effort to help sustain foreign support. By contrast, the enemy had demonstrated considerable adeptness in getting its own message out.

An initial Pentagon attempt in 2002 to develop a more aggressive communications program had turned into a public relations disaster. No sooner had the department's policy branch created an Office of Strategic Influence than reports emerged that consideration was being given to planting false news stories to influence policy makers and public sentiment in friendly as well as unfriendly countries. Rumsfeld called the reports distorted and declared that the military would not be permitted to tell lies to promote U.S. policies or views, but he quickly concluded that the office had been irreparably damaged by the coverage and shut it down.

The existence of the office had been controversial within the Pentagon itself; some senior public affairs officials had eyed it suspiciously as a threat to their efforts to distribute factual information about the U.S. military. An ensuing policy debate over what to do next only deepened the divide between those in public affairs and those in psychological and information operations, who at times rely on propaganda and misleading information to advance military objectives. Arguments about who should control the Pentagon's message, under what circumstances, and toward which audiences went unresolved, leaving Rumsfeld unable to establish a coherent, effective communications policy.

By seeming to blur the lines between transparent spin and clandestine propaganda, the Lincoln Group's activities in Iraq added to the internal Pentagon split. Officials in public affairs pointed to the hypocrisy of trying to promote democratic principles, freedom of speech, and political transparency in Iraq while the U.S. military was paying to disseminate propaganda in Iraqi news media. The psychological operations camp, in turn, defended such operations as necessary to combat the enemy's own intense propaganda efforts.

An internal military assessment cleared U.S. forces of violating any laws or instructions in connection with the Lincoln Group's program.

But Rumsfeld himself remained uncertain about how to proceed. In March 2006, more than three months after the Lincoln Group's operations had come to his attention, he sent another snowflake to half a dozen senior subordinates seeking advice. "We need to sort out what we think about the way the Lincoln Group is going about executing their contract in Iraq, and whether or not that is the right way to accomplish what is needed. I am not convinced that is the case. Please get back to me within a week with a recommendation as to how we should proceed."

Rumsfeld never did manage to define a strategic communications plan that worked. Just before leaving office, when asked at a town hall meeting with Pentagon employees to assess the Defense Department's performance in the war of ideas, he gave it a D-plus.

As he struggled with the war in Iraq in 2005, Rumsfeld faced the next critical juncture in his drive to transform the U.S. military: It was time again for another Quadrennial Defense Review (QDR) of military strategy, weapons, and force structure. The last QDR in 2001, during Rumsfeld's initial months in office, had advanced arguments for a more flexible, adaptable military and had begun to highlight such rising concerns as homeland defense and counterterrorism. But the review had left the structure of U.S. forces and most weapons systems largely intact.

With Rumsfeld settled into a second term, there was much speculation that he would use this next QDR to effect radical change. These periodic assessments were not necessarily binding in their recommendations about which weapons and programs to fund. But given the time and effort devoted to them, the reviews carried great weight, and for a defense secretary like Rumsfeld looking for powerful levers to reshape the Pentagon, they provided an important opportunity to frame strategy and budget decisions for the next four years.

Clearly, the case for change had become even stronger by 2005 than it had been in 2001. Several years into the fight against a troublesome insurgency in Iraq and against elusive terrorist networks like al Qaeda around the world, U.S. forces still appeared at a loss to understand the enemy and seemed to lack the right strategies and capabilities to win. While the Pentagon remained flush with planes, ships, and precision-guided munitions—all useful in large conventional battles—it was desperately short of other kinds of troops, weapons, and specialized skills useful in unconventional conflicts and postwar reconstruction operations.

Moreover, although homeland defense had been identified as the Pentagon's number one mission, how to carry it out had grown increasingly problematic. In the previous QDR, for instance, military planners had assumed that National Guard units would stay at home and serve as the nation's primary domestic security force. By 2005, because of the demands of the war in Iraq, reserve units were nearly tapped out.

Given a huge federal budget deficit and mounting war costs, there was also pressure to make hard budget choices about less relevant weapons systems. Rumsfeld thus seemed to have considerable wind at his back to apply the hard lessons of the previous four years, to challenge service chiefs resistant to having their budgets cut, and to insist on major revisions in strategy and force structure. Indeed, fostering the notion that sweeping change was in store, some defense officials in early 2005 floated the possibility that Rumsfeld would convene a high-level summit similar to that held in Key West in 1948, when James Forrestal brokered an agreement among the service chiefs on their roles and missions.

A classified document setting the "terms of reference" for the QDR and signed by Rumsfeld in March 2005 provided a new, expansive vision for the U.S. military, putting less emphasis on waging conventional warfare and more on dealing with insurgencies, terrorist networks, failed states, and other nontraditional threats. By giving higher priority to a larger set of possible security challenges, the document went beyond notions of military transformation previously touted by the Bush administration. Officials predicted that the shift in strategy could result in a significant reordering of funds, diverting money away from major weapons programs, such as tactical fighter jets and aircraft carriers, and toward more ground troops. Or it could lead to a different mix of troops that would favor specialized areas such as intelligence gathering, foreign-language skills, and civil affairs work. There was also speculation that the review could result in greater investment in new technologies, such as improved drone aircraft, better computer network defenses, and new measures for countering biological or chemical attacks.

But after setting the themes for the QDR, Rumsfeld largely took a back seat, turning over much of the daily management to subordinates. His diminished role was a marked contrast with the hands-on, day-to-day involvement he'd had in the 2001 review. This time, the demands of the war were keeping him otherwise occupied. Talk of a Key West–type summit eventually faded, and signs emerged that the review might not produce such radical change after all.

Rumsfeld did step in during the summer of 2005 to make a decision about the overall force-sizing concept for the military. In the 2001 review, he had decided to stay essentially with the two-war model adopted in the 1990s after the Soviet Union's demise, although he refined it a bit into a metric known as "1–4–2–1." That metric called for a U.S. military large enough and sufficiently well equipped to defend the U.S. homeland ("1"), to conduct smaller-scale peacetime operations in as many as four regions ("4"), and to "swiftly defeat" adversaries in two overlapping military campaigns ("2") while preserving the option to "win decisively" in one of those campaigns by forcing a regime change ("1").

But within days of completion, Rumsfeld's revised model already appeared out-of-date, when the United States found itself fighting a war in Afghanistan that did not fit any of the major conflict scenarios envisioned in the review. Nor had the 2001 QDR adequately provided for a protracted war on terrorism and a prolonged rotation of Army and Marine forces into and out of Iraq. By 2005, it was evident that a new force construct was needed to achieve a better balance among domestic defense, the antiterrorism campaign, and conventional military requirements. Some officials proposed moving to a metric that provided for only one conventional fight in order to make room also for an irregular one like the prolonged counterinsurgency campaign in Iraq. The service chiefs, though, were reluctant to dispense with the two-war model altogether. They argued that the United States, in order to deter aggression, needed to continue asserting its ability to fight in more than one area of the world at the same time.

Rumsfeld agreed. Besides, he didn't like the idea of discarding the 1–4–2–1 metric reached only four years earlier. "He said he'd worked in big corporations, and people there did not like it when strategies were switched on them," recalled a senior strategist in the Pentagon's policy branch. "He said he didn't like to change things just for the heck of changing them, and we were really going to have to convince him that something needed to be changed here.'"

The final QDR report, issued in early 2006, did not explicitly repeat the earlier metric. Rather, it divided U.S. military activities into three areas—homeland defense, irregular warfare, and conventional campaigns—and sought to spell out the requirements for each. But it stipulated that in the conventional category, the Pentagon would be expected to maintain a two-war capability.

In the end, the programmatic changes ordered by the review were relatively modest. Rumsfeld's desire to make the military more mobile and lethal, more capable of dealing with emerging threats from terror groups and insurgents, was plainly visible in such decisions as a 15 percent increase in the size of Special Operations forces. His interest in improving the ability of U.S. forces to strike quickly anywhere in the world could be seen in provisions for doubling the procurement of attack submarines, for arming submarine-launched Trident missiles with conventional warheads, and for starting the development of next-generation long-range strike systems. Investment in new forms of warfare was also evident in a decision to double the number of unmanned aerial vehicles and to begin a $1.5 billion, five-year effort to develop countermeasures against genetically engineered bioterror agents.

But in general, the review was better at defining new threats to U.S. forces and outlining a strategy for dealing with them than at laying out the programs to realize that strategy. Initial hopes that the yearlong assessment would order far-reaching changes in spending priorities had been largely stymied by the resistance of the military services. The review left all the largest acquisition programs—the Air Force's F-35 Joint Strike Fighter, the Army's Future Combat System, and the Navy's DD(X) destroyer—unscathed. Missile defense and space systems were reaffirmed. And no provision was made for a major expansion in ground force numbers. Instead, the final report concluded that the existing size of the force, both the active and reserve components across the services, was "appropriate to meet current and projected operational demands."

The 2005 QDR process was notably more collegial than previous ones, with fewer instances of interservice battles, and the review's recommendations were strongly endorsed by the military services. But the cost of such unanimity was compromise and an essentially cautious outcome on the programs. "I think the QDR was as strong as it could be and still have everybody signing up to it," observed Ryan Henry, who as principal undersecretary for policy played a leading role managing the process.

Rumsfeld, who personally drafted the preface to the final report, seemed to play down the significance of the exercise by portraying it more as just another transformative step than as a major breakthrough. "There is a tendency to want to suggest that documents such as this represent a 'new beginning,'" he wrote. "Manifestly, this document is not a 'new beginning.' Rather, this department has been and is transforming along a continuum that reflects our best understanding of a world that has changed a great deal since the end of the last century. This study reflects the reality that the Department of Defense has been in a period of continuous change for the past five years."

A favorite Rumsfeld notion that featured prominently in the QDR was something defense officials called "building partnership capacity." Shorthand for providing U.S. assistance to partner nations around the world, the phrase represented an indirect approach to fighting terrorism and promoting freedom through collaboration with indigenous forces and local government institutions. Rumsfeld and aides saw it as an alternative to the dreaded "nation building."

The concept has particular significance in the vast, worldwide task of combating terrorism, which requires enlisting host-country police to track and capture terrorists, teaming with foreign militaries, sharing intelligence with foreign partners, and strengthening border surveillance in remote and unpopulated regions. In the long run, an effective counterterrorism campaign depends on convincing entire societies to reject terrorist propaganda and recruitment.

Afghanistan was cited as a prime example of what could be achieved through such leveraging. Iraq was supposed to have been another. Before the war, Rumsfeld and other senior officials spoke enthusiastically of ousting Saddam Hussein in order to enable the Iraqi people to move toward a democratic system, not to build one for them.

In the autumn of 2004, during a series of brainstorming sessions that Rumsfeld held with senior aides on drafts of a strategic plan for the larger war on terrorism, the notion of an indirect approach had come up again. Officials reasoned that the more other countries, particularly in the Middle East, Africa, and Southeast Asia where terrorist networks were rooted, could be leveraged as proxies and surrogates in the counterterrorism campaign, the less the battle could be portrayed as a religious clash between Islamic extremists and the United States. Considering that the fight would probably be a long one, officials figured that the more partners were involved, the less exhausting the struggle would be for America.

But beefing up security assistance to foreign partners involved maneuvering through a patchwork of legal restrictions and complex divisions of responsibilities among U.S. government agencies. It might mean drawing on the Pentagon for military training, the State Department for police training, the Department of Homeland Security for border protection, and the Treasury Department for financial enforcement. Coordinating such efforts often required months of work.

In general, foreign aid programs were traditionally administered by the State Department, not the Pentagon. Rumsfeld was keen to revolutionize the process and invest the Defense Department with authority to deliver aid and training. "The secretary believed that we had this outdated, Cold War set of authorities, which were inappropriate for the twenty-first century," recounted one participant in the deliberations. "The pitch was not just to make some minor adjustments to foreign aid. It was to blow up the entire regime of foreign aid that had come out of the Cold War because it needed to be overhauled for the world we were living in."

In a briefing to Bush in January 2005, Rumsfeld and Feith proposed terminating the existing U.S. foreign aid and security assistance systems and creating a new set of laws and institutions that would feature "building partner capacity," among other approaches. Although the president wasn't ready to attempt such a drastic overhaul, Rumsfeld had already begun to chip away at the old order. At his urging, the Pentagon had received congressional authority and funding to train and equip the militaries and police forces in Iraq and Afghanistan without going through the State Department. It also had gotten approval to reimburse coalition partners for logistical and military support provided in Iraq and Afghanistan.

Throughout 2005, Rumsfeld moved to expand these train-and-equip authorities worldwide. He argued that the new authority was needed for time-sensitive, urgent terrorist threats to the United States that would not wait for the normal budget process under the State Department's authority. Moreover, he contended that the budgets necessary in a post-9/11 world would be impossible to derive from the strapped foreign affairs resources.

Some foreign affairs specialists inside and outside the government, who worried about a creeping militarization of U.S. foreign policy, argued against giving the Pentagon greater train-and-equip authority. They warned it could lead to the growth of a separate military assistance effort not subject to the same constraints applied to foreign aid programs that were administered by the State Department. Such constraints were meant to ensure that aid recipients meet certain standards, including respect for human rights and protection of legitimate civilian authorities.

Many lawmakers, too, were initially cool to Rumsfeld's request. The Armed Services committees in both the House and the Senate declined to write the provision into their original defense authorization bills, citing concerns about a lack of jurisdiction and an absence of detail about where the money would be spent. But the Pentagon pressed its case, with senior commanders helping persuade reluctant congressmen. "This was the most heavily lobbied we've been by the Pentagon in the several years I've been here," one Senate staff member recalled. "They really, really wanted this."

At the State Department, Rice also threw her support behind the measure, overruling lower-ranking staff members who had argued that existing laws were sufficient and cautioned against granting the Pentagon such flexibility. She joined Rumsfeld in a letter to Congress in the summer of 2005 urging passage of the legislation.

The measure passed in December 2005 as part of the 2006 National Defense Authorization Act. Under section 1206, Congress granted unusual authority for the Pentagon to spend as much as $200 million of its own budget to train and equip foreign military forces to carry out counterterrorism operations in their own countries or to join with U.S. forces in operations elsewhere (in Iraq, for instance).

Some strings were attached. Before the money could be spent, the Pentagon had to get approval from the State Department—a dual-key provision to ensure that Pentagon security needs met State Department foreign policy objectives. Moreover, the new authority could not be used to provide any assistance to countries blacklisted by other U.S. laws for human rights abuses or other reasons. And it was allowed for the training and equipping of only military forces, not of police. Further, the authorization was stipulated to expire after two years, far short of the open-ended mandate that Rumsfeld had sought.

Still, it was a precedent-setting victory for Rumsfeld. And in an associated measure (section 1207 of the same act), the defense secretary also received authorization to transfer $100 million in Pentagon funds to the State Department for use in its new office overseeing reconstruction activities in foreign countries. The idea of shifting Pentagon money to the State Department had been almost as controversial as letting the Pentagon spend train-and-equip funds, but the initiative was part of Rumsfeld's same ultimate objective—a more flexible foreign assistance system that would allocate money as needed among whatever agencies were best suited for delivery.

———•———

Also near the end of 2005, Rumsfeld put the finishing touches on a broad directive intended to ensure that the next time U.S. troops went to war, they would be better prepared for its aftermath. The new order required U.S. forces to give the same priority to planning for postconflict stability operations as they did to preparing for the fight.

For a Pentagon leader who had come into office generally averse to U.S. troops getting enmeshed in extensive postwar reconstruction efforts, the directive was a breakthrough. Rumsfeld never acknowledged that he had erred in the Iraq War preparations. But when presented with a 2004 Defense Science Board study that excoriated the U.S. military for its insufficient attention to postconflict operations, the secretary ordered that the board's recommendations be incorporated into a formal directive. Countless previous studies by think tanks had made the same point but had gone unheeded. This time, with the difficulties in Iraq fresh on his mind, Rumsfeld took some action.

"This was a very specific instruction to issue a directive, and I think people were surprised," said Jeffrey "Jeb" Nadaner, the deputy assistant secretary for stability operations. "He could have just said, let's implement this study, or let's harvest a few recommendations and figure out a way to do them. But he was ordering a formal document."

The eleven-page directive assigned long lists of specific responsibilities to the Pentagon's various civilian branches, military services, and regional commands. For instance, it instructed the Pentagon's undersecretary for personnel to develop methods for recruiting people for stability operations and to bolster instruction in foreign languages and cultures. It ordered the undersecretary for intelligence to ensure that "suitable" information for stability operations be available. And it directed the undersecretary for policy to create a "stability operations center" and to submit a semiannual report to the secretary of defense.

Although some of the boldest steps that had been suggested by defense scholars, such as the creation of separate constabulary units and other specialized forces to handle stability operations, were not adopted, the document was an important milestone that bluntly asserted post-conflict planning as a core mission of the Defense Department.

The biggest sticking point in drafting the directive had been a decision over who should monitor compliance. The Army had sought the job, but Rumsfeld made it clear to Nadaner and other staff members that he did not want the Army in the role of executive agent. "He was emphatic about it," Nadaner recalled. "He said at a meeting that when the Army gets things, it runs away with them, and he can't find out what's going on or get to the bottom of things." Nadaner suspected Rumsfeld had in mind the Army's slowness in dealing with the Abu Ghraib scandal. The oversight job for postconflict stability operations was assigned to the Pentagon's policy office.

———•———

Rumsfeld most significantly pushed the boundaries of his authority in expanding the use of military spies abroad. In the process, he trod on the CIA's traditional turf and stepped on some State Department toes as well.

Traditionally, the Pentagon had left the business of collecting human intelligence to the CIA. The special skills required in espionage, plus the years of undercover work, lent themselves more to civilians than to soldiers. Besides, the Pentagon already had a lot of other intelligence to manage. Information gathered through satellite imagery, phone intercepts, and computer monitoring was a normal province of the Pentagon's large intelligence organizations—the National Security Agency, the National Reconnaissance Office, the National Geospatial-Intelligence Agency, and the Defense Intelligence Agency.

But the global battle against terrorist networks had put a new premium on the kind of intelligence that can be gained only by having a spy in the room. Terrorists were less susceptible to overhead surveillance, wiretapping, and other mechanical and electronic means of intelligence gathering. U.S. commanders were confident that they could take out terrorist networks if they knew the hiding spots. The main problem lay in locating them. "This was something that came up in almost every combatant commanders' conference—the need to find, fix, and finish," Rumsfeld recalled in an interview. "We had the ability to finish. We just couldn't find and fix things."

The Pentagon leader considered it problematic that military forces should have to rely on the CIA for on-the-ground information. He and his aides had been frustrated with the lack of timeliness or usefulness to them of some information the agency had provided in the past. Because the CIA serves the information needs of Washington decision makers, it often has different priorities than do military commanders, who want tactical information their forces can use in combat operations. And Rumsfeld was keen to avoid another situation like the invasion of Afghanistan in 2001, where the CIA's better preparatory fieldwork had left U.S. forces reliant on agency operatives. If the military was to take a leading role in the global hunt for terrorists, as Rumsfeld intended, it would have to reduce its traditional dependence on the CIA for intelligence.

For months after the administration declared war on terrorism, the secretary mulled how far he could go in expanding the Pentagon's capabilities to gather intelligence and recruit sources abroad. The Defense Department had established a human intelligence service in 1993, but it was never as expansive as the CIA's operations directorate and tended to leave surreptitious intelligence missions to the agency.

Historically, Pentagon lawyers had contended that the Defense Department lacked authority to conduct such missions. But Rumsfeld's general counsel, Jim Haynes, argued otherwise, as did some in the Special Operations community, who maintained that such authority had long existed but hadn't been exercised as a matter of custom.

Among those insistent on the Pentagon's authority was William G. "Jerry" Boykin, a onetime head of the Army's highly skilled, supersecretive Delta Force. Boykin had been frustrated by the refusal of Pentagon leaders, dating to the U.S. hostage situations in Beirut in the 1980s, to approve clandestine operations. In planning rescue operations then, Boykin recalled, proposals to recruit informants or to infiltrate commandos to conduct surveillance were denied on the grounds that such activities were a CIA responsibility. Similarly, in Mogadishu in the 1990s, U.S. Special Operations forces relied on the CIA for information to target warlords.

In February 2003, Boykin, then a two-star general, interviewed with Rumsfeld for a top job in the newly created office of undersecretary for intelligence—the office that Rumsfeld had set up to get a firmer handle on all the department's intelligence activities and that Cambone had been picked to head. Looking over Boykin's résumé and noting the general's commando experience, Rumsfeld recalled his own annoyance at having had to sign orders in 2001 placing military Special Operations units under CIA authorities for operations in Afghanistan.

"Why did I have to do that?" Rumsfeld asked. "We're going to war, and I'm the secretary of defense. I'm responsible for these people, and I'm being told I have to put them under CIA authorities. That didn't seem right to me."

"I'm not a lawyer, but I don't think you do have to," Boykin replied. "I think you have full authority to do this. I think you have authorities that have not been exercised in this department for many years."

"You know, that's what my general counsel tells me, too," Rumsfeld said.

Boykin went on to serve as a deputy to Cambone in charge of "warfighting support," while Rumsfeld oversaw the formation of small spy teams, each staffed with two or three Special Operations troops and dispatched to countries in the Middle East, North Africa, Asia, and South America where al Qaeda or affiliated groups were suspected of operating. Initially called "operational control elements," the teams were assigned to lay the groundwork for potential military operations, including such clandestine missions as capturing or killing terrorism suspects. They engaged in some of the same spy craft typical of CIA operatives—using false names and nationalities, establishing front companies, recruiting agents, and cultivating sources in government or Islamic groups.

But the teams generated concern at the CIA, where they were regarded as dangerously amateurish and potentially disruptive of the CIA's own operations. Intelligence officials complained that the military units sometimes carried out missions without the knowledge of local CIA station chiefs. Worries about the qualifications and preparation of the military operatives were exacerbated in 2004, when members of a team operating in Paraguay shot and killed an armed assailant who tried to rob them outside a bar. In another incident, members of a team in East Africa were arrested by the local government after their espionage activity was discovered.

CIA officials argued that the military teams should come under the control of agency station chiefs, while State Department officials lobbied for tighter supervision by local U.S. ambassadors. Even the military's own regional commanders were not sure what authority they had over the teams.

"Rumsfeld decided he was going to wage a battle for intel supremacy with CIA, and it caused nothing but problems," said a general who handled intelligence matters for one of the regional commands at the time. "He decided that the Pentagon was going to do whatever it wanted. He didn't want the station chiefs in charge of human intelligence; he didn't want military source operations subordinated to the CIA. He just got into a battle, and it wasn't a healthy battle."

Some lawmakers, too, grew worried that the Pentagon was creating a parallel intelligence-gathering network separate from the CIA and free of congressional oversight. While CIA covert activities must be authorized by a presidential finding, and while the agency must report to the Senate and House intelligence committees, the Pentagon's lawyers determined that no such reporting requirement applied to the military teams. Moreover, there were indications that beyond these teams, even more secretive military groups were engaged in spying without having notified Congress. In early 2005, for instance, journalist Seymour Hersh reported in the *New Yorker* on U.S. military reconnaissance missions inside Iran to gather information on nuclear, chemical, and missile sites.

Alarmed, House lawmakers demanded the Pentagon provide a more detailed account of its military espionage. In closed-door sessions with Cambone in early 2005, they questioned the Pentagon's authority to conduct certain intelligence missions and insisted such activity at least be reported to Congress. In response, Cambone presented a finely parsed argument that had been crafted with Rumsfeld and with Pentagon attorneys, asserting that while the U.S. teams operated clandestinely, they did not engage in covert action.

Under U.S. law, "clandestine" refers to actions that are meant to go undetected; "covert," going a step further, refers to operations for which the U.S. government denies responsibility. Covert action requires notification to senior congressional leaders, but clandestine activity does not. Cambone noted that for an action to be covert, the government must be looking for deniability and the opportunity to influence a foreign government. Both conditions must be met, Cambone stressed.

Similarly artful interpretations were advanced to excuse the military intelligence activities from other disclosure rules. Under Title 10 of the *U.S. Code*, for instance, the Defense Department must report certain actions related to the positioning of forces for war. But if the Pentagon's intelligence activity could be considered preparatory for war, this reporting requirement wasn't applicable. Another section of the *Code*, Title 50, mandates that all executive-branch departments keep Congress informed of intelligence activities. But the law does not cover "traditional" military activities and their "routine support"—terms that could be applied to the military intelligence effort given the broad, limitless scope of the war on terrorism.

Several key House leaders—David Obey (D-WI), John Murtha (D-PA), and Bill Young (R-FL)—found such arguments less than persuasive, even after Rumsfeld personally met with them to argue his case. To compel Rumsfeld to be more forthcoming about the secretive missions, Obey, as the ranking Democrat on the Appropriations Committee, introduced an amendment to the 2006 defense appropriations bill requiring the Pentagon to notify Congress of any "special military activities" (spy missions) being conducted in countries on the State Department's list of state sponsors of terrorism (Iran, North Korea, Sudan, Syria, and Cuba).

Eager to head off the legislation, the White House intervened. Andy Card phoned Obey with a promise to help develop an arrangement with

Rumsfeld that would meet congressional concerns. Obey agreed to withdraw his amendment. But in a November 2005 floor statement, the congressman publicly voiced concern that the Pentagon was engaged in some "highly inappropriate and highly dangerous" missions.

Rumsfeld subsequently agreed to disclose Pentagon spying operations to Congress on a graduated scale—the more sensitive the operation, the fewer people on the Hill would be notified. In addition, the Pentagon promised to submit a quarterly report on its intelligence activities. But defense officials made it clear that they were agreeing to the procedures as a matter of respect and comity, not law.

Rumsfeld also moved to ease strains with the CIA by establishing a set of procedures for resolving disputes over the activities of the spy teams as well as over a separate issue involving the allocation of forces. In July 2005, the secretary signed a two-page memorandum of understanding with Porter Goss, who had replaced George Tenet as CIA director. Under the agreement, the Pentagon stopped short of placing the military field teams under CIA supervision or even giving local CIA station chiefs veto authority over the activities of the teams, but it promised to try to coordinate the activities with station chiefs. And if a chief objected to a particular mission, the issue would be pushed up the chain of command for adjudication.

A similar arrangement for resolving disputes with U.S. ambassadors over spy team activities was worked out between Rumsfeld and Rice. Meanwhile, Rumsfeld changed the name of the intelligence teams to "military liaison elements" to suggest a more cooperative relationship between them and local embassy personnel. And the Pentagon instituted a more rigorous system for selecting and training operatives and for screening proposed military intelligence operations.

The tensions over the deployment of the military intelligence teams was only one of a number of controversies spawned by Rumsfeld's mammoth effort to overhaul the Pentagon's entire intelligence apparatus. The secretary had signaled the importance to him of this undertaking by installing his top troubleshooter, Steve Cambone, as undersecretary for intelligence in 2003. Charged with making the intelligence bureaucracy more responsive to the needs of field commanders, Cambone pushed for greater coordination among existing branches and rearranged spending priorities.

He directed regional commands to set up "joint intelligence operations centers" meant to bring analysts and collectors of intelligence closer together with those who use the information. He instituted a more centralized system for assigning surveillance and reconnaissance assets around the world. He combined what had been separate budgets for strategic and tactical systems into a single Military Intelligence Program and exercised tighter oversight.

Some of the moves brought noticeable improvements in intelligence support for combat forces, but they also stirred resentment and resistance among those who regarded Cambone as overly controlling and inexperienced in the intelligence world. Enamored with space-age technology, Rumsfeld and Cambone invested heavily in new satellite programs, including a Space-Based Radar system promising the capability to spot moving targets on the ground in any weather—a very expensive proposition that skeptics warned could not be done at reasonable cost. The project was canceled after Rumsfeld left.

Other initiatives reinforced perceptions among some in the intelligence community that the Pentagon's new intelligence directorate intended to compete with rather than complement the CIA. The Defense Intelligence Agency, for instance, substantially increased its human intelligence branch, expanding the ranks of case officers, linguists, interrogators, and technical specialists. Defense officials explained that the swelling intelligence corps was necessary to provide technical and administrative support for growing numbers of Special Operations forces engaged in counterterrorism missions abroad.

On the domestic front, the Pentagon also stepped up intelligence gathering and became embroiled in allegations of unwarranted snooping on U.S. citizens. A program called the Counter-Intelligence Field Activity, set up in early 2002 to coordinate military counterintelligence operations, was revealed in late 2005 to have collected information on antiwar protestors after the invasion of Iraq. The disclosure prompted outcries from civil liberties groups and from some Democratic lawmakers, who charged that the Pentagon had crossed the line from justified force-protection activities to unacceptable spying on legitimate political action. A subsequent internal investigation concluded that a database for storing threat reports had indeed been improperly used. Defense officials promised to tighten rules governing the collection and retention of such domestic threat reports, but the Pentagon program was eventually shut down in 2008.

The biggest threat to Rumsfeld's intelligence designs came in 2004 when Congress, responding to the recommendations of the 9/11 Commission, moved to establish a new spymaster office to oversee the nation's intelligence community. The initiative could have drained the Pentagon's new intelligence office of much of its authority. But Rumsfeld and Cambone argued successfully against weakening the defense secretary's control over the Pentagon's intelligence agencies, contending that ceding authority to the new director of national intelligence would stand in the way of getting timely information to soldiers on the ground.

Some senior military intelligence officers considered such claims exaggerated. Both James Clapper, a retired Air Force lieutenant general who headed the National Geospatial-Intelligence Agency, and Air Force general Michael Hayden, who then ran the National Security Agency, testified secretly before Congress in the summer of 2004 that putting their agencies under the new director's control would not harm their work. Shortly after the testimony, Rumsfeld called the men to the Pentagon for lunch, where he told them they were out of line because their agencies provide combat support and should be solely under the Pentagon's authority. When Clapper's five-year job contract was up in mid-2006, Rumsfeld didn't renew it.

Ultimately, the need for an undersecretary for intelligence was accepted within the Defense Department and credited with providing a more coordinated Pentagon position on intelligence matters. But the position's development under Rumsfeld owed much to the secretary's close relationship with Cambone, which had both positive and negative implications for what was accomplished.

As a result of Rumsfeld's strong backing, Cambone was able to get things done faster and more effectively. At the same time, some programs were pushed through with such corner cutting that they failed to receive the kind of thorough vetting they would have received under other circumstances. "I think Rumsfeld got what he wanted in terms of having somebody he could turn to and trust on a daily basis in the intelligence area," said Rich Haver, who advised the secretary on intelligence matters for two years. "But the very strength of his relationship with Steve became a crutch."

Indeed, the secretary often turned to Cambone for help on a number of the department's most sensitive issues, whether detainee affairs, missile defense, or cross-border operations in Pakistan. Even Gordon England, the deputy secretary, was not always privy to what transpired between the two.

"When Steve left and I took his job for a few months," recalled Robert Andrews, who had been one of Cambone's deputies, "the first person I talked to was Gordon England, and Gordon said, 'You know, there were a lot of things between Steve and the secretary that I never knew about. Sometimes Steve would tell me and sometimes he wouldn't.'"

Cambone's exceptional status lent his undersecretary's post an extra dimension. Although the job called essentially for setting policy and budgets, not for running operations, Cambone became intimately involved in helping shape some of the military's most secretive missions. Before seeking Rumsfeld's approval for such missions, officers planning them often reviewed details with Cambone, whose support could make all the difference in persuading the secretary to sign off on them.

"It became apparent that the way to get to Rumsfeld was through Cambone," said Andrews, who worked on Special Operations issues in the Pentagon's policy branch before joining the intelligence office in 2006. "So what happened was, the unconventional war, the Special Operations war, started being run through the undersecretary for intelligence."

In December 2005, Rumsfeld formally designated Cambone next in line to take charge of the Defense Department in the event the secretary and deputy secretary died or were incapacitated. Previously, the secretary of the Army had been the department's third in line, but this struck Rumsfeld as inconsistent particularly with wartime reality, where the Army secretary tended to be a less central player. "Steve was the person most intimately involved in operations," Rumsfeld explained. "So I just rearranged the pecking order, or what they call the order of succession."

CHAPTER 17

Toward the Abyss

More than four years after the September 11 attacks, the Bush administration was still trying to define who should be doing what in the war on terrorism. For months, top officials had attempted to draft a presidential directive that would clarify agency responsibilities. Taking the initiative to craft a conceptual framework, Rumsfeld and Feith had presented Bush with a plan in May 2004 for formalizing many of the ad hoc approaches launched by various parts of the U.S. government to thwart al Qaeda and other terrorist networks. Pleased with the Pentagon's outline, Bush had ordered the drafting of a directive that would put the plan into action, but the move stalled.

Rumsfeld renewed efforts in June 2005, delivering another briefing to the president that laid out a comprehensive counterterrorism strategy. Underscoring what had become a common refrain, the brief emphasized that rooting out terrorist networks was not just a military fight but required "all elements of national power and influence," meaning greater involvement by other government agencies, including the departments of State, Justice, and Homeland Security.

Rumsfeld stressed that the main strategic aim should be to promote freedom, democracy, and economic prosperity around the world, thereby mitigating the conditions that terrorists sought to exploit. In discussions with his staff, he pointedly expressed his desire to avoid language that defined the U.S. goal as *defeating* terrorism, placing the focus instead on protecting freedoms. "He was very insistent about that," recalled Jeb Nadaner, a deputy assistant secretary of defense who helped draft the strategy. "He would say that since the terrorists can't defeat us, their aim is to get us to do things like clamp down on civil liberties, in which case we've lost."

Again, Bush signed off on the idea of a formal directive, but the departments of Defense and State disagreed over how to assign responsibilities for the three main pillars of the strategy, which were defined as attacking terrorists abroad, defending the homeland, and supporting mainstream Muslim efforts to reject violent extremism.

To ensure accountability, Pentagon officials favored having one government department in charge of each strategic pillar. They proposed that the Defense Department oversee attacks on terrorist networks, the Department of Homeland Security oversee defense of U.S. territory, and the Department of State oversee initiatives to bolster mainstream Muslim efforts to counter extremist ideology. But State Department officials took issue with this approach, arguing for more of a partnering than a division of responsibilities. The single-department-in-charge model, they argued, could bias planning in each area.

Rumsfeld countered that State's idea of shared leads was unworkable and amounted to a prescription for stagnation. Unity of command had been a persistent refrain of his, and it was a central management principle for the U.S. military as well—even though, as some State Department officials observed, the Pentagon itself functioned with a complex web of command arrangements. Regional commanders who reported to Rumsfeld, for instance, often also interacted with the chairman of the Joint Chiefs of Staff and with senior officers on the Joint Staff. And in Baghdad, responsibility for American activities was divided between a four-star general and an ambassador. A great deal of U.S. government effort relied on teamwork.

Nonetheless, at a meeting of principals on January 5, 2006, Rumsfeld, participating by video teleconference from the Pentagon, made his case for having a single department in charge of each major element of the counterterror effort. Rice objected and, highlighting her concern that agencies might dominate certain areas if they were made principally responsible, noted the Pentagon's predilection for military action.

"I don't really think that's the case, Condi," Rumsfeld asserted.

Unhappy with the direction of the meeting and offended by the portrayal of his department as a brutish bunch whose first instinct was always to kick down doors, Rumsfeld signed off before the session adjourned. A week later, he sent a memo to Steve Hadley, Bush's national security adviser, urging settlement of the issue and arguing against a shared-lead approach:

> My recommendation is that you put the Department of State, the Department of Homeland Security and anyone else you want in charge of all of them. But whatever you do, do not put the Department of Defense in as a "co-chair" or a "blended lead" or a "rotating lead." My view is that the president ought to be able to know who he should hold accountable, and only if you put somebody in charge is that going to be possible. In the DoD we are comfortable working in a "supporting" role with others, as opposed to a "supported" role where others support us. We understand the concept, we can do it and we can certainly work comfortably with others in the lead of all those groups.

On February 6, Rumsfeld wrote Hadley a more general note about the global war on terrorism in which he criticized what he regarded as the general lack of attention by the NSC to the subject. "If there is a global war on terror, why do we not have National Security Council meetings on that subject?" Rumsfeld asked. "Instead, we have meeting after meeting on Iraq. There must be a good reason. Possibly it's because there isn't any coordinated work going on with respect to the global war on terror that lends itself to briefings and meetings. If that is the case, then one would think we need to figure out a way to change that. Let me know if I can be helpful."

Hadley had received similar memos from Rumsfeld in the past and had twice written back disputing the assertion and pointing to the meetings on the war on terrorism that had been held by the NSC, the Principals Committee, the Deputies Committee, and the Counterterrorism Steering Group. At other times, Hadley had addressed the matter in conversation with Rumsfeld. But it never seemed to matter. The defense secretary, Hadley thought, had a tendency to get fixated on certain ideas and never let them go.

At least part of Rumsfeld's sense that inadequate attention had been given to the broader strategy, Hadley figured, was just a matter of the secretary's defensiveness about his own performance. Rumsfeld must have regarded every session on Iraq as in effect a review of his work, and it was natural for him then to press for meetings to review other people's work in turn.

In any case, when Bush's directive on the war on terrorism was finally issued in March 2006, it avoided stipulating any lead-agency responsibilities. Instead, it identified about five hundred tasks, assigning them to various agencies. Rumsfeld and his staff were dismayed. "The result was scattered accountability for a myriad of subtasks," said Robert Andrews, one of those at the Pentagon who had spent months working on the issue. "There was no defined accountability to the president for implementing his strategic guidance."

———————

Meanwhile, in Iraq, the election of a 275-member legislature in December 2005 had gone smoothly, with Iraqi forces in charge of much of the security. Rumsfeld was particularly proud of the top U.S. military commanders who were overseeing the war. In early January 2006, he congratulated Abizaid, Casey, and Army lieutenant general Martin Dempsey, who had taken over command of the Iraqi training effort from Petraeus, praising them for the "first-rate" briefing they had recently given the president. "It is a pleasure to watch the three of you interact," Rumsfeld wrote in a January 4 memo. "I know the President left the Pentagon feeling he has the A-team on the job in Iraq. I'm delighted you are leading the fight for our country in the most important set of challenges we face."

The briefing, which provided a general update on the situation in Iraq, was decidedly upbeat. It noted that the election of the new Iraqi government and recent military operations had set the United States up well for "decisive action in 2006." And although it predicted continued insurgent violence and intimidation of the new political order, it anticipated that significant reductions in U.S. forces were possible by the end of the year.

In the wake of the elections, the Pentagon was aiming to trim the number of combat brigades from seventeen to fifteen, which would bring the overall troop level to about 130,000. The briefing outlined three options for further cuts. One, dubbed "baseline," envisioned dropping to ten brigades by October 2006, with an eleventh brigade stationed in Kuwait as a reserve. A second plan, named "stretch," called for a reduction to eight brigades by December. And a third, "exploitation," proposed slimming to eight by September. No options for keeping troop numbers steady or raising them in 2006 were included.

Army lieutenant general Pete Chiarelli, then just taking over in Baghdad as second in command, was convinced that one way or another, the U.S. troop level was going down, as was the number of bases, then at 110. "I was told, 'Your goal, Chiarelli, is to be down to fifty forward operating bases,' and we started the process of closing them," he recalled.

In the January briefing, the generals cautioned Bush, Rumsfeld, and other senior officials against a rush toward withdrawal. They warned that the impact of the election would not be seen immediately, that political wrangling would continue, and that violence and intimidation would persist. One of the briefing pages listed a handful of "bad things that could happen," among them: a new Shia government could pursue a sectarian agenda, Sunni insurgents could link even more tightly with al Qaeda as a hedge against Shia/Iranian influence, the Iraqi government could prove to be unable to establish control over armed groups, Iraqi security forces could fracture along ethnic lines, and the sectarian violence could bubble over into civil war.

But for the most part, the message from the generals highlighted the positive: that the insurgency would not extend beyond the provinces in which it was concentrated; that the political process could diminish Sunni rejectionist sentiments in the insurgency; that Iran, while attempting to influence events in Iraq, would remain deterred from direct action; and that Iraqi security forces would strengthen in ability and in number over time.

About 80 percent of Iraqi army divisions were projected to be able to lead military operations by the fall of 2006. Police development still lagged badly, beset by corruption, ineptitude, and infiltration, but Casey had declared 2006 the "year of the police," signaling a major push to embed military advisers with police units, as had been done in 2005 with Army units.

Statistics tracking violence in Iraq had shown a decrease in the second half of 2005, although the figures had still recorded significant upward spikes along the way. Total casualties had fallen from a little more than 3,000 in May to about 1,500 in December; monthly suicide attacks had dropped from about 70 to 30. Foreign fighters captured or killed had declined from about 130 to 50 per month. And car bombs had decreased from just under 100 to just over 20 per month.

Eager to capitalize on the encouraging indicators and to solidify plans for further U.S. troop reductions, Rumsfeld wrote Pace on January 20 asking for "a schedule for the rest of this year" showing the "decision points" for additional cuts. Casey responded three days later outlining a "conditions-based, off-ramp strategy" that called for "decision points at three month intervals," beginning in March 2006.

———•———

But hopes that the election could defuse sectarian tensions and mark a definite turning point were shattered on February 22 with an attack on the al-Askari Mosque in Samarra, about eighty miles north of Baghdad. Dressed as Iraqi police officers, insurgents entered the shrine just before 7:00 a.m., captured five guards, and detonated two bombs, which collapsed the mosque's golden dome and badly damaged an adjoining wall. Although no one died, the assault on one of the holiest sites in Shiite Islam triggered a wave of sectarian violence that swept across central Iraq, killing hundreds and dramatically underscoring Iraq's religious divide.

Among Iraqis, the mood darkened immediately. Shiites who had waited patiently to see whether U.S. forces could ensure their security turned to militias for protection, and retaliatory religious warfare between Sunni and Shia escalated.

Initially, after the attack on Samarra, Rumsfeld and his commanders were encouraged by indications that Iraqi security forces had stepped in and seemed to contain the violent response to the bombing. The Iraqi government, too, held together. Pace expressed the official U.S. view when, on March 5, he declared that the Iraqis had looked into the abyss of all-out civil war and had pulled back.

A few weeks after the bombing, Casey sent a confidential memo to Rumsfeld titled "Some Thoughts on Civil War in Iraq." In the general's estimation, civil war hadn't yet broken out and was by no means inevitable. Casey doubted that the Iraqis could be pushed into civil war while U.S. forces remained in large numbers and while Iraqis continued to believe in a political process.

But should a violent, protracted civil war erupt, Casey warned that it would "put the accomplishment of our objectives off for another generation" and open Iraq as "a terrorist safe haven." In such a case, the United States would, in Casey's view, have to either reinforce and reoccupy the country or leave. "The first option," Casey wrote, "would acknowledge that the accomplishment of our strategic objectives for Iraq will be significantly delayed, but that we have not given up. The second acknowledges strategic defeat. I favor the former."

The debate over whether Iraq teetered on the brink of civil war intensified through the spring, and as negotiations over the formation of a new Iraqi government stretched from weeks into months, a more pessimistic outlook took hold even among senior Bush administration officials. With the U.S. military facing the additional burden of containing Shiite militias—on top of countering the insurgency and training Iraqi security forces—it became harder and harder for U.S. commanders to argue that they had enough troops.

Reflecting growing concern in Congress, a ten-person bipartisan panel was set up in March to assess the situation in Iraq and to make policy recommendations. Dubbed the Iraq Study Group, it was chaired by James A. Baker III, secretary of state under George H. W. Bush, and Lee H. Hamilton, a Democrat and former chairman of the Committee on Foreign Affairs.

Long-simmering resentment toward Rumsfeld in the military community boiled into the open in March and April when retired generals, freer to express their views than were active-duty officers, voiced their distress at the secretary's handling of the Iraq War.

The public attacks began with Paul Eaton, a recently retired two-star Army officer who had been the first general in charge of training Iraqi forces in 2003 and 2004. In an opinion piece for the *New York Times*, he called Rumsfeld "incompetent strategically, operationally and tactically" and appealed for the secretary's resignation. Soon after, in a *Time* magazine essay, retired Marine lieutenant general Gregory Newbold, director of operations on the Joint Staff from 2000 to 2002, highlighted a series of grave mistakes made in Iraq and termed them "McNamara-like micromanagement." He, too, called for replacing Rumsfeld. Retired Army major general John Batiste, who had commanded the 1st Infantry Division in Iraq in 2004 and 2005 and who had served earlier as Wolfowitz's senior military assistant, also urged replacing Rumsfeld. In interviews and an op-ed article in the *Washington Post*, Batiste denounced a "pattern of poor strategic decisions" and appealed for new Pentagon leadership "that respects the military."

What bothered Rumsfeld the most wasn't the criticism of his decisions but that of his style. "This idea that he didn't brook dissent—it just bugged him," recalled Di Rita. Pentagon officials sought to blunt the attacks by denying the characterizations and suggesting that the retired generals represented no more than a disgruntled few.

A number of other senior retired officers—Mike DeLong, the former CENTCOM deputy commander; Jack Keane, the former Army vice chief; and Vern Clark, the former chief of naval operations—were enlisted to offer a more positive view of the Pentagon leader. Some civilian specialists on the military also entered the fray, expressing concern that criticism of a sitting defense secretary, even by retired officers, could inhibit civilian-military relations and pointing out that the military was not blameless for what had gone wrong in Iraq.

But the appeals from the generals for Rumsfeld to step down constituted an exceptional affront. Earlier criticism from such retired generals as Anthony Zinni, the former Marine head of Central Command, had been easier for Rumsfeld to dismiss as griping from those who had opposed the war from the start and who had never worked under the Bush administration. This latest condemnation, though, was coming in large part from more recently retired officers who had experience preparing for or serving in Iraq, even if they hadn't been close to Rumsfeld. And while they constituted only a tiny fraction of all retired generals, the important positions these officers had once held and the pointedness of their remarks about the defense secretary made for an extraordinary protest.

———•———

With the critiques of his wartime performance in the headlines, Rumsfeld asked his staff, on April 14, to organize a meeting with a group of military analysts. The use of a select group of analysts, many of them retired military officers, to counter attacks on the administration's wartime activities and to generate positive coverage had become a favorite tool of Rumsfeld and his staff since 2002. Invited periodically to private briefings with the defense secretary and other high-ranking Pentagon officials, the analysts received privileged access and often came away with talking points they could use in media interviews or op-ed articles.

When a group of seventeen analysts assembled with Rumsfeld and Pace on April 18, the first question for the secretary was what impact he thought the latest criticisms would have on his credibility, the military, and the administration. "It is clearly a distraction and unhelpful, but our democracy has lots of distractions and things that are unhelpful," Rumsfeld said.

Seeming to brush off the appeals for his removal, Rumsfeld reminded his audience that he had been unpopular before. Rather than seeing the recent backlash as a particular criticism of his performance, he considered it symptomatic of the general unpopularity of war.

Addressing some of the complaints against him, Rumsfeld turned to the issue of troop levels in Iraq and spoke of the need to strike a balance between having too many and too few U.S. forces there. He argued that having too many troops risked being too intrusive, thereby feeding the insurgency and creating among Iraqis an overdependence on U.S. assistance. Too few troops risked insecurity, which could jeopardize the establishment of a stable government.

"There's no guidebook. You don't get taught this in war college," Rumsfeld said. "This is tough stuff. It's an art. It isn't a science." Taking a shot at the qualifications of his critics and comparing them to the generals advising him, Rumsfeld added, "I look at the shallowness of a lot of the people who were opining about this and opining about that and I say to myself, any day, I'd take Casey and Abizaid's opinion."

Much of the rest of the discussion turned into a kind of pep rally for the secretary, with the analysts—clearly members of Rumsfeld's shrunken fan base—urging him to go on the offensive and shore up waning public support for the war. They spoke of the need to communicate more explicitly the purpose of the war, to stress the consequences of losing in Iraq, to explain how victory there could help strengthen the U.S. struggle against neighboring Iran. They urged Rumsfeld to cite new milestones for the Iraq War, given that the several election milestone dates for 2005 had been met. And they advised that he talk more about the need for sacrifice and about Iraq in the context of the longer, global war on terrorism.

Strategically, a more aggressive public affairs response made sense to Rumsfeld. Increasingly, he had come to see the battle against Islamic extremism as more an ideological than a strictly military struggle. Rumsfeld took two pages of notes during the meeting. The next day, he wrote a memorandum distilling the collective guidance he had received into fifteen bullet points.

He seemed to take to heart the suggestion that he go on the offensive and talk about the "dire consequences" of failure in Iraq. "Get some bumper sticker statements and some battle cries," he had jotted down. He also liked the idea of putting the Iraq conflict in a larger context by casting it as "only one battleground" in the larger global war on terrorism that included Somalia, the Philippines, and other trouble spots. And he made a note to himself to "link Iraq to Iran" by stressing that the more the United States were to succeed in Iraq, the more Iran would be disadvantaged.

There was no mention of acknowledging mistakes or conceding any personal responsibility for the war's difficulties. Instead, Rumsfeld's mind went to the inherently messy nature of war and to the waging of the Iraq War in particular in a much more intense media environment. Preparing for a speech in May, he sent a memo to Matt Latimer, his speechwriter, suggesting that it include a discussion of "modern war" and its new realities.

"Today's warfighters are conducting battles in an era of digital cameras, satellite phones, the Internet, twenty-four-hour news, blogs, and because of these new technologies the American people are seeing things they never saw before about the realities of conflict and of post-war violence," Rumsfeld told graduating cadets at the Virginia Military Institute on May 16.

Rumsfeld also harkened back to previous conflicts, trying as he had on previous occasions when he was under attack to find some reassurance in the notion that even the greatest military operations had had their setbacks. "Today, for example, we remember the D-Day invasion in World War II as a great American victory," he said to the cadets. "That's how it's taught. But many historians also remember it for a series of strategic and tactical errors and decisions based on imperfect intelligence, difficulties that cost lives and delayed the Allied advance. Actually, it was undoubtedly both of those things, which of course is often the nature of warfare."

After a few weeks, the volleys of criticism from the retired generals subsided. But the damage had been done. With Rumsfeld's reputation further eroded, calls for replacing him became rooted not in arguments about the need to atone for mistakes of the past but, far more urgently, in assertions about the need to work out a new way forward. "Put simply, the failed strategies in Iraq and Afghanistan cannot be fixed as long as Rumsfeld remains at the epicenter of the chain of command," Richard Holbrooke, who was U.S. ambassador to the United Nations in the Clinton administration, wrote in the *Washington Post*. "Unless the secretary of defense is replaced, the policy will not and cannot change."

———•———

Privately, Bush was weighing whether to let Rumsfeld go. Individuals far more influential than a few retired generals had been urging the president to drop the defense secretary. On Capitol Hill in particular, many senior Republicans had no more tolerance for Rumsfeld and had told Andy Card so in meetings with him earlier in the year. "Rumsfeld was in the crosshairs," Card recalled. "I heard comments like, 'He's just terrible. He won't even listen to us. We can't talk to him. He's so arrogant.' And it was from our friends. I went back to the president and said, 'Hey, up on the Hill, the drums are beating pretty loudly for change. I think they're serious, and you should think about it.'"

The extent to which Rumsfeld had allowed his relations with key members of Congress to deteriorate baffled even some of his closest associates at the Pentagon. Not only did Rumsfeld appear unwilling to do what was necessary to cultivate better ties, but he seemed at times to antagonize needlessly with his confrontational style. "He'd be behind closed doors with a group of fifty members or so, and he'd be asked a question, and there'd be other ways to answer it but he'd go with the most confrontational," said an officer who was present at a number of Hill meetings with Rumsfeld.

At a strategy session in April with nearly a dozen top aides and outside advisers, the president aired the question of what to do about Rumsfeld. The majority of the group was inclined to cut the secretary loose. But Bush worried that Rumsfeld's departure would look like a concession to the protesting retired generals. He was also reluctant to invite a confirmation hearing for a new defense secretary during a midterm campaign. In public, the president issued strong affirmations of "full support" for the embattled defense secretary.

For his part, Rumsfeld gave no hint that resignation might be on his mind. To the contrary, he told all the political appointees at the Pentagon that if any were planning to leave in the coming months, he wanted to know, and if he didn't hear from them, he would assume they were staying until the end of the Bush administration in January 2009. The implication was that he intended to do so as well.

While inclined to dismiss the protests by the retired generals as a political stunt, Rumsfeld recognized that some of their arguments had resonance. The episode renewed his long-standing concern that the department had not done enough to correct what he saw as distortions about the war and other aspects of his tenure. Indeed, since his snowflake in May 2004 decrying "myths" that had sprung up, Rumsfeld had continued to gripe about perceived inaccuracies. Now, with a fresh wave of accusations being hurled at him, he appeared determined to respond more aggressively.

On February 6, 2006, he fired off a memo titled "Rebuttal" to several senior aides. "Seems to me that we ought to pull together a list of the major dramatic criticisms of the department over the last five years and develop a file of responses," he wrote. "The list could include such things as: there was no plan; there weren't enough troops; that type of thing. We have most of this pulled together. Please assign someone to do that. Then we can begin engaging people outside the department on those issues and systematically rebut them before they become urban legends."

More memos followed. On March 10, he wrote an aide demanding that the Pentagon issue a response to the claim that the military had lacked a plan for postinvasion Iraq. "That is utter nonsense," Rumsfeld declared. "We need to knock it down hard." Ten days later, Rumsfeld demanded "a point-by-point analysis" of the mistakes listed in an opinion article in the *Philadelphia Inquirer* by Trudy Rubin headlined "Mistakes Harm U.S. Efforts in Iraq." Three weeks later, when a critical opinion piece by Clarence Page appeared in the *Washington Times*, Rumsfeld instructed that letters setting the record straight be sent to both Page and the paper.

By that point, the secretary's appeals for a more rapid-fire Pentagon rebuttal effort fell mostly on Dorrance Smith, who had taken over as the assistant secretary for public affairs at the start of 2006. A onetime producer for ABC News who had worked as a senior media adviser for Paul Bremer in Baghdad, Smith beefed up a "rapid response" team to deal with media reports discovered to be spreading what, in the Rumsfeldian view, were lies, mischaracterizations, or inaccuracies.

When an accused newspaper, magazine, or broadcast network rebuffed the demands of Smith's office to issue a correction, Smith printed the correction at the top of the Pentagon's *Early Bird*, a compilation of important news issued daily by the Defense Department and read widely by the Pentagon's brass. On some days, the number of items deemed worthy of correction reached half a dozen or so. Although intended to highlight the extent of misinformed coverage, the list may have had an unintended effect—to reinforce the impression of the besieged Rumsfeld and his aides being frequently on the defensive.

On a vacation in Key West, Florida, with his three grown children and seven grandchildren in February 2006, Rumsfeld visited the "little White

House," the two-story waterfront dwelling used by Harry Truman for working vacations while he was president. Rumsfeld admired what Truman had been able to accomplish, presiding over the creation of a range of institutions and programs that proved critical in the ensuing Cold War struggle between the United States and the Soviet Union. The Marshall Plan, Radio Free Europe, the CIA, the International Monetary Fund, the World Bank, NATO, even the Department of Defense—all emerged on Truman's watch.

If only there could be a similar surge of new institution building now, Rumsfeld thought. For while much of what had arisen in Truman's day had served the United States well for decades, the main threat had changed and required other approaches. America's primary enemy was no longer a superpower but small terrorist cells.

Rumsfeld had tried chipping away at pieces of the Cold War institutional edifice, proposing, for instance, a wholesale revision of the U.S. approach to foreign aid and a revamping of America's apparatus for communicating its policies and intentions to the rest of the world. But by the spring of 2006, he had concluded that a much broader overhaul was needed, one as sweeping and profound as what Truman had achieved at the dawn of the Cold War. His pitch for such large-scale reform began with a trip to the Truman Library in Independence, Missouri, in March for a speech that paid tribute to the former president and emphasized similarities between Truman's efforts to contain communism and the Bush's administration's battle against terrorism.

"Both required our nation to gird for a long, sustained struggle, punctuated by periods of military conflict," Rumsfeld asserted. "Both required the use of all elements of national power to defeat the enemy. Both required a transition from arrangements that were successful in the previous war to arrangements that were much better suited for this new and different era. And above all, both required perseverance by the American people and by their leadership, to be sure."

Picking up on two of his favorite themes, Rumsfeld noted the importance given in Truman's day to bolstering the capacity of partner nations through major aid programs, whether in western Europe or Asia, and to countering Soviet propaganda with an aggressive effort by such operations as the Voice of America and Radio Free Europe.

But Rumsfeld stopped short of providing a detailed plan for managing a long counterterrorism struggle. His purpose appeared largely to be just to lay out the case for such a plan and to establish the Truman era as a reference point. Much of the rest of the speech was devoted to recalling the policies and programs established by Truman and pursued by his successors during the Cold War that had provoked controversy, had run into difficulty, and had hardly been assured of success. In those years, political parties quarreled, allies bickered, and the media criticized. The right way ahead often wasn't clearly marked or linear or the first way chosen.

"No path is straight," Rumsfeld observed. Truman, Eisenhower, Kennedy, Reagan—"they did what they did without a road map. There was no guidebook they could pick up in the morning and tell them what to do when they got up to serve the country."

The parallels with the present were evident, Rumsfeld's suggestion being that government leaders in such momentous times often must endure the kind of second-guessing and lambasting that had been heaped on him and the Bush administration. Rumsfeld noted that the question asked during the Cold War about when it would end had an echo in the question being asked about America's new struggle. There was no clear answer then, Rumsfeld said, "and there isn't one today."

———•———

Rumsfeld continued to think about the kinds of new institutions necessary to deal more effectively with the new global threats—not just terrorism, but others including weapons proliferation, cybercrime, narcotics, piracy, hostage taking, and criminal cartels. In late April, he wrote one of his concept papers on the subject, proposing in six pages a sweeping makeover of world institutions that was both an indictment of the existing order and a pie-in-the-sky attempt to define a new world.

He spared few of the major international organizations of the day. The United Nations, NATO, the Organization of American States, the African Union, the Economic Community of West African States, the Association of Southeast Asian Nations, the European Union—all "were designed at a time when the world's challenges were notably different," he wrote. As he saw them, these institutions, faced with a changed world and different goals, had "failed to adapt sufficiently."

Rumsfeld proposed a high-level commission to make recommendations for restructuring existing international organizations or for creating new ones. Among the suggested entities were a "global peace operations and governance corps" that would have peacekeepers standing by to respond rapidly to crises and to provide military and police assistance; a maritime group to help track shipments of drugs, illegal arms, and weapons of mass destruction; a cooperative structure for governing cyberspace operations; and an organization to address key issues of biotechnology and bioengineering.

In a separate section titled "Regional Challenges," Rumsfeld voiced particular concern about the threat posed by Iran, noting that the time might have come "to form a new collective security arrangement" for the Middle East. He spoke of the need to strengthen ties with key allies in the region—notably, Egypt and Saudi Arabia—and to "bolster all Arab moderates now while they are viable."

And Rumsfeld didn't stop there, offering another set of ideas for overhauling the U.S. government. Recalling the 1986 Goldwater-Nichols legislation that reworked the Pentagon's command structure to improve coordination among the military services, he suggested a similar process be applied to the government's national security side.

"The broader USG structure is still in the industrial age, and it is not serving us well," he wrote. "Only a broad, fundamental reorganization can enable the federal departments and agencies to function with the speed and agility the times demand. The charge of 'incompetence' against the U.S. Government should be easy to rebut, were people to understand the extent to which the current system of government makes competence next to impossible."

Calls for a national security overhaul had been mounting from many experts who argued the current structure was outdated. For more than half a century, the departments of Defense and State had been accustomed to operating mostly independently of one another. But the battle against insurgents and terrorists had demonstrated an urgent requirement to better blend the strengths of the two departments and to incorporate the capabilities of other government agencies as well.

Rumsfeld advised establishing a "commission of statesmen" modeled after the Hoover Commission of the late 1940s, set up by Truman to recommend administrative changes in the federal government. The commission, he said, should look at revamping foreign assistance, organizing it into a single "national security account" rather than the multiple accounts currently overseen by various congressional committees and subcommittees. The basic problem with the current approach, Rumsfeld went on, was that "DoD has resources but not authorities, while State has authorities but not resources." This limited the president's ability to respond. "A modest change will not do it," he wrote. "The only choice is to trash the current laws and undertake a total overhaul of the current systems."

To help the United States get its message out around the world, Rumsfeld advised establishing a "U.S. Agency for Global Communication" that "could serve as a channel to inform, educate and compete in the battle for ideas." This battle, he argued, was as important as any physical one. "Today the centers of gravity of the conflict in Iraq and the Global War on Terror are not on battlefields overseas; rather, they are in the centers of public opinion in the U.S. and in the capitals of free nations," he wrote. Al Qaeda's leaders understood this and consistently responded more quickly than U.S. authorities, Rumsfeld lamented. "When the USG does try to compete in the communications arena, it runs up against a lack of national consensus and understanding about what means are acceptable to the media and to the Congress, and disagreements as to what is legal."

In its expression of frustration with all the constraints imposed by the current order, the paper echoed the anchor chain memo that Rumsfeld had drafted in his first weeks in office. Then the target of his ire was Congress and the myriad legislative restrictions and demands that weighed the Pentagon down. Now Rumsfeld was setting his sights on the rest of the federal government, and indeed, the rest of the world.

———•———

The difficulty of getting the departments of Defense and State to work together was highlighted again in a clash over efforts to establish provincial reconstruction teams in Iraq. The teams were intended to join military and civilian development experts in helping bolster provincial governments. A similar initiative had met with some success in Afghanistan, and Zalmay Khalilzad brought the idea with him when he moved from there in mid-2005 to become the U.S. ambassador in Iraq.

Rice and other State Department officials were enthusiastic about the plan. By deploying civil-military teams into the provinces, their hope was to reenergize a U.S. reconstruction effort that had been hobbled by the concentration of civilian political and economic specialists in Baghdad's heavily guarded Green Zone and only four regional outposts.

But Rumsfeld was wary, seeing the new teams as likely to place greater demands for security on U.S. troops at a time when he was trying to reduce force levels in Iraq. In his view, the teams had more to do with reconstruction than with combating terrorism and didn't warrant either Defense Department funds or military manpower. He also doubted whether the State Department would be able to recruit sufficient numbers of qualified people, and he worried that the military would be called on to fill the gap in both staffing and security. "He felt this was State signing up for another level of stuff that they wouldn't be able to deliver on," Casey recalled in an interview.

More fundamentally, the teams pointed to a shift in strategy that Rumsfeld was not prepared to embrace. His focus remained on transferring responsibility to the Iraqis as soon as possible and pulling out U.S. troops. By contrast, Rice and others in her department had begun to question the wisdom of rushing to hand over security responsibilities to provinces that were at best only marginally ready to meet them. They favored greater emphasis on stability operations and saw the proposed teams as a way of more tightly integrating civil and military efforts. Rice inaugurated the first team in Mosul during a visit to Iraq in November 2005, and initial plans called for a total of sixteen teams by the summer of 2006, each staffed with about a hundred political, development, legal, and civil-military specialists.

But the initiative set off months of haggling that occupied top Pentagon and State Department officials. Rumsfeld raised question after question about how the teams would be funded, staffed, and secured. State officials wanted the Pentagon to provide military units to protect the teams when they traveled; defense officials suggested using private security details instead. State hoped Defense would pay for the teams that were located on forward operating bases, while State agreed to pay for those located at regional embassy office sites. But military lawyers ruled that because State was responsible for the mission, no Pentagon operational funds could be used.

Eventually, with his top military commanders supporting the basic concept of the teams, Rumsfeld gave some ground. In April 2006, the State Department announced that U.S. military forces would provide security for the teams. Assorted memoranda of agreement, cables, and military orders—many of them at cross-purposes—evolved to codify policy for the new groups. But more than a year elapsed before basic issues of budgets, staffing, security, and command-and-control relationships were resolved, delaying the full deployment of the teams and limiting their early effectiveness in the field.

Even more difficult to settle was a disagreement involving how best to apportion U.S. troops in Iraq to guard Iraq's energy infrastructure. Insurgent attacks on oil, power, water, rail, bridge, and gas facilities had plagued the U.S. occupation of the country from the outset. By early 2006, oil production had declined from its postwar peak of 2.55 million barrels per day in September 2004 to just over 1.7 million. At prevailing prices, Iraq had lost about $4.5 billion in oil export revenue during 2005, jeopardizing its ability to secure financing from the International Monetary Fund and threatening a national economic collapse. In Baghdad, electricity was available for only three to five hours a day, and the city was averaging less than three days' supply of diesel and gasoline.

Attacks on oil pipelines weren't the only cause of the problem. Corruption contributed as well. So did the dilapidated condition of the pipes and pumps. But without improved security, repairs couldn't be made, nor could more orderly accounting systems be imposed.

Primary responsibility for protecting the pipelines lay with local, often tribal forces. The new Iraqi government had created special units, known as Strategic Infrastructure Battalions, to augment these efforts. But the battalions were poorly vetted and notoriously corrupt; some were known to have facilitated pipeline attacks themselves.

Rice and her State Department staff wanted the U.S. military to do more. They argued that securing Iraq's oil flow, a key part of the country's economic lifeline, was a vital part of the counterinsurgency campaign.

Rumsfeld and the military command in Baghdad wanted Iraqis to take more responsibility. They were skeptical that throwing more U.S. troops at the problem would really make a difference, given the tendency of pipeline equipment to break down regardless of the attacks.

"It didn't do us any good to go out and put a guy every fifty meters on the pipelines if that would cause only a 10 or 20 percent increase in electricity," Casey said, recalling the debate. Said a White House official also involved in the deliberations, "There were a lot of different thoughts about what do to. And there was probably not a silver-bullet solution. It was going to have to be a combination of things."

But what was particularly frustrating for those in the interagency discussions outside the Pentagon was the persistent resistance from Rumsfeld to taking on an expanded mission. Rumsfeld's argument that the Iraqis should do more themselves contained an important qualifier that further limited U.S. options. He wanted to minimize not only the role of U.S. forces in pipeline security missions but also the role of Iraqi soldiers working with the Americans in combating the insurgency. If those Iraqi forces were to be ruled out for pipeline duty, it was unclear to other senior U.S. officials which Iraqis Rumsfeld had in mind when he argued that Iraqis had to take on the task.

Finally, Hadley stepped in to try to bridge the differences between Rice and Rumsfeld. The plan that eventually emerged sought to satisfy everybody by addressing both the security and the maintenance issues. It called for the creation of rapid-repair crews to patch pipeline damage caused by attacks and to speed the restoration of service. Modeled after something the Colombian government had tried against insurgents in its country, the units would be drawn from the strategic infrastructure battalions, with U.S. troops providing training and oversight. In addition, the plan provided for hardening pipelines, adding secondary pipelines, cracking down on corruption in the oil and electrical ministries, and improving intelligence coordination.

Rumsfeld's tensions with Rice involved not just policy but message. In England in late March, in response to a question, Rice acknowledged that the Bush administration had made "tactical errors, thousands of them, I am sure" in Iraq and perhaps elsewhere. Her spokesman later said she was speaking figuratively.

But Rumsfeld was incensed, viewing the comments as blatant finger-pointing at the Pentagon. Fuming at his stand-up desk as he met with several senior aides the next morning, Rumsfeld wondered aloud what Rice could have possibly intended. He objected to the idea that top administration officials needed to make concessionary comments about errors having been made. Better in his view to say simply that lessons are always being learned. And for Rice to have made the comment overseas in a time of war aggravated the defense secretary all the more.

Rumsfeld spoke with Hadley about Rice's remarks. But the secretary didn't leave it there. Asked about the comments five days later in a radio interview, the Pentagon leader said, "I don't know what she was talking about, to be perfectly honest." War plans always change once the fighting begins, he added, so tactics adjust constantly. "If someone says, 'Well, that's a tactical mistake,' then I guess it's a lack of understanding, at least my understanding, of what warfare is about," he said pointedly.

Bush stepped in to try to arrange at least the surface appearance of calm between his quarreling secretaries, ordering them on a mutual mission to Baghdad. In part, the president intended to put on a public display of U.S. support for Nouri al-Maliki, Iraq's new prime minister, but the joint mission also provided an opportunity to show that Rumsfeld and Rice could set aside their differences and work together. As things turned out, however, the visit in late April did more to highlight the strain between the two secretaries than to erase it.

At a news conference in Baghdad, the Pentagon leader looked tense and impatient, seemingly irritated about having to share the spotlight with Rice. Asked about the flap over Rice's thousands of errors comment, Rumsfeld answered tightly, "I said I hadn't seen it and I wasn't aware of what she meant. But she's right here, and you can ask her." Rice reiterated that her reference to tactical errors hadn't been made "in the military sense." But as she spoke, Rumsfeld alternately doodled and stared absent-mindedly at the ceiling.

Throughout the spring of 2006, Rumsfeld and his commanders continued to complain that other U.S. government agencies were failing to provide the necessary civilian personnel and assistance. State Department officials, often the focus of the Pentagon's lament, frequently countered by citing the lack of security in Iraq as a major obstacle to progress on the political and economic fronts. But Bush was sympathetic to the argument that U.S. government departments other than the Pentagon needed to do more.

In a cabinet meeting in April, the president tried to energize department heads to provide additional support in Iraq, particularly staff to advise Iraqi ministries and to fill slots in the new provincial reconstruction teams. He told the assembled officials that all their agencies needed to contribute more personnel.

A few weeks later, at an NSC meeting on May 26, Rice reported to Bush that an additional forty-eight people had signed up from the State Department and other government agencies for duty in Iraq. But Casey couldn't believe Rice was representing the addition of a mere four dozen people as a sign of significant progress. Hundreds, even thousands, more people were needed.

"Excuse me," Casey ventured. "Did you say forty-eight?"

"Yes," Rice replied.

"Ma'am, that's a paltry number," the general remarked.

Rice exploded. It wasn't Casey's place to be commenting on cabinet contributions. That was her job, she asserted in what others who were present later characterized as a tirade. Bush promptly adjourned the meeting.

Later that day, Rumsfeld sent a note to Casey. "My apologies to you for the comments that were made in the NSC meeting this morning," Rumsfeld wrote. "It is a pattern. There is not much anyone seems to be able to do about it. I thought the President summed it up pretty well when he said, 'On that happy note, we will adjourn.' Thanks for all you are doing out there, and for your patience today as well."

——•——

Around the same time as he was pressing for more support from other government agencies, Rumsfeld presided over one of the periodic gatherings in Washington of all the four-star regional commanders. Held two or three times a year, the conferences were also attended by the service chiefs and high-ranking Pentagon civilians. But for the meeting that May, Rumsfeld had also invited officials from the NSC staff, the State Department, the CIA, and elsewhere to engage in a broad discussion about how the government could pull together more effectively to wage the global fight against terrorism.

After the meeting, several participants noted that the remarks making the most impact had come from Philip Zelikow, Rice's counselor. Zelikow, a onetime lawyer who had taught public policy at Harvard and history at the University of Virginia, had spoken frankly about the State Department's own shortcomings.

He said the State Department was still organized around a country-team model, while the Defense Department had a regional model, with regional strategies, that was more appropriate for conducting a worldwide campaign against terrorism. Further, Zelikow noted, the State Department had little knowledge of counterinsurgency strategies and, with few individual exceptions, it had no effort under way to train its people in such strategies.

According to Zelikow, both the State Department and the Pentagon lacked ideas for how to provide the kind of security assistance to foreign partners that was critical to waging effective counterinsurgency campaigns. This involved not just military training but police and judicial assistance and help with economic development and political operations. Additionally, Zelikow explained, the basic State Department approach to work in foreign countries was one of "passive report," meaning officials tended to observe and report back to Washington what was going on. Increasingly, though, U.S. diplomatic personnel were being called on to help shape the policies and institutions of host countries.

Zelikow thought it crucial that the State Department recognize its changing role and teach its staff new skills—chief among them, how better to manage policing functions and judicial assistance. Zelikow further pointed to the department's need for an expeditionary capability—a kind of civilian reserve corps—to be deployed in crises and to be ready to assume charge of local police, courts, banks, and other entities when a nation collapses or a government is ousted.

Effecting this kind of change at State, Zelikow continued, would require closer partnering in the field between State's country teams and the Pentagon's regional commands. It would require new attitudes on Capitol Hill, where committees responsible for military and diplomatic programs tended to be highly protective of their own turfs. And it would involve major shifts in funds. To this end, Zelikow suggested that Rumsfeld and Rice consider sitting side by side in testimony before Congress on a more integrated agenda and in support of each other's budget plans.

Rumsfeld offered no specific response that Zelikow could later recall. But Hadley detected a softening of the secretary's tone in subsequent weeks and months. Instead of complaining about a lack of will and commitment, Rumsfeld started acknowledging that a lack of capacity might be the core issue. The Pentagon leader would remark that the State Department and other agencies simply did not have the extensive planning processes and rapidly deployable resources that the Pentagon did.

"I think in the end he recognized that these other departments weren't organized to be expeditionary and they did not have, as he said, the deliberative planning process that they needed in order to take on these kinds of tasks," Hadley said. "And he was very good about suggesting that one of the challenges we had was to develop this capacity in other departments, and he offered—and I think other agencies took him up on—sending people from DoD to help other agencies develop this kind of capacity."

For a time, too, in 2006, a number of cabinet secretaries—from Agriculture, Energy, Transportation, and Justice—flew to Iraq to meet with their ministerial counterparts and look at ways of assisting. But there was little follow-up, according to James Jeffrey, then the senior adviser to the secretary of state for Iraq, who viewed the visits as more theatrical than practical. Part of the problem was the very different nature of the U.S. and Iraqi positions. "Iraq is a typical centralized country where, say, the minister of energy actually runs all of the oil wells, whereas the Department of Energy in Washington is a regulatory agency," Jeffrey said. "Most of our cabinet departments are regulatory agencies in a federalized, privatized system. So even if they knew each other and their translators were good and such, they tended to talk past each other."

These periodic meetings of the four-star commanders had gone through a noteworthy evolution under Rumsfeld. Historically, the conference sessions had been organized by the chairman of the Joint Chiefs of Staff, with the secretary of defense making an appearance generally toward the end of two or three days of other meetings in which the regional commanders and service chiefs were able to confer among themselves. But over time, Rumsfeld had exerted greater and greater influence over the meetings.

Myers resisted Rumsfeld's growing role in shaping agendas and attending meetings, insisting that as chairman he continue to run the sessions. But Rumsfeld pushed back, and eventually assumed control of the agendas. "Rumsfeld completely took them over," said Jim Jones, the retired former Marine commandant and ex-NATO commander, who later became the national security adviser to President Barack Obama. Even the name of the gatherings was changed to reflect the shift. Instead of "commanders' conferences," they were officially designated Defense Senior Leadership Conferences.

It was only in the final year of Rumsfeld's tenure, after Pace had taken over as chairman, that the commanders were able to carve out some meeting time without Rumsfeld in the room. "I remember the first such meeting we had," Jones said. "It was thirty minutes before the start of the full day with everybody else. The emotion in the room—I mean, the fact that they could talk freely, or felt that they could say things they wouldn't otherwise say—it was palpable. And the chairman said, 'Well, we've got to do this again.' And I said, 'Amen.'"

———•———

By May, Rumsfeld and his top military commanders were receiving alarming new reports about a situation in Iraq they had been watching with growing concern for some time: Iran's role in fostering attacks on U.S. and coalition forces by supplying explosive devices to Shia militants. In a memo to Rumsfeld, Abizaid cited a list of items—armor-piercing shells, C-4 plastic explosives, infrared triggering devices, and electronic transmitter/receiver components—believed to be coming from the Qods Force of the Iranian Revolutionary Guard Corps (IRGC-QF).

"While there is no evidence IRGC-QF provides specific targeting guidance, I believe Iran is fully aware of EFP [explosively formed projectile]

use against Coalition targets," Abizaid wrote. Asserting that Iranian supreme leader Ali Khamenei was "cognizant" of the support to Shia militants, Abizaid recommended that the United States issue a "forceful
demarche" to Iran regarding its contribution to attacks in Iraq. Rumsfeld
quickly forwarded the memo to Hadley and Rice, recommending that the
issue be addressed "directly and quickly" by all the relevant agencies.

But at the State Department, U.S. policy toward Iran was moving in a
different direction. Following the failure of European negotiations aimed
at dissuading Iran from its nuclear ambitions, Rice had decided to push
for a dramatic shift in approach in which the United States would enter
into broad-based talks with Iran. The move was conditioned on Iran
ceasing its enrichment and reprocessing efforts.

Rumsfeld was very skeptical about the plan, wondering what the
United States would get out of the concession. But Rice had managed to
bring Bush along on the idea, and even Cheney appeared willing to ac-
cede to it.

Over Memorial Day weekend, Eric Edelman, the Pentagon's civilian
policy chief, received a call from one of Rice's top aides inviting him to a
Monday meeting at Rice's residence to discuss the idea of a diplomatic
overture to Iran. Given Rumsfeld's opposition to the measure, Edelman
did not want his attendance to be construed as Pentagon support. A senior Rice subordinate assured him that there would be no decisions,
only discussion. On his arrival, however, he found a large cast of interagency representatives being presented with a fait accompli. The deal
had been developed by Rice and her team in great secrecy.

When Edelman reported on the meeting to Rumsfeld the next day,
the secretary told him not to worry. Rumsfeld said he had spoken to
Bush and had been told that Rice would not be going forward immediately with the initiative. But she did, announcing on May 31 that the
United States would join European talks with Iran over its nuclear program, provided the Iranian government suspended efforts to enrich
uranium and reprocess spent nuclear fuel. Iran quickly dismissed the offer, but Rice received praise for a smart diplomatic maneuver and for
getting the administration's hawks and doves to agree, however briefly,
on a common approach to Iran.

Still, Rumsfeld hadn't dropped the idea of a demarche to make Iran
stop its efforts to destabilize Iraq by arming violent groups. He raised it

again in early June with Hadley. At around the same time, Edelman discussed with Casey the possibility of officially designating the Qods Force in Iraq as "hostile"—a move that would enable U.S. troops to take action against the Iranian operatives rather than waiting for them to attack.

Casey went public with the U.S. military's concerns in June, telling a Pentagon news conference that Iranian support for extremists inside Iraq had shown a "noticeable increase" during the year. But after Edelman invited Casey to come forward with a recommendation, the general never pushed for it. Casey and his staff debated the issue but determined that there was not enough intelligence information to make the case.

Despite growing impatience with what the Iranians were doing in Iraq, the interagency meetings about what to do failed to come to any resolution. Whenever the issue came before the principals, Hadley would remand it for more paper writing.

Throughout this period in 2005 and into 2006, some consideration was also given to possible military action against Iran. The planning by a highly compartmented group within U.S. Central Command was much more secretive even than discussions along the diplomatic track, and at the upper levels of the U.S. military, at least, there seemed to be little enthusiasm for it. Abizaid in particular was concerned about the prospect of miscalculation that would push the United States into a war with Iran. On his own initiative in late 2005, he prepared a briefing for Rumsfeld and top White House officials intended to provide a heavy dose of reality.

"The rhetoric was increasing about the need to go blow up the Iranian nuclear facilities, and I just wanted to make sure everybody understood, before they said go do it, what it might entail," Abizaid recalled. "Frequently, the strategic choices that have to be considered by the civilian leadership are not adequately seen, and I was very concerned that the Iranian problem was not adequately understood."

A senior officer on Abizaid's staff said that Rumsfeld was given a series of briefings beginning in late 2005 that sketched Iranian military capabilities and described potential U.S. military courses of action. "It was sort of iterative, which is a way the secretary liked to consider things—logically, sequentially, one step at a time, giving himself some time to think and consider between sessions," the officer said.

"We went into details like potential nuclear facilities—where are they, how one could take them out. But it wasn't going to be clean—we wanted to disabuse people of that. And the plans never got to what we call execution-level detail—that is, the point at which you could order this or that and something would happen tomorrow. What Abizaid wanted to show was, 'Hey look, we need to be very sober about this, there's no surgical strike option here that's going to lead us anywhere.' And I think it had the intended effect, which was to calm the waters in Washington and preclude or at least diminish the potential for a rash misstep."

———•———

Larry Di Rita, one of Rumsfeld's first hires and closest aides, left the Pentagon in May 2006 for a job in banking. A frequent squash partner of the secretary's, Di Rita delivered a PowerPoint presentation at his farewell on Rumsfeld's distinctive squash-playing style. Rumsfeld had become a devoted enthusiast after picking up the game in his fifties, and he was known to duck away in the early evening to the Pentagon gym. In typical fashion, he played aggressively, relentlessly—and by his own rules.

Rumsfeld opted for power over finesse, hitting the ball hard and fast. "Every time he'd hit one by me, he'd say, 'Speed kills,'" Di Rita remarked. Rumsfeld preferred "hardball" squash, although it had largely been replaced by a version of the game that uses a softer ball and a wider court. And he had no patience for "lets" (allowing players to take a point over when there is interference), which he thought were for losers.

If hit with a ball, Rumsfeld continued to play and request a point on his behalf. While blood on a player is supposed to bring an immediate halt to a squash game, it didn't for him, especially if the blood was his own. "Squash rules are designed to reflect a kind of Old-World clubbiness, but that's just not his deal," Di Rita explained. "His deal is to be focused and hypercompetitive."

The energy and fierceness with which Rumsfeld played were testament to his good health and vigor even as he approached his seventy-fourth birthday. But some officials who dealt regularly with him saw occasional memory lapses and signs of fatigue suggesting that either the pressures of the job were wearing him down or the years were catching up with him, or both. "There were times when I was sure that I had told him something very important and that I thought had registered, but at a later meeting he'd say, 'Well, I hadn't heard that before,'" Abizaid remarked.

———•———

On June 7, Air Force jets dropped two five-hundred-pound bombs on a house in the village of Hibhib near the city of Baqubah. A bearded man pulled from the rubble was identified as Abu Musab al-Zarqawi, the leading foreign terrorist in Iraq. Still clinging to life when Iraqi and American forces arrived at the scene, al-Zarqawi soon died. His death marked perhaps the greatest triumph for U.S. forces in their bloody campaign against Iraq's three-year-old insurgency.

Encouraged by the elimination of al-Zarqawi and by the swearing-in two and a half weeks earlier of Iraq's first constitutional government under al-Maliki's leadership, Rumsfeld proceeded with a reduction in the number of combat brigades in Iraq from fifteen to fourteen, trimming the troop total to 127,000. The move suggested that whatever concerns Rumsfeld had about civil war, he was confident enough to withdraw some forces. "He knew there was sectarian violence, but he said Iraqis have to sort it out," Edelman said.

At Rumsfeld's request, the Joint Staff and the Pentagon's civilian policy branch had spent some time during the spring looking at the question of what to do in the event of full-scale civil war. "There were a bunch of briefings done, we discussed it with the secretary a couple of times, but nothing really came of it," Edelman recalled. "I didn't regard it as a terribly serious exercise."

After deciding to remove a combat brigade, Rumsfeld asked Edelman to notify Rice of the move. She regarded any drawdown at that time as unwise, given the risk that a fresh spike in violence could undermine the new al-Maliki government. But force-level decisions were not something Rumsfeld tended to put before the principals for consent. His practice had been to make such decisions with the president and then to inform his colleagues after the fact.

Rice erupted at receiving the news from Edelman. "What are you guys doing! You're going to destabilize Maliki!" she exclaimed.

"Look, Madame Secretary, I'm the messenger here; it's not my decision," Edelman replied, weakly.

It wasn't the first time Rumsfeld had used Edelman as a buffer with
the secretary of state. Not infrequently, Rumsfeld would send Edelman
to Principals Committee meetings when he expected some Pentagon
position or action to be in for a tongue-lashing from Rice. "There was a
part of him that was very amused that I would go and take this beating
from her," Edelman recalled.

In the few months after the Samarra bombing in February, Rumsfeld
and his commanders wrestled with whether the nature of the conflict in
Iraq had changed and, if so, whether U.S. strategy should adjust. By
June, the secretary was informed by Casey that the situation had indeed
become more complicated. While Sunni insurgents and other extremist
elements were still a problem, the general concluded that the main security challenge had shifted from an insurgency against U.S. and allied
forces to a struggle among Iraqis for political and economic power.

Casey, speaking by video teleconference, delivered that message to
Rumsfeld, Bush, and other top administration officials gathered at
Camp David on June 12 to assess the situation in Iraq. "The diversity of
violent groups in Iraq has blurred the precision of the term 'The Insurgency' and has increased the complexity of the security environment,"
said the top line of a military briefing chart titled "Strategic Assessment"
presented at the meeting.

Casey outlined the U.S. military's successes to date: the buildup of Iraqi
security forces had progressed, al Qaeda networks in the country had been
weakened, and the resistance fighters had not expanded geographically.
But he also cited disturbing shortcomings: there had been no reduction in
the levels of attacks, al Qaeda networks had shown persistent ability to
carry out high-visibility mass-casualty attacks, the Iraqi government had
demonstrated little will to curb militias, and kidnappings were fueling sectarian fears and diminishing confidence in the new Iraqi government.

Still, Casey recommended staying on course. He reiterated plans to
continue transitioning responsibility to Iraqi forces and reducing the
level of U.S. troops during the year. "Stabilization" had become the

stated operational aim in Iraq, according to the briefing charts, not total victory or elimination of violence. And despite the intensifying blood-shed, Casey anticipated that within a year, Iraq would be mostly stable, with the bulk of American combat troops headed home.

Rumsfeld, too, favored sticking with the plan and showed no inclination to second-guess his main military commanders. But elsewhere in the U.S. government, some senior officials were having serious second thoughts about the U.S. approach. On the NSC staff, Meghan O'Sullivan, the deputy national security adviser for Iraq, had concluded that the military drawdown strategy was out of sync with the new realities in Iraq and was indefensible in the face of the intensified sectarian conflict. A member of her staff, who kept a file tracking violence levels in individual Baghdad neighborhoods, had traced a direct correlation between the violence and the movement of U.S. forces.

"It was the same story over and over again," O'Sullivan recalled. "As soon as we turned a neighborhood over to Iraqi forces and left, the militias would sweep in, the Iraqi forces would prove unreliable, and the violence would go up dramatically."

The emphasis that Rumsfeld and his generals put on ceding control to Iraqis might have made sense in other circumstances, O'Sullivan thought. But not with weakened Iraqi security forces riven by the same sectarian tensions that were tearing the country apart.

At the State Department, Philip Zelikow also questioned the Pentagon's focus on transitioning responsibility. He had delivered a memo in March 2006 calling for a "massive effort to improve security in Baghdad and surrounding areas, and a reckoning with the most violent Shia/Sadrist militias." Working with James Jeffrey, Zelikow drafted a paper for the Camp David meeting that outlined an illustrative new military strategy, a "selective counterinsurgency" that would focus on securing "a few selected areas" and might involve additional American forces in the near term.

NSC and State Department officials had hoped the Camp David meeting might trigger a major reassessment of the U.S. strategy in Iraq. But with the new al-Maliki government just forming in Baghdad, Bush spent only a day at the Maryland retreat with his national security team before departing for a surprise visit to Iraq.

Later in the month, Casey traveled to Washington to present a formal recommendation for a further reduction in U.S. troop levels. Several other high-ranking U.S. commanders in Iraq—among them, Pete Chiarelli and Major General J. D. Thurman, who headed the division responsible for Baghdad and several neighboring provinces—had reservations about proceeding with the cuts, given how unsettled conditions were in Iraq.

Chiarelli warned Casey and the general's senior planners that conditions had changed for the worse since the drawdown plan had been devised. He argued that the al-Maliki government had taken much longer to form than anticipated and that whether it would prove willing and able to overcome sectarian divisions had yet to be seen. "I made strong arguments, saying, 'Hey, maybe we ought to hold off here a little bit longer and see what happens after the new government comes in,'" he said in an interview. But Chiarelli found stiff resistance to delaying the withdrawal schedule.

For his part, Casey does not recall hearing any objection when he met with his commanders in June before heading to Washington. "I said, 'Okay, does everybody have enough troops?' And they all said yes," Casey recounted.

In a series of meetings in Washington with Rumsfeld, Bush, and the Joint Chiefs of Staff, Casey proposed sending two more combat brigades home within a few months, which would have brought the total to twelve brigades, or about 120,000 troops, counting support units. He projected that by the end of 2006, the number of combat brigades would drop to as few as ten, and by the end of 2007, to five or six brigades.

But Casey also noted that it would take another six months to see whether the new al-Maliki government could make a difference, and he cautioned that the sectarian violence and a mounting confrontation with militia groups could well complicate the drawdown plans.

Briefing Rumsfeld on June 21, Casey outlined how the basic assumptions about Iraq had changed in recent months. Instead of having a new government early in 2006, he said, six months had passed without fresh leadership, and the security situation had worsened. Greater Sunni participation in the political process had been expected, but no such effect was yet evident. Instead of Shia military violence being contained by

Iraqi security forces, a confrontation with al-Sadr was looming, and there were doubts about the new Iraqi government's will and capability to deal with that threat. Additionally, although Iraqi security forces had been projected to grow and strengthen, fresh concerns had arisen about police loyalty in some areas, and ministerial capacity was developing more slowly than anticipated. Moreover, amid troublesome evidence of clandestine Iranian activity in support of attacks on U.S. and government forces, it could no longer be assumed that Iran would refrain from direct action in Iraq.

Casey's revealing then-and-now comparison starkly showed just how much conditions in Iraq had fallen short of optimistic U.S. predictions. Yet the general and his staff did not favor any change in course. Nor was Rumsfeld pressing for one. Some of Rumsfeld's readiness to look past the evident warning signs may be explained, at least in part, by the encouragement he had taken in al-Zarqawi's death earlier in the month and in the long-awaited establishment of a legitimately elected Iraqi government. Rumsfeld was so eager, moreover, to diminish America's exposure and involvement in Iraq that he may have not let himself absorb the full implications of the shift in basic assumptions noted by Casey.

But his failure at this critical point to appreciate the need for a new strategy marked a grave misjudgment. It underscored the ultimate failure of his management of the Iraq War and effectively doomed his tenure, leaving Bush little choice before the year was out but to remove him and pursue a different path.

Even before Casey left Washington and returned to Iraq, a surge of car bombs and suicide attacks across the country elevated the sectarian conflict to a new high. On July 1, a truck bomb killed at least sixty-six people and injured more than a hundred on a market street in the Shiite Muslim heart of Baghdad. On July 6, a green minibus loaded with explosives detonated in a group of Iranian pilgrims visiting a Shiite Muslim shrine in southern Iraq on the outskirts of Kufa, killing fourteen and injuring thirty-eight. On July 10, a barrage of bombings and gunfire killed at least forty people.

The fresh spate of attacks came despite a tightened security plan for Baghdad instituted in June that had included a curfew, increased checkpoints, and restrictions on carrying weapons. Already at a high in June, violence against civilians rose further in July, with much of the killing attributed to death squads. The intensified violence revealed a startling geographic pattern, with Shia groups seeking to consolidate territorial control over local neighborhoods.

As attacks in the Iraqi capital threatened to spiral out of control, Chiarelli urged Casey on July 23 to call off the departure of the 172nd Stryker Brigade combat team, which was heading home to Alaska after a yearlong deployment. Chiarelli wanted the unit, with its 3,700 soldiers and agile armored Stryker vehicles, shifted from Mosul to Baghdad as part of a second concerted attempt that summer to bolster security in the Iraqi capital.

Casey received Rumsfeld's approval to extend the brigade's tour in Iraq for another four months, and he shelved plans for any further cuts in the U.S. force level. News of the brigade's delayed departure provoked anger and disappointment among soldiers and their families. Hundreds of brigade members who had already left the country were called back.

In a scolding note to Casey on August 2, Rumsfeld wrote that the late request to keep the brigade had "hurt" and caused "difficulties in Alaska and Congress." The secretary told his commander, "We have to do a better job looking around corners to the extent it is humanly possible."

Later that month, Rumsfeld met in Alaska with family members of the troops deployed. "The question came up frequently as to when they are going to come back," Rumsfeld recounted afterward in a memo to Pace. "They asked if there is any danger that they would be extended beyond the 120 days, or would they be home for Christmas. I told them I did not have a 'magic wand' that I could promise something like that, but that I would do everything humanly possible and within my power to see that they were not extended and that they would be home for Christmas. It would be a wonderful thing if we could get them home for Thanksgiving instead of Christmas."

The 172nd was finally permitted to leave in late fall and did make it home in time for Christmas, though not for Thanksgiving.

By the time the Stryker brigade was delayed, Hadley had begun to harbor some of the same doubts about the U.S. course in Iraq that had been expressed by O'Sullivan and several others on the NSC staff. But embarking on a fundamental reexamination of the strategy was tricky. Rumsfeld and his commanders had shown no inclination to rethink what they were doing, and with midterm congressional elections coming in the fall, the administration could not be seen to be questioning its own approach to such a controversial war.

Hadley figured that the NSC format, with its set agendas and frequent interagency strains, was not conducive to initiating the kind of freewheeling reassessment of war strategy that he had in mind. His idea was to brainstorm with a smaller group, one that included those directly involved with the Iraq War.

After consulting with Bush, Hadley received permission to proceed with a meeting limited to Rumsfeld, Pace, Casey, and Khalilzad. His plan was to present them with a range of blunt questions about the situation in Iraq and existing U.S. strategy, hoping to prompt their realization of the need for change. "I called up Don Rumsfeld and said, 'This is what I'd like to do, the president thinks it would be a good idea, and I will of course report faithfully the answers to the president,'" Hadley recalled. "And Don Rumsfeld said fine, and he participated in it actively."

At the meeting on July 22, Hadley reviewed a list of more than fifty questions, many of which seemed to second-guess past decisions by Rumsfeld and Casey. They asked whether security forces should take more aggressive action in Baghdad, whether there should be more troops in the capital, and whether the transition of security responsibilities to the Iraqis was occurring at the right pace. Queries were raised, too, about whether the sectarian violence had become "self-sustaining," whether the political process could really be expected to help stem the violence, and whether shifts were needed in existing strategies for dealing with the Sunnis, Shias, and Kurds.

The session ended with no shift in course, although, according to the official minutes, general agreement was reached that the conflict had become more complex and that stabilizing Baghdad would be central to success. "Our strategy is the best course of action when compared to the radical alternatives, although we need constantly to assess it and make necessary operational and tactical adjustment," the minutes said.

"Alternatives, such as suspending Iraq's democratic experiment or dividing the country along ethnic lines, are not attractive, particularly feasible or desired by Iraqis. We will continue to need to make adjustments as the situation in Iraq evolves. For now, we recognize that stabilizing the security environment and stimulating more reconciliation are prerequisites for further progress."

Hadley and O'Sullivan took some comfort in the belief that they had at least sparked an internal administration debate. But Rumsfeld and Abizaid, appearing twelve days later before the Senate Armed Services Committee, asserted that while sectarian violence had worsened and the fight against extremists in Iraq and elsewhere would probably last a long time, it should not stop U.S. troops from leaving.

"The Cold War lasted forty-plus years," Rumsfeld noted. "And the struggle against violent extremists who are determined to prevent free people from exercising their rights as free people is going to go on a long time and it's going to be a tough one. That does not mean that we have to spend the rest of our lives as the United States armed forces in Iraq. The Iraqis are going to have to take that over. We can't want freedom more for the Iraqi people than they want for themselves."

Security conditions in Baghdad continued to deteriorate through August even with the modest increase in U.S. forces there. The hope had been that the influx of troops from the 172nd would help clear the insurgent- and militia-infested neighborhoods in the Iraqi capital and that Iraqi forces would then secure them. But the Iraqi forces were not proving effective.

On August 17, Bush expressed his own concerns about the lack of security to Rumsfeld and other senior national security advisers at a White House meeting and called for a "clear way forward" by Labor Day. With the latest Gallup poll showing that 56 percent of Americans considered the war a mistake, the president emphasized the need to "fight off the impression that this is not winnable."

Casey assured Bush that the current level of U.S. troops was sufficient but expressed some uncertainty about whether the Iraqis could do their part in securing the neighborhoods. Bush suggested that if the Iraqis couldn't combat the enemy, the United States would have to step back in and help. "If they can't do it, we will," the president said. "If the bicycle teeters, we're going to put the hand back on. We have to make damn sure we cannot fail. If they stumble, we have to have enough manpower to cope with that."

Bush's use of Rumsfeld's favorite bicycle metaphor was intentional and represented a direct challenge to the defense secretary. Casey replied, "I've got it. I understand your intent."

CHAPTER 18

Not Well Enough or Fast Enough

By the summer of 2006, the U.S. military's rating of the preparedness of forces to fight confirmed a disturbing deterioration in the Army. Not only were troops and equipment in the field being battered by the wars in Iraq and Afghanistan, but forces back home in the United States were hurting as well with so many of their resources going to augment units sent abroad.

The military rating system measured three major factors: whether units had the personnel they needed, whether their equipment requirements had been met, and whether they had received adequate training. The grades, which ranged from a high of C-1 to a low of C-4, were classified, but Congress was privy to them, and lawmakers grew alarmed when they saw only C-3s and C-4s across the board in the Army.

"There is not a single non-deployed Army brigade combat team in the United States that is ready to deploy," Senator Jack Reed, a Rhode Island Democrat and former Army captain, declared in August. "The bottom line is that we have no ready strategic reserve." Addressing Rumsfeld during a session of the Senate Armed Services Committee, Reed called the low ratings "a stunning indictment of your leadership."

Other reports also showed a U.S. Army badly strained by the burdens of two prolonged overseas wars. An assessment issued by two leading

House defense experts, Democratic representatives David Obey of Wisconsin and John Murtha of Pennsylvania, noted growing personnel shortages, particularly in the National Guard and Army Reserves. To provide enough military police and civil affairs specialists, the congressmen observed, the Army was cobbling together units from different reserve outfits. Plans to allow units to train at home for two years between each yearlong deployment to Iraq or Afghanistan had been scrapped, with some troops being sent back overseas after less than a year of rest and retraining.

Shortfalls in tanks, Humvees, and other equipment were even more problematic. About 20 to 30 percent of all Army equipment was not in service because it was either in transit or in mounting backlogs at depots awaiting maintenance. The Army, in the words of the congressmen, had become an organization that was living "hand-to-mouth."

The slump in military readiness was a particular embarrassment for Rumsfeld and the Bush administration. As a presidential candidate in 2000, Bush had attacked the Clinton administration for low readiness ratings. At that time, though, only two of ten divisions had had poor scores. Now, all nondeployed units did.

Publicly, Rumsfeld maintained that the Army was in better shape than the ratings suggested. He insisted that Army forces were better trained and better equipped than when he took office. Further, the size of the "operational" Army, he noted, had been increased during his tenure as a result of an internal restructuring. Recruiting had picked up (due in part, though, to a decision to lower standards), and reenlistment rates remained high, especially among troops who had served in Afghanistan and Iraq.

Rumsfeld explained the decrease in readiness ratings as a direct result of increased requirements for the force. The secretary had been pushing to adopt a different rating system, one that would allow commanders to set narrower requirements based on the missions that units were most expected to carry out. Such a system would have yielded higher readiness scores for the Army.

But even the Army's leadership had reached the point of acknowledging that they could no longer make ends meet. In an extraordinary show of defiance, General Pete Schoomaker, the Army chief of staff, had refused to submit a new budget plan earlier in 2006 after being told to limit the request to $114 billion. Estimating that he needed nearly $139 billion, he indicated to Rumsfeld that if he had to send in a plan based on the lower figure, he would find savings by proposing a drastic reduction in Army troop strength—a move sure to raise objections in Congress and to generate headlines disastrous for the administration.

Some senior subordinates, including Deputy Secretary Gordon England, were privately critical of Army leaders for having failed to do enough on their own to cut costs. The Army had greatly underestimated the cost and time necessary to overhaul its brigade structure, and it had failed to shift as many soldiers from administrative to operational positions as Rumsfeld and his staff thought possible.

But Rumsfeld could not afford a major clash with Schoomaker. The secretary's relations with the Army chief had been much better than his relations with Shinseki. For one thing, Schoomaker had proven especially supportive of Rumsfeld's effort to hold the line against a permanent increase in the Army's overall size. "South of Pete Schoomaker, there was no real support in the Army's leadership for holding the line," recalled David Chu, the undersecretary of defense for personnel. "The barons were saying to Pete, 'You're in the wrong place, you're knuckling under to Rumsfeld.'"

Rumsfeld agreed to reconsider the Army's budget limit, and ultimately he helped persuade Bush to raise the Army's total by $7 billion, to $121 billion. It wasn't as much as Schoomaker had sought, but it showed some sensitivity to the Army's plight and was enough to avoid a bruising public fight with Army leaders.

———————

Adding to Rumsfeld's setbacks in the summer of 2006, the Supreme Court ruled against him and other administration officials in a case with his name on it. *Hamdan v. Rumsfeld* challenged the system of military commissions established to try suspected terrorists captured in military operations in Afghanistan and elsewhere. The commissions, initially conceived as a means of delivering swift and certain punishment by operating outside traditional rules of evidence and without judicial review or congressional oversight, had become mired in arguments about their legality and lack of due process for defendants.

According to the U.S. government, Salim Ahmed Hamdan, a Yemeni captured in Afghanistan in November 2001 and taken to Guantánamo in June 2002, had served as a driver and bodyguard for Osama bin Laden. In July 2004, he was charged with conspiracy to commit terrorism. Hamdan filed a petition for a writ of habeas corpus, arguing that the military commission convened to try him was illegal and lacked the protections required under the Geneva Conventions and the U.S. Uniform Code of Military Justice. At the time the Supreme Court acted on his case, he was among only ten out of 450 prisoners at Guantánamo who had been charged before the military commission system. None of the trials had progressed beyond preliminary hearings.

In late June, a five-justice majority ruled that the commissions were not authorized by Congress, not required by military necessity, and not in keeping with international law. Under Common Article 3 of the Geneva Conventions, the Court held, Guantánamo detainees were entitled to more protections than the commissions afforded. The applicability of Common Article 3, which requires humane treatment of captured combatants and prohibits trials except by "a regularly constituted court," had been a source of intense dispute among administration officials for months. The Court's ruling faulted the commissions for failing to guarantee defendants the right to attend their trials and for allowing the prosecution to introduce hearsay evidence, unsworn testimony, and evidence obtained through coercion.

The day after the Court's decision, Rumsfeld convened a meeting of his senior staff. Seated at a conference table, his arms behind his head, the secretary leaned back in his chair and, sporting a mischievous grin, asked Jim Haynes, his general counsel, "So, Jim, *Hamdan v. Rumsfeld*—who won?"

"I haven't read the whole case yet but . . . ," Haynes began.

"You haven't read the whole case yet? Didn't it come out yesterday?" Rumsfeld shot back.

Haynes appeared unperturbed. "Yeah, I haven't read the whole case yet but of course I've talked to people in DoJ about it," he replied, referring to the Department of Justice. The consensus legal view, Haynes explained, was that Common Article 3 must apply as a matter of treaty law.

Rumsfeld leaned forward, pressing his palms on top of the table. "So I'm going to go down in history as the only secretary of defense to have lost a case against a terrorist?" the secretary queried.

"I wouldn't look at it as a loss," Haynes answered.

"Really?" Rumsfeld asked in disbelief.

Haynes explained that the Court had identified the lack of congressional authorization as a principal flaw in the commissions. He argued that the administration needed simply to press Congress to pass legislation that would allow the commissions to proceed as the Pentagon had planned.

But Charles "Cully" Stimson, who had replaced Matt Waxman as Rumsfeld's senior adviser on detainee matters, took issue with that approach. He contended at the staff meeting that in the face of strong support of detainee rights from such influential Republican senators as John McCain of Arizona and Lindsey Graham of South Carolina, an attempt to seek congressional authorization for the previous plan wouldn't stand a chance on Capitol Hill. Stimson lobbied instead for discarding the special-commission rules and relying, with only several adjustments in procedures, on the Uniform Code of Military Justice—the military's legal rule book.

In the weeks that followed, Cheney and Alberto Gonzales touted draft legislation that would reverse the Court's decision, while Rice appealed for action to affirm it. Faced with conflicting advice from his in-house attorneys, Rumsfeld appeared to take a backseat in the discussion.

A further consequence of the ruling in the *Hamdan* case was to put growing pressure on Rumsfeld to take custody of the high-value detainees that the CIA had been holding at secret sites outside the United States—a responsibility that the defense secretary had been resisting for months. Since public disclosure of the sites by the *Washington Post* in November 2005, several countries had asked the CIA to close prisons on their soil, while others refused requests to host new secret sites. The *Hamdan* decision meant the CIA could no longer handle suspects outside the boundaries of the Geneva Conventions.

Rice pressed Bush for a change in policy, arguing that it was important to settle the issue, both as a matter of foreign policy and on moral grounds. The issue of the secret sites was, she pointed out, having a corrosive effect on the nation's ability to win cooperation on a range of intelligence issues.

On September 6, Bush announced the transfer of fourteen suspected terrorists from the CIA's foreign sites to the military's Guantánamo facility. On the same day, after months of contentious internal debate, the

Pentagon issued Directive 2310 setting new policy on detention operations, and the Army made public a new interrogation manual restoring the standards of the Geneva Conventions. The manual incorporated Common Article 3, listed nineteen approved interrogation techniques, and specifically prohibited eight others, some of which had been in evidence at Abu Ghraib—among them, placing hoods over prisoners' heads, using dogs, or forcing a prisoner to be naked or to perform sexual acts.

In September, Jack Keane, the retired general who had been the Army's vice chief and who was originally Rumsfeld's pick to succeed Shinseki, went to see the secretary. He had grown increasingly worried about what he regarded as a disconnect between the course being pursued by the U.S. military in Iraq and what he knew about the situation there from his own contacts in the field and from intelligence briefings he had received as a member of the Defense Policy Board.

Keane had come to the conclusion that the only way forward in Iraq required a sharp change in U.S. strategy, involving a major escalation of U.S. forces and a new focus on protecting Iraqi civilians. He was also convinced that a new strategy would require different military leadership, meaning the removal of Generals John Abizaid and George Casey. Uncertain about approaching Rumsfeld with so radical a proposal, Keane first sounded out Paul Wolfowitz and Newt Gingrich, both of whom encouraged Keane to talk to Rumsfeld.

Keane met with Rumsfeld and Pace on September 19 and laid out his plan. "I'm reluctant to be here," he told them at the outset. "I just don't want to be another critic, another burden to you. I hate armchair-general know-it-alls who think they have a better idea. That's just not me." But Keane indicated his deep concern about the situation in Iraq. "We're edging toward strategic failure," he warned. He then proceeded to review the three-year U.S. involvement in Iraq. Reading from notes written on yellow legal pages, he succinctly catalogued how the operation had gone wrong early and never righted itself.

In the first year after the invasion, from mid-2003 to mid-2004, Keane explained, U.S. forces had pursued an offensive strategy aimed essentially at killing and capturing insurgents. "Our conventional Army is very well trained for big wars but it's ill-prepared for counterinsurgencies, and what we were doing in '03 and '04 was executing what they knew," Keane said. Under the senior U.S. commander in Iraq at the time, Army lieutenant general Ricardo Sanchez, "there was no unifying strategy and no campaign plan."

Rumsfeld asked Keane to explain.

"Sanchez essentially delegated to his division commanders—they were like warlords in a sense," Keane recounted. "They had the autonomy to do what they thought was right. There was no unifying strategy that was uniting them all toward a common purpose and a common goal." Keane got the distinct impression this was news to Rumsfeld.

When Casey took command of the operation in mid-2004, Keane continued, a campaign plan was put in place that spelled out a program not only for security but for, in military parlance, other "lines of operation"—"governance," aimed at establishing a legitimate Iraqi government; "economic development," geared to ensuring basic needs were met; and "communications," intended to blacken the image of insurgents and improve the perception of U.S. and coalition forces.

"But it is really a defensive strategy," Keane declared. "It relies heavily on establishing an effective government, enfranchising the Sunnis, isolating the insurgents, and bringing them into the political process. There is plenty of logic to it—I thought it made some sense and believed in it as did many others. But it is flawed, and fundamentally so, in the view of what we know now, two years later."

The main point of the plan, he noted, had been to transition as quickly as possible to Iraqi control. "It really is a short-war strategy designed to get us out of there as quickly as possible," Keane said. "Nowhere in it is there a plan to defeat the insurgency ourselves."

Rumsfeld stopped him there. "What do you mean, no plan to defeat the insurgency?" the secretary asked.

"We have never had that as a mission," Keane replied.

"Explain that to me," Rumsfeld said. He seemed interested but dubious.

Keane said the strategy being pursued by Casey and Abizaid had been focused on turning over the fight to Iraqi forces and gradually withdrawing U.S. troops. It did not call for U.S. forces to eliminate the enemy.

"I made him uncomfortable when I told him that, as if he was hearing it for the first time or internalizing it for the first time," Keane recalled.

As Keane spoke, Rumsfeld took notes diligently.

The Iraqi campaign hadn't been without its successes, and Keane noted a few: the capture of Saddam Hussein, the killing of Hussein's two sons, the holding of three elections, the writing of a constitution, the installation of a permanent government, the training of Iraqi security forces, the killing of al-Zarqawi. Even so, Keane observed, the level of violence had increased everywhere in Iraq.

"The fact is, security and stability are worse," he asserted. "It threatens the survival of the government and the success of our mission."

What was needed, from Keane's point of view, was a strategy that would put more emphasis on ensuring the safety of Iraqis in order to win their support against the insurgents. Simply trying to kill and capture enemy fighters would not be sufficient. More enemy fighters would just follow, as the history of other insurgent wars had shown.

As long as insurgents controlled the population in Iraq, Keane told Rumsfeld, efforts at political and economic reform would fail. The United States had been wrong to try to institute such reforms without first ensuring security. "We have to decide if we're really serious about winning," he said. "If so, then we have to match our policies and resources with our rhetoric."

Making security the top priority in Iraq would require more U.S. troops. Keane estimated another five to eight combat brigades—roughly 17,500 to 28,000 troops—on top of the 130,000 troops already in the country.

"Where are we going to get that from?" Rumsfeld asked. Keane could tell the idea of a troop increase was a nonstarter with the secretary.

"We'll have to increase the length of our tours or we will have to make the tours indefinite," Keane said. "We have gone to war in the past where we have stayed for years until we won." Keane knew the system of rotating Army troops in and out of Iraq every twelve months was something that the Pentagon had imposed on itself. As he reminded Rumsfeld, he had accompanied the secretary to brief Bush on the plan when it was devised.

"Why would more troops be decisive?" Rumsfeld asked.

Keane explained that what he had in mind wasn't simply adding more forces but using them differently. They needed to be concentrated in Baghdad and in western Anbar Province, and they had to be positioned in neighborhoods, not holed up in large bases, which had been the trend. "Stop the plans to move to the mega-bases," Keane urged. "We have to de-centralize further."

He stressed the need to widen the "clear, hold, build" approach. Although the approach had been tried only intermittently until then, Keane said it had worked when applied well. He cited the experience in 2005 of Colonel H. R. McMaster's 3rd Armored Cavalry Regiment in stabilizing Tal Afar, a town of about 250,000 in far northwestern Iraq near the Syrian border. Rumsfeld was familiar with the story there and considered it a success. McMaster's troops had driven out the insurgents, set up static patrol bases in the town, earned the trust of Iraqis there, helped organize local elections, and promoted an economic recovery.

To fulfill the new strategy, Keane also proposed that U.S. forces be more judicious about turning over security responsibilities to unready Iraqi forces; that the size of military advisory teams embedded with Iraqi forces be doubled, from ten members each to twenty; and that the planned number of Iraqi security forces be increased from 325,000 to 600,000.

As he outlined his plan, he made sure to cite a serious shortfall in intelligence personnel. In the CIA, he noted, there were fewer analysts assigned to work on Iraq than there were to watch China. The intelligence division of the Pentagon's Joint Staff, which was supposed to have 156 analysts on Iraq, had only 61, he added.

"The result is, we are not mapping the networks," Keane said. "This is hard, tough homicide detective work, where you must read the tactical reports, read the interrogations of our detainees, exploit the captured documents, and then put together a completed mosaic of this network. We've been there three years and we still don't have it."

Keane knew he was treading on particularly sensitive ground when he proposed replacing Abizaid and Casey. Indeed, the suggestion did not sit well with Rumsfeld, who was fond of both generals and had relied heavily on them.

"These are very good men," Rumsfeld said. "They've sacrificed."

"I agree with you that they're good men," Keane replied. "I'm not suggesting that they're not. Heck, they're my friends. But George has already been extended twice, and John also has been extended. If we're going to change the strategy, it makes more sense to put new players in to do this."

Keane had other points to make about Iraqi political and economic reform. But Rumsfeld was running short of time. As a final bit of advice, Keane urged Rumsfeld to read *Counterinsurgency Warfare: Theory and Practice*. Written in a clear, simple style by retired French army lieutenant colonel David Galula, the book, published in 1964, is widely regarded as a classic primer on how to fight guerrilla campaigns. Nearly forgotten within the U.S. military at the start of the Iraq War, it had since become a best seller in Army schools, but Rumsfeld appeared unfamiliar with it. He asked Keane to repeat Galula's name and the book's title as he wrote it down.

Keane left feeling that he had said what he had come to say. He had sensed a certain resignation about Rumsfeld that he hadn't seen in him before, but he detected no change in the secretary's mind. "I walked out of there knowing that he was not going to do what I had asked him to do," Keane recounted, "and feeling that I had added to his burden."

———•———

Rumsfeld's evident resistance to a major change in course was shared by his top military commanders. What the secretary didn't know, however, was that his top civilian policy adviser had developed some of the same worries as had Keane and other critics. Through late 2005 and into early 2006, with the passage of Iraq's constitutional referendum, the election of a National Assembly, and the training of Iraqi forces, Edelman had remained hopeful. But the formation of the new Iraqi government had ushered in doubts. He wondered, for instance, whether the United States should have pushed so hard to get rid of the former interim prime minister, Ibrahim al-Jaafari, who was widely regarded within the Bush administration as having led an ineffective sectarian government. Rumsfeld himself had been adamant that al-Jaafari not emerge to lead the new government. "He must have said a half a dozen times, 'We need someone who has steel up his butt, we need someone with a spine, we need someone who's not a wind sock'—that was his expression, he would call Jaafari a wind sock," Edelman recalled.

If Rumsfeld had a preference for a replacement, it was Ayad Allawi, the secular Shia Muslim who had been prime minister of Iraq's interim government in the second half of 2004. Edelman had preferred Adel Abdul-Mahdi, another leading Shia politician. The choice instead of al-Maliki, an experienced political operator but also a strong advocate for Iraq's Shiite Muslims, was proving more difficult for Iraqi's Sunni minority to accept.

Edelman's deeper concerns emerged from personal research into the history of counterinsurgency efforts, particularly during the Vietnam War. He questioned whether the U.S. approach in Iraq was placing sufficient emphasis on population security. The focus on training Iraqi forces and transferring responsibility to them as fast as possible was fine as far as it went, Edelman thought. But important also was securing the safety of Iraqis.

In the press, parallels being drawn between America's experiences in Iraq and in Vietnam were likening Rumsfeld to Robert McNamara and Casey to Army general William Westmoreland, who had commanded military operations in Vietnam in the 1960s when they were at their peak and who had insisted the war was being won even as communist insurgents continued to make gains. A couple of friends kidded Edelman that he could end up in history books being likened to John McNaughton, an assistant secretary of defense and influential policy adviser to McNamara. The idea of being portrayed as a latter-day McNaughton did not appeal to Edelman.

Even in the important post of undersecretary for policy, Edelman felt marginalized by Rumsfeld in setting Iraq strategy and frustrated by his inability to persuade the secretary to consider an alternative approach. Rumsfeld tended to listen chiefly to Abizaid and Casey, who favored little change in course. The defense secretary had made it clear that he didn't want his civilian policy adviser getting between him and his military commanders—not just on Iraq policy but on most matters. In fact, one of the biggest surprises for Edelman after assuming the Pentagon job had been discovering the considerable deference that Rumsfeld showed the regional four-star officers.

The conventional view of Rumsfeld was that he ran roughshod over the uniformed military. Clearly, he had diminished the role of the military service chiefs and could be very tough on the Joint Staff. But his treatment of the combatant commanders was more respectful and yielding—too much so, in Edelman's view. From where Edelman sat, it seemed that all a commander had to do was send a personal message to the secretary, and Edelman would promptly receive a snowflake from Rumsfeld instructing him to attend to whatever the commander was requesting.

Rumsfeld's insistence that the commanders report directly to him and that no one get in the way made things difficult for Edelman. He had come to loathe the periodic gatherings in Washington of all the combatant commanders, when he was frequently the butt of complaints about how little the rest of the U.S. government was doing to help in Iraq and in the war on terrorism. As head of the policy branch, one of Edelman's main tasks was to lead the Pentagon's coordination efforts with other agencies.

Most often at the conferences, Abizaid would be the one to get the complaint going. "You know, Mr. Secretary," he would say, "we're the only department in the government that's at war. Where the hell is the State Department? Where's the rest of the government?"

This would set Rumsfeld off on his own tirade about the lack of interagency support, particularly from the State Department but also from Justice and Agriculture and the rest. Agitated, Rumsfeld would turn to Edelman and press: "Why can't we get the interagency to do this stuff? Why can't we do that?"

Edelman shared the belief that the rest of the government needed to be doing more, that the agencies were all too often missing in action in Iraq and Afghanistan. But he also regarded the venting by Rumsfeld and the commanders as a form of scapegoating that conveniently ignored worrisome shortcomings in the Pentagon's own efforts.

To Edelman, Rumsfeld was a larger-than-life figure who could be absolutely brilliant in dissecting information. He had a keen sense for imperfections and flaws. He also had a very charming side and, for the most part, had treated Edelman with considerable decency. One of Rumsfeld's redeeming qualities, in Edelman's eyes, was the secretary's level of self-awareness. Rumsfeld knew he was an impatient perfectionist who could drive others crazy. Even so, Rumsfeld couldn't seem to stop himself from savaging people in ways that undercut his own effectiveness and created deep resentments. Even after two years of working closely with him, Edelman found Rumsfeld ultimately enigmatic.

By September, Edelman's frustrations with Rumsfeld and with his own inability to influence military strategy had driven him to consider resigning. He told his wife and a couple of close friends that he was no longer sure he could help Rumsfeld, although he never shared this doubt with the secretary.

———•———

While the proposed solution for getting U.S. troops out of Iraq had been to turn the fight over to Iraq's fledgling security forces, the plan in Afghanistan was supposed to be a transfer of responsibility from the U.S. military to NATO. The alliance's role in Afghanistan had increased gradually. After first assuming military command in the relatively quiet regions of the north and west by mid-2005, NATO had since expanded its control to the south.

In 2006, Rumsfeld faced a decision on whether to approve the last step—the handover of full command to NATO. U.S. troops would remain engaged in the fight in the eastern part of the country, which borders Pakistan and where much of the enemy activity was still concentrated, but NATO would have overall responsibility.

While Rumsfeld had long favored letting NATO take the lead in Afghanistan, his willingness was always conditioned on the alliance's readiness to handle the counterinsurgency fight. As he weighed whether to cede full command, he worried about NATO's ability to resource the effort sufficiently and to reconcile widely differing rules among individual member states, some of which permitted their troops to engage in combat operations, others of which did not.

Violence was again on the rise, evidence of a resurgent Taliban movement that was taking advantage of safe havens in neighboring Pakistan and profiting from Afghanistan's extensive opium trade. Compounding matters, the close cooperative relationship that had existed between top U.S. military and diplomatic authorities in Afghanistan had eroded with the departures of Army lieutenant general David Barno and Ambassador Zalmay Khalilzad.

When Khalilzad was reassigned to Iraq in 2005, Rumsfeld fretted over who would replace him. As a native Afghani, Khalilzad had brought a deep understanding of the culture as well as the clout of a presidential envoy and the personality of an activist. "They're going to send us some poet from Harvard to run this place," Rumsfeld lamented during one video teleconference with the command in Kabul.

Ronald Neumann, a veteran diplomat whose father had been ambassador to Afghanistan, replaced Khalilzad. Barno's successor, Army lieutenant general Karl Eikenberry, was also a seasoned professional with experience in the country. But the two men never established the synergy that had existed between their predecessors, and at the Pentagon, the focus on Afghanistan was allowed to drift. "Afghanistan writ large didn't receive the kind of attention that it had while Barno and Khalilzad were there," said Mary Beth Long, then the principal deputy assistant secretary of defense for international security affairs, "in part because people thought, at least in the beginning, that things were on track and chugging right along, so we just needed to keep going and doing more of the same."

The advice to Rumsfeld from several of his most senior military commanders was to proceed with the handover to NATO. Eikenberry, Abizaid, and Jim Jones, NATO's top military commander at the time, all favored the move. So did the Pentagon's Joint Staff. But a strong dissenting voice came from Rumsfeld's civilian policy office, notably from Edelman and Long, both of whom questioned whether NATO was prepared to take over the counterinsurgency mission.

Long wrote a series of memos to Rumsfeld in which she expressed doubts that the alliance could be adequately resourced and noted that some of America's European partners expected to rely more on economic and development projects than on military action to stabilize Afghanistan. She questioned whether the NATO contingent would be divided essentially between committed fighters and those enjoined by their governments from engaging in combat. She cautioned that NATO forces could end up still largely dependent on the United States and unable to sustain their operations over the long term.

Long also challenged the wisdom of reducing U.S. forces in such a strategic region, so near Iran and Pakistan. She suggested expanding the U.S. military presence in Afghanistan and turning an air base outside the southern city of Kandahar into a second major hub of operations in addition to Bagram Air Base north of Kabul.

Rumsfeld, who shared a number of Long's concerns, used her memos to challenge his military commanders on whether the handover to NATO had been entirely thought through. "The more pointed my memos got, the more, at the end, he would just fold over the first page and put them in front of various people who were advocating the turnover and say, 'Answer these questions,'" Long recalled.

But the secretary also appeared reluctant to go against the advice of his military commanders. At a meeting in his office in August, Rumsfeld received assurances from Jones and Eikenberry, as well as from Admiral Ed Giambastiani, vice chairman of the Joint Chiefs of Staff who was standing in for Pace, that NATO was up to the assignment. Abizaid concurred by phone. The officers contended that the move was right not only for Afghanistan but also for NATO, which would be conducting its first major extended commitment outside its traditional European area of operation.

The idea of getting NATO to do something new appealed to Rumsfeld. He had been interested in transforming the military alliance in much the same way that he had sought to transform U.S. forces. During his term, NATO had significantly evolved, consolidating its military headquarters and establishing a Rapid Response Force. With the growing pressure of having to manage more of the war in Afghanistan, the alliance would need to embrace more change.

Still, Rumsfeld was wary of the risks involved in giving up U.S. control. He had spent hours working with Pace fashioning a NATO-led command structure in Afghanistan that he hoped would work. "I think Rumsfeld agreed to the change reluctantly," said Long, who attended the meeting with the secretary and the commanders. "He told the officers something like, 'Okay, if this is your best military judgment, I guess we're going to go with it.' It wasn't exactly a ringing, 'Let's do it!'"

———•———

In October 2006, the U.S. command in Iraq officially declared that two concentrated efforts—dubbed "Operation Together Forward I" and "II"—to beef up security in Baghdad over the summer with additional U.S. and Iraqi forces had done little to quell the violence. Publicly, Rumsfeld and Casey continued to assert that progress was being made—in the training of Iraqi security forces, in the strengthening of Iraqi ministries of Defense and Interior, and in the gradual closure of U.S. bases. But even stalwart administration supporters were concluding that the existing approach wasn't working. When Republican senator John Warner, the Senate Armed Services Committee chairman, returned from a visit to Iraq, he told reporters that the "situation is simply drifting sideways."

By that point, the NSC staff had quietly launched its own review of Iraq strategy. Pace also had chartered a small, highly confidential group of some of the brightest colonels he could find to reassess the situation in Iraq and examine the options.

For his part, Rumsfeld focused on drafting a new set of "benchmarks" against which to measure progress in Iraq. The U.S. campaign plan approved in mid-2004 had looked ahead only eighteen months, through the election of a new government in December 2005. In Rumsfeld's view, a revised set of political, economic, and military tasks was needed to frame the way ahead in Iraq and to define more clearly how Iraqi authorities could address the sectarian divisions and take on greater responsibility for their own security.

Among senior American military officers and civilian officials in Iraq and at the Pentagon, frustration with the al-Maliki government was growing following al-Maliki's failure to move decisively in a number of key areas to stabilize the country and to advance the process of political reconciliation. Under Rumsfeld's plan, Iraqi officials would be asked to agree to a schedule of milestones in such areas as disarming sectarian militias, holding provincial elections, and passing laws on amnesty and on sharing oil revenue.

Rumsfeld had discussed drawing up new benchmarks with Abizaid and Casey over the summer, and Bush had given the go-ahead. The plan offered the political benefit of signaling renewed flexibility on the part of the administration, and it could serve to preempt the forthcoming recommendations of the independent Iraq Study Group set up in the spring. Although it stopped short of setting a firm date for beginning phased U.S. troop withdrawals—something many Democrats were advocating—it was a move in that direction. Rumsfeld preferred not to think of his plan as prescribing a fixed timetable; rather, he saw it as a collection of projections for various tasks.

On October 10, Rumsfeld sent a memo to Pace and Edelman titled "A New Construct for Iraq" to let them know that Casey had been directed to come up with specific "benchmarks and projections" for Iraq. He noted that U.S. policy up until that time had been capsulated in several refrains uttered repeatedly by the administration:

- "The U.S. will stay in Iraq until we have won (succeeded)."
- "The U.S. will stay as long as we are needed."
- "We oppose a set timetable because it would advantage the enemy, since they could simply wait us out."
- "U.S. military commanders will determine the number of U.S. troops, not politicians in Washington, D.C."
- "Conditions on the ground will determine the pace at which U.S. and Coalition forces are withdrawn."

To measure progress toward establishing a new government, Rumsfeld stated, U.S. authorities had relied on a series of milestones, starting with the establishment of an Iraqi Governing Council in 2003 and running through the appointment of a new cabinet under al-Maliki. But such metrics, Rumsfeld added, had been overshadowed by attacks and casualty figures. "At present, Coalition progress is being measured not against those types of benchmarks but instead by the level of violence in Baghdad which, of course, is determined by the enemy," he wrote.

In contrast, the new approach promised to outline a set of goals for the Iraqi government to meet in the following twelve months, although no specific date for withdrawal would be given. Mindful that once any projections were set, the administration would be held to account for them, Rumsfeld stressed the need to hedge with careful qualifications about uncertainties, particularly the ability of the Iraqis to meet the targets. But he highlighted the advantages of a plan that could inspire confidence, both in Iraqis and in coalition countries, that the United States was determined to cede control while doing so in a rational, measured way.

Ten days later, Rumsfeld alluded to the secret discussions about benchmarks during a Pentagon news conference and emphasized the urgency of transferring more security and governing responsibilities to the Iraqis. "It's their country," he said. "They're going to have to govern it, they're going to have to provide security for it, and they're going to have to do it sooner rather than later."

But Rumsfeld was quick to play down expectations. "There's no doubt in my mind but that some of those projections we won't make; it will be later, or even earlier in some instances," he said. "And in some cases, once we meet the projection, we may have to go back and do it again."

———•———

Many of Rumsfeld's longtime relationships had survived his stormy tenure as defense secretary, with most of his oldest friends and close former associates either sharing his views or putting aside their differences in the interest of camaraderie. But during his last weeks in office, two of Rumsfeld's oldest relationships were shattered.

Ken Adelman had first worked for Rumsfeld in the Nixon administration and then in the Pentagon under Ford. In later years, their families had vacationed together, and Rumsfeld continued to call on Adelman for advice. In 2001, Rumsfeld appointed him to the Defense Policy Board. But Adelman had turned increasingly critical of Rumsfeld, confronting him at board meetings about the course of the Iraq War and about efforts to transform the military.

Rumsfeld asked Adelman to his office on Friday afternoon, September 22. He began warmly, recalling their long friendship and expressing his desire that they remain friends. Then he jumped to his main point, saying, "It might be best if you got off the board."

"If you want me off the board, write me a letter and I'll get off the board," Adelman replied. "It's your choice."

"I'm not telling you I want you off the board. I'm saying, it might be best," Rumsfeld went on.

"It wouldn't be best for me," Adelman countered, intent on not making it easy for Rumsfeld. He asked why Rumsfeld no longer wanted him as a board member.

"Because you're disruptive and negative," the secretary explained.

Adelman agreed with the negative part but took issue with being called disruptive.

"You interrupt briefings; you don't let people finish," Rumsfeld told him.

"Yeah, but you know where I learned that? I learned that right in this room, thirty years ago," Adelman remarked, motioning to where Rumsfeld sat. "I learned it from the master."

Rumsfeld laughed, and the two men went back and forth for some minutes more. Adelman accused Rumsfeld of all too often deflecting responsibility. Rumsfeld insisted he accepted responsibility all the time. But Adelman noted that when things went wrong, Rumsfeld tended to blame the military commanders, the State Department, or the Iraqis.

When Adelman also took his old boss to task for what he called the "abysmal quality" of his decisions, Rumsfeld pressed him for some examples. Adelman cited Rumsfeld's poor handling of the Abu Ghraib scandal and his dismissive "stuff happens" remark in response to the extensive looting in Iraq immediately after the fall of the Saddam Hussein regime. To Adelman's disbelief, Rumsfeld claimed not to remember having said "stuff happens," which had become one of his most infamous comments. The secretary remarked that U.S. troops had been given orders to stop the looting, although he could not say who had issued the orders or why U.S. forces still made little effort to pursue looters.

On Abu Ghraib, Adelman blamed Rumsfeld for not doing more to deal with the fallout from the case once he learned of it in January 2004. Rumsfeld insisted he hadn't realized initially how serious it was or even that photographs existed. He argued that had he tried looking into the case, he would have risked being accused of command influence. Adelman saw Rumsfeld's response as another example of the secretary's evasiveness and tendency to deflect blame.

Ending the meeting, Rumsfeld walked Adelman out of the office. Adelman expressed his appreciation for having had the chance to talk; Rumsfeld offered a quick goodbye. A few weeks later, Rumsfeld sent Adelman a letter saying that, as they had discussed, plans were under way to reorganize the Defense Policy Board and a replacement would soon be named for Adelman, and he expressed appreciation for Adelman's cooperation.

Rumsfeld's long-standing friendship with Steve Herbits, who had served as a special assistant to him at the Pentagon during the Ford years and who returned in 2001 to help on personnel and organizational matters, similarly disintegrated. The October publication of Bob Woodward's State of Denial about the Bush administration revealed that Herbits had secretly shared criticisms of Rumsfeld and memos he had written disparaging Rumsfeld's management style and choice of key subordinates.

Just a few months earlier, during the revolt of the generals, Herbits had publicly come to Rumsfeld's defense, writing a letter to the *Washington Times* urging news media to dig deeper into the backgrounds of those retired generals who were assailing the secretary. Herbits had acted on his own, without prompting from anyone at the Pentagon. But he had already spoken to Woodward for the book, deciding to do so in the interest, he said in a later interview, of trying to explain how the United States had gotten into such a mess in Iraq—and particularly how Rumsfeld had contributed.

"I think Rumsfeld's behavior from the summer of 2003 on was unusual for him," Herbits said. "All his worst instincts came to the fore. And the impact of his leadership was just of such consequence that it couldn't be ignored."

For Rumsfeld to lose a close friend or associate was rare. Perhaps his only other public rupture comparable to the breaks with Herbits and Adelman had occurred with Al Lowenstein in 1970, when Rumsfeld backed Lowenstein's opponent in a congressional election, alienating his friend. "Did we love our friendship with Al? Absolutely," said Joyce Rumsfeld, when asked about the severed ties. "Did we love our friendship with Kenny? Absolutely. Did we love our friendship with Steve? Yes. And it's over."

———•———

With the U.S. congressional elections approaching in November, it was becoming clear that the Republicans would probably lose control of one and possibly of both chambers of Congress. Rumsfeld had resolved that if at least one of the chambers switched to the Democrats, he would have to leave and had signaled his willingness to do so to Bush, although the two men had not explicitly discussed the prospect of Rumsfeld stepping down.

A deeply unpopular figure in the country and around the world, Rumsfeld had sought in the final weeks of the election to cut back on news conferences and other public appearances in an effort to reduce his own drag on the Republican Party's chances at the polls. But it didn't much matter whether he was visible or not. He had become such a target of criticism by those attacking the administration's handling of Iraq, Afghanistan, detainees, the U.S. military, and relations with allies that he remained a significant political liability for Republican candidates.

"Unfortunately, as a result of the political divisiveness that existed, everything Rumsfeld did got criticized," recalled Gene Renuart, who as a three-star Air Force general was the secretary's senior military assistant at the time. "He was the lightning rod for political arguments, and he was very aware of that. He was very concerned that he not put the administration in a difficult position by being out there as that lightning rod."

Before the vote, Rumsfeld was eager to send Bush a memo with some suggestions and thoughts on the way ahead in Iraq. He didn't intend the memo to be prescriptive or definitive, but he hoped it would at least help provoke further debate. Dated November 6, one day before the elections, the memo, titled "Iraq—Illustrative New Courses of Action," showed Rumsfeld accepting the need for "a major adjustment" and acknowledging that "what U.S. forces are currently doing in Iraq is not working well enough or fast enough."

But he stopped far short of proposing a coherent new plan. Instead, he merely provided a laundry list of twenty-one "illustrative options," many purely tactical and all written in the pithy, sentence-fragment form of his snowflakes. The options that Rumsfeld favored most tended to amount to an intensification or acceleration of the existing strategy—more U.S. trainers, more U.S. equipment for Iraqi forces, and more resources for the Iraqi ministries of Defense and Interior. The basic thrust was to draw down U.S. troops and shift to an advisory mission.

Less appealing to Rumsfeld were options that had been pushed by those favoring a more aggressive approach. They included shifting more U.S. forces into Baghdad to control it, sending additional U.S. forces to Iraq, staging a Dayton-like peace process like the one used in the Balkans conflict in 1995, partitioning Iraq, and setting a firm withdrawal date.

The memo indicated frustration with the pace at which responsibility was being turned over to Iraqi authorities and urged tougher action to get the Iraqis to do their part. Rumsfeld suggested, for instance, punishing provinces that failed to cooperate with the Americans by withdrawing economic assistance and security. Indicative of his own exasperation with much of the rest of the U.S. government in filling jobs advising Iraqi officials, Rumsfeld raised the possibility of using military retirees and re-servists to "aggressively beef up" Iraqi government ministries. "Give up on trying to get other USG Departments to do it," he asserted.

Reflecting his lack of confidence that any one option would work, Rumsfeld advised limiting the political fallout from any shift by portray-ing the new course as a trial run. To reduce expectations further, he rec-ommended that U.S. goals and the American military's mission in Iraq be recast in "minimalist" terms.

The same weekend that Rumsfeld was completing his memo, Bush interviewed Robert Gates, the head of Texas A&M University, for the po-sition of defense secretary. After months of consideration, Bush had de-cided to replace Rumsfeld. Although Bush had not yet settled on a new strategy for the war, it had become clear to him that a change in strategy was necessary and that a new defense secretary should oversee it.

Gates and Bush had met only in passing before, but Gates was no stranger to the Bush family, having served as CIA director under Presi-dent George H. W. Bush. He had Washington experience, had shown himself capable of managing large institutions, and had studied the Iraq situation as a member of the Iraq Study Group, where he had concluded that some shifts in approach were needed.

In many ways, Gates was Rumsfeld's antithesis—low-key, self-effacing, nonconfrontational. Hadley had worked with Gates and spoke glowingly of him when Bush floated his name as a possible replacement for Rums-feld. Rice also enthusiastically recommended Gates, who had been her su-perior as deputy national security adviser during the administration of the senior Bush.

The president had told several senior members of his staff that before replacing Rumsfeld, he needed to find a successor with whom he would feel comfortable. His talk with Gates in the private study of his Crawford ranch on November 5 reassured him, and he offered Gates the job on the spot. After being informed of the president's decision by Cheney, Rumsfeld drafted a resignation letter on November 6 and delivered it to Bush on November 7 as voters went to the polls.

In an election widely viewed as a referendum on the Iraq War, Democrats gained majorities in both the Senate and the House of Representatives for the first time in a dozen years. Bush called the results a "thumping." His abrupt announcement the next day that Rumsfeld would be leaving was greeted with relief by many people. But many Republicans, confident they could have retained more congressional seats had Bush acted earlier, were angered that he had waited until after the election to let Rumsfeld go.

Later on the day of his resignation, when Rumsfeld returned to his house in Washington, Margaret Robson, an old friend, found him in an unusually contemplative mood. "He was quiet and reserved and sort of taking it all in," she said. "He was very pensive and thoughtful. It was just as though it was still sinking in." Asked if he had seemed surprised by the turn of events, Robson said no. And if he was angry, he wasn't showing it. "He was having a glass of wine; he was relaxing; he was thinking about the day, just kind of sitting there observing."

Rumsfeld lay low in the nearly six weeks between the announcement he was leaving and his actual departure from the Pentagon. He gave few interviews, made few public appearances, and avoided major decisions.

Even in areas that had been a high priority for him and for the administration, such as missile defense, he deferred significant action to his successor. Edelman tried to nudge Rumsfeld to approve an initiative for missile-defense sites in Europe. Discussions had been under way for months to place silos for interceptor missiles in Poland and a tracking radar in the Czech Republic, expanding the Pentagon's fledgling system for knocking down missiles headed toward the United States. Pentagon officials were eager to lock in the planned expansion before the clock ran out on the Bush administration.

But Rumsfeld had repeatedly postponed a decision during the fall. He had imagined for a time that some sort of larger strategic deal with Russia could be worked out, combining agreement on the new antimissile sites with action on intermediate-range nuclear weapons and other strategic systems. No bigger accord materialized, and Edelman worried that valuable time to secure European involvement in the U.S. antimissile project was being lost. "We must have briefed him four or five times," Edelman recalled. "I couldn't tell whether he had some complicated endgame in mind with the Russians—you know, whether he was playing three-dimensional chess and was several moves ahead—or whether he just didn't want to take responsibility for something that he felt might be controversial." The real reason, according to another official familiar with Rumsfeld's thinking, was that he didn't want to take any action that might box in his successor.

In the several speeches he made before leaving, Rumsfeld offered no regrets or acknowledgment of mistakes. He addressed what he described as some of the lessons learned during the previous six years, but he avoided the specific issues that had brought so much controversy—the management of the wars, the handling of detainees, his strained relations with senior military officers and with members of Congress. Instead, he focused his remarks on the challenges still at hand, reiterating several of the themes he had stressed in recent months—that the terrorist threat involved a kind of enemy the United States had not faced before, that the threat was still not well understood, and that victory would require all U.S. government agencies to work together in new ways.

"To the extent possible we can no longer afford to have Defense and State Departments, CIA and Homeland Security, Treasury and Justice, Agriculture and Commerce each waging their own campaign, with their own rules, their own restrictions, each overseen by separate Congressional committees and subcommittees," Rumsfeld told an audience at Kansas State University. "Defense, diplomacy and development cannot fit neatly into separate compartments today. Success requires that security, governance and development programs progress together."

Rumsfeld also emphasized that the struggle was not something the United States could win on its own; rather, it would need to find better means of enlisting allies. Addressing the Philadelphia Union League Club, he encouraged more thought about alternatives to the United Nations, citing a recent university study by his old friend George Shultz that recommended a "concert of democracies"—a self-selected forum that would allow the world's free and responsible nations to authorize collective action, including the use of force. Short of forming new organizations, Rumsfeld also urged looking at ways to make existing institutions, such as NATO, operate more effectively in providing deployable combat forces and trained peacekeepers.

To the end, Rumsfeld kept making the case for change and talking about shaking up institutions. "And as we know," he said in Philadelphia, "change is hard and change is resisted. Change is uncomfortable for people, and I suppose that's understandable. It upsets constituencies; it upsets interests at home; it upsets interests abroad. But our time requires boldness and vision if we're to strengthen or replace the more familiar, but antiquated, institutions today."

Rumsfeld's resignation, meanwhile, had opened the way to a more candid assessment within the administration itself of the Pentagon's mistakes in Iraq and alternate military strategies. Two days after making Rumsfeld's removal official, Bush launched a formal sweeping review of Iraq policy, pulling together the separate efforts that had been under way in the NSC, the Joint Staff, and the State Department.

But Rumsfeld was not a major player in the process, and the Pentagon was divided on how to proceed on Iraq. While the civilian policy staff favored a major change in approach, the service chiefs, along with Abizaid and Casey, strongly opposed adding significant numbers of troops to the fight. They warned that a surge could lead to more attacks by al Qaeda, provide more targets for Sunni insurgents, and fuel the jihadist appeal for more foreign fighters eager to join the battle against the U.S. superpower. Any short-term benefit that might accrue, they argued, would only set the United States up for bigger problems later.

Rumsfeld shared the concerns of the uniformed military. He worried particularly that an increase in forces would simply reinforce the notion that the war could be won with military might. It would still leave the Pentagon holding the bag. But he also knew that support for the surge was growing at the White House. "He was torn initially," recalled Peter Rodman, who represented the Pentagon in the interagency group conducting the review. "He was torn because the military was against the surge, but it was pretty clear to us that the president wanted this as an option; he wanted this on the table. I think Rumsfeld understood that."

Eventually, Rumsfeld came around privately to endorsing an increase in forces, but he stressed that it would need to be accompanied by surges from other U.S. government agencies in the form of greater diplomatic and economic efforts. Publicly, he continued to caution against creating a dependency in Iraq on U.S. forces.

"The more troops you have, the greater the risk that you will be seen as an occupier and that you will feed an insurgency," he said in one of the rare interviews he granted during his final days in office. "The more troops you have—particularly American troops, who are so darn good at what they do—the more they will do things and the more dependent the Iraqis will become." He also viewed an increase in troops as risking a rise in U.S. casualties, which could undermine public support for the war. "Do I know that the right number is there? No," he said. "Do I think it is? Yes. Is there anyone who is smart enough to prove it is or isn't? No."

———•———

In a final town hall meeting at the Pentagon on December 8, Rumsfeld bade farewell to Defense Department employees with typical showmanship. Smiling broadly, he strode into the Pentagon's main auditorium to loud applause and took his position on a stage with troops from each military service and a few civilian Pentagon employees seated behind him. As he mused about his legacy as one of the nation's longest-serving defense secretaries, he ranged from serious and emotional to humorous and sarcastic.

Always the record keeper, he told the crowd this was his forty-second town hall–style meeting—thirteen had been at the Pentagon, twenty-eight with troops overseas. He ran through a list of accomplishments during his term—the deployment of an initial missile-defense system, the establishment of a new Northern Command for defending the United States, the most significant worldwide repositioning of U.S. forces since World War II, the expansion of Special Operations forces, and the development of a more agile Army based more on brigades than on divisions. He also mentioned, in a positive light, the prison camp at Guantánamo, where he said troops stood guard "over some of the world's most dangerous terrorists while suffering grossly uninformed and irresponsible charges in the media from almost every quarter."

In reference to the criticisms and controversies that had marked his tenure, Rumsfeld suggested that much of the tension was due to the unprecedented nature and large number of the challenges that he had faced during an extremely difficult time. "I wish I could say that everything we've done here has gone perfectly, but that's not how life works, regrettably," he said. "When thousands of people make dozens of difficult decisions on hundreds of pressing issues—for the most part, matters that are new and unfamiliar, where there's no road map, no guidebook that says here's exactly how you should do something—the hope has to be not perfection but that most decisions, with the perspective of time, will turn out to be the right ones, and that the perspective of history will judge the overwhelming majority of those decisions favorably."

For the most part, the questions from department employees were gentle. When asked what he hadn't been able to accomplish in his drive to transform the military from a Cold War organization to a more nimble and adaptive force, Rumsfeld replied first by claiming high marks for having changed the department's attitude and culture. But he admitted that concrete gains had been harder to achieve, rating progress there under his leadership only five on a scale of ten.

His worst day, he said somberly in answer to another question, had been learning about what had gone on at Abu Ghraib. His greatest day, he joked, would come ten days later, when Gates was due to be sworn in as his successor. He went for another punch line when asked how he wanted history to remember him. "My goodness. Better than the local press," he quipped. But he also admitted that he would miss his jousting with reporters. "The stakeouts, the briefings—I'm told it was something like 613 over six years, all across the globe," he said. "Now, you know, we've not always seen eye to eye, I haven't, with the press, but I still hold out hope that over time, they'll get it close to right."

Concluding, Rumsfeld offered his belief that the struggles in Iraq and Afghanistan would pay off in the end, although he stressed that the wars could not be won with military force alone. "In every conflict in our country's history, there have been those who said, 'Toss in the towel. It isn't working,'" he noted. "But by golly, it—something important isn't easy, and this isn't easy. And by golly, it's important, and we'd better do it right."

Following the town hall meeting, Rumsfeld embarked on a surprise trip to Iraq, his fifteenth since the start of the war. This time, he received no briefings and held no news conferences. The purpose of his visit, he explained at the time, was simply to meet with troops. While in Iraq, he made a point of seeing members from each military service and every function in Iraq—F-18 jet pilots in a maintenance control hangar at Al Asad Air Base, medical crews and Special Operations forces at Balad, Army soldiers in Baghdad and Mosul.

He found the audiences reassuringly supportive, particularly if any in their midst ventured a question with a critical tone. In Mosul, for instance, when a reservist pointed out the contradictory message of counseling troops to have patience after the Bush administration's invasion of Iraq had seemed to signal a lack of patience, Rumsfeld received a rousing ovation for pointing out that Saddam Hussein had disregarded seventeen U.N. resolutions over many years prior to the U.S. military operation.

On the plane ride back to Washington, Rumsfeld reminisced with several aides about his life in public service and answered correspondence. One letter in his pile was from the father of a Marine whose son had been killed two years earlier during the battle for Fallujah and whose nephew—his brother's only son—had recently died in the war as well. The letter thanked Rumsfeld for his service to the nation, commending his leadership and the example he had set of accepting the bad as well as the good in life "with dignity, grace, compassion and strength."

"He gave me the letter saying, 'This one is tough,'" recalled Will Grimsley, then an Army colonel serving as one of Rumsfeld's military assistants. "Rumsfeld wanted to answer but couldn't find the words. He was having great emotional difficulty coming up with the right words. What do you say?"

The day after returning from Iraq, Rumsfeld held a farewell session with the Joint Chiefs of Staff. The meeting, which lasted less than an hour, was largely cordial, as Rumsfeld mixed some recollections of his time as secretary with some advice for the future. One of the chiefs summarized the secretary's message as essentially an appeal for the service leaders to present a united front with the rest of the department and not try to circumvent the defense secretary by lobbying members of Congress for their own service interests. "He was a little reflective and he was a little prescriptive," said General Michael "Buzz" Moseley, then the Air

Force chief of staff. "I regarded it as a guy who's been in government a long time sitting down and just having a heart-to-heart talk."

The day after Rumsfeld resigned, Dick Myers, the former chairman, had paid tribute to Rumsfeld, praising him for his perseverance and vision in trying to change the Pentagon bureaucracy and rejecting the view of Rumsfeld as dismissive of military advice. Introducing the secretary before a speech at Kansas State University, Myers's alma mater, the retired general said Rumsfeld had spent more time with senior military leaders than any secretary that Myers had worked with. He also praised Rumsfeld for having remained loyal to subordinates.

"He has had many opportunities to deflect the arrows coming his way to the military, many opportunities," Myers said. "He has never taken one of those opportunities." Citing the Abu Ghraib scandal as an example, Myers noted, "It would have been easy for the secretary of defense to deflect to the department, to individuals. He never did that. He sucked up all those arrows and continued to lead the department in the way that he knew was right."

This portrait of Rumsfeld taking arrows ran counter to the accounts of others depicting Rumsfeld as conveniently ducking responsibility. And the former chairman's description of Rumsfeld spending so much time with the military leadership was belied by the frustration of a number of the chiefs. In fact, some of service leaders took the opportunity of their final meeting with the secretary to express their disappointment at not having had more occasion to meet with him as just the Joint Chiefs of Staff. "I told him that I wished we could have had more time to have these kinds of talks because it's important for us," Moseley recalled. "From my experience in Afghanistan and Iraq, to have these kinds of talks is very useful for all of us."

But to the end, Rumsfeld considered his 2001 decision to incorporate the chiefs into the Senior Level Review Group to be one of his greatest organizational innovations. During his last town hall meeting at the Pentagon, he had pointed to the SLRG as having helped pull together the military services and the department's senior civilians. "There's almost nothing of any major importance that hasn't been thoroughly discussed, digested, masticated by the SLRG, and in many cases with the combatant commanders as well," he said. "And by golly, this department isn't worth anything if all the services are going off in every different direction, working their own little projects and harming the other services."

The chiefs felt otherwise. By and large, they had found the SLRG meetings too big and not conducive to direct dealings with the secretary. They suspected that Rumsfeld had used the SLRG, with its mix of civilians and military officers, to buffer himself from more-direct conversation with the four-star officers.

From time to time, Moseley had spoken privately to Rumsfeld about reviving chiefs-only meetings with the secretary. So had other chiefs. But Rumsfeld wasn't interested. "He said he liked the SLRG because it had more people and provided him a wider intellectual dialogue," Moseley recalled.

In his final days, Rumsfeld heard a similar complaint about the diminished role of the chiefs from another commander he respected: General Jim Jones, who as commandant of the Marine Corps had been a member of the Joint Chiefs during Rumsfeld's first two years. After remarks by Jones disparaging Rumsfeld's treatment of the chiefs were quoted in Bob Woodward's *State of Denial*, Jones met with Rumsfeld.

"We had a pretty direct conversation," recalled Jones, who at the time was leaving his post as NATO's top commander. "I reminded him that he had come in early on and said to the Joint Chiefs that we weren't terribly useful, which made me feel the chiefs were pretty emasculated—or if not emasculated, then at least marginalized." During the run-up to the Iraq War, Jones went on, with not only Rumsfeld but Franks not conferring much with the chiefs, "we had to work very hard to find out what was going on, and it was painful."

When Rumsfeld tried to defend his practice of meeting with the chiefs in larger forums that included civilian staff, Jones told him these forums actually interfered with the flow of military advice. "Mr. Secretary," he remembered saying, "it's a fallacy to think that you're going to get guys like me to walk into a room with forty people in there—about a fourth of them you don't even know—and you're going to get focused military advice, critical military advice. Many times there were things that I wanted to say and I looked around and I wasn't sure who was in the room, I didn't know these people. Now, you can tell me I could have come and seen you and all of that, and frequently I did. But what if ten of us feel this way? Are you going to have ten focused meetings on this? And I know my colleagues also feel like this."

As a result of insisting on the larger, mixed forums, Jones added, political influence was far too often brought to bear on military advice too early in the deliberative process. "In my view," he told Rumsfeld, "the way the system should work is that military advice is developed largely independent of the political consequences, and then it's up to you and the president to apply your political judgment and tell us to execute it. But to seek that advice in a forum where everybody in a civilian suit is thinking the way you are, and we don't know what the rules of the game are, and sometimes we get the impression this is already a done deal—well, you're not getting pure military advice."

———•———

By the time he stepped down, Rumsfeld had served 2,585 days as defense secretary, combining his time in the job under both Ford and Bush—just ten days short of McNamara's record 2,595 days as longest-serving secretary. For his send-off, Rumsfeld received full honors on the Pentagon grounds on December 15. He strode to the ceremony from the steps of the Pentagon accompanied by Bush and Cheney, the three men abreast in dark suits. The grandiose event began with a nineteen-gun salute as Rumsfeld walked the grounds to inspect representatives from all service branches gathered in formation and in full military regalia.

Farewell speeches praised Rumsfeld's accomplishments and character. Pace commended his courage and compassion and, echoing the remarks Myers had made at Kansas State, cited Rumsfeld for a willingness to accept blame for misdeeds by subordinates. Cheney, who was losing one of his closest allies in the administration, extolled Rumsfeld as his best boss and best friend, as an "ideal" public servant, and as "the finest secretary of defense this nation has ever had." Bush characterized Rumsfeld as a comrade in arms through the devastation of September 11 and the planning of complicated wars in Afghanistan and Iraq.

"In these and countless other moments, I have seen Don Rumsfeld's character and his integrity," the president said. "He has always ensured I had the best possible advice. . . . He spoke straight. It was easy to understand him." Bush also noted that the Defense Department had experienced "more profound change" during Rumsfeld's tenure "than at any time since the department's creation in the late 1940s."

Rumsfeld had the last words of the day. Stepping to the podium, he declared his intention to "break with convention one more time." Instead of commenting on the achievements of his six-year tenure, he said he would focus on the future. He spoke of the "sense of urgency" he felt about the challenges ahead, and he highlighted the dangers. "Ours is a world of unstable dictators, weapons proliferators, and rogue regimes," he noted. "And each of these enemies seeks out our vulnerabilities. And as free people, we have vulnerabilities."

He noted grimly the declining defense investments and capabilities of U.S. allies, suggesting that the United States would have to invest more in its own defense. He warned against allowing the United States to be weak. "Today it should be clear that not only is weakness provocative, but the perception of weakness on our part can be provocative as well," he said. "A conclusion by our enemies that the United States lacks the will or the resolve to carry out missions that demand sacrifice and demand patience is every bit as dangerous as an imbalance of conventional military power."

Although he did not mention Iraq explicitly, there could be no mistaking his reference when, in a forceful tone, he argued against backing down. "This is a time of great consequence," he said. "It may well be comforting to some to consider graceful exits from the agonies and, indeed, the ugliness of combat. But the enemy thinks differently." A moment later, he added, "Our country has taken on a bracing and difficult task. But let there be no doubt: It is neither hopeless nor without purpose."

Rumsfeld's voice wavered as he remarked in closing that he would remember the troops in the field and in the military hospitals he had visited. "And I will remember the fallen," he concluded.

Later that day, the last of Rumsfeld's snowflakes was sent out to all Pentagon personnel. "The blizzard is over!" Rumsfeld announced. "Thank you for all you do for our wonderful country. Well done!" A general amnesty was declared for anyone who had left any of the former defense secretary's snowflakes unanswered.

Epilogue

For a few months after his departure, Rumsfeld occupied a suite of government-provided transition offices in a high-rise building in Rosslyn, Virginia, up the Potomac River a short way from the Pentagon. There he began sorting his papers for a memoir and charting his next course.

His roots were in Chicago, where he and Joyce still enjoyed an extensive network of friendships and where he had returned after his first stint as secretary. But this time he chose to remain in Washington, eventually renting space in a downtown office building, hiring a staff of several people, and setting up a new headquarters not far from his house in the city. On the walls of the office, Rumsfeld hung photos of Teddy Roosevelt and Harry Truman, framed certificates marking his own years of service under several presidents, and other mementos. In a corner stood a parting gift from the Joint Chiefs of Staff: a bronze bust of Winston Churchill with a cigar in his mouth. The inscription, quoting Churchill, read, "Victory is never final. Defeat is never fatal. It is courage that counts."

Rumsfeld explained his decision to stay in Washington as a matter of convenience that allowed him ready access to his Pentagon files and facilitated work with the Library of Congress to archive his personal papers. It also kept him near friends and former associates and afforded a close sidelines view of the capital's political scene, although as the Bush administration ran out its term, he purposefully maintained a low profile, giving few public speeches or media interviews and spending large chunks of his time at two other homes outside Washington—the old manor in St. Michaels, Maryland, and the farm in Taos, New Mexico.

One public ceremony at which he did speak was the 2008 dedication of the Pentagon memorial to the victims of 9/11. He showed up with his right arm in a blue sling from recent shoulder surgery. Occasionally when he surfaced elsewhere, there were shows of opposition. He drew street protests outside closed-door appearances in California and France, and more than 2,600 faculty and students at Stanford University signed a petition objecting to his appointment as a distinguished fellow at the Hoover Institution, where he was to play a limited role advising a panel on ideology and terrorism several times a year. John McCain, running as the Republican nominee in the 2008 campaign for the presidency, continued to hammer the former Pentagon leader for mismanaging the Iraq War, telling audiences that Rumsfeld would be remembered as the worst defense secretary in history.

Several longtime friends who visited Rumsfeld in the weeks after he left office described him as somewhat subdued initially, but it wasn't long before the former secretary was exhibiting his customary exuberance in private gatherings. "He's extraordinarily resilient," said Frank Carlucci. "You could bash him all you want and he'll bounce back right away. It rolls off him."

Another longtime friend reported that Rumsfeld was not happy with how abruptly his removal had come about. A former subordinate who spent several days with Rumsfeld in Taos heard him fume about disagreements with other top administration officials, particularly Rice. But whatever grumbling he did, Rumsfeld remained very careful not to be heard sounding critical of Bush. "I have a friend who is totally convinced that Don was the scapegoat and that he must be bitter towards the president," said Margaret Robson, whose late husband was one of Rumsfeld's best friends. "I told him, 'You don't understand Don. He's never going to say anything critical about the president of the United States.'"

In my own early contacts with him for this book after he returned to private life, Rumsfeld wanted to be sure I saw the many letters of praise and kind words he had received following the announcement of his resignation. He had sorted the letters according to source—members of Congress, foreign dignitaries, U.S. military personnel, former associates, friends—and filed them in large, three-ring binders. The correspondence noted Rumsfeld's contributions to the war on terrorism, commended him for his drive to transform the U.S. military, and expressed thanks for his public service.

John Howard, the Australian prime minister, singled out the example Rumsfeld had set by his "good humor and willingness to engage the news media." Even Jim Jones, the retired Marine Corps general who had publicly carped about Rumsfeld's leadership, offered supportive parting words. "Those of us who were privileged to serve with you during the entire length of your appointment have not only been fortunate to participate in the outcome of the important issues of our time, but we have also benefited enormously by your unsurpassed example of commitment, energy and dedication," Jones wrote in a letter dated November 20, 2006. "Your loyalty and ability to clearly articulate the enormous complexities of the problems facing the nation ensured that the president was well prepared for the uniquely difficult decision only he can make. I can't imagine a more reliable or more dedicated secretary of defense. If integrity stands as an asset in today's arena, you can be certain that yours is intact as you leave your post."

Such letters seemed to give Rumsfeld some solace amid media commentary that tended to focus on all that had gone wrong—the mistakes made in the Iraq War, the difficult relations with the military chiefs, the tensions with Congress, the quarrels with other NSC members. As low as his popularity was when he left office—Gallup/Harris polls showed him at 34 percent—Rumsfeld still found that when he dined out at a restaurant or walked along a street, people approached him eager to shake his hand.

Over the course of his life, when Rumsfeld had faced criticisms and denunciations, a sense of certainty in his own rightness had helped sustain him. And although public opinion of him now was as negative as it had ever been, he seemed largely unrattled. Instead, he held fast to an abiding belief that he had done what he thought best and had served honorably. "Don Rumsfeld is a throwback to a breed of public man who judge themselves not relative to their peers but relative to the standard they have set for themselves, a standard closely equated to the public good," Steve Cambone remarked.

Contemplating his next move, Rumsfeld sought opinions from a number of friends and former associates. In the past, he had dismissed the idea of writing a memoir. He had spoken critically of memoirs that involved events in which he had participated and that, in his mind, failed to rightly capture how things had unfolded.

Rumsfeld worried about writing a book that risked criticism from others as unfair or inaccurate and that therefore could result in people thinking less of him. Despite his tendency to be harsh on subordinates privately, he had a longtime aversion to speaking unkindly in public about former colleagues or sharing details of conversations with presidents and other top officials. And he wasn't much accustomed to introspection. In mulling whether to write his autobiography, Rumsfeld read Katharine Graham's Pulitzer Prize–winning work and confessed that the book's frankness scared him.

But Joyce told him it was time to tell his own life's story, and so did others whose judgment he respected. George Shultz, who had helped Rumsfeld rise through the Nixon administration and who remained a booster for years afterward, stressed the contribution that Rumsfeld would be making to history by providing his perspective on events. Early in 2008, Rumsfeld signed with a publisher and began dictating his recollections. His first entry dealt not with his childhood years or his recent Pentagon service but with the period in 1974 when he took over as Ford's chief of staff—a time he considers the most challenging of his life.

Rumsfeld also decided to establish a new charitable foundation. He and Joyce had maintained a family foundation since 1985 that had grown in value to about $20 million and made grants to dozens of groups a year. But there was little pattern to the charitable giving, and Rumsfeld wanted something more focused.

The new trust, which was funded by a grant from Rumsfeld's previous foundation as well as by contributions from his own assets, had several aims: to provide fellowships for graduate students interested in public service, to fund charitable organizations that support troops and their families, to help finance loans to "micro-enterprises" in developing countries, and to back programs aimed at assisting the once-Soviet-controlled republics of Central Asia—countries such as Uzbekistan, Tajikistan, and Kazakhstan—which have not enjoyed the kind of U.S.-based support groups that benefited the eastern European states in their transition from communist rule. The foundation's assorted missions, while a bit of a hodgepodge, reflect Rumsfeld's longtime interests in promoting government service and in venturing into new frontiers of both government and business.

----·----

At the Pentagon, Robert Gates, the new secretary of defense, ushered in a noticeably different approach and personal style. Almost every move he made at the outset seemed, whether deliberately or not, to be a repudiation of what had gone before. He began meeting with the chiefs once a week in the Tank, which Rumsfeld had shunned, and he vowed several times to rely heavily on advice from the uniformed military. In a further concession to the military leaders, he let go of Staser Holcomb, who had been brought in by Rumsfeld to review the appointment of senior officers, and allowed the Joint Chiefs to reclaim greater control over the promotion process.

Gates also relaxed the grip that Rumsfeld had exerted over deployment orders. Rather than insisting on checking every instruction, Gates set some overall parameters for dispatching troops and allowed the movement of small units with no controversial issues to go forward without his personal review.

He let the department's senior civilian staff know that he had no intention of cleaning house, and while some officials chose to leave, most stayed. Eric Edelman, the department's top policy adviser, was among those who agreed to remain, but only after receiving assurances that the combatant commanders would be instructed to work with him more closely. Gates made a point of bringing Edelman along on trips to see the commanders. Relations quickly improved between the regional military commands and the policy branch. "It changed my life dramatically and made things a lot easier," Edelman said.

Even journalists were treated more kindly. Gates preferred a less combative dialogue, without the gleeful sparring that had characterized

Rumsfeld's encounters. "The press is not the enemy, and to treat it as such is self-defeating," Gates asserted in the spring of 2007, declaring an armistice of sorts.

On key policy matters, too, Gates endorsed new ways forward. He readily backed the surge in U.S. forces for Iraq that Bush announced in January 2007. He also recognized that the U.S. Army needed to expand and enthusiastically supported a permanent increase in overall end strength for the service of 65,000 troops, boosting it to a total 547,000, something Rumsfeld had strongly resisted.

Gates did pledge to continue making military transformation a top priority, but it wasn't for him the signature issue it had been for Rumsfeld, and he didn't invest anywhere near the same amount of energy and ambition in it. Instead, he made it very clear that fixing Iraq would be his overriding mission.

In time, Gates also demonstrated a strong commitment to accountability, taking action against top officials with a firmness that Rumsfeld had lacked. He demanded the resignation of Army secretary Francis J. Harvey in 2007 after a slow Army response to reports about substandard care at Walter Reed Army Medical Center. He declined to nominate Pete Pace for a second two-year term as chairman of the Joint Chiefs of Staff amid concerns that a Democratic-controlled Congress would grill the general on Iraq. He managed the removal of Admiral William Fallon, Abizaid's successor at Central Command, after weeks of rifts between the admiral and White House officials over Iran and Iraq. And he fired the top civilian and military leaders of the Air Force—Secretary Michael Wynne and General Michael Moseley, the chief of staff—over their unsatisfactory response to disclosures that nuclear weapons had been flown around the country improperly.

Gates attracted favorable notices as well for a series of thoughtful speeches that argued for a higher level of coordination in administration policy, rejecting any hint of parochialism and setting an example for others in the national security arena. Additionally, he warned against what he called the "next-war-itis" that had dominated the thinking during Rumsfeld's reign, the system's preference for what might be needed in future wars over what was immediately needed. He repeatedly urged the military to focus on current war demands, even if that meant devoting less time and money to planning for speculative future conflicts.

Perhaps most significantly, Gates brought a sense of balance to a Pentagon that Rumsfeld had kept in a swirl. His lack of flare and self-promotion were a relief after the theatrics of his predecessor, and there was noticeably less carping between Defense and State. But in his quieter way, Gates, in the Rumsfeld tradition, persisted in prodding the military to think outside its box, and after being in the job a while, he was heard expressing more than a little sympathy for what his predecessor had gone through in trying to effect change. "Gates said several times that every day he's here, he understands more and more why Rumsfeld was the way he was," remarked Ryan Henry, the second-ranking official in the Pentagon's policy branch.

———•———

For much of his adult life, Rumsfeld never met an organization he didn't want to change. Although his politics were mainstream conservative, his instincts both in government and business were to shake things up. At once a revolutionary and a conservative, he was a living contradiction, a human oxymoron. "I would tell him he's a funny kind of conservative in that conservatives tend to want to preserve things," recalled Doug Feith, who referred to Rumsfeld as a "radical conservative."

The sheer number of initiatives that Rumsfeld undertook as defense secretary, and the long time he served, assure that his impact on the Pentagon will last far beyond the Iraq War. In his six-year tenure, he launched a dizzying list of reforms, all aimed at getting the Pentagon to think about warfare differently and to develop more-flexible plans for dealing with a world of heightened uncertainty, of small wars as well as possible big ones, of multiple contingencies, and of unconventional threats.

"There has in fact been a change in attitudes and cultures over the last decade," said a former official who worked on strategy issues in the department's policy branch. "The Pentagon has become far more receptive to change now than when I came in the early 1990s. We used to base contingency plans on a very small set of scenarios. Now there's a much bigger set. Rumsfeld's theme about contending with surprise and uncertainty and having the agility to adapt has, I think, over time been embraced by the bureaucracy and has led to far more resilience and capacity within the department than there was before 9/11."

But as Rumsfeld himself recognized, his record on transformation is mixed. While his efforts brought noticeable changes in thinking, they were slower to translate into actual changes in weapons programs. Some initiatives, too, like the supercharging of Special Operations Command into a worldwide manhunt force, proved too hard to push past entrenched interests. Although he grew SOCOM's budget by 80 percent and added thirteen thousand troops, Rumsfeld never did get the SOCOM he wanted—one that would have been devoted more to direct-action missions and less to the kind of community engagement practiced by civil affairs teams and psychological operations units. Additionally, the regional commanders never fully accepted Rumsfeld's attempt to hand SOCOM the lead in the war on terrorism, refusing to cede control over activities conducted in the areas of the world they oversee.

Other Rumsfeld projects were scaled back in the months after he was gone. The withdrawal of U.S. forces from Germany was slowed. Plans to build two satellite systems—one the Space-Based Radar, the other a classified system—were deemed unaffordable and canceled. The Pentagon's intelligence directorate was restructured to align more closely with the office of the director of national intelligence, and the controversial Counter-Intelligence Field Activity program, which had attracted criticism for spying on antiwar protestors, was eliminated.

Concerned as he was about saving taxpayer money, far more federal funds were being spent on defense by the end of Rumsfeld's tenure. Even without direct war costs, the defense budget grew from $366 billion to $654 billion between fiscal years 2001 and 2006. Rumsfeld argued that the nation could afford to spend more on its military and should do so, particularly to offset reductions in defense spending by partner nations. "Ours is also a world of many friends and allies," he said in his farewell address. "But sadly, realistically, friends and allies with declining defense investment and declining capabilities, and, I would add, as a result, with increasing vulnerabilities. All of which requires that the United States of America invest more."

To this day Rumsfeld maintains that the wars in Iraq and Afghanistan energized his transformation campaign rather than delaying or distracting it. In his view, the wars gave impetus to what had to be done. "People said there's no way you can have a major transformation program and simultaneously be involved in a war. I said just the opposite," Rumsfeld recalled in an interview. "That's the time you've got the best opportunity to make the changes. When things are in motion, it's a lot easier to make adjustments." In a peacetime environment, Rumsfeld added, nowhere near the same kind of progress could have been made. "The forces would have been marshaled against you much more than they even were, and they were significant even in a time of war." Asked if there was ever a time he thought about slowing up, Rumsfeld replied, "Nope. I thought about hurrying up."

Rumsfeld's initial notion for how the military should change rested on an abiding belief in technological advances, including dramatic improvements in information management and precision weaponry. These advances, he contended, should make it possible for the military to generate considerably more combat capability with the same, or in some cases, fewer, numbers of weapons platforms and with lower levels of manning.

The invasions of Afghanistan and Iraq were triumphs that seemed, at first, to confirm Rumsfeld's vision of a transparent battlefield, long-range precision strikes, and rapid, decisive operations. But the picture changed as the enemy continued to fight back and proved to be different from what had first been imagined. As impressive as the overthrows of the Taliban and Saddam Hussein regimes had been, they ended up far from decisive. U.S. forces found themselves battling not Iraq's elite Republican Guard divisions and Taliban militias but mongrel bands of insurgents and foreign fighters. It was a different kind of twenty-first-century conflict, one where speed and precision weapons mattered less than patience and constructive community relations.

Rumsfeld resisted the idea that combating shadowy, resourceful insurgents could require more forces on the ground, not just alternative tactics. At times he seemed, even to close associates, to treat the Iraq War more as an irritating diversion from his main mission of transforming the military than as the defining challenge of his time in office.

"It's my belief that he had an expectation of what his job would be as secretary of defense, and it probably centered around transformation—building a foundation that a Defense Department could stand on for the next forty years," said Andy Card. "And then a war got in the way. Transformation had been a labor of love for him. The war became a labor of

responsibility. It was the beautiful siren of transformation that had attracted him to the job, but the shoals ended up being the shoals of war."

———•———

War is what saved Rumsfeld in the Bush administration's first year
when his impolitic ways got him into trouble with Congress and the
military brass, and war is what ultimately brought him down. He had
never bought into the rhetoric of implanting democracy abroad that
was touted by others in the administration, but he had favored removing the regime in Baghdad, figuring any change would be an improvement both for the Iraqi people and for U.S. interests in the region.

The war plan he developed with Tommy Franks succeeded in its aim
of swiftly toppling Saddam Hussein. But in war, the hard part often
comes after the fighting ends. And here Rumsfeld proved neglectful. He
failed to ensure adequate preparation for the postwar phase. He couldn't
imagine the enemy's ability to launch a follow-up war of its own. He
claims to have been unaware of the decision to assign command of military operations in Iraq to Ricardo Sanchez, the Army's most junior three-
star general. And when Paul Bremer, the senior U.S. civilian in Baghdad,
appeared increasingly to skirt the Pentagon and deal directly with the
White House and the State Department, Rumsfeld largely washed his
hands of responsibility for all but the security aspect of the mission.

Given the frequent criticism that Rumsfeld micromanaged too much,
it was odd to see him not micromanaging more. Indeed, even after Bremer
and Sanchez were gone, he left the drafting of a new counterinsurgency
plan largely in the hands of the new Baghdad commander, George Casey,
and then held fast to many of its basic assumptions despite mounting
evidence indicating that the nature of the war was changing into a more
sectarian fight and required new assumptions and revised approaches.

Adamant about having Iraqis assume responsibility for their own security, Rumsfeld resisted the idea of pouring more U.S. troops into the
country, even as it became increasingly apparent that Iraqi forces were
not yet capable of securing neighborhoods cleared by American soldiers.
This minimalist approach might have made sense in a more benign environment. But under combat conditions, when the general rule is to

bring as much as possible to the fight because there's no knowing what might be needed, it was an especially risky strategy.

Army colonel Bill Hix, who advised Casey on strategy, recalled that in August 1941, before the United States entered World War II, President Franklin D. Roosevelt asked Henry Stimson, the secretary of war, what sorts of support would be needed to help the British, Russians, and other Allies defeat Germany and Japan. "It wasn't a question of what can you do with what you've got," Hix said. "It was a question of what does it take to win. But Rumsfeld seemed inclined to go the other way—you know, How little can I use to try to win?"

It may be that Rumsfeld's business experience, considered an advantage in his transformation drive, handicapped his thinking when it came to planning for a war and managing it. The initial success, too, of the war in Afghanistan, which showed the power of a relatively small number of U.S. ground forces using precision air strikes and working with indigenous militias, seems to have reinforced Rumsfeld's commitment to the minimalist model.

"I think his fundamental flaw in being secretary of defense in time of war was that he appeared to equate efficiency with effectiveness," Hix said. "War is an inherently inefficient exercise, particularly on the scale of Iraq; it wastes everything. Surprise and uncertainty are inherent components of it, and one important way you deal with that is to prepare for as many things as possible. You can spend ridiculous amounts of money and find out in the end that you didn't need everything—and people will criticize you afterward. But that's just the way it is. If you end up needing something you don't have, its absence can put at risk everything you are fighting for and demand more lives, treasure and political capital. That's where we were in Iraq."

———————

Asked to assess Rumsfeld's tenure, James Schlesinger gave him high marks as a secretary of defense trying to revamp the U.S. military, but scored Rumsfeld low as a secretary of war. The same, Schlesinger added, was true of Robert McNamara, the only other Pentagon leader whose term rivaled Rumsfeld's for controversy.

Both Rumsfeld and McNamara came to the Pentagon from the corporate world exhibiting arrogance and impatience, and both showed similar characteristics in office: keen analytical minds, insatiable appetites for data, predilections for new methods and approaches to problem solving. McNamara may have been more soullessly analytical, and Rumsfeld more intuitive, but both sought tighter civilian control of the military and ordered reappraisals of U.S. strategy. Both brought with them contingents of civilian aides who shared their determination to shake things up and a propensity to clash with the Joint Chiefs. And both became embroiled in unpopular wars.

Where they differed significantly was in how they ultimately viewed their own tenures. Despite his public cheerleading for the Vietnam War, McNamara privately became dubious about its wisdom and effectiveness while still in office. In later years, he increasingly recognized that he had failed as defense secretary because of mistakes he and others had made in Vietnam.

By contrast, Rumsfeld did not leave office doubting his handling of the Iraq War. He has acknowledged no major missteps or shown any remorse on the subject to date. To the contrary, he contends that the strategy he pursued in Iraq from 2003 through 2006 succeeded in large part—inflicting substantial enemy losses, developing capable Iraqi forces, and establishing a new Iraqi government. The shift in strategy and surge in U.S. forces after he left that is credited with pulling Iraq back from the brink of total disaster would not have worked had it been tried earlier, Rumsfeld has argued, because conditions were not right. The problem with this thinking is that it overestimates what the old strategy accomplished and underestimates what a better-run counterinsurgency program could have achieved.

Asked in our final interview whether he harbored any regrets, Rumsfeld was dismissive. "Oh, that's the favorite press question: What was your biggest mistake?" he remarked. Nor was he interested in being drawn out on the question of how, having come into office so well prepared for the job, he had run into so much difficulty. "I wouldn't be in a position to tell you how to explain it," he said. "You'll have to divine it."

Part of the answer lies in the circumstances. He and the rest of the Bush administration were confronted with extraordinary challenges for which, as Rumsfeld often said, no guidebook or blueprint existed. (Although, in the case of counterinsurgency warfare, there was a wealth of established doctrine that, while out of use for decades, was readily available on the Army's shelves to be dusted off.) And Rumsfeld was hardly alone in his misjudgments. It is both incorrect and unfair to heap singular blame on him for the disaster that Iraq became. Many wrong shots were called by Bremer and the Coalition Provisional Authority. Sanchez proved inadequate to his assignment. And Casey and Abizaid readily concurred with the notion of trying to fight in Iraq with as few U.S. forces as possible. The generals tended to reinforce Rumsfeld's thinking, not challenge it.

"The military was a full-blown partner in this," observed Michael Vickers, a former CIA officer and Special Forces member who played a key role in arming the Afghan resistance to the Soviets in the 1980s and who joined the Bush administration in its last year and a half as an assistant secretary of defense for Special Operations. "The notion that Rumsfeld was managing the war and that the generals were just cowed and going along is just wrong."

Other top administration officials were complicit as well. Bush was exceedingly deferential toward Rumsfeld and failed to question the Iraq strategy sufficiently until late 2006. Cheney consistently lobbied to keep his old friend in power and, in the case of detainee policy, led him down a path of dubious legality and damaging morality. And the rest of the U.S. government, as Rumsfeld frequently complained, was unable to muster the personnel and resources needed to supplement the Pentagon's security measures with economic reconstruction and diplomatic assistance. The administration was trying to fight a twenty-first-century adversary using a dysfunctional twentieth-century interagency structure, one that lacked strong mechanisms to integrate the work of separate departments or a clear precedent for how to coordinate postwar operations of the magnitude required in Iraq. Critical decisions about such central matters as whether, after the invasion of Iraq, to establish an interim Iraqi government or a longer-term U.S. occupation authority were made without full discussion with all the principals.

But much of what befell Rumsfeld resulted from his own behavior. With him it was often hard to divorce style from substance. He is apt to be remembered as much for how he did things as for what he did. And here, too, he was an internal contradiction. Capable of genuine charm, kindness, and grace, he all too frequently came across as brusque and domineering, often alienating others and making enemies where he needed friends. His bullying manner and cutting humor made it difficult for him to draw loyalty from people and make others want to work for him. He kept many people around him and under him on edge.

In an interview in the spring of 2008, Cheney strongly defended Rumsfeld's rough approach. "I liked his style, the way he dug in and asserted civilian control at the Department of Defense," the vice president explained. "It's easy to go over there and just sort of sit on top and float on top of the organization. A lot of people keep you happy in the secretary's office. Don was a bulldog for work and for digging into the organization in major ways and making his presence felt."

Addressing arguments that Rumsfeld's bull-in-a-china-shop manner was needlessly harsh, Cheney maintained that such tough tactics were necessary to shake up a bureaucracy as hidebound as the Pentagon's. "He broke china, which I think is important to do as secretary," Cheney said. "If you're not doing that, especially under the circumstances, then I don't think you're doing your job."

But others, even some who remain largely sympathetic to Rumsfeld, acknowledge that the former secretary too often undercut himself. "He wielded a courageous and skeptical intellect," Feith wrote of Rumsfeld. "He challenged preconceptions and assumptions—including his own—and drove colleagues as well as subordinates to take a long view and to evaluate honestly whether their work was actually producing results. His ideas and ambitions for the Defense Department and the United States were high-minded, his contributions extensive and influential. But his style of leadership did not always serve his own purposes: He bruised people and made personal enemies, who were eager to strike back at him and try to discredit his work."

Stuart Rochester, a senior Pentagon historian, recalled receiving several research requests from Rumsfeld asking whether, as secretary, he had the authority to take a particular action—to merge some Joint Staff functions with those in the secretary's office, for instance, or to combine the operations centers of each of the military services into a single center. "He had no patience for moving in a consensual way," Rochester said. "He felt he needed to act in a decisive way. He'd always be asking, 'Can I do this without having to consult with the service chiefs and with Congress?' A lot of what Rumsfeld was trying to achieve made sense, a lot of his instincts were right, but the problem was the way he went about things. In the end he had to settle for less because he'd alienated so many."

Even Pace, the even-tempered, ramrod-straight Marine general who as chairman sought to appear in lockstep with Rumsfeld, couldn't avoid a blunt judgment months after leaving office when asked what he thought of his former boss. "I'm not an apologist for Secretary Rumsfeld. He's a son of a bitch. And I told him that," Pace remarked before an audience at the Naval Postgraduate School in Monterey, California, in May 2008. In a later interview, Pace said he had not meant to sound derogatory. "He's just a very demanding leader," Pace explained, adding that Rumsfeld "demands more of himself than of anybody else."

For all his grousing that other government agencies didn't do enough in Iraq and in the larger war on terrorism, Rumsfeld did not make it easy to work with his Pentagon. His own lack of collegiality and his strained relations with other cabinet members inhibited interagency cooperation. "Unfortunately, he was not collaborative with the rest of the government," Abizaid said. "He closely guarded so many of his prerogatives as secretary. That, I think, contributed to a sense that the Pentagon itself wasn't approachable."

Rumsfeld could be at his most obstinate when he wasn't getting his way. "When he grew frustrated with how something was going, he was inclined to check out or throw up some kind of roadblock," Card said. "He might decide not to attend a meeting, or he would come and say he hadn't seen the documents being presented. It was as if he was both spurning involvement and demanding attention at the same time. Sometimes, if he didn't agree with something, he would say, 'It's not our job.' Other times he would say, 'If you're telling me it's my job, then this is how we're going to do it, but I only have so many resources so we're going to have to take resources away from here to do it. So what are your priorities?'"

Even the commanders with whom Rumsfeld got along best found him trying. "He's a very complicated guy, and my feelings are mixed," Abizaid remarked months after retiring. "He'd drive me nuts at times, and there were days I wanted to kill either him or myself. There were probably ten times I wrote out a letter of resignation, although I never sent it. On the other hand, I have great respect for Rumsfeld's courage and his tenacity."

———•———

Rumsfeld has tended, even in retrospect, to write off much of the criticism of his style as a function of the mission he was asked to do. "Change is hard" has remained a frequent refrain of his. Chosen to lead the Defense Department as the agent of change, Rumsfeld said he expected that he would come under attack. "People in uniform resisted, and people in civilian clothes resisted; the Congress resisted," he recounted in an interview. "They don't call it the Iron Triangle for nothing, between the permanent bureaucracy and the defense contractors and the Congress. They're permanent, and the people coming in are temporary. And if you try to change that interaction in the Iron Triangle, you're going to catch some shrapnel."

In fact, Rumsfeld has continued to relish his image as a no-nonsense reformer. Coming across a description of himself as someone who dragged the Defense Department into the twenty-first century "with no bedside manner," Rumsfeld said he liked the phrase, joking that it would make a good title for a book.

Convinced that many of his critics didn't really know him, he believes he got along well with those with whom he spent the most time. "The people who I worked with for the most part, I think, were fairly comfortable working with me," he said. "It's the people three layers down who would get the ripple effect."

Told that even some senior officers who dealt closely with him found him difficult, Rumsfeld said it was the work itself that was difficult, and he defended his own manner as nothing the officers shouldn't have been able to tolerate. "The idea that guys with three and four stars on their shoulders can't take tough questions—well, then, they shouldn't have three or four stars on their shoulders."

Rumsfeld has ascribed much of the negative perception of him and the Bush administration to distorted media coverage. Complaints about what he views as inaccurate, biased reporting came up frequently in the series of interviews conducted for this book, and he returned to the issue again in our final meeting in November 2008.

"The intellectual dishonesty on the part of the press is serious," he asserted. He groused about "a strong incentive to be negative and dramatic" that had infused much of the coverage. "It's a formula that works. It gets Pulitzers; it gets promotions; it gets name identification on the front page above the fold."

Part of the formula, Rumsfeld added, involved pillorying him along with Bush and Cheney but sparing Powell and Rice. As an example, he noted accusations that Bush and Cheney had lied about Saddam Hussein's possession of weapons of mass destruction in making the case for the invasion of Iraq. "They never say Colin Powell lied," Rumsfeld asserted. "They don't say Condi lied."

Rumsfeld attributed many of the distortions to self-serving accounts provided by State Department and NSC officials. He said that although other top administration officials knew such leaking was going on, they did nothing about it. Even out of office, Rumsfeld has sought to nudge his erstwhile colleagues to correct the record. He wrote Powell, for instance, objecting to statements by Lawrence Wilkerson, a retired U.S. Army colonel who served as Powell's chief of staff, in which Wilkerson alleged that senior defense officials had quietly encouraged Taiwanese politicians to move toward a declaration of independence from mainland China—an act that the Communist regime has repeatedly warned would provoke a military strike.

Rumsfeld's decision while in office not to tell his side of things and to ban his staff from providing insider accounts was motivated, he said, out of a sense of loyalty to the president. He wanted to be able to look Bush in the eye and assert that neither he nor any of his aides were behind any of the stories disclosing the administration's secret discussions. But he has had second thoughts about having kept as mum as he did.

———•———

Some associates who served with Rumsfeld during both his stints as defense secretary think he changed over the years. "I refer to him as Don

One and Don Two," said James Roche, who was a Navy officer doing strategic planning under the first Don and secretary of the Army under the second. "Don One was a leader, Don Two was a bureaucrat. Don Two was worried about what the White House was doing, what Condi was doing, what Colin was doing."

Ken Adelman, who greatly admired the earlier Rumsfeld but grew increasingly disillusioned with him during the Bush years, wonders whether Rumsfeld fundamentally changed or just appeared different to him. "Maybe he was better before, or maybe I was just wrong about him," Adelman said. "Maybe it's the challenges that were different later. I don't know."

The second time around, Rumsfeld was clearly more driven than he had been in the mid-1970s. He spoke at his farewell ceremony of having felt "an enormous sense of urgency," particularly in the wake of the September 11 attacks, to identify U.S. vulnerabilities and to fortify the military against them. "Get your eyes off your shoelaces!" he often instructed his staff, advising them to be alert to problems, to remain vigilant, and to think longer term. "Stir the pot" was another of his favorite sayings, reflecting his incessant drive for improvement.

But just what the stirring was supposed to produce wasn't always clear. The recipe was a constant work in progress, and the cooking was compounded by a tendency on Rumsfeld's part to prolong it, to delay decisions, or to cede responsibility to others. At times he appeared less the head cook than the health inspector, closely examining the ingredients and challenging the kitchen's methods.

Rumsfeld was at his best—and seemingly most comfortable—when he was questioning things. Decisions came harder. Although he projected an aura of the man-in-command, he frequently led not by direct orders but by the power of strong suggestion. In the planning for the invasion of Iraq, for instance, he didn't tell Franks to do it this way or that; he kept saying, "Well, are you sure you want to do it this way? What about this option or that option?"

The same could be said of his approach to decisions on major new weapons systems. Apart from the Crusader system, which he was nudged by Wolfowitz and others into canceling, and Comanche, which the Army itself offered up for elimination, Rumsfeld remained reluctant to cancel any big program.

"On decisions he was very wary," said Paul Gebhard, who served as a special assistant in Rumsfeld's first months and continued to consult for several years afterward. "He didn't want people to box him in. He didn't want the fingerprints. He would roll the stuff around forever."

NSC officials also found him frustratingly evasive on a number of issues, tossing out options but resisting being pinned down. "I think he's a man who keeps everybody bouncing around wondering what to do, and then kind of acquiesces to a situation when people have tried to figure out what he wants," remarked John Hamre, a deputy secretary of defense under Clinton. "The service chiefs tell you that when they went to him with a presentation to try to get an answer, they'd never get one. They'd ask themselves, What does he want? Finally, they'd try to package something as close as they could to what they thought he wanted, and he'd look at it and say, 'Well if that's what you want, okay.' That was his basic MO."

So much of Rumsfeld's own energy as defense secretary was taken up dealing with tiny details—wordsmithing briefing charts, examining the smallest deployment orders, nitpicking the schedules of commanders, snowflaking about dining table settings. In his own efforts to probe, he would often get down to a level of minutiae that struck some officials as inappropriate for a defense secretary.

"I look at him as a tragic hero, like a Forrestal or McNamara, who tried to do the right thing but got overwhelmed by it all," said a former Pentagon official who had worked closely with Rumsfeld for a time.

Most tragic of all was the human loss that occurred on Rumsfeld's watch. The tally of U.S. troops who had died in the Iraq War had reached 2,939 on the day of his farewell ceremony, and the number of wounded in action had exceeded twenty-two thousand. Countless others were mentally and emotionally traumatized from the nightmarish conflict. Aside from the toll in human lives, billions of dollars had been spent on the war. And the U.S. military's honor had been tarnished by the Abu Ghraib revelations and other scandals involving the treatment of detainees in the custody of American troops. These are the deepest scars of Rumsfeld's time as secretary.

Rumsfeld is in many respects an honorable man, deeply patriotic, a good friend to many, and unfailingly loyal to those he has served and to a number who have served him. He is smart, cunning, and capable of great geniality, all highly desirable qualities in a leader with such power.

The challenges he faced were extraordinary—waging a counterinsurgency campaign long after the U.S. military had forgotten the lessons of the last one it fought, attempting to transform a Pentagon bureaucracy notoriously resistant to change, coping with a U.S. government deficient in civilian capacity to assist in postwar stabilization and reconstruction.

But in the end, Rumsfeld's biggest failings were personal—the result of the man himself, not simply of the circumstances he confronted. While he was unwilling to profess regrets to me, it is unlikely that he is without any. Nor do I expect him simply to fade away. That has never been his style. Withdrawal is not a Rumsfeld rule.

Acknowledgments

When I initially approached Donald Rumsfeld about this book, he made it clear that he did not want to assist in a way that might be interpreted as a stamp of approval. This is not an authorized biography. But Rumsfeld did do more to help than perhaps he originally intended, and I thank him for his cooperation. To my knowledge, he raised no objection when friends or former associates checked with him before agreeing to talk to me. He provided access to many memos, correspondence, and other documents in his files. And he granted me eight interviews, sometimes engaging in discussion for hours at a stretch.

Joyce Rumsfeld was also exceedingly accommodating. She spoke at length during five interviews, opened the way for me to talk with a number of old friends, and encouraged her husband to see me. I am deeply indebted to her, although she, like her husband, will undoubtedly object to some of what I have written.

Several of Rumsfeld's closest Pentagon associates, including Steve Cambone and Larry Di Rita, as well as Keith Urbahn, who works for the former secretary now, spent hours answering my questions and explaining Rumsfeld's methods and motivations. I am grateful to all three for their efforts. Special thanks as well to Nancy Pardo, a longtime assistant to Rumsfeld who provided much useful material about his ancestry and early years.

Few people interviewed for this book were dispassionate about Rumsfeld. For some, talking about him was a pleasure. His numerous longtime friends were eager to set the record straight and offer stories of Rumsfeld's genial, considerate side. For many others, though, recalling Rumsfeld produced a painful array of angry, bitter, and unforgiving emotions. My thanks to all who took the time to share recollections and judgments about this complex and paradoxical character.

My agent, Esther Newberg, was instrumental in getting the book launched, backing my effort to undertake the project with an open mind. Among those approached about publishing the book, no one expressed more enthusiasm or believed more in its potential than Peter Osnos, the founder of PublicAffairs and now an editor-at-large. He, along with Susan Weinberg, the publisher, allowed me leeway to do the kind of book that I wanted and to let deadlines slip until it was done.

The skillful, patient editing of Morgen Van Vorst greatly improved the text. Melissa Raymond guided me through the production process. Whitney Peeling developed the publicity plan. I am also indebted to Pete Garceau for creating the jacket, Trish Wilkinson for designing the text, Cliff Corcoran for checking facts, Kathy Delfosse for copyediting the manuscript, Ella Hoffman for compiling the notes, Chrisona Schmidt for copyediting the notes, and Cheryl Rivard for proofreading.

My eternal appreciation goes to the editors at the *Washington Post* who gave me the opportunity over fourteen years to report on the Pentagon. The list includes: Len Downie, Bob Kaiser, Steve Coll, Phil Bennett, Liz Spayd, Mike Abramowitz, Bob McCartney, Alan Cooperman, Matt Vita, and Scott Vance. While working on this book, I benefited greatly from the advice and encouragement of current and former *Post* colleagues. Early on, David Maraniss and Karen DeYoung offered tips on writing a biography. Glenn Kessler, Robin Wright, Josh White, Ann Scott Tyson, and Sally Quinn shared knowledge and insights. Many helpful comments on the manuscript came from Rick Atkinson, Dana Priest, Vernon Loeb, Tom Ricks, Valerie Strauss, and Bob Woodward. And Lucy Shackelford provided invaluable research assistance.

My deep gratitude as well to Eliot Cohen and Tom Keaney, who, while I researched and wrote the book, arranged for a home away from home at Johns Hopkins University's School of Advanced International Studies. Tom also served as an insightful reader of the manuscript, as did James Mann, David Martin, Michael O'Hanlon, Thom Shanker, and Bryan Whitman—all of whom contributed to strengthening the final product and none of whom bear any responsibility for its weaknesses. A note of acknowledgment, too, to Sandy Cochran, an occasional lunch mate and sounding board.

Above all, I am grateful to my family. To my brother, Russell, who took an interest and made thoughtful suggestions. To my wife, Lissa, whose smart counsel, unfailing support, and abiding love sustained me. And to our children, Wynne, Cole, and Max, who corrected my grammar, kept me laughing, and continue to fill my life with delight.

Notes

This book is based on more than three hundred interviews, as well as on many memoranda, briefing charts, notes of meetings, reporting cables, correspondence, calendars, and other primary documents. In a number of instances, people were interviewed more than once, so multiple dates may appear below for interviews with the same person. Many of the documents cited in the book remain classified or privately held, but I have provided titles and dates for them whenever possible. Full transcripts for relevant Defense Department news conferences can be found on the Pentagon's Web site, www.defenselink.mil/transcripts. Transcripts of Donald Rumsfeld's speeches as defense secretary are posted at www.defenselink.mil/speeches. One extraordinary aspect of the Bush period was the amount of reporting that quickly emerged in books and news stories, providing near-contemporaneous accounts of previously secret deliberations and decisions. This work by others, cited frequently in the notes below, contributed significantly to my telling of the Rumsfeld story.

Introduction

2   "We said there's no way": Interview with Joyce Rumsfeld, April 23, 2007.

2   Sitting with Bush: Interview with a senior presidential aide who was present at the meeting, March 27, 2008.

2   "In the president's mind": Interview with a former senior White House official, October 5, 2007.

4   As Bush started looking: This account of internal White House deliberations is based on interviews with three White House officials.

4   A White House rump group: Robert Draper, *Dead Certain: The Presidency of George W. Bush* (New York: Free Press, 2007), 398; Elisabeth Bumiller, *Condoleezza Rice: An American Life* (New York: Random House, 2007), 298.

5   "I thought, What is that about?": Joyce Rumsfeld interview, April 23, 2007.

5   "He really got frantic": Interview with Delonnie Henry, June 6, 2007.

5   Dated November 6: Rumsfeld memorandum to Bush, "Iraq—Illustrative New Courses of Action," November 6, 2006; first disclosed in Michael R. Gordon and David S. Cloud, "Rumsfeld Memo Proposed 'Major Adjustment' in Iraq," *New York Times*, December 3, 2006.

7   "I thought there was": Interview with General (retired) Jack Keane, February 29, 2008.

8   "He clearly was more thoughtful": Interview with then-Lieutenant General Victor E. "Gene" Renuart Jr., December 4, 2006.

8   Rumsfeld remembers responding: Interview with Donald Rumsfeld, November 19, 2008.

9   "He looked like": Delonnie Henry interview, June 6, 2007.

9   "You've been a star": Interview with Matt Latimer, January 18, 2007.

10   "The president, at least": Former senior presidential aide interview, March 27, 2008.

10   "I think they both understood": Former senior White House official interview, October 5, 2007.

10   Rumsfeld, for his part, was wary: Donald Rumsfeld interview, November 19, 2008.

Chapter 1: A Bit of a Rascal

16   Some histories show him: Heinrich Meyerholz, "The Rumsfelds Came from Niedersachsen," *Old North German Families Journal*, January 1977; English translation in Donald Rumsfeld's personal files. Copy obtained by author.

16   An alternate history: Wolfgang Buesing, *The Buesing at Ofen: History of an Oldenburg Family and Its Farm* (Oldenburg, 1960), 26; English translation in Donald Rumsfeld's personal files. Copy obtained by author.

16   The manifest for the SS *Donau*: See www.immigrantships.net/v8/1800v8/donau18760624.html.

16   After reaching America: A number of details about Rumsfeld's parents were taken from a brief history prepared for the Rumsfelds by Nancy Pardo, "George and Jeannette Rumsfeld: A Brief Introduction." Copy obtained by author.

17   As Baird recalled the moment: Letter from Warner G. Baird to Jeannette Rumsfeld, January 3, 1978, Donald Rumsfeld's personal files. Copy obtained by author.

18   While studying Native Americans: Tales of Rumsfeld's early childhood mischief provided by Joan Ramsay in an unpublished paper of recollections dated May 17, 2002. Copy obtained by author.

18   By his own account: Trudi McC. Osborne, "A Winnetka Boy in the War Room," *Chicago Magazine*, January 4, 1976.

18   "If it doesn't go easy": "Rumsfeld's Rules"; also cited in Rowan Scarborough, *Rumsfeld's War: The Untold Story of America's Anti-Terrorist Commander* (Washington, DC: Regnery, 2004), 64.

19   "The intensity of a young": Joyce Rumsfeld interview, May 25, 2006.

19   "I remember asking him": Interview with Judy Koch Merrifield, July 19, 2006.

20   He remembered his dad: Donald Rumsfeld, interview by Rowan Scarborough, October 18, 2003.

20   George Rumsfeld also had a reputation: Interview with Ned Jannotta, April 18, 2006.

21   In Don Rumsfeld's eyes: Donald Rumsfeld, eulogy, September 20, 1974. Copy obtained by author.

21   "She kept cleaning up my language": Donald Rumsfeld, town hall meeting in Mosul, Iraq, December 10, 2006.

21   "I think his mother was": Interview with Myles Cunningham, May 9, 2006.

21   *Life* magazine featured: Special education issue, *Life*, October 16, 1950.

21   "He was smart": Interview with Betty Christian, April 24, 2006.

21   "He was a very good student": Cunningham interview, May 9, 2006.

22   "I think he liked that": Interview with Brad Glass, April 17, 2006.

22   "George and I weren't particularly": Eleanor Randolph, "From Melons to Men, Rumsfeld's a 'Mover,'" *Chicago Tribune*, November 9, 1975.

22   "I marveled at what": Cunningham interview, May 9, 2006.

23   "He came to me": Interview with Lenny Vyskocil, July 13, 2006.

23   "You can get into trouble": Interview with Bob Nellis, June 2, 2006.

23   "That's the way Don wrestled": Cunningham interview, May 9, 2006.

23   "He was the most aggressive wrestler": Interview with Lex Irvine, June 2, 2006.

23   "We would put a half-dollar": Vyskocil interview, July 13, 2006.

24   "Don now says": Interview with Carolyn Twiname, April 25, 2006.

24   "They just both": Nellis interview, June 2, 2006.

24   Pearson was declared the winner: Pearson says he won on a technicality involving "riding" time, the amount of time a wrestler is in control of the opponent. One minute of riding time is worth a point, and Pearson recalls having just under a minute but being given the extra point anyway. Rumsfeld says the match actually ended in a tie and the victory went to Pearson because he was the defending champion.

24   "The guy was a bull": Interview with Fred Pearson, June 1, 2006.

25   "Don was determined": Cunningham interview, May 9, 2006.

25   "There was an inspection": Interview with John Madigan, June 2, 2006.

26   "There was a very distinct sign": Interview with Bill Ryno, June 1, 2006.

26   one of the most competitive people: Interview with John Griesser, May 1, 2006.

26   "He was good-looking": Christian interview, April 24, 2006.

26   "I was aware": Joyce Rumsfeld interview, May 25, 2006.

26   "She was kind of a little pixie": Interview with Barbara Mayberry, July 19, 2006.

27   "So mine was more": Joyce Rumsfeld interview, May 25, 2006.

27   "He'd say things like": Vyskocil interview, July 13, 2006.

27   Griesser recalled Rumsfeld saying: Griesser interview, May 1, 2006.

27   "When he said that": Christian interview, April 24, 2006.

28   "The point is": Joyce Rumsfeld interview, May 25, 2006.

28   "My dad sent a note back": Donald Rumsfeld, speech to the Boy Scout National Meeting Breakfast, May 26, 2006.

29   A friend's father: Madigan interview, June 2, 2006.

29   "We definitely worked him over": Jannotta interview, April 18, 2006.

29   "We had a hard time": Interview with Jim Otis, April 18, 2006.

29   Decades later, he told an interviewer: Donald Rumsfeld, interview for video marking 100th anniversary of the Princeton wrestling team.

29   "I just thought": Joyce Rumsfeld interview, May 25, 2006.

29   In the 1950s Princeton: Jerome Karabel, *The Chosen: The Hidden History of Admission and Exclusion at Harvard, Yale, and Princeton* (Boston: Houghton Mifflin Harcourt, 2005), 298.

30   "Back in my day": Mark F. Bernstein, "Rumsfeld's Princeton," *Princeton Alumni Weekly*, October 6, 2004.

30   "He was an unhappy camper": Otis interview, April 18, 2006.

30   "I worked hard": Bernstein, "Rumsfeld's Princeton."

30   Recruiters for the Reserve: *The Nassau Herald*, Class of 1954, 398.

30   "I remember him saying": Joyce Rumsfeld interview, May 25, 2006.

31   "There was camaraderie": Interview with Michael Weatherly, June 15, 2006.

31   Rumsfeld also knew how: Interview with Dick Stevens, June 15, 2006.

31   "Rumsfeld was a very strong individual": Interview with Somers Steelman, June 15, 2006.

31   "Rumsfeld was never one": Weatherly interview, June 15, 2006.

31   "As close as we all were": Steelman interview, June 15, 2006.

32   Academically, Rumsfeld by his account: Donald Rumsfeld interview, August 29, 2007.

32   "He wasn't an intellectual giant": Interview with Sid Wentz, June 20, 2006.

32   When asked years later: Bernstein, "Rumsfeld's Princeton."

32   At the time, Rumsfeld characterized: *The Nassau Herald*, Class of 1954, 295.

32   "He was not swayed": Wentz interview, June 20, 2006.

33   "We were just glued to it": Bernstein, "Rumsfeld's Princeton."

33   The sport had a long: Peter Jarow, "Wrestling Program Boasts Storied History," *Daily Princetonian*, March 3, 2005.

33   "He was very quick": Interview with Carlton MacDonald Jr., June 20, 2006.

34   In the final match: Ben McGrath, "Rummy Meets His Match," *New Yorker*, April 14, 2003.

34   Rumsfeld "would go in for this so-called takedown": McGrath, "Rummy Meets His Match."

34   "They've always built Rumsfeld up": McGrath, "Rummy Meets His Match."

35   "There is much to be said": Donald Rumsfeld, "The Steel Seizure Case of 1952 and Its Effects on Presidential Powers" (senior thesis, Princeton University, April 26, 1954), 135.

35   "With an eye toward": Rumsfeld, "Steel Seizure Case," 138.

35   "You dare not, if I may say so": Adlai Stevenson, speech to the senior class banquet at Princeton University, March 22, 1954.

36   In later years: See, for instance Donald Rumsfeld, town hall meeting in Mosul, Iraq, December 10, 2006.

36   in a passage Rumsfeld liked to cite: See, for instance, his speech to the Boy Scouts National Meeting Breakfast, May 26, 2006.

36   "A lot of guys": Interview with Julie Sherman Whitaker, July 18, 2006.

36   "That's not usually": Joyce Rumsfeld interview, May 25, 2006. All other quotes attributed to her about visiting Princeton in the spring of 1954 and getting engaged come from this interview.

37   "He said, 'I'm going'": Stevens interview, June 15, 2006.

38   "He'd call them 'reversible names'": Interview with Ken Adelman, November 16, 2006.

38   "Don always says": Joyce Rumsfeld interview, April 3, 2007.

Chapter 2: Developing His Own Tune

39   "Coordination was required": Interview with Alan Halkett, July 19, 2006.

39   "I was about as disappointed": Donald Rumsfeld interview, August 29, 2007.

40   "Flying attack jets": Interview with Charles Kinnaird, August 21, 2006.

40   "I think he would have stayed in": Joyce Rumsfeld interview, May 25, 2006.

40   "It was the only way": Interview with Walt Halperin, July 18, 2006.

40   a "spunky" and skillful wrestler: Interview with Joe Gattuso, December 12, 2007.

41   "He taught formation flying": Joyce Rumsfeld interview, May 25, 2006.

41   Rumsfeld had his own close call: Donald Rumsfeld interview, November 19, 2008.

41   "Self-assurance, he always had that": Walt Halperin interview, July 18, 2006.

42   "I remember Rummy": Interview with Willa Halperin, July 18, 2006.

42   Rumsfeld told an interviewer: John Osborne, "The President and the Poor," *New Republic*, May 24, 1969.

42   As he tells the story: Donald Rumsfeld interview, August 29, 2007.

42   "I was so excited": Donald Rumsfeld, speech to the United States Association of Former Members of Congress, March 4, 2003.

43   "He had been a wrestler": Donald Rumsfeld in a town hall meeting with troops in Mosul, Iraq, December 10, 2006.

43   "Going from being a naval aviator": Donald Rumsfeld, interview by Dr. Alfred Goldberg and Dr. Roger Trask, OSD Historical Office, July 12, 1994. Copy obtained by author.

43   "No member of Congress": "Re-elect Rep. Dennison," *Warren Tribune Chronicle*, October 21, 1958.

44   Rumsfeld insists there was nothing: Donald Rumsfeld interview, August 29, 2007.

44   Himself a rising star: Interview with Robert Griffin, August 31, 2006.

44   "I wanted to learn": Osborne, "Winnetka Boy."

45   "I remember seeing Rumsfeld": Kinnaird interview, August 21, 2006.

45   "I was in the advertising business": Weatherly interview, June 15, 2006.

45   "He would take you to task": Stevens interview, June 15, 2006.

46   "Immediately Don decided to run": George Rumsfeld to Ben and Ida [no last name given in letter], September 10, 1962. Copy obtained by author.

46   "We were at a Christmas party": Interview with John Mabie, June 1, 2006.

46   "The idea of him getting elected": Otis interview, April 18, 2006.

46   "We were all so young then": Twiname interview, April 25, 2006.

47   "He looked like": Jannotta interview, April 18, 2006.

47   "If elected, at age thirty": Statement announcing candidacy, Rumsfeld for Congress Committee.

47   A campaign flyer: Rumsfeld campaign flyer, Rumsfeld for Congress Committee.

47   He warned against: Campaign literature titled "This Is What I Believe," Rumsfeld for Congress Committee.

48   "Get your chin up!": Jannotta interview, April 18, 2006.

48   Rumsfeld campaigned tirelessly: "Candidate to Shake Hands for Four Days," *Chicago Daily Tribune*, March 19, 1962.

48   "We did not know": Mabie interview, June 1, 2006.

48   "I remember one committeeman": Jannotta interview, April 18, 2006.

49   "Rumsfeld's Republicanism is sound": "Rumsfeld for Congress," *Chicago Sun-Times*, January 27, 1962.

49   "If the Republican party": George Tagge, "Hint Rumsfeld Is Choice of Rep. Church for House," *Chicago Daily Tribune*, February 14, 1962.

50   On March 9: "The Evidence," *Chicago Sun-Times*, March 9, 1962.

50   When Burks saw: "Burks Remembers Signing Checks," *Chicago Sun-Times*, March 21, 1962.

50   The allegations against Burks: Andrew Cockburn, *Rumsfeld: His Rise, Fall, and Catastrophic Legacy* (New York: Scribner, 2007), 14.

50   "I learned from the incident": Osborne, "Winnetka Boy."

50   "We took a sleepy": Otis interview, April 18, 2006.

51   "Listen to this": Donald Rumsfeld, speech to the United States Association of Former Members of Congress, March 4, 2003.

51   "We looked to Don": Griffin interview, August 31, 2006.

51   "You'd better be careful": Henry Z. Scheele, "Prelude to the Presidency: An Examination of the Gerald R. Ford-Charles A. Halleck House Minority Leadership Contest," *Presidential Studies Quarterly* 25 (Fall 1995): 770; also cited in Robert V. Remini, *The House: The History of the House of Representatives* (New York: HarperCollins, 2006), 398.

52   "That congressional class": Interview with Barbara Ludden, September 29, 2006.

52   "I told him": Interview with Mel Laird, October 6, 2006.

52   "He didn't look much older": Willard Edwards, "Freshman Rep. Rumsfeld: A Space Expert," *Chicago Tribune*, August 18, 1963, 6.

53   "genetically impatient": Donald Rumsfeld, speech to newspaper editors, April 22, 2004.

53   "From the very beginning": Ludden interview, September 29, 2006.

53   With a group of five other: Associated Press, "6 in GOP Criticize U.S. Space Program," *New York Times*, July 28, 1963, 49.

54   He won approval in: "4.5 Million Noise Fund," *Chicago Tribune*, March 11, 1964.

54   He also fought, unsuccessfully: "Dems Deserts in New Bid for Space Center," *Chicago Tribune*, March 26, 1964; John Finney, "House Votes $5.19 Billion Authorization for Space," *New York Times*, March 26, 1964, 11.

55   Nitze never quite got over: Strobe Talbott, *The Master of the Game: Paul Nitze and the Nuclear Peace* (New York: Knopf, 1988), 86–88.

55   "I don't think he": Jannotta interview, April 18, 2006.

55   "Let's face it": Ludden interview, September 29, 2006.

55   "He wasn't an ideologue": Interview with Robert Ellsworth, February 9, 2007.

56   "He hadn't made $10,000": Ludden interview, September 29, 2006.

56   "It was button-down": Interview with Bruce Ladd, August 28, 2006.

56   Rumsfeld was intent on: Michael Pakenham, "Rep. Rumsfeld a Real Cutup for Supporter," *Chicago Tribune*, March 11, 1963.

56   "He had a policy": Interview with Sue Sittnick, September 22, 2006.

57   On one trip: Jerry Landauer, "Some in Congress Reap Extra Expense Money on Overseas Junkets," *Wall Street Journal*, January 14, 1967, 1.

57   "He was very punctilious": Interview with Frank Carlucci, February 22, 2007.

57   "He was never about": Sittnick interview, September 22, 2006.

57   "He was tremendously careful": Ladd interview, August 28, 2006.

57   "This is for Don": Ludden interview, September 29, 2006.

58   He accused Rumsfeld: Robert Sherrill, "De-escalator of the War on Poverty," *New York Times Magazine*, December 13, 1970.

58   Years later, Williams recalled: Sherrill, "De-escalator."

59   Rumsfeld has credited Tom Curtis: Remini, *The House*, 403.

59   "Don Rumsfeld was a catalyst": Tom Curtis, interview by Robert L. Peabody, Robert L. Peabody research interviews, February 3, 1965, Gerald R. Ford Library.

59   At that point, by his account: Donald Rumsfeld, interview by Robert L. Peabody, Robert L. Peabody Research Interviews, Box 1, January 30, 1964, Gerald R. Ford Library.

59   A party conference was convened: Rowland Evans and Peter Novak, "The December Caucus," *Washington Post*, November 30, 1964, A17.

59   "I've only got one life to live": Donald Rumsfeld, interview by Robert L. Peabody, Robert L. Peabody Research Interviews, Box 1, December 30, 1964, Gerald R. Ford Library.

60   "It looked like something was on": Donald Rumsfeld, interview by Robert L. Peabody, Robert L. Peabody Research Interviews, Box 1, December 30, 1964, Gerald R. Ford Library.

60   "We worked hard on it": Remini, *The House*, 404.

60   The contest wasn't really about: Remini, *The House*, 404; also, E.W. Kenworthy, "Ford Will Oppose Halleck in House," *New York Times*, December 19, 1964, 14.

60   "Rumsfeld's Raiders": Remini, *The House*, 405; also, Philip Warden, "Rep. Ford Wins Halleck Job as GOP leader," *Chicago Tribune*, January 5, 1965, 1.

61   "Perhaps behind the scenes": Donald Rumsfeld, interview by Robert L. Peabody, Robert L. Peabody research interviews, April 9, 1965, Gerald R. Ford Library.

61   "My position, I suppose": Donald Rumsfeld, interview by Dr. Alfred Goldberg and Dr. Roger Trask, OSD Historical Office, July 12, 1994.

61   "Does the concept of declaring war": Testimony before the Joint Committee on the Organization of the Congress, June 2, 1965, entered into the *Congressional Record*, June 3, 1965, 12418–12421; cited in George C. Wilson, "Different View on Defense," *Washington Post*, November 9, 1975.

62   He joined a group: John W. Finney, "52 in House Seek a Congress Study of Policy on War," *New York Times*, September 26, 1967, 1.

62   The logistical management of the war: "War in Viet Hit by Rumsfeld," *Chicago Tribune*, April 13, 1966, 8.

62   A visit he made: William C. Selover, "Congressmen See U.S. Aid Dollars Straying in Vietnam," *Christian Science Monitor*, August 8, 1966.

62   the Pentagon and State Department tightened controls: William C. Selover, "Vietnam Pilfering, Graft Muzzled," *Christian Science Monitor*, August 8, 1966.

63   "The trip was an eye-opener": Ladd interview, August 28, 2006.

63   "I was floored": Donald Rumsfeld, interview by Dr. Alfred Goldberg and Dr. Roger Trask, OSD Historical Office, July 12, 1994.

63   He told newspaper editors: "Editors Told White House Seeks Secrecy," *Chicago Tribune*, February 22, 1966.

63   Rumsfeld became a cosponsor: Bruce Ladd, *Crisis in Credibility* (New York: New American Library, 1968), 204–206.

64   "I inserted anything": Ladd, *Crisis in Credibility*, 209.

64   Rumsfeld "believed in openness": Ladd interview, August 28, 2006.

64   In a speech: Ladd, *Crisis in Credibility*, 212.

66   "My vote today": Donald Rumsfeld, speech on the floor of the U.S. House of Representatives, April 10, 1968, *Congressional Record.*

66   "I don't think he was": Ladd interview, August 28, 2006.

67   "I think his thinking was": Ludden interview, September 29, 2006.

67   She portrayed herself: Margaret Mohan, "Politics Split Family," *Chicago Tribune*, September 30, 1964, N3.

68   "Certain members stand out": "Quality in the House," *New York Times*, November 4, 1966, 38.

68   "red hot fight": Philip Warden, "Mrs. Reid Receives Appropriations Post," *Chicago Tribune*, January 26, 1967, 12.

69   Recalling the moment: Donald Rumsfeld, foreword to *The All-Volunteer Force: Thirty Years of Service*, ed. Barbara A. Bicksler, Curtis L. Gilroy, and John T. Warner (Dulles, VA: Brassey's, 2004).

70   Acknowledging the challenge: Aldo Beckman, "Rumsfeld Won't Give Up Efforts to Reform Procedures in House," *Chicago Tribune*, September 15, 1968.

71   "I'm no intellectual giant": Ladd interview, August 28, 2006.

71   "You've worked like hell": Osborne, "The President and the Poor."

71   "The legislative process is too slow": Ellsworth interview, February 9, 2007.

Chapter 3: Tough Enough

74   Headquartered on the nineteenth: "G.O.P. Team Calmly Views Dem Struggle," *Chicago Tribune*, August 28, 1968, 10.

74   "Nixon had the idea": Ellsworth interview, February 9, 2007.

74   Nixon considered naming: Rowland Evans and Robert Novak, "Nixon's Plans to Replace Bliss Hint Changing Times," *Los Angeles Times*, November 28, 1968.

74   He was "rough and ready": Rudy Abramson, "Rumsfeld: Achiever Seeking Challenges," *Los Angeles Times*, November 4, 1975.

75   But Rumsfeld thought: Jannotta interview, April 18, 2006; "Poverty Agency Chief: Donald Rumsfeld," *New York Times*, April 22, 1969.

75   Rumsfeld wanted assurances: John Osborne, "The President and the Poor," *The New Republic*, May 24, 1969.

75   Flown to Florida: Robert B. Semple Jr., "Rumsfeld to Head Poverty Agency,"
        New York Times, April 22, 1969.

75   Others, though, expected: Charles Clapp, interview by A. James Reichley,
        August 25, 1977, Gerald R. Ford Library.

75   "He's not the kind of guy": Jannotta interview, April 18, 2006.

76   A way to circumvent this: James Mann, *Rise of the Vulcans: The History of
        Bush's War Cabinet* (New York: Viking, 2004), 10.

76   Nixon had spelled out: Richard Nixon, message to Congress about OEO,
        February 19, 1969; "Redirection of the Office of Economic Opportunity,"
        White House Central Files, Subject Files, Federal Government-OEO (FG
        6–7); Nick Thimmesch, "Federal Anti-Poverty Program No Smaller, On
        Sounder Basis," *Los Angeles Times*, June 30, 1970.

76   "Rumsfeld called me in": Carlucci interview, February 22, 2007.

77   Rumsfeld also proved: Ehrlichman memorandum to Nixon, November
        25, 1969, White House Central Files, Subject Files, Federal Government-
        OEO (FG 6–7); Jonathan Spivak, "New Antipoverty Chief Plays Down
        Militancy and Stresses Research, *Wall Street Journal*, January 7, 1970.

77   Rumsfeld's staunch defense: Donald Rumsfeld, interview by A. James
        Reichley, January 25, 1978, Gerald R. Ford Library.

77   When Rumsfeld held: Donald Rumsfeld, address to the National Press
        Club, December 16, 1969; also cited in Mann, *Rise of the Vulcans*, 13.

78   "He wasn't an ideologue": Interview with Terry Lenzner, June 22, 2007.

78   "One of the most gratifying things": Laurence Leamer, *Playing for Keeps in
        Washington* (New York: Dial, 1977), 152.

79   Cheney maintains that his interview: Eric Schmitt, "Cheney Tells of Meet-
        ing Rumsfeld 35 Years Ago," *New York Times*, May 14, 2003.

79   Rumsfeld remembers thinking: Donald Rumsfeld interview, November
        19, 2008.

79   "Cheney didn't seek": Lenzner interview, June 22, 2007.

79   "Rumsfeld took to Cheney": Carlucci interview, February 22, 2007.

80   "We've got about two-thirds": Sherrill, "De-escalator."

80   Rumsfeld, according to his critics: See remarks by William Bechtel, a Sen-
        ate staff director, cited in Sherrill, "De-escalator."

80   "The cumulation of events": Sherrill, "De-escalator."

80   "I guess what happens is": Sherrill, "De-escalator."

81   The president had taken: H. R. Haldeman, *The Haldeman Diaries: Inside
        the Nixon White House* (New York: Putnam's, 1994), 169.

81   "Gradually I could see": Lenzner interview, June 22, 2007.

81   In the summer of 1970: Haldeman, *The Haldeman Diaries*, 194.

82   One suggestion was for: Haldeman, *The Haldeman Diaries*, 208.

82   The next month: Haldeman, *The Haldeman Diaries*, 216, 221.

82   "A trained ape could": Donald Rumsfeld interview, February 5, 2008.

82   "I didn't want": Carlucci interview, February 22, 2007.

83   "You know, we've got": Lenzner interview, June 22, 2007.

83   In a statement: "Legal Aid Director Ousted by Rumsfeld; Aide Also Dropped," *New York Times*, November 21, 1970.

83   Lenzner charged that: John P. MacKenzie, "OEO Firings Are Called Political," *Washington Post*, November 22, 1970.

83   "I don't think either": Lenzner interview, June 22, 2007.

83   "It was a very tough job": Judy Bachrach, "Silent Choreographer of White House Ballet," *Washington Post*, December 22, 1974.

84   "Nixon decided he wanted him": John Ehrlichman, *Witness to Power: The Nixon Years* (New York: Simon & Schuster, 1982), 102–103.

84   As a former congressman: Mann, *Rise of the Vulcans*, 6.

84   He wrote Haldeman: Rumsfeld memoranda to Haldeman, January 4, 1971, White House Special Files, Haldeman Files, Box 72, National Archives.

85   "An excellent briefing paper": Nixon conversation with Haldeman, February 22, 1971, Conversation 455–1, Nixon Tape Collection, National Archives.

85   Rumsfeld argued in a memo: Rumsfeld memorandum, February 27, 1971, Security Files, National Security Council Files, Box 833, National Archives.

85   "I don't think you should": Nixon conversation with Rumsfeld, March 8, 1971, Conversation 463–6, Nixon Tape Collection, National Archives.

87   "I need a man": Nixon conversation with Haldeman, March 9, 1971, Conversation 464–12, Nixon Tape Collection, National Archives.

88   "I cautioned him": Donald Rumsfeld, interview by Dr. Alfred Goldberg and Dr. Roger Trask, OSD Historical Office, July 12, 1994.

88   "Come on, Henry": Donald Rumsfeld interview, February 5, 2008.

88   "They don't want to": Nixon conversation with Kissinger, April 6, 1971, Conversation 1–4, Nixon Tape Collection, National Archives.

88   Afterward, Kissinger grumbled: Nixon conversation with Kissinger and Haldeman, April 7, 1971, Conversation 246–7, Nixon Tape Collection, National Archives.

89   "I think Rumsfeld may be": Nixon conversation with Kissinger and Haldeman, April 7, 1971, Conversation 246–7, Nixon Tape Collection, National Archives; also cited in Mann, *Rise of the Vulcans*, 1.

90   "I mean, they're all cowering": Nixon conversation with Kissinger, April 7, 1971, Conversation 1–39, Nixon Tape Collection, National Archives.

90   They did not mistake it: Mann, *Rise of the Vulcans*, 4; Cockburn, *Rumsfeld*, 22.

90   "Eventually the senior staff": Ehrlichman, *Witness to Power*, 103.

90   Kissinger appraised Rumsfeld: Kissinger conversation with Rockefeller, May 25, 1971, Telephone Conversation Transcripts, Box 10, National Archives.

91   "Confidence in the president": "Report on the European Visits of Counselors to the President," National Security Files, National Security Council Files, Box 833, National Archives.

91   "stiff, unpleasant, and cocksure": Nixon conversation with Rumsfeld, May 19, 1971, conversation 501–29, Nixon Tape Collection, National Archives.

91   "I've really been moving around": Nixon conversation with Rumsfeld, July 22, 1971, conversation 542–5, Nixon Tape Collection, National Archives.

92   "You've got so much ease": Nixon conversation with Rumsfeld, March 8, 1971, conversation 463–6, Nixon Tape Collection, National Archives.

93   "uplifting in its international message": Nixon conversation with Rumsfeld, July 22, 1971, conversation 542–5, Nixon Tape Collection, National Archives.

93   As Rumsfeld was waiting: James Warren, "Nixon Looked Out for Ambitious Rumsfeld, Tape Reveals," *Chicago Tribune*, January 7, 2001.

93   "It doesn't help": Nixon conversation with Rumsfeld, July 22, 1971, Conversation 542–6, Nixon Tape Collection, National Archives.

94   "The tape seems": Donald Rumsfeld testimony before the Senate Armed Services Committee, January 11, 2001.

94   But he did play a role: Donald Rumsfeld's involvement in Nixon's political operations is discussed in Mann, *Rise of the Vulcans*, 5, 17–18.

95   He provided Mitchell: White House Special Files: SMOF: H. R. Haldeman: Political Analyses—Rumsfeld, Dent, Richard, Davies 1971, Box 23, Folder 6, National Archives.

95   "a file of bad stuff": Nixon conversation with Rumsfeld, May 19, 1971, conversation 501–29, Nixon Tape Collection, National Archives.

95   "He's young, he's 39 years old": Nixon conversation with Haldeman, July 23, 1971, conversation 544–4, Nixon Tape Collection, National Archives.

96   "assume personal responsibility": Haldeman memorandum to Rumsfeld, July 17, 1971; Rumsfeld memorandum to Haldeman, September 22, 1971; both memos in White House Special Files, Haldeman Files, Box 85, National Archives.

96   "I mean, if the figures": Nixon conversation with Colson, July 23, 1971, Conversation 6–197, National Archives.

96   "I kind of want": Nixon conversation with Rumsfeld, October 19, 1971, Conversation 11–135, Nixon Tape Collection, National Archives.

96   "I can't believe that Gallup": Nixon conversation with Haldeman, February 15, 1972, Conversation 672–2, Nixon Tape Collection, National Archives.

96   Asked about the Gallup connection: Donald Rumsfeld interview, September 12, 2007.

96   "cultivation and promotion": Ehrlichman memorandum to Haldeman, January 9, 1971, White House Special Files, Haldeman Files, Box 72, National Archives.

97   "It would not be workable": Rumsfeld memorandum to Haldeman, February 4, 1971, White House Special Files, Haldeman Files, Box 74, National Archives.

97   "I think he was": Donald Rumsfeld interview, February 5, 2008.

97   "It wasn't a friendship": Joyce Rumsfeld interview, November 6, 2006.

98   Rumsfeld agreed reluctantly: Donald Rumsfeld, interview by Dr. Alfred Goldberg and Dr. Roger Trask, OSD Historical Office, July 12, 1994.

98   "He can't run stuff": Nixon conversation with Shultz, August 17, 1971, Conversation 566–7, Nixon Tape Collection, National Archives.

98   "He's doing beautifully": Nixon conversation with Colson, October 25, 1971, Conversation 12–115, Nixon Tape Collection, National Archives.

98   "Everything I was dealing with": Donald Rumsfeld interview, February 5, 2008.

99   "Is the system now perfect?": Philip Shabecoff, "Controls at 6 Months: Inflation Rate Curbed," *New York Times*, February 14, 1972.

99   "The controls program": Donald Rumsfeld, "Everything's Under Control," *New York Times*, August 29, 1972.

99   "I told my wife": Reuters, "Rumsfeld's Wife Sets Him Straight," *Washington Post*, August 13, 1972.

99   He recalled only one: Donald Rumsfeld interview, February 5, 2008.

100   As he explains: Osborne, "Winnetka Boy."

100   Colson had called: Donald Rumsfeld interview, September 12, 2007.

100   "I went to George Shultz": Donald Rumsfeld, interview by Dr. Alfred Goldberg and Dr. Roger Trask, OSD Historical Office, July 12, 1994.

100   "a complete shock": Haldeman, *The Haldeman Diaries*, 540.

100   "I am not one of Rumsfeld's admirers": Kissinger conversation with Shultz, December 1, 1972, Kissinger Phone Transcripts, National Security Archive.

101   "She thought it would be nice": David Broder, "Rumsfeld Says New Job Rounds Out Education," *Washington Post*, December 5, 1972.

101   "kind of a wild card": Broder, "Rumsfeld Says."

102   "Everything in Rummy's life": Robert T. Hartmann, *Palace Politics: An Inside Account of the Ford Years* (New York: McGraw-Hill, 1980), 274.

102   The move to NATO: Louise Hutchinson, "Trembling on the Brink of Senate Race," *Chicago Tribune*, February 11, 1973.

102   But later, when the: David Binder, "Nation's New Defense Chief: Donald Henry Rumsfeld," *New York Times*, November 4, 1975.

102   "I still don't know": Osborne, "Winnetka Boy."

102   Rumsfeld initially came across: Richard Neff, "Rumsfeld Won Respect of Nato Diplomats," *Christian Science Monitor*, September 26, 1974.

102   "When Don first arrived": Interview with François de Rose, September 27, 2006.

103   "He drove his troops": David Binder, "Nation's New Defense Chief: Donald Henry Rumsfeld," *New York Times*, November 4, 1975.

103   The job gave Rumsfeld: Donald Rumsfeld, interview by Dr. Alfred Goldberg and Dr. Roger Trask, OSD Historical Office, July 12, 1994.

103   Rumsfeld found himself: Marilyn Berger, "Battle Looms on GIs in Europe," *Washington Post*, July 9, 1973.

103   He was part of: Leslie H. Gelb, "U.S. Jets for Israel Took Route Around Some Allies' Position," *New York Times*, October 31, 1973.

104   "This was really important": De Rose interview, September 27, 2006.

104   "My impression was that": Interview with William G. Hyland, February 23, 2007.

104   He was acutely discomfited: Osborne, "Winnetka Boy."

104   "He moved around a lot": Interview with Étienne Davignon, July 7, 2006.

105   "Don Rumsfeld called": Richard Nixon, *The Memoirs of Richard Nixon* (New York: Grosset & Dunlap, 1978), 1042.

105   Rumsfeld denies ever: Donald Rumsfeld interview, February 5, 2008.

105   "I think people tend": Aldo Beckman, "Rumsfeld's Chipper, the Future's Vague," *Chicago Tribune*, June 30, 1974.

Chapter 4: Keep Your Eye on Rummy

107   In early August 1974: Donald Rumsfeld, interview by Dr. Alfred Goldberg and Dr. Roger Trask, OSD Historical Office, July 12, 1994; Osborne, "Winnetka Boy."

108   Ford wanted to retain: Gerald R. Ford, *A Time to Heal: The Autobiography of Gerald R. Ford* (New York: Harper & Row, 1979), 148.

109   "Rumsfeld and the others": Ford, *Time to Heal*, 131.

109   Ford himself added: Barry Werth, *31 Days: The Crisis That Gave Us the Government We Have Today* (New York: Nan A. Talese/Doubleday, 2006), 94.

109   His scant party support: Hartmann, *Palace Politics*, 226.

109   "the clearly coordinated planting": Hartmann, *Palace Politics*, 225,

109   "He'd picked Rockefeller": Interview with Richard Cheney, November 20, 2007.

110   "I said it just wasn't feasible": Donald Rumsfeld, interview by Dr. Alfred Goldberg and Dr. Roger Trask, OSD Historical Office, July 12, 1994; the meeting is also recounted in Ford, *Time to Heal*, 186.

111   "Clearly the toughest job": Donald Rumsfeld interview, February 5, 2008.

112   "staff coordinator": John Herbers, "4 Months After Nixon, His Legacy Haunts the New President," *New York Times*, December 19, 1974.

112   "There are people": Rudy Abramson, "Rumsfeld: Achiever Seeking Challenges," *Los Angeles Times*, November 4, 1975.

112   He spent more time: "King of the Castle," *Newsweek*, November 17, 1975.

113   Simon later remarked: Bill Simon, interview by A. James Reichley, October 18, 1977, Gerald R. Ford Library.

113   "He is strikingly": Leslie H. Gelb, "Successor Haig: Donald Rumsfeld," *New York Times*, September 25, 1974.

113   noted "strong support": James Reston, "Keep an Eye on 'Rummy,'" *New York Times*, October 4, 1974.

113   Rumsfeld's initial struggles: Leamer, *Playing for Keeps*, 168; Ron Nessen, *It Sure Looks Different from the Inside* (Chicago: Playboy Press, 1978), 150.

114   "I had the uneasy feeling": Nessen, *Sure Looks Different*, 132; also cited in Mann, *Rise of the Vulcans*, 61.

114   Rumsfeld worried particularly: Donald Rumsfeld interview, February 5, 2008.

114   When Rockefeller proposed: Leamer, *Playing for Keeps*, 170.

115   If there is one aspect: Donald Rumsfeld, interview by Trevor Armbrister in 1977, James. M. Cannon Papers, Box 34, 1977, Gerald R. Ford Library.

115   "He was a tough": Interview with Jerry Jones, January 8, 2007.

115   "Don generates much more paper": Richard Cheney, interview by James F.C. Hyde Jr. and Stephen J. Wayne, Hyde/Wayne Oral History Collection, Box 1, Richard Cheney, February 8, 1977, Gerald R. Ford Library.

115   "Come back when": "These Are My Guys," *Time*, November 17, 1975.

115   Rumsfeld could be charming: "King of the Castle," *Newsweek*, November 17, 1975.

116   "going around puffing": Leamer, *Playing for Keeps*, 172.

116   "I'll reflect on a decision": Clare Crawford, "For Man-in-Motion Donald Rumsfeld, the Talk Is About Vice-President," *People*, April 19, 1976.

116   "His active hands move": John Hersey, *The President: A Minute-by-Minute Account of a Week in the Life of Gerald Ford* (New York: Knopf, 1975), 164–165; John Hersey, "The President," *New York Times*, April 20, 1975.

117   "I don't badmouth": Osborne, "Winnetka Boy."

117   "I am not going": Crawford, "Man-in-Motion."

117   "There is something distant": Judy Bachrach, "Silent Choreographer of White House Ballet," *Washington Post*, December 22, 1974.

117   "To this day": Interview with Brent Scowcroft, April 16, 2007.

118   "sloppy and inaccurate": Leamer, *Playing for Keeps*, 175.

118   "As a youngster": Donald Rumsfeld interview, October 16, 2007.

118   The first mention of them: Allen L. Otten, "Politics and People: Rumsfeld's Rules," *Wall Street Journal*, December 9, 1976.

119   An abridged version: Donald Rumsfeld, "The White House Work Rules," *Washington Post*, January 23, 1977.

119   "Don had some class": Hartmann, *Palace Politics*, 283.

119   "If you are lost": Donald Rumsfeld interview, October 16, 2007.

121   "I think Rumsfeld is": Richard Nixon dictation, April 14, 1971; cited in Richard Reeves, *President Nixon: Alone in the White House* (New York: Simon & Schuster, 2001), 314.

122   Although Ford maintained: Lou Cannon, "Rumsfeld: Silent Architect," *Washington Post*, November 4, 1975.

122   Ford had been uncomfortable with Schlesinger: Henry Kissinger, *Years of Renewal* (New York: Simon & Schuster, 1999), 323–324.

123   In a memo to Ford: Memorandum to the President, July 10, 1975, Richard B. Cheney Files, Box 5, Intelligence—Appointment of CIA Director, 1975, Gerald R. Ford Library. The ten other names that Rumsfeld put forward, without listing their first names, were Bork, Dillon, Foster, Hauge, Iacocca,

McGee, Resor, Roosa, White, and Wriston. The seven other people, in addition to Rumsfeld, who provided recommendations were Philip Buchen, Richard Cheney, Roderick Hills, Henry Kissinger, John Marsh, David Packard, and Nelson Rockefeller.

123   "The president sat Kissinger": Donald Rumsfeld interview, February 5, 2008.

123   Rumsfeld also objected to: Donald Rumsfeld, interview by A. James Reichley, January 25, 1978, Gerald R. Ford Library.

124   "First of all": Donald Rumsfeld interview, February 5, 2008.

124   The Pentagon's top officers: John W. Finney, "Uncertain Pentagon Asks What Rumsfeld's Policy Is," *New York Times*, November 5, 1975; Guy Halverson, "Pentagon Mood Joyless As Rumsfeld Sworn In," *Christian Science Monitor*, November 21, 1975; "These Are My Guys," *Time*, November 17, 1975.

125   He was expected to be: George C. Wilson, "Different View on Defense," *Washington Post*, November 9, 1975.

125   Indeed, Kissinger was anticipating: Kissinger, *Years of Renewal*, 840.

125   After his confirmation hearing: Rumsfeld memorandum to Gerald Ford, November 18, 1975, Richard Cheney Files, Box 3, Defense—Hearings on Donald Rumsfeld's Nomination, Gerald R. Ford Library; also cited in Mann, *Rise of the Vulcans*, 69.

126   "I hope we can": Memorandum of conversation, November 26, 1975, in National Security Adviser: NSC Meeting File, Box 16, Folder "NSC Meeting, November 26, 1975," Gerald R. Ford Library.

126   "Rumsfeld afforded me": Kissinger, *Years of Renewal*, 175.

126   "They were just totally": Interview with Vice Admiral (retired) Staser Holcomb, February 8, 2007.

126   "Schlesinger was basically": Kissinger, *Years of Renewal*, 177.

126   Schlesinger thought of: Hyland interview, February 23, 2007.

127   "He had the technique": Scowcroft interview, April 16, 2007.

127   "The Pentagon had been effectively": Donald Rumsfeld, interview by Dr. Alfred Goldberg and Dr. Roger Trask, OSD Historical Office, July 12, 1994.

128   "I had no choice but": Memorandum, January 22, 1976, in National Security Adviser: Kissinger reports on USSR et al., January 22, 1976, Box 1, Folder "January 21–23, 1976—Kissinger Moscow Trip (2)," Gerald R. Ford Library.

128   In Kissinger's view: Kissinger, *Years of Renewal*, 850.

128   "I would be like the skunk": Donald Rumsfeld, interview by Dr. Alfred Goldberg and Dr. Roger Trask, OSD Historical Office, July 12, 1994.

128   In his memoir, Ford: Ford, *Time to Heal*, 358.

128   "He handed me his book": Donald Rumsfeld interview, February 5, 2008.

129   But in the Ford administration: Mann, *Rise of the Vulcans*, 68.

129   "He wanted to be": Adelman interview, March 6, 2007.

129   "There was no political calculation": Donald Rumsfeld interview, February 5, 2008.

129   Scowcroft saw Rumsfeld: Scowcroft interview, April 16, 2007.

130   "I think it was about": Hyland interview, February 23, 2007.

130   What had worried Kissinger: Mann, *Rise of the Vulcans*, 63–64.

130   "As a veteran": Kissinger, *Years of Renewal*, 175.

131   In January 1976: John W. Finney, "Rumsfeld Calls for More Funds, Citing Increasing Soviet Power," *New York Times*, January 27, 1976.

131   Rumsfeld's new twist: John W. Finney, "Defense Policy Debate," *New York Times*, April 6, 1976.

131   Among them: Scowcroft memorandum on Soviet military trends and capabilities briefing, April 24, 1976, in National Security Adviser, Presidential Country Files for Europe and Canada, Box 19, File "USSR (34)," Gerald R. Ford Library.

131   "Hughes didn't have to": Holcomb interview, December 14, 2006.

131   In playing up the specter: Leamer, *Playing for Keeps*, 184–185.

132   "In a preeminently": Leamer, *Playing for Keeps*, 185.

132   By the autumn of 1976: John O. Marsh memorandum, October 18, 1976, John O. Marsh Files, Box 5, file "Briefings—Department of Defense Briefings by Malcolm Currie and John Hughes, March 1976–October 1976," Gerald R. Ford Library.

132   For his part, Kissinger: Finney, "Defense Policy Debate."

132   "It's a different era": Donald Rumsfeld, Interview by Dr. Alfred Goldberg and Dr. Roger Trask, OSD Historical Office, August 2, 1994.

133   Rumsfeld, while not a: Mann, *Rise of the Vulcans*, 73–74; Cockburn, *Rumsfeld*, 40–42.

133   "I would describe him": Interview with Admiral (retired) Bobby R. Inman, March 22, 2007.

134   As a precedent: Mann, *Rise of the Vulcans*, 74.

134   "It bothered me": Donald Rumsfeld, interview by Dr. Alfred Goldberg and Dr. Roger Trask, OSD Historical Office, July 12, 1994.

134   "I was in the middle": Scowcroft interview, April 16, 2007.

134   "He didn't credit Bush": Holcomb interview, December 14, 2006.

134   "All of us were": Ellsworth interview, February 9, 2007.

135   "As far as I know": William P. Clements, interview by Dr. Alfred Goldberg and Dr. Roger Trask, OSD Historical Office, May 16, 1996.

135   Rumsfeld also used: George C. Wilson, "U.S. May Need $30 Billion Missile Program," *Washington Post*, January 28, 1976; John W. Finney, "Long-Term Rise in 'Real' Outlay Projected with No Cut in Forces," *New York Times*, January 22, 1976.

136   But Rumsfeld has denied: Richard Mendel, "The First Chrysler Bail-Out," *Washington Monthly*, February 1987.

136   In his second term: Donald Rumsfeld, interview on PBS *News Hour*, February 14, 2001; Pentagon News Conference, April 18, 2006.

137   "He'd be out": Interview with Robin West, January 25, 2007.

137   "I stood by the desk": Holcomb interview, December 14, 2006.

137   "That's getting pretty precise": Interview with Admiral (retired) James Holloway, February 5, 2007.

138   "I was working": Bob Woodward, *Plan of Attack* (New York: Simon & Schuster, 2004), 411.

138   Power was respected: Rowland Evans and Robert Novak, "The Rumsfeld Influence," *Washington Post*, January 29, 1976.

138   In a memoir: James L. Holloway III, *Aircraft Carriers At War: A Personal Retrospective of Korea, Vietnam, and the Soviet Confrontation* (Annapolis, MD: Naval Institute Press, 2007), 362–366.

138   "If you ever do": Holloway interview, February 5, 2007.

139   "It was a very rocky relationship": Inman interview, March 22, 2007.

139   But Ford subsequently: James Coates, "Rumsfeld Curtails Trips to Key States," *Chicago Tribune*, October 14, 1976.

140   During Rumsfeld's tenure: The officer was Samuel L. Gravely Jr., who was made commander of the U.S. Third Fleet on August 18, 1976.

140   He appeared with: John W. Finney, "Ford and Rumsfeld Endorse Brown to Continue as Head of Joint Chiefs of Staff," *New York Times*, October 19, 1976.

141   Resisting calls in: John W. Finney, "Defense Officials Censured for Rockwell Lodge Visits," *New York Times*, March 17, 1976.

141   A subsequent *New York Times*: John W. Finney, "Furor over Missile Decision Reflected Pitfalls of Policy-Making Jobs in the Pentagon," *New York Times*, April 5, 1976.

141   Rumsfeld cleared Currie: John W. Finney, "Rumsfeld Clears Pentagon Aide of Conflict of Interest in Missile Program, Eagleton Charges a 'Whitewash,'" *New York Times*, June 9, 1976. A later report by the Democratic majority of the investigating subcommittee of the Joint Congressional Committee on Defense Production found that Currie had cooperated with Rockwell in supporting the missile program, although the panel stopped short of saying he had violated the department's conflict of interest rules. The minority GOP members of the committee said that while there may have been a "mutuality of interest" between Currie and Rockwell in pushing development of the missile, there was no evidence that Currie gave preferential treatment to the contractor. See John W. Finney, "Aid to Contractor by Currie Reported," *New York Times*, October 15, 1976.

141   "It was a period": Donald Rumsfeld, Interview by Dr. Alfred Goldberg and Dr. Roger Trask, OSD Historical Office, August 2, 1994.

142   He appeared to offer: Woodward, *Plan of Attack*, 16–18.

142   The Pentagon press corps: *Armed Forces Journal International* 116, no. 12 (August 1979): 20–21. At the time the Pentagon press corps consisted of

thirty-seven men and one woman representing fourteen daily newspapers, eight magazines, and thirteen news agencies, plus all three major television networks and one radio network.

142   Bill Greener, Rumsfeld's spokesman: Interview with Bill Greener, September 18, 2006.

Chapter 5: A Politician in the Corporate World

143   After the end of: Stephen F. Hayes, *Cheney: The Untold Story of America's Most Powerful and Controversial Vice President* (New York: HarperCollins, 2007), 123.

143   In his final weeks: Jannotta interview, April 18, 2006.

143   "He viewed the private": Joyce Rumsfeld interview, April 23, 2007.

144   But a series of: Joann Lublin, "Brash Don Rumsfeld Tries His Prescription to Turn Searle Around," *Wall Street Journal*, January 25, 1978; Donald Rumsfeld, "A Politician in the Corporate World," *Fortune*, September 10, 1979.

144   Although they were reluctant: Interview with Daniel Searle, August 22, 2006.

145   "If I felt I had": Searle interview, August 22, 2006.

145   Even Rumsfeld's mother: Midge Decter, *Rumsfeld: A Personal Portrait* (New York: Regan, 2003), 81.

145   "If you look": *Daily Northwestern*, cited in Aldo Beckman, "A Political Maze for Rumsfeld," *Chicago Tribune*, April 4, 1977.

145   He had yet to: Steve Neal, "Donald Rumsfeld Gets Down to the Business of Running for President," *Chicago Tribune*, January 26, 1986.

145   "What I was looking": Thomas M. Chesser, "It Was Tough Medicine, but G.D. Searle Breathes Easier Now," *New York Times*, January 31, 1982.

146   "Don hit the ground running": Joyce Rumsfeld interview, April 23, 2007.

146   In his first days: Lublin, "Brash Don Rumsfeld"; Donald Rumsfeld, "A Politician in the Corporate World," *Fortune*, September 10, 1979; Sandy Graham, "When the Going Gets Tough at Searle, 'Snowflakes' Descend from Rumsfeld," *Wall Street Journal*, May 20, 1980; Chesser, "It Was Tough Medicine."

146   "There were some instances": Searle interview, August 22, 2006.

147   "You had to have": Sittnick interview, September 22, 2006.

147   "I remember a meeting": Interview with Jim Denny, June 1, 2006.

147   The article described: "The Ten Toughest Bosses," *Fortune*, April 21, 1980.

148   "They say I use": Graham, "When the Going Gets Tough."

148   And while Rumsfeld's friends: Sittnick interview, September 22, 2006; Denny interview, June 1, 2006.

148   "because it's just": Donald Rumsfeld interview, October 16, 2007.

149   He reflected on the: Donald Rumsfeld, "A Politician in the Corporate World," *Fortune*, September 10, 1979.

151   "In going through": Denny interview, June 1, 2006.

151   Although Rumsfeld had refocused: William Robbins, "Rumsfeld's Remedy for Searle," *New York Times*, March 16, 1979; Janet Kev, "Rumsfeld Turns Searle Around with Bottom-Line Management," *Chicago Tribune*, April 1, 1981.

151   "We were struggling": Denny interview, June 1, 2006.

151   The product, aspartame: According to Searle lore, a company laboratory chemist, James Schlatter, had happened on the substance by accident in 1965 in the course of conducting ulcer research. Licking his finger to turn a page in a book, he inadvertently tasted some aspartame that was on the finger. See Joseph E. McCann, *Sweet Success: How NutraSweet Created a Billion Dollar Business* (Homewood, IL: Business One Irwin, 1990), 24.

152   "I said, look, here's a big company": Donald Rumsfeld interview, September 12, 2007.

152   "We had a very good": Interview with James Turner for an online documentary, www.soundandfury.tv/pages/Rumsfeld2.html.

153   An investigative report: Gregory Gordon, "Did Searle Ignore Early Warning Signs?" United Press International, October 13, 1987.

153   Hayes himself had left: Melanie Warner, "The Lowdown on Sweet?" *New York Times*, February 12, 2006.

154   "The patent extension for aspartame": Interview with Bill Timmons.

154   Several key lawmakers: Gordon, "Did Searle Ignore."

155   "It turns out that": Donald Rumsfeld interview, September 12, 2007.

155   One assignment he undertook: Mann, *Rise of the Vulcans*, 138–145; Cockburn, *Rumsfeld*, 84–88; William Arkin, "Shadow Government," *Washington Post*, June 4, 2006.

156   Embracing the mission enthusiastically: Adelman interview, March 6, 2007.

156   "Particularly as the years": Denny interview, June 1, 2006.

157   "Rumsfeld was plugged into": George P. Shultz, *Turmoil and Triumph: My Years as Secretary of State* (New York: Scribner's, 1993), 435.

157   Instead, Rumsfeld concentrated: Howard Teicher and Gayle Radley Teicher, *Twin Pillars to Desert Storm: America's Flawed Vision in the Middle East from Nixon to Bush* (New York: Morrow, 1993), 268.

158   "I can't help but": Details of the unreleased memo were provided to the author by a source with access to it.

159   The Iraqi leader, greeting: Cable from Charles H. Price II to Department of State, "Rumsfeld Mission: December 20 Meeting with Iraqi President Saddam Hussein," December 21, 1983, National Security Archive.

160   During his meeting with Aziz: Cable from Charles H. Price II to the Department of State, "Rumsfeld One-on-One Meeting with Iraqi Deputy Prime Minister," December 21, 1983, National Security Archive.

160   "When the elevator doesn't": Donald Rumsfeld, interview by Scarborough, October 18, 2003.

160   "We were looking at it": Donald Rumsfeld, interview by Scarborough, October 18, 2003.

160   But the purpose of: George P. Shultz, Department of State Cable to the United States Embassy in Sudan, "Briefing Notes for Rumsfeld Visit to Baghdad," March 24, 1984, National Security Archive.

160   Rumsfeld was also carrying: Teicher and Teicher, *Twin Pillars*, 299–300.

161   When Rumsfeld raised: Teicher and Teicher, *Twin Pillars*, 299.

161   His hope was to expand: Teicher and Teicher, *Twin Pillars*, 294, 297.

161   "a bigger disaster": Shultz, *Turmoil and Triumph*, 235.

161   By the end of: Teicher and Teicher, *Twin Pillars*, 262.

162   "He was deeply analytical": Interview with George Shultz, February 12, 2008.

162   "When I was Middle East envoy": Donald Rumsfeld, interview by Dr. Alfred Goldberg and Dr. Roger Trask, OSD Historical Office, July 12, 1994.

162   "a healthy respect for the complexities": Donald Rumsfeld interview, October 16, 2007.

163   "I said, 'The Searle family'": Denny interview, June 1, 2006.

163   "It would haunt him": Jannotta interview, April 18, 2006.

164   "I could if I'd thought about it": Denny interview, June 1, 2006.

164   As he was closing: This account of the sale of Searle was provided in interviews with Denny and Jannotta.

164   Under the terms of: Steven Greenhouse, "Monsanto to Acquire G.D. Searle," *New York Times*, July 19, 1985.

164   A *Chicago Tribune* profile: Steve Neal, "Donald Rumsfeld Gets Down to the Business of Running for President," *Chicago Tribune*, January 26, 1986.

164   He had kept his: Lublin, "Brash Don Rumsfeld."

164   "We just hung out": Joyce Rumsfeld interview, April 23, 2007.

165   "I expect that at some point": Donald Rumsfeld, "A Politician in the Corporate World," *Fortune*, September 10, 1979.

165   But he dropped the idea: Steve Neal, "Juices Stir for Rumsfeld," *Chicago Tribune*, April 29, 1979; Teicher and Teicher, *Twin Pillars*, 285.

166   "To his admirers": Steve Neal, "Donald Rumsfeld Gets Down to the Business of Running for President," *Chicago Tribune*, January 26, 1986.

167   "He didn't want": Joyce Rumsfeld interview, April 23, 2007.

167   He viewed the front-runners: Robert W. Merry, "Rumsfeld, with a Resume to Rival That of Bush, Prepares to Seek GOP Nomination for President," *Wall Street Journal*, May 30, 1986.

168   His political action committee: William Safire, "3 Coins in the Fountain," *New York Times*, February 19, 1987.

168   "If Republican presidential nominees": Mann, *Rise of the Vulcans*, 167.

168   "might be a more comfortable": Kissinger, *Years of Renewal*, 177.

168   "His campaign style is": Stephen Chapman, "Can Rumsfeld Add Another Line to a Strong Resume?" *Chicago Tribune*, February 15, 1987, prospective section, 3; also cited in Mann, *Rise of the Vulcans*, 167.

168   "Elected officials keep": Steelman interview, June 15, 2006.

169   "That was a big surprise": Joyce Rumsfeld interview, April 3, 2007.

169   "The last thing I needed": Cheney interview, November 20, 2007.

169   "I am unwilling to proceed": Donald Rumsfeld to contributors, supporters, and friends, April 2, 1987. Copy obtained by author.

170   "I never lost": Joyce Rumsfeld interview, April 23, 2007.

170   "Everyone was emotional": Joyce Rumsfeld interview, April 23, 2007.

Chapter 6: A Friendly Hawkish Guy

171   He had entered into: One troublesome venture in which Rumsfeld took part involved a merchant banking firm in Dallas, Mason Best Company. With Rumsfeld providing advice on defense-related acquisitions, the firm set up a holding company, Westmark Systems, Inc., to acquire electronics firms. But it started off with a badly timed purchase of Tracor, a maker of military electronics systems. Financed with a large amount of debt, the $700 million deal closed just a few days after Wall Street's deep plunge in October 1987, leaving Westmark, on whose board Rumsfeld served, struggling for years to salvage its investment.

172   "Don had a reputation": Interview with Steve Klinsky, October 15, 2007.

173   its sales dropped: Jacqueline S. Gold, "Deal of the Decade," *Financial World*, September 1, 1992.

173   Once, in a pique: Interview with Rick Friedland, December 12, 2007.

173   He displayed a capacity: Klinsky interview, October 15, 2007.

173   "You could see": Friedland interview, December 12, 2007.

174   "For almost three years": Klinsky interview, October 15, 2007.

174   The system was in contention: Jacqueline S. Gold, "Deal of the Decade," *Financial World*, September 1, 1992.

175   To promote the GI/MIT: John Burgess, "Tuning In to a Trophy Technology," *Washington Post*, March 24, 1992; Carl Weinschenk, "Mr. Rumsfeld Goes Back to Washington," *Cable World*, March 30, 1992.

175   He spent some time: GI and MIT had already entered a royalty-splitting agreement with Zenith and AT&T should any of their proposals be chosen. By then, another competitor, the Japanese broadcasting company NHK, had fallen out of the competition because it had put forward an analog system and the FCC wanted digital. The final entry had come from a consortium that included NBC, the David Sarnoff Research laboratories, and two European consumer electronics manufacturers—the Dutch firm Phillips and France's Thomson.

176   The impressive return: Richard Ringer, "General Instrument Moves to Pay Off Its Debt Early," *New York Times*, July 1, 1993; William Gruber, "Rumsfeld Reflects on Politics, Business," *Chicago Tribune*, October 20, 1993; "How a High-Tech Bet Paid Off Big," *Fortune*, November, 1, 1993.

177   "There was some feedback": Friedland interview, December 12, 2007.

177   "I wouldn't say": Klinsky interview, October 15, 2007.

177   "I remember the response": Madigan interview, June 2, 2006.

179   "I'd been around big companies": Donald Rumsfeld interview, October 16, 2007.

179   "Don is a very high energy guy": Interview with John Martin, February 25, 2008.

180   By June, Rumsfeld had: Michael Wines, "For Its Stretch Drive, Dole Campaign Turns to a Turnabout Artist," *New York Times*, September 26, 1996.

180   "At first, it was just": Interview with Robert Dole, December 8, 2006.

180   Working with the campaign staff: Fred Barnes, "The Rumsfeld Factor," *Weekly Standard*, August 5, 1996.

181   "It's just a matter": Interview with Paul Wolfowitz, May 18, 2008.

181   With the advice of: Mann, *Rise of the Vulcans*, 231–233.

182   "Our view was that Rummy": Dole interview, December 8, 2006.

182   "Scott Reed is the executive": Wines, "For Its Stretch Drive."

183   Rumsfeld proved an especially: Mann, *Rise of the Vulcans*, 239.

183   "This is a guy who": Interview with Marshall Billingslea, May 8, 2007.

183   "We all thought of him": Interview with William Kristol, May 27, 2008.

184   "He sees a world": Billingslea interview, May 8, 2007.

184   "They were friends and he associated": Interview with Peter Rodman, January 9, 2007.

184   The letter, dated: Elliott Abrams et al., "Open Letter to President Bill Clinton," *Project for the New American Century*, January 26, 1998, www.newamericancentury.org/iraqclintonletter.htm.

185   A few weeks after: Douglas J. Feith, *War and Decision: Inside the Pentagon at the Dawn of the War on Terrorism* (New York: Harper, 2008), 194–196.

185   It was the issue of: Much of this account of Rumsfeld's involvement with the missile threat commission was taken from the author's earlier book, *Hit to Kill: The New Battle over Shielding America from Missile Attack* (New York: PublicAffairs, 2001), 30–51.

185   The 1995 estimate: "Emerging Missile Threats to North America During the Next 15 Years," PS/NIE 95–19, November 1995.

186   "I liked Rumsfeld": Interview with Newt Gingrich, October 31, 2007.

186   the nine-member commission: In addition to Rumsfeld, the commission members included Barry Blechman, General (retired) Lee Butler, Richard Garwin, William Graham, William Schneider Jr., General (retired) Larry Welch, R. James Woolsey, and Paul Wolfowitz.

188   "The answer I got back": Interview with William Graham, April 13, 2000.

189   While the basic notion: For an example of one such riff, see Donald Rumsfeld's news conference at the Pentagon on February 12, 2002.

190   The foreword says: Thomas C. Schelling, foreword to *Pearl Harbor: Warning and Decision*, by Roberta Wohlstetter (Stanford, CA: Stanford University Press, 1962).

192   "The threat to the United States": *Report of the Commission to Assess the Ballistic Missile Threat to the United States: Executive Summary* (Washington, DC: U.S. Government Printing Office, July 15, 1998).

192   At a news conference: Bradley Graham, "Iran, North Korea Missile Gains Spur Warning," *Washington Post*, July 16, 1998.

194   The letter presented: An unclassified version of the letter was issued in March 1999.

196   "I am not making": Interview with John E. McLaughlin, October 31, 2007.

197   The report, released: James Risen, "U.S. Should Improve Defense of Satellites, Panel Advises," *New York Times*, January 9, 2001.

Chapter 7: Operating from the Outbox

199   "What about George W.?": Jannotta interview, April 18, 2006.

199   Bush considered Rumsfeld: Woodward, *Plan of Attack*, 16; Woodward, *State of Denial*, xii–xiii.

199   Rumsfeld had come to regard: Bob Woodward, "Bush's Wild Card," *Washington Post*, January 12, 2001.

199   And while the senior Bush: Scowcroft interview, April 16, 2007.

200   "just a nice old guy": Interview with John Hillen, March 2, 2007.

200   search for a vice presidential candidate: Cheney interview, November 20, 2007.

201   Since Rice, a much younger: Karen DeYoung, *Soldier: The Life of Colin Powell* (New York: Knopf, 2006), 290–300; Mann, *Rise of the Vulcans*, 267; Woodward, *State of Denial*, xi.

201   George Shultz lobbied: Shultz interview, February 12, 2008; also cited in Mann, 268.

201   "He's capable and smart": Scowcroft interview, April 16, 2007.

201   the Cheney/Rumsfeld relationship: Joyce Rumsfeld interview, April 3, 2007.

202   During a meeting in Austin: Donald Rumsfeld, interview by Rowan Scarborough, October 18, 2003.

202   Bush left the meeting: Interview with Andrew Card, January 11, 2008.

202   "They clicked and": Cheney interview, November 20, 2007.

202   "All I'm going to say": Draper, *Dead Certain*, 282; Barton Gellman, *Angler: The Cheney Vice Presidency* (New York: Penguin, 2008), 37.

202   The president-elect made it clear: Card interview, January 11, 2008.

202   when Cheney phoned: Donald Rumsfeld interview, November 19, 2008.

202   "He's going to be": Bush press conference, December 28, 2000.

204   "Performance has tended to": Interview with Stuart Rochester, June 11, 2008.

204   "General Powell's a strong figure": Bush press conference, December 28, 2000.

204   Initially, Powell did not regard: Interview with a former senior administration official, July 14, 2008.

204   "It is clearly not": Bush press conference, December 28, 2000.

204   Rumsfeld met with: This account of the Cohen-Rumsfeld meeting was provided by two participants.

206   "Mr. Secretary, I'd like for": Interview with General (retired) Hugh Shelton, September 21, 2006.

206   Shelton had received a letter: Shelton interview, September 21, 2006; also cited in Woodward, *State of Denial*, 19.

207   "help is on the way": Cheney speech at Valley Forge Military Academy, Pennsylvania, September 6, 2000.

208   Bush had called for: Bush speech at The Citadel, South Carolina, September 23, 1999.

208   "While Rumsfeld knew": Interview with Andy Hoehn, November 21, 2006.

209   "He didn't give me": Interview with Andrew Marshall, October 30, 2006.

209   "Rumsfeld was sort of": Interview with Paul Gebhard, January 16, 2007.

210   "There was no cohesion": Interview with General (retired) Jim Jones, May 10, 2007.

210   "He did not want to": Gebhard interview, January 16, 2007.

211   "Most of the senior military": Shelton interview, September 21, 2006.

211   "He came in with": Interview with Admiral (retired) Vernon E. Clark, February 7, 2007.

212   Had Coats become defense secretary: Mann, *Rise of the Vulcans*, 263; DeYoung, *Soldier*, 299–300.

212   the other candidate suggested by the White House: Donald Rumsfeld interview, November 19, 2008.

212   "Somewhat to my surprise": Wolfowitz interview, May 18, 2008.

213   "Normally, the deputy secretary": Interview with Dov Zakheim, January 25, 2007.

213   "Rumsfeld didn't treat Wolfowitz": Interview with a former senior defense official, January 17, 2008.

215   "There was a lot of resistance": Interview with Robert Soule, December 14, 2006.

215   "grab hold of this building": Delonnie Henry interview, June 6, 2007.

216   "You'd put stuff in his inbox": Delonnie Henry interview, June 6, 2007.

216   "I want to run this department": Interview with Ray Dubois, December 13, 2006.

216   "He had a philosophy": Interview with Steve Herbits, February 27, 2007.

217   "That's the Secretary of State's job": Gebhard interview, January 16, 2007.

217   "You know, you have a plane": Michael R. Gordon and Bernard E. Trainor, *Cobra II: The Inside Story of the Invasion and Occupation of Iraq* (New York: Pantheon, 2006), 6.

218   While the White House had been advised: Woodward, *Plan of Attack*, 14; DeYoung, *Soldier*, 317–318.

218   He fumed at Shelton: Shelton interview, September 21, 2006.

219   "His point was that": Hoehn interview, November 21, 2006.

219   "Shelton came back": Interview with Chris Williams, March 16, 2007.

220   "Because Fry works for me": Shelton interview, September 21, 2006; also cited in Woodward, *State of Denial*, 32.

220   with the help of Saudi Arabia: Woodward, *State of Denial*, 28–29.

221   "It was obviously meant": Zakheim interview, January 25, 2007. Rumsfeld's visit to China also cited in Scarborough, *Rumsfeld's War*, 106.

221   "It was laborious": Shelton interview, September 21, 2006.

222   "Their input about": Interview with Rich Haver, March 20, 2007.

222   "I couldn't get Jim Deane's": Haver interview, March 20, 2007.

223   "He was saying early on": Hoehn interview, November 21, 2006.

224   He often invoked the analogy: Interview with Steve Cambone, January 19, 2007.

224   "SecDef Levers for Implementing Decisions": Viewed by author.

224   "We basically just showed": Soule interview, December 14, 2006.

224   "Strategy to Programs": Viewed by author.

225   "This was an attempt to say": Interview with a former defense official, September 20, 2006.

225   "Rumsfeld had this reputation": Soule interview, December 14, 2006.

226   Cambone disputed this characterization: Cambone interview, January 31, 2009.

226   "I tried to explain to him": Soule interview, December 14, 2006.

227   "He gave us sort of a Business 101": Soule interview, December 14, 2006.

227   "I've seen this with": Soule interview, December 14, 2006.

227   Rumsfeld told associates: Interview with Barry Watts, May 31, 2007.

228   Rumsfeld had accumulated assets: Donald Rumsfeld public financial disclosure report, January 18, 2003.

228   "I find it excessively complex": Donald Rumsfeld to Amy Comstock, Government Ethics Office, May 14, 2002.

228   "Make major weapon systems decisions": Donald Rumsfeld, memorandum, "Possible Directions from the DoD Strategy Review and Studies—Standards to Be Planted Down the Road from Defense Guidance, the QDR and Building DoD Budgets for 2002 and 2003," May 21, 2001. Viewed by author.

229   "He's a guy who": Interview with a former defense official, September 20, 2006.

229   "I am often briefed": Donald Rumsfeld, memorandum, "Assumptions," October 18, 2002. Viewed by author.

230   Rumsfeld lashed out: Watts interview, May 31, 2007.

230   The zipper rule: Interview with a former senior defense official, April 3, 2008.

230   "I didn't know anything": Interview with General (retired) John Abizaid, February 2, 2007.

231   "I understand that you're": Interview with then vice admiral Stan Szemborski, May 29, 2007.

232   "He came down to my office": Soule interview, December 14, 2006.

232   "He used to joke": Douglas J. Feith, *War and Decision: Inside the Pentagon at the Dawn of the War on Terrorism* (New York: Harper, 2008), 72.

232   "His management style": Gebhard interview, January 16, 2007.

232   "He was very much a paper person": Delonnie Henry interview, June 6, 2007.

233   "He was very single-subject": Delonnie Henry interview, June 6, 2007.

233   a memo listing the cost-cutting measures: Donald Rumsfeld, memorandum, "Cost-Cutting," July 11, 2001. Viewed by author.

235   "I wanted to make sure": Interview with William J. "Jim" Haynes II, June 22, 2007.

Chapter 8: Lots of Battlefronts

238   "While the Hill group": Interview with Robert Rangel, January 19, 2007.

238   "He kept sending up": Rangel interview, January 19, 2007.

239   "And I swear, members": Interview with Torie Clarke, November 17, 2006.

239   "Defense establishment is tangled": Donald Rumsfeld, memorandum, "The DoD Challenge," June 25, 2001.

240   "A lot of people": Interview with Powell Moore, June 26, 2007.

240   "They'd be asked something like": Moore interview, June 26, 2007.

241   "Hell, I'm not going to cave": Moore interview, June 26, 2007.

241   tensions with the service chiefs: Thomas E. Ricks, "Rumsfeld, Joint Chiefs Spar Over Roles in Retooling Military," *Washington Post*, May 25, 2001.

242   "No one knew what": Gebhard interview, January 16, 2007.

243   "The current strategy isn't working": Rumsfeld testimony before Senate Armed Services Committee, June 21, 2001.

244   the White House announced: Thomas E. Ricks, "Bush Seeking Defense Increase '02 Budget Request Adds 18.4 Billion," *Washington Post*, June 23, 2001.

245   "Here's the problem that": Shelton interview, September 21, 2006.

245   "So far, there's been more storm": Ken Adelman, "Stop Reviewing; Start Reforming," *Wall Street Journal*, July 13, 2001.

246   "He came up to me": Adelman interview, March 6, 2007.

246   "The president has asked me": Hoehn interview, November 21, 2006.

246   "It happened a number of times": Shelton interview, September 21, 2006.

246   "The Tank leaks": Evan Thomas, "Rumsfeld's War," *Newsweek*, September 16, 2001.

246   "He was very upset about it": Jim Jones interview, May 10, 2007.

246   "The secretary didn't stay long": Jim Jones interview, May 10, 2007.

247   "There was a reluctance": Donald Rumsfeld interview, April 8, 2008.

247   "It was very Socratic": Interview with Ken Krieg, January 5, 2007.

247   "It just frustrated him no end": Hoehn interview, November 21, 2006.

248   "It worked," he wrote. "We were able": Donald Rumsfeld, memorandum to Aldridge, Chu, White, England, and Roche (copy to Wolfowitz), Subject: Joint Chiefs, November 12, 2001. Viewed by author.

248   conservatives were complaining: Thomas E. Ricks, "For Rumsfeld Many Roadblocks, Miscues, and Resistance Mean Defense Review May Produce Less Than Promised," *Washington Post*, August 7, 2001.

248   "This is one of the most": Michael Duffy, "Rumsfeld: Older but Wiser," *Time*, August 27, 2001.

248   "I was not in the rhythm": Duffy, "Rumsfeld."

249   As Cheney remarked: Ricks, "For Rumsfeld Many Roadblocks,"

250   The bomber decision: James Dao, "Much Maligned B-1 Bomber Proves Hard to Kill," *New York Times*, August 1, 2001; Stan Crock, "Why the Hawks Are Carpet-Bombing Rumsfeld," *BusinessWeek*, August 6, 2001.

250   "It's going to be tough": Ricks, "For Rumsfeld Many Roadblocks."

250   "Good grief. It's nothing": Wils S. Hylton, "Dick and Don Go to War," *Esquire*, February 1, 2002.

251   "He felt that the chairman's position": Shelton interview, September 21, 2006.

251   "He was very, very closed": Abizaid interview, February 2, 2007.

252   "We've done a lot": Shelton interview, September 21, 2006.

253   "Congress may want the last word": Alfred Goldberg, memorandum to Donald Rumsfeld, "OSD-JCS Staff Considerations," November 27, 2002.

253   "I would watch Rumsfeld": Hoehn interview, November 21, 2006.

253   "He felt that he was doing": Interview with Vice Admiral (retired) Staser Holcomb, February 8, 2007.

254   "You just got this clear feeling": Shelton interview, September 21, 2006.

254   "Clark would come in": Interview with Steve Bucci, October 18, 2006.

255   "I don't think Rick ever recovered": Keane interview, February 29, 2008.

256   "That's what we thought": Interview with General (retired) Kevin Byrnes, February 1, 2007.

256   "One day a war game": Byrnes interview, February 1, 2007.

257   Wolfowitz had come around: Wolfowitz interview, May 21, 2008.

257   "Aren't you glad now": Wolfowitz interview, May 21, 2008.

258   "Ultimately, Doug was Paul's decision": Herbits interview, February 27, 2007.

259   "He always cared deeply": Adelman interview, November 16, 2006.

260   "Cambone exhibited a lot": Holcomb interview, February 8, 2007.

260   Cambone was hard-pressed: Cambone interview, June 28, 2007.

260   "We reflected different sides": Interview with Doug Feith, March 15, 2007.

261   "He would ask, 'What is it'": Interview with Ryan Henry, March 24, 2007.

262   "Bush had a great deal": Shelton interview, September 21, 2006.

262   "I don't take guidance from staff": Gebhard interview, January 16, 2007.

263   In public, Rumsfeld and Powell: At one point in the summer of 2001, Rumsfeld sparred with reporters on the subject. In response to one question, he asked, "Are you trying to find some daylight between Colin and me?" When another reporter asked, "Do you always agree on everything?" Rumsfeld replied, "Except for those few cases where Colin is still learn-

ing." Jane Perlez, "Reporter's Notebook: Two Mates Clown a Bit for the Aussies," *New York Times*, July 31, 2002.

263   He saw his own staff: DeYoung, *Soldier*, 354.

263   Powell was bothered: Interview with a former senior administration official, July 14, 2008.

264   "I want to talk to the senior staff": Donald Rumsfeld, memorandum, September 6, 2001. Viewed by author.

264   more coordinator than director: Gordon and Trainor, *Cobra II*, 147.

265   "We have all of these meetings": John R. Bolton, *Surrender Is Not an Option: Defending America at the United Nations and Abroad* (New York: Threshold, 2007), 60.

265   "He would call me up": Card interview, January 11, 2008.

266   As the administration set its sights: For a fuller discussion of the administration's internal deliberations about the ABM treaty, see Bolton, *Surrender*, 54–74.

267   One approach was to work out: Feith, *War and Decision*, 44.

267   Rumsfeld ran into sharp: James Dao, "Skeptical Senators Question Rumsfeld on Missile Defense," *New York Times*, June 22, 2001.

268   "We told them basically": Soule interview, December 14, 2006.

268   Instead, the department's missile defense: Graham, *Hit to Kill*, 366.

268   "I want a story": Haver interview, March 20, 2007.

269   "This was supposed to be": Haver interview, March 20, 2007.

271   "We put together a helluva brief": Interview with Newt Gingrich, October 31, 2007.

271   "Why am I reviewing": Interview with Admiral (retired) Ed Giambastiani, October 11, 2007.

272   "He understood that war plans": Giambastiani interview, October 11, 2007.

272   Rumsfeld arranged to meet: Woodward, *Plan of Attack*, 31–35.

273   "If you get the assumptions right": Feith, *War and Decision*, 111.

273   "He didn't believe anyone": Feith, *War and Decision*, 110.

273   "They were just briefing": Donald Rumsfeld, interview by Bob Woodward, September 20, 2003.

273   "He almost laughed": Shelton interview, September 21, 2006.

274   "He's not a pound-on-the-table guy": James Dao, "A Low-Key Space Buff: Richard Bowman Myers," *New York Times*, August 25, 2001.

274   Rumsfeld had also looked: Woodward, *State of Denial*, 57.

275   "My position was, I would do this": Clark interview, February 7, 2007.

275   "I knew that Rumsfeld": Shelton interview, September 21, 2006.

276   "He just didn't see why": Holcomb interview, February 8, 2007.

277   "We had to prepare people": Interview with General (retired) Montgomery Meigs, August 19, 2005.

277   "The topic today is an adversary": Donald Rumsfeld speech to Pentagon employees, September 10, 2001.

279   "He was looking for a council": Krieg interview, January 5, 2007.

279   "He never showed up to a single meeting": Interview with James Roche, January 17, 2007.

280   "I think there are a thousand": Krieg interview, January 5, 2007.

Chapter 9: A Defining Moment

282   He ran to an aide's office: Admiral (retired) Ed Giambastiani, interview by OSD historian, OSD Historical Office, July 18, 2002.

282   When an emergency worker: Cockburn, *Rumsfeld*, 1.

282   Rumsfeld joined a conference call: National Commission on Terrorist Attacks upon the United States, *The 9/11 Commission Report: Final Report of the National Commission on Terrorist Attacks upon the United States* (New York: Norton, 2004), 38.

283   played no part: *The 9/11 Commission Report*, 40–41.

283   Critics later considered: Cockburn, *Rumsfeld*, 4.

283   "quiet, deadly serious": Torie Clarke, *Lipstick on a Pig: Winning in the No-Spin Era by Someone Who Knows the Game* (New York: Free Press, 2006), 221.

283   Cheney advised Rumsfeld: *The 9/11 Commission Report*, 43.

283   Pulling out a yellow legal pad: Clarke, *Lipstick*, 222.

284   concluded he had the authority: *The 9/11 Commission Report*, 554 n. 8.

284   informed the president: *The 9/11 Commission Report*, 465 n. 234.

284   tried to firm up the rules: Torie Clarke, interview by Pentagon historians, OSD Historical Office, July 2, 2002.

284   until sometime in the afternoon: *The 9/11 Commission Report*, 465 n. 234.

284   in search of better air: Clarke, *Lipstick*, 223.

284   "I want to tie up": Clarke, *Lipstick*, 225.

284   "We're going to need": Clarke, *Lipstick*, 225.

285   the secretary told Myers: *The 9/11 Commission Report*, 334–335.

285   "This is the defining moment": Bob Woodward, *Bush at War* (New York: Simon & Schuster, 2002), 25–26.

285   when Rumsfeld confronted: Feith, *War and Decision*, 47–48.

285   "We were talking about that": Giambastiani interview by OSD historian, August 1, 2002.

285   talking points summarized: Woodward, *Bush at War*, 25–26.

286   "A desk sat alone": Clarke, *Lipstick*, 229.

286   "The Pentagon's functioning": Rumsfeld news conference, September 11, 2001.

286   "The fire went through": Interview with Barbara Starr, February 19, 2009.

286   Clearly, the level of reporting: *The 9/11 Commission Report*, 257.

286   an elaborate ruse or deception: George Tenet, *At the Center of the Storm* (New York: HarperCollins, 2007), 154; *The 9/11 Commission Report*, 259.

287   "It was not a case": Cambone interview, January 19, 2007.

287   Rumsfeld could not recall: *The 9/11 Commission Report*, 208.

287   raised a slew of questions: Feith, *War and Decision*, 44; Tenet, *Center of the Storm*, 160.

288   But the military didn't: *The 9/11 Commission Report*, 208

288   He wondered aloud: *The 9/11 Commission Report*, 330.

288   He questioned how soon to act: Woodward, *Bush at War*, 32–33.

288   very little for U.S. forces to do: Feith, *War and Decision*, 49–50.

288   strongly favored making Iraq: Woodward, *Bush at War*, 48–49.

289   They wanted action: Feith, *War and Decision*, 51.

289   The Pentagon did not have: *The 9/11 Commission Report*, 331–332.

290   a meeting of Bush's war council: Woodward, *Bush at War*, 79–80, 84; DeYoung, *Soldier*, 351–352.

290   The Defense Department paper: *The 9/11 Commission Report*, 334–335; Feith, *War and Decision*, 51–52.

290   also favored the idea: Wolfowitz interview, May 21, 2008.

290   "Paul had a passion": Interview with John McLaughlin, October 31, 2007.

291   skirted the matter: Woodward, *Bush at War*, 88–89.

291   Rumsfeld never offered: Interview with a senior participant at the Camp David meeting, July 14, 2008; Woodward, *Bush at War*, 86–91; DeYoung, *Soldier*, 352.

291   the Pentagon went ahead: Sean Naylor, *Not a Good Day to Die: The Untold Story of Operation Anaconda* (New York: Berkley, 2005), 85; Gordon and Trainor, *Cobra II*, 19–21.

292   In a message to regional commanders: Feith, *War and Decision*, 55–56.

292   "a marathon, not a sprint": Feith, *War and Decision*, 56–57.

292   Rumsfeld recognized that Franks: Feith, *War and Decision*, 63.

292   Rumsfeld wanted to show: Feith, *War and Decision*, 67.

293   concerned that singling out bin Laden: Woodward, *Bush at War*, 81, 105, 136, 216, 222.

293   "If the initial U.S. military": Feith, *War and Decision*, 66. The memo is also cited in *The 9/11 Commission Report*, 559–560 n. 75.

293   in several NSC meetings: Woodward in *Bush at War* cites one meeting on September 25 (p. 137) and another on September 26 (p. 153).

293   A couple of times in late September: Feith, *War and Decision*, cites memorandums on September 20 and September 30, 66, 81–83.

293   Some of the president's: Woodward, *Bush at War*, 153.

293   He and his top aides saw: Feith, *War and Decision*, 59.

294   he was having trouble: *9/11 Commission Report*, 336.

295   "Well, when can we get these guys": Interview with Robert Andrews; also cited in Scarborough, *Rumsfeld's War*, 3–4.

295   "When CIA gives us": Andrews interview, November 12, 2007.

296   The remark was an expression: Cambone interview, May 4, 2007.

296   "However, the attack on": Donald Rumsfeld, preface to *The Quadrennial Defense Review Report*, September 30, 2001.

298   He had raised the issue: Donald Rumsfeld, interview by Bob Woodward and Daniel J. Balz, January 9, 2002.

298   "If people could be killed": Donald Rumsfeld, memorandum, "Guidelines When Considering Committing U.S. Forces," March 2001; cited in Thomas Shanker, "Rumsfeld Favors Forceful Actions to Foil an Attack," *New York Times*, October 14, 2002.

299   The diagram had caught: Hoehn interview, January 18, 2007.

301   "Not too well yet": Feith, *War and Decision*, 96.

301   Rumsfeld was anxious: Feith, *War and Decision*, 97.

301   But Rumsfeld could not generate: Woodward, *Bush at War*, 217–218.

301   lack of "actionable" proposals: Memorandum to General Richard Myers and General Peter Pace, "What Will Be the Military Role in the War on Terrorism"; cited in Feith, *War and Decision*, 112–113.

301   Rumsfeld ordered Feith: Feith, *War and Decision*, 104.

302   "This is the CIA's strategy": Woodward, *Bush at War*, 243–244.

302   Rice told Rumsfeld: Woodward, *Bush at War*, 245.

303   In the strategy paper: Feith, *War and Decision*, 105.

303   "I do not see": Tommy Franks, *American Soldier* (New York: Regan, 2004), 296.

303   "you have my complete confidence": Franks, *American Soldier*, 300.

303   "He felt like": Interview with Lieutenant General (retired) John Campbell, November 1, 2007.

304   But the document never went: Tenet, *Center of the Storm*, 216.

304   neither side was ready: Campbell interview, November 1, 2007.

304   "a flawed plan": William Kristol, "The Wrong Strategy," *Washington Post*, October 30, 2001.

305   "half-measures": Charles Krauthammer, "Have They Nothing Better to Do?" *Washington Post*, October 30, 2001.

305   another "military quagmire": R. W. Apple Jr., "A Military Quagmire Remembered: Afghanistan as Vietnam," *New York Times*, October 31, 2001.

305   a barrage of questions: Feith, *War and Decision*, 119.

305   the need for patience: Woodward, *Bush at War*, 262.

305   Rumsfeld pressed for ways: Feith, *War and Decision*, 120.

305   Rumsfeld ordered Pace and Feith: Feith, *War and Decision*, 120.

305   Some of the ideas: Feith, *War and Decision*, 122; Woodward, *Bush at War*, 282–283.

306   "I think that what was": Rumsfeld news conference at Central Command, Tampa, FL, November 27, 2001.

306   At first, the execution: Franks, *American Soldier*, 289–296; Thomas E. Ricks, "Rumsfeld's Hands-On War: Afghan Campaign Shaped by Secretary's Views, Personality," *Washington Post*, December 9, 2001.

307   "a different kind of war": Bush news conference, October 11, 2001.

307   not with conventional capabilities: Rumsfeld news conference, October 18, 2001.

308   Franks had rejected: Ron Suskind, *The One Percent Doctrine: Deep Inside America's Pursuit of its Enemies Since 9/11* (New York: Simon & Schuster, 2006), 58–59, 74.

308   He feared losing: Paul Wolfowitz testimony before the Senate Foreign Relations Committee, June 26, 2002.

309   The decision to have Rumsfeld: Clarke, *Lipstick*, 161–162.

309   the word "kill" nine times: Jeffrey A. Krames, *The Rumsfeld Way: Leadership Wisdom of a Battle-hardened Maverick* (New York: McGraw-Hill, 2003), 12–13.

309   He justified the use: Rumsfeld news conference, November 1, 2001.

309   "perfectly legitimate": Rumsfeld news conference, November 13, 2001.

309   "If you're chasing a chicken": Rumsfeld news conference, November 11, 2001.

309   "There's been a good deal": Rumsfeld news conference at Central Command, Tampa, FL, November 27, 2001.

310   which aides said were unscripted: Eric Schmitt, "Talking the Talk His Own Way, by Golly," *New York Times*, June 26, 2002.

310   "The Rock Star and the Goat": Joyce Rumsfeld interview, April 23, 2007.

311   "They were pretty painful": Abizaid interview, February 2, 2007.

311   "Those daily video conferences": Interview with Rear Admiral (retired) Jim Robb.

311   "When the SecDef started": Naylor, *Not a Good Way*, 153.

311   "Numbers became so important": Naylor, *Not a Good Way*, 153.

312   "He said to me": Interview with Vice Admiral (retired) Albert M. "Bert" Calland, October 1, 2007.

312   "The impression I got was": Calland interview, October 1, 2007.

313   "leaves us with a responsibility": Rumsfeld news conference, October 9, 2001.

313   Rumsfeld didn't want: Feith, *War and Decision*, 101–102.

313   At an NSC meeting: David Rohde and David E. Sanger, "How a 'Good War' Went Bad," *New York Times*, August 12, 2007.

314   "We were by no means": Feith, *War and Decision*, 157–158.

314   In April 2002, a test case emerged: Feith, *War and Decision*, 140–145.

314   "I didn't think it": Donald Rumsfeld interview, November 19, 2008.

315   "The last thing you're": Rumsfeld news conference, April 22, 2002.

316   it was then Cheney who spearheaded: For a full discussion of Cheney's role, see Barton Gellman, *Angler: The Cheney Vice Presidency* (New York: Penguin, 2008), 162–173.

316   But these facilities were: Jack L. Goldsmith, *The Terror Presidency: Law and Judgment Inside the Bush Administration* (New York: Norton, 2007), 107–108.

317   Rumsfeld was deeply reluctant: Interview with Roger Pardo-Maurer, August 15, 2007.

317   "some radioactive rock": Pardo-Maurer interview, August 15, 2007.

317   "the least worst place": Rumsfeld news conference, December 27, 2001.

317   "He went out of his way": Pardo-Maurer interview, August 15, 2007.

318   "He basically thought": Interview with Matthew Waxman, December 12, 2007.

318   about four hundred detainees: Feith, *War and Decision*, 160.

318   A forty-two-page draft memorandum: John Yoo and Robert J. Delabunty, memorandum to William J. Haynes II, "Application of Treaties and Laws to al Qaeda and Taliban Detainees," January 9, 2002.

319   "handled not as prisoners of war": Rumsfeld news conference, January 11, 2002.

319   Rumsfeld issued written instructions: Rumsfeld memorandum to Myers, "Status of Taliban and Al Qaeda," January 19, 2002.

319   Angered, Myers went to see: Interview with General (retired) Richard Myers, April 5, 2007.

320   Rumsfeld didn't argue for: Feith, *War and Decision*, 161.

320   Rumsfeld liked the argument: Feith, *War and Decision*, 162.

320   an executive order: Bush memorandum to Cheney et al., "Humane Treatment of al Qaeda and Taliban Detainees," February 7, 2002.

320   Feith continued to insist: Feith interview, August 20, 2008.

321   the caveat about "military necessity": Jane Mayer, *Dark Side: The Inside Story of How the War on Terror Turned into a War on American Ideals* (New York: Doubleday, 2008), 124–125.

321   "The implication of that being": Waxman interview, December 12, 2007.

321   "Whenever it came time": Waxman interview, December 12, 2007.

322   "All of a sudden": Donald Rumsfeld interview, November 19, 2008.

Chapter 10: Iterative Planning

323   change would have to slow: James R. Blaker, *Transforming Military Force: The Legacy of Arthur Cebrowski and Network Centric Warfare* (Westport, CT: Praeger Security International, 2007), 62.

323   He knew that if: Blaker, *Transforming Military Force*, 23–24.

324   "Rumsfeld didn't care": Blaker, *Transforming Military Force*, 23.

325   "Frankly, the debates about": Krieg interview, March 12, 2007.

325   "People were inclined just to say": Krieg interview, March 12, 2007.

325   "a process that shapes": Briefing to Pentagon leadership, "U.S. Defense Priorities: Next Steps in Transformation," May 2002. Briefing slides viewed by author.

326   "As a result, the United States": Donald Rumsfeld, *Annual Report to the President and the Congress*, 2002.

327   presented Rumsfeld with another chance: Gordon and Trainor, *Cobra II*, 21–23, 52–53.

327   when Rumsfeld received: Woodward, *Plan of Attack*, 1–2.

327   "Rather than issuing orders": Feith, *War and Decision*, 111–112.

328   Rumsfeld was looking not to just: Gordon and Trainor, *Cobra II*, 28.

328   His concept called for: Gordon and Trainor, *Cobra II*, 29; Woodward, *Plan of Attack*, 58.

328   the "Generated Start": Gordon and Trainor, *Cobra II*, 36; Woodward, *Plan of Attack*, 96, 98–99.

328   the "Running Start": Gordon and Trainor, *Cobra II*, 50, 89.

329   the "Hybrid": Gordon and Trainor, *Cobra II*, 67–68; Woodward, *Plan of Attack*, 146.

329   Keane had been designated: Thomas E. Ricks, "Bush Backs Overhaul of Military's Top Ranks," *Washington Post*, April 11, 2002.

330   Herbits put together a briefing: Herbits interview, February 27, 2007.

331   the Crusader had drawn controversy: Thom Shanker and James Dao, "Army Digs In Its Heels and Saves Howitzer Plan, for Now," *New York Times*, May 2, 2002.

332   "That for me was the final straw": Wolfowitz interview, May 18, 2008.

333   "We were basically told": Interview with a former senior Pentagon official, January 17, 2008.

333   tried to get Rumsfeld: Interview with Barry Blechman, May 4, 2007.

334   "I don't understand what": Giambastiani interview, October 11, 2007.

334   "I'd say to the Army": Interview with General Bantz John Craddock, March 27, 2007.

335   Clark presented a briefing: Clark interview, February 7, 2007.

336   "That was the first": Clark interview, February 7, 2007.

337   "His main point was": Feith interview, September 15, 2006.

337   his favorite picture: Rumsfeld news conference, October 11, 2006.

338   Same people, same resources: Rumsfeld news conference, November 1, 2005; October 11, 2006.

338   a relatively amateurish operation: Ricks, *Fiasco*, 53–55.

338   An investigation by the: David S. Cloud and Mark Mazzetti, "Prewar Intelligence Unit at Pentagon Is Criticized," *New York Times*, February 9, 2007.

339   "The role of Wolfowitz": Interview with Peter Rodman, May 1, 2007.

339   "As a student of intelligence": Feith, *War and Decision*, 99.

339   a major interagency struggle: Nora Bensahel et al., *After Saddam: Prewar Planning and the Occupation of Iraq* (Santa Monica, CA: Rand Arroyo Center, 2008), 26–27.

339   position on Chalabi was grossly distorted: Feith, *War and Decision*, 254.

340   "But I was told by": Ryan Henry interview, March 10, 2007.

340   "Although he opposed trying": Feith, *War and Decision*, 252.

341   Rumsfeld took issue with: Rumsfeld memorandum to Rice, "Subject: National Security Presidential Directive 8," November 1, 2001. Viewed by author.

341   "I can remember him": Interview with General (retired) Wayne Downing, June 7, 2007.

342   He knew Rumsfeld: Interview with a former senior administration official, July 14, 2008.

342   "It was most obvious": Card interview, January 11, 2008.

343   "Powell versus Cheney and Rumsfeld": DeYoung, *Soldier*, 416.

343   Particularly frustrating for Powell: Interview with a former senior administration official, January 14, 2008.

343   "I was constantly having to": Interview with Beth Jones, September 12, 2007.

344   "I don't think that Rumsfeld": Card interview, January 11, 2008.

345   "He was toxic": Downing interview, June 7, 2007.

345   "He would say to me": Beth Jones interview, September 12, 2007.

345   "try to help us deal": Rumsfeld memorandum to Rice, "Subject: Interagency Process," August 20, 2002. Viewed by author.

347   "I like to be prepared": Rumsfeld memorandum to Rice, "Subject: NSC Meetings," October 30, 2003. Viewed by author.

347   "There must be a way": Rumsfeld memorandum to Rice, "Subject: Agendas and Schedules for PC and NSC Meetings," November 5, 2003. Viewed by author.

348   "My view is that": Rumsfeld memorandum to Bush, "Subject: Alternative Approaches to Operate the NSC—Consensus v. Options for POTUS," April 1, 2004. Viewed by author.

348   the staff devoted much of its effort: Donald P. Wright and Timothy R. Reese, *On Point II: Transition to the New Campaign: The United States Army in Operation Iraqi Freedom, May 2003–January 2005* (Fort Leavenworth, KS: U.S. Army Combined Arms Center, 2008), 66.

349   "You pay attention to": Franks, *American Soldier*, 423, 441.

349   "I give no credit to": Bensahel et al., *After Saddam*, 18, citing an interview with Lieutenant General William Wallace for "Frontline: The Invasion of Iraq."

349   "We were extraordinarily focused": Wright and Reese, *On Point II*, 76.

350   "We had the wrong assumptions": Wright and Reese, *On Point II*, 79.

350   "I told him it was": Interview with Admiral (retired) Lowell E. "Jake" Jacoby, October 11, 2007.

350   "The secretary's notion": Abizaid interview, February 2, 2007.

351   advanced in an influential paper: Peter W. Rodman memorandum to Rumsfeld, "Subject: Who Will Govern Iraq?" August 15, 2002. Copy published in Feith, *War and Decision*, 546–547.

351   Drawing on Rodman's work: Feith, *War and Decision*, 253.

351   "They're not more nationalistic": Abizaid interview, February 2, 2007.

352   Two U.S. intelligence estimates: The estimates, made public by the Senate Intelligence Committee in 2007, were titled "Principal Challenges in Post-Saddam Iraq" and "Regional Consequences of Regime Change in Iraq."

352   Rumsfeld listed twenty-nine pitfalls: Rumsfeld memorandum, "Iraq: An Illustrative List of Potential Problems to Be Considered and Addressed," October 15, 2002. Viewed by author.

353   did not regard the chances: Wright and Reese, *On Point II*, 73; Bensahel et al., *After Saddam*, 14.

353   War games run by: Bensahel et al., *After Saddam*, 13, 16.

353   Rumsfeld cited his: Examples of Rumsfeld recalling his memo include an interview with the *New York Times* five weeks before the invasion and with the *Washington Post* in 2005.

354   "There's no question": Donald Rumsfeld, interview by Bob Woodward, October 23, 2003.

354   "If you look at": Feith interview, October 5, 2007.

354   "It is clear that": Defense Science Board, *Defense Science Board Summer Study on Transition to and From Hostilities* (Washington, DC: Office of the Under Secretary of Defense for Acquisition, Technology, and Logistics, December 2004).

355   inconsistent Pentagon participation: Bensahel et al., *After Saddam*, 23, 28.

356   quietly shared their information: Gordon and Trainor, *Cobra II*, 148; Bob Woodward, *The War Within: A Secret White House History, 2006–2008* (New York: Simon & Schuster, 2008), 154–156.

356   a number of unflattering references: Franks, *American Soldier*, 207, 277, 278, 383, 545.

356   with decades of varied military experience: Gordon and Trainor, *Cobra II*, 46–47.

357   "His presumption was": Interview with General (retired) John Jumper, August 20, 2007.

358   "I'd never worked for": Clark interview, February 7, 2007.

358   "You had the marginalization": Billingslea interview, June 20, 2007.

359   "Rumsfeld did not want": Feith interview, October 5, 2007.

359   "properly guarded the chain": Feith, *War and Decision*, 371.

360   how much he echoed Rumsfeld: Woodward, *State of Denial*, 72.

360   could not recall an instance: Card interview, January 11, 2008.

360   "The secretary would think": Craddock interview, June 23, 2007.

360   "tried very hard": Abizaid interview, February 2, 2007.

361   The case involved a three-star: Vernon Loeb and Thomas E. Ricks, "Rumsfeld's Style, Goals Strain Ties in Pentagon," *Washington Post*, October 16, 2002; Woodward, *State of Denial*, 73.

361   Asked about the Keys case: Myers interview, April 5, 2007.

361   "It was sort of a joke": Jumper interview, August 20, 2007.

361   so "tied up": Clark interview, February 7, 2007.

362   "and probably the ones": Myers interview, February 26, 2009.

362   "He didn't like the way": Interview with Larry Di Rita, February 19, 2007.

363   He was not pleased: Woodward, *Plan of Attack*, 231–234.

363   marked the first time: Gordon and Trainor, *Cobra II*, 99.

364   "It turned into an": Interview with Peter Chiarelli, December 20, 2007.

364   "We often joked": Gordon and Trainor, *Cobra II*, 99–100.

365   "No one had told the secretary": Craddock interview, June 23, 2007.

365   "I don't know how": Chiarelli interview, December 20, 2007.

366   "And if it did": Scowcroft interview, April 16, 2007.

367   "George, I don't want": Haver interview, March 20, 2007.

367   "I've been thinking about this": Haver interview, March 20, 2007.

368   The answer he got back: Robert Andrews memorandum to Rumsfeld, "Subject: Manhunts," July 11, 2002. Viewed by author.

369   Andrews had been discussing this issue: Scarborough, *Rumsfeld's War*, 14–16.

369   He called them "showstoppers": Classified at the time, the list of showstoppers later appeared in Richard H. Shultz Jr., "Showstoppers," *The Weekly Standard*, January 26, 2004.

369   a highly compartmentalized special-access program: Seymour M. Hersh, "The Gray Zone," *New Yorker*, May 24, 2004.

370   Rumsfeld directed Myers: Rumsfeld memorandum to Myers, "Subject: Terrorist Organizations," July 22, 2002. Viewed by author. Also cited in Scarborough, *Rumsfeld's War*, 21–22.

371   "General, I want you to call": Interview with Robert Andrews, October 20, 2007.

372   "I've found that when": Andrews interview, November 12, 2007.

372   several such examples: Mayer, *Dark Side*, 187–188.

373   "It was one of those areas": Di Rita interview, February 8, 2009.

373   "Perhaps I was somewhat": Lieutenant Colonel Diane Beaver testimony before the Senate Armed Services Committee, June 17, 2008.

374   in a note to Myers: Mayer, *Dark Side*, 201.

374   he did little additional research: Jim Haynes testimony before the Senate Armed Services Committee, June 17, 2008.

374   "In hindsight, I cannot": Beaver testimony, June 17, 2008.

374   Haynes intervened: Jane Dalton and Jim Haynes testimony before the Senate Armed Services Committee, June 17, 2008.

374   "When Rumsfeld appointed Haynes": Herbits interview, February 27, 2007.

375   "And my understanding": Dalton testimony, June 17, 2008.

375   Rumsfeld was "personally involved": "Testimony of Lieutenant General Randall M. Schmidt," Department of the Army Inspector General, Investigations Division, August 24, 2005, 25; cited in Michael Scherer and Mark Benjamin, "What Rumsfeld Knew," *Salon*, April 14, 2006.

Chapter 11: Too Many Hands on the Wheel

377   hadn't directly managed: Gordon and Trainor, *Cobra II*, 141.

378   a system with divided command: Wright and Reese, *On Point II*, 80.

378   "He immediately felt": Craddock interview, June 23, 2007.

379   crossed off eight or nine names: Feith, *War and Decision*, 387.

379   Powell, incensed, threatened: Interview with a former senior administration official, July 14, 2008.

379   "would have been better served": Wright and Reese, *On Point II*, 71.

379   Cheney's office blacklisted: Interview with Eric Edelman, June 18, 2007.

379   "appears to have suffered": Wright and Reese, *On Point II*, 77.

380   In a private conversation: Interview with James Schlesinger, March 15, 2007.

380   a joint study: Edward Djerejian and Frank G. Wiser, co-chairs, "Guiding Principles for U.S. Post-Conflict Policy in Iraq," Council on Foreign Relations and the James A. Baker II Institute for Public Policy, Rice University, December 2002, 1.

380   "will be judged more": Frederick D. Barton and Bathsheba N. Crocker, "A Wiser Peace: An Action Strategy for a Post-Conflict Iraq," Center for Strategic and International Studies, January 2003, 6.

381   "the possibility of the United States": Conrad C. Crane and W. Andrew Terrill, "Reconstructing Iraq: Insight, Challenges and Missions for Military Forces in a Post-Conflict Scenario," U.S. Army War College, Strategic Studies Institute, February 2003, 42.

381   feared that too few troops: Gordon and Trainor, *Cobra II*, 116–117, 151–152.

381   A fourteen-page memo: Feith, *War and Decision*, 362–364.

381   To the extent that: Franks, *American Soldier*, 366, 419.

381   "was behind the power curve": Craddock interview, June 23, 2007.

381   "I'll say to Rumsfeld's credit": Interview with General George Casey Jr., April 3, 2007.

382   "culture of dependence": Rumsfeld speech, "Beyond Nation-Building," New York, February 14, 2003.

382   both were misleading: Gordon and Trainor, *Cobra II*, 152.

383   McKiernan, the land commander: Gordon and Trainor, *Cobra II*, 98.

383   offerered a qualified assessment: Interview with a former senior NSC official.

383   "It was the opinion": Jumper interview, August 20, 2007.

384   "met repeatedly during": Rumsfeld memorandum for files, "Subject: Military Advice to POTUS," September 29, 2004.

384   "something on the order of": General Eric Shinseki testimony before the Senate Armed Services Committee, February 25, 2003.

385   "I am reasonably certain": Wolfowitz testimony before the House Budget Committee, February 27, 2003.

385   "My personal view": Rumsfeld news conference, February 28, 2003.

385   "Anecdotal evidence suggests": Bensahel et al., *After Saddam*, 18.

386   he had meant to say: Rumsfeld offered this explanation, for instance, during a speech at the Eisenhower National Security Conference in Washington, D.C., on September 25, 2003.

386   Britain's role was "unclear": Rumsfeld news conference, March 11, 2003.

387   "I remember one of": Edelman interview, September 24, 2007.

388   "The Turks say": Edelman interview, September 24, 2007.

388   Rumsfeld met with some: Interviews with three participants; also cited in Woodward, *Plan of Attack*, 325–327.

390   "The enemy we're fighting": Rick Atkinson, "General: A Longer War Likely," *Washington Post*, March 28, 2003; Jim Dwyer, "A Gulf Commander Sees a Longer Road," *New York Times*, March 28, 2003.

390   "Their assumptions were wrong": Michael R. Gordon, "A New Doctrine's Test," *New York Times*, April 1, 2003.

390   the war plan had taken significant risks: Vernon Loeb, "Rumsfeld Faulted for Troop Dilution," *Washington Post*, March 30, 2003.

390   "It was playing internal politics": Ryan Henry interview, March 24, 2007.

391   Myers did not remember: Myers interview, April 5, 2007.

391   He called the complaints "bogus": Rumsfeld/Myers news conference, April 1, 2003.

391   "I couldn't take it any longer": Myers interview, April 5, 2007.

392   "I keep getting credit": Rumsfeld/Myers news conference, April 1, 2003.

392   "There has been no small number": Rumsfeld memorandum to Myers, "Subject: The Iraq War Plan and the TPFD," April 1, 2003. Viewed by author.

395   "Never, from the first day": Boyer, "Downfall."

395   "It's the same picture": Rumsfeld news conference, April 11, 2003.

396   destroyed almost three-quarters: Bensahel et al., *After Saddam*, 69.

396   found that seventeen of twenty-three: Jay Garner interview with *Frontline*, July 17, 2003.

396   "Some senior officials in Washington": Fred Charles Ikle, preface to *Every War Must End* (New York: Columbia University Press, 2005); also cited in Ricks, *Fiasco*, 136.

396   McKiernan considered declaring: Office of the Special Inspector General for Iraq Reconstruction, "Hard Lessons: The Iraq Reconstruction Experience," February 6, 2009, 59.

397   "The president and the secretary of defense": Wright and Reese, *On Point II*, 141.

397   But after discussing the matter: Wright and Reese, *On Point II*, 142.

397   "ineffective and incoherent": Glenn Kessler, "Gingrich to Urge Overhaul of Powell's Department," *Washington Post*, April 22, 2003; Edward Walsh and Juliet Eilperin, "Gingrich Lying Low After Attack on State Dept. Leaves Some Conservatives Fuming," *Washington Post*, April 26, 2003.

399   Bremer was an odd choice: Charles H. Ferguson, *No End in Sight: Iraq's Descent into Chaos* (New York: PublicAffairs, 2008), 143–144.

399   Rumsfeld told Feith: Feith, *War and Decision*, 422.

399   someone they could talk to: DeYoung, *Soldier*, 465.

399   There had been complaints about Garner's: DeYoung, *Soldier*, 464.

399   "The neocons were saying": Ryan Henry interview, May 12, 2007.

400   "The interagency process": Interview with L. Paul "Jerry" Bremer III, January 22, 2009.

401   "the only one there": Interview with a former senior administration official, July 14, 2008.

401   Rumsfeld, too, professes: Donald Rumsfeld interview, August 30, 2007.

402   Bremer sent a draft: L. Paul "Jerry" Bremer III, "How I Didn't Dismantle Iraq's Army," *New York Times*, September 6, 2007.

403   His staff had collected: Gordon and Trainor, *Cobra II*, 481.

403   "I told him, and he agreed": Abizaid interview, July 20, 2007.

403   He persuaded Rumsfeld: Wright and Reese, *On Point II*, 438; Gordon and Trainor, *Cobra II*, 483–485.

404   "Sometime after March 10": Bremer interview, January 22, 2009.

404   In memos in May: L. Paul Bremer III, "Facts for Feith," *National Online*, March 19, 2008.

404   Feith recalls Rumsfeld: Feith, *War and Decision*, 438.

405   no recollection of Bremer: Donald Rumsfeld interview, November 19, 2008.

406   "If Rumsfeld says": Bremer interview, January 22, 2009.

406   Bremer outlined seven steps: L. Paul Bremer, "Iraq's Path to Sovereignty," *Washington Post*, September 8, 2003.

407   "If you have six or eight": Donald Rumsfeld interview, August 30, 2007.

407   "I want to make": Gordon and Trainor, *Cobra II*, 486.

408   "Rumsfeld never forgot that": Holcomb interview, February 8, 2007.

409   "The lateness of this decision": Bensahel et al., *After Saddam*, 14.

410   "I thought it was sufficient": Wright and Reese, *On Point II*, 145.

410   "I said, 'Jesus Christ, John'": Wright and Reese, *On Point II*, 146.

410   The changes, he insists, were never: Donald Rumsfeld interview, November 19, 2008.

410   Sanchez writes of two meetings: Ricardo S. Sanchez with Don T. Phillips, *Wiser in Battle: A Soldier's Story* (New York: HarperCollins, 2008), 418–422; 439–443.

411   "possible but not likely": Myers interview, February 26, 2009.

411   "You must love those you lead": Shinseki farewell address, June 11, 2003. Transcript available at www.army.mil/features/ShinsekiFarewell/farewell remarks.htm.

412   some "closing thoughts": Shinseki memorandum to Rumsfeld, "Subject: End of Tour Memorandum," June 10, 2003; cited in Thomas E. Ricks, "Scolding Donald Rumsfeld," *Washington Post*, July 29, 2008.

414   "The secretary feels": Thom Shanker, "Retired Commando Chief Is Chosen to Lead the Army," *New York Times*, June 11, 2003.

414   to persuade Rumsfeld to pace himself: Craddock interview, June 23, 2007.

415   Legend attributes the name: Peter T. Kilborn, "Weekends with the President's Men," *New York Times*, June 30, 2006.

Chapter 12: Long, Hard Slog

418   "It's amazing how much": Interview with Ian Brzezinski, May 3, 2007.

418   why the secretary of defense: Beth Jones interview, September 12, 2007.

420   "Normally, Rumsfeld would take": Feith interview, July 26, 2007.

421   trade-offs in assigning forces: Wright and Reese, *On Point II*, 167.

422   but never received a response: L. Paul Bremer III with Malcolm Mc-Connell, *My Year in Iraq: The Struggle to Build a Future of Hope* (New York: Simon & Schuster, 2006), 10.

422   "Basically we were telling them": Interview with an Army officer, October 31, 2007.

422   "It wasn't no": Interview with John Hamre, October 2, 2007.

422   "the security situation is difficult": Hamre memorandum to Rumsfeld, "Subject: Preliminary Observations Based On My Recent Visit to Baghdad," July 2003. Viewed by author.

423   "Because I had known": Hamre interview, October 2, 2007.

424   "It probably means a protracted war": Peter J. Boyer, "Downfall," *The New Yorker*, November 20, 2006.

424   on a visit to Romania: Wolfowitz interview, May 18, 2008.

424   "There's a guerrilla war there": Wolfowitz testimony before the House Armed Services Committee, June 18, 2003.

424   "guerrilla and insurgency operations": Boyer, "Downfall."

424   "My issue was": Donald Rumsfeld interview, November 19, 2008.

425   "I guess the reason": Rumsfeld news conference, June 30, 2003.

425   "a classical guerrilla-type campaign": Abizaid news conference, July 16, 2003.

425   "Attached are the definitions of 'guerrilla warfare'": Rumsfeld memorandum to Abizaid, July 23, 2003.

426   "He sent me a series": Abizaid interview, July 20, 2007.

426   he provided a definition of "counter-insurgency": Abizaid memorandum to Rumsfeld, November 11, 2003; a copy appeared in the *New Yorker*, November 20, 2006.

426   "We are seeing the establishment": Woodward, *State of Denial*, 266; Tenet, *Center of the Storm*, 437–438.

426   "As we discussed": Rumsfeld memorandum to Abizaid, "Subject: Terminology," January 7, 2004. Viewed by author.

427   he compiled eleven examples: Rumsfeld memorandum to Di Rita, "Subject: Firsts," September 3, 2003.

428   "But they did not have": Interview with an Army officer, October 31, 2007.

429   "It was creating": Giambastiani interview, November 26, 2007.

430   "What I found really stunning": Interview with Representative David Obey, June 6, 2008.

430   "It is impossible to review": David Firestone, "Senior House Democrats Urges Top Defense Hands to Resign," *New York Times*, September 6, 2003.

431   "Twenty-five years ago": Rumsfeld speech at the Eisenhower National Security Conference, Washington, DC, September 25, 2003.

433   The situation in Afghanistan: Pamela Constable, "Afghans' Goals Facing Renewed Threats," *Washington Post*, September 8, 2003.

433   "They needed somebody": "How a 'Good War' in Afghanistan Went Bad," *New York Times*, August 12, 2007.

434   "He's not someone who": Interview with Marin Strmecki, December 6, 2007.

436   "He commented favorably": Feith, *War and Decision*, 443.

436   "It was uncharacteristic of him": Holcomb interview, February 8, 2007.

437   "He never liked nation building": Rodman interview, May 1, 2007.

437   "That's a very classic Rumsfeld": Herbits interview, February 27, 2007.

437   "I think he had a deep view": Feith interview, July 26, 2007.

438   "Rumsfeld spoke protectively": Feith, *War and Decision*, 442–443.

438   But Bremer was never sure: Bremer interview, January 22, 2009.

438   "Don terrifies his civilian subordinates": Bremer with McConnell, *My Year*, 208.

438   "I think there were things": Holcomb interview, February 8, 2007.

438   "a very long leash": Donald Rumsfeld interview, November 19, 2008.

439   announcing the creation: David Sanger, "White House to Overhaul Iraq and Afghan Missions," *New York Times*, October 6, 2003.

439   "I was not consulted": Rumsfeld memorandum to Card, "Iraq Stabilization Phase Reporting Relationship," October 6, 2003; also cited in Feith, *War and Decision*, 470.

440   According to Pentagon notes: The notes were read to the author.

440   "winning or losing": Rumsfeld memorandum to Myers, Wolfowitz, Pace, and Feith, "Global War on Terrorism," October 16, 2003.

441   Feith's office drafted a paper: Bremer with McConnell, *My Year*, 170.

442   In a meeting with Bremer in Washington: Bremer with McConnell, *My Year*, 171.

442   "We know where they are": Rumsfeld interview with ABC's *This Week*, March 30, 2003.

443   "There is a tension": Rumsfeld memorandum, "Subject: Risk and the Way Ahead in Iraq," October 28, 2003. Viewed by author. Also cited in Woodward, *War Within*, 22–23.

443   Rumsfeld weighed in: Feith, *War and Decision*, 463.

444   he now was estimating: Bremer with McConnell, *My Year*, 205.

444   Feith credits Rumsfeld: Feith, *War and Decision*, 466.

444   Bremer in his account: Bremer interview, January 11, 2009.

444   "It may be that": Interview with Meghan O'Sullivan, July 17, 2008.

445   A Pentagon review: Feith, *War and Decision*, 461.

445   A counterargument was advanced: Bremer with McConnell, *My Year*, 207.

445   During a visit to Iraq: Bremer with McConnell, *My Year*, 156.

445   "We need to array": Rumsfeld memorandum to Abzaid and Bremer, "Subject: Reporting on Security Issues," September 12, 2003; also cited in Bremer with McConnell, *My Year*, 162.

445   He told Wolfowitz: Bremer with McConnell, *My Year*, 171.

446   a passive or reactive mode: Bremer with McConnell, *My Year*, 221.

446   "I've been asking": Bremer with McConnell, *My Year*, 222.

446   "I told him": Rumsfeld memorandum for the files, "Private Conversation with Bremer," December 10, 2003; also cited in Woodward, *State of Denial*, 273–274.

446   "Rumsfeld was clearly": Bremer with McConnell, *My Year*, 245.

447   Rice asked Rumsfeld: Woodward, *State of Denial*, 274.

447   "Do you know what": Interview with a former senior administration official, July 14, 2008.

447   "He was really ecstatic": Interview with Larry Silberman, May 19, 2008.

447   Rumsfeld phoned Sanchez: Sanchez with Phillips, *Wiser in Battle*, 300–301.

447   "Well, dammit, you guys": Sanchez with Phillips, *Wiser in Battle*, 306.

Chapter 13: The Thought of Resigning

450   "Are current U.S. military": Rumsfeld memorandum, "Subject: Stress on the Force," September 2003.

452   "Schoomaker worked his relationship": Casey interview, April 3, 2007.

452   "We should take advantage": Schoomaker testimony before the House Armed Services Committee, January 28, 2004.

453   "an overarching security strategy": Iraq Security Forces Assessment Team Final Report, 8. Viewed by author.

453   Rumsfeld approved the plan: Wright and Reese, *On Point II*, 437, 441.

454   Wolfowitz reported to: Wolfowitz memorandum to Rumsfeld, "Accelerating the Buildup of Iraqi Security Forces," November 12, 2003. Viewed by author.

454   receive the "highest priority": Rumsfeld memorandum to Abizaid and Bremer, "Iraqi Security Forces," February 20, 2004.

455   "If people are looking": Rumsfeld memorandum to Feith with copies to Myers and Wolfowitz, "Subject: Foreign Troops," February 20, 2004.

455   "He told me": Keane interview, February 29, 2008.

456   "He was drifting more": Card interview, January 11, 2008.

456   "I don't think it": Interview with Dan Bartlett, October 5, 2007.

457   "I am concerned about": Rumsfeld memorandum to all the undersecretaries, some assistant secretaries, and military and civilian heads of the services, "Subject: Updating Systems and Procedures," March 17, 2004.

457   "To get where we are": Rumsfeld memorandum, "Subject: Goldwater-Nichols for the USG," February 8, 2004.

458   "The United States has one": Rumsfeld memorandum, "Subject: Role of the U.S. Military," March 26, 2004.

460   he was twice prevented: Bremer with McConnell, *My Year*, 136, 192.

460   An internal Pentagon review: The review was conducted by Peter Rodman. His results were conveyed to Rumsfeld in a short memo that was read to the author by a senior defense official.

460   Rumsfeld initially resisted: Abizaid interview, July 20, 2007.

461   "Oh, come on. People are fungible": Rumsfeld news conference, April 15, 2004.

461   "Fighting him was not quite": Abizaid interview, July 20, 2007.

461   "I told Myers and Abizaid": Rumsfeld memorandum to himself, "Subject: Military Advice," April 26, 2004. Viewed by author.

462   Cheney had resisted: Abizaid interview, July 20, 2007.

462   the secretary echoed: Feith, *War and Decision*, 483.

463   He found that: David Petreaus, interview by Steven Clay, the Combat Studies Institute at Fort Leavenworth, November 21, 2006.

464   "sadistic, blatant, and wanton": Major General Antonio Taguba, "Article 15–6 Investigation of the 800th Military Police Brigade," March 2004.

464   "perhaps 10 soldiers": Seymour M. Hersh, "The General's Report," *New Yorker*, June 25, 2007.

464   neither he nor Keating: Craddock interview, June 23, 2007.

464   informed both Rumsfeld and Myers: Abizaid interview, February 14, 2008.

465   "the general nature of the photos": General Richard Myers, testimony before the Senate Armed Services Committee, May 7, 2004.

465   "There were rumors": Rumsfeld testimony before the Senate Armed Services Committee, May 7, 2004.

465   "I suspect that": Holcomb interview, February 8, 2007.

465   "It's my hypothesis": Herbits interview, February 27, 2007.

466   "I had to call": Craddock interview, June 23, 2007.

466   "He told a small group": Ryan Henry interview, March 10, 2007.

466   "Cabinet secretaries and staff": Bartlett interview, October 5, 2007.

466   "It was inconsistent": Rumsfeld testimony before the Senate Armed Services Committee, May 7, 2004.

467   "You are courageously leading": Bush appearance at the Pentagon, May 10, 2004.

467   "The question now is": Richard W. Stevenson and Carl Hulse, "President Backs His Defense Chief in a Show of Unity," *New York Times*, May 11, 2004.

467   "My worst nightmare": Rumsfeld memorandum to himself, "Subject: Nightmare," May 10, 2004.

468   announced the news: Rumsfeld appearance on *Larry King Live*, February 3, 2005.

469   fundamental shortcomings in the investigations: Bradley Graham, "Some Seek Broad, External Inquiry on Prisoner Abuse," *Washington Post*, May 27, 2004.

469   "Frankly, I think one": Interview with Pete Geren, May 14, 2007.

470   no U.S. "policy of abuse": Final Report of the Independent Panel to Review DoD Detention Operations, August 2004.

470   had reached 842: Office of the Inspector General of the Department of Defense, "Review of DoD-Directed Investigations of Detainee Abuse," August 25, 2006, i.

471   Other Pentagon investigations: Reports by Lieutenant General Anthony R. Jones and Major General George Fay, Brigadier General Charles Jacoby Jr., Vice Admiral Albert T. (Tom) Church III, and the office of the Pentagon's inspector general all speak to this migration problem.

472   no longer effective: Office of the Inspector General of the Department of Defense, "Review of DoD-Directed Investigations of Detainee Abuse," August 25, 2006, 27.

472   three times in less than thirty days: Major General George Fay and Lieutenant General Anthony Jones, "Investigation of Intelligence Activities At Abu Ghraib," Department of Defense, August 23, 2004, 42.

472   "Dave, I want to talk": Interview with Colonel (retired) David Lamm, August 31, 2007.

473   "He thought that with two": Ryan Henry interview, March 10, 2007.

473   "He thought that the policy": Waxman interview, December 17, 2007.

473   "direct" and "indirect" responsibility: Schlesinger panel news conference, August 24, 2004.

473   "The secretary of defense": Schlesinger interview, March 15, 2007.

474   "You had the Army saying": Di Rita interview, May 11, 2007.

475   "He was very frustrated": Geren interview, May 14, 2007.

476   "The length of time": Department of Defense, "A Report on Detention Operations," draft copy, November 29, 2006. Viewed by author.

476   "Unfortunately, that division": Waxman interview, December 17, 2007.

477   "of all the myths": Rumsfeld memorandum to Di Rita, May 18, 2004. Viewed by author.

478   a lengthy article: David Barstow, "Behind TV Analysts, Pentagon's Hidden Hand," *New York Times*, April 20, 2008.

478   A subsequent investigation: Office of the Inspector General of the Department of Defense, "Examination of Allegations Involving DoD Public Affairs Outreach Program," January 14, 2009.

479   "against a false standard": Rumsfeld memorandum to Bush, "Some thoughts on Iraq and how to think about it," June 8, 2004. Viewed by author.

479   "You would need to": Rodman memorandum to Rumsfeld, June 10, 2004. Viewed by author.

480   "I do believe that": Rumsfeld memorandum to Bush, "Subject: What Are We Fighting? Is It a Global War on Terror," June 18, 2004. Copy obtained by author.

481   "Our problem is": Abizaid memorandum to Rumsfeld and Myers, July 16, 2004. Viewed by author.

481   considered naming his military assistant: Craddock interview, March 27, 2007.

482   "I don't know of a tougher job": Casey confirmation hearing before the Senate Armed Services Committee, June 24, 2004.

482   "Our guys are trying": Casey interview, October 14, 2007.

484   "Your job as you knew it": Interview with Arlene Nestel, June 11, 2007.

484   "His behavior from": Herbits interview, February 27, 2007.

485   a seven-page report: Woodward, *State of Denial*, 316–317.

485   "This is a guy who": Herbits interview, February 27, 2007.

486   "He worked with": Feith, *War and Decision*, 72.

486   But little got done: Hamre interview, October 2, 2007.

486   "He didn't use people": Interview with John Young, May 28, 2008.

Chapter 14: Framework for Iraq

487   "His eyes filled up": Starr interview, February 19, 2009.

488   often argumentative negotiations: DeYoung, *Soldier*, 506–507; Woodward, *State of Denial*, 312.

489   "We regularly have PCs": Rumsfeld memorandum to Myers, Wolfowitz, Pace, Feith, and Craddock, "Subject: "PCs and NSCs on Iraq," June 26, 2004. Viewed by author.

489   "efforts to widen the coalition": Rumsfeld memorandum to Bush, "Subject: Some Thoughts for Agenda Items for NSC and PC Meetings," November 13, 2004.

491   a series of briefing charts: Briefing by Casey to Rumsfeld, "Framework for Iraq," July 8, 2004. Charts viewed by author.

492   "Nobody had really identified": Interview with Colonel Will Grimsley, October 18, 2006.

492   "He kept saying no one": Casey interview, April 3, 2007.

493   "get Petraeus off the net": Casey interview, April 3, 2007.

493   "Rumsfeld was really pushing": Grimsley interview, October 18, 2006.

493   intention to reduce: Bradley Graham, "U.S. Forces Plan Lower Profile," *Washington Post*, June 21, 2004.

494   "force levels appropriate": Rumsfeld memorandum to Myers with copy to Wolfowitz, "Subject: Force Estimate for Iraq," May 21, 2004. Viewed by author.

494   "adequate to perform": Myers memorandum to Rumsfeld, July 13, 2004. Viewed by author.

494   "The number of brigades": Lieutenant General Norton A. Schwartz, "Iraq Force Estimate," June 17, 2004. Viewed by author.

494   Abizaid would have approached: Abizaid interview, February 14, 2008.

495   the "red lines" for talks: Myers and Wolfowitz memorandum to Casey, "Subject: Talking Points Discussed During Today's SVTC," October 8, 2004. Viewed by author.

496   "Rumsfeld was actually pretty good": Casey interview, October 14, 2007.

496   "a great battle buddy": Abizaid interview, February 2, 2007.

496   Myers described Rumsfeld as: Myers interview, February 26, 2009.

497   four of the country's eighteen provinces: Included in the four were the two most populous provinces, Baghdad and Ninewa. The other two were Al Anbar and Salah ad Din.

497   citing them publicly: Rumsfeld news conference, October 11, 2004.

498   "I went to Don": Wolfowitz interview, May 18, 2008.

498   "Listen, fourteen of the eighteen": Bush news conference, January 7, 2005.

498   "He kept pushing us": Casey interview, October 14, 2007.

499   Only the screen: Interview with a senior military officer, June 4, 2007.

499   asked his speechwriter: Rumsfeld memorandum to Latimer, August 30, 2004.

499   "Directions have been given": Winston Churchill, BBC broadcast, October 1, 1939.

500   "He emphasized points": Latimer interview, January 27, 2007.

500   Touring the devastated cities: John Dos Passos, "Americans Are Losing the Victory in Europe," *Life*, January 7, 1946.

500   personal reading list: Rumsfeld remarks at Pentagon town hall meeting, December 8, 2006.

501   "if the extremists won": Rumsfeld memorandum to Latimer, September 28, 2004.

501   "salutary neglect": David S. Cloud, "Afghan Warlords Slowly Come in from the Cold," *Wall Street Journal*, March 14, 2005.

501   "I'd frequently find": Abizaid interview, July 20, 2007.

502   "When are you going": Lamm interview, June 12, 2007.

502   "Just be focused": Interview with Lieutenant General (retired) David Barno, April 26, 2007.

502   "By God, Barno": Lamm interview, June 12, 2007.

503   "It was all about": Barno interview, April 26, 2007.

503   "Rumsfeld wanted to look": Lamm interview, June 12, 2007.

504   "He usually was convinced": Barno interview, April 26, 2007.

504   "It was very, very rare": Feith interview, September 15, 2006.

505   waiting for just such an opening: Interview with Colonel Greg Lengyel, October 24, 2006.

505   "He used to play": Edelman interview, September 24, 2007.

506   "The snowflakes were an issue": Beth Jones interview, September 12, 2007.

506   "You don't need to": Interview with Stephen Hadley, May 10, 2008.

507   "He wanted to move quickly": Hoehn interview, January 18, 2007.

508   "There were indeed some": Lincoln P. Bloomfield Jr., "Politics and Diplomacy of the Global Defense Posture Review," in *Reposturing the Force: U.S. Overseas Presence in the Twenty-first Century*, ed. Carnes Lord (Newport, RI: Naval War College, 2006), 50.

508   it wouldn't be worth doing: Hoehn interview, November 21, 2006.

508   Deadpan, Powell said: Bloomfield, "Politics and Diplomacy," 51–52.

509   "We want to have our forces": Rumsfeld media stakeout in Singapore with Australian minister of defense Robert Hill on June 5, 2004.

509   "little long-term strategic sense": "Misconceived Military Shuffle," *New York Times*, August 17, 2004.

509   "In Rumsfeld's view": Hoehn interview, November 21, 2006.

510   seemed more comfortable: Robert D. Kaplan, "What Rumsfeld Got Right," *Atlantic Monthly*, July-August 2008.

510   "I think, in his heart": Hoehn interview, November 21, 2006.

512   "We invited the senator": Moore interview, June 26, 2007.

513   "My plan is to be": Rumsfeld memorandum to Gonzales with copies to Wolfowitz and Haynes, "Subject: Document and E-mail Request," June 9, 2004.

514   a turbulent exchange of views: Rowan Scarborough, "Rumsfeld-McCain Feud Grew After Summer Lunch," *Washington Times*, January 10, 2005.

514   placed principal blame: Office of the Inspector General of the Department of Defense, "Management Accountability Review of the Boeing KC-767A Tanker Program," May 13, 2005.

515   "My time basically": Office of the Inspector General of the Department of Defense, Deputy Inspector General for Investigations, tape transcription, interview of Donald Rumsfeld, April 1, 2005; cited in R. Jeffrey Smith, "Tanker Inquiry Finds Rumsfeld's Attention Was Elsewhere," *Washington Post*, June 20, 2006.

516   "Don asked that": Office of the Inspector General of the Department of Defense, "Management Accountability Review of the Boeing KC-767A Tanker Program," May 13, 2005, 18.

516   "How could such major": Rumsfeld memorandum to leadership, "Subject: Darlene Druyun and Corruption in the Air Force Acquisition," November 2, 2004.

517   the "vacancy rate": Rumsfeld memorandum to Dina Powell with copies to Cheney, Card, and Rice, "Subject: Turbulence in Key Positions," November 4, 2004.

517   "If you look at": Interview with Dan Stanley, November 6, 2006.

518   "Just because something": Delonnie Henry interview, June 6, 2007.

519   may have run its course: Card interview, January 11, 2008.

519   had urged the president: Woodward, *State of Denial*, 360–363, 367–368.

521   "Why don't we have": Rumsfeld's town hall meeting in Kuwait, December 8, 2004.

522   he had given Di Rita authority: Di Rita interview, February 8, 2009.

523   "arrogant buck-passing": William Kristol, "The Defense Secretary We Have," *Washington Post*, December 15, 2004.

523   "If this Department is not capable": Rumsfeld memorandum to Myers with copies to Abizaid, Casey, England, Harvey, and Schoomaker, "Subject: Meeting OAR Needs," December 14, 2004. Viewed by author.

524   "I need a date certain": Rumsfeld memorandum to Myers and Pace, with copies to Abizaid, Casey, Harvey, and Schoomaker, "Subject: Armored Vehicles," December 21, 2004. Viewed by author.

524   "gotten better organized": Casey briefing to Rumsfeld, "Post-Election Posture," December 15, 2004. Briefing slides viewed by author.

524   "broadly on track": Briefing to Bush, "Iraq Update," December 16, 2004. Briefing slides viewed by author.

525   a study ordered by Casey: Ricks, *Fiasco*, 393–394.

525   "The average counterinsurgency": Casey testimony before the Senate Armed Services Committee, September 29, 2005.

526   "The secretary was just": Casey interview, October 14, 2007.

526   "He's one of the world's toughest guys": Abizaid interview, July 20, 2007.

527   "One of the things I learned": Interview with J. D. Crouch, October 24, 2007.

527   "I don't want to know": Interview with a senior defense official, September 28, 2006.

528   "The conversation got a little dicey": Krieg interview, March 12, 2007.

529   "It was one of those moments": Krieg interview, March 12, 2007.

Chapter 15: Second Thoughts

531   "I don't need to know": Rumsfeld memorandum to Pace with a copy to Myers, "Subject: Views from generals," January 4, 2005. Viewed by author.

533   "The question was": Interview with Colonel Bill Hix, October 31, 2007.

533   "George, this line": Hix interview, October 31, 2007.

533   "He was always pushing": Casey interview, October 14, 2007.

534   "bridge force": Rumsfeld memorandum to Feith and Myers, August 2, 2004. Viewed by author.

534   Myers responded that: Myers memorandum to Rumsfeld, August 12, 2004. Viewed by author.

534   possibilities for employing Kurdish fighters: Rumsfeld memorandum to Casey, October 20, 2004. Viewed by author.

534   plan to remove Special Operations: Rumsfeld memorandum to Abizaid and Casey, February 14, 2005. Viewed by author.

534   Casey proposed either: Casey memorandum to Rumsfeld, March 4, 2005. Viewed by author.

535   "We must avoid": Abizaid memorandum to Rumsfeld and Myers, January 9, 2005. Viewed by author.

535   Casey could recall: Casey interview, October 14, 2007.

536   "You have to understand": Abizaid interview, July 20, 2007.

537   "It is a task not": Rumsfeld memorandum to senior Pentagon staff, "Subject: A Nation and the Civilized World at War in the 21st Century," January 18, 2005. Copy obtained by author.

538   "The amount of material": Interview with a former senior defense official, January 17, 2008.

539   "We had an understanding": Interview with Gordon R. England, April 11, 2008.

539   For himself Rumsfeld: The division of responsibilities between Rumsfeld
      and England described here comes from a one-page list dated July 6, 2005.
      Copy obtained by author.

540   "The frustration with Wolfowitz": Interview with a former senior Penta-
      gon official, December 12, 2007.

541   Over the weekend of: Interviews with England (April 11, 2008) and Philip
      Zelikow (April 15, 2008); Tim Golden, "Detainee Memo Created Divide
      in White House," *New York Times*, October 1, 2006; Gellman, *Angler*,
      347–350; Mayer, *Dark Side*, 316–319.

542   "He didn't like this idea": Interview with a former senior Pentagon offi-
      cial, December 12, 2007.

542   England gathered three dozen: Interviews with Cambone (November 12,
      2007) and Waxman (December 12, 2007); Golden, "Detainee Memo";
      Gellman, *Angler*, 351–352.

543   "I never felt like": England interview, April 11, 2008.

543   "Aside from the legal merits": Waxman interview, December 12, 2007.

544   assailed Waxman: Tim Golden and Eric Schmitt, "Detainee Policy Sharply
      Divides Bush Officials," *New York Times*, November 2, 2005.

544   "Rumsfeld's attitude": Cambone interview, November 12, 2007.

545   "Any who say we have lost": Rumsfeld testimony before the Senate Armed
      Services Committee, June 23, 2005.

546   The general warned: Casey briefing to Rumsfeld, "State of the Iraqi Insur-
      gency: June 2005 Assessment," June 23, 2005. Briefing slides viewed by
      author.

547   in a follow-up to service chiefs: Briefing to Joint Chiefs of Staff, "Iraq
      Campaign: Way Ahead," June 27, 2005. Briefing slides viewed by author.

547   "He said the terminology": Feith interview, October 5, 2007.

548   began testing the new phrase: Eric Schmitt and Thom Shanker, "U.S. Offi-
      cials Retool Slogan for Terror War," *New York Times*, July 26, 2005.

548   no fewer than five times: Richard W. Stevenson, "President Makes It Clear:
      Phrase Is 'War on Terror,'" *New York Times*, August 4, 2005.

548   "There has been": Rumsfeld speech to the Dallas Chamber of Commerce,
      August 2, 2005.

550   "England knew instinctively": Interview with Paul McHale, November 21,
      2006.

550   "Certain folks at the White House": Rangel interview, January 30, 2007.

551   invoked only a few times: Nicholas Lemann, "The Talk of the Town: In-
      surrection," *The New Yorker*, September 26, 2005.

551   "Look at the chain": Card interview, January 11, 2008; also cited in Wood-
      ward, *State of Denial*, 427–428.

551   "I felt that": England interview, April 16, 2008.

552   "He became very uneasy": McHale interview, November 21, 2007.

553   acknowledged as much: Bradley Graham, "War Plan Drafted to Counter
      Terror Attacks in U.S.," *Washington Post*, August 8, 2005.

553   the "gaps and seams" briefing: McHale interview, November 21, 2007.

554   "DHS had some issues": Interview with a Pentagon official, January 3, 2007.

554   "To the extent that": Rumsfeld memorandum to Chertoff with copies to Cheney, Card, Hadley, and Townsend, "Subject: Katrina After-action Lessons Learned Recommendation that DOD and DHS Determine When the Department of Defense Would Be Involved in a Catastrophic Event— Natural or Man Made," March 7, 2006. Viewed by author.

554   Chertoff wrote back: Chertoff memorandum to Rumsfeld, March 10, 2006. Viewed by author.

555   Edelman was frustrated: Edelman interview, September 24, 2007.

555   "a very robust network": Richard A. Oppel Jr., Eric Schmitt, and Thom Shanker, "Baghdad Bombings Raise Anew Questions About U.S. Strategy in Iraq," *New York Times*, September 17, 2005.

556   like "oil spots": Andrew F. Krepinevich Jr., "How to Win in Iraq," *Foreign Affairs*, September-October 2005.

556   he dictated a memo: Rumsfeld memorandum to Abizaid and Casey with a copy to Myers, September 21, 2005. Viewed by author. The article attached was: Joe Klein, "Saddam's Revenge," *Time*, September 18, 2005.

557   "Please take a look": Rumsfeld memorandum to Casey with a copy to Myers, September 22, 2005. Viewed by author.

557   "That was in the back": Bartlett interview, October 5, 2007.

557   "We started asking": O'Sullivan interview, July 17, 2008.

558   "We were all a little nervous": Crouch interview, October 24, 2007.

558   "We were presenting this": O'Sullivan interview, July 17, 2008.

559   "I think that it would": Crouch interview, October 24, 2007.

559   Casey briefed Hadley: Casey briefing to Hadley, "Iraq Campaign Plan," September 16, 2005. Briefing slides viewed by author.

560   "There was a tension": Casey interview, October 14, 2007.

560   Bush in particular: Woodward, *War Within*, 4–6.

560   "clear, hold and build": Rice testimony before the Senate Foreign Relations Committee, October 19, 2005.

560   "Anyone who takes": Rumsfeld news conference, November 29, 2005.

560   started using it himself: See, for example, Bush's speech at a luncheon of military wives at Bolling Air Force Base in Washington on October 25, 2005, or his Veterans Day speech in Pennsylvania on November 11, 2005.

561   "I'm looking forward to": Rumsfeld memorandum to Abizaid and Casey, "Subject: Upcoming Schedule," September 23, 2005. Viewed by author.

561   "might be better spent": Rumsfeld memorandum to Abizaid and Casey with a copy to Myers, September 26, 2005. Viewed by author.

561   "It's always a bumpy road": Rumsfeld memorandum to Abizaid and Casey with a copy to Pace, "Subject: Thanks for a Good Job in DC," October 5, 2005. Viewed by author.

562   "It was clear that people": Abizaid interview, February 14, 2008.

Chapter 16: A Period of Continuous Change

564   no serious competitors: Holcomb interview, February 8, 2007.

564   "With Rumsfeld during this period": Di Rita interview, February 8, 2009.

565   "I don't think": Rumsfeld news conference, November 29, 2005.

565   "That made the secretary": Interview with General (retired) Peter Pace, July 8, 2008.

565   a three-page secret assessment: CIA Red Cell Report, no. 200, "Preempting Damage from a 'Tet Offensive' in Iraq," September 30, 2005. Viewed by author.

566   a memo congratulating them: Rumsfeld memorandum to Casey and Vines with copies to Pace and Abizaid, "Subject: Good Job on the Constitutional Referendum," October 17, 2005. Viewed by author.

566   a "strategic opportunity": Casey briefing to Rumsfeld, "Potential Off-Ramp Decisions," October 21, 2005. Viewed by author.

566   Casey testified that only: Casey testimony before the Senate Armed Services Committee, September 29, 2005.

567   a twenty-seven-page report: The survey on which the report was based was done in August 2005 and led by Colonel Bill Hix, Casey's chief strategist, and Dr. Kalev Sepp, a professor at the Naval Post Graduate school. Casey sent a copy of the report to Rumsfeld on November 12. The report was viewed by the author.

567   "We clearly need": Rumsfeld memorandum to Casey with copies to Pace, Edelman, and Haynes, "Subject: The Counterinsurgency Survey," November 15, 2005. Viewed by author.

568   "I'd try to explain": Casey interview, October 14, 2007.

569   "Early on, General Casey": Hix interview, October 31, 2007.

570   Harvey had traveled: Woodward, *War Within*, 23.

571   "The interesting thing is": Interview with Derek Harvey, May 9, 2008.

571   the briefing in December 2004: Ricks, *Fiasco*, 408–409.

571   "There was an antipathy": Harvey interview, May 9, 2008.

572   would be a "cakewalk": Ken Adelman, "Cakewalk in Iraq," *Washington Post*, February 13, 2002.

572   argued with the secretary: Adelman interview, March 6, 2007; also cited in Woodward, *State of Denial*, 433–434.

572   "Mr. Secretary, there's just": Schlesinger interview, March 15, 2007.

573   "I think towards": Williams interview, March 16, 2007.

573   secretly paid Iraqi newspapers: Borzou Daragahi and Mark Mazzetti, "U.S. Military Covertly Pays to Run Stories in Iraqi Press," *Los Angeles Times*, November 30, 2005.

573   "The attached article": Rumsfeld memorandum to Casey with copies to Pace, Edelman, Abizaid, and Di Rita, "Subject: Information Operations," November 30, 2005. Viewed by author.

574   an Office of Strategic Influence: James Dao and Eric Schmitt, "Pentagon Readies Effort to Sway Sentiment Abroad," *New York Times*, February 20, 2002.

575   "We need to sort out": Rumsfeld memorandum to Dorrance Smith with copies to England, Pace, Abizaid, Casey, and Edelman, "Subject: Lincoln Group Work in Iraq," March 6, 2006. Viewed by author.

575   gave it a D-plus: Rumsfeld town hall meeting, December 8, 2006.

576   the "terms of reference": Bradley Graham, "Pentagon Prepares to Rethink Focus on Conventional Warfare," *Washington Post*, January 25, 2005.

577   "He said he'd worked": Interview with a former senior defense official, September 28, 2006.

578   "appropriate to meet": Department of Defense, *Quadrennial Defense Review Report*, February 6, 2006, 41.

579   "I think the QDR": Ryan Henry interview, April 14, 2007.

579   "There is a tendency to want": Donald Rumsfeld, preface to *Quadrennial Defense Review*, 2005, v.

580   "The secretary believed": Interview with a former senior defense official, September 28, 2006.

580   In a briefing to Bush: Feith, *War and Decision*, 511–513.

581   a creeping militarization: See, for instance, Senate Foreign Relations Committee, "Embassies as Command Posts in the Anti-terror Campaign," December 15, 2006.

581   "This was the most heavily lobbied": Bradley Graham, "Pentagon Can Now Fund Foreign Militaries," *Washington Post*, January 29, 2006.

581   threw her support: Bradley Graham, "U.S. Directive Prioritizes Post-Conflict Stability," *Washington Post*, December 1, 2005.

583   "This was a very specific instruction": Interview with Jeffrey "Jeb" Nadaner, September 12, 2006.

583   The eleven-page directive: Department of Defense Directive 3000.05, "Military Support for Stability, Security, Transition, and Reconstruction Operations," November 28, 2005.

583   "He was emphatic about it": Nadaner interview, September 12, 2006.

584   "This was something that": Donald Rumsfeld interview, April 8, 2008.

585   "Why did I have to": Interview with William G. "Jerry" Boykin, May 30, 2007.

586   a team operating in Paraguay: Greg Miller, "U.S. Seeks to Rein In Its Military Spy Teams," *Los Angeles Times*, December 18, 2006.

586   "Rumsfeld decided": Interview with a senior military intelligence officer, February 26, 2007.

586   missions inside Iran: Seymour Hersh, "The Coming Wars: What the Pentagon Can Now Do in Secret," *New Yorker*, January 17, 2005.

587   Cambone noted that: Cambone interview, February 5, 2007.

587   Similarly artful interpretations: Bart Gellman, "Secret Unit Expands Rumsfeld's Domain," *Washington Post*, January 23, 2005.

587   less than persuasive: Obey interview, June 6, 2008.

588   "highly inappropriate and highly dangerous": Representative David Obey floor statement, November 3, 2005.

588   signed a two-page memorandum: Contents of the memorandum were described to the author in an interview with several officials in the office of the undersecretary of defense for intelligence.

589   the swelling intelligence corps: To train and manage this enlarged force, DIA set up a new branch. Originally called the Strategic Support Branch, or Strategic Support Operations Group, it was later given the more benign name of the Defense HUMINT Management Office after some unwanted publicity, including Gellman's "Secret Unit Expands Rumsfeld's Domain."

590   told them they were out of line: Siobhan Gorman, "Imagery Intelligence Agency Chief Being Forced from Post," *Baltimore Sun*, January 6, 2006.

590   credited with providing: Center for Strategic and International Studies, "Transitioning Defense Organizational Initiatives: An Assessment of Key 2001–2008 Defense Reforms," Project Director: Kathleen H. Hicks, November 2008.

591   "I think Rumsfeld": Haver interview, May 5, 2007.

591   "When Steve left": Andrews interview, November 12, 2007.

591   "Steve was the person": Donald Rumsfeld interview, April 8, 2008.

Chapter 17: Toward the Abyss

593   Bush had ordered: Feith, *War and Decision*, 510–511.

594   "He was very insistent": Nadaner interview, September 12, 2006.

595   "I don't really think": Andrews interview, November 12, 2007.

595   "My recommendation is that": Rumsfeld memorandum to Hadley with copy to Crouch, "Subject: The circular PC meeting on 'lead departments,' 'blended leads' and 'co-leads' and the like," January 12, 2006. Viewed by author.

595   "If there is a global war": Rumsfeld memorandum to Hadley, "Subject: NSC Meeting on GWOT," February 6, 2006. Viewed by author.

595   had twice written back: Hadley interview, May 10, 2008.

596   directive on the war on terrorism: This was designated National Security Presidential Directive 46.

596   "The result was scattered": Andrews interview, November 12, 2007.

596   "It is a pleasure": Rumsfeld memorandum to Abizaid, Casey, and Dempsey with a copy to Pace, "Subject: Briefings to the President," January 4, 2006. Viewed by author.

596   "decisive action in 2006": Briefing to Bush, "MNF-I Update," January 4, 2006. Briefing slides viewed by author.

597   "I was told": Chiarelli interview, December 20, 2007.

598   "year of the police": Eric Schmitt, "2000 More M.P.'s Will Help Train the Iraqi Police," *New York Times*, January 16, 2006.

598   "a schedule for the rest of this year": Rumsfeld memorandum to Pace, with copies to Edelman, Abizaid, and Casey, "Subject: Iraq Force Level Discussion," January 20, 2006. Viewed by author.

598   "conditions-based, off-ramp strategy": Casey memorandum to Rumsfeld, January 23, 2006. Viewed by author.

599   looked into the abyss: Peter Pace, *Meet the Press*, March 5, 2006.

599   "put the accomplishment": Casey memorandum, "Some Thoughts on Civil War in Iraq," n.d. Viewed by author.

600   "incompetent strategically": Major General (retired) Paul D. Eaton, "A Top-Down Review for the Pentagon," *New York Times*, March 19, 2006.

600   "McNamara-like micromanagement": Lieutenant General (retired) Gregory Newbold, "Why Iraq Was a Mistake," *Time*, April 9, 2006.

600   "pattern of poor strategic decisions": Major General (retired) John Batiste, "A Case for Accountability," *Washington Post*, April 19, 2006; Thomas E. Ricks, "Rumsfeld Rebuked by Retired Generals," *Washington Post*, April 13, 2006.

600   "This idea that": Di Rita interview, May 26, 2006.

601   "It is clearly a distraction and unhelpful": Transcript of meeting first made available with article by David Barstow, "Behind TV Analysts, Pentagon's Hidden Hand," *New York Times*, April 20, 2008.

602   a memorandum distilling: Rumsfeld memorandum, "Subject: Thoughts on Meeting with the Military Analysts on April 18," April 19, 2006. Viewed by author.

602   a discussion of "modern war": Rumsfeld memorandum to Latimer, April 19, 2006. Viewed by author.

603   "Today's warfighters are": Rumsfeld speech to graduating cadets at the Virginia Military Institute, May 16, 2006.

603   "Put simply, the failed strategies": Richard Holbrooke, "Behind the Military Revolt," *Washington Post*, April 16, 2006.

603   "Rumsfeld was in the crosshairs": Card interview, January 11, 2008.

604   "He'd be behind": Interview with a retired general, April 5, 2007.

604   at a strategy session: Among those present at the evening meeting, which took place in the White House Yellow Oval Room, were Dan Bartlett, Karl Rove, Josh Bolten, Andy Card, Condoleezza Rice, Steve Hadley, Ken Mehlman, Karen Hughes, Margaret Spellings, and Ed Gillespie. Only three (Bartlett, Hadley, and Rove) argued for keeping Rumsfeld, at least for the time being, according to interviews with two participants. The meeting was first reported in Draper, *Dead Certain*, 398.

604   "Seems to me that": Rumsfeld memorandum to Di Rita, Rangel, and Dorrance Smith, "Subject: Rebuttal," February 6, 2006. Viewed by author.

605   "That is utter nonsense": Rumsfeld memorandum to Smith, "Subject: A Better Presentation to Allegations of 'No Plan,'" March 10, 2006. Viewed by author.

605   a "point-by-point analysis": Rumsfeld memorandum to Smith, "Subject: Response to Clarence Page and *Washington Times*," April 10, 2006. Viewed by author.

606   "Both required our nation": Rumsfeld speech at the Harry S. Truman Presidential Library, Independence, Missouri, March 2, 2006.

607   "were designed at a time": Rumsfeld paper, "Illustrative New 21st Century Institutions and Approaches," April 21, 2006. A May 1, 2006, version was obtained by Bob Woodward and excerpted in the *Washington Post* on October 8, 2006.

609   a clash over efforts: Glenn Kessler and Bradley Graham, "Rice's Rebuilding Plan Hits Snags," *Washington Post*, January 15, 2006; Bradley Graham and Glenn Kessler, "Iraq Security for U.S. Teams Uncertain," *Washington Post*, March 3, 2006; Bradley Graham, "Military to Protect U.S. Aid Teams in Iraq," *Washington Post*, April 14, 2006.

610   "He felt this was State": Casey interview, April 14, 2007.

611   Even more difficult: Woodward, *State of Denial*, 440–443.

612   "It didn't do us any good": Casey interview, April 14, 2007.

612   "There were a lot of": Crouch interview, October 24, 2007.

613   "tactical errors, thousands of them": Joel Brinkley, "Rice, in England, Concedes U.S. 'Tactical Errors' in Iraq," *New York Times*, April 1, 2006.

613   Rumsfeld was incensed: Di Rita interview, May 26, 2006.

613   "I don't know what": Rumsfeld interview with Scott Hennen, WDAY Radio, Fargo, ND, April 4, 2006.

613   looked tense and impatient: Glenn Kessler, *The Confidante: Condoleezza Rice and the Creation of the Bush Legacy* (New York: St. Martin's, 2007), 179–180; Bumiller, *Condoleezza Rice*, 287–288.

614   "Excuse me": Casey interview, October 14, 2007.

614   "My apologies to you": Rumsfeld memorandum to Casey with copy to Pace, "Subject: Comments in This Morning's NSC," May 26, 2006. Viewed by author. Also cited in Woodward, *War Within*, 53.

615   He said the State Department: Zelikow interview, April 15, 2008.

616   "I think in the end": Hadley interview, April 17, 2008.

616   "Iraq is a typical": Interview with James Jeffrey, May 10, 2008.

617   "Rumsfeld completely took": Jim Jones interview, May 10, 2007.

617   "While there is no evidence": Abizaid memorandum to Rumsfeld, "Subject: Iranian Involvement in Anti-Coalition Violence in Iraq," May 8, 2006. Viewed by author.

618   But Rice had managed: Kessler, *Confidante*, 197; Bumiller, *Condoleezza Rice*, 290.

618   told him not to worry: Edelman interview, October 29, 2007.

619   a "noticeable increase": Casey news conference, June 22, 2006.

619   "The rhetoric was increasing": Abizaid interview, July 20, 2007.

619   "It was sort of iterative": Interview with a senior military officer, April 4, 2007.

620   "Every time he'd hit": Di Rita interview, May 26, 2006.

621   "There were times when": Abizaid interview, July 20, 2007.

621   "He knew there was": Edelman interview, September 24, 2007.

621   "What are you guys doing": Edelman interview, September 24, 2007.

622   "The diversity of violent groups": "Strategic Assessment: Camp David Briefing," June 12, 2006. Briefing slides viewed by author.

623   "It was the same story": O'Sullivan interview, July 17, 2008.

623   "massive effort to improve": Zelikow interview, April 15, 2008; also cited in Michael R. Gordon, "Troop 'Surge' Took Place Amid Doubt and Debate," *New York Times*, August 30, 2008.

623   "selective counterinsurgency": Zelikow interview, April 15, 2008.

624   "I made strong arguments": Chiarelli interview, December 20, 2007.

624   "I said, 'Okay, does": Casey interview, October 14, 2007.

624   Casey proposed sending: Casey briefing at the Pentagon, "Iraq Update and the Way Ahead: Tank Update," June 21, 2006. Briefing slides viewed by author. Also cited in Michael R. Gordon, "Top U.S. General in Iraq Outlines Sharp Troop Cut," *New York Times*, June 25, 2006.

624   Casey outlined how: Casey briefing to Rumsfeld, "Iraq Update: SECDEF," June 21, 2006. Briefing slides viewed by author.

626   Chiarelli urged Casey: Chiarelli interview, December 20, 2007; also cited in Linda Robinson, *Tell Me How This Ends: General David Petraeus and the Search for a Way Out of Iraq* (New York: PublicAffairs, 2008), 17; Woodward, *War Within*, 65.

626   "We have to do a better job": Rumsfeld memorandum to Casey with copies to Abizaid and Pace, "Subject: Decision on Stryker Brigade," August 2, 2006. Viewed by author. Also cited in Woodward, *War Within*, 66.

626   "The question came up frequently": Rumsfeld memorandum to Pace with copies to Schoomaker, Abizaid, and Casey, "Subject: 172nd Stryker Brigade," August 26, 2006.

627   "I called up Don Rumsfeld": Hadley interview, April 17, 2008.

627   "Our strategy is the best": Summary of July 22, 2006, meeting prepared by Meghan O'Sullivan and sent to Rumsfeld by Hadley on August 12, 2006. Viewed by author.

628   "The Cold War lasted": Rumsfeld testimony before the Senate Armed Services Committee, August 3, 2006.

628   a "clear way forward": Woodward, *War Within*, 89; Bumiller, *Condoleezza Rice*, 299.

Chapter 18: Not Well Enough or Fast Enough

631   "There is not a single": Senator Jack Reed, Senate Armed Services Committee hearing, August 3, 2006.

632   "hand-to-mouth": Joint statement by Representatives David R. Obey and John Murtha, September 13, 2006.

632   Publicly, Rumsfeld maintained: Rumsfeld testimony before the Senate Armed Services Committee, August 3, 2006.

633   he indicated to Rumsfeld: Szemborski interview, May 29, 2007.

633   "South of Pete Schoomaker": Interview with David Chu, January 16, 2008.

634   "So, Jim, *Hamdan v. Rumsfeld*": Interview with Charles "Cully" Stimson, November 27, 2007.

635   Rice pressed Bush: Dafna Linzer and Glenn Kessler, "Decision to Move Detainees Resolved Two-Year Debate Among Bush Advisors," *Washington Post*, September 8, 2006.

636   "I'm reluctant to be here": Keane interview, February 29, 2008. Accounts of the meeting between Keane, Rumsfeld, and Pace also appear in Woodward, *War Within*, 129–138, and Thomas E. Ricks, *The Gamble: General Petraeus and the American Military Adventure in Iraq, 2006–2008* (New York: Penguin, 2009), 88–91.

640   "He must have said": Edelman interview, September 24, 2007.

642   "You know, Mr. Secretary": Edelman interview, September 24, 2007.

644   "They're going to send us": Lamm interview, June 12, 2007.

644   "Afghanistan writ large": Interview with Mary Beth Long, October 26, 2007.

645   continued to assert: See, for instance, Rumsfeld and Casey news conference on October 11, 2006.

646   "simply drifting sideways": Anne Plummer Flaherty, "Sen. Warner Casts Dismal View of Iraq," *Associated Press*, October 5, 2006.

647   "benchmarks and projections": Rumsfeld memorandum to Pace and Edelman, "A New Construct for Iraq—Establish a public plan (benchmarks) to turn over any responsibility for governance and security to the Iraqis and thereby permit a reduction of Coalition forces," October 10, 2006. Viewed by author. Also cited in Woodward, *War Within*, 169.

647   "It's their country": Rumsfeld news conference, October 20, 2006.

648   "It might be best": Adelman interview, March 6, 2007. Accounts of the meeting between Rumsfeld and Adelman also cited in Jeffrey Goldberg, "The End of the Affair," *The New Yorker*, November 20, 2006, and Woodward, *War Within*, 147–151.

650   Herbits had publicly come: Stephen Herbits, letter to the editor, *Washington Times*, April 30, 2006.

650   "I think Rumsfeld's behavior": Herbits interview, February 27, 2007.

650   "Did we love our friendship": Joyce Rumsfeld interview, April 23, 2007.

651   "Unfortunately, as a result": Renuart interview, March 12, 2007.

651   "a major adjustment": Michael R. Gordon and David S. Cloud, "Rumsfeld Memo Proposed 'Major Adjustment' in Iraq," *New York Times*, December 3, 2006.

652   spoke glowingly of him: Draper, *Dead Certain*, 399.

652   Rice also enthusiastically: Bumiller, *Condoleezza Rice*, 300–301; Woodward, *War Within*, 197.

653   "He was quiet and reserved": Interview with Margaret Robson, August 28, 2007.

654   "We must have briefed him": Edelman interview, June 18, 2007.

654   "To the extent possible": Rumsfeld speech at Kansas State University, Landon Lecture, November 9, 2006.

655   "And as we know, change is hard": Rumsfeld speech to the Philadelphia Union League Club, Gold Medal Award Ceremony, December 1, 2006.

655   "He was torn initially": Rodman interview, March 14, 2008.

656   "The more troops you have": Rumsfeld interview with Cal Thomas of Fox *News Watch*, December 7, 2006.

656   "I wish I could say": Rumsfeld town hall meeting at the Pentagon, December 8, 2006.

658   received a rousing ovation: Rumsfeld town hall meeting in Mosul, December 10, 2006.

658   "He gave me the letter": Grimsley interview, December 12, 2006.

658   "He was a little reflective": Interview with General Michael "Buzz" Moseley, July 2, 2007.

659   "He has had many opportunities": General (retired) Richard Myers remarks, introducing Rumsfeld at Kansas State University, November 9, 2006.

659   "I told him that I wished": Moseley interview, July 2, 2007.

660   "We had a pretty direct conversation": Jim Jones interview, May 10, 2007.

662   "Ours is a world": Rumsfeld speech at farewell parade, December 15, 2006.

662   "The blizzard is over!": "Rumsfeld Declares End to Memo 'Blizzard,'" *Associated Press*, December 15, 2006.

Epilogue

664   the worst defense secretary: Associated Press, "McCain Blasts Rumsfeld for War," *Philadelphia Inquirer*, February 20, 2007.

664   "He's extraordinarily resilient": Carlucci interview, February 22, 2007.

664   "I have a friend who": Robson interview, August 28, 2007.

665   "Don Rumsfeld is a throwback": Cambone interview, February 1, 2007.

666   The new trust: Bradley Graham, "Rumsfeld Foundation to Encourage Public Service," *Washington Post*, September 17, 2007.

667   "It changed my life dramatically": Edelman interview, October 29, 2007.

668   "The press is not the enemy": David S. Cloud, "At Pentagon, a New Personality Faces the Same Tough Calls," *New York Times*, December 22, 2006.

669   "Gates said several times": Ryan Henry interview, March 24, 2007.

669   "I would tell him": Feith interview, March 15, 2007.

669   "There has in fact been": Interview with a former senior defense official, September 28, 2006.

670   "Ours is also a world": Rumsfeld speech at farewell parade, December 15, 2006.

670   "People said there's no way": Donald Rumsfeld interview, November 19, 2008.

671   "It's my belief that": Card interview, January 11, 2008.

673   "It wasn't a question of": Hix interview, October 31, 2007.

673   scored Rumsfeld low: Schlesinger interview, March 15, 2007.

674   he contends that the strategy: Donald Rumsfeld, "One Surge Does Not Fit All," *New York Times*, November 23, 2008.

674   "Oh, that's the favorite": Donald Rumsfeld interview, November 19, 2008.

675   "The military was a full-blown": Interview with Michael Vickers, November 22, 2006.

676   "I liked his style": Cheney interview, December 24, 2007.

676   "He wielded a courageous": Feith, *War and Decision*, 509.

676   "He had no patience": Rochester interview, June 11, 2008.

677   "I'm not an apologist": Pace appearance in a panel discussion, "Role of Military and Intelligence in National Security," sponsored by the Panetta Institute in Monterey, California, May 9, 2008.

677   "He's just a very demanding leader": Pace interview, July 8, 2008.

677   "Unfortunately, he was not collaborative": Abizaid interview, February 2, 2007.

677   "When he grew frustrated": Card interview, January 11, 2008.

677   "He's a very complicated guy": Abizaid interview, February 2, 2007.

678   "People in uniform resisted": Donald Rumsfeld interview, November 19, 2008.

679   "I refer to him as": Roche interview, January 17, 2007.

680   "Maybe he was better before": Adelman interview, November 16, 2006. Similar quotations in Goldberg, "The End of the Affair."

681   "On decisions he was very wary": Gebhard interview, January 16, 2007.

681   "I think he's a man who": Hamre interview, October 2, 2007.

681   "I look at him as a tragic hero": Interview with a former senior Pentagon official, March 7, 2008.

Bibliography

Books

Bensahel, Nora, et al. *After Saddam: Prewar Planning and the Occupation of Iraq.* Santa Monica, CA: Rand Arroyo Center, 2008.

Blaker, James R. *Transforming Military Force: The Legacy of Arthur Cebrowski and Network Centric Warfare.* Westport, CT: Praeger Security International, 2007.

Bloomfield, Lincoln P. Jr. "Politics and Diplomacy of the Global Defense Posture Review." In *Reposturing the Force: U.S. Overseas Presence in the Twenty-first Century.* Edited by Carnes Lord. Newport, RI: Naval War College Newport Paper, 2006.

Bolton, John R. *Surrender Is Not an Option: Defending America at the United Nations and Abroad.* New York: Threshold Editions, 2007.

Bremer, L. Paul III, with Malcolm McConnell. *My Year in Iraq: The Struggle to Build a Future of Hope.* New York: Simon & Schuster, 2006.

Brinkley, Douglas. *The Great Deluge: Hurricane Katrina, New Orleans, and the Mississippi Gulf Coast.* New York: Morrow, 2006.

Buesing, Wolfgang. *The Buesing at Ofen: History of an Oldenburg Family and Its Farm.* Oldenburg, 1960. Translated into English in Donald Rumsfeld's personal files.

Bumiller, Elisabeth. *Condoleezza Rice: An American Life.* New York: Random House, 2007.

Bush, George, with Victor Gold. *Looking Forward.* Garden City, NY: Doubleday, 1987.

Cannon, James M. *Time and Chance: Gerald Ford's Appointment with History.* New York: HarperCollins, 1994.

Carroll, James. *House of War: The Pentagon and the Disastrous Rise of American Power.* Boston: Houghton Mifflin, 2006.

Chandrasekaran, Rajiv. *Imperial Life in the Emerald City: Inside Iraq's Green Zone.* New York: Knopf, 2006.

Clarke, Richard A. *Against All Enemies: Inside America's War on Terror.* New York: Free Press, 2004.

Clarke, Torie. *Lipstick on a Pig: Winning in the No-Spin Era by Someone Who Knows the Game.* New York: Free Press, 2006.

Cleveland, James C. *We Propose: A Modern Congress.* New York: McGraw-Hill, 1966.

Cockburn, Andrew. *Rumsfeld: His Rise, Fall, and Catastrophic Legacy.* New York: Scribner, 2007.

Cohen, Eliot A. *Supreme Command: Soldiers, Statesmen, and Leadership in Wartime.* New York: Free Press, 2002.

Creed, Patrick, and Rick Newman. *Firefight: Inside the Battle to Save the Pentagon on 9/11.* New York: Presidio/Ballantine, 2008.

Decter, Midge. *Rumsfeld: A Personal Portrait.* New York: Regan, 2003.

DeYoung, Karen. *Soldier: The Life of Colin Powell.* New York: Knopf, 2006.

Dickinson, Lora Townsend. *The Story of Winnetka.* Winnetka, IL: Winnetka Historical Society, 1956.

Donnelly, William M. *Transforming an Army at War: Designing the Modular Force, 1991–2005.* Washington, DC: Center of Military History, U.S. Army, 2007.

Draper, Robert. *Dead Certain: The Presidency of George W. Bush.* New York: Free Press, 2007.

Ehrlichman, John. *Witness to Power: The Nixon Years.* New York: Simon & Schuster, 1982.

Fallows, James M. *Blind into Baghdad: America's War in Iraq.* New York: Vintage, 2006.

Feith, Douglas J. *War and Decision: Inside the Pentagon at the Dawn of the War on Terrorism.* New York: Harper, 2008.

Ferguson, Charles H. *No End in Sight: Iraq's Descent into Chaos.* New York: PublicAffairs, 2008.

Firestone, Bernard J., and Alexej Ugrinsky, eds. *Gerald R. Ford and the Politics of Post-Watergate America.* Westport, CT: Greenwood, 1993.

Fontenot, Gregory, E. J. Degen, and David Tohn. *On Point: The United States Army in Operation Iraqi Freedom.* AUSA Institute of Land Warfare book. Annapolis, MD: Naval Institute Press, 2005.

Ford, Gerald R. *A Time to Heal: The Autobiography of Gerald R. Ford.* New York: Harper & Row, 1979.

Franks, Tommy. *American Soldier.* New York: Regan, 2004.

Galbraith, Peter. *The End of Iraq: How American Incompetence Created a War Without End.* New York: Simon & Schuster, 2006.

Gellman, Barton. *Angler: The Cheney Vice Presidency*. New York: Penguin, 2008.

Goldsmith, Jack L. *The Terror Presidency: Law and Judgment Inside the Bush Administration*. New York: Norton, 2007.

Gordon, Michael R., and Bernard E. Trainor. *Cobra II: The Inside Story of the Invasion and Occupation of Iraq*. New York: Pantheon, 2006.

Graham, Bradley. *Hit to Kill: The New Battle Over Shielding America from Missile Attack*. New York: PublicAffairs, 2001.

Grayson, C. Jackson, and Louis Neeb. *Confessions of a Price Controller*. Homewood, IL: Dow Jones-Irwin, 1974.

Greenberg, Karen J., and Joshua L. Dratel. *The Torture Papers: The Road to Abu Ghraib*. New York: Cambridge University Press, 2005.

Haldeman, H. R. *The Haldeman Diaries: Inside the Nixon White House*. New York: Putnam's, 1994.

Harnsberger, Caroline Thomas. *Winnetka: The Biography of a Village*. Evanston, IL: Schori, 1977.

Hartmann, Robert T. *Palace Politics: An Inside Account of the Ford Years*. New York: McGraw-Hill, 1980.

Hashim, Ahmed. *Insurgency and Counter-Insurgency in Iraq*. Crises in World Politics. Ithaca, NY: Cornell University Press, 2006.

Hayes, Stephen F. *Cheney: The Untold Story of America's Most Powerful and Controversial Vice President*. New York: HarperCollins, 2007.

Heilbrunn, Jacob. *They Knew They Were Right: The Rise of the Neocons*. New York: Doubleday, 2008.

Hersey, John. *The President*. New York: Knopf, 1975.

Herspring, Dale R. *The Pentagon and the Presidency: Civil-Military Relations from FDR to George W. Bush*. Lawrence: University Press of Kansas, 2005.

Holloway, James L. *Aircraft Carriers at War: A Personal Retrospective of Korea, Vietnam, and the Soviet Confrontation*. Annapolis, MD: Naval Institute Press, 2007.

Ikle, Fred Charles. *Every War Must End*. New York: Columbia University Press, 2005.

Isikoff, Michael, and David Corn. *Hubris: The Inside Story of Spin, Scandal, and the Selling of the Iraq War*. New York: Crown, 2006.

Karabel, Jerome. *The Chosen: The Hidden History of Admission and Exclusion at Harvard, Yale, and Princeton*. Boston: Houghton Mifflin Harcourt, 2005.

Kernell, Samuel, and Samuel L. Popkin, eds. *Chief of Staff: Twenty-five Years of Managing the Presidency*. Berkeley: University of California Press, 1986.

Kessler, Glenn. *The Confidante: Condoleezza Rice and the Creation of the Bush Legacy*. New York: St. Martin's, 2007.

Kettl, Donald F. *Team Bush: Leadership Lessons from the Bush White House*. New York: McGraw-Hill, 2003.

Kissinger, Henry. *Years of Renewal*. New York: Simon & Schuster, 1999.

Kitfield, James. *War and Destiny: How the Bush Revolution in Foreign and Military Affairs Redefined American Power*. Washington, DC: Potomac, 2006.

Krames, Jeffrey A. *The Rumsfeld Way: Leadership Wisdom of a Battle-hardened Maverick*. New York: McGraw-Hill, 2003.

Krepinevich, Andrew F. *An Army at the Crossroads*. Washington, DC: Center for Strategic and Budgetary Assessments, 2008.

Ladd, Bruce. *Crisis in Credibility*. New York: New American Library, 1968.

Leamer, Laurence. *Playing for Keeps in Washington*. New York: Dial, 1977.

Mabry, Marcus. *Twice As Good: Condoleezza Rice and Her Path to Power*. New York: Modern Times, 2007.

Mann, James. *Rise of the Vulcans: The History of Bush's War Cabinet*. New York: Viking, 2004.

Mayer, Jane. *Dark Side: The Inside Story of How the War on Terror Turned into a War on American Ideals*. New York: Doubleday, 2008.

McCann, Joseph E. *Sweet Success: How NutraSweet Created a Billion Dollar Business*. Homewood, IL: Business One Irwin, 1990.

McClellan, Scott. *What Happened: Inside the Bush White House and Washington's Culture of Deception*. New York: PublicAffairs, 2008.

McNamara, Robert S., with Brian VanDeMark. *In Retrospect: The Tragedy and Lessons of Vietnam*. New York: Times Books, 1995.

Medved, Michael. *The Shadow Presidents: The Secret History of the Chief Executives and Their Top Aides*. New York: Times Books, 1979.

Mount, Graeme S., with Mark Gauthier. *895 Days That Changed the World: The Presidency of Gerald R. Ford*. Montreal: Black Rose, 2006.

Nagl, John A. *Learning to Eat Soup with a Knife: Counterinsurgency Lessons from Malaya and Vietnam*. Chicago: University of Chicago Press, 2005.

National Commission on Terrorist Attacks upon the United States. *The 9/11 Commission Report: Final Report of the National Commission on Terrorist Attacks upon the United States*. New York: Norton, 2004.

Naylor, Sean. *Not a Good Day to Die: The Untold Story of Operation Anaconda*. New York: Berkley, 2005.

Nessen, Ron. *It Sure Looks Different from the Inside*. Chicago: Playboy Press, 1978.

Osborne, John. *White House Watch: The Ford Years*. Washington, DC: New Republic Book Co., 1977.

Packer, George. *The Assassins' Gate: America in Iraq*. New York: Farrar, Straus & Giroux, 2005.

Peabody, Robert L. *Leadership in Congress: Stability, Succession, and Change*. Boston: Little, Brown, 1976.

Ratner, Michael. *The Trial of Donald Rumsfeld: A Prosecution by Book*. New York: New Press, 2008.

Reeves, Richard. *President Nixon: Alone in the White House*. New York: Simon & Schuster, 2001.

Remini, Robert Vincent. *The House: The History of the House of Representatives*. New York: Smithsonian Books/HarperCollins, 2006.

Ricks, Thomas E. *Fiasco: The American Military Adventure in Iraq*. New York: Penguin, 2006.

———. *The Gamble: General David Petraeus and the American Military Adventure in Iraq, 2006–2008*. New York: Penguin, 2009.

Robinson, Linda. *Tell Me How This Ends: General David Petraeus and the Search for a Way Out of Iraq*. New York: PublicAffairs, 2008.

Rodman, Peter W. *Presidential Command: Power, Leadership, and the Making of Foreign Policy from Richard Nixon to George W. Bush*. New York: Knopf, 2009.

Rothstein, Hy S. *Afghanistan and the Troubled Future of Unconventional Warfare*. Annapolis, MD: Naval Institute Press, 2006.

Rumsfeld, Donald. Foreword to *The All-Volunteer Force: Thirty Years of Service*. Edited by Barbara A. Bicksler, Curtis L. Gilroy, and John T. Warner. Dulles, VA: Brassey's, 2004.

Sanchez, Ricardo S., with Don T. Phillips. *Wiser in Battle: A Soldier's Story*. New York: HarperCollins, 2008.

Scarborough, Rowan. *Rumsfeld's War: The Untold Story of America's Anti-Terrorist Commander*. Washington, DC: Regnery, 2004.

Schelling, Thomas C. Foreword to *Pearl Harbor: Warning and Decision*, by Roberta Wohlstetter. Stanford, CA: Stanford University Press, 1962.

Seely, Hart, and Donald Rumsfeld. *Pieces of Intelligence: The Existential Poetry of Donald H. Rumsfeld*. New York: Free Press, 2003.

Shapley, Deborah. *Promise and Power: The Life and Times of Robert McNamara*. Boston: Little, Brown, 1993.

Shultz, George Pratt. *Turmoil and Triumph: My Years as Secretary of State*. New York: Scribner's/Maxwell Macmillan International, 1993.

Stevenson, Charles A. *SECDEF: The Nearly Impossible Job of Secretary of Defense*. Washington, DC: Potomac, 2006.

Suskind, Ron. *The One Percent Doctrine: Deep Inside America's Pursuit of Its Enemies Since 9/11*. New York: Simon & Schuster, 2006.

———. *The Way of the World: A Story of Truth and Hope in an Age of Extremism*. New York: Harper, 2008.

Talbott, Strobe. *The Master of the Game: Paul Nitze and the Nuclear Peace*. New York: Knopf, 1988.

Teicher, Howard, and Gayle Radley Teicher. *Twin Pillars to Desert Storm: America's Flawed Vision in the Middle East from Nixon to Bush*. New York: Morrow, 1993.

Tenet, George. *At the Center of the Storm*. New York: HarperCollins, 2007.

Trask, Roger R., and Alfred Goldberg. *The Department of Defense, 1947–1997: Organization and Office*. Washington, DC: Office of the Secretary of Defense, 1997.

Werth, Barry. *31 Days: The Crisis That Gave Us the Government We Have Today*. New York: Nan A. Talese/Doubleday, 2006.

West, Bing. *No True Glory: A Frontline Account of the Battle for Fallujah*. New York: Bantam, 2005.

———. *The Strongest Tribe: War, Politics, and the Endgame in Iraq*. New York: Random House, 2008.

Woodward, Bob. *The Choice*. New York: Simon & Schuster, 1996.

———. *Bush at War*. New York: Simon & Schuster, 2002.

———. *Plan of Attack*. New York: Simon & Schuster, 2004.

———. *State of Denial*. New York: Simon & Schuster, 2006.

————. *The War Within: A Secret White House History, 2006–2008*. New York: Simon & Schuster, 2008.

Wright, Donald P., and Timothy R. Reese. *On Point II: Transition to the New Campaign: The United States Army in Operation Iraqi Freedom, May 2003–January 2005*. Fort Leavenworth, KS: US Army Combined Arms Center, 2008.

Articles

Abramson, Rudy. "Rumsfeld: Achiever Seeking Challenges." *Los Angeles Times*, November 4, 1975.

Adelman, Ken. "Stop Reviewing; Start Reforming." *Wall Street Journal*, July 13, 2001.

————. "Cakewalk in Iraq." *Washington Post*, February 13, 2002.

Apple, R. W. Jr. "A Military Quagmire Remembered: Afghanistan as Vietnam." *New York Times*, October 31, 2001.

Arkin, William. "Shadow Government." *Washington Post*, June 4, 2006.

Associated Press. "6 in GOP Criticize U.S. Space Program." *New York Times*, July 28, 1963.

————. "Rumsfeld Declares End to Memo 'Blizzard.'" *Washington Post*, December 15, 2006.

————. "McCain Blasts Rumsfeld for War." *Philadelphia Inquirer*, February 20, 2007.

Atkinson, Rick. "General: A Longer War Likely." *Washington Post*, March 28, 2003.

Bachrach, Judy. "Silent Choreographer of White House Ballet." *Washington Post*, December 22, 1974.

Barnes, Fred. "The Rumsfeld Factor." *Weekly Standard*, August 5, 1996.

Barnes, Julian E. "Influence of Joint Chiefs Starting to Rebound." *Los Angeles Times*, February 18, 2007.

Barnes, Julian E., and Peter Spiegel. "A Pentagon Battle over the Next War." *Los Angeles Times*, July 21, 2008.

Barstow, David. "Behind TV Analysts, Pentagon's Hidden Hand." *New York Times*, April 20, 2008.

Batiste, John. "A Case for Accountability." *Washington Post*, April 19, 2006.

Beckman, Aldo. "Rumsfeld Won't Give Up Efforts to Reform Procedures in House." *Chicago Tribune*, September 15, 1968.

————. "Rumsfeld's Chipper, the Future's Vague." *Chicago Tribune*, June 30, 1974.

Berger, Marilyn. "Battle Looms on GIs in Europe." *Washington Post*, July 9, 1973.

Bernstein, Mark F. "Rumsfeld's Princeton." *Princeton Alumni Weekly*, October 6, 2004.

Binder, David. "Nation's New Defense Chief: Donald Henry Rumsfeld." *New York Times*, November 4, 1975.

Boyer, Peter J. "Downfall." *New Yorker*, November 20, 2006.

Bravin, Jess. "Divisions Persist on Detainee Policy." *Wall Street Journal*, July 12, 2006.

Bremer, L. Paul III. "Facts for Feith." *National Review Online*, March 19, 2008.

———. "Iraq's Path to Sovereignty." *Washington Post*, September 8, 2003.

Broder, David. "Rumsfeld Says New Job Rounds Out Education." *Washington Post*, December 5, 1972.

———. "The Danger of Holdovers." *Washington Post*, December 4, 2008.

Burgess, John. "Tuning In to a Trophy Technology." *Washington Post*, March 24, 1992.

Cannon, Lou. "Rumsfeld: Silent Architect." *Washington Post*, November 4, 1975.

Chapman, Stephen. "Can Rumsfeld Add Another Line to a Strong Resume?" *Chicago Tribune*, February 15, 1987.

Chesser, Thomas M. "It Was Tough Medicine, but G.D. Searle Breathes Easier Now." *New York Times*, January 31, 1982.

Chicago Daily Tribune. "Candidate to Shake Hands for Four Days," March 19, 1962.

Chicago Sun-Times. "Rumsfeld for Congress," editorial, January 27, 1962.

Chicago Sun-Times. "The Evidence," editorial, March 9, 1962.

Chicago Sun-Times. "Burks Remembers Signing Checks," March 21, 1962.

Chicago Tribune. "4.5 Million Noise Fund," March 11, 1964.

Chicago Tribune. "Dems Desert in New Bid for Space Center," March 26, 1964.

Chicago Tribune. "Editors Told White House Seeks Secrecy," February 22, 1966.

Chicago Tribune. "War in Viet Hit by Rumsfeld," April 13, 1966.

Chicago Tribune. "G.O.P. Team Calmly Views Dem Struggle," August 28, 1968.

Cloud, David S. "Afghan Warlords Slowly Come in from the Cold." *Wall Street Journal*, March 14, 2005.

———. "Pentagon Review Calls for No Big Changes." *New York Times*, February 2, 2006.

———. "U.S. to Hand Iraq a New Timetable on Security Role." *New York Times*, October 22, 2006.

———. "At Pentagon, A New Personality Faces the Same Tough Calls." *New York Times*, December 22, 2006.

Cloud, David S., and Mark Mazzetti. "Prewar Intelligence Unit at Pentagon is Criticized." *New York Times*, February 9, 2007.

Coates, James. "Rumsfeld Curtails Trips to Key States." *Chicago Tribune*, October 14, 1976.

Constable, Pamela. "Afghans' Goals Facing Renewed Threats." *Washington Post*, September 8, 2003.

Crawford, Clare. "For Man-in-Motion Donald Rumsfeld, the Talk Is About Vice-President." *People*, April 19, 1976.

Crock, Stan. "Why the Hawks Are Carpet-Bombing Rumsfeld." *BusinessWeek*, August 6, 2001.

Dao, James. "Skeptical Senators Question Rumsfeld on Missile Defense." *New York Times*, June 22, 2001.

———. "Much Maligned B-1 Bomber Proves Hard to Kill." *New York Times*, August 1, 2001.

———. "A Low-Key Space Buff: Richard Bowman Myers." *New York Times*, August 25, 2001.

Dao, James, and Eric Schmitt. "Pentagon Readies Effort to Sway Sentiment Abroad." *New York Times*, February 20, 2002.

Daragahi, Borzou, and Mark Mazzetti. "U.S. Military Covertly Pays to Run Stories in Iraqi Press." *Los Angeles Times*, November 30, 2005.

Donnelly, John. "A Transformer in Disguise." *Weekly Standard*, June 23, 2008.

Dos Passos, John. "Americans Are Losing the Victory in Europe." *Life*, January 7, 1946.

Duffy, Michael. "Rumsfeld: Older but Wiser." *Time*, August 27, 2001.

Dwyer, Jim. "A Gulf Commander Sees a Longer Road." *New York Times*, March 28, 2003.

Edwards, Willard. "Freshman Rep. Rumsfeld: A Space Expert." *Chicago Tribune*, August 18, 1963.

Evans, Rowland, and Peter Novak. "The December Caucus." *Washington Post*, November 30, 1964.

———. "Nixon's Plans to Replace Bliss Hint Changing Times." *Los Angeles Times*, November 28, 1968.

———. "The Rumsfeld Influence." *Washington Post*, January 29, 1976.

Finney, John W. "House Votes $5.19 Billion Authorization for Space." *New York Times*, March 26, 1964.

———. "52 in House Seek a Congress Study of Policy on War." *New York Times*, September 26, 1967.

———. "Uncertain Pentagon Asks What Rumsfeld's Policy Is." *New York Times*, November 5, 1975.

———. "Long-Term Rise in 'Real' Outlay Projected with No Cut in Forces." *New York Times*, January 22, 1976.

———. "Rumsfeld Calls for More Funds, Citing Increasing Soviet Power." *New York Times*, January 27, 1976.

———. "Defense Officials Censured for Rockwell Lodge Visits." *New York Times*, March 17, 1976.

———. "Furor over Missile Decision Reflected Pitfalls of Policy-Making Jobs in the Pentagon." *New York Times*, April 5, 1976.

———. "Defense Policy Debate." *New York Times*, April 6, 1976.

———. "Rumsfeld Clears Pentagon Aide of Conflict of Interest in Missile Program, Eagleton Charges a 'Whitewash.'" *New York Times*, June 9, 1976.

———. "Aid to Contractor by Currie Reported." *New York Times*, October 15, 1976.

———. "Ford and Rumsfeld Endorse Brown to Continue as Head of Joint Chiefs of Staff." *New York Times*, October 19, 1976.

Firestone, David. "Senior House Democrats Urge Top Defense Hands to Resign." *New York Times*, September 6, 2003.

Flaherty, Anne Plummer. "Sen. Warner Casts Dismal View of Iraq." *Associated Press*, October 5, 2006.

Fortune. "The Ten Toughest Bosses," April 21, 1980.

Fortune. "How a High-Tech Bet Paid Off Big," November 1, 1993.

Gelb, Leslie H. "U.S. Jets for Israel Took Route Around Some Allies' Position." *New York Times*, October 31, 1973.

———. "Successor Haig: Donald Rumsfeld." *New York Times*, September 25, 1974.

Gellman, Bart. "Secret Unit Expands Rumsfeld's Domain." *Washington Post*, January 23, 2005.

Gold, Jacqueline S. "Deal of the Decade." *Financial World*, September 1, 1992.

Goldberg, Jeffrey. "The End of the Affair." *New Yorker*, November 20, 2006.

Golden, Tim. "Detainee Memo Created Divide in White House." *New York Times*, October 1, 2006.

Golden, Tim, and Eric Schmitt. "Detainee Policy Sharply Divides Bush Officials." *New York Times*, November 2, 2005.

Gordon, Gregory. "Did Searle Ignore Early Warning Signs?" *United Press International*, October 13, 1987.

Gordon, Michael R. "A New Doctrine's Test." *New York Times*, April 1, 2003.

———. "Top U.S. General in Iraq Outlines Sharp Troop Cut." *New York Times*, June 25, 2006.

Gordon, Michael R. "Troop 'Surge' Took Place Amid Doubt and Debate." *New York Times*, August 30, 2008.

Gordon, Michael R., and David S. Cloud. "Rumsfeld Memo Proposed 'Major Adjustment' in Iraq." *New York Times*, December 3, 2006.

Gorman, Siobhan. "Imagery Intelligence Agency Chief Being Forced from Post." *Baltimore Sun*, January 6, 2006.

Graham, Bradley. "Iran, North Korea Missile Gains Spur Warning." *Washington Post*, July 16, 1998.

———. "Some Seek Broad, External Inquiry on Prisoner Abuse." *Washington Post*, May 27, 2004.

———. "U.S. Forces Plan Lower Profile." *Washington Post*, June 21, 2004.

———. "War Plan Drafted to Counter Terror Attacks in U.S." *Washington Post*, August 8, 2005.

———. "Pentagon Prepares to Rethink Focus on Conventional Warfare." *Washington Post*, January 25, 2005.

———. "U.S. Directive Prioritizes Post-Conflict Stability." *Washington Post*, December 1, 2005.

———. "Pentagon Can Now Fund Foreign Militaries." *Washington Post*, January 29, 2006.

———. "Military to Protect U.S. Aid Teams in Iraq." *Washington Post*, April 14, 2006.

————. "Rumsfeld Foundation to Encourage Public Service." *Washington Post*, September 17, 2007.

Graham, Bradley, and Glenn Kessler. "Iraq Security for U.S. Teams Uncertain." *Washington Post*, March 3, 2006.

Graham, Sandy. "When the Going Gets Tough at Searle, 'Snowflakes' Descend from Rumsfeld." *Wall Street Journal*, May 20, 1980.

Greenhouse, Linda. "Justice, 5–3, Broadly Reject Bush Plan to Try Detainees." *New York Times*, June 30, 2006.

Greenhouse, Steven. "Monsanto to Acquire G.D. Searle." *New York Times*, July 19, 1985.

Gruber, William. "Rumsfeld Reflects on Politics, Business." *Chicago Tribune*, October 20, 1993.

Halverson, Guy. "Pentagon Mood Joyless As Rumsfeld Sworn In." *Christian Science Monitor*, November 21, 1975.

Herbers, John. "4 Months After Nixon, His Legacy Haunts the New President." *New York Times*, December 19, 1974.

Herbits, Stephen. Letter. *Washington Times*, April 30, 2006.

Hersey, John. "The President." *New York Times*, April 20, 1975.

Hersh, Seymour M. "The Gray Zone." *New Yorker*, May 24, 2004.

————. "The Coming Wars: What the Pentagon Can Now Do in Secret." *New Yorker*, January 17, 2005.

————. "The General's Report." *New Yorker*, June 25, 2007.

Holbrooke, Richard. "Behind the Military Revolt." *Washington Post*, April 16, 2006.

Hutchinson, Louise. "Trembling on the Brink of Senate Race." *Chicago Tribune*, February 11, 1973.

Hylton, Wils S. "Dick and Don Go to War." *Esquire*, February 1, 2002.

Jarow, Peter. "Wrestling Program Boasts Storied History." *Daily Princetonian*, March 3, 2005.

Kaplan, Robert D. "What Rumsfeld Got Right." *Atlantic Monthly*, July-August 2008.

Kenworthy, E. W. "Ford Will Oppose Halleck in House." *New York Times*, December 19, 1964.

Kessler, Glenn. "Gingrich to Urge Overhaul of Powell's Department." *Washington Post*, April 22, 2003.

Kessler, Glenn, and Bradley Graham. "Rice's Rebuilding Plan Hits Snags." *Washington Post*, January 15, 2006.

Kev, Janet. "Rumsfeld Turns Searle Around with Bottom-Line Management." *Chicago Tribune*, April 1, 1981.

Kilborn, Peter T. "Weekends with the President's Men." *New York Times*, June 30, 2006.

Klein, Joe. "Saddam's Revenge." *Time*, September 18, 2005.

Krauthammer, Charles. "Have They Nothing Better to Do?" *Washington Post*, October 30, 2001.

Krepinevich, Andrew F. Jr. "How to Win in Iraq." *Foreign Affairs*, September-October 2005.

Kristol, William. "The Wrong Strategy." *Washington Post*, October 30, 2001.

Landauer, Jerry. "Some in Congress Reap Extra Expense Money on Overseas Junkets." *Wall Street Journal*, January 14, 1967.

Lane, Charles. "High Court Rejects Detainee Tribunals." *Washington Post*, June 30, 2006.

Lemann, Nicholas. "The Talk of the Town: Insurrection." *New Yorker*, September 26, 2005.

Life. Special education issue, October 16, 1950.

Linzer, Dafna, and Glenn Kessler. "Decision to Move Detainees Resolved Two-Year Debate Among Bush Advisors." *Washington Post*, September 8, 2006.

Loeb, Vernon. "Rumsfeld Faulted for Troop Dilution." *Washington Post*, March 30, 2003.

Loeb, Vernon, and Thomas E. Ricks. "Rumsfeld's Style, Goals Strain Ties in Pentagon." *Washington Post*, October 16, 2002.

Lublin, Joann. "Brash Don Rumsfeld Tries His Prescription to Turn Searle Around." *Wall Street Journal*, January 25, 1978.

MacKenzie, John P. "OEO Firings Are Called Political." *Washington Post*, November 22, 1970.

Meyerholz, Heinrich. "The Rumsfelds Came from Niedersachsen." *Old North German Families Journal*, January 1977. English translation in Donald Rumsfeld's personal files.

McC. Osborne, Trudi. "A Winnetka Boy in the War Room." *Chicago Magazine*, January 4, 1976.

McGrath, Ben. "Rummy Meets His Match." *New Yorker*, April 14, 2003.

Mendel, Richard. "The First Chrysler Bail-Out." *Washington Monthly*, February 1987.

Merry, Robert W. "Rumsfeld, with a Resume to Rival That of Bush, Prepares to Seek GOP Nomination for President." *Wall Street Journal*, May 30, 1986.

Miller, Greg. "U.S. Seeks to Rein In Its Military Spy Teams." *Los Angeles Times*, December 18, 2006.

Mohan, Margaret. "Politics Split Family." *Chicago Tribune*, September 30, 1964.

Neal, Steve. "Juices Stir for Rumsfeld." *Chicago Tribune*, April 29, 1979.

————. "Donald Rumsfeld Gets Down to the Business of Running for President." *Chicago Tribune*, January 26, 1986.

Neff, Richard. "Rumsfeld Won Respect of Nato Diplomats." *Christian Science Monitor*, September 26, 1974.

Newsweek. "King of the Castle," November 17, 1975.

New York Times. "Quality in the House," editorial, November 4, 1966.

New York Times. "Poverty Agency Chief: Donald Rumsfeld," April 22, 1969.

New York Times. "Legal Aid Director Ousted by Rumsfeld; Aide Also Dropped," November 21, 1970.

New York Times. "Misconceived Military Shuffle," August 17, 2004.

Oppel, Richard A. Jr., Eric Schmitt, and Thom Shanker. "Baghdad Bombings Raise Anew Questions About U.S. Strategy in Iraq." *New York Times*, September 17, 2005.

Osborne, John. "The President and the Poor." *New Republic*, May 24, 1969.

Otten, Allen L. "Politics and People: Rumsfeld's Rules." *Wall Street Journal*, December 9, 1976.

Pakenham, Michael. "Rep. Rumsfeld a Real Cut-up for Supporter." *Chicago Tribune*, March 11, 1963.

Perlez, Jane. "Reporters Notebook: Two Mates Clown a Bit for the Aussies." *New York Times*, July 31, 2002.

Randolph, Eleanor. "From Melons to Men, Rumsfeld's a 'Mover.'" *Chicago Tribune*, November 9, 1975.

Reuters. "Rumsfeld's Wife Sets Him Straight." *Washington Post*, August 13, 1972.

Reston, James. "Keep an Eye on 'Rummy.'" *New York Times*, October 4, 1974.

Ricks, Thomas E. "Rumsfeld, Joint Chiefs Spar Over Roles in Retooling Military." *Washington Post*, May 25, 2001.

———. "Bush Seeking Defense Increase '02 Budget Request Adds 18.4 Billion." *Washington Post*, June 23, 2001.

———. "For Rumsfeld Many Roadblocks, Miscues, and Resistance Mean Defense Review May Produce Less Than Promised." *Washington Post*, August 7, 2001.

———. "Rumsfeld's Hands-on War Afghan Campaign Shaped by Secretary's Views, Personality." *Washington Post*, December 9, 2001.

———. "Rumsfeld Rebuked by Retired Generals." *Washington Post*, April 13, 2006.

———. "Scolding Donald Rumsfeld." *Washington Post*, July 29, 2008.

Ringer, Richard. "General Instrument Moves to Pay Off Its Debt Early." *New York Times*, July 1, 1993.

Risen, James. "U.S. Should Improve Defense of Satellites, Panel Advises." *New York Times*, January 9, 2001.

Robbins, William. "Rumsfeld's Remedy for Searle." *New York Times*, March 16, 1979.

Rohde, David, and David E. Sanger. "How a 'Good War' Went Bad." *New York Times*, August 12, 2007.

Rumsfeld, Donald. "Everything's Under Control." *New York Times*, August 29, 1972.

———. "The White House Work Rules." *Washington Post*, January 23, 1977.

———. "A Politician in the Corporate World." *Fortune*, September 10, 1979.

———. "One Surge Does Not Fit All," *New York Times*, November 23, 2008.

Rutenberg, Jim. "In Farewell, Rumsfeld Warns Weakness is 'Provocative.'" *New York Times*, December 16, 2006.

Safire, William. "3 Coins in the Fountain." *New York Times*, February 19, 1987.

Sanger, David. "White House to Overhaul Iraq and Afghan Missions." *New York Times*, October 6, 2003.

Scarborough, Rowan. "Rumsfeld-McCain Feud Grew After Summer Lunch." *Washington Times*, January 10, 2005.

Scheele, Henry Z. "Prelude to the Presidency: An Examination of the Gerald R. Ford–Charles A. Halleck House Minority Leadership Contest." *Presidential Studies Quarterly* 25 (Fall 1995).

Scherer, Michael, and Mark Benjamin. "What Rumsfeld Knew." *Salon*, April 14, 2006.

Schmitt, Eric. "Talking the Talk His Own Way, by Golly." *New York Times*, June 26, 2002.

———. "Cheney Tells of Meeting Rumsfeld 35 Years Ago." *New York Times*, May 14, 2003.

———. "2,000 More M.P.'s Will Help Train the Iraqi Police." *New York Times*, January 16, 2006.

Schmitt, Eric, and Thom Shanker. "U.S. Officials Retool Slogan for Terror War." *New York Times*, July 26, 2005.

Selover, William C. "Congressmen See U.S. Aid Dollars Straying in Vietnam." *Christian Science Monitor*, August 8, 1966.

———. "Vietnam Pilfering, Graft Muzzled." *Christian Science Monitor*, August 8, 1966.

Semple, Robert B. Jr. "Rumsfeld to Head Poverty Agency." *New York Times*, April 22, 1969.

Shabecoff, Philip. "Controls at 6 Months: Inflation Rate Curbed." *New York Times*, February 14, 1972.

Shanker, Thom. "Rumsfeld Favors Forceful Actions to Foil an Attack." *New York Times*, October 14, 2002.

———. "Retired Commando Chief Is Chosen to Lead the Army." *New York Times*, June 11, 2003.

Shanker, Thom, and James Dao. "Army Digs In Its Heels and Saves Howitzer Plan, for Now." *New York Times*, May 2, 2002.

Shanker, Thom, and Eric Schmitt. "Rumsfeld Seeks Leaner Army and a Full Term." *New York Times*, May 11, 2005.

———. "Pentagon Weights Strategy to Change to Deter Terror." *New York Times*, July 5, 2005.

Sherrill, Robert. "De-escalator of the War on Poverty." *New York Times Magazine*, December 13, 1970.

Shultz, Richard H. Jr. "Showstoppers." *Weekly Standard*, January 26, 2004.

Smith, R. Jeffrey. "Tanker Inquiry Finds Rumsfeld's Attention Was Elsewhere." *Washington Post*, June 20, 2006.

Spivak, Jonathan. "New Antipoverty Chief Plays Down Militancy and Stresses Research." *Wall Street Journal*, January 7, 1970.

Stevenson, Richard W. "President Makes It Clear: Phrase Is 'War on Terror.'" *New York Times*, August 4, 2005.

Stevenson, Richard W., and Carl Hulse. "President Backs His Defense Chief in a Show of Unity." *New York Times*, May 11, 2004.

Stout, David. "Rumsfeld Bids Farewell to Pentagon." *New York Times*, December 8, 2006.

Tagge, George. "Hint Rumsfeld Is Choice of Rep. Church for House." *Chicago Daily Tribune*, February 14, 1962.

Thimmesch, Nick. "Federal Anti-Poverty Program No Smaller, on Sounder Basis." *Los Angeles Times*, June 30, 1970.

Thomas, Evan. "Rumsfeld's War." *Newsweek*, September 16, 2001.

Thomas, Cal. "For Rumsfeld, 'War on Terror' Is Misleading Label." *Chicago Tribune*, December 12, 2006, 23.

Time. "These Are My Guys," November 17, 1975.

Tyson, Ann Scott. "Rumsfeld Discusses Successes, Failures." *Washington Post*, December 9, 2006.

————. "The Curtain Is Drawn on the Rumsfeld Era." *Washington Post*, December 16, 2006.

Walsh, Edward, and Juliet Eilperin. "Gingrich Lying Low After Attack on State Dept. Leaves Some Conservatives Fuming." *Washington Post*, April 26, 2003.

Warden, Philip. "Rep. Ford Wins Halleck Job as GOP leader." *Chicago Tribune*, January 5, 1965.

Warden, Philip. "Mrs. Reid Receives Appropriations Post." *Chicago Tribune*, January 26, 1967.

Warner, Melanie. "The Lowdown on Sweet?" *New York Times*, February 12, 2006.

Warren, James. "Nixon Looked Out for Ambitious Rumsfeld, Tape Reveals." *Chicago Tribune*, January 7, 2001.

Warren Tribune Chronicle. "Re-elect Rep. Dennison," editorial, October 21, 1958.

Weinschenk, Carl. "Mr. Rumsfeld Goes Back to Washington." *Cable World*, March 30, 1992.

Wilson, George C. "Different View on Defense." *Washington Post*, November 9, 1975.

————. "U.S. May Need $30 Billion Missile Program." *Washington Post*, January 28, 1976.

Wines, Michael. "For Its Stretch Drive, Dole Campaign Turns to a Turnabout Artist." *New York Times*, September 26, 1996.

Public Remarks

Abizaid, John. News conference, July 16, 2003.

Bush, George W. Speech at The Citadel, South Carolina, September 23, 1999.

————. News conference, October 11, 2001.

————. News conference, January 7, 2005.

————. Speech at a luncheon of military wives at Bolling Air Force Base, Washington, October 25, 2005.

————. Veteran's Day speech, Pennsylvania, November 11, 2005.

————. Farewell speech for Donald Rumsfeld, The Pentagon, December 15, 2006.

Casey, George. News conference, June 22, 2006.

Cheney, Richard. Speech at Valley Forge Military Academy, Pennsylvania, September 6, 2000.

Myers, Richard. Speech at Kansas State University, November 9, 2006.

Pace, Peter. Appearance on NBC's *Meet the Press*, March 5, 2006.

———. Speech, Naval Postgraduate School, Monterey, CA, May 2008.

Rumsfeld, Donald. Speech on the floor of the U.S. House of Representatives, April 10, 1968, *Congressional Record*.

———. Speech in Chicago, November 1974.

———. Speech to Pentagon employees, September 10, 2001.

———. News conference, September 11, 2001.

———. News conference, October 9, 2001.

———. News conference, October 18, 2001.

———. News conference, November 1, 2001.

———. News conference, November 11, 2001.

———. News conference, November 13, 2001.

———. News conference at Central Command, Tampa, FL, November 27, 2001.

———. News conference, December 27, 2001.

———. News conference, January 11, 2002.

———. News conference at the Pentagon on February 12, 2002.

———. News conference, April 22, 2002.

———. Speech, "Beyond Nation-Building," New York, February 14, 2003.

———. News conference, February 28, 2003.

———. Speech to the United States Association of Former Members of Congress, March 4, 2003.

———. News conference, March 11, 2003.

———. News conference, April 1, 2003.

———. News conference, April 11, 2003.

———. News conference, April 15, 2003.

———. News conference, June 30, 2003.

———. Speech, Eisenhower National Security Conference, Washington, DC, September 25, 2003.

———. Speech to the Newspaper Association of America/American Society of Newspaper Editors, J. W. Marriott Hotel, Washington, DC, April 22, 2004.

———. News conference, October 11, 2004.

———. Remarks at town hall meeting in Kuwait, December 8, 2004.

———. Speech to the Dallas Chamber of Commerce, August 2, 2005.

———. News conference, November 1, 2005.

———. News conference, November 29, 2005.

———. Speech at the Harry S. Truman Presidential Library, Independence, Missouri, March 2, 2006.

———. News conference, April 18, 2006.

———. Speech to graduating cadets at the Virginia Military Institute, May 16, 2006.

———. Speech to the Boy Scout National Meeting Breakfast, May 26, 2006.

———. News conference, October 11, 2006.

———. News conference, October 20, 2006.

————. Speech at the Landon Lecture at Kansas State University, Manhattan, KS, November 9, 2006.

————. Speech to the Philadelphia Union League Club, Gold Medal Award Ceremony, December 1, 2006.

————. Remarks at Pentagon town hall meeting, December 8, 2006.

————. Remarks at town hall meeting in Mosul, Iraq, December 10, 2006.

————. Speech at farewell parade, December 15, 2006.

————. Speech to journalists at a seminar in Colorado Springs sponsored by the Heritage Foundation, May 13, 2008.

Rumsfeld, Donald, and George Casey. News conference, October 11, 2006.

Rumsfeld, Donald, and Richard Myers. News conference, April 1, 2003.

Schlesinger, James, and members of the Independent Panel to Review Department of Defense Detention Operations. News conference, August 24, 2004.

Shinseki, Eric. Farewell address, June 11, 2003.

Stevenson, Adlai. Speech to the Senior Class Banquet at Princeton University, March 22, 1954.

Congressional Hearings and Testimony

Joint Committee on the Organization of the Congress, June 2, 1965, entered into the *Congressional Record*, June 3, 1965, 12418–12421.

Senate Armed Services Committee, January 11, 2001.

Senate Armed Services Committee, June 21, 2001.

Senate Armed Services Committee, June 2002.

Senate Armed Services Committee, February 25, 2003.

House Budget Committee, February 27, 2003.

House Armed Services Committee, June 18, 2003.

House Armed Services Committee, January 28, 2004.

Senate Armed Services Committee, May 7, 2004.

Senate Armed Services Committee, June 23, 2005.

Senate Armed Services Committee, September 29, 2005.

Senate Foreign Relations Committee, October 19, 2005.

Senate Armed Services Committee, August 3, 2006.

Senate Armed Services Committee, June 17, 2008.

Reports

Barton, Frederick D., and Bathsheba N. Crocker. *A Wiser Peace: An Action Strategy for a Post-Conflict Iraq*. Center for Strategic and International Studies, January 2003.

Crane, Conrad C., and W. Andrew Terrill. *Reconstructing Iraq: Insight, Challenges and Missions for Military Forces in a Post-Conflict Scenario*. U.S. Army War College, Strategic Studies Institute, February 2003.

Defense Science Board. *Defense Science Board Summer Study on Transition to and From Hostilities.* Washington, DC: Office of the Under Secretary of Defense for Acquisition, Technology, and Logistics, 2004.

Fay, George, and Anthony Jones. *Investigation of Intelligence Activities at Abu Ghraib.* Department of Defense, August 23, 2004.

Final Report of the Independent Panel to Review DoD Detention Operations. August 2004.

Office of the Special Inspector General for Iraq Reconstruction. *Hard Lessons: The Iraq Reconstruction Experience.* February 6, 2009.

Office of the Inspector General of the Department of Defense. *Review of DoD–Directed Investigations of Detainee Abuse.* August 25, 2006.

_____. *Examination of Allegations Involving DoD Public Affairs Outreach Program.* January 14, 2009.

Rumsfeld, Donald, et al. *Report of the Commission to Assess the Ballistic Missile Threat to the United States: Executive Summary.* Washington, DC: U.S. Government Printing Office, 1998.

Taguba, Antonio. *Article 15–6 Investigation of the 800th Military Police Brigade.* March 2004.

Manuscript Collections

Donald Rumsfeld, personal files.

Gerald R. Ford Presidential Library and Museum, Ann Arbor, MI.

National Archives, Washington, DC.

Miscellaneous

Manifest for the SS *Donau.*

Rumsfeld, Donald. "The Steel Seizure Case of 1952 and Its Effects on Presidential Powers." Senior thesis, Princeton University, April 26, 1954.

Donald Rumsfeld. Three interviews conducted by the OSD Historical Office: July 12, 1994; August 2, 1994; September 12, 1994.

Memoranda

Abizaid, John. Memorandum to Rumsfeld, November 11, 2003.

_____. Memorandum to Rumsfeld and Myers, July 16, 2004.

_____. Memorandum to Rumsfeld and Myers, January 9, 2005.

_____. Memorandum to Rumsfeld, "Subject: Iranian Involvement in Anti-Coalition Violence in Iraq," May 8, 2006.

Andrews, Robert. Memorandum to Rumsfeld, "Subject: Manhunts," July 11, 2002.

Bush, George W. Memorandum to Cheney et al., "Humane Treatment of al Qaeda and Taliban Detainees," February 7, 2002.

Casey, George. Memorandum to Rumsfeld, March 4, 2005.

———. Memorandum to Rumsfeld, January 23, 2006.

———. Memorandum, "Some Thoughts on Civil War in Iraq," n.d.

Chertoff, Michael. Memorandum to Rumsfeld, March 10, 2006.

Goldberg, Alfred. Memorandum to Donald Rumsfeld, "OSD-JCS Staff Considerations," November 27, 2002.

Hamre, John. Memorandum to Rumsfeld, "Subject: Preliminary Observations
Based on My Recent Visit to Baghdad," July 2003.

Myers, Richard. Memorandum to Rumsfeld, July 13, 2004.

Myers, Richard, and Paul Wolfowitz. Memorandum to Casey, "Subject: Talking
Points Discussed During Today's SVTC," October 8, 2004.

Rodman, Peter W. Memorandum to Rumsfeld, "Subject: Who Will Govern Iraq?,"
August 15, 2002.

———. Memorandum to Rumsfeld, June 10, 2004.

Rumsfeld, Donald. Memorandum, "Guidelines When Considering Committing
U.S. Forces," March 2001.

———. Memorandum, "Possible Directions from the DoD Strategy Review and
Studies—Standards to Be Planted Down the Road from Defense Guidance,
the QDR, and Building DoD Budgets for 2002 and 2003," May 21, 2001.

———. Memorandum, "Cost-Cutting," July 11, 2001.

———. Memorandum to Rice, "Subject: National Security Presidential Directive 8,"
November 1, 2001.

———. Memorandum to Aldridge, Chu, White, England, and Roche with a copy
to Wolfowitz, "Subject: Joint Chiefs," November 12, 2001.

———. Memorandum to Myers, "Status of Taliban and Al Qaeda," January 19,
2002.

———. Memorandum to Myers, "Subject: Terrorist Organizations," July 22, 2002.

———. Memorandum to Rice, "Subject: Interagency Process," August 20, 2002.

———. Memorandum, "Iraq: An Illustrative List of Potential Problems to Be
Considered and Addressed," October 15, 2002.

———. Memorandum, "Assumptions," October 18, 2002.

———. Memorandum to Myers, "Subject: The Iraq War Plan and the TPFD,"
April 1, 2003.

———. Memorandum to Abizaid, July 23, 2003.

———. Memorandum, "Subject: Stress on the Force," September 2003.

———. Memorandum to Di Rita, "Subject: Firsts," September 3, 2003.

———. Memorandum to Abzaid and Bremer, "Subject: Reporting on Security
Issues," September 12, 2003.

———. Memorandum to Card, "Iraq Stabilization Phase Reporting Relationship," October 6, 2003.

———. Memorandum to Myers, Wolfowitz, Pace, and Feith, "Global War on Terrorism," October 16, 2003.

———. Memorandum, "Subject: Risk in the Way Ahead in Iraq," October 28,
2003.

_____. Memorandum to Rice, "Subject: NSC Meetings," October 30, 2003.

_____. Memorandum to Rice, "Subject: Agendas and Schedules for PC and NSC Meetings," November 5, 2003.

_____. Memorandum, "Private Conversation with Bremer," December 10, 2003.

_____. Memorandum to Abizaid, "Subject: Terminology," January 7, 2004.

_____. Memorandum, "Subject: Goldwater-Nichols for the USG," February 8, 2004.

_____. Memorandum to Abizaid and Bremer III, "Iraqi Security Forces," February 20, 2004.

_____. Memorandum to Feith with copies to Myers and Wolfowitz, "Subject: Foreign Troops," February 20, 2004.

_____. Memorandum to all the undersecretaries, some assistant secretaries, and military and civilian heads of the services, "Subject: Updating Systems and Procedures," March 17, 2004.

_____. Memorandum, "Subject: Role of the U.S. Military," March 26, 2004.

_____. Memorandum to Bush, "Subject: Alternative Approaches to Operate the NSC—Consensus v. Options for POTUS," April 1, 2004.

_____. Memorandum, "Subject: Military Advice," April 26, 2004.

_____. Memorandum, "Subject: Nightmare," May 10, 2004.

_____. Memorandum to Di Rita, May 18, 2004.

_____. Memorandum to Myers with a copy to Wolfowitz, "Subject: Force Estimate for Iraq," May 21, 2004.

_____. Memorandum to Bush, "Some Thoughts on Iraq and How to Think About It," June 8, 2004.

_____. Memorandum to Gonzales with copies to Wolfowitz and Haynes, "Subject: Document and E-mail Request," June 9, 2004.

_____. Memorandum to Bush, "Subject: What Are We Fighting? Is It a Global War on Terror," June 18, 2004.

_____. Memorandum to Myers, Wolfowitz, Pace, Feith, and Craddock, "Subject: "PCs and NSCs on Iraq," June 26, 2004.

_____. Memorandum to Feith and Myers, August 2, 2004.

_____. Memorandum to Latimer, August 30, 2004.

_____. Memorandum to Latimer, September 28, 2004.

_____. Memorandum for files, "Subject: Military Advice to POTUS," September 29, 2004.

_____. Memorandum to Casey, October 20, 2004.

_____. Memorandum, "Subject: Darlene Druyun and Corruption in the Air Force Acquisition," November 2, 2004.

_____. Memorandum to Dina Powell with copies to Cheney, Card, and Rice, "Subject: Turbulence in Key Positions," November 4, 2004.

_____. Memorandum to Bush, "Subject: Some Thoughts for Agenda Items for NSC and PC Meetings," November 13, 2004.

_____. Memorandum to Myers with copies to Abizaid, Casey, England, Harvey, and Schoomaker, "Subject: Meeting OAR Needs," December 14, 2004.

————. Memorandum to Myers and Pace, with copies to Abizaid, Casey, Harvey, and Schoomaker, "Subject: Armored Vehicles," December 21, 2004.

————. Memorandum to Pace with a copy to Myers, "Subject: Views from generals," January 4, 2005.

————. Memorandum to senior Pentagon staff, "Subject: A Nation and the Civilized World at War in the 21st Century," January 18, 2005.

————. Memorandum to Abizaid and Casey, February 14, 2005.

————. Memorandum to Chertoff with copies to Cheney, Card, Hadley, and Townsend, "Subject: Katrina After-action Lessons Learned Recommendation That DOD and DHS Determine When the Department of Defense Would Be Involved in a Catastrophic Event—Natural or Man Made," March 7, 2006.

————. Memorandum to Abizaid and Casey with a copy to Myers, September 21, 2005.

————. Memorandum to Casey with a copy to Myers, September 22, 2005.

————. Memorandum to Abizaid and Casey, "Subject: Upcoming Schedule," September 23, 2005.

————. Memorandum to Abizaid and Casey with a copy of Myers, September 26, 2005.

————. Memorandum to Abizaid and Casey with a copy to Pace, "Subject: Thanks for a Good Job in DC," October 5, 2005.

————. Memorandum to Casey and Vines with copies to Pace and Abizaid, "Subject: Good Job on the Constitutional Referendum," October 17, 2005.

————. Memorandum to Casey with copies to Pace, Edelman, and Haynes, "Subject: The Counterinsurgency Survey," November 15, 2005.

————. Memorandum to Casey with copies to Pace, Edelman, Abizaid, and Di Rita, "Subject: Information Operations," November 30, 2005.

————. Memorandum to Abizaid, Casey, Dempsey with a copy to Pace, "Subject: Briefings to the President," January 4, 2006.

————. Memorandum to Hadley with a copy to Crouch, "Subject: The circular PC meeting on 'lead departments,' 'blended leads' and 'co-leads' and the like," January 12, 2006.

————. Memorandum to Pace, with copies to Edelman, Abizaid, and Casey, "Subject: Iraq Force Level Discussion," January 20, 2006.

————. Memorandum to Di Rita, Rangel, and Dorrance Smith, "Subject: Rebuttal," February 6, 2006.

————. Memorandum to Hadley, "Subject: NSC meeting on GWOT," February 6, 2006.

————. Memorandum to Dorrance Smith with copies to England, Pace, Abizaid, Casey, and Edelman, "Subject: Lincoln Group Work in Iraq," March 6, 2006.

————. Memorandum to Smith, "Subject: A Better Presentation to Allegations of 'No Plan,'" March 10, 2006.

————. Memorandum to Smith, "Subject: Response to Clarence Page and *Washington Times*," April 10, 2006.

_____. Memorandum, "Subject: Thoughts on Meeting with the Military Analysts on April 18," April 19, 2006.

_____. Memorandum to Latimer, April 19, 2006.

_____. Memorandum to Casey with a copy to Pace, "Subject: Comments in This Morning's NSC," May 26, 2006.

_____. Memorandum to Pace with copies to Schoomaker, Abizaid, and Casey, "Subject: 172nd Stryker Brigade," August 26, 2006.

_____. Memorandum to Pace and Edelman, "A New Construct for Iraq—Establish a public plan (benchmarks) to turn over any responsibility for governance and security to the Iraqis and thereby permit a reduction of Coalition forces," October 10, 2006.

_____. Memorandum to Bush, "Iraq—Illustrative New Courses of Action," November 6, 2006.

_____. Memorandum, "The DoD Challenge," June 25, 2001.

_____. Memorandum to General Richard Myers and General Peter Pace, "What Will Be the Military Role in the War on Terrorism," October 10, 2001.

Shinseki, Eric. Memorandum to Rumsfeld, "Subject: End of Tour Memorandum," June 10, 2003.

Wolfowitz, Paul. Memorandum to Rumsfeld, "Accelerating the Buildup of Iraqi Security Forces," November 12, 2003.

Yoo, John, and Robert J. Delabunty. Memorandum to William J. Haynes II, "Application of Treaties and Laws to al Qaeda and Taliban Detainees," January 9, 2002.

Briefings and Other Unpublished Material

Briefing to Pentagon leadership, "U.S. Defense Priorities: Next Steps in Transformation," May 2002.

Briefing to Bush, "Iraq Update," December 16, 2004.

Briefing to Joint Chiefs of Staff, "Iraq Campaign: Way Ahead," June 27, 2005.

Briefing to Bush, "MNF-I Update," January 4, 2006.

Casey, George. Briefing to Rumsfeld, "Framework for Iraq," July 8, 2004.

_____. Briefing to Rumsfeld, "Post-Election Posture," December 15, 2004.

_____. Briefing to Rumsfeld, "State of the Iraqi Insurgency: June 2005 Assessment," June 23, 2005.

_____. Briefing to Hadley, "Iraq Campaign Plan," September 16, 2005.

_____. Briefing to Rumsfeld, "Potential Off-Ramp Decisions," October 21, 2005.

_____. Briefing at the Pentagon, "Iraq Update and the Way Ahead: Tank Update," June 21, 2006.

_____. Briefing to Rumsfeld, "Iraq Update: SECDEF," June 21, 2006.

"Strategic Assessment: Camp David Briefing," June 12, 2006.

Summary of July 22, 2006, meeting prepared by Meghan O'Sullivan and sent to Rumsfeld by Hadley on August 12, 2006.

Index

Note: Throughout this index, the initials *D.R.* are used to indicate references to Donald Rumsfeld in subentries.

771

Bradley Graham has spent more than thirty years working for *The Washington Post* in various reporting and editing assignments focused on foreign and military affairs. The author of *Hit to Kill: The New Battle Over Shielding America from Missile Attack*, he lives in Bethesda, Maryland.

PublicAffairs is a publishing house founded in 1997. It is a tribute to the standards, values, and flair of three persons who have served as mentors to countless reporters, writers, editors, and book people of all kinds, including me.

I. F. Stone, proprietor of *I. F. Stone's Weekly*, combined a commitment to the First Amendment with entrepreneurial zeal and reporting skill and became one of the great independent journalists in American history. At the age of eighty, Izzy published *The Trial of Socrates*, which was a national bestseller. He wrote the book after he taught himself ancient Greek.

Benjamin C. Bradlee was for nearly thirty years the charismatic editorial leader of *The Washington Post*. It was Ben who gave the *Post* the range and courage to pursue such historic issues as Watergate. He supported his reporters with a tenacity that made them fearless and it is no accident that so many became authors of influential, best-selling books.

Robert L. Bernstein, the chief executive of Random House for more than a quarter century, guided one of the nation's premier publishing houses. Bob was personally responsible for many books of political dissent and argument that challenged tyranny around the globe. He is also the founder and longtime chair of Human Rights Watch, one of the most respected human rights organizations in the world.

·   ·   ·

For fifty years, the banner of Public Affairs Press was carried by its owner Morris B. Schnapper, who published Gandhi, Nasser, Toynbee, Truman, and about 1,500 other authors. In 1983, Schnapper was described by *The Washington Post* as "a redoubtable gadfly." His legacy will endure in the books to come.

Peter Osnos, *Founder and Editor-at-Large*